AN INTRODUCTION TO SHI'I ISLAM
The History and Doctrines of Twelver Shi'ism

An Introduction to Shi'i Islam

The History and Doctrines of Twelver Shi'ism

by

Moojan Momen

YALE UNIVERSITY PRESS
New Haven and London

First published in the United Kingdom by George Ronald Publisher
Published in the United States by Yale University Press

Typeset by Sunrise Setting, Torquay, Devon
Printed and bound in Great Britain by Billing & Sons Limited, Worcester

Library of Congress catalogue card number: 85–40438

International standard book number: 0–300–03499–7
0–300–03531–4 (pbk.)

10 9 8 7 6 5 4 3 2

This book is dedicated to all those who have died for the cause of Truth in Iran

Contents

List of Illustrations

Maps

Foreword

To introduce such a book is not an easy task. Like most Western Islamologists, my training and research have been concentrated on Sunni Islam and so Shiʿism is not my main field. However, this book has been researched and presented in such a truly scientific manner that it does not suffer from the biases apparent in many such works.

There is now much interest in the question of the differences between Sunni and Shiʿi Islam. I used to discuss this matter often with my students in the Islamic Studies department of the Faculty of Literature of Rome University. But nowadays the question is also frequently raised on television and in the newspapers. Indeed, many are now beginning to be more familiar with the differences between Shiʿi and Sunni Islam. If this is the result of the 'Islamic Revolution' in Iran, then we have Khomeini to thank for it. However, unfortunately the presentations of this subject are often ill-informed and misleading. One frequently finds journalists referring to Shiʿi Islam as the most 'revolutionary' form of Islam. Dr Momen has, in this book, brought out well the evidence for the fact that the development of Shiʿism has been evolutionary and he has put into perspective its so-called 'revolutionary' aspects.

This book clarifies the reality of Shiʿi Islam, and can now be considered the best available description of the aforementioned differences between it and Sunni Islam. In spite of the fact that the author has concentrated on the Ithnā-ʿAsharī (Twelver) Shiʿis who form the majority of the population of Iran today, he also describes other forms of Shiʿism such as the Ismāʿīlīs and the *Ghulāt*. There is even a chapter on Sufism and ʿIrfān (Gnosis). Some Iranian writers of recent years have leaned too far towards the notion that, of the two forms of Islam, Shiʿism is the more favourable environment for Sufism; whereas the fact is that Sufism, in its earliest years, was more accepted by the Sunnis and continues to the present to be more widespread among them.

To sum up, this book is a major contribution towards a clearer and more comprehensive definition of Shiʿi Islam and its differences from Sunnism and may be recommended to everyone who wishes to understand these matters better.

Prof. Alessandro Bausani
Director, Department of Islamic
Studies of the University of Rome

March 1985

Preface

The majority of books written in the West on Islam are concerned with Sunni Islam and have tended to ignore or minimise the importance of Shi'i Islam. This is not surprising in view of the fact that Sunni Islam represents the belief of the majority of Muslims and is the state religion of most of the countries of the Middle East and North Africa.

However, the Shi'is are the next largest group after the Sunnis in the Muslim world and are the largest religious community in several countries: Iran, Iraq, Bahrain and Lebanon. In Iran Twelver Shi'i Islam is the state religion. There are important Shi'i communities in several other countries also: India, Pakistan, the Gulf states and the USSR, while Shi'ism of the Zaydī sect is prominent in North Yemen and that of the Ismā'īlī sect in India, Pakistan and East Africa.

The rise to economic importance of the Persian Gulf region (where most of the important oil deposits are in areas with Shi'i populations) has led in the West to a renewed interest in this area, while the recent revolution in Iran has caused many to realise the importance of trying to obtain a deeper understanding of the religious undercurrents in the area.

This book is an attempt to present to a Western audience a general outline of Shi'i Islam. While I have not assumed that the reader already has a knowledge of Sunni Islam, I have tended to concentrate on explaining those areas in which Shi'i Islam differs most greatly from Sunni Islam: such matters as the question of the succession to Muhammad, the nature of the Imamate, the Twelfth Imam, etc. Because of this, the reader may form the impression that these two communities are a long way apart in their view of Islam and this would be an unfortunate conclusion since in fact the two are much closer to each other than many Christian sects are. There is no disagreement between the two in the matter of the station and centrality of the Prophet Muhammad in the religion, nor on most of the historical details of his life. There are no major differences in the ritual observances of daily life, and on many doctrinal and theological matters there is also a broad consensus.

It is in order to outline and confirm this large area of agreement between Sunni and Shi'i Islam that the first chapter is included in this book. Any readers who are already well versed in the basic facts of Islam may wish to omit this chapter, while readers who wish to have detailed information about those areas covered in the first chapter will need to refer to other books on Islam.

The main intention of this book is to present both modern critical research on Shi'ism and also the traditional way that Shi'is see themselves. Critical scholarship has produced some interesting research on Shi'i Islam, particularly concerning its early history, and this has tended to throw considerable doubt on the traditional Shi'i accounts. However, this research, interesting as it may be for the intellectual, has had no impact at all on Shi'i Islam itself, neither on the Shi'i religious leaders nor on the Shi'i masses. They care little for what Western scholars may be writing about their religion and indeed many are deeply suspicious of the motives behind such research. Therefore, in this book, I have given the outlines of the results of modern research but also I have tried to present the orthodox traditional accounts of Shi'i history, since it is this that is the reality of the religion for the Shi'is themselves and it is this that raises the passions of the crowds during the great Shi'i commemorations. Thus for anyone trying to achieve an understanding of the world of Shi'i Islam, it is these traditional accounts that are more relevant and important. And so, for example, the reader will find in Chapter 4 an account of the history of early Shi'ism as it has emerged from modern critical scholarship. But in Chapter 3, the same period has already been examined giving the traditional account of the lives of the Shi'i Imams and, in particular, the Karbalā episode that looms so large in Shi'i history and in the minds of the Shi'is that its importance can hardly be overestimated.

Research is, of course, continually throwing up new facts or new ways of looking at the material presented in this book. The reader will appreciate that, in order to keep this a readable introductory book, I have, at times, needed to examine several controversial viewpoints and present one of them as though this was established fact. Some readers will also notice that I have tended to present the evolution of Shi'ism as a history of ideas and I have not gone into the social and economic factors that may have shaped these developments. This is partly because to have gone into such matters would have expanded the book greatly and partly because, for many periods of Shi'i history, a great deal more work needs to be done in this field before any reliable statements can be made.

One of the problems in writing this book has been to decide what to call the sect of Islam that is being described, since it is known by a variety of names. It is often referred to by Sunnis by the derogatory title of Rāfiḍī (the Repudiators, see p. 73). The name Ja'farī is strictly a designation of the Shi'i school of jurisprudence (see p. 125), but this name has also been used for the whole sect, especially by the ulama and by Sunnis. In Lebanon the Shi'is have traditionally been called Mutawālī (plural: Mutāwila), while in Afghanistan and India the name Qizilbāsh is used. A name that has found favour among Western scholars is Imāmī. Although it is used among Arab Shi'is, it has little currency among Iranians or Indians and has the further disadvantage of being often used loosely to include Ismā'īlīs. Probably the most accurate and most widely-accepted, although less elegant, designation is Ithnā-'Asharī (Twelver) and this is the usage that has been preferred in this book. The Shi'a often refer to themselves as al-Khāṣṣa (the Select, as against the Sunnis who are referred to as al-'Āmma, the generality of the people).

When Shi'i Islam is being referred to in this book, it is the Uṣūlī school of Ithnā-'Asharī (Twelver) Shi'i Islam (i.e. the mainstream of Twelver Shi'i Islam to which the majority of Shi'is belong today) that is meant unless specifically noted otherwise. The reader will find notes on some of the other sects of Shi'i Islam in the second half of Chapter 3, while in Chapter 12 may be found a description of the other schools within Twelver Shi'ism.

It will be apparent to the reader that use has been made of a number of Islamic terms in the text of this book. Among these the reader will note the use of the phrase 'the Prophet' to refer to Muhammad, while other frequently-used words such as ulama, mujtahid, etc. are defined in the Glossary.

A Note on Transliteration, Pronunciation and Technical Terms

Those with sufficient knowledge to care about transliteration will be able to work out for themselves the system used in this book. The following are a few notes to assist others with pronunciation and with technical terms. On the question of pronunciation, the following table is intended to assist the reader to work out how words are pronounced in Arabic and Persian:

Letter	*Arabic*	*Persian*
a	b*a*t	b*a*t
end -a	Coca-Col*a*	l*e*t
ā	b*a*r	b*a*r
b	*b*at	*b*at
ch	not used	*ch*at
d	*d*og	*d*og
ḍ	stressed, explosive *d*	*z*ebra
dh	*th*is	*z*ebra

f	*f*at	*f*at
g	not used	*g*irl
gh	gargling sound similar to French *r*	*k* sound at back of throat
h	*h*at	*h*at
ḥ	stressed, guttural *h*	*h*at
i	h*i*t	b*e*t
ī	h*ee*l	h*ee*l
j	*j*ump (*g*irl in Egypt)	*j*ump
k	*k*ing	*k*ing
kh	as in Scottish lo*ch* or German ma*ch*en	as in Scottish lo*ch* or German ma*ch*en
l	*l*et	*l*et
m	*m*an	*m*an
n	ma*n*	ma*n*
p	not used	*p*ut
q	*k* sound at back of throat	*k* sound at back of throat
r	*r*at	*r*at
s	*s*ad	*s*ad
ṣ	stressed explosive *s*	*s*ad
sh	*sh*ine	*sh*ine
t	*t*ell	*t*ell
ṭ	stressed, explosive *t*	*t*ell
th	*th*ink	*s*ad
u	b*u*ll	sh*o*rt
ū	b*oo*t	b*oo*t
v	not used	*v*ery
w	*w*all; also in diphthong ‘aw’ as in gro*w*l	not used except in diphthong ‘aw’ as in gro*w*l
y	*y*et; also in diphthong ‘ay’ as in m*ai*n	*y*et; also in diphthong ‘ay’ as in m*ai*n
z	*z*ebra	*z*ebra
ẓ	stressed, explosive *z*	*z*ebra
zh	not used	trea*s*ure or as in French *j*
’	glottal stop	glottal stop
	(an apostrophe is also used as in English to indicate a dropped letter as in Sayfu’d-Dīn for Sayf ad-Dīn elided together)	
‘	strong, guttural sound with compressed throat	glottal stop in mid-word or end-word; not sounded at beginning of word

I have allowed myself a certain amount of freedom in that, for most names and titles, where the second word is a noun (i.e. the construct or genitive form), I have elided together component parts of the Arabic such as: 'Abdu'llāh instead of 'Abd Allāh; and Sayfu'd-Dīn instead of Sayf ad-Dīn. But for the sake of clarity I have not done this for technical terms and names of books, thus: *marja' at-taqlīd* not *marja'u't-taqlīd*; and *Jawāhir al-Kalām* not *Jawāhiru'l-Kalām*, nor in names and titles where the second word is an adjective, e.g. Shaykh al-Mufīd.

As for the technical terms themselves, it has been difficult to decide whether to give them in their Persian or Arabic form since most of the important books are written in Arabic, but Persian is the language of the largest and most influential group in the Shi'i world. To have given both would have cluttered up the text unduly. I have mostly used the Arabic forms, the only exceptions being those terms that have predominantly been used in their Persian form, e.g. *Vilāyat-i Faqīh*. However, Arabic terms or names consisting of two words can usually be converted to their Persian form by use of the following manœuvres:

1. Remove the article al , at , as , ash
2. Insert -i after the first term (or -yi if last letter of first term is a vowel)
3. Change letter w, if it occurs, to v
4. A terminal -a should usually be changed to -ih (although the final h is not pronounced)

Thus, for example:

marja' at-taqlīd	becomes	*marja'-i taqlīd*
wilāyat al-faqīh	becomes	*vilāyat-i faqīh*
al-Futūḥāt al-Makkiyya	becomes	*Futūḥāt-i Makkiyyih*

Certain words and names commonly occurring in the book carry no transliteration marks. These words, with their fully transliterated form in parentheses, are:

Shi'i (Shī'ī)	ulama ('ulamā)
Shi'a (Shī'a)	Imam (Imām)
Sunni (Sunnī)	Mulla (Mullā)
Sufi (Ṣūfī)	

The names in the following list are treated as being anglicised and therefore carry no transliteration marks (original transliterated form in parentheses):

'Abbasid ('Abbāsī)	Mirdasid (Mirdāsī)
Buyid (Būya)	Safavid (Ṣafavī)
Hamdanid (Ḥamdānī)	Sarbadarid (Sarbadārī)
Ilkhanid (Īlkhānī)	Timurid (Tīmūrī)
Mazyadid (Mazyādī)	'Uqaylid ('Uqaylī)

The names: Muhammad, 'Ali, Hasan and Husayn have not been transliterated (Muḥammad, 'Alī, Ḥasan, Ḥusayn) where they refer to the Prophet himself and the First, Second and Third Imams respectively but do carry transliteration marks when they occur as part of another name, e.g. Muḥammad Bāqir Majlisī. The names of the more well-known cities such as Tehran, Isfahan and Baghdad have also not been transliterated.

Since any single Islamic (Hijrī) year overlaps with two Christian years, where only the Hijrī year of an event is known, the equivalent Christian (Georgian) date is given as the first of the two years partially covered by that Hijrī year.

Acknowledgements

In preparing a book of this nature one must rely upon the assistance of many people. In particular, I must thank Prof. Alessandro Bausani for agreeing to write a Foreword for this book, and Prof. Wilferd Madelung who kindly agreed to look through the whole manuscript and gave his valuable suggestions. Others who helped over particular aspects of the subject (and I must apologize to many whom I have omitted) are: Prof. Nikki Keddie, University of California, Los Angeles; Prof. Emrys L. Peters, Manchester University; Todd Lawson, McGill University Montreal; Dr Juan R. Cole, University of Michigan, Ann Arbor; Stephen Lambden, Newcastle University; and Dr Peter Smith, University of Lancaster. It is only the generous lending policy of a number of libraries that has enabled the research necessary for this book to be done. In particular, I would like to thank the staff of the following libraries for their helpfulness: Library of the School of Oriental and African Studies, London; Cambridge University Library; Oriental Faculty Library, University of Cambridge; and Sandy Public Library. I am grateful to Dr Gustav Thaiss for permission to publish the quotation from his Ph.D. thesis on p. 237 and to Longman for permission to publish the quotation from Jafri, *Origins and Early Development of Shi'a Islam*, on pp. 31–2. I am also grateful to the following for permission to use various photographs: Peter Carapetian, fig, 61; The MacQuitty International Photographic Collection, figs. 11, 27, 32, 38, 52, 68; the Middle East Centre, St. Antony's College, Oxford, figs. 3, 9, 10, 14; Dr Javad Nurbakhsh, fig. 36. Photographs were also kindly supplied by the Embassy of the Islamic Republic of Iran, London; Islamic Republic News Agency, London; the Iraqi Cultural Centre, London; N. Askew and several other individuals. I must also thank May Ballerio, Mark Hofman and Russ Busey for their careful work and useful suggestions, and Dr Wendi Momen for the Index.

Glossary

'Abbasid ('Abbāsī) – descendant of al-'Abbās, uncle of the Prophet Muhammad. This family seized the Caliphate in 132/750

akhbār (sing. *khabar*) – Traditions, sayings attributed to Muhammad and to the Imams. They are composed of two parts: the names of the transmitters of the Tradition (*isnād*) and the text of the Tradition (*matn*). In this book where the word 'Tradition' with a capital 'T' occurs, a *khabar* or *ḥadīth* is meant

ākhūnd – appears to have been originally used to designate high-ranking members of the ulama but is now used as an equivalent to mulla to denote any member of the ulama and is often used slightly pejoratively

Āl –family of. Not to be confused with the Arabic definite article *al*

'Alid ('Alawī) – a descendant of 'Alī ibn Abī Ṭālib, the cousin and son-in-law of the Prophet and the First Imam of the Shi'is

'Allāma – very learned member of the ulama; learned in every branch of the Islamic sciences

Amīr – commander, chief, leader

Anṣār (lit. the helpers) – the Medinan followers of Muhammad

Āqā (lit. lord or master) – used to designate persons in positions of power and authority. In modern Persian when prefixed to a name is the equivalent of 'Mr'

Āyātu'llāh (lit. sign of God) – modern description of *mujtahid* (see below)

Bāb (pl. *abwāb*, lit. gate) – one of the designations of the four representatives of the Hidden Imam

Caliph (*Khalīfa*, pl. *khulafā*, lit. successor) – title given to those who held power over the Islamic Empire after Muhammad

faqīh (*fuqahā*) – an expert in *fiqh* (see below); used in the Shi'i world as equivalent of *mujtahid*

fiqh – religious jurisprudence, elucidation and application of the *Sharī'a*

furū' (lit. branches) – subsidiary principles (applied to religious law, as opposed to *uṣūl*), see pp. 175–6

ghayba – occultation or concealment

ghulāt (sing. *ghālin*) – followers of *ghuluww*, see below

ghuluww, ghāliyya – extremism, holding doctrines that are so heretical as to put those holding them outside the pale of Islam, see pp. 45, 65–7

ḥadīth – as for *akhbār*

Ḥā'irī – related to the *ḥā'ir*, the sacred enclosure around the Shrine of Husayn at Karbalā; designation of ulama from Karbalā

ḥajj – the pilgrimage to Mecca undertaken according to the prescribed ritual during the month of Dhu'l-Ḥijja. *Ḥājjī* or *al-Ḥājj* – one who has performed the Ḥajj

Hasanid (Ḥasanī) – descendant of the Imam Hasan

ḥāshiyya – gloss or marginal notes on a book. e.g. *Ḥāshiyya al-Kifāya* is a gloss on Ākhūnd Khurāsānī's *Kifāyat al-Uṣūl*

Ḥikma (*Ḥikmat-i Ilāhī*) – Divine Wisdom or Philosophy, Theosophy, see pp. 216–19

Husaynid (Ḥusaynī) – descendant of the Imam Husayn

ibn – son of

ijāza (lit. permission) – certificate permitting a pupil to transmit his master's teaching or testifying to his ability to exercise *ijtihād*

ijtihād (lit. exertion) – the process of arriving at judgements on points of religious law using reason and the principles of jurisprudence (*uṣūl al-fiqh*)

Imam (Imām) (lit. the one who stands in front) – principal meaning for Twelver Shi'is is as designation of one of the twelve legitimate successors of the Prophet Muhammad. Also used to designate a religious leader of the community

Imām-Jum'a – leader at the Friday communal prayer (usually, in Iran, the government appoints one main Imām-Jum'a in each city, often a hereditary position)

'irfān – gnosis, mystic knowledge

jihād – holy war undertaken to expand the boundaries of Islam or to defend it against an attacker

kalām – speculative theology

khums (lit. one-fifth) – religious tax originally paid to the Prophet and, by Shi'is, to the Imam from certain categories of goods and income. Now paid to the believer's *marja' at-taqlīd* in his capacity as *nā'ib al-Imām*

kitāb – book

madrasa (Persian *madrasih*) – religious college (where the Islamic sciences are taught)

Mar'ashī – descendant of Abu'l-Ḥasan 'Alī al-Mar'ashī, a fifth-generation descendant of the Fourth Imam, Zaynu'l-'Ābidīn

marja' at-taqlīd (plur. *marāji'at-taqlīd*, Persian *marja'-i taqlīd*, lit. reference point for emulation) – one who through his learning and probity is qualified to be followed in all points of religious practice and law by the generality of Shi'is *mawla* (plur. *mawālī*) – (1) lord or master; (2) client of one of the Arab tribes (in early Islam all converts had to become clients of one of the Arab tribes, a socially-inferior position)

Mīr (contraction of *Amīr*) – usually means the same as Sayyid, i.e. a descendant of Muhammad, but can also be used as equivalent of *Amīr*

Mīrzā (contraction of *Amīrzāda*) – originally meant prince, later usually indicates an educated man if placed before a name and prince if placed after

Muhājirūn (lit. emigrants) – those who left Mecca and migrated to Medina during the lifetime of the Prophet. Later used to designate those who migrated to the borders of the Islamic Empire in order to participate in *jihād*

Muḥaqqiq – one who conducts research or investigation of religious matters

mujtahid – one who has studied sufficiently and achieved the level of competence necessary to obtain permission (*ijāza*) to practise *ijtihad*

mulla (*mullā*, derived from *mawla*) – usual Persian term for one of the ulama

Mūsawī (Persian *Mūsavī*) – descendant of the Imam Mūsā al-Kāẓim

Mu'tazilī – adherent of a school of theology (*Mu'tazila*) that emphasised certain key issues: the unity and justice of God, the createdness of the Qur'an and the free will of man. It evolved into a theology on the basis of rationality

Nā'ib – deputy, representative; *Nā'ib al-Imām* (Persian *Nā'ib-i Imām*) – representative of the Imam; *Nā'ib al-Khāṣṣ* – special or specific representative (of the Hidden Imam); *Nā'ib al-'Āmm* – general representative (of the Hidden Imam)

nabī – prophet

naṣṣ – specific designation, usually used in relation to the designation of 'Ali by Muhammad or of one Imam by his predecessor

qāḍī – judge

Raḍawī – descendant of the Imam 'Alī ar-Riḍa

rasūl (plur. *rusul*) – apostle or messenger of God (not to be confused with the Christian use of the word apostle to denote one of the disciples of Christ)

rawḍa (Persian *rawḍih*, *rawḍih-khānī*) – gathering for the recital of the sufferings of the Imams; *rawḍih-khān* – reciter of the *rawḍa*

rijāl – the study of the biographies of the ulama and the transmitters of the *ḥadīth*

Ṣāḥib – used in conjunction with a name of a book to mean 'author of'. In this form it is a frequent way of referring to ulama who have written important works; thus, for example, Shaykh Muḥammad Ḥasan an-Najafī (see p. 318) is often referred to as Ṣāḥib al-Jawāhir, the author of the *Jawāhir (al-Kalām)*

Sayyid – in Shi'i areas this is the designation of descendants of the Prophet Muhammad, but in the Arab world in general it is now also used as an equivalent of 'Mr'. Descendants of the Prophet are entitled to wear green turbans, but ulama who are Sayyids usually wear black turbans, a practice that is said to have derived from the Musha'sha'

Shahīd – martyr

Shar', Sharī'a – the religious law

sharḥ (lit. explanation) – commentary or interpretation of another work

shaykh (lit. an elder) – designation sometimes used for leading ulama. In the Arab world in general it is more commonly used for tribal leaders

Shaykh al-Islām – official title given, in Iran, to a member of the ulama appointed to preside over the *Sharī'a* court in each major town

sūra (Persian *sūrih*) – chapter of the Qur'an

Ṭabāṭabā'ī – descendant of Ibrāhīm aṭ-Ṭabāṭabā, a fourth-generation descendant of the Second Imam, Hasan

tafsīr – commentary or exegesis of whole or part of the Qur'an

taqiyya – dissimulation about one's religious beliefs in order to protect one's self, family or property from harm, see p. 183

taqlīd – emulation, imitation or following; denotes the following of the dictates of a mujtahid

ṭullāb (sing. *ṭālib*) – religious student at a *madrasa*

ulama (*'ulamā*, lit. learned persons) – the religious class. The singular of this word, *'ālim*, can be used of a person learned in any branch of knowledge but the plural is restricted to the religiously learned

uṣūl – principles; *uṣūl ad-dīn* – principal elements of religion (as distinct from *furū'*, see p. 175); *uṣūl al-fiqh* – principles of jurisprudence – principles used for arriving at a judgement in *fiqh*

vazīr (Arabic *wazīr*) – minister (to a king or governor)

vilāyat-i faqīh (Arabic *wilāyat al-faqīh*) – the concept that government belongs by right to those who are learned in jurisprudence

walī – (1) guardian, helper or defender, a title used of the Imams; (2) saint – a title often used of eminent Sufis

wilāya (Persian *vilāyat*) – a term which can indicate temporal government or power (as in *vilāyat-i faqīh*) and also spiritual guidance and sanctity

zakāt – a religious tax payable by believers on certain categories of property and wealth and intended to assist the poor and needy, travellers and debtors. It is considered that the *zakāt* 'purifies' the remaining property and wealth of the one who pays it. It is usually paid to the *marja' at-taqlīd*

1

An Outline of the Life of Muhammad and the Early History of Islam

This chapter is intended to set the background for the emergence of Shiʻi Islam. It will consist mostly of a survey of the life of Muhammad and a brief outline of the early history of Islam as well as some of the fundamental elements of the teachings contained in the Qur'an. The outline presented in this introductory chapter is intended to be a presentation of what is held in common by both Shiʻis and Sunnis. The specifically Shiʻi aspects of the history and teachings will be presented in subsequent chapters.

The emergence of Muhammad and the religion of Islam must be seen against the background of the Arabian Peninsula in the seventh century AD. Whether nomads or settled in towns, the people of Arabia were divided into tribes and the individual's loyalty was first and foremost to the tribe or the clan within the tribe to which he belonged. Honour, marriage, social status and friendship were all determined by one's tribe and one's position in the tribe. These tribes were frequently at war with one another and feuds could go on for generations with tribal honour demanding that blood revenge or blood money should be obtained for each death caused by the conflict. Bearing arms and fighting for one's tribe were the greatest marks of honour for men. If one did not belong to a powerful tribe, then it was necessary to obtain the protection of a powerful tribe, otherwise one's life was at risk. Sometimes one tribe would ally itself with another against its enemies.

The majority of the inhabitants of the peninsula were engaged in pastoral or agricultural pursuits, either as nomads or settled in one of a small number of towns. The other important economic factor was the presence of a trade route along the western side of the peninsula linking India with Syria and Byzantium.

Most of the tribes had a primitive form of worship and prayed to deities in the form of idols made of stone and wood. Both Christianity and Judaism had, however, made some inroads in the peninsula and a number of Jewish tribes existed.

Among the Arab tribes there were certain places that were regarded as shrines and each had a sanctuary around it. Within the sanctuary, usually at a particular time of the year, the tribes would gather and put aside their feuding for a time while they celebrated a festival related to that shrine. These festivals were important occasions for trade, cultural activities such as poetry reading and for the settlement of disputes and feuds. The custodians of these shrines thus became prominent persons and were frequently used to settle blood feuds by acting as arbitrators.

One such shrine in Arabia was the Ka'ba in Mecca. The Ka'ba became the repository for the idols of many of the tribes and a yearly festival was held at 'Ukāẓ nearby. Muhammad himself came from the family of the custodians of the Ka'ba. His ancestor, Qusayy, was said to have seized the Ka'ba from its previous custodians and established his tribe, Quraysh, as the most important tribal group in Mecca and his family as the most important family among Quraysh. In his family was vested the custodianship of the Ka'ba together with the responsibility for providing with food and water the pilgrims who came to the shrines.

The sons and grandsons of Qusayy extended and increased the influence of their family and of Mecca. They instituted two great trade journeys, one in the winter to the Yemen in the south to trade with the ships coming from India on the Monsoon winds and one in the summer to the north to trade in Syria with the Byzantines. In order to do this, they had to establish a number of treaties and alliances with other tribes through whose territory they needed to pass. This process greatly increased the importance of Mecca as the focal point of the trade route.

By the time of Muhammad's birth, Mecca was a very important centre and the power of the Quraysh tribe paramount. Muhammad's own family line, although retaining some of its ancestral privileges, had, however, lost much of its power and influence to other clans within Quraysh such as the Umayya and Makhzūm families.

Muhammad was born in AD 570 in Mecca. His father died a few months before Muhammad was born and his mother died when he was six. He was placed under the care of his grandfather and two years later, when this grandfather died, Muhammad entered the household of his uncle Abū Ṭālib, the father of 'Ali and the head of the Banū Hāshim family. Thus 'Ali was not only a cousin but also virtually a foster-brother of Muhammad (although there was a considerable age difference between the two).

As Muhammad grew up, he became known for his honesty and reflective nature. He assisted his uncle in his trading ventures, but the family was not a rich one and its fortunes were in decline. Later a rich widow, Khadīja, engaged Muhammad to manage her trading concerns.

When he was twenty-five, Muhammad married Khadīja, who was fifteen years his senior, and while she lived he took no other wives. They had eight children, but only four daughters grew to adulthood. Also in Muhammad's household lived his cousin, 'Ali, and his adopted son, a freed slave named Zayd.

It was when Muhammad was aged forty (i.e. in AD 610) that the first revelation came to him. Muhammad himself has related that, one day, while he was meditating on Mount Hirā, near Mecca, as was his custom, the Angel Gabriel appeared to him and instructed him three times to read. Then the *Sūra* of al-'Alaq was revealed: 'Recite in the name of thy Lord who created; created man of congealed blood . . .'

Muhammad fled in terror at this revelation, but his wife Khadīja comforted him and became the first believer. His cousin 'Ali who was only nine or ten years old at the time became the second to believe and Zayd, the other member of his household, was next. The first from outside Muhammad's household to believe was Abū Bakr. A number of others also gathered around Muhammad at this time although the details of how these earliest of his followers became believers are not, for the most part, available.

Then after about four years came the moment when Muhammad made a public announcement of his mission. Once at a gathering of his own clan of the Hāshim family and once at a general meeting of Meccans on Mount Ṣafā, Muhammad proclaimed his mission and called on the people to abandon idolatry and to worship the one true God. This public announcement aroused the fiercest opposition from the Meccan notables, for any abandonment of idol-worship threatened the position of the Ka'ba as the foremost centre of idol-worship in Arabia which in turn meant the destruction of Mecca as a commercial centre. Muhammad's followers at this stage were mostly young men of no influence in the community. Some were members of powerful clans but could exert no influence because of their youth. Others were slaves. All of the Meccan nobility combined against the new Prophet and only the protection of Abū Ṭālib (who stood by his nephew on account of kinship and not because he was a believer) saved Muhammad from death while several of his followers endured the cruellest tortures and many faced abuse and insults.

At this earliest stage, Muhammad appears to have taught a very simple religious doctrine: that there is only one God who has sent Muhammad as His messenger to mankind; that idol-worship is prohibited as are various other practices such as the burying alive of baby daughters; and that man must purify his thoughts and actions in preparation for the Day of Judgement.

So harsh did the persecution become that in 615 Muhammad ordered a group of his followers to migrate to Ethiopia and seek there the protection of its Christian king. The Quraysh leaders even sent emissaries to Ethiopia to try to persuade the king to return the refugees but the king refused.

The following year, a deputation of leading members of Quraysh from the Umayya and Makhzūm families called on Abū Ṭālib asking him to restrain his nephew or alternatively to withdraw his protection but Abū Ṭālib refused. The Quraysh imposed a boycott on the members of the Hāshim and the related Muṭṭalib families who supported Muhammad, although the majority of them were not Muslims. The boycott lasted three years but eventually it collapsed, mainly because it was not achieving its purpose and Muhammad was continuing to preach his message.

Although the boycott ended in 619, two events in that year caused Muhammad great sorrow and plunged him into great danger. The first was the death of Khadīja who had been his main support and the second was the death of Abū Ṭālib, his uncle and protector. Leadership in the house of Hāshim now passed to Abū Lahab who was another uncle of Muhammad but his inveterate enemy. Abū Lahab soon found a pretext for withdrawing clan protection from Muhammad and this placed the latter in great peril for he could now be killed with impunity (withdrawal of clan protection meant that blood revenge or blood money would not be exacted) and such a person could not expect to survive long. It was now a priority for Muhammad to find a protector. He travelled to the nearby town of Ṭā'if to seek the protection of the leading clan there but he was ridiculed and rejected. Finally Muhammad was forced to accept the protection of the chief of the Banū Nawfal and suffered the humiliation of returning to Mecca under the protection of a tribe that was not his own and a chief who was an idolator.

It was just at this time when matters seemed at their bleakest for the Prophet that an event occurred that was to be the key to his eventual triumph. In 620, at the yearly pilgrimage season, Muhammad met some six or seven men from the tribe of Khazraj of the town of Yathrib and converted them to his teachings. The following year, five of them returned and together with another seven received instruction from Muhammad at secret meetings at a pass called 'Aqaba near Mecca. They pledged that they would refrain from idolatry, murder of their off-spring, adultery, theft and calumny and would obey the Prophet. Their pledge did not, however, include a promise to take up arms on behalf of the Prophet. When it was time for them to return to Yathrib, Muhammad sent one of his Meccan disciples with them.

In Yathrib Muhammad's message achieved some measure of success so that the following year, AD 622, 72 men and 3 women came to Mecca to pledge their allegiance to Muhammad. Since these represented prominent members of both Aws and Khazraj, the two major rival tribes of Yathrib, and they now promised to protect Muhammad with arms if necessary, Muhammad decided to move to Yathrib. First of all he instructed his followers to leave for Yathrib until the time came when only Muhammad, 'Ali, Zayd and Abū Bakr were left in Mecca. The Meccan leaders were alarmed at the departure of the Muslims, both frightened at the thought of what Muhammad might do next and dismayed at the disregard shown by the Muslims for the ties of kinship. Some forty of the Meccan notables gathered in the council chamber of the town and decided that Muhammad must be killed. That night, however, Muhammad slipped away from the town with Abū Bakr and hid in a nearby cave. 'Ali slept that night in the Prophet's bed in order to fool the assassins who were keeping watch. In the morning, the attackers were furious when they discovered that their prey had evaded them and, for a time, 'Ali's life was in danger. Despite a thorough search for him and the placing of a reward upon his head, Muhammad slipped through the net of the Meccans and reached Yathrib, which was henceforward called Madīnat an-Nabī, the City of the Prophet, or just Medina for short. This move of the Prophet from Mecca to Medina signalled the turnabout in his fortunes. That year, AD 622, the year of the Hijra (Hegira) or Emigration, is the starting point of the Islamic calendar.

When Muhammad first arrived in Medina, his followers were still a minority among the inhabitants but Muhammad himself had been invited there as an arbitrator between the feuding tribes of Aws and Khazraj and therefore his personal prestige was high. His role in the first few years of his presence in Medina was mainly a political one. He was a builder of bridges between the rival factions in the town. In the first year, he set up a confederation of all the groups who lived in Medina. This alliance involved a commitment to fight together against outside enemies, not to make a separate peace with the enemy and not to give refuge to anyone who had committed a crime or an act of aggression or had stirred up dissension. The treaty of alliance made the city of Medina a sanctuary and Muhammad the arbitrator in any disagreements. The Jewish tribes of Medina were included in the alliance with full rights.

In order to strengthen ties between his own followers, Muhammad caused each of those who had come with him from Mecca, the *Muhājirūn* (the emigrants), to adopt one of his followers in Medina, the *Anṣār* (the helpers), as blood-brothers.

The next few years saw Muhammad engaged in two conflicts, an external conflict with the Meccans and an internal conflict with his opponents within Medina. Inside Medina, there was a faction who in Muslim histories are called the *Munāfiqūn* (the dissemblers) who had entered the Medinan confederation but only reluctantly and were now working to destroy it and to bring Muhammad's power and influence to an end. Their leader was 'Abdu'llāh ibn Ubayy who had had great influence in Medina prior to Muhammad's arrival. The Jews of Medina, who had at first welcomed the arrival of a prophet who taught monotheism, later began to resent the growth of his power and also the trading losses that they were incurring due to Meccan enmity. They were reluctant when asked to contribute to the public purse and urged others not to do so either for they saw no obligation on their part to participate in Muhammad's conflict with the Meccans. It has been suggested that due to the increasing hostility of the Jews, some sixteen months after his arrival in Medina, Muhammad changed the direction in which prayer was to be said from Jerusalem to the Ka'ba in Mecca.

The war with the Meccans began as a series of skirmishes and raids upon their caravans. The first real battle was at Badr in 623. The Meccans came out in force to protect a caravan of theirs led by Abū Sufyān of the Umayya family. Although the caravan reached Mecca safely, the Meccans pressed forward aggressively. At Badr, the forces of the Prophet defeated them decisively and many of the leading men of Mecca were killed on that day.

In AD 625, after further raids and hostilities, a Meccan army marched on Medina. Muhammad's forces advanced to Mount Uḥud where they awaited the Meccans. A measure of the strength of the Munāfiqūn in Medina may be made from the fact that, at this critical juncture, 'Abdu'llāh ibn Ubayy deserted the Medinan army and almost one-third of the army went with him back to Medina. At first the Battle of Uḥud went well for the Medinans and the Meccans were on the point of defeat when a portion of the Medinan army broke ranks in search of booty and this exposed their flank. The flow of the battle was reversed and the Medinans were forced to retreat although the victors themselves had been so badly mauled that they were unable to press home their advantage and withdrew.

Muhammad's prestige was now at a low ebb; the Munāfiqūn were jubilant and openly encouraged the Jews to revolt. One tribe of Jews had already provoked Muhammad into expelling it from Medina prior to the Battle of Uḥud and now another tribe were encouraged to resist the order to leave and barricaded themselves into their quarter of the town. Eventually, the Munāfiqūn having failed to come to their aid, this Jewish tribe was forced to capitulate and also left Medina. The Muhājirūn were given their houses.

In AD 627 there occurred the final effort of the Meccans to break the growing power of Muhammad. Allying themselves to the Jewish tribes that had been expelled from Medina and to several other tribes, an army of 10,000 was put into the field. Muhammad could only muster 3,000 men and, because of the activities of the Munāfiqūn, he could not even be sure of all of these. On the advice of Salmān, a Persian convert, however, Muhammad caused a trench to be dug around the town. This novel form of defence discomfited the attackers and after an inconclusive siege they withdrew. During the siege, the last major tribe of Jews left in Medina broke ranks and began negotiations with the Meccans, exposing one of the flanks of the town. After the siege was over, Muhammad turned his attention to this treacherous tribe. They eventually agreed to surrender themselves and Muhammad set as judge over them the chief of one of the clans of the Aws tribe. They were expecting to receive leniency from that quarter because in former days they had been allies of Aws. But the stern chief of the Aws decreed the death of all male members of the tribe. Their women and children were sold into slavery.

Over the next few years, a series of raids and skirmishes increased Muhammad's prestige among the nomadic tribes of the area. Then in AH 6 (AD 628) Muhammad decided to set out for Mecca on pilgrimage. He departed from Medina during one of the months set aside for pilgrimages and each of his companions was armed only with a sword. At Ḥudaybiyya the path of the pilgrims was blocked by the Meccans, who were wary of allowing Muhammad into their town although this was the traditional month of truce and pilgrimage. Eventually, after negotiations, a ten-year truce was agreed under which Muhammad would leave the area but would return the following year and perform the pilgrimage.

Later in the same year, Muhammad launched an attack on a large settlement of Jews at Khaybar who had been active in opposing him and were even trying to set up an alliance to attack Medina. The fortified settlements at this oasis were taken one after another. During that year a number of other expeditions consolidated Muhammad's position.

In February 629, seven years after the emigration, Muhammad returned to Mecca in fulfilment of the previous year's treaty. Most of the Meccans left town, but a few such as his uncle, al-'Abbās, who until this time had been sitting on the fence neither supporting nor opposing his nephew, now extended to him a warm welcome.

An expedition sent by Muhammad to the far north faced disaster when it came across a vastly superior Byzantine army. It was saved from total annihilation by the skilful leadership of Khālid ibn Walīd who in later years was to lead the Muslim armies to important victories.

In late 629, the truce agreed at Ḥudaybiyya was broken through an attack by some of the allies of the Meccans upon some of the allies of the Medinans in Mecca. The Meccans came to the assistance of their allies and so Muhammad decided to raise an army and put an end to the

Meccan threat. It was in early 630 that Muhammad arrived before Mecca with a large army. The Meccans had been unable to raise a significant force. The chief of the Umayya family came to proffer Muhammad his allegiance and the rest of the Meccans soon submitted, although a handful did fight to the bitter end. Muhammad thus entered Mecca in triumph only eight years after fleeing it in danger of his life. His first act was to enter the Ka'ba with 'Ali and destroy the idols therein (see Fig. 1). Shortly afterwards, at Ḥunayn, Muhammad defeated two tribes who had united against him.

The following year, the ninth year of the Hegira, is known as the 'Year of Delegations' for it was in that year that deputations came from all over Arabia tendering their submission to Muhammad. From Yemen in the south and Bahrain in the east they came. It must have been especially pleasing to Muhammad to see the submission of the town of Ṭā'if that had rejected him so contemptuously years before. To each of these places Muhammad sent one of his close disciples to teach them Islam. Even the Christian tribes of the north came to acknowledge Muhammad's suzerainty and to pay the poll-tax which Islam decreed for non-Muslim subjects.

That year Muhammad decided not to perform the pilgrimage to Mecca but entrusted to 'Ali the task of warning those who were still polytheists that they would no longer be allowed access to the Ka'ba. The following year Muhammad performed what came to be known as the 'Farewell Pilgrimage' to Mecca. This pilgrimage became the model for all subsequent pilgrimages to Mecca.

Shortly after his return to Medina, in the summer of 632, Muhammad fell ill, and after a few weeks of ill-health he died.

As we have already noted, during the Meccan phase of his ministry, Muhammad taught a very simple religious ethic centred on the need to put aside idol-worship and turn to the one true God. Later in Medina these teachings were expanded. Three fundamental tenets remained at the core of the religion:

1. Belief in one God and rejection of all idols;
2. Belief in Muhammad as the messenger of God;
3. Belief in the Day of Judgement.

But to these were added a number of obligatory ritual observances:

1. Obligatory Prayer, five times a day;
2. Fasting for the month of Ramaḍān;
3. Paying of alms;
4. Pilgrimage to the Ka'ba;
5. *Jihād*, or Holy War against idolators.

To these were added a number of laws regulating social transactions such as marriage, divorce, inheritance, etc. as well as a moral and ethical code enjoining chastity, honesty, tolerance, forgiveness, etc. These in brief were the teachings enshrined in the Qur'an and promulgated by Muhammad. They were to become the foundations of the Islamic community.

The major social achievement of Muhammad's ministry was the welding together of a hundred or more disparate and feuding tribes into one nation, a union that overrode the ties of kinship and the enmity of blood-feuds. So united was this people that the might of neither Byzantium nor Persia could stand before it. So powerful was the impetus given to this nation by Islam that within one generation it had conquered territory stretching from Tunisia to the borders of India and within a few generations this backward and primitive people became the centre of civilisation in the Western world and remained thus for almost four hundred years.

As to Muhammad's personal life, he led a simple existence. Although by the end of his life he was a powerful and rich ruler, he contented himself with plain clothing, simple food and austere surroundings. His judgement was renowned both in dealing with his adversaries and in settling disputes between individuals and clans. In his political dealings he never used force where negotiations would suffice nor did he initiate aggression but only moved against those who had already demonstrated their hostile intentions. He was a gentle man, to whom the sight of human suffering caused sorrow and pain and he would grieve if ever his followers went beyond what was immediately necessary in the process of fighting and killing. The few executions that were carried out on his orders were of men who had continually striven to undermine his position over a long period of time despite many warnings or who had professed Islam and then betrayed their fellow believers. To other enemies he was often magnanimous in victory to such an extent that his own followers sometimes complained that he treated his enemies better than he treated his followers.

The fact that Muhammad took more than a dozen wives has at times occasioned critical comment in the West. But a number of facts should be realised in connection with this. Muhammad at first took only one wife, Khadīja, and he was happy with her and took no other wife until she died after twenty-five years of marriage. Muhammad himself was fifty years of age by this time. It should not be imagined that Muhammad's later marriages were out of sexual desire. They were contracted mostly for political or humanitarian reasons. These later wives were either widows of followers of his who had been killed in battle and had been left without a protector, or they belonged to important families or clans whom it was necessary to honour in order to strengthen alliances. Many were of advanced years and only one had not been married previously – 'Ā'isha, the daughter of his close companion, Abū Bakr, whom the Prophet wished to honour. Indeed, that his later marriages were not due to a voluptuous nature is indicated by the fact that although his first wife, Khadīja, bore a total of eight children, only one more child was born to Muhammad after Khadīja's death.

After the death of the Prophet, an *ad hoc* assembly of Muslims chose Abū Bakr to be the leader of the Islamic community, the *Khalīfa* (Caliph). Abū Bakr's Caliphate only lasted two years (AD 632–4) during which the most important event was the suppression of a revolt of many Arab tribes who had apostasised from Islam immediately upon the Prophet's death.

Abū Bakr appointed as his successor 'Umar. During 'Umar's Caliphate (AD 634–44) the Muslim armies achieved the most remarkable victories against both the Persian and Byzantine Empires. The succession to 'Umar was decided by a council of six appointed by the Caliph. This council made 'Uthmān of the Umayya family Caliph. 'Uthmān ruled for twelve years (AD 644–56) but became very unpopular towards the end of his life. He was assassinated in 656 and 'Ali was acclaimed Caliph. But Mu'āwiya of the Umayya family rose in revolt. 'Ali's assassination in 661 paved the way for Mu'āwiya to become Caliph.

Mu'āwiya moved the capital of the Islamic Empire to Damascus and instituted the Umayyad dynasty. This dynasty held sway until AH 132/AD 750* with a total of fourteen rulers. They are generally considered by many Muslim historians to have been corrupt, irreligious and treacherous. Only 'Umar II (AD 717–20) is generally regarded in a favourable light.

The revolt of Abū Muslim in Khurāsān overturned the Umayyad dynasty and put into power the 'Abbasid Caliphs, who were descended from the Prophet's uncle al-'Abbās (Spain remained in the hands of the Umayyads, however). The 'Abbasids made Kūfa in Iraq their capital, but later in 763 they began the construction of a new capital, Baghdad. The 'Abbasids wielded real power for about 150 years but thereafter came increasingly under the control of their Turkish mercenaries and then under the power of a succession of dynasties that controlled Baghdad, the seat of the Caliphate.

The Islamic lands were split up with different dynasties controlling the various parts. For a brief period, one ruler might control a large part of the Islamic lands but only with the rise of the Ottoman Empire and the conquests of Selim the Grim in the early 16th century did most of the Islamic lands (excluding Iran, India and Central Asia) come under a lengthy period of stable unified rule. The Ottoman Empire was broken up at the end of the First World War and the Ottoman Caliphate terminated in 1924.

* Henceforth dates will be given as Hijrī dates first, followed by Gregorian dates, thus: 132/750.

2

The Question of the Succession to Muhammad

The succession to Muhammad is clearly the key question in Shi'i Islam and the principal factor separating Shi'is from the Sunni majority. The question is not only who was the successor of Muhammad but also the nature of the role of this successor, for it is on both these points that Shi'is and Sunnis disagree.

On the death of Muhammad, an *ad hoc* assemblage of a number of the notables in Islam elected, by general consensus, Abū Bakr to be the Caliph or successor to Muhammad. This was envisaged as being a temporal appointment designed to continue the position of Muhammad as the head of the city of Medina and of a confederacy of tribes, which was the emerging Muslim state. A conspicuous absentee at this meeting of election was 'Ali, the Prophet's cousin and son-in-law. There were a number of persons who considered that in view of a number of statements made by Muhammad in his lifetime, 'Ali should have occupied the leading position – not only as temporal head (Caliph) but also as spiritual head (Imam).

In order to understand the personality of 'Ali and his position it is necessary to return to the very beginning of Islamic history and trace, firstly, 'Ali's part in it and, secondly, the close relationship between the Prophet and 'Ali. Thirdly, it is also necessary to examine those Traditions, many accepted by both Sunnis and Shi'is, that are considered by Shi'is to mean that 'Ali was the rightful successor of Muhammad.

The Prophet was brought up in the house of Abū Ṭālib, 'Ali's father, and thus Muhammad was very close to his young cousin from the time of the latter's birth. Indeed, the two may be regarded as foster-brothers, despite the difference in age between them.

'Ali was only nine years old[1] when Muhammad first became aware of his prophetic mission. After Khadīja, the Prophet's wife, 'Ali was the first person to acknowledge the Prophet's mission and become a believer.[2] After 'Ali's conversion Zayd became a Muslim and then Abū Bakr and others.

It was three years after the onset of Muhammad's mission that he decided to make a public announcement of it. The occasion he chose was a gathering of his own clan. For Shi'is this meeting has a further significance, for, according to both Sunni and Shi'i sources, at this meeting Muhammad made a significant statement regarding 'Ali's relationship to himself. The following is an account of that episode according to the history of Ṭabarī, who is regarded by both Sunnis and Shi'is as one of the most reliable of the chroniclers of the life of the Prophet. Ṭabarī describes how, after the revelation of the Qur'anic verse: 'Warn your closest relatives',[3] Muhammad prepared a meal and invited some forty members of the clan of 'Abdu'l-Muṭṭalib (i.e. the Banū Hāshim). After the meal Muhammad was about to address the company when Abū Lahab made a jest and dispersed the gathering. And so Muhammad invited them again the following evening to a meal. The following is a description of what occurred after the meal in the words of 'Ali as recorded by Ṭabarī:

> Then the Apostle of God addressed them saying: 'O family of 'Abdu'l-Muṭṭalib, by God, I do not know of anyone among the Arabs who has brought his people anything better than what I have brought you. I have brought you the best of this world and the next. God Almighty has ordered me to call you to Him. And which of you will assist me in this Cause and become my brother, my trustee and my successor among you.' And they all held back from this while I ['Ali], although I was the youngest of them in age, the most diseased in eyesight, the most corpulent in body and thinnest in the legs, said: 'I, O Prophet of God, will be your helper in this matter.' And he put his arm around my neck and said: 'This is my brother, my trustee and my successor among you, so listen to him and obey.' And so the people arose and they were joking, saying to Abū Ṭālib ['Ali's father]: 'He has ordered you to listen to your son and obey him.'[4]

This passage is interpreted by Shi'is as indicating that from this early stage in Muhammad's career and at a time when 'Ali was only about thirteen years old, Muhammad had already picked 'Ali out as his successor.

Over the ensuing years 'Ali was constantly at Muhammad's side. When the night came for the flight from Mecca to Medina, it was 'Ali who took on the dangerous task of sleeping in the Prophet's bed and thus fooling the assassins that had been sent to murder the Prophet. After Muhammad's successful escape, 'Ali remained in Mecca long enough to settle the Prophet's debts and then together with some of the Muslim women he too slipped away to Medina.

A short while after the arrival of the exiles in Medina another significant event occurred. Muhammad decreed that each Muslim should become the brother of another Muslim. Thus Abū Bakr and 'Umar became brothers, as did Ṭalḥa and Zubayr, and 'Uthmān and 'Abdu'r-Raḥmān ibn Awf. All authorities, whether Sunni or Shi'i, are agreed that Muhammad singled out 'Ali to be his own brother. The following is the account as given in the *Saḥīḥ* of at-Tirmidhī, a collection of Traditions accepted as authoritative by the Sunnis:

The Apostle of God made brothers between his companions, and 'Ali came to him with tears in his eyes crying: 'O Apostle of God! You have made brethren among your companions but you have not made anyone my brother.' And the Apostle of God said to him: 'You are my brother in this world and the next.'[5]

During the Medinan period 'Ali acted as Muhammad's secretary and deputy. Whenever there were important documents to be written, such as the treaty of Ḥudaybiyya, it was 'Ali who wrote them. The Prophet's daughter, Fāṭima, was given in marriage to 'Ali and the children of this marriage, Hasan and Husayn, were the only grandchildren of the Prophet to survive into adult life.

'Ali was one of the most courageous and able men in the Muslim army. He was appointed the standard-bearer at the battles of both Badr and Khaybar. At Khaybar (AH 7) the following Tradition is related by several Sunni and Shi'i histories. This is the version found in a Sunni collection of Traditions, the *Saḥīḥ* of Muslim:

The Apostle of God said on the day of Khaybar: 'I shall certainly give this banner to a man who loves God and his Apostle and through whom God will give victory.' 'Umar ibn al-Khaṭṭāb said: 'I never wished for leadership except on that day.' And he also said: 'And so I leapt up towards it hoping to claim it as a right.' And the Apostle of God summoned 'Ali, the son of Abū Ṭālib, and gave it to him and said: 'Go! And do not turn aside until God gives you victory.'[6]

When the Prophet left to go on his longest expedition, to Tabūk, 'Ali was left in charge at Medina. According to some accounts, 'Ali felt insulted to be left with the women and children while, according to others, rumours were spread that 'Ali had been left behind because it was feared he would bring misfortune to the expedition. In any case, 'Ali went to the Prophet voicing his discontent at being left behind. It was at this time, according to numerous Sunni and Shi'i Traditionists, that the famous *Ḥadīth* of *Manzilat Hārūn* (position of Aaron) was revealed. According to this Tradition, Muhammad said to 'Ali: 'Are you not content to be with respect to me as Aaron was to Moses, except that after me there shall be no other Prophet.'[7] The implication was that 'Ali was to be Muhammad's chief assistant in his lifetime and his successor after him.

An episode that has been given great prominence in Shi'i works is called the episode of the *Mubāhala*. The usual Shi'i accounts of this episode are as follows: Muhammad in the ninth year of the Hegira sent out a series of letters to nearby rulers, summoning them to accept Islam. At Najrān, which was a Christian town on the route between Medina and the Yemen, the leaders assembled to decide what they should do.

After some discussion it was pointed out that Jesus had prophesied the Paraclete or Comforter, whose son would conquer the Earth. However, it was felt this could not refer to Muhammad who had no son. Then a great book called *al-Jāmi'* was consulted which contained the writings and traditions of all the prophets. In this book reference was found to how Adam had seen a vision of one brilliant light surrounded by four other lights and was told by God that these were five of his descendants. Similar things were found in the writings of Abraham, Moses and Jesus. And so it was decided to send a deputation of their learned men to Medina to ascertain the truth. At Medina, after a great debate, it was decided to engage in *Mubāhala* (mutual cursing), referring the matter to God and calling down God's curse on whomever was the liar. It was at this time that the verse of *Mubāhala* (Qur'an 3:61) was revealed. The contest was set for the next day and all the people of Medina came out to witness it. Muhammad came out with only 'Ali, Fāṭima, Hasan and Husayn and they stood under a cloak. The Christians asked Muhammad why he had not brought the leaders of his religion and Muhammad replied that God had commanded this. Then the Christians remembered what they had read in *al-Jāmi'* and became convinced that Muhammad was the figure prophesied by Jesus. The Christians withdrew from the contest and agreed to pay tribute. From this episode, Muhammad, 'Ali, Fāṭima, Hasan and Husayn became known as *Ahl al-Kisā* (the people of the cloak).

When the Qur'anic *Sūra* of Bara'a was revealed towards the end of the year AH 9 and Abū Bakr was sent to read it to the people of Mecca, Muhammad sent 'Ali out after him and caused him to return. Then the *Sūra* was given to 'Ali to take to Mecca to read. When questioned regarding this, the Prophet is reported, in both Sunni and Shi'i sources, to have said: 'Gabriel came to me and said: "Do not let it [the reading of the *Sūra*] be performed by anyone other than yourself or someone from you [i.e. your family] on your behalf."'[8]

'Ali's many personal qualities are amply attested to in various histories and collections of Traditions. Among the statements regarding 'Ali and his family made by the Prophet and accepted as authentic by both Sunnis and Shi'is are the following:

1. There is no youth braver than 'Ali.[9]
2. No-one but a believer loves 'Ali and no-one but a hypocrite (*munāfiq*) hates 'Ali.[10]
3. I am from 'Ali and 'Ali is from me.[11]
4. The truth circulates with him ('Ali) wherever he goes.[12]
5. I am the City of Knowledge and 'Ali is its Gate (*Bāb*).[13]
6. On one occasion the Prophet was about to eat some poultry and he said: 'O God! Send me the man you love most among mankind to eat this

bird with me.' And 'Ali came and ate with him.[14]

7. The Prophet said in reply to someone who had complained about 'Ali: 'What do you think of one who loves God and his Prophet and who in turn is loved by God and his Prophet?' Also: 'The most loved of women to the Prophet of God is Fāṭima and the most loved of men is 'Ali.'[15]

8. On one occasion, the Prophet called 'Ali and began whispering to him. After a time those present began saying: 'He has been a long time whispering to his cousin.' Later, the Prophet said: 'It was not I that was whispering to him but God.'[16]

9. The Prophet took the hand of Hasan and Husayn and said: 'Whoever loves me and loves these two and loves their mother and father, will be with me in my station on the Day of Resurrection.'[17]

10. The Prophet said: 'Hasan and Husayn are the chiefs of the youths of paradise.'[18]

It was during the last year of the Prophet's life that, according to Shi'is, he confirmed 'Ali's position as his successor. The occasion was the Farewell Pilgrimage when the Prophet performed the pilgrimage to Mecca for the last time. Having completed the rites of the Pilgrimage, the Prophet set out on the return journey to Medina, accompanied by a large concourse of the Muslims, including all of his leading disciples. At a place called Ghadīr Khumm, Muhammad caused the caravan to be stopped and from an improvised pulpit delivered an address. Once again, the principal Sunni and Shi'i sources show no disagreement over the facts of the episode. The following is the account given in Ibn Ḥanbal, a Sunni collection of *ḥadīth*:

> We were with the Apostle of God in his journey and we stopped at Ghadīr Khumm. We performed the obligatory prayer together and a place was swept for the Apostle under two trees and he performed the mid-day prayer. And then he took 'Ali by the hand and said to the people: 'Do you not acknowledge that I have a greater claim on each of the believers than they have on themselves?' And they replied: 'Yes!' And he took 'Ali's hand and said: 'Of whomsoever I am Lord [*Mawla*], then 'Ali is also his Lord. O God! Be Thou the supporter of whoever supports 'Ali and the enemy of whoever opposes him.' And 'Umar met him ['Ali] after this and said to him: 'Congratulations, O son of Abū Ṭālib! Now morning and evening [i.e. forever] you are the master of every believing man and woman.'[19]

Finally there is the highly controversial episode in the last days of Muhammad's life which is usually called the Episode of Pen and Paper. Muhammad, while in his terminal illness and only days before his death, called for pen and paper. The following is the account related by al-Bukhārī, the Sunni Traditionist, on the authority of Ibn 'Abbās:

> When the Prophet's illness became serious, he said: 'Bring me writing materials

that I may write for you something, after which you will not be led into error.' 'Umar said: 'The illness has overwhelmed the Prophet. We have the Book of God and that is enough for us.' Then the people differed about this and spoke many words. And he [the Prophet] said: 'Leave me! There ought not to be quarrelling in my presence.' And Ibn 'Abbās went out saying: 'The greatest of all calamities is what intervened between the Apostle and his writing.'[20]

Shi'is claim that what Muhammad wished to write down was the confirmation of 'Ali's successorship. Sunnis have advanced various alternative explanations. Shi'is also claim that the Prophet died with his head in 'Ali's lap. Some Sunni Traditions support this while others state that the Prophet's head was on the lap of his wife, 'Ā'isha.

To 'Ali was given a number of privileges not accorded to the other companions of the Prophet. Apart from the fact that the Prophet's daughter was given to 'Ali in marriage, when many others including Abū Bakr and 'Umar had been suitors, 'Ali was the only man allowed to come and go as he pleased in the Prophet's house. At one stage the Prophet ordered all the doors of the various houses opening onto the Mosque of the Prophet in Medina to be blocked off, except for the doors from his own house and from that of 'Ali.[21]

There are also a number of other statements which both Sunni and Shi'i sources agree were made by Muhammad and to which Shi'is point as evidence of the position of 'Ali and his family and the fact that 'Ali was Muhammad's successor:

1. *Ḥadīth* of the Two Weighty Matters *(ath-Thaqalayn)*

This is a very widely reported statement of Muhammad. The following is the version in the Sunni collection of *Ḥadīth* by Ibn Ḥanbal: 'The Apostle of God said: "I have left among you two weighty matters which if you cling to them you shall not be led into error after me. One of them is greater than the other: The Book of God which is a rope stretched from Heaven to Earth and my progeny, the people of my house. These two shall not be parted until they return to the pool [of Paradise]."'[22]

This *ḥadīth*, which is repeated in many slightly variant forms, is reported by some Traditionists to have been uttered by Muhammad on the road between Mecca and Medina. There has been some disagreement as to exactly who is meant by the phrase 'the people of my house' (*Ahl al-Bayt)*. Some Sunni sources state that Muhammad's wives should be included. But Shi'i writers point to several Traditions that can be found in Sunni as well as Shi'i sources that confine the meaning of this phrase to 'Ali, Fāṭima, Hasan and Husayn. For example, when the verse of *al-Mubāhala* was revealed (see above), several Sunni sources record that the Prophet then defined the people of his house as being the four persons under his cloak.[23] Similarly, when the verse of purification (Qur'an 33:33, see p. 155) was revealed, according to the Sunni

Traditionist, at-Tirmidhī, its meaning was confined to these four persons.[24]

2. The *ḥadīth* of the Safīna (Noah's Ark)

Once again many Sunni sources have reported this Tradition in various forms: 'My family among you are like Noah's Ark. He who sails on it will be safe, but he who holds back from it will perish.'[25]

3. On one occasion when four of the Muslims complained to the Prophet concerning something that 'Ali had done, the Prophet grew angry and said: 'What do you want from 'Ali? 'Ali is from me and I am from 'Ali. He is the guardian [*walī*] of every believer after me.'[26] And in another context: 'You are my successor [i.e. guardian of the religion, *walī*] in this world and the next.'[27]

4. The Prophet is reported to have said: 'No one may execute my affairs except myself and 'Ali.'[28]

5. The Prophet said: 'As for 'Ali, Fāṭima, Hasan and Husayn, I am at war with whoever fights against these and at peace with whoever is at peace with these.'[29]

Apart from these and the previously-quoted Traditions which are accepted by both Sunnis and Shi'is, the Shi'is have numerous other Traditions extolling 'Ali:

1. The Fourth Imam is reported to have said: "The Apostle of God taught 'Ali a matter [*harf*] which opened up one thousand matters each of which in turn opened up a thousand matters.'[30]

2. 'Ali said: 'I am Muhammad and Muhammad is I.'[31]

3. 'Ali said in the *Ḥadīth an-Nūrāniyya*: 'Muhammad is the Seal of the Prophets [*khātim al-anbiyā*] and I am the Seal of the Successors [*khātim al wasiyyīn*].'[32]

In addition to these *ḥadīth*, certain verses of the Qur'an are held to relate to 'Ali and his succession to Muhammad:

1. 'You are a warner and to every people there is a guide.'[33] Many sources, including even Sunni ones such as as-Suyūṭī, acknowledge that when this verse was revealed, Muhammad said: 'I am the warner and you, O 'Ali, are the guide and through you will be guided those who are to be guided.'[34]

2. 'Your guardian [*walī*] can only be God, His apostle and those who say their prayers, pay alms [*zakāt*] and bow down before God'[35] The word *walī* can mean either friend, helper or master. Many of the commentators both Sunni and Shi'i are agreed that this verse refers to 'Ali and was revealed after 'Ali had given his ring away to someone in need who had entered the mosque while prayers were in progress.[36] The verse itself can be translated: 'Those who pay alms while bowing down before God,' thus referring more closely to this episode.

The Events at the Saqīfa

If, as the Shi'is assert, Muhammad had clearly indicated his desire that 'Ali should be his successor, how did it come about that Abū Bakr was elected the first Caliph? This is a very complex matter and central to the whole issue is what occurred at the Saqīfa (Portico) of the Banū Sā'ida, a branch of Khazraj tribe of Medina. The facts of what happened are, in broad terms, agreed by the most reliable of both Sunni and Shi'i writers.[37] When Muhammad died, his daughter, Fāṭima, her husband, 'Ali, and the rest of the family of Hāshim, gathered around the body preparing it for burial. Unbeknown to them, two other groups were gathering in the city. One group consisted of Abū Bakr, 'Umar, Abū 'Ubayda and other prominent Meccans (the *Muhājirūn*) and the second of the most important of the Medinans (the *Anṣār*). This second group was gathering in the portico of the Banū Sā'ida. It was reported to Abū Bakr that the Anṣār were contemplating pledging their loyalty to Sa'd ibn 'Ubāda, chief of the Khazraj. And so Abū Bakr and his group hurried to the Saqīfa. One of the Anṣār spoke first saying that as the Anṣār had been the ones who supported and gave victory to Islam and since the Meccans were only guests in Medina, the leader of the community should be from the Anṣār. Abū Bakr replied to this very diplomatically. He began by praising the virtues of the Anṣār, but then he went on to point out that the Muhājirūn (the Meccans) were the first people in Islam and were closer in kinship to the Prophet. The Arabs would accept leadership only from Quraysh and so Quraysh should be the rulers and the Anṣār their ministers. One of the Anṣār proposed: 'Let there be one ruler from us and one ruler from you. For we do not begrudge you this matter but we fear to have ruling over us a people whose fathers and brothers we have killed (in fighting between Mecca and Medina before the conquest of Mecca by Muhammad).'[38] And so the argument went back and forth until Abū Bakr proposed: 'Give your allegiance to one of these two men: Abū 'Ubayda or 'Umar.' And 'Umar replied: 'While you are still alive? No! It is not for anyone to hold you back from the position in which the Apostle placed you. So stretch out your hand.' And Abū Bakr stretched out his hand and 'Umar gave him his allegiance. One by one, slowly at first, and then rushing forward in a mass, the others did likewise.

A pro-Shi'i historian, Ya'qūbī, has recorded that one of the Anṣār did briefly advance the claim of 'Ali during the discussions at the Saqīfa but even from Ya'qūbī's account it is clear that there was no real discussion of this claim.[39]

It is possible to speculate as to the reasons why Abū Bakr was elected to the leadership. Certainly clan rivalry played a great part. Within

Quraysh there was a certain amount of envy and enmity towards the prestige enjoyed by the house of Hāshim. Thus 'Umar is reported to have said to 'Ali's cousin at a later date: 'The people did not like having the Prophethood and Caliphate joined together in your house.'[40] Abū Bakr, however, came from a relatively insignificant clan which had no pretensions to power. The Anṣār had been contemplating choosing the chief of Khazraj as their leader and so when Abū Bakr came forward as a candidate, the Aws tribe who had been the great rival of Khazraj in Medina were only too eager to have this alternative. Khazraj themselves were not totally united and several leading men of that tribe were among the first to pay obedience to Abū Bakr, presumably having some grudge against their chief. And so, all in all, Abū Bakr was an expedient choice for the majority, although it cannot be denied that he enjoyed considerable prestige in the community anyway.

With respect to the above speech by Abū Bakr at the Saqīfa, in which he refuted the claims of the Anṣār to the leadership and advanced the claims of Quraysh, Shi'i historians have pointed out that with respect to each of the points which Abū Bakr mentioned, 'Ali was superior to Abū Bakr. Thus if Quraysh were closer in kinship to the Prophet than the Anṣār, then 'Ali was closer than Abū Bakr. If Quraysh were first to accept Islam, then 'Ali was the first of them to do this. If Quraysh were more entitled to leadership among the Arabs than the Anṣār on account of their nobility, then 'Ali and the house of Hāshim were the most noble clan within Quraysh. And 'Ali's services to Islam and his close personal companionship with the Prophet, were at least equal, if not superior, to Abū Bakr's. Moreover, if selection of the leader was to have been by consensus, then why was the house of Hāshim, the house of the Prophet, not consulted? The best that can be said of the affair at the Saqīfa is that, in the words of 'Umar, it was a *falta*, which means an affair concluded in haste and without reflection.[41]

Both Sunni and Shi'i sources are agreed that after allegiance had been given to Abū Bakr at the Saqīfa and at the mosque, 'Umar with a crowd of armed men marched to 'Ali's house demanding that he also pledge his allegiance to Abū Bakr. It is even indicated that a threat was made to burn down 'Ali's house if he refused. Words were exchanged, and according to some accounts, even blows, until Fāṭima, 'Ali's wife and the daughter of the Prophet, appeared and put the attackers to shame by threatening to make a personal public appeal.

Both Sunni and Shi'i sources agree that 'Ali was urged by such persons as his uncle al-'Abbās, and even Abū Sufyān of the house of Umayya, to set himself up as an alternative leader and to have allegiance paid to him. Abū Sufyān even offered to fill Medina with armed men to enforce 'Ali's leadership.[42] It is impossible to assess, however, how strong the party that looked to 'Ali at this time was. But 'Ali refused to split the community, particularly when, shortly after Abū Bakr assumed the Caliphate, a large number of the Arabs apostatised from Islam and a campaign had to be waged against them. Under the Caliphates of 'Umar and of 'Uthmān also, 'Ali did not advance his claim.

There is disagreement between Sunni and Shi'i historians as to 'Ali's attitude to the Caliphate of Abū Bakr and later to those of 'Umar and 'Uthmān. Sunni historians are anxious to portray 'Ali as having been loyal to the leadership of the first three Caliphates and indeed a trusted adviser in their councils. Some of these sources even state that 'Ali gave his allegiance to Abū Bakr on the day of the Saqīfa. The Shi'i historians, of course, completely reject this view. They portray 'Ali as feeling deeply hurt that his rights had been usurped in this underhand manner and only refraining from open rejection of Abū Bakr in order to avoid dissension and strife at a critical time. Shi'i sources maintain that 'Ali did not in fact give his allegiance to the new Caliph until after Fāṭima's death, which occurred six months after the death of the Prophet.

Conflict between the Prophet's family and the new Caliph began from the day after the death of the Prophet. Fāṭima laid claim to the estate of Fadak, which had been the personal property of the Prophet and had come to him out of the booty of the expedition to Khaybar. Abū Bakr refused this claim, stating that the property belonged to the whole community, the Prophet having said: 'No one shall inherit from me, but what I leave is for alms.'

During the brief two-year period of Abū Bakr's Caliphate, whatever initial support there may have been for 'Ali's candidature melted away in the face of 'Ali's own refusal to advance a claim. However, despite this, there was a handful of men who steadfastly refused to give their allegiance to Abū Bakr or to anyone other than 'Ali. Four of these men, 'Ammār, Miqdād, Abū Dharr and Salmān were acclaimed by Shi'is as the first four of their number and, according to many Traditions, these four were shortly joined by another three.

Shi'i historians scornfully point out that whereas the theoretical justification for the choice of Abū Bakr as Caliph was that this was the consensus of the Muslims, even this claim cannot be made for 'Umar's succession to Abū Bakr. Abū Bakr, on his death-bed, appointed 'Umar as his successor and secured his succession by obtaining pledges of support for 'Umar from several prominent persons. Once again, 'Ali was passed over and was not even consulted.

Under 'Umar's Caliphate, 'Ali remained withdrawn from public affairs but still refusing to encourage sedition by advancing an alternative claim. The Sunni historians once again minimise the disagreements,[43] whereas the Shi'is show 'Ali openly disagreeing with some of 'Umar's decisions and publicly showing his contempt for the Caliph on several occasions.[44]

'Umar appointed a council of six men to decide the leadership after him. Although the council included 'Ali, it was weighted in such a way as to make it unlikely that he would be elected. Two of the members of the council, Sa'd and 'Abdu'r-Raḥmān who were cousins, were naturally inclined to support 'Uthman, who was 'Abdu'r-Raḥmān's brother-in-law, and moreover, under 'Umar's terms for setting up a council, the casting vote was to be given to 'Abdu'r-Raḥmān.

The most commonly quoted Traditions state that the result of the deliberations of the council in 644 was that 'Abdu'r-Raḥmān offered the Caliphate to 'Ali on the condition that he should rule in accordance with the Qur'an, the example of the Prophet and the precedents established by the first two Caliphs. 'Abdu'r-Raḥmān must have known of 'Ali's disagreement with some of the policies of the first two Caliphs and so it was inevitable that 'Ali would refuse to bind himself to follow their precedents. 'Abdu'r-Raḥmān then offered the Caliphate to 'Uthmān on the same condition and he accepted.

Even those historians who are staunchly Sunni can scarcely disguise the fact that 'Uthmān's Caliphate was something of a disaster for Islam. In place of the strict piety, simplicity and probity that had characterised the leadership of the community under Muhammad and the first two Caliphs, 'Uthmān's leadership was marked by nepotism and a love of wealth and luxury. He was a weak-minded man who allowed his relative, Marwān, to dominate him and to run the affairs of the community. 'Uthmān was of the house of Umayya and soon members of this family were placed in the highest positions in the community, despite the fact that, in former days, this family had been the most implacable and the most powerful of the enemies of the Prophet in Mecca and had led the Meccans against the Prophet once he was established in Medina.

Soon there was disaffection in the provinces of the rapidly expanding Muslim empire. In Egypt there was a rising against their Governor, a foster-brother of 'Uthmān, who was one of the few people that the Prophet himself had condemned to death at the conquest of Mecca for the crime of interpolating the Qur'an and apostatising (he had been saved by 'Uthmān's intervention). In Kūfa (Iraq), the Governor, 'Uthmān's half-brother, was disgracing himself by appearing drunk in public. Delegations from Egypt and Iraq arrived in Medina in 656 voicing strong protests to the Caliph. They found support among many of the prominent citizens of Medina such as Zubayr and Ṭalḥa, who each had aspirations for the Caliphate, and 'Ā'isha, the wife of the Prophet, who supported Ṭalḥa.

'Ali was placed in a difficult position. The rebel delegations appealed to him to support their protests and he certainly sympathised with their grievances. But 'Ali, also, was not one to foment discord or to support rebellion. 'Uthmān appealed to him to placate the rebels and 'Ali did his best to mediate, urging the Caliph, at the same time, to alter his policies. However, in the end, after the rebels found themselves betrayed by the Caliph, 'Uthmān's house was attacked and he was killed.

Immediately after the murder of 'Uthmān, a crowd surrounded 'Ali urging him to accept the Caliphate. 'Ali was at first reluctant to accept, given the circumstances, but he was urged to do so from all sides. The Muhājirūn, the Anṣār and the delegations from the provinces were all urging acceptance upon him. So eventually he consented. The year was 656; it was 24 years since the death of the Prophet of Islam; after almost a quarter of a century in the wilderness, 'Ali had come to the position that he had considered rightfully his all along.

3

The Lives of the Imams and Early Divisions among the Shi'is

In considering Shi'i history, especially in the early period, it is necessary to differentiate between the traditional history as recorded by the Shi'i writers and the results of modern critical scholarship. In this chapter the traditional view will be examined and the results of the research of modern scholars will be found in the next chapter. The first part of the life of 'Ali has already been dealt with in the previous chapter and what historical information is available regarding the Twelfth Imam will be found in Chapter 8.

Although a great number of histories of the Imams have been written by the Shi'is of every generation, many of them are of little use in constructing biographies of the Imams for they were written with a different purpose than the conveying of biographical information. They are largely anecdotal and apologetic in nature, seeking to prove certain points about the Imams. Among the specific points that Shi'i writers sought to prove about each Imam were: that their births were miraculous, the baby Imam being born already circumcised and with his umbilical cord already severed; that they spoke immediately on birth (and sometimes from within their mother's womb) praising God; that each was specifically designated by the preceding Imam (or in the case of 'Ali by Muhammad); and that each performed miracles and was possessed of supernatural knowledge. Most Shi'i writers consider that the Imams were all martyred but this is evidently a late view since some of the earliest works specifically refute this with regard to some of the Imams.[1] Since most of the Imams do not appear in the standard non-Shi'i histories either, the Imams have tended to become quasi-legendary rather than historical figures.

The Imamate of 'Ali

The early life of the fourth Caliph and first Shi'i Imam, Abu'l-Ḥasan

ʿAlī ibn Abī Ṭālib, known as Amīru'l-Mu'minīn, and his actions under the first three Caliphs have been recorded in the previous chapter. The turbulent years of his brief ministry as Caliph will be considered in this chapter.

It can be said that ʿAli's succession to the Caliphate was approved of and accepted by the vast majority of Muslims in Medina and also in most of the provinces of the Empire. He was truly a Caliph chosen by a consensus of all the Muslims. After the initial euphoria wore off, however, it became clear that he was faced with grave internal problems. During ʿUthmān's Caliphate, all the important governorships of the Muslim Empire had gone to members of the Umayyad family, and now this family, led by its most able member, Muʿāwiya, the Governor of Syria, refused to accept ʿAli's Caliphate, urging vengeance for ʿUthmān and implying that ʿAli was giving shelter to the murderers and was therefore guilty of complicity. In another direction, Ṭalḥa and Zubayr, two of the most prominent companions of the Prophet, were galled at the accession to the Caliphate of a younger man, and realising that they would now never have a chance to accede to that position withdrew to Mecca and linked up with ʿĀ'isha, the daughter of Abū Bakr and widow of the Prophet, who had a long-standing grudge against ʿAli. These three proceeded to Baṣra and raised a rebellion, again in the name of vengeance for ʿUthmān, although all three were as much responsible for the murder as anyone.

At first, all went well for ʿAli. He was, after all, a great military leader and was able to defeat the Baṣran rebels at the Battle of al-Jamal (the camel). Zubayr and Ṭalḥa were killed in the fighting and ʿĀ'isha captured and sent back to Medina with the honour due to the widow of the Prophet.

However, soon the tide of events began to turn against ʿAli. One of the problems that beset him was his own forthright nature. He refused to allow political expediency to dictate to him where he felt a matter of principle was at stake. He set about immediately trying to put right every aspect of the life of the community that he felt had deviated from the intention of the Prophet. He pressed ahead with this regardless of the fact he was making powerful and influential enemies among many who had benefited under the previous Caliphs. These persons went over to Muʿāwiya who now came out in open revolt in Syria.

It was at this point, in 36/656, after the Battle of the Camel, that ʿAli moved his headquarters from Medina to Kūfa in Iraq. From this time until the middle of the second Islamic century (mid-8th century AD) when Baghdad was built, Kūfa was to remain the main centre of Shiʿism in the Islamic world. However, Kūfa's support for the Shiʿi cause was to prove a mixed blessing. The vacillating nature of the Kūfans was to cause

Shiʻism as many problems as it was to bring benefits.

In 37/657 Muʻāwiya marched towards Kūfa. Reluctantly, ʻAli came forward to meet him and battle was joined at Ṣiffīn. Of the two armies, ʻAli's was filled with veteran companions of the Prophet, particularly the Medinan Anṣār, and pious readers of the Qur'an, while Muʻāwiya's side could only boast a handful of companions of the Prophet and consisted for the most part of Arab tribes who had joined Islam late and had been drawn to the frontier provinces by the prospect of rich booty. Also, Muʻāwiya was an expert intriguer and gladly paved the way for a defection to his side with promises of money.

The Battle of Ṣiffīn was prolonged, bloody and inconclusive. It ended in a call for arbitration. But ʻAli, hampered by the fickle nature of the Kūfans, was unable to have the man of his choice represent him, and, although accounts of the arbitration are confused, it seems clear that ʻAli did not come out of it well. In the meantime, a perverse fate dictated that ʻAli, who had been most reluctant to submit to arbitration, was now being blamed by part of his Kūfan army for having done so. 'Judgement is God's alone', they chanted and separated themselves from ʻAli's army, thus becoming known as the Khawārij (Kharijites) or 'Seceders'.

ʻAli found himself hard pressed on all sides. The arbitration process was clearly providing Muʻāwiya with an opportunity to regroup and strengthen his position. In Egypt ʻAli's governor was overthrown through Muʻāwiya's machinations and the province came under Syrian control. Finally the Khawārij were committing atrocities close to ʻAli's capital and posed a serious threat.

ʻAli was forced to put aside plans for attacking Syria and advanced against the Khawārij. They were routed at the Battle of Nahrawān. But they had their revenge in that it is said to have been one of their number, ʻAbdu'r-Raḥmān ibn Muljam, who assassinated ʻAli, wounding him in Kūfa on 19 Ramaḍān 40/27 January 661. ʻAli died two days later.

To attempt to draw a portrait of the personal qualities of ʻAli is indeed a difficult task, for he has assumed, even in the eyes of Sunni Muslims, an almost legendary dimension as a paragon of virtues and a fount of knowledge. His courage in battle, his magnanimity towards his defeated opponents, his sincerity and straightforwardness, his eloquence and his profound knowledge of the roots of Islam cannot be questioned, for they are matters of historical record. He is also attributed with having been the founder of the study of Arabic grammar through his disciple, Abu'l-Aswad al-Dū'alī, and the originator of the correct method of reciting the Qur'an. His discourses and letters (especially as compiled in the *Nahj al-Balāgha*, which is considered by many Muslims as second only to the Qur'an in importance) are considered the earliest examples of Muslim writings on philosophy, theology and ethics, while through disciples such as Ḥasan al-Baṣrı and Rabı' ibn Khaytham he is considered to have given the initiative to Sufism in Islam. He was regarded even by such persons as the second Caliph, 'Umar, as the 'best of judges' and his judicial decisions are highly regarded both by Sunni and Shi'i experts in jurisprudence. For Shi'is the brief period of his Caliphate is looked upon as a Golden Age when the Muslim community was directed as it always should be directed, by the divinely-chosen Imam.

Although Najaf is the place where the Shrine of 'Ali is located, there must remain some doubt as to whether the remains of 'Ali are in fact there, for some Traditions state that he was buried in Kūfa and others that he was buried in Medina, or that his burial-place is unknown. However, the vast majority of Shi'is accept Najaf as the place of 'Ali's burial, and in consequence a large town has grown around this spot. The first building to have been erected over this location was commissioned by the 'Abbasid Caliph Hārūn ar-Rashīd. Several further buildings were built and destroyed, at least one of which was destroyed on the orders of the anti-Shi'i Caliph Mutawakkil. The Buyid ruler 'Aḍudu'd-Dawla built a shrine in the 4th/10th century that lasted until 755/1354 but the main part of the present structure was built by the Safavid monarch, Shāh Ṣafī in about 1045/1635 and the dome was gilded by Nādir Shāh. In the course of the last 400 years, Najaf has become the residence of some of the most eminent ulama of the Shi'i world and the site of some of the most important religious colleges.

Hasan, The Second Imam

Abū Muḥammad Ḥasan ibn 'Alī, known as al-Mujtabā (the chosen) is considered by Shi'is to have become the Imam after the death of 'Ali. Hasan was born in the year AH 3 in Medina and was brought up in the household of the Prophet himself until the latter's death when Hasan was aged about 7. There can be no doubt that the Prophet had a great fondness for his two grandchildren, Hasan and Husayn, whom he referred to as the 'chiefs of the youths of paradise'[2] and about whom he had been widely quoted as saying 'he who has loved Hasan and Husayn has loved me and he who has hated them has hated me'.[3] Most of the companions of the Prophet still alive could remember how the Prophet used to caress and kiss these two grandchildren of his and how he had even interrupted his sermon on one occasion because Hasan had tripped and fallen.

Hasan was thirty-seven years old when his father fell at the hands of the assassin at Kūfa. It is known that many of the surviving companions of the Prophet, both of the Medinan Anṣār and the Meccan Muhājirūn, were in 'Ali's army. So they must have been in Kūfa at the time of 'Ali's assassination and therefore must have assented to Hasan being acclaimed Caliph in succession to his father a few days later, for there is no record of any dissent to this in Kūfa, nor indeed of any dissent in Mecca and Medina.

Of all the twelve Shi'i Imams, Hasan is the one who has been disparaged most harshly by Western historians. He has been derided for having given up the Caliphate to Mu'āwiya without a fight. He has been described as uxorious, unintelligent, incapable and a lover of luxury. This harsh criticism is rejected by Shi'i historians. They point out that Hasan's abdication was not an act of feeble cowardice but a realistic and compassionate act. Following the assassination of 'Ali, the Kūfan army had rallied around Hasan to face the advancing Syrian army led by Mu'āwiya. But Mu'āwiya's spreading of false reports, his secret agents and liberal bribes had wreaked such havoc among Kūfans that Hasan had seen his army melt away. In this situation abdication was the only realistic course of action open to Hasan and avoided pointless bloodshed.

In the correspondence between Mu'āwiya and Hasan that led to the abdication, it is interesting to note that Mu'āwiya brushed aside Hasan's objections that Mu'āwiya had no precedence in Islam and indeed was the son of the most prominent opponent of Islam by asserting that the situation between him and Hasan now was the same as that between Abū Bakr and 'Ali after the death of the Prophet, that Mu'āwiya's military strength, political abilities and age were of more importance than Hasan's claim to religious precedence. In other words, as Shi'i historians point out, political power was to become the arbitrator of leadership in Islam rather than religious considerations.

The Kūfans, by their wavering, their disunity and their fickleness, had let Hasan down badly, as they had his father 'Ali, and as they were going to do with his brother Husayn some twelve years later. Part of the Kūfan army rebelled against Hasan, part of it went over to the Syrians and the rest melted away. Even Hasan's own tent was plundered, he himself wounded. Small wonder then that he felt he had no choice but to abdicate.

Mu'āwiya needed Hasan's abdication to lend some plausibility and justification to his own seizure of power; a mere military victory would not have been enough. Therefore, he was happy to offer Hasan generous terms including general amnesty for Hasan's followers, a large financial settlement for Hasan himself, and, according to some accounts, a further condition that the Caliphate would revert to Hasan on Mu'āwiya's death.

Hasan, after his abdication in 41/661, retired to Medina and led a quiet life. He refused to involve himself in any political activity – which was a very pragmatic action, in that although delegations came to him to offer him their support if he would rise up, Mu'āwiya had such a firm grip on the Empire that any uprising would have been doomed to failure. And, in any case, Hasan had given his word and signed an agreement.

Hasan died in 49/669 at the early age of forty-six. It is stated by the Shi'i historians and confirmed in some of the Sunni histories that he was poisoned by his wife at the instigation of Mu'āwiya. Certainly nothing could have suited Mu'āwiya's purposes more since it paved the way for his plan to ensure the succession of his son, Yazīd.

Hasan was buried in Medina in al-Baqī' cemetery next to his mother, Fāṭima.

Husayn, the Third Imam

After Hasan, his younger brother Husayn became the head of the House of 'Ali and, according to the Shi'is, the Third Imam. Abū 'Abdu'llāh Ḥusayn ibn 'Alī, who is given by Shi'is the title Sayyid ash-Shuhadā (Prince of Martyrs), was born in Medina in 4/626. The great love of the Prophet for his two grandsons has been referred to in the previous section and, according to some reports, 'Ali preferred Husayn to Hasan.

While his brother Hasan was alive Husayn played a secondary role, but after the death of his brother he became the head of the family and the focus of the aspirations of the Kūfans, who were growing increasingly restive under the stern Syrian rule. While Mu'āwiya ruled, however, Husayn made no move, considering himself bound, it is said, by the terms of Hasan's treaty with Mu'āwiya.

The Umayyads had instituted the public cursing of 'Ali from the pulpit, motivated, it is said, by a desire to provoke staunch Shi'i elements into open revolt. The first to fall foul of this policy was Ḥujr ibn 'Adī al-Kindī. He raised a revolt in Kūfa in 51/671. The revolt was easily overcome and Ḥujr with six of his companions were executed in Damascus by Mu'āwiya. These seven are regarded by Shi'is as the first of their martyrs.

Mu'āwiya died in 60/680, but prior to his death he had arranged for his son, Yazīd, to succeed him. If the rule of Mu'āwiya, the son of the Prophet Muhammad's most powerful enemy in Mecca, had been offensive to some pious Muslims, the accession of Yazīd, a drunkard who openly ridiculed and flouted the laws of Islam, was an outrage. In Kūfa the people began to stir once more and soon letters and messengers were arriving in Medina urging Husayn to come to Kūfa and assume leadership there.

Because of pressure from the Governor of Medina to declare allegiance to Yazīd, Husayn had moved from Medina to Mecca and it was from there that he sent an emissary, his cousin Muslim ibn 'Aqīl, to

Kūfa to assess the situation. On Muslim's arrival in Kūfa, large meetings were held at which thousands pledged their support for Husayn.

Despite the enthusiastic reports sent by Muslim, Husayn was warned by several persons against going to Kūfa whose inhabitants had proved so fickle in their support of his father and brother, but Husayn decided to press on and left Mecca in the company of some fifty armed men and a number of women and children.

But the situation was changing rapidly in Kūfa. Yazīd, fully aware of the situation, had instructed the energetic 'Ubaydu'llāh ibn Ziyād to take control of Kūfa. 'Ubaydu'llah had instigated a reign of terror, dealing harshly with any manifestations of revolt. He had reinforced these measures by threatening the tribal leaders with death if their tribes were found to be fomenting rebellion. These measures had already resulted in Muslim being captured and executed and now 'Ubaydu'llāh assigned military units to all the routes to Kūfa from the south in order to intercept Husayn.

Although Husayn received warnings of the state of affairs in Kūfa, he pressed ahead, declining alternative proposals that would have ensured his safety. A few of his supporters succeeded in slipping out of Kūfa and joining up with his forces but others were arrested and the vast majority of Kūfans were overtaken with either terror of 'Ubaydu'llāh's sword or greed for 'Ubaydu'llāh's money and forgot their pledges of support for Husayn.

It fell to al-Ḥurr at-Tamīmī, the young commander of a military detachment numbering one thousand, to intercept Husayn's party as it approached Kūfa. Al-Ḥurr's instructions were to prevent Husayn approaching any town or village in Iraq and he explained this to Husayn. The latter replied by showing him the sackful of letters from the people of Kūfa that he had received. Seeing that al-Ḥurr's men were overcome with thirst, Husayn magnanimously offered them water from his party's supplies and later al-Ḥurr and his men lined up behind Husayn as he led them in prayer.

Eventually after negotiations Husayn agreed to proceed in a direction away from Kūfa while al-Ḥurr sent for further instructions. Husayn's party travelled on, shadowed by al-Ḥurr's detachment until they reached the plain of Karbalā. It was the second day of Muḥarram in the year AH 61 (2 October 680). On the following day some four thousand men under 'Umar ibn Sa'd arrived with instructions from 'Ubaydu'llāh that they should not allow Husayn to leave until he had signed a pledge of allegiance to Yazīd. Ibn Sa'd's men surrounded Husayn's party and even cut them off from the river which was their only source of water.

Husayn began negotiations with Ibn Sa'd pointing out that he had no desire to initiate bloodshed and asking to be allowed to withdraw to

Arabia. But Ibn Sa'd refused to relent, having been promised by 'Ubaydu'llāh the governorship of Rayy if he accomplished his mission. Meanwhile the situation in Husayn's camp was becoming desperate due to shortage of water.

Then 'Ubaydu'llah sent his final orders through Shimr (or Shamir). Ibn Sa'd was either to attack Husayn immediately or hand over command to Shimr. On the evening of 9 Muḥarram, Ibn Sa'd drew up his forces and advanced them towards Husayn's camp, ready for battle the next day. That night, Husayn addressed his companions, asking them to withdraw and leave him to face the enemy. They refused to desert him.

And so there dawned the fateful day of 10 Muḥarram AH 61 (10 October 680), which is known as *'Āshūrā*.[4] At dawn Husayn once more approached the camp of the Umayyads and addressed them with such emotive words that several were visibly moved and al-Ḥurr at-Tamīmī, who had first intercepted Husayn, threw in his lot with Husayn's tiny band and was one of the first to fall when the fighting began.[5]

Husayn's companions on that day are traditionally said to have numbered 72 armed men (18 of the family of 'Ali and 54 supporters) and the women and children. The fighting appears to have been of a sporadic nature consisting of single combat and brief forays. The steady fire maintained by the Umayyad archers on Husayn's camp took its own toll. One by one Husayn's supporters fell and then the members of his family until only he and his half-brother 'Abbās, the standard-bearer on that day, were left of the fighting men. 'Abbās was killed trying to obtain water for the thirsty women and children and the army converged on the lone figure of Husayn.

Carrying his infant son in his arms, Husayn pleaded for water for the babe but an arrow lodged in the baby's throat killing him. As the troops closed around him, Husayn fought valiantly until at last he was struck a severe blow that caused him to fall face down on the ground. Even then the soldiers hesitated to deal the final blow to the grandson of the Prophet until Shimr ordered them on, and, according to some accounts himself came forward and struck the blow that ended Husayn's life.

The Umayyad army looted the tents, decapitated the bodies of all Husayn's companions and raised these on spears to lead their procession back to Kūfa. The women and children who had been taken prisoner included 'Alī, the only surviving son of Husayn, who had been too ill to participate in the fighting.

At Kūfa 'Ubaydu'llāh convened a great assembly and ordered the head of Husayn to be brought to him on a tray and also the captives. When the head was placed before him, 'Ubaydu'llāh struck the lips with his cane and taunted the captives. Some of those witnessing this scene were intensely moved and one of them spoke up saying: 'Remove your cane from those lips, for, by God, many a time have I seen the lips of the Prophet of God on those lips.'[6]

Zaynab, the sister of Husayn, bore herself with dignity and answered 'Ubaydu'llāh firmly and fearlessly. At first, 'Ubaydu'llāh wanted to put 'Alī to death also, but Zaynab protested, saying: 'O Ibn Ziyād! You have spilt enough of our blood', and then she put her arms around 'Alī's neck and said: 'By God! I will not be parted from him, and so if you are going to kill him, then kill me with him.'[7] And so 'Ubaydu'llāh imprisoned the captives and after a while sent them on to Damascus with the head of Husayn.

At Damascus Yazīd gloated over the head of Husayn and insulted 'Alī and Zaynab. Later, however, no doubt fearing that a popular outcry might threaten his throne, Yazīd sought to appease the captives and released them, allowing them to return to Medina.

Thus ended the tragedy of Karbalā. It has been given here in detail, because, of all the episodes of Islamic history, it has had a greater impact than any on the Shi'a down the ages. A brief consideration must be given to the question of Husayn's intentions and ambitions in setting out for Kūfa. Some historians have dismissed it as mere political adventuring that went wrong, but, of course, Shi'i historians disagree.

Husayn had received plenty of warning of the collapse of the Shi'i revolt in Kūfa as he approached Iraq. Indeed, the Shi'i histories record that at one of the staging-posts on the journey, after receiving grim news from Kūfa, Husayn addressed his companions and told them of the death and destruction that awaited them ahead. Husayn could, at this point, have retired to Medina or even have accepted the offer which was made to him of refuge in the mountain strongholds of the Tayy tribe. However, he refused these courses of action and even addressed his companions urging them to leave him as he pressed on towards Kūfa and certain destruction.

S. H. M. Jafri, a modern Shi'i historian, has written:

> . . . it is clear that Ḥusayn was fully aware of the dangers he would encounter and that he had a certain strategy and plan in mind to bring about a revolution in the consciousness of the Muslim community. Furthermore, it is also very clear from the sources, as has been stated before, that Ḥusayn did not try to organise or mobilise military support, which he easily could have done in the Hijaz, nor did he even try to exploit whatever physical strength was available to him . . .
>
> Is it conceivable that anyone striving for power would ask his supporters to abandon him? . . . What then did Ḥusayn have in mind? Why was he still heading for Kūfa?
>
> It is rather disappointing to note that Western scholarship on Islam, given too much to historicism, has placed all its attention on the discrete external aspects of the event of Karbalā and has never tried to analyse the inner history and agonising conflict in Ḥusayn's mind . . . A careful study and analysis of the

events of Karbalā as a whole reveals the fact that from the very beginning Ḥusayn was planning for a complete revolution in the religious consciousness of the Muslims. All of his actions show that he was aware of the fact that a victory achieved through military strength and might is always temporal [sic], because another stronger power can in course of time bring it down in ruins. But a victory achieved through suffering and sacrifice is everlasting and leaves permanent imprints on man's consciousness . . . The natural process of conflict and struggle between *action* and *reaction* was now at work. That is, Muḥammad's progressive Islamic *action* had succeeded in suppressing Arab conservatism, embodied in heathen pre-Islamic practices and ways of thinking. But in less than thirty years' time this Arab conservatism revitalised itself as a forceful *reaction* to challenge Muḥammad's *action* once again . . . The strength of this *reaction*, embodied in Yazīd's character, was powerful enough to suppress or at least deface Muḥammad's *action*. Islam was now, in the thinking of Ḥusayn, in dire need of reactivation of Muḥammad's *action* against the old Arabian *reaction* and thus required a complete shake-up . . .

. . . Ḥusayn's acceptance of Yazīd, with the latter's openly reactionary attitude against Islamic norms, would not have meant merely a political arrangement, as had been the case with Ḥasan and Mu'āwiya, but an endorsement of Yazīd's character and way of life as well . . .

. . . Ḥusayn prepared his strategy . . . He realised that mere force of arms would not have saved Islamic *action* and consciousness. To him it needed a shaking and jolting of hearts and feelings. This, he decided, could only be achieved through sacrifice and sufferings. This should not be difficult to understand, especially for those who fully appreciate the heroic deeds and sacrifices of, for example, Socrates and Joan of Arc, both of whom embraced death for their ideals, and above all of the great sacrifice of Jesus Christ for the redemption of mankind.

It is in this light that we should read Ḥusayn's replies to those well-wishers who advised him not to go to Iraq. It also explains why Ḥusayn took with him his women and children, though advised by Ibn 'Abbās [his father's cousin] that should he insist on his project, at least he should not take his family with him. Aware of the extent of the brutal nature of the reactionary forces, Ḥusayn knew that after killing him, the Umayyads would make his women and children captives and take them all the way from Kūfa to Damascus. This caravan of captives of Muḥammad's immediate family would publicise Ḥusayn's message and would force the Muslims' hearts to ponder on the tragedy. It would make the Muslims think of the whole affair and would awaken their consciousness. This is exactly what happened. Ḥusayn succeeded in his purpose. It is difficult today to evaluate exactly the impact of Ḥusayn's action on Islamic morality and way of thinking, because it prevailed. Had Ḥusayn not shaken and awakened Muslim consciousness by this method, who knows whether Yazīd's way of life would have become standard behaviour in the Muslim community, endorsed and accepted by the grandson of the Prophet. No doubt, even after Yazīd kingship did prevail in Islam, and the character and behaviour in the personal lives of these kings was not very different from that of Yazīd, but the change of thinking which prevailed after the sacrifice of Ḥusayn always served as a line of distinction between Islamic norms and the personal character of the rulers.[8]

It would be difficult to exaggerate the impact and importance of the martyrdom of Husayn for Shi'is. Although it was the usurpation of

'Ali's rights that is looked upon by Shi'is as the event initiating their movement and giving it intellectual justification, it was Husayn's martyrdom that gave it its impetus and implanted its ideas deep in the heart of the people. To this day it is the martyrdom of Husayn that is the most fervently celebrated event in the Shi'i calendar. During the first ten days of Muḥarram, the whole Shi'i world is plunged into mourning. For details of the observances during this time see pp. 240–43.

Above all, the martyrdom of Husayn has given to Shi'i Islam a whole ethos of sanctification through martyrdom. Although the Shi'is were persecuted all through their early history and, according to their traditions, every single one of the Imams suffered martyrdom, it is above all the martyrdom of Husayn that has given this characteristic to Shi'i Islam; a characteristic that recent events in Iran have demonstrated to be as strong as ever.

In his physical appearance, Husayn is said to have been very handsome and strikingly like the Prophet himself. He was of medium height with olive-brown skin and is said to have possessed great serenity and charm.

His body had more than thirty wounds from swords, lances and arrows upon it and was then trampled under the hooves of the horses of Ibn Sa'd's troops. After the troops had left, some of the tribesmen from a nearby village came and buried the bodies.

In later years a shrine was built over this spot. The first shrine was destroyed by the 'Abbasid Caliph Mutawakkil in 235/850 and the site ploughed over. After the death of this Caliph, a shrine of some sort was again erected but the bulk of the present shrine probably dates from the time of 'Aḍudu'd-Dawla, the Buyid prince, 369/979. The building was subjected to several further depredations including having the dome burnt down in the 11th century and the whole town of Karbalā was sacked by the Wahhābīs in 1801 and by the Ottoman army under Najīb Pāshā in 1843. The last important restoration of the shrine was carried out at the behest of Nāṣiru'd-Dīn Shāh in the 1850s when the dome was gilded and other important structural work carried out. The enclosed area round the shrine is called the *Ḥā'ir* and is forbidden to non-believers.

Apart from the Shrine of Husayn, Karbalā contains the equally-imposing Shrine of 'Abbās, the half-brother of Husayn, where 'Abbās and the other members of the family of 'Ali are said to be buried. The town of Karbalā has, of course, become an important religious centre, being both a point of pilgrimage and also a seat of learning with numerous theological colleges.

Until recent political changes made this impossible, it was customary for important men in Iran to have their bodies brought to Karbalā to be buried there and enormous graveyards around the town attest to this custom.

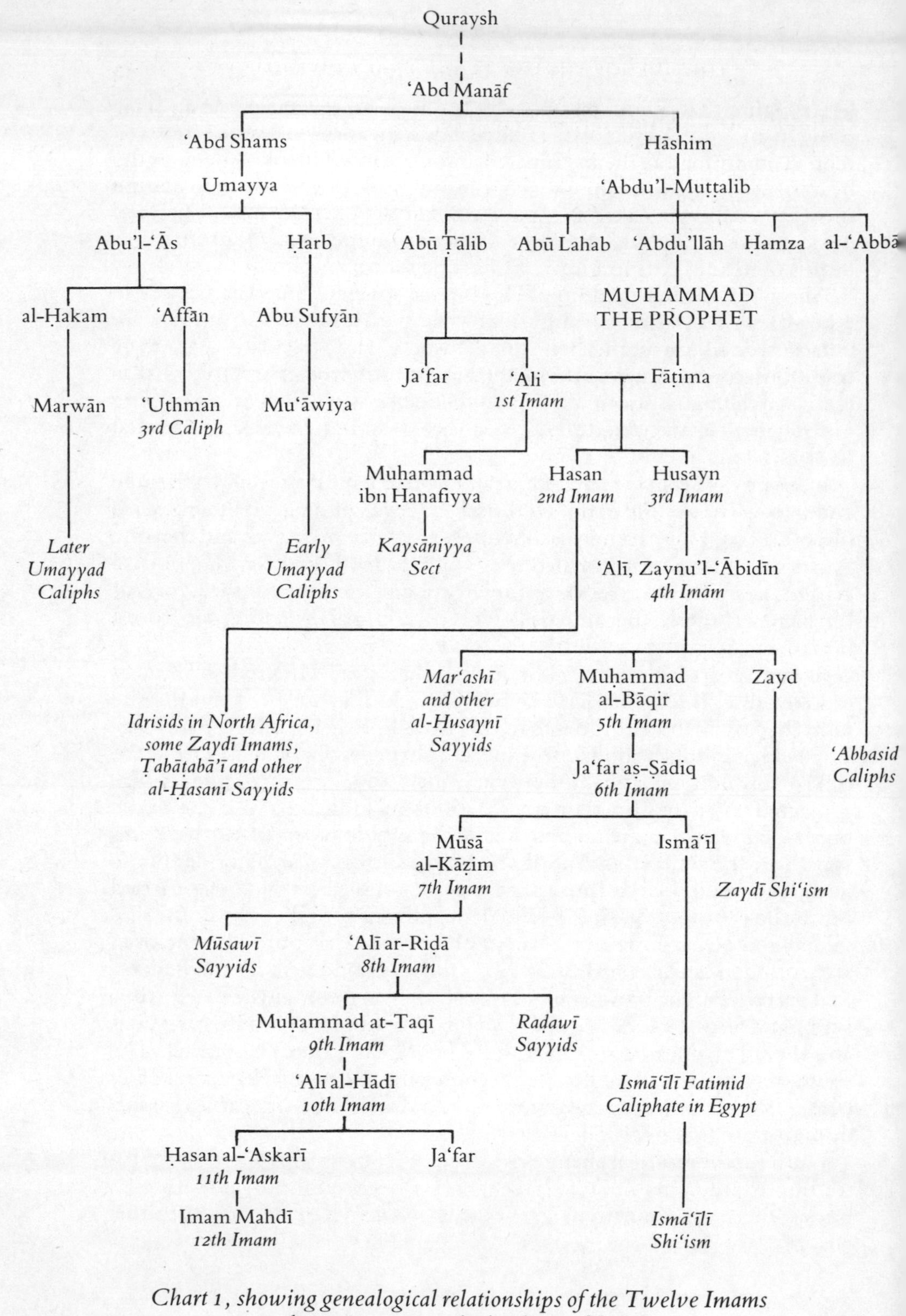

Chart 1, showing genealogical relationships of the Twelve Imams to dynasties, sects and other lines of descent

'Alī, Zaynu'l-'Ābidīn, the Fourth Imam

Abū Muḥammad 'Alī ibn Ḥusayn, known as Zaynu'l-'Ābidīn (the ornament of the worshippers) and also by the titles as-Sajjād (the prostrator) and az-Zakī (the pure), is regarded as the Fourth Imam by Twelver Shi'is. He had been born in the year 38/658[9] in Medina. His father was the Third Imam, Husayn, and, according to Shi'i tradition, his mother was Shahrbānū, the daughter of Yazdigird, the last Sassanian king of Iran.

In the previous section it has already been related that 'Ali was the only son of Husayn to survive the slaughter at Karbalā because he had been too weak and sick to fight. It has also been related that he was sent a captive to Damascus and then freed by Yazīd and allowed to retire to Medina.

Husayn's martyrdom in 61/680 had a profound effect on the Shi'a. In Kūfa, towards the end of the same year, a group of Shi'a began to meet in order to discuss what they could do to atone for their failure to come to Husayn's assistance. They elected as their leader Sulaymān ibn Ṣurad to whom they gave the title *Shaykhu'sh-Shī'a* (the leader of the Shi'a). Their movement, which became known as the *Tawwābūn* (the penitents) remained underground for four years. Then in 65/684 the Tawwābūn came into the open and 3,000 of them marched against an Umayyad army of 30,000 and were killed.

In 64/683, shortly before the Tawwābūn uprising, Yazīd the Umayyad Caliph died. There followed the brief six-month reign of his sickly son and then the Umayyads fell into disarray with factional fighting. This created a chance for all those factions that had been opposed to the Umayyads. In Kūfa, the leaders of the different tribal factions met and decided to invite 'Abdu'llāh ibn Zubayr, who had already in 61/680 proclaimed his Caliphate in the Hijaz, to send his representative to govern the city. Thus Iraq came under the rule of Ibn Zubayr. However, there also arrived in Kūfa at this time Mukhtār ath-Thaqafī who was advancing a propaganda among the Shi'is in favour of Muḥammad ibn al-Ḥanafiyya, the First Imam 'Ali's third son by a woman of the tribe of Ḥanīfa (i.e. not by Fāṭima, the daughter of the Prophet). The Tawwābūn who were about to set off on the road to martyrdom refused to ally themselves with Mukhtār, but after their defeat Mukhtār's cause grew as there was no alternative leadership among the Shi'a of Kūfa. Eventually, in 66/686, Mukhtār was strong enough to seize possession of Kūfa.

Whereas the Tawwābūn and indeed Shi'ism itself had been primarily an Arab movement up to this time, Mukhtār was the first to mobilise for the Shi'i cause the large numbers of Iranians who, in the social structure of the Islamic Empire, held an inferior status as *Mawālī* (clients of the Arab tribes). Mukhtār in his propaganda emphasised the role of Ibn al-Ḥanafiyya as the Mahdī (the rightly-guided one) who would deliver the Muslims from oppression and restore justice. Mukhtār's uprising was put down in 67/686 or 68/687 and Mukhtār himself killed, but the propaganda on behalf of Ibn al-Ḥanafiyya continued, and when the latter died in 81/700 a group of his followers considered that he had not died at all but had gone into occultation and would return. Mukhtār and the supporters of Ibn al-Ḥanafiyya were thus the first to bring into prominence two key ideas that were henceforth to be of great importance in the development of Shi'i thought; the idea of Mahdī and the concept of occultation and return.

During these turbulent years, the Fourth Imam Zaynu'l-'Ābidīn kept very much in the background, not involving himself in the politics and upheavals of the period. So completely did he set himself apart from an active role that neither 'Abdu'llāh ibn Zubayr nor later al-Ḥajjāj, when he defeated 'Abdu'llāh, felt it necessary to place any restriction on Zaynu'l-'Ābidīn's movements nor to extract from him any pledge of obedience.

From what is recorded of Zaynu'l-'Ābidīn's life, it would appear that he led a very secluded pious life with only a handful of close associates. It is recorded that he spent a great deal of time weeping over the martyrs of Karbalā. His name as-Sajjād (the prostrator) bore witness to the numerous times that he prostrated himself before God and it is said that the resulting calluses on his forehead needed to be shaved down twice a year.

Although he kept himself apart from the people and although much of the support of the Shi'is was diverted to Muḥammad ibn al-Ḥanafiyya, there is no doubt that Zaynu'l-'Ābidīn was held in great respect by all. Several leading jurists of the time, such as az-Zuhrī and Sa'īd ibn al-Musayyib, were counted among his close associates. As for followers and disciples, it is difficult to be sure of their number. It seems fairly certain that there were hardly any until the collapse of Mukhtār's revolt and the end of Ibn Zubayr's Caliphate in 73/692. There is, however, the famous story told that when Hishām, the son of the Caliph 'Abdu'l-Mālik came on pilgrimage to Mecca, he found that because of the crowds, he was unable to approach the Ka'ba but, to his annoyance, the crowd parted allowing another to approach with ease. When he asked who it was for whom the crowd parted so respectfully while he, the son of the Caliph, was ignored, he was told it was Zaynu'l-'Ābidīn. It is also reported that the Caliph 'Abdu'l-Mālik brought Zaynu'l-'Ābidīn to Damascus and held him in prison briefly.

According to various sources, Zaynu'l-'Ābidīn died in 94/712 or 95/

713 aged either fifty-seven or fifty-eight. He was buried in al-Baqīʻ cemetery. According to Shiʻi historians he was poisoned on the orders of the reigning Caliph, Walīd, or his brother Hishām.

Muḥammad al-Bāqir, the Fifth Imam

Abū Jaʻfar Muḥammad ibn ʻAlī, known as al-Bāqir ('the splitter open', i.e. of knowledge; also said to mean 'the ample' in knowledge) was born in 57/676. His mother, Fāṭima, was a daughter of the Second Imam, Hasan. Thus, al-Bāqir joined in himself the two lines of descent from Fāṭima and ʻAli. He was about thirty-seven years of age when his father died.

Like his father, Muḥammad al-Bāqir was politically quiescent and refrained from openly putting forward any claim. As during his father's time with Ibn al-Ḥanafiyya, there was a rival claimant for the allegiance of the Shiʻis during al-Bāqir's time. This was al-Bāqir's half-brother, Zayd, who advocated a more politically active role for the Imam and was prepared to accommodate to a certain extent the view-point of the majority of Muslims by acknowledging the Caliphates of Abū Bakr and ʻUmar and by accepting their legal practices.

It is reported that the Caliph Hishām summoned al-Bāqir and his son Jaʻfar to Damascus and debated with them concerning the question of whether ʻAli, the First Imam, possessed knowledge of the unseen (*ʻilm al-ghayb*). Hishām is said to have been defeated in argument and to have sent al-Bāqir home.

Pressed by the rival claim of Zayd, al-Bāqir emphasised the doctrine of *naṣṣ* (specific designation of an Imam by the preceding Imam, see p. 153). However, al-Bāqir's supporters and disciples were in a minority compared with those of Zayd and of Abū Hāshim, the son of Ibn al-Ḥanafiyya.

A further important development during this period, as seen in the Shiʻi sources, was the beginning of an independent stance by the Shiʻis on matters of law and ritual practices. The Shiʻis began to rely only on the guidance of their Imams on these matters and to reject the rulings of ʻUmar and other Traditionists on whom the rest of the Muslim world was becoming dependent.

As with the other Imams, Shiʻis claim al-Bāqir as a martyr but there is no concurrence as to the manner of his death, some saying he was poisoned by Hishām, others that it was Ibrāhīm ibn Walīd who arranged his death. There is also a wide discrepancy regarding the date of death with variations from 114/732 to 126/743. Most sources appear to settle for 117/735 but this would preclude one historian's account of how al-Bāqir warned Zayd against his open revolt which occurred in 122/740.[10]

He was about fifty-seven years old at the time of his death and lies buried at al-Baqī' cemetery in Medina.

Ja'far aṣ-Ṣādiq, the Sixth Imam

Abu 'Abdu'llāh Ja'far ibn Muḥammad known by the title aṣ-Ṣādiq (the truthful) was the eldest son of Muḥammad al-Bāqir, while his mother was a great-granddaughter of the first Caliph, Abū Bakr. His date of birth is variously given as 80/699, 83/702 or 86/705. He was therefore about thirty-seven years old when his father died.

Apart from the First Imam 'Ali, no other Imam of the Twelver line achieved as great a renown in the Muslim world for piety and learning as Ja'far aṣ-Ṣādiq did in his own lifetime. Many of those who sat in aṣ-Ṣādiq's circle of students later went on to become renowned scholars and jurists. Abū Ḥanīfa, the founder of the Ḥanafī School of Law in Sunni Islam, is said to have been one of his students, and Mālik ibn Anas, the founder of the Mālikī School of Law, was also evidently closely associated with aṣ-Ṣādiq and transmitted Traditions from him. However, it must not be imagined that more than a few of the thousands of students who are reported to have studied under aṣ-Ṣādiq were Shi'is or accepted his claim to the Imamate. Indeed, it cannot be certain that he openly advanced such a claim.

During aṣ-Ṣādiq's Imamate there were stirring events throughout the Muslim world. The Shi'a of this time appear to have been desperately looking for any 'Alid (descendant of 'Ali – see Glossary) who could establish his authority and take over the Caliphate. Thus they supported, in turn: Zayd's revolt in 122/740; the rebellion of 'Abdu'llāh ibn Mu'āwiya (a descendant of Ja'far, 'Ali's brother) in 127/744; the 'Abbasid rising beginning in 129/747, which received a great deal of Shi'i support, at least while the real purpose of the rising was concealed under the claim to be acting for 'one who shall be chosen from the family of the Prophet'; and the revolt of Muḥammad an-Nafs az-Zakiyya (the pure soul) in 145/762 against the 'Abbasids. Throughout all these turbulent events, aṣ-Ṣādiq followed the policy of his father and grandfather and remained politically quietist. Even when Abū Salama, the political leader of the 'Abbasid revolt, reportedly offered him the Caliphate, aṣ-Ṣādiq declined it.

The Imamate of aṣ-Ṣādiq may be said to consist of two parts. During the first part, while the Umayyads were in power, aṣ-Ṣādiq taught quietly in Medina and succeeded in establishing his considerable reputation. During this phase he was relatively free from molestation by the authorities. Once the 'Abbasids came to power, and particularly during the reign of the second 'Abbasid Caliph, al-Manṣūr, aṣ-Ṣādiq began to be harassed. On several occasions he was summoned to Kūfa and held in prison, and Shi'i histories describe several attempts by al-Manṣūr to kill him. Husain Jafri has suggested that it was under aṣ-Ṣādiq that the doctrine of *naṣṣ* (designation of the Imam by the preceding Imam, see p. 153) as an essential pre-requisite for the Imamate, and the doctrine of *'ilm* (the special knowledge of the Imam, see p. 155) were fully developed.[11] This may well have been so, for there was certainly a profusion of claims and counter-claims at this time and it was the doctrine of *naṣṣ* that both distinguished the Twelver line from other 'Alid claimants and also provided the justification for the quietist line taken by these Imams. The doctrine of *taqiyya* (religious dissimulation) was also developed at this time. It served to protect the followers of aṣ-Ṣādiq at a time when al-Manṣūr was conducting a brutally repressive campaign against 'Alids and their supporters.

Most authorities agree that aṣ-Ṣādiq died in 148/765. As usual, Shi'i historians have attributed his death to poisoning, on this occasion by the Caliph al-Manṣūr.

Mūsā al-Kāẓim, the Seventh Imam

The Seventh Imam of the Twelver Shi'is was Abu'l-Ḥasan Mūsā ibn Ja'far known as al-Kāẓim (the forbearing). He was born in 128/745 (or according to other accounts 120/737 or 129/746) on the road between Mecca and Medina. His mother was a Berber slave called Ḥamīda. He was about twenty years of age at the time of his father's death.

The first years of his Imamate were concerned with a dispute over the succession to the Imamate. It appears that most of the followers of aṣ-Ṣādiq were expecting the latter's eldest son, Ismā'īl, whose mother was a granddaughter of Zaynu'l-'Ābidīn, the Fourth Imam, to succeed to the Imamate. Then Ismā'īl died during his father's lifetime and Mūsā's followers claimed that aṣ-Ṣādiq had then designated Mūsā, but there was some confusion among the ranks of Shi'a. Although for later generations, the most important group that split off at this time were those who considered the Imamate transferred from Ismā'īl to Muḥammad, Ismā'īl's son (i.e. the Ismā'īlīs), it would appear from the reports that Mūsā was most strongly challenged by the claim of 'Abdu'llāh al-Afṭaḥ, the oldest surviving son of aṣ-Ṣādiq. A number of influential followers of aṣ-Ṣādiq are recorded to have at first followed 'Abdu'llāh and then later changed their allegiance to Mūsā.

Throughout the whole of his life, Mūsā was faced with hostility and harassment from the 'Abbasid Caliphs. During the Caliphate of al-Manṣūr which overlapped with the first ten years of Mūsā's Imamate, the opposition was not so intense, but then came the ten years of the

Caliphate of al-Mahdī. Spies were planted in Medina to watch for any sign of disloyalty emanating from Mūsā, and at least once during this period he was arrested, brought to Baghdad and imprisoned for a while. It was, however, during the Caliphate of Hārūn ar-Rashīd that the persecution of 'Alids reached a climax. This Caliph is reported to have had hundreds of 'Alids killed. On one occasion Mūsā was arrested and brought to Baghdad. The Caliph was determined on his execution but then set him free as a result, it is said, of a dream.

In the last half of Mūsā's lifetime, many of the Shi'is who had split off from him at the beginning of his ministry returned their allegiance to him. New followers were gained and important new centres established in Egypt and north-west Africa.

The cause of Mūsā's final arrest and murder is said to have been the result of the plotting of Hārūn ar-Rashīd's vizier Yaḥyā ibn Khālid of the Barmakī family. When Hārūn put his son and heir Amīn into the charge of Ja'far ibn Muḥammad of the al-Ash'ath family, Yaḥyā grew fearful that when Hārūn died, the influence of the Barmakī family would come to an end, and so he began to plot against Ja'far ibn Muḥammad. Ja'far was secretly a Shi'i and a believer in the Imamate of Mūsā and so Yaḥyā began to feed information to Hārūn about the fact that Ja'far considered Mūsā to be the real sovereign and sent him the *khums* (see p. 179). These reports were designed to raise the wrath of the jealous and easily-influenced Caliph and to that end a relative of Mūsā's was suborned into giving further evidence about the influence of Mūsā and how money came to him from all parts of the Empire.

That year, 177/793, when Rashīd went on pilgrimage, he caused Mūsā to be arrested and sent him to Baṣra and then to Baghdad. There, Mūsā was kept in prison and eventually killed by poisoning. This occurred in the year 183/799.

Since there were rumours among the Shi'a that Mūsā, the Seventh Imam, would also be the last Imam and would not die but would be the Mahdī, Hārūn made a public display of Mūsā's body in Baghdad (this was also to show people there were no marks on his body and that he had not met a violent death). Mūsā al-Kāẓim was buried in the cemetery of the Quraysh.

In later years the Shrine of Mūsā al-Kāẓim and of his grandson, the Ninth Imam Muḥammad at-Taqī, became the centre of a separate suburb of Baghdad called Kāẓimayn (the two Kāẓims) and a shrine has stood over the site of these graves since the time of the Buyid dynasty. The present magnificent shrine dates from the early 16th century when it was built by Shāh Ismā'īl, the Safavid ruler of Iran. The domes were tiled with gold in 1796 by Āghā Muḥammad Shāh, the first of the Qājār dynasty of Iran. They were later re-tiled by Nāṣiru'd-Dīn

Shāh in the 1850s and most recently in the last decade by the Iraqi government.

'Alī ar-Riḍā, the Eighth Imam

Abu'l-Ḥasan 'Alī ibn Mūsā, known as ar-Riḍā (the approved or acceptable) was born in Medina in 148/765. Various names are given to his mother in the historical sources but what is certain is that she was a slave. He was thirty-five years old when his father died.

It was during the Imamate of ar-Riḍā that the Caliph Hārūn ar-Rashīd died and the Empire was split between his two sons: Amīn, who was born of an Arab mother and controlled Iraq and the West with his Arab vizier al-Faḍl ibn Rabī'; and Ma'mūn, who was born of a Persian mother and controlled Iran and the East with his Iranian vizier, al-Faḍl ibn Sahl. Amīn attempted to interfere with the arrangements for the succession that had been agreed upon and soon there was a civil war in which Amīn was defeated and Ma'mūn's army under the Iranian General, Ṭāhir, occupied Baghdad. Ma'mūn, however, remained for the time being in Marv in Khurāsān.

It was at this point that Ma'mūn suddenly and somewhat unexpectedly summoned 'Alī ar-Riḍā from Medina to join him at Marv. On ar-Riḍā's arrival he was appointed, somewhat reluctantly it is said, to be Ma'mūn's heir-apparent.

There has been much conjecture as to what caused Ma'mūn to adopt this course of action. Some have suggested that the revolts in the West of the Empire – some of them under a Shi'i banner led by Zaydī Imams – were becoming serious and this was a political move designed to give Ma'mūn the support of a body of the Shi'a and a respite. Some have suggested that it was the work of his powerful vizier, al-Faḍl ibn Sahl, who had Shi'i proclivities.

It was while ar-Riḍā was in Marv that his sister, Fāṭima, known as Ma'sūma (the immaculate) set out from Medina to see him. She died at Qumm *en route* and it is her shrine which is the religious focus of the city of Qumm. Qumm had been founded as a Shi'i town when, in 94/712, Aḥwaṣ ibn Sa'd al-Ash'arī had fled from Kūfa as a result of the persecutions of Shi'is being carried out by the Umayyad Governor, al-Ḥajjāj. The present imposing shrine was constructed mainly by Shāh Bīgum, the daughter of Shāh Ismā'īl, in 925/1519 and additions were made throughout the Safavid and Qājār eras. Gold tiles were placed on the roof by the Qājār monarch Fatḥ 'Alī Shāh. A number of the most important theological colleges in the Shi'i world have grown up around this shrine.

Whatever may have been the cause of Ma'mūn's nomination of ar-

Riḍā (which occurred in the year 201/816) there can be no doubt that it caused a great stir. Everywhere the black standards and uniforms of the 'Abbasids were changed to the green of the 'Alids. In Iraq, the 'Abbasid family rebelled and set up a rival Caliph.

In order to quell these rebellions, Ma'mūn set out with his court and army towards Iraq. At Ṭūs, on the way to Iraq, 'Alī ar-Riḍā suddenly took sick and died. The year was 203/818. The suddenness of his death has caused most writers to state that he was poisoned and the Shi'i writers accuse the Caliph Ma'mūn of doing this out of jealousy for the affection with which the people held ar-Riḍā, but there were other parties, especially the deposed 'Abbasids, who had reason to hate ar-Riḍā.

'Alī ar-Riḍā was buried near the tomb of Hārūn ar-Rashīd near Ṭūs. A tomb was built over the grave but this was destroyed and the present building dates from the early 14th century AD when the Mongol Sulṭān Muḥammad Oljeitu converted to Shi'ism and rebuilt the shrine. Most of the elaborate decorative work dates from Safavid and Qājār times and gold tiles were placed on the roof by Shāh 'Abbās I (completed in 1016/1607). In AD 1673 an earthquake destroyed the dome of the building and this was repaired by the Safavid Shāh Sulaymān. The city of Ṭūs was forgotten and a new city called Mashhad (place of martyrdom) grew around the shrine. Shi'i pilgrims flock to this site and there is a prescribed ritual for the pilgrimage. Adjacent to the shrine itself is another magnificent building which is the Mosque of Gawhar-Shād, the wife of Shāh-Rukh (see p. 98). This building, completed in 797/1394, is one of the finest in Iran. A number of theological colleges have been built around the shrine, the most famous of which is that of Mīrzā Ja'far Khān.

Muḥammad at-Taqī, the Ninth Imam

Abū Ja'far Muḥammad ibn 'Alī, known by the titles at-Taqī (the God-fearing) and al-Jawād (the generous), was born in 195/810. There are differences as to the identity of his mother but most sources seem to state that she was a Nubian slave. Muḥammad at-Taqī's father 'Alī ar-Riḍā had been married to Ma'mūn's daughter but no children resulted from that marriage.

Muḥammad at-Taqī was born in Medina and remained there when his father went to join Ma'mūn in far-off Marv. He was only seven years old when his father died and he succeeded to the Imamate. His youth became a cause of controversy among the Shi'a, some asking how such a boy could have the necessary knowledge to be the Imam. Shi'i writers have countered such suggestions by relating numerous stories about his extraordinary knowledge at a young age and by referring to the fact that the Qur'an states that Jesus was given his mission while still a child.

The Caliph Ma'mūn had changed his colour from the 'Alid green back to the 'Abbasid black shortly after arriving in Baghdad but he maintained his friendly attitude towards the Shi'is and the 'Alids and Muḥammad at-Taqī was to benefit greatly from this.

Muḥammad at-Taqī had apparently come to Baghdad shortly after his father's death and had been warmly received by Ma'mūn who was greatly impressed with the boy. Ma'mūn decided to give his daughter Umm al-Faḍl in marriage to at-Taqī. Members of the 'Abbasid family were opposed to this but it is related that Muḥammad at-Taqī proved his worth in public debate with one of the leading scholars of Baghdad. A magnificent wedding was arranged. It has been suggested that a revolt in the important Shi'i centre of Qumm, which began in 210/825 and flared up again in 214/829 and 216/831, caused Ma'mūn to arrange this wedding in order to placate Shi'i sentiment.[12] But it would appear that Ma'mūn had little to fear from this revolt.

After eight years in Baghdad, Muḥammad at-Taqī and his bride retired to Medina. Some of the histories report that Umm al-Faḍl was not altogether happy as at-Taqī's wife and wrote to her father complaining but the Caliph defended at-Taqī.

Ma'mūn died in 218/833 and was succeeded by his brother, Mu'taṣim. Muḥammad at-Taqī was summoned back to Baghdad in 220/835 and he died there in that same year. Since most Shi'i writers have felt it necessary to demonstrate that all the Imams were martyred, they have attributed at-Taqī's death to poisoning by his wife, Umm al-Faḍl, on the instigation of Mu'taṣim. However, there is little evidence of this and Shi'i writers differ among themselves as to how the poisoning was accomplished. Moreover, early Shi'i writers, such as Shaykh al-Mufīd, have declined to give credence to the story of the poisoning.[13]

Muḥammad at-Taqī was buried in the cemetery of the Quraysh at Baghdad, close to his grandfather. The grave is now contained in the double shrine of Kaẓimayn.

'Alī al-Hādī, the Tenth Imam

Abu'l-Ḥasan 'Alī ibn Muḥammad, who is known by the titles al-Hādī (the guided) and an-Naqī (the distinguished), was born in 212/827 or 214/829 in Medina. His mother was a Moroccan slave called Samāna. He was seven years old when his father died. Once again the Shi'is were faced with the problem of a child Imam.

During the remaining years of the Caliphate of Mu'taṣim and the five-year Caliphate of Wāthiq, al-Hādī and the Shi'is were relatively free and unmolested. All this was to change, however, with the Caliphate of

Mutawakkil which began in 232/847. During this reign, both Shi'is and Mu'tazilīs (see Glossary) came under an intense persecution.

In 233/848 Mutawakkil summoned al-Hādī to Sāmarrā, the new 'Abbasid capital north of Baghdad. Although received hospitably and given a house in which to live, al-Hādī was in reality a prisoner of the Caliph. The quarter of the city where al-Hādī lived was known as al-'Askar since it was chiefly occupied by the army (*'askar*) and, therefore, al-Hādī and his son Ḥasan are both referred to as 'Askarī or together as 'Askariyayn (the two 'Askarīs). Al-Hādī lived in Sāmarrā for twenty years, always under the observation of the Caliph's spies. It is reported that at least once Mutawakkil attempted to kill al-Hādī but was frustrated by a miracle. Al-Hādī continued to live in Sāmarrā after the death of Mutawakkil in 247/861 and during the brief reign of Muntaṣir and the four-year reign of Musta'īn until his death in 254/868 during the Caliphate of Mu'tazz. Real power was, by this time, in the hands of the Turkish Generals of the Caliphs and so it is difficult to see what advantage there would have been to the Caliph in poisoning the Imam as most Shi'i histories claim. Shaykh al-Mufīd, among the early Shi'i writers, does not state that the Imam was poisoned.[14]

'Alī al-Hādī and his son Ḥasan al-'Askarī are buried in the twin shrines called 'Askariyayn in Sāmarrā. The first substantial building over this site was constructed by Nāṣiru'd-Dawla, the Hamdanid ruler of Mosul in 333/944. The building was enlarged and ornamentation added by the Buyids and Safavids and the dome was gilded by Nāṣiru'd-Dīn Shāh Qājār in about 1868.

Ḥasan al-'Askarī, the Eleventh Imam

The Eleventh Imam was Abū Muḥammad Ḥasan ibn 'Alī, known as al-'Askarī on account of his almost life-long detention in Sāmarrā. He was born in 232/846 (or 230/844 or 231/845) in Medina and was therefore only two years of age when his father was summoned to Sāmarrā. His mother was a slave who is named as Ḥadīth.

Ḥasan al-'Askarī was twenty-two years old when his father gave him a slave-girl who is usually called Narjis or Ṣaqīl and who is named as the mother of Muḥammad, the Twelfth Imam.

The period of Ḥasan's Imamate was brief, only six years. During this time he was under intense pressure from the 'Abbasids and access to him for his followers was restricted. He therefore tended to use agents to communicate with the Shi'is who followed him.

Ḥasan al-'Askarī died on either 1 or 8 Rabī' al-Awwal 260 (25 December 873 or 1 January 874). The Shi'i histories maintain that he was poisoned by the Caliph Mu'tamid.

Muḥammad al-Mahdī, the Twelfth Imam

Abu'l-Qāsim Muḥammad ibn Ḥasan, known as al-Mahdī (the guided), al-Muntaẓar (the awaited), al-Ḥujja (the proof), al-Qā'im (the one who will arise), Baqiyatu'llāh (the remnant of God), is identified as the Twelfth Imam. After the death of Ḥasan al-'Askarī there was a great deal of confusion among the Shi'a, with some saying that al-'Askarī had had no son and others asserting that he had (see pp. 59–60). Those who were to go on to become the main body of the Twelver Shi'a believed that Ḥasan's son Muḥammad had gone into occultation. Further details of the Twelfth Imam can be found in Chapter 8.

EARLY DIVISIONS AMONG THE SHI'IS

The traditional accounts of the history of the Shi'a are mostly a recital of the various sects that split off from the main body of the Shi'a at different times, starting from the time of 'Ali. It is difficult to determine how many of these sects really existed as historical entities and how many are inventions of later writers. What is certain is that even if these sects did exist, the majority died out within a century. A few have survived to the present day and a brief description of the later developments of these sects is given below.

In considering the traditional account of these sects, it would be useful to examine briefly a number of general terms used about them as these terms crop up frequently in the following accounts:

a. *Ghulāt* (the extremists) and *Ghuluww* (extremism): those sects which hold either the opinion that any particular person is God or that any person is a prophet after Muhammad, are called by this title. Certain other doctrines such as *tanāsukh* (transmigration of souls), *ḥulūl* (descent of God or the Spirit of God into a person) and *tashbīh* (anthropomorphism with respect to God) are also usually ascribed to these groups. They are generally considered to be outside the pale of Islam.

b. *Wāqifa* or *Wāqifiyya* (those who hesitate or stop). This term is applied to any group who deny or hesitate over the death of a particular Imam and, therefore, stop at that Imam and refuse to recognise any further Imams. Most often it refers specifically to the group considering Mūsā al-Kāẓim to be the last Imam.

c. *Qaṭ'iyya* (those who are certain). This term applies to those who are certain of a death of a particular Imam and therefore go on to the next Imam.

During the Caliphate of 'Ali

1. *The Sabā'iyya*

'Abdu'llāh ibn Sabā al-Ḥimyarī, a semi-legendary figure known as Ibn as-Sawda, is generally considered to have started the tendency to *ghuluww* (extremism in matters of doctrine). He is said to have been a Jew converted to Islam. He is described as a devoted follower of 'Ali and during 'Uthmān's Caliphate travelled from place to place agitating in 'Ali's favour. Indeed, he is considered by some Sunni writers as the originator of Shi'ism itself, although on account of his extremism this is considered by Shi'is as a mere insult.[15] During 'Ali's Caliphate, however, he was banished by 'Ali to Madā'in on account of his saying to 'Ali: 'Thou art God.' According to many accounts, moreover, 'Ali even caused some of the followers of Ibn Sabā to be burned.[16]

After the assassination of 'Ali, 'Abdu'llāh ibn Sabā is said to have stated that he had not died at all. He was alive in the clouds and would return to fill the earth with justice.[17] If these reports are true, the Sabā'iyya would be, within the traditional schema, the first group of Wāqifiyya[18] and the first to have introduced the doctrines of *ghayba* (occultation or concealment) and *raj'a* (return).[19] However, the doctrine for which Ibn Sabā is best remembered and which caused Muslim writers to account him as one of the *ghulāt* is his attribution of divinity to 'Ali (and according to some sources, his own claim to be the prophet of 'Ali).

Groups who were active at a later period but who are considered to have been derived from the Sabā'iyya are:

a. *'Ulyāniyya* or *'Alyā'iyya* named after 'Ulyān (or 'Alyā) ibn Dhirā' as-Sadūsī (or ad-Dawsī or al-Asdī) who appear to have been active around AD 800 and are also called adh-Dhammiyya (the blamers) because they stated that 'Ali was God with Muhammad as his Apostle and that Muhammad was to be blamed in that he was sent to call the people to 'Ali but called them to himself. Others of this group assigned divinity to both Muhammad and 'Ali.

b. *Isḥāqiyya* or *Ḥamrawiyya* named after Isḥāq ibn Muḥammad an-Nakha'ī al-Aḥmar of Kūfa, who died in 186/802. This group evidently had close links with the previous group as Isḥāq is named as the leading dogmatist of the previous group by some writers.[20] They stressed that both Muhammad and 'Ali were divine and shared in the prophethood.

c. *Muḥammadiyya* or *Mīmiyya*. This sect are a counterpart to the 'Ulyāniyya and stressed the divinity of Muhammad. Their leading champion was al-Fayyāḍ.

d. *Ahl-i Ḥaqq ('Alī Ilāhīs, 'Aliyu'llāhīs).* The 'Ulyāniyya are traditionally linked to a Shi'i sect that has survived to the present day, the 'Aliyu'llāhīs as the Ahl-i Ḥaqq are often erroneously called. The historical connection is however tenuous and the Ahl-i Ḥaqq sect appear to have originated among the tribes in the Qarā-Quyūnlū Empire in the 15th century. There is no uniform set of beliefs among the Ahl-i Ḥaqq. Rather they form a loose network of groups each with its own beliefs. The twelve Imams of the Twelver line are revered but are not central to their beliefs. Their organisation and rituals are not unlike those of the Sufi orders. They are most numerous among the Kurds in west Iran and among the Turkomans and Kurds in north Iraq (especially around Sulaymāniyya and Kirkūk) and south-east Turkey.

After the Martyrdom of Husayn

2. *The Kaysāniyya*

The Kaysāniyya began (see p. 35) as a movement started by Mukhtār ibn Abū 'Ubayd ath-Thaqafī, claiming to represent Muḥammad ibn al-Ḥanafiyya (the son of 'Ali by a Ḥanafī woman). The name is thought to be derived from Kaysān, the leader of the *Mawālī* under Mukhtār.

Mukhtār himself is said to have taught that the Imamate was transferred to Muḥammad ibn al-Ḥanafiyya after Husayn. Doctrinally the Kaysāniyya stood halfway between the later Zaydī and Twelver positions concerning the nature of the Imamate in that while denying *naṣṣ* (designation) and emphasising that the Imam's claim is based on his personal qualifications, they also stressed the innate supernatural knowledge of the Imam. Mukhtār is said to have introduced the doctrine of *badā* (changeability of God's will) when he was defeated in a battle that he had prophesied he would win.

The Kaysāniyya survived the defeat and death of Mukhtār but after the death of Ibn al-Ḥanafiyya himself they split up into a number of groups:

a. *Karibiyya,* named after Abū Karib aḍ-Ḍarīr; this group held to the doctrines of *ghayba* (concealment) and *raj'a* (return). They considered that Ibn al-Ḥanafiyya had not died but was concealed on Mount Rawḍa (some seven days' journey from Medina) and would return to fill the earth with justice. Because they believed that prior to the return of the Imam, the drawing of swords was forbidden, they fought with sticks and were therefore called the Khashabiyya. Two of the most famous of Arab poets belonged to this sect, Sayyid al-Ḥimyarī and Kuthayyir.

b. *Hāshimiyya,* who held that Ibn al-Ḥanafiyya did die and that he taught all of his knowledge to his son, Abū Hāshim, to whom the Imamate passed. This sect is said to have introduced the allegorical interpretation of the Qur'an and the idea that beneath the *ẓāhir* (exoteric) there is a *bāṭin* (esoteric meaning).

Abū Hāshim died in Humayma (Palestine) in about 98/717. Upon his death several further factions arose.

c. *'Abbāsiyya*. The 'Abbasids originally claimed that Abū Hāshim passed the Imamate on to Muḥammad ibn 'Alī (the great-grandson of 'Abbās, the uncle of the Prophet) at his death-bed in Ḥumayma and that the Imamate was transferred to the descendants of 'Abbās. Thus initially the 'Abbasid propaganda was in reality a branch of the Hāshimiyya. Later, once the 'Abbasids had overthrown the Umayyads and assumed the Caliphate, they changed the basis of their claim to the Caliphate by stating that 'Abbās was the rightful successor to the Prophet.

d. *Rawandiyya*. Despite this change of emphasis by the 'Abbasids following their overthrow of the Umayyads, there remained a sect called the Rawandiyya who believed in the Imamate of the 'Abbasids and it is even said that some of them believed in the divinity of al-Manṣūr, the second 'Abbasid Caliph. However, the 'Abbasids, wishing to secure a more orthodox basis for their Caliphate, found such a heterodox movement extremely embarrassing and al-Manṣūr is even reported to have had some of the sect killed.

e. *Rizāmiyya* or *Muslimiyya*. There is also recorded a group called in one source the Rizāmiyya after Rizām ibn Razm.[21] What appears to have been an almost identical sect is called Muslimiyya in another source.[22] This sect considered Abū Muslim, the 'Abbasid General, as having inherited the Imamate from 'Abdu'llāh as-Saffāḥ, the first 'Abbasid Caliph, and some of the heresiographers include this group among the *ghulāt* on account of their believing in Abū Muslim's divinity or claiming that he was greater in rank than Gabriel. In any case, this sect did not believe Abū Muslim had died but rather that he was in concealment and would return to fill the earth with justice. One writer calls the sect Barkūkiyya and asserts that they were to be found in Herat and Marv and that they believed that the man who was killed by al-Manṣūr was not Abū Muslim but a devil who took on his shape.[23] What appears to be the same sect is called in other sources the Khurramiyya, Khurramdīniyya and Isḥāqiyya. They were active in Khurāsān and Transoxania and are linked in several sources with Zoroastrianism and Mazdakism (the Isḥāqiyya, for example, were held to believe that Abū Muslim was in fact a prophet sent by Zoroaster to revive his religion).

A group of this sect under the leadership of Hāshim ibn Ḥakīm al-Muqanna' (the veiled one) arose in revolt in 159/775 during the reign of the Caliph al-Mahdī. They believed that God had existed in the form of all the prophets from Adam to Muhammad and then in 'Ali and his sons and finally in Abū Muslim from whom it had passed to al-Muqanna'.[24]

This group were called Muqanniyya or Mubayyaḍa and are considered part of a wider belief in the descent of the spirit of God into the form of a man which is called Ḥulūliyya.

f. *Al-Kaysāniyya al-Khullaṣ* or *Mukhtāriyya*. This group considered the Imamate to be passed down among Muḥammad ibn al-Ḥanafiyya's descendants: from Abū Hāshim to his brother, 'Alī, and to 'Alī's son, Ḥasan, and to Ḥasan's son, 'Alī. The mothers of this succession of Imams were also descendants of Ibn al-Ḥanafiyya.

g. *Bayāniyya*. The followers of Bayān ibn Sam'ān at-Tamīmī who maintained that the divinity passed from 'Ali to his sons and then through Abū Hāshim to Bayān. Among the beliefs attributed to this group are anthropomorphism with respect to God. Bayān's relationship with the Fifth Imam, Muḥammad al-Bāqir, appears to have varied quite markedly. At one time he is reported to have been advancing claims of a *ghuluww* nature with respect to al-Bāqir; at another time he is reported to have sent a message summoning al-Bāqir to accept his prophethood. Bayān was put to death by Khālid ibn 'Abdu'llāh al-Qasrī, Hishām's governor in Iraq.

After the Imamate of Zaynu'l-'Ābidīn

3. *The Zaydiyya*

Zayd, the son of the Fourth Imam, Zaynu'l-'Ābidīn, asserted a claim to the Imamate on the basis that it belonged to any descendant of 'Ali and Fāṭima who is learned, pious and comes forward openly to claim the Imamate (i.e. raises a revolt). Zayd is said to have studied under Wāṣil Ibn 'Aṭā, the reputed founder of the Mu'tazila (see p. 77ff.), and so the Zaydiyya came to incorporate Mu'tazilī theology and a large number of this school joined the movement. In order to widen the basis of his support yet further, some Zaydīs propounded the doctrine of *Imāmat al-Mafḍūl* – that it was possible for a man of lesser excellence to be appointed Imam during the lifetime of a man of greater excellence. Through this doctrine, they justified the Caliphates of Abū Bakr and 'Umar stating that these were matters of expediency while 'Ali was of greater excellence. A corollary of this was the acceptance that the companions of the Prophet were not blame-worthy or sinful in rejecting 'Ali (an important point for the Traditionists who depended on the authority of these companions for the transmission of the Traditions).

Zayd and his half-brother, the Fifth Imam Muḥammad al-Bāqir, came to open disagreement over several points of doctrine. Initially, Zayd's activist approach attracted many of the Shi'is, but later as Zayd compromised more and more with the Traditionists many of the Shi'a turned their backs on him and returned to al-Bāqir.

Zayd raised his revolt in Ṣafar 122/January 740 but was unsuccessful and was killed in Kūfa by the Caliph Hishām. Zayd's son, Yaḥyā, then fled to Khurāsān and started a revolt there but was overcome and killed in 125/743.

Since the Zaydīs recognised no designation for the Imamate nor any strict hereditary principle (beyond the fact that the Imam must be of the descendants of Hasan and Husayn), a number of other revolts are held to be Zaydī rebellions. The first of these was that of Muḥammad ibn 'Abdu'llāh, An-Nafs az-Zakiyya (the pure soul) who was descended from Hasan. He claimed the Imamate and rose in rebellion against the 'Abbasid Caliph al-Manṣūr. He was killed in 145/762. After his death, a number of his followers, called the Muḥammadiyya, said that he had not been killed but was in concealment and would return to fill the earth with justice. Those who accepted the death of an-Nafs az-Zakiyya transferred the Imamate to Muḥammad ibn al-Qāsim, one of the descendants of the Imam Husayn, who lived in Ṭālaqān. He was arrested on the orders of the Caliph Mu'taṣim in 219/834 and died in prison, although some of his followers in Daylām and Ṭabaristān (north Iran) continued to await his return. An even later revolt which is considered to be in the line of Zaydiyya is that of Yaḥyā ibn 'Umar who was of Husaynid descent. He arose in rebellion during the Caliphate of Musta'īn and was killed in 250/864. The same year, Ḥasan ibn Zayd succeeded in founding a Zaydī state in Ṭabaristān in north Iran. A few decades later in 301/913, Ḥasan ibn 'Alī al-Uṭrush, Nāṣir al-Ḥaqq, a Zaydī Imam, made his way to Daylām and Gīlān in north Iran where the people had resisted the adoption of Islam. Here he was successful in converting the people to Zaydī Shi'ism and a succession of 'Alid Zaydī rulers ruled over them until about 424/1032. In 288/901 another Zaydī state was established in Yemen, centred on Sa'da and, in more modern times, in San'a. This state, although over-run on numerous occasions during its history, managed to retain its Zaydī identity and on the dismemberment of the Ottoman Empire after the First World War, the Zaydī Imam, Yaḥyā al-Mutawakkil, succeeded in bringing the area under his control and establishing a Zaydī state which survived until a revolution in 1962. Thus this sect has survived to the present day. In its early history it was, however, recorded as having divided into a number of sub-groups:

a. *Jārūdiyya.* This group of the Zaydiyya named after Abu'l-Jārūd Ziyād ibn Abī Ziyād, was opposed to the approval of the companions of the Prophet. They held that although there was no specific designation of 'Ali by the Prophet, there was a sufficient description given so that all should have recognised him. They therefore considered the companions sinful in failing to recognise 'Ali. They also denied the legitimacy of Abū Bakr and 'Umar. This sect was active during the late Umayyad and early 'Abbasid period and its views predominated among the later Zaydīs.

b. *Sulaymāniyya* or *Jarīriyya.* This group, led by Sulaymān ibn Jarīr, held that the Imamate should be a matter to be decided by consultation. They felt that the companions, including Abū Bakr and 'Umar, had been in error in failing to follow 'Ali but this did not amount to sin. 'Uthmān, however, was attacked for the innovations that he introduced.

c. *Butriyya* or *Ṣālihiyya.* These two groups, named respectively after Kathīr an-Nawa al-Abtar and Ḥasan ibn Ṣālih, seem to have held identical doctrines. They agreed with the Jarīriyya on the matter of Abū Bakr and 'Umar and suspended judgement with respect to 'Uthmān. It is stated by one author that they followed the Mu'tazila in theology and the Ḥanafī school in most questions of law, though in some matters they agreed with ash-Shāfi'ī and the Shi'is.

During the Imamates of Muḥammad al-Bāqir and Ja'far aṣ-Ṣādiq

This period was a very turbulent one both in the Islamic world in general, with the overthrow of the Umayyads and establishment of the 'Abbasid Caliphate, and in the Shi'i community. We have already noted the 'Abbasid movement which grew out of the Kaysāniyya during this time and the rebellions of Zayd and an-Nafs az-Zakiyya. A number of other groups were also active during this period.

4. *The Janāḥiyya*

In 127/744 'Abdu'llāh ibn Mu'āwiya rose in revolt against the last Umayyad Caliph. 'Abdu'llāh was a descendant of Ja'far ibn Abū Ṭālib, the brother of the Imam 'Ali. Ja'far was known as Dhu'l-Janāḥayn (the possessor of two wings). 'Abdu'llāh is accused of holding a number of extreme opinions: the incarnation of God in a succession of Prophets and Imams passing eventually through Muḥammad ibn Ḥanafiyya and Abū Hāshim to 'Abdu'llāh ibn Mu'āwiya; transmigration of souls; and the allegorical interpretation of the Qur'an. 'Abdu'llāh was forced to flee from Kūfa and established his rule over the province of Fārs until defeated by Abū Muslim. Some of his followers asserted that he had not died but was concealed in the mountains of Isfahan and would appear again.

5. *The Mughīriyya*

The followers of Mughīra ibn Sa'īd al-'Ijlī are sometimes accounted among the *ghulāt* of the Imamiyya and sometimes among the Zaydiyya. In fact it would appear that Mughīra changed his allegiance over the years several times. Initially he was a follower of Muḥammad al-Bāqir but the latter repudiated him and anathematised him on account of his assertion of al-Bāqir's divinity. Mughīra believed in anthropomorphism with respect to God. After al-Bāqir's death, Mughīra claimed the Imamate and even prophethood for himself. However, he told his followers to await the return of al-Bāqir who would raise the dead. Mughīra was put to death in 119/737 by Khalīd ibn 'Abdu'llāh al-Qasrī, on the same day as Bayān ibn Sam'ān (see above) according to some writers.[25] Indeed, Bayān and Mughīra were closely linked in many ways including their *ghuluww* tendencies with respect to al-Bāqir. After Mughīra's death his followers attached themselves to Muḥammad an-Nafs az-Zakiyya.

6. *The Manṣūriyya or Kisfiyya*

A third group linked to the Bayāniyya and the Mughīriyya were the followers of Abū Manṣūr al-'Ijlī. Abū Manṣūr also initially claimed to be a follower of al-Bāqir but was repudiated by the latter on account of *ghuluww* tendencies. Later Abū Manṣūr claimed the Imamate had passed to him. The name Kisfiyya arose because Abū Manṣūr believed himself to be the piece (*kisf*) of heaven falling down which is mentioned in Qur'an (52:44). He maintained that the first thing created by God was Jesus and then after him 'Ali. He held to an allegorical interpretation of the Qur'an which among other things meant that those things forbidden in the Qur'an were nothing but allegory for the names of certain evil men. Thus his followers are accused of all manner of immorality and sin. It is also said that they killed their enemies by strangling or breaking the skull with wooden clubs.

After Abū Manṣūr's death, leadership of the group passed to his son, Ḥusayn, although some of the Manṣūriyya went over to the supporters of an-Nafs az-Zakiyya.

7. *The Khaṭṭābiyya*

Abu'l-Khaṭṭāb Muḥammad ibn Abū Zaynab al-Asadī al-Ajda' was yet another figure who was at first connected with the main line of Twelver Imams. At first he claimed to be the representative of Imam Ja'far aṣ-Ṣādiq and to have been taught by him knowledge of the Greatest Name of God. But he was repudiated and anathematised by aṣ-Ṣādiq. Then Abu'l-Khaṭṭāb claimed the Imamate for himself while elevating aṣ-Ṣādiq to the level of prophethood and divinity. Central to Abu'l-

Khaṭṭab's doctrines appears to have been an allegorical interpretation of the Qur'an. His followers also believed that they would not die but would be lifted up to heaven. They are accused of having disregarded all religious observances and regarded everything as lawful. Abu'l-Khaṭṭāb was executed in Kūfa in 138/755. His followers, who appear to have been numerous, split among several leaders:

a. *Bazīghiyya.* The followers of Bazīgh ibn Mūsā, the weaver, who followed Abu'l-Khaṭṭāb's doctrines and claimed that a man who had reached perfection should not be said to have died and that the best of his followers were superior to the angels.

b. *Mu'ammariyya.* The followers of Mu'ammar ibn Khaytham, the corn dealer, who claimed prophethood in succession to Abu'l-Khaṭṭāb and asserted that the present world would never come to an end but that both paradise and hell were to be experienced here.

c. *'Umayriyya* or *'Ijliyya.* The followers of 'Umayr ibn Bayān al-'Ijlī, the straw dealer of Kūfa.

d. *Mufaḍḍaliyya.* The followers of Mufaḍḍal aṣ-Ṣayrafī who is said to have believed in the lordship of aṣ-Ṣādiq but repudiated the apostleship or prophethood of Abu'l-Khaṭṭāb.

e. *Ghurābiyya.* The followers of this group, who in one source are accounted as part of the Khaṭṭābiyya, are said to have held that since Muhammad and 'Ali were as indistinguishable from each other as one raven (*ghurāb*) is from another, when the angel Gabriel was sent with the divine revelation from God for 'Ali, he gave it by mistake to Muhammad. One Muslim writer has commented on the beliefs of this sect that even were it to be accepted that Gabriel could not distinguish between an eleven-year-old boy and a forty-year-old man, can it really be accepted that God would not have corrected the error?[26]

In many of the sources, the Khaṭṭābiyya are closely linked with the emergence of the Ismā'īlīs. Mufaḍḍal ibn 'Umar al-Ju'fī, a member of this sect, is said to have been closely associated with and perhaps even a teacher of Ismā'īl ibn Ja'far and is accused of having led Ismā'īl astray in several Traditions attributed to the Imam Ja'far aṣ-Ṣādiq.[27] Some Ismā'īlī doctrines are said to have been derived from the Khaṭṭābiyya. A group of the Khaṭṭābiyya are said to have transferred their allegiance directly to Muḥammad ibn Ismā'īl after the death of Abu'l-Khaṭṭāb. Even in some Ismā'īlī books, Abu'l-Khaṭṭāb is accounted as one of the founders of the Ismā'īliyya.[28] In other Ismā'īlī books, however, Abu'l-Khaṭṭāb is condemned as a heretic.

8. *The Bāqiriyya*

This is one of the sects known under the more general name Wāqifiyya

– those who hesitate over the death of a particular Imam in contradistinction to the Qaṭ'iyya – those who are certain about the death of the Imam. In the case of the Bāqiriyya, they believed the Imamate ceased with al-Bāqir and that he was in concealment and would return.

After the Imamate of Ja'far aṣ-Ṣādiq

The death of Ja'far aṣ-Ṣādiq marks an important turning-point in the history of the Shi'a, for it is at this point that one of the most important fragmentations of the Shi'i community occurred according to the traditional histories. Apart from the line of what would become the Ithnā-'Ashariyya or Twelver sect (who appear at this time to have been called the Qaṭ'iyya or the ones who were certain about the death of the previous Imam and went on to the next Imam) and the *ghulāt* sects of the Khaṭṭābiyya, Mughīriyya, etc. mentioned in the previous section, the following sects must also be noted:

9. *The Ja'fariyya or Nāwusiyya*

These are the Wāqifiyya with respect to aṣ-Ṣādiq, believing that the latter did not die but is concealed and will return as the Mahdī. Nāwus of Baṣra was a prominent exponent of this idea. There was also a group to whom no particular name appears to have been assigned who believed that after aṣ-Ṣādiq the Imamate ceased.

10. *The Afṭaḥiyya or Faṭaḥiyya*

These maintained that after the Third Imam, Husayn, the succession should always be through the eldest surviving son of the previous Imam. The eldest surviving son of aṣ-Ṣādiq was 'Abdu'llāh al-Afṭaḥ (the flat-footed or flat-headed). It is claimed that al-Afṭaḥ disagreed with his father during his lifetime over matters of doctrine and was inclined to the opinion of the Murji'ites.[29] However, according to one tradition, al-Afṭaḥ survived his father by only seventy days leaving no sons and according to another tradition he was found to be lacking in knowledge by the learned ones among the Shi'a. Therefore, although there was a great deal of support for his claim to the Imamate initially, it fell away rapidly. Some of his followers felt that the Imamate finished with him, while others believed that he had a son who was living in concealment but who was the Mahdī. Most of them turned to the Imam Mūsā al-Kāẓim; but some, however, continued to regard al-Afṭaḥ as the rightful Imam before Mūsā.

11. *The Shumaytiyya or Sumaytiyya*

The followers of Yaḥyā ibn Abī Shumayt (or Sumayt) who asserted the Imamate of aṣ-Ṣādiq's fourth son, Muḥammad, known as ad-Dībāj (the handsome). According to at least one account this Muḥammad believed in a Zaydī type of Imamate and came forward against the Caliph Ma'mūn in 199/814. He was defeated but Ma'mūn treated him considerately and made him part of his court in Khurasān.[30] This sect believed in the Imamate remaining in the family of Muhammad ad-Dībāj and that the Mahdī would come from among them.

12. *The Ismā'īliyya or Sab'iyya*

There seems general agreement among the Shi'i sources that, at first, aṣ-Ṣādiq had intended his eldest son Ismā'īl to succeed him. But then Ismā'īl died and this had disturbing implications for both the question of the nature of the Imamate and for the doctrine of designation (*naṣṣ*). Apart from the groups mentioned above who believed that Ismā'īl's death annulled his Imamate and who therefore transferred their allegiance to other members of aṣ-Ṣādiq's family, there were a number who denied that it was possible to annul designation. These split into several groups:

a. *Pure Ismā'īliyya.* These held that Ismā'īl did not in fact die but was concealed by aṣ-Ṣādiq out of fear for his safety and that he will return as the Mahdī.

b. *Mubārakiyya.* The followers of Mubārak, a servant or *mawla* of Muḥammad ibn Ismā'īl, who maintained that since the Imamate was designated to Ismā'īl and since after Hasan and Husayn the Imamate could not pass between brothers but only to sons, the Imam after aṣ-Ṣādiq should be Muḥammad, the son of Ismā'īl, but these then stop with Muḥammad's Imamate.

c. *Fatimid Ismā'īlīs, Qarāmiṭa (Carmathians), Bāṭiniyya and Ta'līmiyya.* The Fatimid Ismā'īlīs believed that following on from Muḥammad ibn Ismā'īl there were several hidden Imams and that from these came the Fatimid dynasty in Egypt (297/909–567/1171). Simultaneous to the rise of the Fatimid dynasty, there were groups of Ismā'īlīs active along the southern shores of the Persian Gulf who did not recognise the Fatimids as their Imams. These were called Qarāmiṭa (Carmathians). Because of their belief that there is a hidden meaning (*bāṭin*) behind every literal or external meaning (*ẓāhir*) of all revealed scripture, the Ismā'īlīs were often called Bāṭiniyya. Another sub-group of the Ismā'īlīs were the Druse, who had deified the Fatimid Caliph al-Ḥākim and broken off from the main body of the Ismā'īlīs forming a distinct group in Syria that has survived to the present day.

The Fatimid Ismā'īlīs split in 487/1094 into two major divisions, the Nizārī and Musta'līan in favour of two opposing claimants to the Imamate. The majority of the Musta'līan branch continued to recognise the Caliphs in Egypt until 526/1132 and then their Imam and Caliph Abu'l-Qāsim Ṭayyib went into occultation and this branch has had no revealed Imam ever since. Leadership of the movement was transferred to the Yemen under a series of *Dā'ī Muṭlaqs* (missionaries in charge of the movement). There was a further split in 999/1590 with one line of *dā'īs*, the Sulaymānī, remaining in Yemen with a few followers in India, and another line, the Dā'ūdī, resident in India claiming the majority of Indian Musta'līan followers who are called Bohras. Musta'līan Ismā'īlīs are predominantly to be found in the Indian province of Gujarat but also in south Arabia, the Persian Gulf, East Africa and Burma, numbering several hundred thousand in all.

The other main division of the Ismā'īlīs, the Nizārīs, became centred on Alamut in Iran under Ḥasan aṣ-Ṣabbāḥ. Initially Ḥasan's successors regarded themselves as *dā'īs* of an occulted Imam, but the fourth *dā'ī* proclaimed himself Imam, claiming to be in fact a descendant of Nizār who had been ousted from the Fāṭimid Caliphate in 487/1094. The Nizārīs became famous in history as the Assassins. They are also called Ta'līmīs because of their doctrine that the Imam is the dispenser of divinely-ordained teaching (*ta'līm*). Their centre at Alamut was destroyed by Hulagu Khan in 654/1256 and after this the Nizārī Imams went into hiding, changing their residence from place to place in Iran. It is only in the 19th century that the Nizārī Imams re-emerge as historical figures in the form of the first Agha Khān who in 1840 fled from Iran to India where Nizārī missionary efforts over many centuries had created a large community. The Agha Khān established himself in Bombay, which has remained the centre of the Nizārīs in India. The Agha Khān's successors have become international figures. The community is most numerous in India (where they are called Khojas) but there are also important communities in East Africa, Pakistan, Syria, Iran, Afghanistan and Central Asia, numbering several millions in all.

After the Death of Mūsā al-Kāẓim

After Mūsā the main line of Shi'is who eventually went on to become the Twelvers turned to Mūsā's son, 'Alī ar-Riḍā, and were again called the Qaṭ'iyya (those who were certain of the death of Mūsā). But a number of other groups arose:

13. *The Mūsawiyya or Mamṭūra*

These denied or were uncertain of the death of Mūsā and therefore did not accept the continuation of the Imamate beyond Mūsā, and are again called by the general name of Wāqifiyya. Some of them believed that he had not died but escaped from prison and was now in concealment; others considered he had died and was raised again to life and is in concealment; yet others believed he was raised to heaven like Jesus and will return. All these groups believe in the return of Mūsā as the Imam Mahdī to fill the earth with justice. By their enemies these people were called the Mamṭūra (the rained-upon).[31]

14. *The Bajaliyya*

Ibn Warsand al-Bajalī took the Mūsawiyya doctrine to Morocco and Spain in the first part of the 3rd/9th century. He and his descendants had some success in propagating this doctrine among the people of this area and some of the Idrisid amirs were also converted. The sect probably eventually died out in the 6th/12th century with the advent of the Almohad movement.

15. *The Bashīriyya*

The followers of Muḥammad ibn Bashīr of Kūfa maintained that Mūsā was not imprisoned and did not die. He was in concealment and had appointed Ibn Bashīr as his representative and given him his seal. Therefore, all the followers of Mūsā had now to obey Ibn Bashīr for he was the Imam and the Imamate would remain with him and his successors until the return of Mūsā as the Mahdī. 'Alī ar-Riḍā and others who claimed the Imamate after Mūsā were of base birth and were falsely claiming descent from Mūsā. Only the five daily prayers and fasting were obligatory and the validity of all other religious laws were denied. The Bashīriyya were said to have believed in the transmigration of souls, holding that there has only ever been one Imam whose soul goes from one body to the next. They also held to the doctrine of *tafwīḍ* (see p. 66). They believed in holding all goods in common. After Ibn Bashīr, leadership of this group fell to his son, Samī'.

After the Imamate of 'Alī ar-Riḍā

The main line of Twelver Shi'ism continued after 'Alī ar-Riḍā with his son, Muḥammad at-Taqī, but as the latter was only seven years old there were groups who dissented from this:

16. *The Aḥmadiyya*

This group believed that 'Alī's father, Mūsā, had decreed that after 'Alī the Imamate should go to Mūsā's next son, Aḥmad (it is he who is said to be buried in the shrine of Shāh Chirāgh in Shiraz).

17. *The Mu'allifa*

This group adopted a position of being Wāqifiyya over the death of Mūsā and awaiting his return.

18. *The Muḥadditha*

These are stated to have been a group of Murj'ites and others from the main stream of Islam who came to believe in the Imamate of Mūsā and 'Alī (in the hope of political favour it is said) but after 'Alī's death returned to their former belief. Similarly some of the Zaydiyya are said to have attached themselves to 'Alī but returned to their former beliefs when he died.

After the Imamate of 'Alī al-Hādī

19. *The Namīriyya, Nuṣayriyya, 'Alawiyya*

This group began as followers of Muḥammad ibn Nuṣayr an-Namīrī. There is considerable variation in the sources regarding the teachings of this man. Some state that he was a follower of the teachings of Abu'l-Khaṭṭāb; some say that he considered 'Alī al-Hādī, the Tenth Imam, to be God and that he, Ibn Nuṣayr was his prophet; some state that he considered 'Alī al-Hādī to be the Imam and 'Alī's son Muḥammad who died in 249/863 was the Mahdī while he proclaimed himself in 245/859 to be the Bāb (Gate) to 'Alī al-Hādī. The later writers of the sect relate his claims regarding the Mahdī to the son of Ḥasan al-'Askarī, the Eleventh Imam, and thus acknowledge all twelve Imams of the Twelver line. The man who is mostly responsible for the establishment of the sect was Ḥusayn ibn Ḥamdān al-Khaṣībī (d. 346/957 or 358/968). Under the patronage of the Hamdanid dynasty, he greatly extended the influence of the sect at Aleppo. After the fall of the Shi'i dynasties of Aleppo, the sect faced great persecution over the centuries at the hands successively of the Crusaders, the Mamluks and the Ottomans. They were also rent by civil wars between their various clans. After the First World War the French attempted to set up a separate 'Alawī state centred on Lattakia but later this was abandoned. At present the 'Alawīs are politically dominant in Syria under President Hafiz al-Assad. The 'Alawī community now numbers several millions living in a band of land stretching from Lattakia in Syria to Antakya (Antioch) in Turkey.

20. *The Muḥammadiyya*

During the lifetime of 'Alī al-Hādī, one of his sons, Muḥammad, died. However, a group of 'Alī's followers maintained that 'Alī had designated Muḥammad as the next Imam and that the latter had not died but this had been a ruse to put off their enemies. Muḥammad was now concealed and would return as the Mahdī.

21. *The Pure Ja'fariyya*

These maintained that 'Alī al-Hādī had in fact nominated his son, Ja'far, as the next Imam.

After the Death of Ḥasan al-'Askarī

After the death of Ḥasan al-'Askarī, the Shi'is were thrown into confusion and fragmented into a large number of groups. According to al-Mas'ūdī, the Shi'i broke up into twenty sects at this time;[32] Sa'd al-Qummī describes fifteen sects;[33] and an-Nawbakhtī, fourteen sects.[34] These sects may be divided into the following broad groupings:

a. *The Wāqifiyya at Ḥasan al-'Askarī*

These stopped at the Imamate at Ḥasan al-'Askarī who was considered the Mahdī. Some of these thought that he had not died but had gone into occultation while another group thought he had died but had been raised to life again. Both of these groups considered that al-'Askarī had left no son. A third group stopped at al-'Askarī because although they acknowledged his death and recognised that the earth could not be without an Imam, they could not be sure who was al-'Askarī's successor.

b. *The Cessation of the Imamate*

These considered that just as prophecy had ceased with Muhammad, so it was possible for the Imamate to have ceased with al-'Askarī who had neither son nor successor. One group maintained that there could be no Mahdī, while another held that the Mahdī would arise from among the descendants of the Imams in the last days.

c. *The Muḥammadiyya*

These maintained that al-Hādī had designated his son Muḥammad, who predeceased him, as the Imam (since neither Ḥasan al-'Askarī, because of his childlessness, nor Ja'far, because of his immorality, fulfilled the conditions required for the Imamate). One group maintained Muḥammad had not died but was the Mahdī in concealment.

d. *The Ja'fariyya*

These considered that al-'Askarī had died without a son and that the Imamate belonged to his brother Ja'far. One group of this faction considered that since al-Askarī died without issue, the Imamate must belong to Ja'far; another group held that al-'Askarī had formally designated Ja'far; another group that as al-Askarī had died without issue, he had not fulfilled the condition for the Imamate and thus the true Imam after al-Hādī was Ja'far (see number 21 above); yet another group claimed that the Tenth Imam had designated his son Muḥammad as Imam but as Muḥammad predeceased him, the Imamate was transferred to Ja'far through an intermediary, a slave called Nafīs (this group is called the Nafīsiyya).

e. *The Qaṭ'iyya*

This is the group who as with the previous Imams was certain of the death of the previous Imam, al-'Askarī, and went on to al-'Askarī's son as the next Imam. One group considered that his name was Muḥammad and that he was of mature years at the death of al-'Askarī; another that his name was 'Alī; another that his name was Muḥammad but that he had been born eight months after the Imam's death; and finally there was the group who held that al-'Askarī had had a son, he was four years of age at the time of the death of his father, he had gone into occultation until the last days and it was forbidden to seek him out.

This last-described group, the fifteenth sect described by Sa'd al-Qummī, was, of course, the one that went on to become the orthodox Ithnā-'Asharī (Twelver) or Imāmī sect of Shi'i Islam. The other groupings died out within one hundred years or so.

The reason that a fairly lengthy description of all these various Shi'i groupings (most of which became rapidly extinct) has been given is that this was the milieu out of which Twelver Shi'ism emerged in the early 4th/10th century. Many of the doctrines and concepts first used by these groups were to become incorporated into Twelver Shi'ism (e.g. the Mahdī, occultation and return, esoteric exegesis, etc.; see next chapter).

4

Early History of Shi'i Islam, AD 632–1000

In the whole field of Islamic studies, Shi'i Islam has probably received less than its fair share of attention and effort from Western orientalists. However, in recent years, there have been some studies in this very important field and the 1979 revolution in Iran has undoubtedly focused attention on Shi'i Islam. In surveying the whole of Shi'i history, it is without doubt the early period in which modern, mainly Western, critical scholarship has presented a picture which differs most markedly from that found in the books of the traditional Muslim historians, whether Shi'i or Sunni.

At the start, one problem that is conceived by modern scholars to beset the study of Islam (whether Sunni or Shi'i) is the problem of the historicity of the sources. For Muslims the ideal society was the one in which the Prophet ruled over men with infallible wisdom and judgement. For Shi'is this period is extended to the period of the Imam 'Ali. This was an ideal 'Golden Age' which each generation of Muslims tries to recreate. Therefore there is little concept of change and development having occurred in Islamic theology, jurisprudence or constitutional theory. If most Muslims in any age were to have been asked in what way their theology differed from that of the orthodox of an earlier period, their answer would be that there is no difference. This, of course, is a fundamental difference from Western insistence that all such matters are continuously in a state of change and development. However, the result of this Muslim conceptualisation of a static, unchanging Islam is that when later Shi'i writers write of early periods, and especially of the period of the Prophet and the Imams, they unconsciously and retrospectively impose their own views and formulations onto that earlier period. Thus works that purport to examine the history or teachings of an earlier period are in reality more a reflection of the period in which they are written than true expositions of that earlier period. Also, since we have very few Shi'i works surviving from much before the 4th/10th century, it is very difficult to examine the earliest period and, to a great extent, reliance has been placed on the works of opponents of Shi'ism from that early period.

Modern historians have rejected much of the picture that the Muslim historical works attempt to create. These early historical works, whether written from the point of view of Twelver Shi'is, Ismā'īlīs, Mu'tazilites or orthodox Sunnis, all present a picture of the Shi'is as a single main body following a line of Imams from which, at different times, groups have split off over the question of the succession to the Imamate. This picture is thought by modern scholars to have been retrospectively imposed over the facts of the history of the early period by historians of the 3rd and 4th Islamic centuries for doctrinal reasons.[1] Because of this it is very difficult to go through the sources back to what the Imams and their followers actually said and did.

One writer has suggested that the traditional account of the differences between the various Shi'i sects was, in fact, a surreptitious method of conducting political debate during the later 'Abbasid period. By referring their arguments to events that allegedly occurred in the past, those conducting this debate avoided the wrath of the autocratic 'Abbasid government.[2]

Having discarded the traditional account of early Shi'i history, it is, of course, difficult to replace this with a complete alternative picture. But by a close analysis of the earliest sources, some idea has been built up by modern critical scholarship of the circumstances in which Shi'ism arose.

The First Four Caliphs and the Umayyad Dynasty (AD 632–750)

Even the standard Shi'i sources admit that as a religious group the Shi'a of 'Ali were an extremely small group. They were limited to four persons initially and Western scholars have even cast doubt on this number. However, it would be difficult to deny, on an objective assessment of the source material, that 'Ali evidently felt that he had some claim to the leadership on the death of the Prophet and had been unfairly passed over in the election of Abū Bakr. Why else would a man who had been in the forefront of the military and political affairs of the Muslim community suddenly retire from all participation in the affairs of the community? In a straight-forward election by consensus, as would have occurred after the death of a tribal leader, 'Ali's youth would have precluded any realistic expectation of election, while by Arab customs of inheritance, Muhammad's uncle, al-'Abbās, would have inherited his position. Therefore 'Ali's retirement from active public life seems to support the idea that he felt that he had received some specific designation by Muhammad. This is all that can be gleaned from the sources. Beyond that, it is a matter of opinion whether one chooses to believe that 'Ali claimed for himself the type of religio-political leadership implied in the Shi'i concept of the Imamate or to believe that this is a retrospective imposition by Shi'i historians. Probably the vast majority of those who later flocked to 'Ali's side after he had assumed the Caliphate were Shi'a of 'Ali only in the political sense and not in the religious sense.

Much confusion has arisen due to the use of the word Shi'i to describe persons of very widely differing opinions. There has been a tendency to imagine that when someone from the early period is described as Shi'i this means that he held the same opinions as a modern Shi'i. To demonstrate this more clearly, two terms should be defined. Firstly, political Shi'ism: this indicates a belief that the members of the house of Hāshim are the people most worthy of holding political authority in the Islamic community, but no belief in any particular religious station for this family. Secondly, religious Shi'ism: this indicates a belief that particular members of the house of Hāshim are in receipt of divine inspiration and are thus the channel of God's guidance to men whether or not they hold *de facto* political authority.

Although during the lifetimes of 'Ali and Hasan, there were many who could be numbered as political Shi'i, few can confidently be counted as religious Shi'i. Even in the celebrated case of Ḥujr ibn 'Adī al-Kindī and his thirteen companions whom Shi'is count as the first of their martyrs, it is difficult to see in the charges drawn up against them any firm indication that they were partisans of 'Ali in any but a political sense.[3]

The next indication of a religious aspect to the movement that is described as Shi'i in the historical sources comes with the martyrdom of Husayn. His action has been interpreted by Shi'i writers as an act of self-sacrifice resulting from a desire to jolt the consciences of the Muslims and to reactivate the ethos of the Islamic community as created by Muhammad, an ethos which was in danger of being submerged by the worldliness of the Umayyads.[4] Some Western writers, however, have tended to look upon Husayn as an ill-fated adventurer who misjudged the reliability of Kūfan promises and over-estimated his own inviolability as the grandson of the Prophet. But this rather cynical view of Husayn belies some of the historical evidence such as Husayn's refusal to take the safe option of turning back or turning aside to the hills held by his supporters when apprised of the hopelessness of his situation, and his refusal to compromise even when certain death was the alternative.

It is, however, with the advent of the *Tawwābūn* (the penitents) following the martyrdom of Husayn that the first unequivocally religious manifestation of the Shi'i movement appeared. There can be little doubt that the self-sacrifice of this band of men must be ascribed to religious zeal for the house of 'Ali rather than any political considerations.

Although almost all Shi'i groups were agreed on the succession passing from 'Ali to Hasan and thence to Husayn,[5] after the last-named, there appears to have been something of a split. Certainly the vast majority of those who have been referred to above as political Shi'a went on to support Mukhtār who arose in the name of Muḥammad ibn al-Ḥanafiyya. The mass of the Shi'a of Kūfa followed Mukhtār and, indeed, it is doubtful whether Zaynu'l-'Ābidīn, the Imam of the Twelver line, had any followers at all, at least until the collapse of Mukhtār's revolt in Iraq and perhaps not until after the end of Ibn az-Zubayr's Caliphate in the Hijaz in 73/692.[6] Some Western historians even doubt whether Zaynu'l-'Ābidīn put forward any claim to religious leadership (i.e. the Imamate) at all.

In the same way, Muḥammad al-Bāqir, the Fifth Imam of the Twelver line, who was during his lifetime eclipsed by the support among the Shi'a for Abū Hāshim, the son of Muḥammad ibn al-Ḥanafiyya, and the increasing support for his own half-brother, Zayd, is represented by some Western writers as having made no claims at all but rather as having had claims retrospectively imposed upon him by later Shi'i writers.

The fact that Muḥammad ibn al-Ḥanafiyya, who was a son of 'Ali by a Ḥanafī woman (i.e. not by Fāṭima, the daughter of the Prophet); Muḥammad an-Nafs az-Zakiyya, who was a descendant of Hasan; 'Abdu'llāh ibn Mu'āwiya, who was not a descendant of 'Ali at all but of 'Ali's brother, Ja'far; and the 'Abbasids, who were descendants of the uncle of both Muhammad and 'Ali; were all able to lay claim to Shi'i sympathy and to obtain considerable Shi'i support shows that some at least of the Shi'is of that time placed no particular emphasis on either descent from the Prophet through Fāṭima or even descent from 'Ali – any claimant from the house of Hāshim would do. This is a clear indication that political considerations such as the overthrow of Umayyad-Syrian domination and the status of the *mawālī** were dominant over the religious issue of the station and identity of the Imam and the rights of the house of 'Ali. Therefore any claimant who looked as though he could be successful was able to obtain support. However, despite the above evidence, there is equally no proof that a small number of persons did not exist who may be considered as proto-Twelvers and who looked to those who were to become identified as the Twelver line of Imams for religious guidance.

It is only with the Sixth Imam, Ja'far aṣ-Ṣādiq (d. 148/765), that there is any firm evidence that any form of religious leadership was being

* During this period, when non-Arabs wished to become Muslims, they were made to become clients (*mawla*, plural *mawālī*) of one of the Arab tribes. This gave them an inferior social status and in some cases made them liable to exploitation in direct contradiction of the Qur'an and Sunna.

claimed by the Twelver Imams. Aṣ-Ṣādiq was a well known and influential figure in the Islamic world. His circle of students included several who were later to go on to become prominent jurists and Traditionists in their own right among non-Shi'i Muslims. It is almost certain that aṣ-Ṣādiq did not make an open claim to religious leadership among his circle of students, but the existence of a number of prominent religious figures such as Hishām ibn al-Ḥakam, 'Alī al-Maythamī and Muḥammad ibn Nu'mān, Mu'min aṭ-Ṭāq, who evidently looked to aṣ-Ṣādiq as Imam, as well as several other leading figures such as Abu'l-Khaṭṭāb, who held beliefs of a *ghuluww* (extremist)* nature regarding him, all tends to indicate that aṣ-Ṣādiq was a focus of religious speculation and leadership in his own time.

The names of *ghulāt* groups, especially in Kūfa, increase dramatically in number during aṣ-Ṣādiq's lifetime. Indeed, from the sources it would appear that a sizeable proportion of the population of Iraq was involved in speculation of a *ghuluww* nature at this time. It is therefore necessary to digress for a moment to consider the origin of the *ghulāt*.

The Ghulāt

When the Arabs invaded the Fertile Crescent in the years following the death of the Prophet, they encountered ancient civilisations with sophisticated religious systems. The religion of Islam by comparison was as yet simple and undeveloped. The Prophet himself was already dead and so there was no one to whom the Muslims could turn for a binding answer to the sophisticated religious questions being posed by these ancient civilisations. There thus arose a ferment of discussion around some of the concepts introduced by these older religious systems.

Initially the Arabs in their camp cities managed to avoid much disturbing religious speculation but as assimilation increased and more of the native population embraced Islam, more and more discussion arose. This was probably particularly true of Iraq which was already the seat of intense religious ferment even before the Arab invasion. In Iraq the ancient Babylonian religious systems, Zoroastrianism, Mazdakism, Manichaeism, Judaism and various forms of Christianity all contributed to a kaleidoscope of religious debate and speculation probably unequalled in the ancient world. From this variegated background ideas were injected into the Muslim community and intensively discussed by groups of people interested in such matters. These groups of people, discussing what the majority of Muslims would consider heterodox concepts which they had imbibed from the religious milieu of Iraq,

* For a fuller explanation of this term see Glossary and the following pages.

became known to later generations of Muslims by the name *ghulāt* or extremists. Among the ideas that were injected into the debate were such concepts as *tanāsukh* (transmigration of souls), *ghayba* (occultation), *raj'a* (return), *ḥulūl* (descent of the Spirit of God into man), *imāma* (Imamate, divinely-inspired leadership and guidance), *tashbīh* (anthropomorphism with respect to God), *tafwīḍ* (delegation of God's powers to other than God), and *badā* (alteration in God's will). The *ghulāt* were, however, in need of a priest-god figure onto which to project their ideas of *ḥulūl*, *ghayba*, etc., a role admirably suited to the figure of 'Ali. In the rest of the discussion in this chapter the term *ghuluww* will be used as a convenient label for theological speculation based on the above doctrines.*

The linking of *ghuluww* speculation to the Shi'a or party of 'Ali was probably a historical and geographical accident. Syria and Iraq had been rivals and antagonists from long before the Arab invasion. In the period immediately before the Muslim onslaught, Syria representing Byzantine Christianity gazed across a hostile frontier at Iraq representing Zoroastrian Iran. Following the Arab invasion it did not take long before the old rivalry resurfaced. When Mu'āwiya made Syria his base for a bid for the Caliphate, it was only natural for 'Ali to go to Iraq and set up his headquarters there. When Mu'āwiya, representing the party (*Shi'a*) of 'Uthmān (or 'Uthmāniyya), overcame Hasan, representing the party (*Shi'a*) of 'Ali and Syria came to dominate Iraq, it was only natural for the party of 'Ali to come to represent Iraq's political aspirations and its desire to overthrow eventually Syrian domination.

Thus fortuitously there came together in Iraq the *ghulāt* and the Shi'a of 'Ali. The *ghulāt* adopted the family of 'Ali as the embodiment of their religious speculation but the Shi'a of 'Ali always looked on the *ghulāt* with a certain amount of suspicion and distaste. However, one event above all others probably served as a catalyst to fuse together the *ghulāt* and the political Shi'a of 'Ali so that later historians came to look upon them as one. This event was the martyrdom of Husayn. The pathos of this event gave the family of 'Ali a cultic significance and thus gave the Shi'a of 'Ali, which had previously been primarily a political party, a thrust into a religious orientation directing it firmly in the direction of the *ghulāt*, while at the same time giving those engaged in *ghuluww* speculation a hero-martyr and a priestly family with which they could associate much of their speculation. That the *ghulāt* were only loosely attached to the family of 'Ali is proved by the ease with which such figures as Abū Manṣūr and Abu'l-Khaṭṭāb felt they could transfer the Imamate from the family of 'Ali onto themselves and their descendants.

Although this type of speculation is now called *ghuluww*, i.e.

* A number of Western scholars have attempted to attribute the origin of these Shi'i-*ghuluww* ideas to Yemeni (South Arabian) religious traditions.

extremism, this is only really a statement by later Muslim writers who compared this speculation with the fully-evolved orthodox position. It does not necessarily follow that the holding of these opinions was considered extreme at that time. As one writer has put it:

> . . . there is no reason to be shocked when the *Ghulât* looked to others than Muḥammad's descendants as messianic figures – one might equally say the extremist is the one who exalts persons purely on account of their birth. Nor is there anything more extreme in expecting a man to return whom others regard as dead – as some of the early *Ghulât* did – than in the expectation of the so-called moderate Shi'a that a man will return whom others doubt was ever born [i.e. the Twelfth Imam].[7]

The major factor that caused groups to be labelled as *ghulāt* by later writers was their attribution of either divinity to anyone other than God or prophethood to anyone after Muhammad.[8] However, as the same writer has pointed out, the idea that Muhammad was the last prophet from God is not explicitly stated in the Qur'an and was almost certainly a doctrine developed quite late in the evolution of orthodox Muslim theology.[9] Thus there is nothing to indicate that *ghulāt* speculation was considered extremist or immoderate by the Muslims in the 2nd century (AD 718–815). One indication of the widespread acceptability of *ghuluww* views is the fact that it is embarrassingly difficult for Shi'i writers to find eminent religious figures of this period who can be claimed to be Shi'i but who are not tainted by some degree of *ghuluww* heterodoxy. For example, of Hishām ibn al-Ḥakam, and Muḥammad ibn Nu'mān, Mu'min aṭ-Ṭāq, the two leading Shi'i theologians of aṣ-Ṣādiq's time, the first is credited with believing that God has a finite three-dimensional body, that He does not know things before they come into being, that He does change His decisions (*badā*) and that parts of the Qur'an have been suppressed and corrupted, while the latter is accused of anthropomorphism towards God – all of these opinions being contrary to the positions later adopted by the Twelver Shi'i theologians. It would seem, therefore, that the *ghuluww* doctrines were in fact the doctrine of the majority of the Shi'a at this time, including the followers of aṣ-Ṣādiq. The many Traditions ascribed to aṣ-Ṣādiq specifically refuting *ghuluww* views may well be later inventions, for it is doubtful whether men such as Hishām ibn al-Ḥakam would go against the explicit teachings of their Imam.

If Ja'far aṣ-Ṣādiq did try to make any doctrinal modifications to what the Shi'a were thinking at this time, it was probably in the sphere of belief in the Imams as incarnations of the Divinity that he exerted his efforts. Both the fact that he expelled Abu'l-Khaṭṭāb who made this claim about him from among his supporters and also the fact that this particular belief, characteristic of the *ghulāt*, appears to have died out among the

Shi'a in the generations succeeding aṣ-Ṣadiq (so that it is not in the list of Shi'i beliefs compiled by al-Khayyāṭ and al-Ash'arī in the 3rd/9th–10th century) indicate that this may have been one area in which aṣ-Ṣādiq and perhaps his son Mūsā al-Kāẓim exerted their influence and succeeded in having this doctrine put aside by their followers. Indeed, it is probable that the very appellation *ghulāt* dates from after aṣ-Ṣādiq. For before that time belief in the descent and incarnation of the Divinity was in the mainstream of ideological speculation, but from the time of aṣ-Ṣādiq this particular belief was gradually classed as being extreme and hence labelled *ghuluww*, a label which was then retrospectively applied to earlier generations because, of course, no one would admit that in those earlier generations such belief had been well accepted and mainstream. The other beliefs characteristic of the *ghulāt*, however, remained within the mainstream of Shi'ism for the time being. It must be noted that Shi'i scholars would maintain that modern critical scholarship has produced very little evidence that, regardless of what their followers may have been thinking, the Imams themselves said and thought anything different to what is ascribed to them by present-day Shi'is.

Other Shi'i Groups

While the *ghulāt* were having a significant influence on the development of Shi'ism from one direction during the lifetime of aṣ-Ṣādiq, another important influence was the political developments of the period. The 'Abbasid revolution had profound implications for the Shi'i movement. The 'Abbasid movement arose from a Shi'i base. Whether true or not, the 'Abbasids claimed that Abū Hāshim, the son of Muḥammad ibn al-Ḥanafiyya, had transferred his Imamate to the 'Abbasid family. The followers of Ibn al-Ḥanafiyya, the Kaysāniyya, were apparently the first of the Shi'a to set up an organised propaganda and the 'Abbasids were able to take over their network of missionaries and agents. The propaganda of the 'Abbasids was skilfully worked so as to attract the widest possible Shi'i support. The call of the 'Abbasid agents was for the people to rise in the name of *'ar-Riḍā min Ahl al-Bayt'* – one who shall be chosen from the family of the Prophet. To the masses this, of course, implied an 'Alid and the deception no doubt contributed to the success of the 'Abbasid uprising. For many of the Kaysāniyya and the Zaydiyya, the success of the 'Abbasid revolt was the fulfilment of their aspirations. The overthrow of the Umayyads, the shift of the centre of power from Syria to Iraq, and the improvement in the social position of the *mawālī*, were sufficient to satisfy many of the political Shi'a even if the 'Abbasid family were not exactly what they had in mind as *'ar-Riḍā min Ahl al-Bayt'*.

While *ghuluww* doctrines may have been the main source of theology for the Shi'a in this period, the 'Abbasid revolution was probably the factor that gave the impetus to the creation of the most fundamental and distinctive doctrine of the religious Shi'is, the doctrine of the Imamate. For the 'Abbasids also, initially at least, claimed a religious type of Imamate. At first they claimed it on the basis of their designation by Abū Hāshim, the son of Muḥammad ibn al-Ḥanafiyya. This ensured the support of large sections of the Shi'a who were inclined to the Zaydī-Kaysānī concept of the Imamate. Later, during the Caliphate of al-Mahdī when the 'Abbasids wanted to widen the basis of their support, they began to assert that their ancestor al-'Abbās, the uncle of the Prophet, should in fact have been regarded as the true successor to the Prophet and they therefore based their claims on that. The presence of a rival branch of the Hashimite clan claiming both Caliphate and Imamate and being successful in establishing their authority must have caused a considerable crisis in the Shi'i community and presented it with a formidable challenge.

It is clear that large numbers of those who had previously been Shi'i (particularly those in the Zaydī and Kaysānī camps) rejoined the mainstream of Islam after the 'Abbasid revolution. Iraq, the population of which had previously been predominantly Shi'i (at least in the political sense), now became a bastion of orthodoxy. Nowhere is this made more clear than in considering the lives of such persons as Abū Ḥanīfa, the founder of one of the four main schools of Sunni law, and Sufyān ath-Thawrī, a prominent jurist. These two citizens of Kūfa had very clear Shi'i leanings in their early life. They are both reported to have studied under aṣ-Ṣādiq; they supported Zayd ibn 'Alī's revolt against the Umayyads; and later, in the period immediately after the 'Abbasid revolt, they are reported to have been against the 'Abbasids and to have supported the revolt of Muḥammad an-Nafs az-Zakiyya, the Hasanid claimant. And yet despite these clear early manifestations of Shi'i leanings, these men went on to become leading members of the *Ahl al-ḥadīth* (the Traditionists), the group out of which Sunni orthodoxy evolved.* The Hijaz is reported to have been predominantly Shi'i before the 'Abbasid revolution and yet one hundred years later there is little Shi'i activity there. This drawing away of support to rival claimants no

* The entrance of large numbers of Shi'is into the ranks of the 'orthodox' *Ahl al-ḥadīth* at this crucial stage in the development of Sunni doctrine no doubt accounts for the fact, observed by Hodgson ('How did the early Shi'a . . .', p. 4), that Sunni Islam came more than half-way towards accommodating the Shi'i viewpoint. This can clearly be seen in the 'canonical' collections of *ḥadīth* that were made at this time. The other time that Shi'i thought came to have a great influence on Sunni Islam was in the 8th/14th century through the vehicle of Sufism. It may be argued that at the present time, through the 1979 Iranian Revolution and the ideology of Āyatu'llāh Khumaynī, Shi'ism is once more having a major impact on the Sunni world.

doubt gave impetus to the remaining Shi'is to formulate and consolidate some of their doctrines, especially with regard to the Imamate. It was undoubtedly a critical time for the Shi'a and this may be why so many of the most important Shi'i *ḥadīth* are referred back to aṣ-Ṣādiq who was the Imam during this period.

The first steps towards the separation of the Shi'is into a distinctive sect within Islam appears to have occurred under Muḥammad al-Bāqir and Ja'far aṣ-Ṣādiq, the Fifth and Sixth Imams. The former is credited with initiating a distinctively Shi'i system of jurisprudence and developments under the latter were even more far-reaching. Aṣ-Ṣādiq came to prominence in a generation that had seen a plethora of Shi'i revolts under a number of 'Alid-Shi'i claimants to the Imamate and Caliphate. The increasing unrest against Umayyad rule made it relatively easy for an 'Alid to put forward a claim and gather followers. Aṣ-Ṣādiq appears to have wished to set himself and his party apart from this trend. He did this by effectively depoliticising the institution of the Imamate through the doctrines of designation (*naṣṣ*) and knowledge (*'ilm*). By making the Imamate dependent only on designation by the previous Imam and by making the Imam the recipient of an esoteric, all-encompassing knowledge, the question of whether the Imam held political power became irrelevant and so there was no need to initiate an armed struggle to bring it about. The process of depoliticising the Imamate was, of course, taken even further one century later when the Imam was occulted. Then the Imamate became a matter for theological debate rather than being of any political or even juridical significance.

In summary, then, Shi'ism during the first one hundred and fifty years of Islam started as a principally political movement focused on the house of 'Ali, centred in Iraq, and antagonistic to Umayyad-Syrian domination. It was neither an organised nor a uniform movement and would perhaps be better described as a sentiment than a movement. From time to time this mist of sentiment would condense around a central figure who laid claim to leadership but most of the time it remained rather vague in its aims and varied from group to group and locality to locality. Towards the end of this period Shi'ism as a mainly political movement became attached to the type of theological speculation known under the label of *ghuluww*, which thus formed a religious wing to the movement. Individual Shi'is would be attracted either in the direction of political involvement (the Zaydī-Kaysānī group who apparently were the most organised and carried out an active propaganda) or of religious speculation (the *ghulāt*). Many of the numerous sects recorded by the Muslim heresiographers were probably more akin to schools of thought centred on the opinions of prominent individuals. The numbers of these sects may have been increased by a desire on the part of the heresiographers to make the facts fit a purported saying of Muhammad that there would be seventy-three sects in Islam.

As to the religious doctrines held by these early Shi'a, it would seem that, apart from those who were only political Shi'a, the majority subscribed to such doctrines as anthropomorphism, transmigration of souls, descent of the divine spirit into men, occultation and return, alteration of the Divine will, etc., i.e. those beliefs typifying the *ghulāt*, together with an emerging concept of the Imamate, although there were varying opinions about the identity of the Imam. Most of these doctrines are of course held to be heretical by the final fully-developed Twelver theology and so it is of great interest to follow how such a revolution in thinking occurred in this group. Whether there existed up to the time of aṣ-Ṣādiq any Shi'is who could be truly held to be proto-Twelvers* (in the sense that they accepted each in turn of the Twelver line of Imams and did not subscribe to *ghuluww* doctrines) is open to serious doubt. If they existed at all (which presupposes that the Twelver line of Imams did in fact lay claim to being Imams), they were only a tiny handful among the large numbers who had Shi'i sympathies and there is almost no objective evidence that they existed at all.

The 'Abbasid Period (132/750–334/945)

Although, as noted above, the 'Abbasid Revolution began as a manifestation of Shi'ism, it quickly took an anti-Shi'i turn. Once in power, the 'Abbasids realised that many of the Shi'a would not accept them as legitimate rulers and so they turned towards the *Ahl al-ḥadīth* (the proto-Sunnis) for their religious support and began to persecute the Shi'is. The series of Zaydī revolts, particularly by 'Alids of the Hasanid line, which had begun towards the end of the Umayyad era, continued into the 'Abbasid period with the revolt of Yaḥyā al-Maḥḍ in 175/791 in Daylām (north Iran) and the more successful rebellion of his brother, Idrīs, who succeeded in setting up a Shi'i state in the Maghrib (north-west Africa) in 172/788.

The Husaynid (Twelver) line also achieved some political importance during aṣ-Ṣādiq's lifetime although disputes about the succession after his death weakened them once more.

During the civil war between Hārūn ar-Rashīd's two sons, al-Amīn and al-Ma'mūn, several Shi'i factions took advantage of the 'Abbasid weakness to come out in open revolt. Most of these Shi'i revolts were Hasanid-Zaydī rebellions but a number of Husaynids also joined and soon a large area of Hijaz, Yemen and Iraq was under Shi'i control. The

* True Twelvers could not of course exist until 260/874 when the Twelfth Imam went into occultation.

THE SHI'I WORLD DURING THE LIFETIMES OF THE IMAMS AND THE LESSER OCCULTATION, AD 632-950

The Umayyad and 'Abbasid Periods

The shaded areas and towns shown are the main areas where followers of the Twelver Imams are reported to have lived during this period. The boundaries shown are those of provinces of the 'Abbasid Empire.

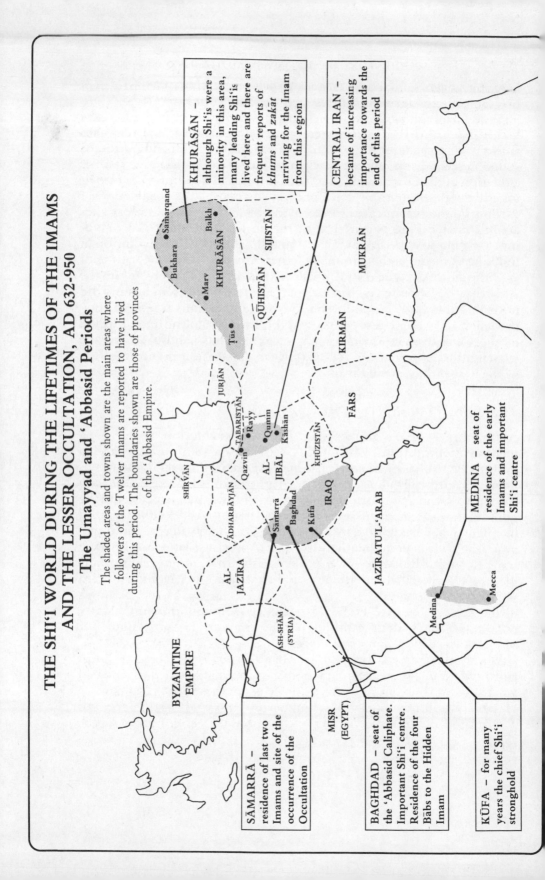

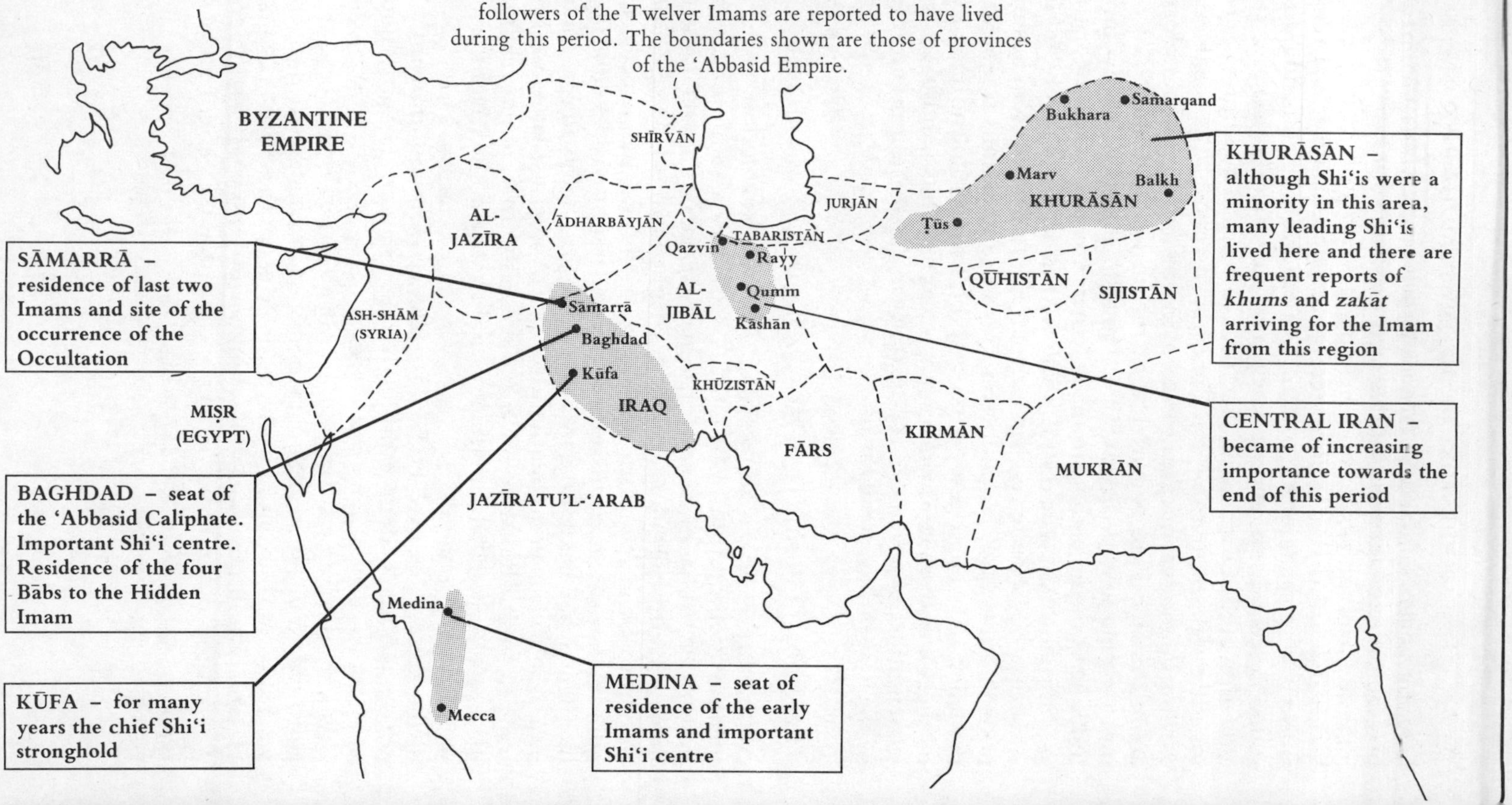

fact that al-Ma'mūn chose 'Alī ar-Riḍa to marry his daughter and become the heir-apparent to the Caliphate has been taken by some to indicate that, at his time, the Husaynid line of Imams was considered the leading line among the 'Alid. It might equally well imply, however, that al-Ma'mūn considered them the most moderate, pliable and quietist group and therefore the most likely to be won over to an alliance with the 'Abbasids and thus split the Shi'i rebellion that was gaining ground in the west of the Empire.

'Alī ar-Riḍa died or was poisoned in 203/818 leaving only a young son, Muḥammad at-Taqī. With this, the Twelver line of Imams plunges back into obscurity and henceforth until the time of the Twelfth Imam plays little role in the wider Muslim community.

What then can be said about their followers – the proto-Twelvers? Although it is clear that there was a group of persons, successors to Hishām ibn al-Ḥakam and his generation, who followed these Imams, their numbers cannot have been substantial as there is almost no mention of them (as distinct from other groups of Shi'a) in contemporary sources. It is only from about AD 880 onwards, i.e. after the Occultation of the Twelfth Imam, that contemporary references to them begin to occur. It is also to this later period that the earliest surviving Twelver Shi'i works are dated.

Only a very tentative picture can be built up of the Twelver community in about the year 880. It appears that they referred to themselves at this time as the Imāmiyya while their opponents called them the Rāfiḍa (the Rejectors). The term Rāfiḍa is said to relate to those who rejected Zayd ibn 'Alī when he began to compromise Shi'i tenets (in an effort to win support from non-Shi'i Muslims). More probably it refers to the rejection by these Shi'is of Abū Bakr, 'Umar and most of the companions of the Prophet. This latter rejection was of fundamental importance since it implied a rejection of the whole body of *ḥadīth*, transmitted by these companions, on which the structure of what was gradually evolving to be Sunni Islam was based. It was probably this point which was decisive in causing the Twelver Shi'is to separate into a distinct sect set apart from what was evolving into the Sunni community.

The Imāmiyya were strong in Iraq and especially in Kūfa and the Karkh or West Bank quarter of Baghdad. Other important communities included Qumm, which by 300/912 had overtaken even Kūfa as the centre of Imāmī scholarship, Rayy, Kāshān and Khurāsān. During the lifetimes of the last few Imams, it would appear that the proto-Twelvers had developed an elaborate network of agents (*wakīl*, plural *wukalā*). This system of agents, the *Wikāla*, was not, as with other similar Shi'i networks, principally for the purpose of fomenting revolt but rather to facilitate communication and to collect the *khums* and *zakāt* (see p. 179). It has been suggested, however, that some of the Shi'i revolts that occurred in 250–1/864–5 in Kūfa, Rayy and Ṭabaristān were linked to the Tenth Imam, 'Alī al-Hādī. It is not clear to what extent these communities were in contact with the communities of other Shi'i sects such as the Zaydiyya, who became established in northern Iran and Yemen at the end of the third century, and the Idrisids in Morocco.

Beliefs of the Shi'a

As may be expected, Shi'i writers present the Shi'is of this period as believing in the same doctrines as later Shi'is, but the objective evidence belies this. The opponents of the Shi'is, such writers as the Mu'tazilī al-Kayyāṭ and al-Ash'arī, writing in the period 269–300/882–912, state that the majority of the Shi'a at that time held to such doctrines as anthropomorphism with respect to God, *badā* (alteration in the Will of God), that God wills every act of sin and disobedience, and that the Qur'an has been altered.[10] These two writers do mention a small number of Imāmī Shi'a who were by this time adhering to doctrines derived from the Mu'tazila (i.e. close to the final Shi'i position) but from their statements it is clear that the majority held the same views as the *ghulāt* of the previous century (with the exception that belief in divine incarnation had now been dropped).

Indeed, it may be surmised from the paucity of Shi'i books of any description surviving from before about 330/941 that the large number of books that are known (from bibliographical works such as Shaykhu'ṭ-Ṭā'ifa's *Fihrist*) to have been written by Shi'is all revealed such glaring differences in matters of doctrine (matters such as the *ghuluww* beliefs discussed above and the Occultation of the Twelfth Imam) from later Shi'i orthodoxy that they were considered unsuitable for onward transmission and thus became lost, whereas numerous Sunni works exist from the mid-2nd century/8th century onwards.

Thus the community that was eventually to become the Twelver Shi'is was at this time holding views almost diametrically opposed to their eventual position. These proto-Twelver Shi'is do not even appear to have agreed as yet on the number and identity of the Imams or on the fact of the Occultation. As late as 342/953 Muḥammad an-Nu'mānī states that most of the Shi'is of his generation were uncertain as to the identity of the Imam and had doubts as to his occultation.[11] And a few years later Ibn Bābūya writes that he found the Shi'is of Naysābūr (Nīshāpūr in Khurāsān) perplexed about the Occultation of the Twelfth Imam.[12] In the earliest extant Shi'i works, which date from this period, there is no reference to the Imams being twelve in number or to the Occultation.[13]

The crystallisation of the doctrine of *Ghayba* (Occultation) occurred in about 300/912. Prior to that date Shi'i books make no reference to this doctrine. A short while later, however, books appear with all twelve Imams listed and the Occultation stated as a fact.[14] As late as 342/953 thirteen years after the start of the Greater Occultation, an-Nu'mānī is undecided as to whether the first *Ghayba* or the second (i.e. Lesser or Greater Occultation, see p. 165) will be the longer.[15]

The exact significance of the Occultation of the Twelfth Imam is not hard to discern. By the 4th/10th century the Islamic world had seen numerous Shi'i revolts headed by various 'Alids (or persons claiming to represent 'Alids) who laid claim to the Imamate. Most important of all was the Ismā'īlī Fatimid movement that had succeeded in establishing a state in Egypt under a person who was claimed to be a living Imam and whose missionaries were penetrating the 'Abbasid realms. Any living Imam was bound to be the centre of Messianic fervour and therefore a potential political rival to the temporal authorities under which the Twelvers lived. On the other hand, the Twelver tradition had already, under the Imam Ja'far aṣ-Ṣādiq, established its theory of the Imamate which included the necessity of the perpetual existence of a living Imam to guide mankind. The problem was neatly resolved by occulting the Imam and thus effectively depoliticising him while not violating the principle that the Imam must always exist.

The Buyid Period (334/945–447/1055)

Political Developments

In 334/945 the Buyid (or Buwayhid) dynasty overcame Baghdad and the 'Abbasid Caliphate came under a Shi'i overlord. Although Buyids were clearly Shi'i and have been called Twelver, it is probable that they were Shi'is of the Zaydi sect initially. The fact that they came from Daylām, an Iranian province along the southern coast of the Caspian, makes it all the more likely that they began as Zaydīs, for that area of Iran had resisted the advances of Islam until finally converted by the Zaydī missionary Ḥasan an-Nāṣir al-Uṭrush in the late 3rd/9th century. There is also evidence, however, that the Buyids had Twelver sympathies; thus, for example, under the Buyids, extensive building was carried out in Kāẓimayn at the shrines of the Seventh and Ninth Imams (these two Imams are not accepted by the Zaydīs). Since the Buyids were not descendants of 'Ali, Zaydī Shi'ism would have required the Buyids, once in power, to install an 'Alid as Imam and for all to obey him. It may be for this reason that after they came to power the Buyids tended towards Twelver Shi'ism which with its occulted Imam was more attractive to them politically. The Buyids did not terminate the 'Abbasid Caliphate in Baghdad, probably because there was no one available who could command the same respect, and they found it useful politically to have a Caliph in Baghdad whom they could manipulate and through whom they could control their subjects.

Almost simultaneous with the rise of the Buyids was the growth in power of another Shi'i dynasty, the Hamdanids. The Hamdanids began as amirs of Mosul and northern Iraq under the 'Abbasids in 293/905–6. From this base they gradually extended their power and in 333/944 (i.e. only one year before the Buyid capture of Baghdad), they moved into northern Syria capturing Aleppo, Antakya and Ḥumṣ. The head of the western branch of the dynasty at this time was 'Alī ibn 'Abdu'llāh, Sayfu'd-Dawla, who made Aleppo his capital. In view of the fact that most of Sayfu'd-Dawla's reign was occupied in campaigning against the Byzantines, it is remarkable that he was able to gather around himself, at his court, some of the most famous names of Islamic culture, the philosopher al-Farābī, the poet al-Mutanabbī and Abu'l-Faraj al-Iṣbahānī, the compiler of a vast treasury of Arab verse and stories. After Sayfu'd-Dawla's death in 356/967, the dynasty went into decline with internal strife and external attacks from the Byzantines until it finally ended in 394/1003. The exact nature of the Shi'ism of the Hamdanids is not entirely clear. It would appear most probable that they were Nuṣayrīs (see p. 58). But since this sect also acknowledges all twelve Imams of the Twelver line, Twelver Shi'is seem to have found the Hamdanid areas congenial and Aleppo soon became an important Twelver centre.

To Shi'is in the mid-4th/10th century it must have seemed that everything was going their way. Almost the whole of the Muslim world was under the control of Shi'is of one sect or another. In Iraq and Iran the Buyids held sway. The Shi'i Hamdanid dynasty controlled Syria. In Egypt and much of north Africa, Shi'is of the Ismā'īlī branch, the Fatimids, were extending their influence, while in north-west Africa the Idrisids maintained an 'Alid state of sorts until overcome by the Fatimids. Zaydī Shi'is controlled parts of northern Iran and the Yemen.

Doctrinal Developments and the Ulama

It has already been briefly stated that the doctrines held by the majority of the Shi'a up to the beginning of the third century were almost diametrically opposed to the final doctrinal position of Twelver Shi'ism. It was at this time, when great changes were occurring in the political fortunes of the Shi'a, that a correspondingly great change appears to have occurred among them in the matter of doctrine.

This great change, when it came, seems to have been very sudden and abrupt – indeed, almost within one lifetime. Its seeds had, however, undoubtedly been sown long before. Even among the band of aṣ-Ṣādiq's followers there is reported to have been a theologian with Mu'tazilī leanings, Abu'l-Ḥasan ibn A'yān known as Zurāra. This small stream of Mu'tazilī thinking survived among the Imāmī Shi'a side-by-side with the mainstream theology which, as has been argued earlier, was based on the earlier *ghuluww* speculation. One hundred and fifty years later (*c.* 269–300/882–912), al-Khayyāṭ and al-Ash'arī were able to report a Mu'tazilī-based school among the Imāmī (i.e. Twelver) Shi'is but still in a minority, while the majority, as these writers state, still adhered to the *ghuluww*-based doctrines. This Mu'tazilī-based school was undoubtedly the group centred on the Nawbakhtī family in Baghdad. It was among this group that the new ideas were formulated and developed. These two groups (the *ghulāt* and *non-ghulāt* followers of the Imams) were, however, even at this stage showing signs of separating into distinct sects in that they appear to have been paying their *khums* and *zakāt* to two different sets of agents both claiming to represent the Hidden Imam.[16] (For a further consideration of the period of the Lesser Occultation see pp. 162–5.)

The change of doctrine that occurred among the Imāmī Shi'a involved an almost complete *volte-face* on most issues. From believing in anthropomorphism with respect to God, the Imāmiyya came to accept the Mu'tazilī view that all those verses in the Qur'an which seem to imply that God has a physical body should be interpreted figuratively. From believing that God does change His mind over matters that He has decreed (the classic case quoted being that Ismā'īl was at first designated aṣ-Ṣādiq's successor and this was changed to Mūsā al-Kāẓim), the Imāmī theologians came to re-interpret the term *badā* so as to render it virtually identical to the concept of abrogation of one verse of the Qur'an by a later verse (*naskh*), which is accepted by all Muslims. From believing that God creates and determines all men's actions, even acts of sin and disobedience, the Twelvers came to accept that men determine and are responsible for their own actions. From believing that the Qur'an has been tampered with and altered so as to exclude evidence of 'Ali's succession, they came to believe that the present version of the Qur'an is complete and unaltered. From a belief that God has delegated certain of his functions such as creation to intermediaries such as the Imams, they came to believe that only God performs these functions. In only two key areas did the Twelvers, after this great revolution in their thinking, differ from the fundamental tenets of the Mu'tazilites: firstly in their conception of the Imamate and secondly in their rejection of both *wa'īd*, the unconditional and permanent punishment of the believing sinner, and its associated doctrine of the intermediate position (between belief and unbelief) of the believing sinner. Their rejection of *wa'īd* was in reality a consequence of the doctrine of the Imamate. So important did the Imamate appear that it seemed inconceivable that a true believer in the Imam would suffer eternal punishment no matter what his sin had been.

The change in Twelver theology from the *ghuluww*-based views to Mu'tazilī-based doctrines appears to have occurred in two stages. The first and more important stage consisted of the rejection of the *ghuluww* doctrines and will be considered here. This stage undoubtedly occurred under the influence of Mu'tazilī thought but it was in the second stage that Mu'tazilī *kalām* (speculative theology) became the basis of Shi'i theology and this will be considered later in this chapter.

The first stage in the change in doctrine seems to have begun in Qumm in the last half of the 3rd/9th century. Qumm had been a Shi'i town from the 2nd/8th century. It was under the rule of the Shi'i family of Sa'd ibn Malik al-Ash'arī from 125/742 to 278/891 and a growing number of Shi'i ulama took up residence there. Here Aḥmad ibn Muḥammad ibn 'Īsā al-Ash'arī, who is described as the Shaykh of Qumm, took the lead in opposing the views of the *ghulāt*. From about 255/869 he succeeded in expelling from Qumm a number of Shi'is who are said to have held *ghuluww* views.[17] Up to this time Baghdad had been the centre of Twelver scholarship with the residence there of the deputies of the Imams. But with this, Qumm increased in importance until eventually it overtook Baghdad with such figures as Sa'd ibn 'Abdu'llah al-Ash'arī (d. 300/912), Ja'far ibn Qūlūya (d. 369/979) and Muḥammad ibn Bābūya (d. 381/991) being the most significant figures in Shi'i Islam in their own time and being regarded as the exponents of what the rest of the Shi'i world gradually came to accept as orthodoxy.

The life of Ibn Bābūya (Ibn Babawayh) probably marks the end of this first stage of change. Ibn Bābūya was a noted Traditionist of Qumm who in his writings was very antagonistic to the discipline of *kalām*, speculative theology, which was the main tool of the Mu'tazilites. From Ibn Bābūya's writings, it is clear that the first stage of the great change was coming to an end during his lifetime. Large parts of his works are devoted to refuting anthropomorphism in a vigorous and thorough manner,[18] thus indicating that the argument was still fresh in his day. His own views regarding determinism (that God determines all men's actions) varied from his early works to his later writings. In his early works he denies that man has the power to choose his own acts and asserts that these are predetermined through God's foreknowledge of them.[19] In his later works, however, Ibn Bābūya has shifted his ground and writes of God's will as His commanding and forbidding rather than predestination.[20] Apart from his early determinist views, Ibn Bābūya has clearly accepted all the other main Mu'tazilī-based doctrines and only differs in his methodology from later writers such as Shaykh al-Mufīd in that he prefers to base his theology on Traditions rather than reason.

From the date of the expulsions in Qumm, the statements of al-Khayyāṭ and al-Ash'arī and a study of Ibn Bābūya's works, it would appear that the first stage of the great change in thinking in Qumm occurred between 260/873 and 360/970, but probably at different times and at different rates in other centres.

After Ibn Bābūya there came the second stage in the great change in Shi'i theology that occurred during this period: the adoption of Mu'tazilī *kalām*. This occurred in Baghdad under the influence of three notable figures who were each both jurists and theologians and who were so prominent that each became considered the leader of the Twelver Shi'is in his own day.

The first of these was Abū 'Abdu'llāh Muḥammad ibn Muḥammad ibn an-Nu'mān known as Ibn al-Mu'allim or more commonly as al-Shaykh al-Mufīd (d. 413/1022). He moved the doctrine of Twelver Shi'ism more towards the camp of Mu'tazilī theology by rejecting Ibn Bābūya's insistence that Traditions should be the basis of doctrine and maintaining that theology should be based on reason and revelation jointly. In his writings al-Mufīd tends to argue from reason and then uses a Tradition or Qur'anic reference as additional evidence. He set forth his doctrinal differences with Ibn Bābūya in *Taṣḥīḥ al-I'tiqād*, a correction to the latter's best-known dogmatic work.

After al-Mufīd came Abu'l-Qāsim 'Alī ibn al-Ḥusayn al-Musawī known as ash-Sharīf al-Murtaḍā or 'Alamu'l-Hudā (d. 436/1044). Whereas al-Mufīd's ideas had been closer to the moderate Baghdādī school of Mu'tazilī thought, 'Alamu'l-Hudā took Shi'i thought closer to the more radically rationalist Baṣran school of Mu'tazilism. Thus while al-Mufīd used reason to defend and justify doctrine, for 'Alamu'l-Hudā reason was itself the starting point of theology. For example, while al-Mufīd restricted God's attributes only to those found in the Qur'an and the Traditions, 'Alamu'l-Hudā allowed other attributes derived from reason. It was to be 'Alamu'l-Hudā's formulation of theology, based on the Baṣran school of Mu'tazilism, that would become the basis of Shi'i theology during the following centuries.[21]

The third of this trio of prominent figures of the 4th–5th Islamic centuries was Abū Ja'far Muḥammad ibn al-Ḥasan ibn 'Alī aṭ-Ṭūsī, known as Shaykhu'ṭ-Ṭā'ifa (d. 460/1067). Shaykhu'ṭ-Ṭā'ifa is best known for his fundamental contributions to Shiʻi law. So authoritative was he in this field that for a hundred years his works were considered definitive. In theology he followed closely the approach of his teacher ʻAlamu'l-Hudā.

It is not at all clear what factors caused this rapid and far-reaching change in doctrine among the Twelver Shiʻis. Several events that occurred during this period may have had an influence in precipitating it. Firstly, with the rise to power and influence of the Nawbakhtī family in the court of the ʻAbbasids, opportunities arose for Shiʻis to be appointed to influential positions in the government. This process reached its peak under the Caliph al-Muqtadir (295/908–320/932). To the Shiʻis who were thus achieving status and influence in society, *ghulāt*-based views, such as anthropomorphism, etc. would have been something of an embarrassment, and they undoubtedly would have encouraged any movement that brought the ideas of the Shiʻa more into line with the mainstream of Islam.

Secondly, to the emerging Twelver Shiʻis, the advent of the Shiʻi Buyid dynasty meant a great change in their circumstances. For the first time they could come out into the open and debate their doctrines publicly without resorting to dissimulation. This circumstance must have caused the Twelvers to examine carefully their doctrines before having them exposed to public scrutiny and may well have contributed to the change in doctrine. Since, up to this time, the Shiʻis had kept their opinions secret, it is probable that there grew up over time a great deal of local variation in doctrine and practice. The bringing out of their doctrine into the open no doubt led to an eradication of these local variations as well as creating pressure to bring their doctrines more closely into line with the Sunni majority.

One further factor that may have influenced the Twelver Shiʻis greatly in this period was the emergence of Ismāʻīlī Shiʻism and, in particular, the establishment of the Fatimid state in Egypt. It is known that the Ismāʻīlī propagandists were active throughout the Muslim world at this time and the emergence of an Ismāʻīlī doctrine together with its own state may well have pushed the Twelvers into reformulating their own doctrines.

At the same time that most aspects of Twelver theology, under the Shiʻi scholars of the Buyid period, were evolving from a Traditionist basis to a rationalist one, the doctrine of the Imamate was moving in the opposite direction. The Nawbakhtīs had, while affirming the sinlessness of the Imams, denied that they could perform miracles. Ibn Bābūya and the Traditionists of Qumm rejected the Nawbakhtī's argument on this point but had allowed that it was possible for the Prophet and the Imams to err through distraction in matters of performing religious ritual.

Indeed, Ibn Bābūya accuses his opponents on this point of being *ghulāt*. Al-Mufīd in turn accuses the Traditionists of Qumm of *taqṣīr* (falling short, i.e. failing to give the Imams and the Prophet their due). All subsequent Shi'i writers have agreed with al-Mufīd on this point and have denied the possibility of any error in the words and actions of the Prophet and the Imams.

With regard to the question of the text of the Qur'an, it has already been noted that the early Shi'is believed that the Qur'an had been altered and parts of it had been suppressed. The Nawbakhtīs are said to have adhered to this view although it went against their usual position of agreeing with Mu'tazilī thought. The compiler of the earliest, authoritative collection of Twelver Traditions, al-Kulaynī, seems to have given some substance to this view in several of the Traditions that he relates.[22] Ibn Bābūya, however, takes the position that the text of the Qur'an is complete and unaltered. Al-Mufīd appears to have wavered somewhat on this point during his lifetime. He seems to have accepted the fact that parts of the Qur'an had been excised by the enemies of the Imams in some of his early writings, although he refused even then to state that anything had been added. In his later writings, however, al-Mufīd has reinterpreted the concept of omissions from the text of the Qur'an to mean that the text of the Qur'an is complete (although he does allow that the order needs to be changed) but that what has been omitted is the authoritative interpretation of the text by 'Ali. In this manner, al-Mufīd and most subsequent Shi'i writers were able to fall into line with the rest of the Islamic world in accepting the text of the Qur'an as contained in the recension of 'Uthmān.

Apart from the field of doctrinal theology, the trio of al-Mufīd, 'Alamu'l-Hudā and Shaykhu'ṭ-Ṭā'ifa also initiated important developments in defining the principles of Shi'i jurisprudence and establishing the theoretical basis for the status and functioning of the doctors of law (the *fuqahā*). However, the steps taken by them were only preliminary and the full development of these fields was left to later generations (see Chapter 10).

The state of the Muslim world differed markedly during the lifetime of Shayku'ṭ-Ṭā'ifa from what has been described above for the middle of the 4th/10th century. By the middle of the 5th/11th century the power of the Shi'i dynasties was on the wane. The staunchly Sunni Seljuq Turks were advancing from the east and by 1055 had overcome the Buyids and occupied Baghdad. The Hamdanid dynasty in Syria had fallen and the Fatimids in Egypt were losing influence. Sunni Islam was slowly but surely re-establishing its control over the Muslim world.

The intellectual centre of Twelver Shi'ism moved from place to place during the period under consideration in this chapter. From the middle of the 3rd/9th century, Baghdad was undoubtedly the centre of Twelver Shi'ism, being both the residence of the four ambassadors of the Hidden Imam (see pp. 162ff.) and the seat of the influential Nawbakhtī family. By the early part of the 4th/10th century the centre of Shi'i activities had shifted to the Traditionist school of Qumm. After the death of Ibn Bābūya, Baghdad once again became the centre of Twelver scholarship. This continued until the close of the period when shortly after the Seljuq capture of Baghdad Shaykhu'ṭ-Ṭā'ifa was forced to leave that city. He settled in Najaf thus establishing it as the centre of the Shi'i world.

The Popular Religion

During the Buyid era there were some important developments in popular religion for Shi'ism. Under the Buyid Mu'izzu'd-Dawla two great Shi'i commemorations were instituted in 351/962 in Baghdad: firstly the martyrdom of the Imam Husayn on 10 Muḥarram and secondly the festival of Ghadīr Khumm commemorating the Prophet's nomination of 'Ali as his successor at Ghadīr Khumm (see p. 15) on 18 Dhu'l-Ḥijja.* It was also during this period that public mourning ceremonies for the Imam Husayn were initiated, shrines were built for the Imams and the custom of pilgrimages to these shrines established. Shi'i propaganda was carried out by *manāqib-khāns*, poets who would recite in praise of 'Ali and his family. These recitations would introduce such Shi'i concepts as the succession of 'Ali, the necessity for an Imam, the infallibility of the Imam, the miracles of the Imams and the justice of God.

The hundred-year period during which the Buyids were in control of Baghdad and Iran, the Hamdanids ruled over Northern Syria and the Fatimids controlled Egypt, Southern Syria and the Hijaz, has been called 'the Shi'i century'. However, Shi'i domination was only political during this time and Shi'ism, despite being given a free hand, was unable to make any substantial inroads on the Muslim masses. This is particularly true of the Islamic cities that were increasingly the focus of life. At no time during this period was the majority of any important city of the Muslim world Shi'i with the exception of Kūfa and possibly of Rayy. Shi'ism was somewhat more successful among the rural population but even this was mostly true of the inaccessible areas or fringes of the Muslim world – such areas as Daylām in northern Iran, the tribes on the fringes of the Arabian desert in Iraq and Syria and the more remote areas in western Iran. The ruling Shi'i dynasties also reflected this tendency,

* In retaliation the Sunnis instituted two commemorations – that of Abū Bakr's stay in the cave with the Prophet, and the death of Mus'ab ibn az-Zubayr who had defeated Mukhtār. These four festivals became the usual occasions for Sunni-Shi'i conflict.

being originally from those fringe areas. Thus Shi'i domination was only superficial in the Islamic heartlands and easily brushed aside at the end of this period.

Geographical Spread

It is difficult to assess the exact strength of Shi'ism at the close of the Buyid period or even its geographical spread. A number of towns and cities may be named as important Shi'i centres but, with the exception of Qumm, Kūfa and possibly Kāshān and Rayy, Shi'is were only a minority in these places. In general terms, in Iran, Khurāsān was predominantly and staunchly Sunni although with important Shi'i centres in the east of the area in such places as Nīshāpūr and Sabzivār; Shīrāz, Isfahan and south-eastern Iran were also Sunni; however, an area resembling an inverted triangle with its base on the south Caspian littoral and its apex at Kāshān and including Qumm, Rayy and all of Daylām (modern Gīlān), Ṭabaristān (modern Māzandarān) and Gurgān was predominantly Shi'i. Western Iran was a mixture of Sunni cities such as Hamadān with many of the tribes in the mountains being extremist Shi'is (*ghulāt*). Northern Iraq and Ādharbāyjān were Sunni while much of southern Iraq with the exception of the city of Baṣra was Shi'i. Baghdad was divided into Karkh, the quarter on the West Bank of the Tigris which was Shi'i and the larger East Bank city which was Sunni. In Syria most of the tribal groups on the fringes of the desert were Shi'i with Ismā'īlīs and extremist Shi'is being most numerous among them. The cities such as Damascus, however, remained Sunni. In Egypt, despite its long period of Ismā'īlī government, the people remained Sunni and Twelver Shi'ism was limited to a very small number. In the Hijaz and Yemen Shi'ism was still important although in the Hijaz it was being absorbed into orthodox Sunnism. In the Gulf area Ismā'īlī Qarmaṭīs were strong but Twelver Shi'is were also to be found in some numbers.

One approach to discovering which were the important Twelver Shi'i areas of this time is to study the place of origin of the Twelver Shi'i ulama of that period – the premiss being that the stronger and more important the Shi'i community, the greater number of ulama it produced. Table 1, which is derived from the *Fihrist* of Shaykhu'ṭ-Ṭā'ifa[23] represents the Twelver Shi'i ulama of the first four centuries of the Islamic era.

The situation in the lifetime of Shaykhu'ṭ-Ṭā'ifa himself had changed somewhat. Table 2, which is derived from the biographical dictionary of Āghā Buzurg Ṭihrānī,[24] one of the most meticulous of modern Shi'i scholars, relates to ulama who died during the fifth Islamic century (AD 1009–1105). It can be seen from this table that Kūfa had declined markedly in importance by the time of Shaykhu'ṭ-Ṭā'ifa while the

Iranian cities had increased in importance. This table confirms that Khurāsān, which is usually regarded as having been staunchly Sunni, did nevertheless have a significant Shi'i community.

Table 1: Geographical origins of Twelver Shi'i ulama of the first four Islamic centuries (to AD 1008)

Kūfa	147	Ahvāz	6
Qumm (and Barqrūd)	43	Qazvīn	4
Baṣra	22	Daylām and Ṭabaristān (north Iran)	4
Baghdad	18	Isfahan	4
Rayy (and Kulayn, Iran)	15	Sijistān (South Afghanistan)	3
Wāsiṭ (Iraq)	12	Aleppo	3
Madā'in (Iraq)	8	Damascus	3
Khurāsān	7	Gurgān	3

Table 2: Geographical origins of Twelver Shi'i ulama who died during the fifth Islamic century (AD 1009–1105)

Nīshāpūr (Khurāsān)	21	Baṣra	8
Qumm	16	Tripoli (Syria)	7
Khurāsān (except Nīshāpūr)	14	Isfahan	6
Qazvīn	14	Damascus	4
Rayy (Iran)	13	Kūfa	3
Baghdad	12	Egypt	2
Daylām & Ṭabaristān (north Iran)	11	Hamadān	2
Gurgān (north Iran)	11	Kāshān	2
Aleppo	9	Egypt	2

THE SHI'I WORLD IN THE MEDIEVAL PERIOD, AD 950-1500

From Buyid times to the eve of the Safavid rise to power

The political boundaries shown are those at the height of Shi'i power in about the year 1000.
The shaded areas indicate the main areas of Twelver Shi'i population.
The towns named are the important Shi'i centres.

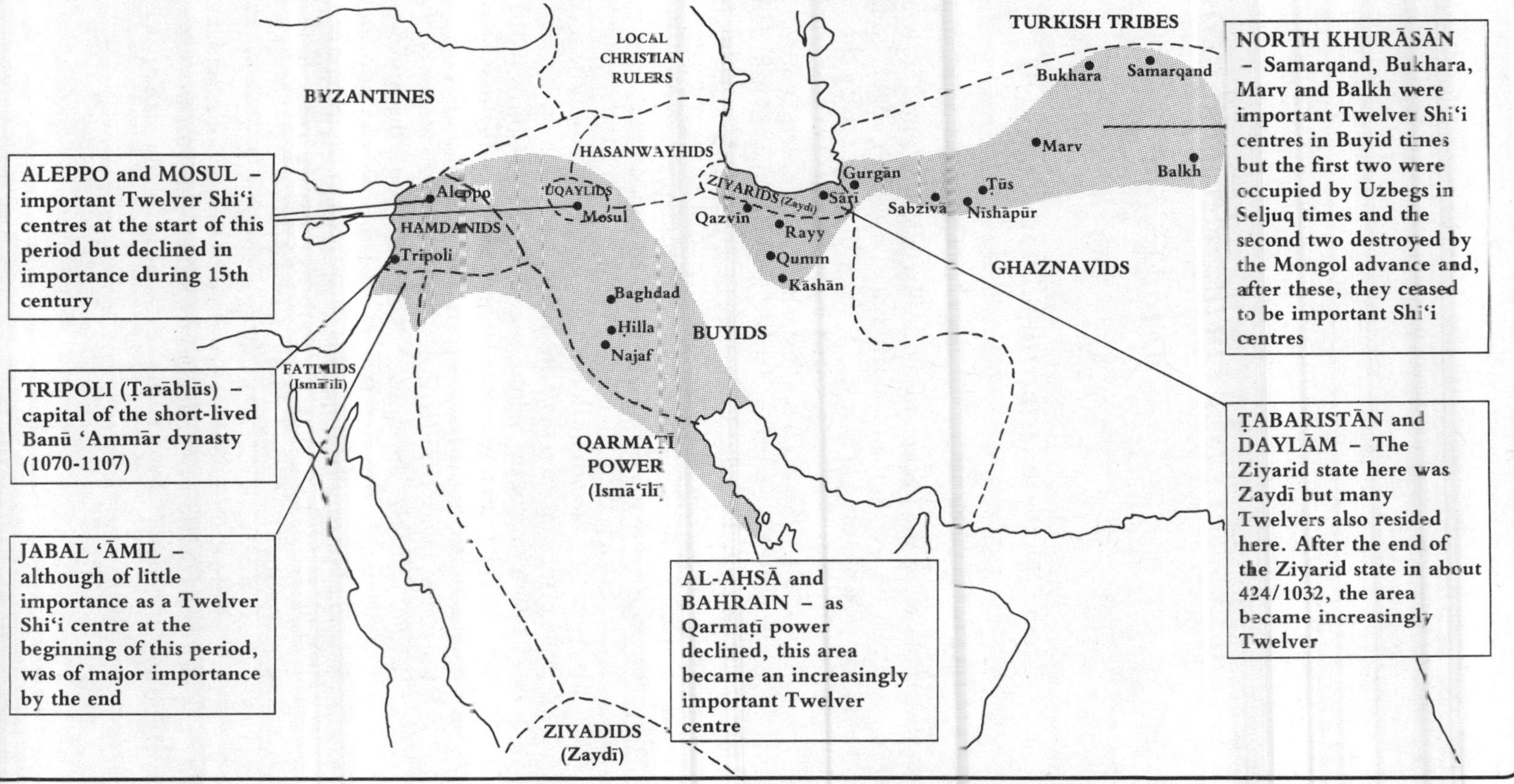
TURKISH TRIBES
LOCAL CHRISTIAN RULERS
BYZANTINES
HASANWAYHIDS
UQAYLIDS
ZIYARIDS (Zaydī)
HAMDANIDS
FATIMIDS (Ismā'īlī)
BUYIDS
GHAZNAVIDS
QARMAṬĪ POWER (Ismā'īlī)
ZIYADIDS (Zaydī)
Bukhara
Samarqand
Marv
Balkh
Tūs
Nishāpūr
Sabziva
Gurgān
Sarī
Qazvīn
Rayy
Qumm
Kāshān
Aleppo
Mosul
Tripoli
Baghdad
Hilla
Najaf
ALEPPO and MOSUL – important Twelver Shi'i centres at the start of this period but declined in importance during 15th century
TRIPOLI (Ṭarāblūs) – capital of the short-lived Banū 'Ammār dynasty (1070-1107)
JABAL 'ĀMIL – although of little importance as a Twelver Shi'i centre at the beginning of this period, was of major importance by the end
AL-AḤSĀ and BAHRAIN – as Qarmaṭī power declined, this area became an increasingly important Twelver centre
NORTH KHURĀSĀN – Samarqand, Bukhara, Marv and Balkh were important Twelver Shi'i centres in Buyid times but the first two were occupied by Uzbegs in Seljuq times and the second two destroyed by the Mongol advance and, after these, they ceased to be important Shi'i centres
ṬABARISTĀN and DAYLĀM – The Ziyarid state here was Zaydī but many Twelvers also resided here. After the end of the Ziyarid state in about 424/1032, the area became increasingly Twelver

5

Shi'i Islam in the Medieval Period

AD 1000–1500

The Seljuq Period (5th/11th–6th/12th Centuries)

Political Developments

Following the decline of the 'Abbasids, Iran and Iraq were for a time under the sway of an Iranian dynasty of Shi'i persuasion, the Buyids. However, at the beginning of the 5th/11th century the empire of this dynasty was gradually seized by waves of Turkish tribes emanating from Central Asia. These Turkish tribes adopted Sunnism in its severest form under the Ḥanafī School. The first of these Turkish dynasties was the Ghaznavids who took over most of Iran, reaching their greatest extent in about 421/1030. They were followed by the Seljuqs who conquered the Ghaznavids in Iran and pressed on into Iraq, finally overthrowing the Buyid control of Baghdad in 447/1055.

The Seljuqs were to remain in power in Iraq and much of Iran until the last years of the 6th/12th century, vanishing from the scene only a few years before the advent of the Mongols.

The coming of the Seljuqs was at first a great blow to the Shi'is. In the previous chapter it was noted that the great Shi'i jurist Shaykhu'ṭ-Ṭā'ifa had his house in the Karkh quarter of Baghdad attacked and his library burned and was forced to flee to Najaf. Shi'ism was publicly cursed from the pulpit in the mosques of Khurāsān,[1] and the Shrine of Husayn at Karbalā was damaged in 489/1095.[2] The powerful minister of the Seljuq Sulṭāns, Niẓāmu'l-Mulk, was the principal opponent of the Shi'is but after his assassination in 485/1092 the pressure on the Shi'is began to lift. The death of Niẓāmu'l-Mulk marks the beginning of the decline of the Seljuqs and from this time on rival factions within the dynasty fought one another. During this period a number of Shi'is achieved prominent positions. Majdu'l-Mulk, a secret Shi'i from Qumm, was minister to the Seljuq Sulṭān, Berk-Yaruk. Aṭ-Ṭughrā'ī of Isfahan was minister to

Sulṭān Mas'ūd but he was charged with being an Ismā'īlī and executed in about 514/1120 after Mas'ūd's defeat at the hands of his brother Sulṭān Maḥmūd. Sulṭān Maḥmūd's minister Anūshīrvān ibn Khālid of Kāshān, who wrote a famous history of the Seljuq period, is reported in several sources to have been a Shi'i.

Also after the death of Niẓāmu'l-Mulk, there was a resurgence of the power of the Abbasid Caliphate. This reached its peak under the Caliphate of an-Nāṣir (576/1180–622/1225). During this period, Shi'i influence at the Abbasid Court also grew. Several ministers to the Caliphs were Shi'is and an-Nāṣir himself was very sympathetic and reconciliatory to the Shi'i. He chose as his minister for a time, Sayyid Nāṣiru'd-Dīn ibn Mahdi, an 'Alid and a Shi'i of Rayy.

The Seljuqs were in control of most of Iran and had Baghdad under their sway for much of this period. But the situation in the rest of Iraq and in Syria was different. Even when the Seljuqs were at their strongest, a number of semi-independent tribal amirates existed in Iraq. The most powerful of these were the Mazyadids, a dynasty of Shi'i amirs who made their capital at Ḥilla on the banks of the Euphrates between Karbalā and Najaf. It was the Buyids who first recognized the Mazyadids as amirs in this area in 403/1012. But it was not until Seljuq times that the Mazyadids came into their own. Ḥilla, their capital, was built in 495/1101 by the greatest of the dynasty, Sayfu'd-Dawla Ṣadaqa (479/1086–501/1108), at a time when most of southern Iraq was under his control and his influence was great even in Baghdad. From the first, Ḥilla was a Shi'i centre of learning. Sayfu'd-Dawla, who is praised in history for his generosity and hospitality, was killed in a battle against the Seljuq Sulṭān Muḥammad, but Dubays, his son and successor, continued to be a powerful factor in the affairs of southern Iraq and Baghdad. The dynasty continued in power until the death of 'Alī, the son and successor of Dubays in 545/1150.

In northern Iraq, the Hamdanid rule was ended by another Shi'i dynasty called the 'Uqaylids who held power in Mosul from 380/990 until about 489/1096.

In Syria also, dynasties of Shi'i amirs held sway for long periods of time. In the previous chapter, the Shi'i Hamdanid dynasty has been noted. Following their collapse another Shi'i dynasty of amirs arose in Aleppo called the Mirdasids. They remained in power until overcome by the 'Uqaylids of Mosul in 472/1079. The 'Uqaylid occupation of Aleppo lasted only until 478/1085 when this region came under the control of the Sunni Seljuqs.

Further south in Syria, at Tripoli (Ṭarāblūs), another Shi'i dynasty of amirs, the Banū 'Ammār, held power until overthrown by the Crusaders in 503/1109.

Several of those who travelled through Syria in the 5th/11th century commented on the large numbers of Shi'is there although it is not always clear to which sect of Shi'ism they are referring. Most of the cities near the Syrian coast had a majority of Shi'is: Aleppo, Tripoli, Ba'ālbakk, Sidon, Tyre and Tiberius, while even the cities further inland had large Shi'i populations: Ḥumṣ, Ḥamā and Damascus.[3] One writer estimated the Shi'is to outnumber the Sunnis throughout Syria.[4]

The declining power of the Fatimids in Egypt resulted in a gradual shrinking of their empire. In Syria, their region of control was steadily decreasing while in north Africa independent states came into being. The setting up of the Zīrid state in Tunis by Mu'izz ibn Bādis resulted in a general massacre of Ismā'īlī Shi'is in 407/1016 and Shi'ism never recovered in that area.

The Ulama

Although Shaykhu'ṭ-Ṭā'ifa (Shaykh Muḥammad aṭ-Ṭūsī) lived on into the early Seljuq period and by transferring his residence from Baghdad to Najaf was responsible for the transfer of the centre of Shi'ism to that city, he himself more properly belonged to the previous Buyid era and should be regarded as the culmination of that period.

The century after Shaykhu'ṭ-Ṭā'ifa has usually been regarded as somewhat sterile in terms of intellectual and religious development within Shi'ism. In the same way that Muḥammad Bāqir Majlisī's overwhelming influence in a later age was to be succeeded by a century in which no-one could emerge from the shadow of his influence, so also Shaykhu'ṭ-Ṭā'ifa's towering achievements (probably in combination with the changed political circumstances) led to a century in which there was little creative development. It has been called in some sources the period of *taqlīd* (imitation, i.e. unquestioned following of Shaykhu'ṭ-Ṭā'ifa's lead).

However, the century after Shaykhu'ṭ-Ṭā'ifa's death must not be totally written off. There were a number of important works written during this period by ulama who, although not of the stature of Shaykhu'ṭ-Ṭā'ifa, were nevertheless of some importance. His son and grandson remained in Najaf maintaining the primacy of that town. However, by the time of the passing of Shaykhu'ṭ-Ṭā'ifa's grandson, Muḥammad ibn Ḥasan ibn Muḥammad aṭ-Ṭūsī, in 540/1145, Aleppo was becoming increasingly important as a Shi'i centre with the presence there of such figures as Abu'l-Makārim Ḥamza ibn 'Alī al-Ḥalabī known as Ibn Zuhra (d. 585/1189) and Muḥammad ibn 'Alī as-Sarawī al-Māzandarānī known as Ibn Shahrāshūb (d. 588/1192). Aleppo was the centre of Shi'i learning for about half a century from 540/1145 to 590/1193.

Another important Shi'i centre of that time was northern Iran, Ṭabaristān (now known as Māzandarān) and the region extending as far south as Qumm. This area also produced some significant scholars during the Seljuq era. The most important of these were Abū Ja'far Muḥammad ibn 'Alī aṭ-Ṭabarī of Āmul (d. 514/1120), who wrote the *Bishārat al-Muṣṭafā*, and Ḍiyā'u'd-Dīn Faḍlu'llāh ibn 'Alī al-Ḥusaynī ar-Rāwandī (d. after 548/1153) and Quṭbu'd-Dīn Sa'īd ibn Hibatu'llāh ar-Rāwandī (d. 573/1178) in Kāshān. In Khurāsān there lived Faḍl ibn Ḥasan aṭ-Ṭabarsī (aṭ-Ṭabrisī, d. 548/1153), who wrote one of the most important Shi'i commentaries on the Qur'an, the *Majma' al-Bayān*.

This period marks an important watershed in Shi'i history. From about the beginning of the 4th/10th century until the middle of the 6th/12th century, the most important ulama of the Shi'i world had been Iranians. There was now a shift and for the next four hundred and fifty years until the late Safavid period, the most important ulama were to be Arabs (with a few notable exceptions such as Khwāja Naṣīru'd-Dīn Ṭūsī).

The Mazyadid capital, Ḥilla, had been established in 495/1101 and was immediately an important Shi'i centre. But it was not until about a century later that it rose to pre-eminence in the Shi'i world, overtaking Aleppo. It was to remain thus for about three hundred years. The scholar responsible for establishing Ḥilla's importance and also for ending the century of *taqlīd* to Shaykhu'ṭ-Ṭā'ifa was Muḥammad ibn Aḥmad, known as Ibn Idrīs al-Ḥillī (d. 598/1202). Ibn Idrīs was the first to dare to express views that were different to those of Shaykhu'ṭ-Ṭā'ifa whom he regarded as having introduced into Twelver Shi'ism a number of innovations which had no basis in the Traditions of the Imams. He was followed by Muḥammad ibn Ja'far (d. 636/1239 or 645/1248) and his son Ja'far ibn Muḥammad (d. 680/1281), both known by the name Ibn Nimā.

The Shi'i ulama of this period directed most of their energies towards polemical works defending their beliefs against Sunni attacks. However, in doing so, they succeeded in defining more clearly many of the theological issues and set the stage for the developments of the Mongol period.

The Popular Religion

In the field of popular religion, the *manāqib-khāns* started in Buyid times continued, but more covertly, to avoid clashes with the Sunni authorities. To counter them and their praise of 'Ali and his family, the Sunnis brought into being *faḍā'il-khāns* who exalted Abū Bakr, 'Umar and the other companions of the Prophet.

It was during this period that Sufism first began to become a medium of religious expression for the masses. Although a great expansion in Sufi orders began during this period, it was principally a phenomenon in Sunni Islam and frowned upon by Shi'is. Indeed, it has been suggested that the growth of Sufism at this time was a direct result of the suppression of Shi'ism by the Seljuqs. Sufism grew, it is postulated, to fill the gap in the field of the esoteric side of Islam left vacant by Shi'ism. But a more powerful stimulus towards the growth of Sufism at this time was probably that Muslims were beginning to despair of ever creating the perfect society through the leadership of the Caliph and began to look to individual morality and the spiritual advancement of the individual. It was not until the Mongol era, however, that Sufism began to make a significant impact on Shi'ism.

One further important development was the espousal by the Caliph an-Nāṣir (who, as has been noted above, was markedly pro-Shi'i) of brotherhoods with chivalrous ideals. These brotherhoods were called *futuwwa* (youths) and were usually modelled on 'Ali as the ideal of Islamic chivalry: 'There is no youth (*fatā*) braver than 'Ali.' The *futuwwa* was to become an important instrument for the development of pro-Shi'i sympathy among the Sunni masses in later centuries.

Geographical Spread

The 5th/11th century saw the ebbing of the tide of Ismā'īlī Shi'ism that, in the previous century, had threatened to engulf Islam. In the Gulf area, the Qarmaṭī state, which had declined since the late 4th/10th century, was destroyed by local tribes in 470/1077 and Ismā'īlī control was never re-established in that region. In Syria, also, the Fatimids were gradually pushed back, starting with the Mirdasid capture of Aleppo in 1023 and later the Seljuq advance to Jerusalem in 1070. In these areas where Ismā'īlī power was ebbing, there suddenly appear large communities of Twelver Shi'is (in Bahrain, al-Aḥsā and the Jabal 'Āmil in Lebanon) where there are no reports of large communities of Twelvers having been before. Although this is a point that requires further investigation, it can tentatively be postulated that the ebbing tide of Ismā'īlī power left behind these large Twelver Shi'i communities as converts from Ismā'īlī Shi'ism. The reasons for such conversions are not hard to discern. The Ismā'īlīs had become feared and hated by the rest of the Muslim world and large numbers were killed wherever the orthodox community could lay its hands on them. This was particularly true of the Qarmaṭīs of the Gulf area, who had committed the sacrilegious act of removing the Black Stone of the Ka'ba. Thus it seems plausible that as the tide of Ismā'īlī power ebbed, large numbers of Ismā'īlīs should convert to the much more acceptable Twelver form of Shi'ism, thus forming the basis of the present-day Twelver communities in Bahrain, al-Aḥsā and the Jabal 'Āmil.

With regard to the distribution of Shi'is in the Muslim world during this period, it was substantially the same as has already been described in the previous chapter for the Buyid period. An analysis of the geographical origins of Shi'i ulama dying in the 6th Islamic century (AD 1106–1202) can be found in Table 3.[5]

Table 3: Geographical origins of Twelver Shi'i ulama who died in the sixth Islamic century (AD 1106–1202)

Rayy (and Varāmīn)	59	Isfahan	9
Qumm (and Āwa)	43	Kūfa	8
Sabzivār	34	Karbalā	8
Qazvīn	32	Daylām (Gīlān)	7
Kāshān (and Rawand)	32	Tafrish (near Qumm)	7
Ṭabaristān (Māzandarān)	27	Baṣra	5
Nīshāpūr	26	Qā'in	4
Mashhad (and Ṭūs)	21	Ṭarāblūs (Tripoli)	3
Aleppo	20	Bahrain	3
Ḥilla	16	Shīrāz	2
Baghdad	14	Egypt	1
Gurgān	13	Mosul	1

The Ilkhanid Period (7th/13th–8th/14th Centuries)

Political Developments

The Mongol invasions of the Islamic world which began in 617/1220 were a great blow to the civilisation of Islam in that the great cities of the eastern Islamic world were devastated to an extent from which they never fully recovered. These invasions were also a blow to the Sunni orthodoxy in that the fall of Baghdad and the subsequent killing of the 'Abbasid Caliph, Musta'ṣim, in 656/1258 removed one of the pillars on which the constitutional theory of Sunnism had been built.

The Mongol invasions were not, however, such a blow to Shi'ism. The rule of the non-Muslim Mongols, who were at this time Shamanists and Buddhists and who treated the Shi'is and Sunnis alike, was a considerable improvement on their former position as an oppressed minority under the Seljuqs. While Baghdad, the centre of Sunni orthodoxy, had been devastated, Ḥilla, the main centre of Shi'ism, submitted to the Mongols and was spared. The killing of the 'Abbasid Caliph threw Sunni theology and constitutional theory (which had over the years built up the theoretical position of the Caliph even as his *de facto* powers were weakening) into some disorder, while the occulted Imam of the Shi'is had not been affected. Thus the weakening of Sunnism led to a relative strengthening of Shi'ism. The presence of the Shi'i scholar Khwāja Naṣīru'd-Dīn Ṭūsī among the chief advisers of the Mongol leader, Hulagu Khan, must also have given comfort to the Shi'is in the midst of the holocaust caused by the Mongols.

Sunni historians have frequently accused Shi'is of having urged and brought about the fall of Baghdad and the murder of the Caliph. This accusation has only very slight justification. Baghdad's fate was sealed by the Caliph's own refusal to submit to the advancing Mongol army. Although it is true that Ibn al-'Alqamī (d. 656/1258), the Shi'i minister to the Caliph, did ask the Mongol force to attack Baghdad, he did this after he had been dismissed as minister and as a consequence of Sunni attacks upon the Shi'is in Baghdad. Nor was Khwāja Naṣīru'd-Dīn's role in the fall of Baghdad anything more than the execution of his duties as astrologer to the Mongol army. Moreover, it is doubtful whether any Shi'i action against an oppressive Sunni regime and in favour of an advancing Mongol army that had Naṣīru'd-Dīn as one of its advisers and could therefore, be presumed to be sympathetic, can be classed as treachery. In the event Hulagu Khan showed no particular favour to the Shi'is on the capture of Baghdad and several prominent Shi'is, including Sharafu'd-Dīn Muḥammad ibn Ṭāwus, the *naqīb* (leader) of the 'Alids in the city, were killed.

As conditions settled in the Middle East under the Mongol Ilkhanid dynasty which controlled most of Iran and Iraq, the Shi'is found the Ilkhanids to be tolerant rulers and even sympathetic to Shi'ism. The first of this dynasty to convert to Islam and enforce Islam in his court was Ghāzān (reigned AD 1295–1304). He turned out the Buddhist priests and built many mosques. He also showed leanings towards Shi'ism in that he frequently visited the Shi'i shrines in Iraq and built hostels called *dār as-siyādas*, for descendants of the Prophet.

The brother and successor of Ghāzān, Oljeitu (reigned AD 1304–1316), took the name Khudābanda when he became a Muslim. His minister, Sa'du'd-Dīn Sāwī, was an ally of the Shi'is and introduced the Shi'i theologian, Tāju'd-Dīn Muḥammad ibn 'Alī Āwī, to the court. The efforts of the latter and 'Allāma al-Ḥillī resulted in Khudābanda's conversion to Shi'ism in 709/1309,[6] Shi'ism became the official religion of the state and even when, in 711/1311, Sa'du'd-Dīn was executed and Tāju'd-Dīn murdered, 'Allama al-Ḥillī was brought from Ḥilla to help consolidate the Shi'i position.[7] However, the Shi'i advantage was cancelled after Khudabanda's death as his son, Abū Sa'īd, was a staunch Sunni.

From AD 1335 onwards the Ilkhanid dynasty gradually crumbled with a succession of feeble aspirants to the throne and much factional fighting. During this period a number of Shi'i states were established. At Sabzivār in Khurāsān, Ḥasan Jūrī, the head of the Shaykhiyya-Jūriyya, a Shi'i-Sufi order, helped the Sarbadārids to establish a small Shi'i state which existed from 1337 to 1386. The Sarbadārids were a series of rulers who maintained a Shi'i republic with a strong emphasis on expectation of the Hidden Imam. The first of them, Amīr 'Abdu'r-Razzāq, was killed by his brother, Amīr Vajīhu'd-Dīn Mas'ūd, in 738/1337 and it was the latter who really founded the state. Mīr Qavāmu'd-Dīn Mar'ashī (d. 781/1379), known as Mīrzā Buzurg, the head of another branch of the Shaykhiyya order, founded a Shi'i state based on Āmul in Māzandarān in 760/1359. His son, Sayyid Kamālu'd-Dīn (d. 820/1417), was defeated by Tīmūr in 794/1391 but confirmed in his governorship and the line continued as semi-independent rulers until the Safavid era. These two small Shi'i states were interesting principally because they were based on Sufi orders, combining a commitment to Shi'ism with military characteristics; the same combination found in the Safavid order that was, two centuries later, to sweep to power and have such a decisive influence on the fortunes of Shi'ism in Iran.

Several of the minor local dynasties that replaced the Ilkhanids are stated to have been Shi'i or sympathetic to Shi'ism. But it is not at all clear whether these dynasties or the Sarbadārids referred to above were Twelver or tended to extremist (*ghuluww*) views. In all probability they were similar to the Safavids in the earliest days of their dynasty, mixing orthodox Twelver views and *ghuluww* ideas. The Jalāyir dynasty in Ādharbāyjān and Iraq, and the Chupanids in Ādharbāyjān were among those dynasties sometimes thought to have Shi'i leanings though the evidence for this is weak.

In Syria, the last Shi'i state, the 'Uqaylids, had fallen before the Seljuqs in AD 1085 and Shi'ism itself was actively suppressed by 'Imādu'd-Dīn Zangī who took Aleppo in 1128. During the next two centuries the area became an arena of constant conflict between the forces of Islam and the Crusaders. Throughout this period Shi'is of all sects, especially the Ismā'īlīs and the Nuṣayrīs ('Alawīs), often sided with the Crusaders against the forces of Sunni Islam. The Shi'is in Syria received two great blows in the last half of the 13th century. The first was the capture of Aleppo by the Mongols in AD 1260 when many thousands of Shi'is were slaughtered. The second was the massacre of Shi'is that occurred at the end of the 13th century when the Crusaders were driven from Syria by the Mamluks of Egypt. The Mamluk Sulṭān, al-Ashraf, in particular was severe on the Shi'is. The Druse and Nuṣayrīs were forced to conform to the outward forms of Sunni Islam. The Ismā'īlī fortresses were reduced one by one, and the Twelvers were driven out of Kisrawān in 1305 and sought refuge in the Biqā' valley of central Lebanon where they remain to this day.

This was a period in which Islam was beginning to spread rapidly in India. At least one dynasty of this period, the Bahmānī Kings of the Deccan, showed Shi'i proclivities but made no attempt to enforce Shi'ism on the populace.

The Ulama

The main trend in Shi'i intellectual life during this period can be summarised as consisting of the integration of philosophy and mysticism (Sufism) into the mainstream of Shi'i thought. The Shi'i theology evolved in this period remains predominant to the present day. There were also important developments during this period in the field of jurisprudence and in the development of the role of the ulama.

The leading Shi'i scholar at the beginning of this period was Abū Ja'far Muḥammad ibn Muḥammad, Khwāja Naṣīru'd-Dīn Ṭūsī (d. 672/1274). It is difficult to say which were his most important intellectual achievements because he made so many major contributions in such a wide variety of fields. He was an important astronomer and mathematician as well as writing on medicine, ethics, history and geography. From the point of view of Shi'ism his most important achievement was to incorporate philosophical concepts, from his study of Avicenna and other philosophers, into Shi'i theology. Until this time philosophy had been viewed with suspicion as it was closely associated with Ismā'īlī thought. But Naṣīru'd-Dīn, who had spent many years in the Ismā'īlī stronghold of Alamūt, revolutionised Twelver Shi'i theology (*kalām*) by expressing it in terms of concepts introduced from philosophy.

At Ḥilla, which was still the main centre of Shi'ism at this time, the Ibn Tāwus family dominated the city for several generations. One of their number, Majdu'd-Dīn Muḥammad, succeeded in negotiating Ḥilla's surrender to the Mongol army without any bloodshed. Another representative of the family, Raḍiyu'd-Dīn 'Alī ibn Mūsā (d. 664/1266), was the leading Shi'i scholar of his time. He was not much interested in legal matters but was rather orientated towards mysticism and asceticism and is credited with performing many miracles (*karāmāt*). He claimed to be in contact with the Imams through dream and vision and also claimed to have met the Hidden Imam.

After Ibn Tāwus, the next important Shi'i scholar at Ḥilla was Ja'far ibn Ḥasan, Muḥaqqiq al-Ḥillī or Muḥaqqiq al-Awwal (d. 676/1277). He was the author of the *Sharā'i' al-Islām* which has remained to this day one of the foremost works in Shi'i jurisprudence. He, together with his nephew, Ḥasan ibn Yūsuf, 'Allāma al-Ḥillī (d. 726/1325) were the most important Shi'i scholars of this period. They introduced important developments in the role of the ulama (see pp. 185–6). 'Allāma al-Ḥillī was responsible for establishing *ijtihād* as the central methodology of Shi'i jurisprudence and for introducing methods of criticism of the *ḥadīth*.

'Allāma al-Ḥillī was succeeded by his son Muḥammad ibn Ḥasan, Fakhru'l-Muḥaqqiqīn (d. 771/1370), who in turn was the teacher of the first of great Shi'i scholars from the Jabal 'Āmil region of Lebanon, Muḥammad ibn Makkī al-'Āmilī, known as Shahīd al-Awwal (the First Martyr). Having studied in Ḥilla, Shahīd al-Awwal returned to Syria where because of the strongly anti-Shi'i climate maintained by the Mamluks, he was forced to maintain dissimulation (*taqiyya*). Shahīd al-Awwal succeeded in establishing the Jabal 'Āmil as an important centre of Shi'i studies, although it did not yet equal Ḥilla in importance. He was arrested and kept in prison in Damascus for one year before being executed on the orders of the Mamluk Sulṭān Barqūq in 786/1384.

During this period, with the tolerance of the Ilkhanid government and the removal of the 'Abbasid Caliphate, tensions between Sunnis and Shi'is decreased markedly especially in the eastern Muslim world. No longer was the polemic between the two an important part of the writings of the scholars. That is not to say that there was no dispute between the two sects. But even though the great Sunni scholar, Ibn Taymiyya, wrote a refutation of one of 'Allāma al-Ḥillī's works, this was combined with respect for his opponent.[8] The majority of Sunni scholars, represented by such figures as Bayḍāwī, refused to enter into the controversy at all.

This easing of the hostility between the Sunnis and the Shi'is allowed each side to adopt a great deal of the thought of the other. Shi'i ulama such as 'Allāma al-Ḥillī borrowed freely from Sunni methods of dealing with the *ḥadīth* literature. But the most important results of this rapprochement were the attempts by several Shi'is to bring Sufism into Shi'ism. Ibn Maytham al-Baḥrānī (d. 679/1280) wrote a commentary on the collection of 'Ali's speeches known as the *Nahj al-Balāgha* (the Path of Eloquence) which interpreted much of the material in a Sufi manner.

Even more important in this respect than Ibn Maytham was Sayyid Ḥaydar ibn 'Alī Āmulī who lived until the closing years of the 8th/14th century in Baghdad. He attempted to bring together Shi'ism and Sufism by stating that Sufis were in reality only Shi'is who were more concerned about the esoteric aspects of religion, while other Shi'is concentrated on the external aspects such as doctrine and religious law. In his principal work on this theme, *Jāmi' al-Asrār* (The Compilation of Mysteries), Sayyid Ḥaydar links the names of the prominent early Sufis with the Twelver Imams. He stresses everything in Sufi writings that indicates that divine knowledge was purveyed to the lines of Sufi Shaykhs through the Imam 'Ali, while at the same time emphasising everything in the writings of previous Shi'i ulama in favour of Sufism.

The Sufi Orders

The rapprochement between Shi'ism and Sunnism was to have an even greater impact on Sunni Islam. Firstly, among Sunnis there developed a tendency to what is called *tashayyu' ḥasan* (good or moderate leaning towards Shi'ism). This meant extolling the virtues of 'Ali and condemning Mu'āwiya and Yazīd but without going to what was considered the extreme of Twelver Shi'ism and rejecting the first three Caliphs and exaggerating the position of 'Ali and the Imams. But, even more importantly, the Sufi orders, which were in the process of being formed into organised schools with chains of successive leaders during this period, also took a pronounced pro-Shi'i turn in their mode of thought and expression. It was an era when the majority of the great Sufi Shaykhs claimed to be descendants of 'Ali – such figures as ar-Rifā'ī (d. 578/1182), al-Badawī (d. 675/1276), and ad-Dasūqī (d. 676/1277). Simultaneously, the Sufi concept of the position of the Shaykh came to parallel increasingly the Shi'i Imamate while 'Ali came to occupy almost as important a position in Sufism as he did in Shi'ism. These changes resulted in several Sufi orders gradually evolving from Sunnism to Shi'ism.

In Khurāsān the Kubrāwiyya order, which had started as an orthodox Sunni order in the early 7th/13th century, gradually adopted an increasingly Shi'i orientation. As-Simnānī (d. 736/1336), a Shaykh of the major line in the order, although still regarding himself a Sunni, regarded 'Ali as superior to the first three Caliphs and the *quṭb* (axis) of his time. Another prominent Shaykh of the Kubrāwiyya, 'Alī Hamadānī (d. 786/1385), although described as a Sunni, greatly venerated 'Ali and the House of the Prophet. He played an important part in taking this Sufi-Shi'i admixture to India. Later several lines in this order became openly Shi'i. The Shaykhiyya-Jūriyya order of Shi'is has previously been referred to (see p. 93).

In Anatolia the *futuwwa* orders, modelled on 'Ali (see p. 90), were very prominent among the Sunni Seljuq Turks and more particularly among the Turkomans, among whom they were called *akhīs*. The Khalwatiyya, one of the principal Sufi orders in Anatolia, had strong pro-Shi'i roots as indicated by the institution of a twelve-day fast for the

Twelver Shi'i Imams. The Bābā'ī order on the other hand showed *ghuluww* influence. The Bābā'īs are of interest also in that they were another example of a Sufi order that became military and eventually in 638/1240 arose against Kaykhusraw, the Seljuq Sulṭān of Qonya.

Geographical Spread

These developments in Sufism and popular religion, important as they may have been for the later evolution in Twelver Shi'ism, were at this stage separate from the mainstream of Twelver Shi'i Islam. Some idea of the geographical spread of Twelver Shi'ism can be obtained from analysis of the geographical origins of the ulama of the period. Table 4 relates to ulama whose deaths occurred during the 7th (1203–1299) and 8th (1300–1396) Islamic centuries.[9]

Table 4: Geographical origins of Twelver Shi'i ulama who died in the seventh (AD 1203–1299) and eighth (AD 1300–1396) Islamic centuries

	7th Century	*8th Century*	*Total*
Ḥilla	34	47	81
Māzandarān	18	12	30
Aleppo	13	15	28
Jabal 'Āmil	4	17	21
Khurāsān	14	6	20
Qumm (and Āwa)	6	12	18
Bahrain	9	6	15
Kūfa	13	3	15
Wāsiṭ (Iraq)	8	7	15
Baghdad	9	5	14
Karbalā	4	6	10
Damascus	0	10	10
Shīrāz	2	7	9
Hamadān	4	4	8
Rayy	5	3	8
Irbil (near Mosul)	4	4	8
Kāshān	1	6	7
Yazd	3	4	7
Isfahan	5	2	7
Qazvīn	5	1	6
Najaf	1	5	6
Mosul	3	3	6
Egypt	5	0	5

The Timurid Period (8th/14th–9th/15th Centuries)

Political Developments

Tīmūr, who is known to Europeans as Tamerlane, led the second wave of Mongols that devastated Iran. This second wave was not as destructive as the first but even so some seventy thousand lost their lives in Isfahan alone, for example.

Having conquered Transoxania, Tīmūr advanced into Iran in 782/1380. By 795/1393 the conquest of Iran and Iraq was complete and Tīmūr turned his attentions to Russia and India. By 803–4/1400–01 Tīmūr had advanced to Syria and Turkey.

Tīmūr was himself a Sunni, but was not unsympathetic to Shi'is. Thus, for example, he allowed the Shi'i Sarbadārids in Sabzivār to continue as his vassals. In particular he favoured 'Alids, descendants of 'Ali, and was lenient towards them even when they rebelled against him. In the massacre at Isfahan, for example, the 'Alids were spared.

Tīmūr died in 807/1405 and after some factional fighting his fourth son, Shāh-Rukh, came to power and reigned until 850/1446. Shāh-Rukh ruled over Khurāsān and much of Iran. He was also sympathetic to Shi'ism, and his wife, Gawhar-Shād, built a magnificent mosque at Mashhad adjacent to the Shrine of the Imam Riḍā. The last of the Timurid rulers, Sulṭān Ḥusayn ibn Bāyqarā (reigned 875/1470–911/1506), maintained a culturally brilliant court at Herat. For a time, early in his reign, he was disposed to making Shi'ism the religion of the state but was dissuaded from this.

To the west of Shāh-Rukh's domain there lay lands controlled by Turkoman tribes, the Qarā-Quyūnlū based around Lake Van and the Aq-Quyūnlū centred on Diyārbakr. Initially it was the Qarā-Quyūnlū who were triumphant when their chief Qarā Yūsuf overcame Sulṭān Aḥmad Jalāyir and conquered Ādharbāyjān in 813/1410. Under Jahān Shāh the Qarā-Quyūnlū spread eastwards to occupy western Iran, Fārs and Kirmān although they failed to overcome Shāh-Rukh's son and successor, Abū Sa'īd, in Khurāsān. Later, however, the fortunes of the two tribes were reversed and the Aq-Quyūnlū came into prominence under Uzūn Ḥasan, overcoming Jahān Shāh in 873/1468. Uzūn Ḥasan was ruler of all of Iran and Iraq until his death in 882/1477.

While the Aq-Quyūnlū were undoubtedly orthodox Sunni, there remains considerable doubt concerning the Qarā-Quyūnlū. A study of the poetry of Jahān Shāh has revealed that the Qarā-Quyūnlū had a pro-Shi'i tendency, albeit Shi'ism of an extremist (*ghuluww*) nature.[10] Ispand, son of Qarā Yūsuf and brother of Jahān Shāh, who was Governor of Baghdad from 836/1432 to 848/1444, is reported to have been converted to Twelver Shi'ism after a religious debate between Sunni ulama and the Shi'i scholar, Ibn Fahd. What is not clear, however, is to what extent the Qarā-Quyūnlū and the other preceding dynasties that showed a pro-Shi'i tendency, such as the Jalāyirs and Chupanids, were genuinely Shi'i in sympathy and to what extent they were using Shi'ism as a political tool to gain the obedience of their subjects.

The Ulama

While Ḥilla remained the most important Shi'i centre of learning during this period, its importance declined so that when at the close of this era the Safavid state was set up, its most prominent ulama were to come from the Jabal 'Āmil in Lebanon and not from Ḥilla. The reason for this decline is almost certainly connected with the harshly intolerant extremist Musha'sha' regime that came to control the area. In 857/1453 Ḥilla was taken by 'Alī, the son of Muḥammad ibn Falāḥ, and was looted, laid waste and burned to the ground. The town remained under the control of the Musha'sha' until 872/1467.

The eminent mujtahid Shahīd al-Awwal lived on into the first few years after Tīmūr's conquest and was invited by the Sarbadarid ruler, 'Alī Mu'ayyad, to go to Khurāsān and establish Twelver Shi'ism there. But the invitation arrived too late for Shahīd al-Awwal; he was already in prison and soon to be executed. However, he wrote his important work, *al-Luma'a ad-Dimashqiyya* for the Khurāsānī ruler.

Under the shadow of Shahīd al-Awwal, the Jabal 'Āmil and especially the village of Karak-Nūḥ became increasingly important while Bahrain was also rising in importance. But, in general, the century following Tīmūr's conquests was devoid of any ulama of the importance of 'Allāma al-Ḥillī and Shahīd al-Awwal of the previous century. The only ulama worth mentioning are al-Miqdād ibn 'Abdu'llāh al-Ḥillī (d. 826/1422) and Aḥmad ibn Muḥammad, known as Ibn Fahd al-Ḥillī (d. 841/1437).

Sufism and the Popular Religion

Perhaps more important for the further development of Shi'ism than the works of scholars in the field of jurisprudence and theology was the further effort to integrate Sufi thought into Shi'ism. Even the eminent scholar of this period, Ibn Fahd, was sympathetic to Sufism and several of his works demonstrate this. But the true successor to Ḥaydar Āmulī of the previous century was Muḥammad ibn 'Alī al-Aḥsā'ī known as Ibn Abī Jumhūr, who died in the opening years of the 10th/16th century. Ibn Abī Jumhūr was an orthodox Shi'i scholar who studied at Najaf and for a time at Karak-Nūḥ, the Shi'i centre in the Jabal 'Āmil. He continued Āmulī's work in integrating Sufism and Shi'ism. But he widened the scope of his endeavours by also attempting to unite and integrate philosophy and Mu'tazilī and Ash'arī theology. He tried to show that all of these led to the Sufi concept of existential monism (*waḥdat al-wujūd*).

Among some Sunni scholars of this period there was also a leaning towards Shi'ism. Huṣayn Wā'iẓ al-Kāshifī, who was a Sunni Traditionist and Qur'an commentator, wrote a book called the *Rawḍat ash-shuhadā* (The Paradise of the Martyrs) eulogising the martyrdom of the Imam Husayn in such moving terms that the book was enthusiastically adopted by Shi'is. He also wrote a work on the *futuwwa* which was another important pro-Shi'i manifestation in Sunnism (see p.90).

While there may not have been much of importance occurring among the ulama of Twelver Shi'ism during this period, this was by no means true of Shi'ism among the people. Although it is difficult to distinguish between extreme Shi'ism (*ghuluww*), Twelver Shi'ism and the pro-Shi'i tendency within Sunni Islam, it is clear that there was a great Shi'i ferment occurring among the people in western Iran, northern Iraq, eastern Anatolia and northern Syria. Into this Shi'i cauldron went the ideas of the Ismā'īlīs, the Ḥurūfīs, the *ghulāt*, as well as the Twelvers. Out of this came a wide variety of movements some of which remained within the mainstream of Islam and some of which moved beyond it. The 'Alawīs (Nuṣayrīs) in northern Syria and the Ahl-i Ḥaqq in western Iran became separate sects (see pp. 46–7, 58). The Bektāshīs were accommodated within the Ottoman Empire as a Sufi order. The Musha'sha' set up as a state in south-east Iran. The Safavids began as a Sufi order but after achieving political power became absorbed into Twelver Shi'ism. All these groups show marked Twelver Shi'i features and, in particular, most of them emphasise devotion to the Twelve Imams.

The Ḥurūfīs were a sect started by Faḍlu'llāh Astarābādī (740/1339–804/1401) who claimed to be a prophet. Much of their doctrine resembles the Ismā'īlī or the early *ghuluww* views, in that Faḍlu'llāh claimed to be able to reveal the true inner meaning of the Qur'an and the religious observances of Islam. This interpretation (*ta'wīl*) involves an elaboration of the mystical significance of numbers, letters and the parts of the body. Although the number seven occurs frequently, there is also a clearly Twelver aspect to these teachings with praise of the Twelve Imams and Faḍlu'llāh even claimed to be the return of the Twelfth Imam.

Faḍlu'llāh began preaching his doctrine in 786/1384 and was executed in 796/1403 on the orders of Tīmūr. But his doctrines continued under his first successor (*Khalīfa*), 'Alī al-A'lā, who, persecuted by Tīmūr and his successors, fled into Anatolia where he had a profound influence on the evolution of the Bektāshī order.

Throughout Iran several of the most prominent Sufi orders were evolving in a more Shi'i-orientated direction. The most important of these, from the point of view of the future history of Iran, was the Safavid order of Sufis. This order was founded by Shaykh Ṣafīyu'd-Dīn (650/1252–735/1334) in Ardibīl in north-west Iran during the Ilkhanid period. He was a Sunni and during his lifetime became sufficiently influential to include most of the inhabitants of Ardibīl among his disciples. He was probably of Kurdish or Turkoman origin but the later Safavid kings concealed their ancestry so as to claim descent from the Seventh Imam, Muṣā al-Kāẓim. Shaykh Ṣafiyu'd-Dīn was succeeded by his son, grandson and great-grandson who each maintained this Sufi order in much the same orientation and were highly respected by the Jalāyir and Timurid rulers. By the end of this period the order had greatly extended its influence, having disciples in most parts of Iran, Iraq, Anatolia and even in some parts of Syria. It was still at this time an orthodox Sunni order.

With the accession of Junayd (the fourth Shaykh after Ṣafīyu'd-Dīn) to the leadership of the order in 851/1447, a new phase of the order's development began. This hitherto peaceful order suddenly became a military one and launched a series of campaigns against neighbouring Christian states. Junayd became the effective ruler of a small state centred on Ardibīl (albeit as a vassal of the Aq-Quyūnlū) and thus came to combine spiritual with temporal authority. Also during Junayd's leadership, the Shaykh of the order became regarded as a manifestation of the divinity and thus the order became identified with extremist Shi'i (*ghulāt*) views. It is not clear at what point the order became openly Shi'i but it was almost certainly at about this time. Although Junayd claimed to be conducting a religious war (*jihād*) against the Georgians of the Caucasus, he could not resist a strike against the Shirvanid territory which bordered on Georgia. He was killed in battle against the Shirvanids in 865/1460. His son Ḥaydar continued his father's aggressive policies and eventually also met the same fate in 893/1488 at the hands of Sulṭān Ya'qūb of the Aq-Quyūnlū who had become alarmed at Ḥaydar's aggression. It was Ḥaydar who organised the movement's followers into a body of troops called Qizilbāsh (redheads: on account of their wearing red hats with twelve points indicating their adherence to the Twelve Imams). It is clear, however, that the Shi'ism of the Qizilbāsh at this period had little resemblance to orthodox Twelver Shi'ism. They regarded their leader as a divine figure and would thus have been classed by Twelver Shi'is as extremists (*ghulāt*). Ḥaydar's sons were exiled to Fārs, but in the increasing anarchy that accompanied the collapse of the Aq-Quyūnlū dynasty, they were able to return to Ardibīl. Ḥaydar's first son 'Alī was killed in 900/1494 by one of the Aq-Quyūnlū, Rustam, leaving the leadership of the order to the youngest son Ismā'īl who was to found the Safavid dynasty.

A movement that in many ways paralleled the Safavids in its early stages was the Musha'sha'. The movement was started by Muḥammad ibn Falāḥ, the foster son of the eminent Twelver scholar, Ibn Fahd. In 840/1436, despite the opposition of Ibn Fahd, Ibn Falāḥ proclaimed himself to be the Mahdī. Later he centred himself at Ḥuwayza in Khuzistān in south-west Iran and managed to obtain the allegiance of several of the Shi'i tribes of the area on the basis of his messianic claims. With the help of his son he was soon in control of the whole area from Ahwaz to the Tigris. All who were not his followers were considered as infidels and therefore there was extensive looting and killing. Najaf and Ḥilla were attacked in 857/1453 and even Baghdad in 860/1456. But then a Qarā-Quyūnlū army was sent against the Musha'sha' which defeated them, killing 'Alī, Ibn Falāḥ's son. Ibn Falāḥ himself died in 866/1461. Ibn Falāḥ's descendants ruled the area with similar extremist (*ghuluww*) doctrines until overcome by the Safavids in 914/1508. The descendants of Ibn Falāḥ remained, however, as Safavid governors of the province. As time went by the Musha'sha' became less and less extremist (much as the Safavids themselves did), until eventually they became orthodox Shi'is. Ḥuwayza became by the 11th/17th century a centre of Twelver Shi'i teaching and Ibn Falāḥ's great-great-grandson was a respected Twelver Shi'i scholar.

The drift towards Shi'ism in several lines of the Kubrāwiyya order has been mentioned in the preceding section. 'Alī Hamadānī's successor, Khwāja Isḥāq, plotted a revolt against Shāh-Rukh. Part of his plan was to put forward one of his disciples, Muḥammad ibn 'Abdu'llāh, who became known as Nūrbakhsh, as the Mahdī. This revolt in 826/1423 failed and Khwāja Isḥāq was executed. Due to the respect for the family of the Prophet which Shāh-Rukh shared with his father, Tīmūr, Nūrbakhsh himself was spared. He attempted a second uprising in Kurdistān and was again defeated and this time detained in Herat until the death of Shāh-Rukh in 851/1447. Nūrbakhsh was then allowed to go to Shahriyār where he established the headquarters of his order and where he lived until his death in 869/1464.

Nūrbakhsh remained a Sunni but with strong Shi'i leanings. He emphasised his own 'Alid lineage, quoted from Shi'i works, visited Shi'i shrines in Iraq and is even said to have studied under Ibn Fahd in Ḥilla. But he also considered the first three Caliphs as Sufi Saints. His Shi'i leanings were essentially an expression of his Sufism. In later years, however, his order became increasingly Shi'i and was to exert a strong influence on many of the Shi'i ulama of the Safavid period as well as playing a major role in the spread of Shi'ism in India.

From the Kubrāwiyya there was also derived the Dhahabiyya which later became openly Shi'i. The Khalwatī orders in Anatolia, which were linked to the Safavid order, also had Shi'i leanings.

In Anatolia the Bābā'ī order, mentioned in the preceding section, gave rise to the Bektāshī order which was to become the order of the Ottoman Janissary troops. This Sufi order contains very strong threads of Shi'ism, albeit of an extremist type in that 'Ali is elevated to a divine trinity of God, Muhammad and 'Ali. It also venerates the Twelve Imams.

Shāh Ni'matu'llāh Walī, who in 762/1360 had gained many disciples at the court of Tīmūr in Herat, settled in Mahān in south-east Iran and made that the centre of his Sufi order, the Ni'matu'llāhīs. Although a Sunni as far as religious observances are concerned, his writings show a great devotion to 'Ali (he himself was from an 'Alid family of Aleppo). He died in 834/1430 and his successors continued his pro-Shi'i line until, during the Safavid era, the order became openly Shi'i.

It is not clear exactly when and how Twelver Shi'ism spread to India. It may well have been that, as a result of the devastation caused by the Mongol invasions, Twelver Shi'is migrated there. The first monarch to have given Twelver Shi'ism support in India is reputed to have been Sulṭān Muḥammad ibn Tughluq (reigned AD 1325–51), but his successors adopted an anti-Shi'i policy. In the Deccan, the Bahmānī kings who ruled from the mid-14th to the early 16th centuries showed some pro-Shi'i inclinations. One of the most important of their ministers, Maḥmūd Gāwān, was a Shi'i. Shāh Ni'matu'llāh Walī (see above) had a strong influence on this dynasty while another major pro-Shi'i Sufi shaykh, 'Alī Hamadānī (see p. 96), travelled in India and Kashmir in 1380.

Nineteenth-century orientalists used to assert that Shi'ism was an Iranian innovation within Islam. As a reaction to this, more recent writers have emphasised the fact that the early Shi'a were Arabs and that the majority of the Iranians were Sunnis until the advent of the Safavid dynasty. However, this later trend has tended to belittle the significance of Iranian Shi'i centres such as Qumm, which were important from the beginning of the emergence of Shi'ism, and also the importance of such early Iranian scholars as Ibn Bābūya and Shaykhu'ṭ-Ṭā'ifa. Moreover, although it is true that the majority of Iranians were Sunnis until the advent of the Safavids, this fact conceals the large number of Shi'is in Qumm, Rayy, Kāshān and much of Khurāsān. It also conceals the important pro-Shi'i influence of Sufi orders such as the Kubrāwiyya, who were predominant in east Iran, and the craft-guilds in the cities, which were modelled on the *futuwwa*. These must have played a key role in preparing the populace for the acceptance of Shi'ism under the Safavids.

Although much of what has been written in this chapter may appear to be the history of extremist (*ghuluww*) Shi'ism rather than Twelver Shi'ism, its relevance will become evident in the next chapter when the fusion of extremist Shi'ism and Twelver Shi'is under the Safavids is described.

6

Shi'i Islam in Modern Times

AD 1500–1900

The Safavid Period (10th/16th–12th/18th Centuries)

Political Developments under Shāh Ismā'īl

The early history of the Safavids has already been described in the previous chapter. When Ismā'īl became the leader of the Safavid order of Sufis in 900/1494, the Aq-Quyūnlū Empire was being seriously weakened by civil war between rival claimants. Rustam, the Aq-Quyūnlū claimant who had killed Ismā'īl's brother, 'Alī, for a time pursued Ismā'īl and the latter went into hiding in Ardibīl and later in Lāhījān. But soon Rustam was embroiled in fighting other claimants and was killed in 1497 leaving Ismā'īl free to organise his followers.

It is clear that Ismā'īl was representing himself to his Turkoman Qizilbāsh followers at this time as not merely the representative of the Hidden Imam, but the Hidden Imam himself and beyond that even claiming divinity for himself. Ismā'īl's followers are said to have gone into battle without armour, confident that no harm would befall them, saying: 'Lā ilāhā ila Allāh, Ismā'īl walīyu'llāh (there is no god but God and Ismā'īl is the Friend of God)', thus equating Ismā'īl with the Imam 'Ali.

Gathering all his men from Anatolia and Syria, Ismā'īl (only twelve years old at this time), set out in 1499 to carve out an empire for himself. The initial campaign was not very successful, but after wintering his troops in Gīlān, Ismā'īl in 1500 attacked the kingdom of Shīrvān whose rulers had killed his grandfather. The king of Shīrvān was defeated and killed and Baku captured. Then one of the Aq-Quyūnlū marched against him with four times as many troops as Ismā'īl had. But Ismā'īl defeated this army and the whole of Ādharbāyjān fell into his hands. In the summer of 1501 Ismā'īl was crowned king in Tabrīz. He proclaimed that the official religion of the new state would be Ithnā-'Ashariyya (Twelver) Shi'ism.

It took Ismā'īl another ten years to conquer all of Iran as far east as Herat as well as Diyārbakr and Baghdad in Iraq. During this time his Qizilbāsh troops served him with fanatical devotion and Ismā'īl incorporated within himself the military, administrative and religious leadership of the country. He instituted the post of *Ṣadr* whose function it was to co-ordinate the propagation of Shi'ism in Iran while the Safavid agents called *Khalīfas* were also busy in Syria and Anatolia.

It is probably insufficiently appreciated how close Ismā'īl came to winning over the Islamic heartlands ideologically. For even while he was conquering Iran, his emissaries were preparing the ground for an extension of his empire westwards. For several generations large numbers of the Turkoman tribes occupying west and central Anatolia had been devotees of the Safavid order and had assisted in the conquest of Iran. The rising Ottoman Empire claimed sovereignty over this area but it was obvious that its hold was shaky with the loyalty of many of the tribesmen leaning towards the newly-emerging Safavid state in Iran. Even the loyalty of the Janissaries, the pre-eminent corps of the Ottoman army, was in doubt since they were followers of the Bektāshī Sufi order and were thus outgrowths of the same religious roots as the Safavid order. Ismā'īl's religious poetry enjoyed wide circulation among the Bektāshīs. In Syria also there were large numbers of followers of the Safavid order and contemporary accounts of Aleppo, for example, speak of a 'party of Ardibīl' within the city[1] while the Mamluk state in Egypt was inclined to an alliance with the Safavids against the Ottomans. Thus Ismā'īl was poised to add eastern Anatolia, Syria and perhaps even Egypt to his domains after completing his conquest of Iran.[2]

So worried were the Ottomans that Sultan Bayazid II ordered large-scale deportations of Shi'is from eastern Anatolia to Morea in AD 1502. In 1511 Bābā Shāh-Qulī began a pro-Safavid revolt among tribesmen in the province of Tekke on the Mediterranean coast of Anatolia. The rebels advanced as far as Brusa before being defeated and driven back. The following year, 1512, Sultan Selim I acceded to the Ottoman throne and determined to act decisively against the danger of the whole of eastern Anatolia seceding to the Safavids. He drew up a list of every known Shi'i in his dominions and massacred them to the reported number of 40,000, deporting and imprisoning large numbers of others. In the same year one of Ismā'īl's close aides raised a force from among the Sufis of the Safavid order in eastern Anatolia and raided the Ottoman domains.

In 1514 Sultan Selim decided to march against Shāh Ismā'īl and reached the plain of Chāldirān in Ādharbāyjān with an army of over 100,000 men against which Ismā'īl could only muster 40,000. Although the Safavid forces had the advantage in the hand-to-hand fighting, the deployment of artillery and hand guns by the Ottomans (when the Safavids had had no experience of these) decided the day. The Ottomans won and occupied Tabrīz. At this stage, instead of pressing home the advantage and overthrowing the Safavid state completely, Selim withdrew. This withdrawal has been attributed to the difficulties of the extended Ottoman lines of communication but may also have had something to do with fears of the effects that a prolonged campaign in Iran might have had on Selim's Janissary troops whose loyalty was under question because of their religious affinities with the Safavids through the Bektāshī Sufi order.

Had Ismā'īl won the day there was probably no other force in the Middle East that could have withstood him, and Anatolia, Syria and perhaps Egypt would have fallen easily to him. Whether Ismā'īl could have imposed Shi'ism on the population of such a large area in the same way as he did in Iran is a question that is as fascinating as it is impossible to answer.

Ismā'īl was a broken man after Chāldirān. He retired to his palace and withdrew from active participation in the affairs of the state, leaving these to his minister, Mīrzā Shāh-Ḥusayn, an Iranian, whose power grew so great that he was eventually assassinated in 1523 by Turkoman Qizilbāsh. In the following year, on 23 May 1524, Shāh Ismā'īl himself died.

Shāh Ismā'īl's Religious Policy

Although Ismā'īl had proclaimed Twelver Shi'ism to be the religion of the state, there were anomalies in his position. The Safavids as a dynasty were greatly concerned by the question of legitimacy. Although in Sunni Islam the legitimacy of the *de facto* ruler had been established by Sunni scholars in the early medieval period, there had been no similar work done in Shi'ism and indeed no comparable circumstance had arisen in Shi'i history. Ismā'īl's own position rested on three bases: firstly, the ancient Persian concept of kingship which was expressed in the concept of the king being the 'Shadow of God on Earth'; secondly, on his position as head of the Safavid order of Sufis thus commanding the absolute obedience of his followers, the Qizilbāsh; thirdly, on the basis of an alleged descent from the Seventh Imam, he and the succeeding Safavids claimed to be the representative of the Hidden Imam, and, as such, to be imbued with infallibility (*'iṣma*).

It is this last claim which is the most interesting for it runs clearly counter to some of the most fundamental tenets of Twelver Shi'ism. Even if the Safavid claim to 'Alid descent is accepted (and most modern scholars consider it to have been a forgery), mere descent from the

Imams confers no spiritual or temporal authority. Twelver Shi'ism is quite clear that in the case of the Imamate, both heredity and designation (*naṣṣ*) are necessary, neither being acceptable without the other. Indeed, in the case of the four representatives of the Hidden Imam that existed during the Lesser Occultation (see pp. 162–5), designation was the only important basis of their authority for none of them was descended from the Imams. Moreover, the doctrines of Twelver Shi'ism are also very clear in stating that after the death of the fourth of these representatives and the start of the Greater Occultation, no-one can claim to be the special representative (*nā'ib al-khāṣṣ*) of the Hidden Imam until the return of the Imam occurs. It was clearly impossible for the Safavids to claim designation (except in visions of the Hidden Imam) and the great stress in their propaganda on their descent from the Imams can only be seen as a smokescreen to hide the fact that this was an irrelevance. In fact, the Safavids were claiming power on the basis of a Zaydī-style Imamate (see pp. 49–50) while claiming to be Twelver Shi'is.

Why then was there no protest at this irreligious claim by Ismā'īl? There appear to be two factors involved in the lack of response by the ulama to his claim. Firstly, there were, by this time, very few prominent native Iranian Twelver ulama. The old Shi'i centres in Iran, such as Qumm, Nīshāpūr, Ṭūs, Kāshān and Rayy were no longer important centres of scholarship and were producing very few ulama and none of any prominence. Among Ismā'īl's own Qizilbāsh forces there appears to have been a profound ignorance of Twelver Shi'ism. When Tabrīz was taken and Twelver Shi'ism proclaimed the religion of the state, for example, there was not a single book on Twelver Shi'ism to be found in Ismā'īl's army and eventually a copy of a book by 'Allāma al-Ḥillī was located in the library of a *qaḍī* of Tabrīz to provide guidance on the new religion of the state. None of those appointed to the office of *Ṣadr* (in charge of the propagation of Shi'ism) in the early period had received formal training as Twelver ulama, and the Shi'ism of one of them was even in doubt.[3] The Arab Twelver ulama resident in Iraq, Syria and Bahrain were the only ones that could have provided informed authoritative opposition to the Safavid claim. These were brought to Iran in increasing numbers, especially during the reigns of Ismā'īl's successors, but they probably felt their position, as immigrants dependent on the largesse of the state, too vulnerable to take on the Shāh and, in any case, it is doubtful if they would have wanted to undermine the newly-emergent state that was propagating Shi'ism and was under attack from Sunni powers. Thus in the early period of the Safavid dynasty there appears to have been an uneasy alliance between the state and the ulama with the state supporting the ulama by enforcing Shi'ism on the populace while the ulama supported the state and kept quiet about the inconsistencies in the religious stance of the monarch.

It is clear that the Shi'ism that Ismā'īl was enforcing throughout his domain at this stage consisted of no more than the Shi'i form of the call to prayer (*adhān*), the acknowledgement of 'Ali's position during the address in the mosque (the *khuṭba*) and the public cursing of 'Ali's enemies. For the majority of the people, it involved no more than exalting 'Ali and cursing his enemies. The tombs of Sunni saints and scholars were desecrated and here and there a few Sunni ulama resisted the change and were dealt with harshly. But there does not appear to have been the major upheaval and opposition that might have been expected in a predominantly Sunni country. This is undoubtedly due to the activities of the Sufi orders and the *futuwwa* brotherhoods who had been inculcating a love of 'Ali and the family of the Prophet among the people for the past two centuries. The religious toleration of the Ilkhanid and Timurid rulers had also served to diffuse much of the old Sunni-Shi'i hatred.

Conscious of the fact that another Sufi order could emulate what the Safavids had done, Ismā'īl set about destroying the organised Sufi orders. The Sunni Naqshbandī and Khalwatī orders were extirpated. The Nūrbakhshī and Dhahabī orders that were pro-Shi'i were initially tolerated but gradually emasculated and lost their influence. Only the Ni'matu'llāhī order, which proclaimed itself Shi'i on the establishment of the Safavid state and allied itself closely to the Safavids, was allowed to continue its activities without opposition.

Shāh Ṭahmāsp

At the time of Ismā'īl's death, his son Ṭahmāsp was only ten years old. There followed a decade of disorder when the various Qizilbāsh factions fought each other for supremacy until in AD 1533 Ṭahmāsp was able to assert his authority. But he was in a perilous position with the state severely weakened and serious incursions being made by the Uzbegs in the East and the Ottomans in the West. Between 1524 and 1538 there were five major Uzbeg attacks and between 1533 and 1553 there were four major Ottoman invasions.

In 1555 Ṭahmāsp signed a peace treaty with the Ottomans and at about the same time moved his capital from Tabrīz to Qazvīn. The rest of his reign was comparatively tranquil.

On the religious side, Ṭahmāsp was still considered a divine figure by his Sufi followers but he had no inclination to assume this role and took steps to suppress the tendency to extremist Shi'ism (*ghuluww*) among his followers. He crushed one Turkoman tribe in 938/1531 for irreligion (*ilḥād*) and another group of Sufis who proclaimed him Mahdī in 1554.

Other manifestations of extremism such as the Nuqṭavi movement (derived from the Ḥurūfīs of the previous century) were also suppressed and a community of them in Kāshān massacred in 983/1575.

On the other side of the coin, Ṭahmāsp did much to encourage the spread of orthodox Twelver Shi'ism. The leading Shi'i scholar of the day, Shaykh 'Alī ibn 'Abdu'l-'Alī al-'Āmilī, known as Muḥaqqiq ath-Thānī or Muḥaqqiq al-Karakī (d. 940/1533), who had visited Iran in Shāh Ismā'īl's time, was now encouraged to settle in Iran. He travelled about the country propagating orthodox Shi'ism, appointing prayer-leaders in each town and village who could teach the people Shi'ism, and openly attacking Sunnism. It is reported that his open cursing of Abū Bakr and 'Umar had repercussions in Mecca and Medina where the Shi'i ulama were persecuted in retaliation.[4]

Ṭahmāsp died in AD 1576 and was succeeded by his son Ismā'īl II. The latter was sympathetic to Sunnism and the fact that he thought it feasible to try to reverse Safavid religious policies and found support for doing so even in the capital city of Qazvīn, shows how superficial conversion to Shi'ism had been in Iran up to this time. But the Qizilbāsh would not tolerate this and Ismā'īl II was assassinated after a reign of only one year. His successor, Sulṭān-Muḥammad Shāh, was a weak and ineffectual ruler who reigned from 1578 until 1588 when he was forced to abdicate in favour of his son, Shāh 'Abbās I.

Shāh 'Abbās I

'Abbās I came to the throne at a critical time in the fortunes of the Safavid Dynasty. The Qizilbāsh chiefs, under his father's weak rule, had lapsed into internecine warfare. The Ottomans and Uzbegs, taking advantage of the situation, had seized Ādharbāyjān and Herat respectively.

'Abbās I, realising that he could no longer rely on the Qizilbāsh, raised a standing army from the *ghulāms*, the Georgian and Circassian slaves which Ṭahmāsp had brought back from his campaigns. Using these, he launched a campaign in 1598 which drove the Uzbegs out of Khurāsān. In 1603 he started a campaign which lasted until 1607 and cleared the Ottomans from Ādharbāyjān. Finally in 1624 Baghdad and the whole of Iraq fell to the Safavid forces. This final victory was of great symbolic importance because of the existence in Iraq of the great Shi'i shrines. In 1597 'Abbās I transferred his capital to Isfahan.

In the field of religion, the policies of Ismā'īl I in suppressing the organised Sufi orders and that of Ṭahmāsp in suppressing expressions of Shi'i extremism (*ghuluww*) while encouraging the growth of orthodox Twelver Shi'ism were continued by 'Abbās I. The Ni'matu'llāhī order of Sufis that had allied itself to the Safavids and had been allowed to continue under the early Safavids was now subjected to pressure and eventually withdrew to India.

The old Sufi organisation of the Safavid order had, by the reign of 'Abbās I, become an empty form. 'Abbās, having seen in his early years how fickle and unreliable was the loyalty of the Qizilbāsh, took every opportunity to undermine and diminish the importance of this aspect of his power base. In 1592 and again in 1614 a number of Sufis of Qarajadāgh, who were among the oldest adherents of the Safavid order, were executed on the charge of collaborating with the Ottomans, thus demonstrating how little was left of the old loyalty. Among the Georgian and Circassian slaves (*ghulāms*) who replaced the Qizilbāsh, the former appeal to *Ṣūfīgarī* (Sufi probity and obedience to the Shaykh) as the basis of loyalty to the Shāh was replaced by *Shāhī-sivanī* (love of the Shāh).

At the beginning of his reign 'Abbās I was attracted by the Nuqṭavī doctrine which was based on the old Ḥurūfī ideas. But in 1593 he turned on this group and had large numbers of them killed in Kashan and Isfahan. From this date on 'Abbās I surrounded himself with orthodox Twelver ulama and worked towards the propagation of that doctrine.

During the reigns of his predecessors Iranians had been sent to Jabal 'Āmil to study Shi'ism. After 'Abbās moved his capital to Isfahan in 1597, he built there a number of theological colleges (*madrasas*) and encouraged ulama from Jabal 'Āmil and Bahrain to come to Iran and particularly to Isfahan. This heralded a major change in the education of Shi'i ulama at the beginning of the 11th/17th century. Whereas Sunnis had since Seljuq times built up a system of education at religious colleges, Shi'i religious students had tended to gather around individual prominent scholars, often being taught in the home of that scholar in the villages of the Jabal 'Āmil or Bahrain or even in the town of Ḥilla. Now with the advent of a Shi'i state that was able to fund such enterprises, the system of religious colleges was started in Iran and particularly in Isfahan. These were the precursors of the religious colleges that were built in Qājār times at Najaf, Qumm and Mashhad and are now the most important such institutions in the Shi'i world.[5]

The principal centre of Shi'i scholarship was thus transferred to Isfahan during the reign of 'Abbās I. A prominent role in this build-up of the importance of Isfahan as a religious centre was played by Mullā 'Abdu'llāh Shushtarī (d. 1021/1612). After spending thirty years studying in Najaf and Karbalā, particularly under Muqaddas Ardibīlī, Shushtarī arrived in Isfahan about one year after Shāh 'Abbās transferred his capital there. He became the principal religious teacher in the town and it is stated that, whereas when he arrived there were only 50 students in Isfahan, by the time of his death, fourteen years later, there were over

1,000. The leading Shi'i scholar of the time was Shaykh Bahā'u'd-Dīn Muḥammad ibn Ḥusayn al-'Āmilī al-Juba'ī, known as Shaykh Bahā'ī (d. 1031/1622). Shaykh Bahā'ī, in the breadth of his knowledge and his achievements in many fields, resembled Khwāja Naṣīru'd-Dīn Ṭūsī. He was an eminent theologian, jurist, philosopher, mystic, astronomer and poet as well as playing a major role in the planning and construction of Isfahan.

By the reign of Shāh 'Abbās I, the claim by the Safavid kings to a semi-divine nature or to being the representative of the Hidden Imam was fading rapidly. 'Abbās I appears himself to have been a pious man. He greatly embellished the holy shrines at Qumm and Mashhad and performed several pilgrimages, on one occasion walking the entire distance from Isfahan to Mashhad on foot. Nevertheless, a few remnants of the old extremist trend remained, such as the custom of prostrating before the monarch (in Islam prostration should only be to God). The role of *Ṣadr*, which was a political appointment, was decreasing in importance, and a new position of *Shaykh al-Islām* was created to which recognised members of the ulama were appointed. This began the process of a separation between the church and the state, but during the days of 'Abbās I the position of the ulama, as newly arrived migrants, was too insecure and the position of the king too strong to allow any real independence to the ulama. For the time being, the state remained in firm control of the ulama.

Shāh 'Abbās died in AD 1629 and was succeeded by his grandson Shāh Ṣafī. This monarch appears to have been addicted to opium and alcohol and to have had little interest in the affairs of state. Under his rule Baghdad was lost to the Ottomans in 1638 and Qandahar to the Moguls of India in the same year. He died in 1642 and was succeeded by his son, 'Abbās II, who was eight-and-half years of age.

'Abbās II had some of the character of his great-grandfather and succeeded in reviving the fortunes of the dynasty to an extent. Qandahar was recaptured in 1648 and the frontiers were maintained intact. Although also addicted to wine, 'Abbās II did not allow affairs to slip from his grasp and was for the most part just and tolerant as a ruler.

The School of Isfahan

The major intellectual development in Islam during this period began during the reign of Shāh 'Abbās I but reached its full flowering in the reigns of his successors. This was the development of *Ḥikmat-i Ilāhī* (*al-Ḥikma al-Ilāhiyya*), divine philosophy or theosophy, under what has come to be called the Ishrāqī (Illuminationist) school of philosophy or the so-called 'School of Isfahan' (see pp. 217–19). The origins of this school within an Islamic context go back to Shihābu'd-Dīn Yaḥyā Suhrawardī (killed in Aleppo in 1191) who believed that to obtain true wisdom it was necessary to develop both the rational and the intuitive aspects of the mind. While the former could be achieved through the philosophy of Aristotle and Ibn Sīnā (Avicenna), the latter required the purification of the soul which could best be achieved through asceticism, mysticism and gnosis. The School of Isfahan also drew on the works of Sayyid Ḥaydar Āmulī and Ibn Abī Jumhūr in bringing together Sufism and the esoteric aspects of Shi'ism.

The founder of the School of Isfahan was Muḥammad Bāqir Astarābādī, known as Mīr Damād (d. 1040/1631). The greatest figure in this school was Ṣadru'd-Dīn Muḥammad ibn Ibrāhīm Shīrāzī, known as Mullā Ṣadrā (d. 1050/1640). Other prominent names in the movement include Abu'l-Qāsim Astarābādī, known as Mīr Findiriskī (d. 1050/1640), and Mullā Rajab 'Alī Tabrīzī (d. 1080/1669). Mullā Ṣadrā retired at one stage of his life to Kahak, a village near Qumm. Subsequently, an important branch of this movement was centred in Qumm with the presence there of Mullā 'Abdu'r-Razzāq Lāhījī (d. 1072/1661), Mullā Muḥsin-i Fayḍ of Kāshān (d. 1091/1680) and Qāḍī Sa'īd Qummī (d. 1103/1691). Mullā Muḥsin-i Fayḍ is of great importance also as a scholar of Shi'i *ḥadīth*. His book, *al-Wāfī*, which is a synthesis and commentary on the four early canonical books of Shi'i *ḥadīth*, is considered one of the most important works on this subject.

So influential became the *Ḥikmat-i Ilāhī* movement that it embraced several prominent individuals from both the state and the orthodox Shi'i ulama. The Grand Vazir of 'Abbās II, Sayyid Husayn, Sulṭānu'l-'Ulamā (d. 1064/1654), was a patron of this circle as indeed was 'Abbās II himself. Mullā Muḥammad Taqī Majlisī (d. 1070/1659), a noted jurist and father of the even more famous Muḥammad Bāqir Majlisī, was connected with this circle, as was Mullā Muḥammad Bāqir Sabzivārī (d. 1090/1679) who was appointed *Shaykh al-Islām* of Isfahan.

Shāh Sulaymān

'Abbās II died in 1666 and under his successor Shāh Sulaymān the decline of the Safavids resumed. Sulaymān abandoned himself to the pleasure of wine and the harem and took no interest in the affairs of state. His successor Sulṭān-Ḥusayn Shāh began his reign in 1694 as a pious and austere man but soon declined into drunkenness and debauchery. He too refused to involve himself in the business of governing the country, leaving this to ministers and the eunuchs of the Court as well as to the increasingly powerful mujtahids.

The only reason that the Safavids remained in power for as long as they did was the fortunate circumstance that the powers on their borders were not in a position to attack them. The Ottoman Empire was embroiled in Europe, the Mogul Empire was in decline and the Uzbegs had disappeared from the scene. When the end came for the Safavids, it was the result of a revolt from within their own borders. The Ghilzāy Afghans rose in rebellion. At first it would appear that they, being Sunnis, only wished to throw off the Shi'i Safavid yoke, but when they saw the Safavid forces collapse before them, they pushed on in anticipation of booty. With an army of only twenty thousand, they penetrated to the heart of the Safavid realm and took Isfahan in October 1722, terminating effective Safavid rule.

The Ulama of the Late Safavid Period

In the religious sphere, the ulama of the late Safavid period, who were mostly Iranians, had a much firmer power base within the country and thus felt secure enough to take an increasingly independent stand *vis-à-vis* the Safavid state. Already by the reign of Shāh Sulaymān, foreign observers such as Chardin noted that the ulama were saying that these immoral Safavid kings were not worthy of kingship and that the mujtahid is the real ruler as representative of the Imam.[6] This must, however, have remained a minority view among the ulama for although the *nā'ib al-'āmm* concept (see p. 190) was developed in this period, there is nothing in the important Shi'i works of this time to indicate that they considered this concept to include political rule. This idea of the mujtahid as the ideal Shi'i ruler had to await Āyatu'llāh Khumaynī in the twentieth century for its full development (see pp. 195–6).

It cannot, however, be denied that the ulama were taking an increasingly prominent role in the affairs of the country and were becoming more assertive with respect to their demands. This process came to a head in the time of Muḥammad Bāqir Majlisī (who became *Shaykh al-Islām* of Isfahan in 1687 and Mullābāshī – Head Mullā – in 1694) and particularly during the reign of Shāh Sulṭān-Ḥusayn, which began in 1694.

It is necessary to take a close look at the activity of Muḥammad Bāqir Majlisī (d. 1110/1699) since he was one of the most powerful and influential Shi'i ulama of all time and since his policies and actions reorientated Twelver Shi'ism in the direction that it was to develop from his day on. Majlisī was an important scholar in his own right. His encyclopaedic collection of *ḥadīth*, the *Biḥār al- Anwār*, would alone have established his reputation but he was one of the most prolific writers and produced numerous other works that have continued to be important. It is, however, in the social and political role that he played rather than in his scholarly work that his importance lies.

The first point that must be noted is that Majlisī was all-powerful in whatever field he chose to initiate his policies. The government of Sulṭān-Ḥusayn Shāh made almost no effort to control his activities. The three inter-related areas in which Majlisī exerted his efforts were: the suppression of Sufism and philosophy, the propagation of a dogmatic legalistic form of Twelver Shi'ism and the suppression of Sunnism and other religious groups.

Sulṭān-Ḥusayn Shāh had come under Majlisī's influence whilst still in the harem. When it came to the coronation ceremony, Sulṭān-Ḥusayn insisted that it be Majlisī who invested him with the symbols of state. He then asked Majlisī what he desired by way of recompense. Majlisī requested royal decrees forbidding the drinking of wine, the practice of faction-fighting and the sport of pigeon-flying. In addition, he asked for the expulsion of all Sufis from Isfahan. The decree forbidding the drinking of wine had later to be revoked when the Shāh himself became addicted to alcohol, but the attack on Sufism continued.

In the preceding chapter and this chapter, it has been seen that up to the time of Majlisī, Shi'ism and Sufism were closely linked and indeed Sufism had been a vehicle for pro-Shi'i sentiment among the Sunnis. Even the most eminent members of the Shi'i ulama in the preceding centuries had come under the influence of Sufism and such persons as Ibn Tāwus, 'Allāma al-Ḥillī, Shahīd al-Awwal, Ibn Fahd al-Ḥillī, Shahīd ath-Thānī and Shaykh Bahā'ī were either sympathetic to Sufism or considered themselves practising Sufis. Even Majlisī's own father, Muḥammad Taqī Majlisī, was a member of the Dhahabiyya Sufi order. In addition, the development of the School of Isfahan could be considered (and was considered by Majlisī) as a form of philosophical or 'high' Sufism.

Majlisī set out to counter and reverse this trend of Sufism and philosophy in Twelver Shi'ism. Sufis, whether they were the wandering dervishes of 'low' Sufism or the philosopher-ulama of 'high' Sufism came under relentless pressure from Majlisī and his Sharī'a-minded colleagues. The Sufi teachings of the mystical union with God and its connotations were stated to be heresy (that 'foul and hellish growth') while the philosophers of the School of Isfahan were considered 'followers of an infidel Greek'.[7]

The process of suppressing Sufism pursued vigorously by Majlisī and his contemporary Shaykh Muḥammad al-Ḥurr al-'Āmilī (d. 1104/1693) was, in fact, an intensification of a trend that had begun in the previous generation of ulama. One of the teachers of both Majlisī and al-Ḥurr al-'Āmilī, Muḥammad Ṭāhir ibn Muḥammad Ḥusayn Shīrāzī (d. 1098/1686) had been active in preaching against Sufis and had written a treatise in refutation of Sufism.[8] This process continued among the succeeding generations of ulama, several of whom distinguished themselves as persecutors and even slayers of Sufis. The ultimate result of this was that Sufism was divorced from Shi'ism and ceased to influence the main stream of Shi'i development. Philosophy was also down-graded and ceased to be an important part of studies at the religious colleges. There was some degree of rehabilitation of these subjects in later years (see p. 218), but for the most part the distrust of and distaste for these subjects engendered by Majlisī has remained the attitude of the majority of the ulama to the present day.

The second area in which Majlisī exerted himself was in the propagation of the 'dry', formal, dogmatic, legalistic style of Shi'ism that he considered to be the true Shi'ism. Up to this time, it would be true to say that Shi'ism had sat lightly on the population of Iran, consisting mostly of mere expressions of love for 'Ali and hatred of the first three Caliphs. Majlisī sought to establish Shi'ism firmly in the minds and hearts of the people. This he did in three main ways. Firstly, he encouraged many specifically Shi'i rituals such as mourning for the Imam Husayn and visitation (*ziyārat*) of the tombs of the Imams and *Imāmzādas* (descendants of the Imams). This last activity he invested with unprecedented importance and was largely responsible for a great elaboration of the rituals involved. Secondly, he emphasised the soteriological aspects of Shi'ism, stressing the concept of the Imams as mediators and intercessors for man with God. Thirdly, he wrote a large number of books on theology, history and manuals of ritual in Persian, thus bringing this knowledge to the level of understanding of ordinary Iranians. Although the writing of books of Shi'i doctrine and law in Persian was begun as early as the reign of Shāh Ismā'īl by Kamālu'd-Dīn Ḥusayn Ardibīlī,[9] Majlisī was the first to write in Persian so much, on such a wide range of subjects and in a manner that could be understood by the ordinary people.

The third direction in which Majlisī exerted his efforts, and which was in obvious parallel to his goal of propagating Shi'ism, was in suppressing Sunnism. Although much of western and central Iran was now Shi'i, the Afghans in Khurāsān remained for the most part obstinately Sunni. Other Sunni strongholds included the Kurds in the west and the Muslims of the Caucasus. Majlisī waged a relentless campaign of persecution wherever he found any Sunnis. But in this aspect of his policies Majlisī failed. Not only did he fail in converting these remaining pockets of Sunnism but he aroused such resentment and hostility that he sparked off the Afghan revolt that toppled the Safavid dynasty and brought Iran back under Sunni rule.

Paradoxically, then, Majlisī's activities both partially caused the revolt that replaced a Shi'i dynasty with Sunni rule and also established

Shi'ism sufficiently firmly within the hearts of the Iranian people to ensure that the efforts made in the post-Safavid period to return Iran to Sunnism would fail. Apart from the two Majlisīs, father and son, the prominent ulama of the late Safavid period were: Mullā Muḥammad Ṣāliḥ ibn Aḥmad Māzandarānī (d. 1081/1670); Mullā Muḥammad Bāqir ibn Muḥammad Mu'min, known as Muḥaqqiq Sabzivārī (d. 1090/1679); Āqā Ḥusayn ibn Muḥammad, known as Muḥaqqiq Khwānsārī (d. 1098/1686); Shaykh Muḥammad ibn Ḥasan al-Ḥurr al-'Āmilī (d. 1104/1693); Sayyid Ni'matu'llāh Jazā'irī (d. 1112/1700); Sayyid Mīr Muḥammad Ṣāliḥ Khātūnābādī (d. 1116/1704), who succeeded Muḥammad Bāqir Majlisī to the position of *Shaykh al-Islām* of Isfahan; and Shaykh Sulaymān ibn 'Abdu'llāh, known as Muḥaqqiq al-Baḥrānī (d. 1120/1708).

The Uṣūlī-Akhbārī Division

It was during the 11th/17th century that another issue came to the fore among the Twelver Shi'i ulama and this was the controversy between the Uṣūlī and Akhbārī Schools. Since it was the Uṣūlīs who eventually won this debate two hundred years later at the end of the 12th/18th century, Shi'i historians have tended to view the struggle from the Uṣūlī point of view which seeks to represent the Akhbārī position as an innovation started by Mullā Muḥammad Amīn Astarābādī (d. 1033/1623) at the beginning of the 11th/17th century. It is clear, however, from the writings of the Akhbārīs themselves (and is probably a closer approximation to the true position) that the Akhbārīs represented a stream of thought that had been present among Shi'i ulama from the earliest days of Twelver Shi'ism and that the controversy only occurred because of the increasing predominance of the mujtahids. The nature of the Akhbārī position is detailed elsewhere in this book (see pp. 222ff.) but can be briefly described here as being against *ijtihād* and the increasingly dominant position of the mujtahids in Twelver Shi'ism. It sought to establish Shi'i jurisprudence on the basis of the Traditions (*Akhbār*) rather than on the rationalist principles (*Uṣūl*) of jurisprudence used in *ijtihād*.

It is probable that there had always existed within Twelver Shi'ism a school of thought that rejected the rationalist ideas of the majority and decried the increasing use of reason rather than Traditions as a source of law. The Akhbārīs themselves pointed to such figures as Kulaynī, Ibn Bābūya, and other eminent Shi'i ulama of previous generations as having been basically in line with their mode of thinking.[10]

The advent of the Safavid dynasty had presented a large number of questions of jurisprudence to the ulama and it may be that too free a use of the licence granted them by the practice of *ijtihād* provoked the Akhbārī reaction. Certainly Muḥaqqiq al-Karakī had been criticised on this score.[11]

Thus rather than being an innovator, it may be that Muḥammad Amīn Astarābādī was merely vocalising a sentiment that had been current among the ulama. Certainly there was no immediate outcry against Astarābādī's attack on *ijtihād* and mujtahids, while several ulama of the first rank either adopted this position or were at least favourably disposed towards it. Thus, for example, of the 'three Muḥammads' of modern times in the field of the study of *ḥadīth* (see p. 174), two (Mullā Muḥsin-i Fayḍ and al-Ḥurr al-'Āmilī) were outright Akhbārīs, while the third, the formidable Muḥammad Bāqir Majlisī, was by no means against the Akhbārī position and even praised Astarābādī in his major work, *Biḥār al-Anwār*.[12] Other prominent ulama who were either Akhbārī or favourable to the Akhbārī position were Sayyid Ni'matu'llāh Jazā'irī (d. 1112/1700), Muḥammad Taqī Majlisī, the father of Muḥammad Bāqir Majlisī (d. 1070/1659), Mullā 'Abdu'llāh Tūnī (d. 1071/1660) and Shaykh Yūsuf al-Baḥrānī (d. 1186/1772).[13] At Bahrain, the leading Shi'i scholar Shaykh 'Alī ibn Sulaymān al-Baḥrānī al-Qadamī (d. 1064/1653), known as Umm al-Ḥadīth, adopted the Akhbārī school and Bahrain became predominantly Akhbārī. The small group of Shi'i ulama at Mecca and Medina which included Mullā Muḥammad Amīn Astarābādī himself were Akhbārī. The Akhbārī doctrines were also well received in Jazā'ir (Shaṭṭ al-'Arab region of southern Iraq),[14] Najaf and Karbalā[15] and, indeed, it is reported that by the end of the Safavid period the Akhbārīs were predominant in the shrine cities of Iraq.

The Popular Religion

With the advent of a Shi'i state under the Safavids and the gradual conversion of most Iranians to Shi'ism, there were, of course, many major developments in the popular religion in Safavid times. Most of these developments occurred towards the end of the Safavid era. The role of Muḥammad Bāqir Majlisī in promoting Shi'ism at the popular level has been noted above.

The main trends in the evolution of the popular religion in this period was the increased importance of pilgrimages made to the shrines of the Imams (in Iraq and at Mashhad) and the descendants of the Imams (called *Imāmzādas*). There was also an increased popular involvement with Muḥarram ritual commemorating the martyrdom of the Imam Husayn at Karbalā (see pp. 240ff.). As mentioned in the previous chapter, Kamālu'd-Dīn Ḥusayn, known as Wā'iẓ Kāshifī (d. 910/1504), although a Sunni, had written a work called *Rawḍat ash Shuhadā* which portrays the events of Karbalā in an emotive manner in the Persian language. During the Safavid period it became popular to organise meetings at which this book was recited to the accompaniment of much weeping and wailing. These meetings became known as *Rawḍa-khānī (*recital of the *Rawḍat ash-Shuhadā*) and the reciters became known as *Rawḍa-khāns,* which soon became a profession in its own right. The Safavids were, of course, not averse to this development since not only did it strengthen the hold of Shi'ism upon the population but increased enmity of the people towards the Ottoman Turks who as Sunnis were identified with Husayn's enemies at Karbalā.

For the ordinary people, the late Safavid period marked an important watershed during which the influence of the Sufi orders and their spiritual leaders, the *murshids*, declined under attack from the ulama. The latter, and especially Muḥammad Bāqir Majlisī, were able to assume some of the aura left vacant by the Sufi *murshids*, but, to a far greater extent, the devotion of the common people was transferred to the persons of the Imams, who now became the spiritual intermediaries and intercessors of the masses. Pilgrimages to their shrines, and the Karbalā mourning ceremonies, of course, greatly facilitated this process.

Shi'ism in the Arab World

To the west of Iran, Shi'ism was on the defensive. In Iraq, Ḥilla, which had been the most important centre of Shi'ism in the pre-Safavid era, declined markedly and there is not one important scholar of this period named as being from that city, although it remained predominantly Shi'i. Similarly, by the early part of this period Mosul in north Iraq and Aleppo in north Syria had ceased to be important Shi'i centres and lost most of their Twelver Shi'i population. Najaf and Karbalā were, however, growing in importance during this period. The residence in Najaf of Muqaddas Ardibīlī (d. 993/1585), one of the foremost Shi'i ulama of his age, drew to that town numerous students from Iran and the Jabal 'Āmil. Although Najaf had been a centre of Shi'i studies since the time of Shaykhu'ṭ-Ṭā'ifa, the building of religious colleges there, as in Iran, dates from this period. Two brief periods of Safavid rule over Iraq resulted in some repair and construction around the holy shrines.

During this period Lebanon, although nominally part of the Ottoman Empire, was effectively controlled by feudal overlords. In 1517, after he overcame the Mamluks, the Ottoman Selim I placed a Turkoman, Amir 'Assāf, in control of the region of Kisrawān (the coastal strip north of Beirut). With their seat in the village of Ghazīr, the 'Assāf family ruled over this area for most of the sixteenth century until the last of them was killed in AD 1590. They are reported to have been Shi'i and under their rule the area prospered and a number of Shi'is from other parts of Syria moved into this region although it remained predominantly Maronite Christian. In the last part of the sixteenth century the coastal strip north of Kisrawān (also predominantly Maronite) gradually came into the control of the Twelver Shi'i Ḥamāda family who are reported to have been Iranian in origin and who also controlled the area around Hirmal in the Biqā' valley. The Shi'i area around Ba'ālbakk in the Biqā' valley was dominated by the Twelver Shi'i Ḥarfūsh family. The first of this family to be appointed as Amir of the Ba'ālbakk region by the Ottomans was 'Alī ibn Mūsā in 1001/1592. The family remained in power in the region, occasionally extending their power as far as Tripoli and Sidon, until the nineteenth century. The Jabal 'Āmil area, for most of the sixteenth century, was, however, controlled by the Druse Ma'n family.

The last third of the 9th/15th century had seen the transfer of the main centre of Shi'i scholarship from Ḥilla to the Jabal 'Āmil in Lebanon. Although the foremost scholar of the early Safavid period, Muḥaqqiq al-Karakī, left the Jabal 'Āmil and took up residence in Iran, the most important teaching was still being done in the villages of the Jabal 'Āmil area such as Juba', Mays and Karak-Nūḥ and students were sent there from Iran. Shaykh Zaynu'd-Dīn ibn 'Alī al-Juba'ī, known as Shahīd ath-Thānī (the Second Martyr, killed 966/1558), was a pupil of Muḥaqqiq al-Karakī and became the most prominent Shi'i scholar after him. Both he and his son, Abū Manṣūr Ḥasan Ṣāḥibu'l-Ma'ālim (the author of the *Ma'ālim ad-Dīn,* d. 1011/1602) remained in Syria and maintained the tradition of learning there despite the relentless pressure against Shi'ism from the Ottoman authorities. There are varying accounts of how Shahīd ath-Thānī was killed and his head presented to the Ottoman court. But after 'Abbās I transferred his court to Isfahan, many of the ulama of this region migrated to Iran and it declined in importance as a centre of scholarship.

The capture of Bahrain by the forces of Shāh 'Abbās I of Iran in 1602 was an important turning-point for the Twelver Shi'is of this island. It allowed them the freedom to establish their religion and to build up centres of scholarship on the island. Shaykh Muḥammad ibn Ḥasan al-Maqabī (d. 1050/1640) was the first to perform the public Jum'a prayers according to the Shi'i formula after the Safavid conquest.

Shi'ism in India

Contemporary to the Safavid dynasty in Iran, there was a great flowering of Shi'ism in India. Out of the disintegrating Bahmanī kingdom several independent Shi'i states arose.

Yūsuf 'Ādil Shāh, probably a Persian or Turkoman from Sāvih and adopted son of Maḥmūd Gāwān, the Shi'i chief minister of the Bahmanī kingdom was made Governor of Bijapur district. After Maḥmūd Gāwān's execution, Yūsuf proclaimed his independence in 1489. In 908/1503, he followed the Safavid precedent and made Shi'ism the official religion of his state. Yūsuf's son Ismā'īl established links with the Safavid dynasty and for a time his troops wore the red, twelve-pointed cap of the Qizilbāsh. The 'Ādil Shāh dynasty lasted until 1686 when it was overrun by the Moguls under Aurangzeb.

Ḥasan, a converted Brahmin prisoner of the Bahmanī kings, seized the opportunity presented by the collapse of the Bahmanī kingdom to set up a Shi'i kingdom of his own centred on Ahmadnagar in 1490. He took the name Aḥmad Niẓām Shāh. The Niẓām Shāh dynasty ruled until overrun by the Mogul Empire in 1633.

Sulṭān Qulī was an Iranian who established his independence of the Bahmanī kingdom in 1512 with Golconda, near Hyderabad, as the seat of his government. This Shi'i dynasty, the Quṭb Shāhs, continued until overrun by the Moguls under Aurangzeb in 1687.

During this period a number of Iranian Twelver Shi'i ulama migrated to India and helped to establish Shi'ism there. Among the most important of these was Shāh Ṭāhir of Qazvīn (d. 1549) who is reported to have converted Burhān Niẓām Shāh to Shi'ism in about 1522, and Qāḍī Nūru'llāh Mar'ashī Shushtarī (1542–1610) who reached India in 1585 and was executed for his Shi'ism by the Mogul Emperor Jahāngīr.

Further north in Kashmir there arrived at Srinagar in AD 1492 Mīr Shamsu'd Dīn 'Irāqī from Gīlān in Iran. He was a follower of Muḥammad Nūrbakhsh (see p. 102) and propagated a strongly pro-Shi'i doctrine. He succeeded in converting a number of the notables of Kashmir and in particular the Chak family (who had arrived in Kashmir at the beginning of the fourteenth century and had gradually been extending their influence) and Mūsā Rayna, a member of the powerful Rayna family. The king, Sulṭān Muḥammad Shāh, became worried at 'Irāqī's success and the ensuing reaction among the Sunnis and so exiled him to Skardo in Baltistan, where 'Irāqī also had success in converting many to his Shi'i-Nūrbakhshī doctrines.

But the Chak family under Shams Chak and Mūsā Rayna conspired to overthrow Sulṭān Muḥammad Shāh in 1505, and for the next thirty-five years there was a constant see-sawing of power with the Chak family sometimes in power, with a puppet king, and sometimes out of power. Then in 1540 Mīrzā Ḥaydar Dughlat with a Mogul army occupied Kashmir. He suppressed Shi'ism and ruled firmly until defeated and killed in battle in 1551 by Ghāzī Chak. After a series of puppet kings, Ghāzī Chak eventually proclaimed himself king in 1561.

There followed a succession of Shi'i Chak kings until 1586 when the Mogul Emperor Akbar overran Kashmir and terminated the dynasty.

During the period of the Chak dynasty and after the Mogul conquest, there were often major episodes of Sunni-Shi'i conflict in Kashmir. Some of the Chak rulers aggressively promoted Shi'ism and during this time a considerable proportion of the peasantry of the area became Shi'i. The Moguls maintained a neutral religious policy. The Afghans, however, who succeeded the Moguls and ruled from 1751 to 1819 were severe on the whole population but particularly on the Shi'is.

The Mogul dynasty itself, although posing for the most part as champions of Sunni Islam, were not without Shi'i influences. Bābur, the first Mogul Emperor, was assisted by the first Safavid monarch, Ismā'īl I, on the condition that he accepted Shi'ism. His troops wore the red, twelve-pointed cap of the Qizilbāsh for a time. Humāyūn, the second of the Mogul dynasty, was at one time driven from India and sought refuge in Iran, where Shāh Ṭahmāsp gave him assistance in recapturing his throne on the condition of his accepting Shi'ism and of his troops wearing the Qizilbāsh cap which was, in those days, a symbol of being Shi'i.

Shi'ism continued to have a marked influence on the Mogul dynasty over the succeeding generations with several princes being either Shi'i or having Shi'i leanings and also with many Shi'is among the ministers and close companions of the Royal Family. The Bārah Sayyids, a Shi'i family, became so powerful that on the death of Aurangzeb in 1118/1707 they were able to place Bahādur Shāh, a Shi'i, on the Mogul throne and dominated the affairs of state until their overthrow in 1737. During the whole of the Mogul period, the court was divided into two factions, Īrānī, which was in effect the Shi'i faction, and Tūrānī, which was the Sunni faction.

Geographical Spread

A noticeable change occurred among the ulama in the late Safavid period. After five centuries when the most prominent of the ulama had been Arabs, there arose the first of a stream of prominent Iranian ulama that has continued to the present day. This change can most clearly be seen by comparing the places of origin of the most prominent ulama who died during the 11th/17th century and the 12/18th century as contained in the biographical work of Mīrzā Muḥammad 'Alī Kashmīrī, *Nujūm as-Samā* (see Table 5).

From this table it can also be seen that apart from those places already mentioned, the region extending from Ḥuwayza and Shushtar in south-west Iran to the Shaṭṭ al-'Arab (Jazā'ir) in south Iraq had by this time become one of the most important centres of Shi'i scholarship.

Table 5: Geographical origins of Twelver Shi'i ulama dying in the eleventh (AD 1591–1687) and twelfth (AD 1688–1784) Islamic centuries

11th/17th Century		*12th/18th Century*	
Jabal 'Āmil	100	Isfahan	22
Bahrain	33	Jazā'ir (S. Iraq)	16
Astarābād	15	Bahrain	15
Jazā'ir (S. Iraq)	11	Māzandarān	13
Khurāsān	10	Gīlān	12
Shīrāz	8	Shīrāz	12
Najaf	8	Qazvīn	9
Ḥuwayza (S.E. Iran)	8	Khurāsān	8
Qazvīn	6	Jabal 'Āmil	6
Māzandarān and Gīlān	6	Khātūnābād (near Yazd)	5
Shushtar (S.E. Iran)	6	India	5
Isfahan	5	Hamadān	4
Kāẓimayn	4	Khwānsār	4
Yazd	3	Burūjird	2
Damascus	3	Qā'in	2
Qumm	2	Kāshān	2
Tafrish (near Qumm)	2	Najaf	1
Hamadān	2	Ḥuwayza	1
Ḥilla	1		
Karbalā	1		
Tabrīz	1		
Kāshān	1		

In surveying the Safavid period of Shi'i history, the following appear to be the major developments:

1. The ending of the relative mutual tolerance between Sunnis and Shi'is that existed from the time of the Mongol conquests onwards and the resurgence of hatred and hostility between the two sects.
2. The change from a broad inclusive church to a narrow outlook concentrating on law and the external observances of the religion, rejecting Sufism and philosophy and minimising the esoteric aspects of the religion.
3. The beginning of a separation between church and state and the emergence of an independent body of ulama capable of taking a political stand different from the policies of the state.
4. The change from Twelver Shi'ism being a predominantly Arab phenomenon with its principal centres of learning in the Arab world to a preponderance of Iranians and the centre of learning moved to Iran.

The Eighteenth Century

Political Developments

For a time after the Afghan capture of Isfahan it seemed as though the country of Iran as a separate entity might cease to exist. Seizing their opportunity, the Russians attacked from the north, the Ottoman Turks from the west, while the Afghans consolidated their position in the south and east. The country was being dismembered.

Ṭahmāsp, the third son of Sulṭān-Ḥusayn Shāh, had broken out of Isfahan during its siege by the Afghans and proclaimed himself Shāh in Qazvīn after the fall of Isfahan. He managed to maintain a nebulous degree of authority in the central and Caspian regions with the assistance of Fatḥ 'Alī Khān, the Qājār chief.

Ṭahmāsp II, who was an ineffectual leader, was saved from being completely overwhelmed by a number of fortunate circumstances. Alarmed at the increasing derangement of the mind of Maḥmūd Khan, the Afghan leader, the Afghans rose and killed him in 1725. This action led to a split between the Afghans in Isfahan and those in Qandahar. As a result of this, Ashraf, the Afghan leader in Isfahan, was left with too few men to pursue an aggressive policy towards Ṭahmāsp. The enmity between Russia and Turkey kept these two powers preoccupied in other places. The death of Peter the Great muted Russia's desire to expand while the Turks did advance into Iran but were defeated by Ashraf in 1726.

It was at this juncture in 1726 that Nādir Khān of the Afshār tribe joined the army of Ṭahmāsp II. Having risen from humble origins to command a small tribal force, Nādir attracted the attention of Ṭahmāsp by his military abilities. Nādir succeeded in ousting Fatḥ 'Alī Khān, the Qājār leader, from his eminent position in the court and indeed in having him executed.

Nādir Khān was made commander-in-chief of the army and proceeded immediately to capture Mashhad and reassert Ṭahmāsp's authority over the rest of Khurāsān. Then in 1729 he took Herat in the east before proceeding against Ashraf in Isfahan. He inflicted several defeats on the Afghans and drove them out of Isfahan and Shīrāz. The following year he drove the Turks out of western Iran and subdued an Afghan uprising in Herat.

In 1731 Ṭahmāsp sought to stem Nādir's rising fortunes by himself taking the field against the Turks. He was soundly defeated. Nādir took advantage of this to depose Ṭahmāsp in 1732 and placed Ṭahmāsp's infant son on the throne as 'Abbās III. Nādir himself, of course, took the position of regent.

Between 1733 and 1735 Nādir succeeded in driving the Turks out of the territory they had occupied in north-west Iran and the Caucasus while the Russians withdrew by agreement from the Iranian provinces they had occupied under Peter the Great.

Then in 1736 Nādir assembled a great conference of the notables of Iran on the plain of Mughān in north-west Iran for the purpose of choosing a monarch. None, of course, dared to oppose him and Nadir was duly crowned as Shāh of Iran. However, one of the conditions that he laid down for accepting the crown was that Iran should abandon Shi'ism and return to the Sunni fold.

It is clear that Nādir was originally a Shi'i. His tribe, the Afshārs, were one of the six Turkoman tribes that had originally enabled the Safavids to come to power and thus establish Shi'ism in Iran. The names of the members of Nādir's family also clearly indicate a Shi'i background. Moreover, so closely was the Safavid dynasty associated with Shi'ism that it is unlikely that Nādir could have risen to the prominent position he held if he had not outwardly, at least, been Shi'i. Nādir is recorded as having worshipped in the Shi'i shrines at Mashhad after he had captured that city and at Karbalā and Najaf after his campaigns against the Turks. Furthermore, one of Nādir's letters written after Ṭahmāsp's defeat by the Turks in 1731 has been preserved in which he writes of his own victories as being to the glory of Shi'ism.[16]

Therefore the question must be asked: why did Nādir, at his coronation, choose to espouse Sunnism and then try to force it upon Iran? The theory that he was trying to appease Turkey by this move is scarcely credible as he had just inflicted several heavy defeats on Turkey and had nothing to fear from that quarter. Much more likely are the following three reasons: firstly, that Shi'ism was firmly linked in people's minds to the Safavid dynasty and Nādir felt that his own position and that of his dynasty would remain under threat as long as Shi'ism remained the religion of the country; secondly, the majority of Nādir's army were Sunni Afghans and this move could have been calculated to ensure loyalty of his troops; thirdly, there is some evidence that Nādir already saw himself as a great Asiatic conqueror and his conversion to Sunnism would, of course, facilitate his rule over the Sunni majority of Muslims as well as the eventual takeover of the Caliphate from the Ottoman Sulṭāns.

From the plain of Mughān, Nādir sent a peace offer to the Turks which included the proposal that Iranians, having given up Shi'ism, should be accepted as a fifth school of Sunni law under the name of Ja'farī. In addition, there was to be a fifth column in the Ka'ba in Mecca for this school of law and an Iranian leader of the Ḥajj in addition to the Egyptian and Syrian ones.

Nādir Shāh made an attempt to impose Sunnism on the people of Iran but Shi'ism was so deeply rooted by this time that he had but limited success, particularly as he himself spent most of his time absent from Iran on military campaigns. He did, however, confiscate much of the *waqf* (pious endowments) properties controlled by the Shi'i ulama, and prohibited the referral of cases to the *shar'* (religious) courts, limiting all legal decision to the *'urf* courts (courts using customary law).

Nādir's Indian campaign in 1730–40 resulted in the capture of Delhi and the obtaining of a large amount of treasure as booty. Following this, Bokhara and Khiva were captured and Iran's eastern boundary now reached to the Oxus and Indus rivers.

Nādir Shāh was now at the height of his achievements. Thereafter his reign degenerated into savage executions and fruitless military campaigns. A campaign in Daghistan in the Caucasus in 1741–2 produced no result. Then after suppressing several revolts, Nādir pursued a further campaign against Turkey in an effort to force upon the Sulṭān his plan for recognising the Ja'farī School within the fold of Sunni Islam. Although the Turks were defeated, Nādir's object was not gained. Massacres and executions followed wherever Nādir went. He even blinded his own son, Riḍā Qulī. At last, in 1747, Nādir was assassinated by two of his own courtiers whom he had threatened to put to death on the following day.

After the death of Nādir Shāh the whole kingdom degenerated into anarchy. There was factional fighting among Nādir's relatives. After 'Alī Qulī, Nādir's nephew, and Ibrāhīm, 'Alī Qulī's brother, had held power briefly, Shāh-Rukh (who was a grandson of both Nādir Shāh and Sulṭān-Ḥusayn Shāh, the last Safavid) attempted to unite the opposing factions under his rule. But he was defeated and blinded by Mīrzā Sayyid Muḥammad (the son of a mujtahid of Mashhad and related through his mother to the Safavids) who claimed that Shāh-Rukh wished to revert to his grandfather's policy of suppressing Shi'ism and promoting Sunnism. After this, there was anarchy until the factional fighting resolved itself into a contest between Muḥammad Ḥusayn Khān, the head of the Qājār tribe in the north, and Karīm Khān of the Zand tribe in the south.

At first Karīm Khān was victorious and ruled from his capital at Shīrāz for twenty-nine years from 1750 to 1779. Karīm Khān was a devout Shi'i and his reign marks the termination of Nādir Shāh's abortive attempt to reimpose Sunnism on Iran. Under Karīm Khān's wise rule, all the areas under his command prospered. But after his death, his family fought among themselves and allowed the Qājārs to gain the upper hand. In 1794 Āghā Muḥammad, the Qājār leader, killed the last of the Zand dynasty, the valiant Luṭf 'Alī Khān, and in 1796 took the throne as the first of the Qājār dynasty.

The Ulama

The ulama of this period were overshadowed by the towering figure of the recently-deceased Muḥammad Bāqir Majlisī. Perhaps because of his overwhelming influence or because of the unsettled condition of the time, there was an interlude of some sixty years when there were no Shiʻi scholars of the first rank.

Initially those scholars of any eminence that there were (mostly the pupils of Majlisī) continued to live in Isfahan. In particular, there were Bahā'u'd-Dīn Muḥammad Iṣfahānī, known as Fāḍil-i Hindī, who died in 1137/1725 shortly after the fall of Isfahan, and Mullā Ismāʻīl ibn Muḥammad Ḥusayn Khajū'ī (d. 1173/1760). However, the quarter-century between the fall of the Safavids and the establishment of Karīm Khān Zand was a troublesome and turbulent period. The occupation of Isfahan by Sunni Afghans and the attempt by Nādir Shāh to impose Sunnism on Iran, although not causing any large-scale conversions to Sunnism, did bring a great deal of pressure to bear on the ulama, some of whom were executed by Nādir Shāh. This hostile atmosphere caused the ulama to flee Iran in increasing numbers and the centre of Shiʻi scholarship moved from Isfahan to the shrine cities of Iraq: Kāẓimayn, Najaf and, particularly, Karbalā which now became the focal point of Shiʻi scholarship. Among the first to move to Karbalā was Shaykh Yūsuf ibn Aḥmad al-Baḥrānī (d. 1186/1772) but it was undoubtedly the presence there of Āqā Muḥammad Bāqir ibn Muḥammad Akmal, known as Vaḥīd Bihbahānī (d. *circa* 1207/1792), the first major scholar to emerge after Majlisī, that established Karbalā as the foremost centre of Shiʻi scholarship of that time.

The period from the middle of the Safavids to the time of Vaḥīd Bihbahānī was the period of the dominance of the Akhbārī School in Twelver Shiʻi Islam. The doctrines of this school are described elsewhere in this book (see pp. 222ff.). Although this controversy had begun as a comparatively minor disagreement on a few points, it grew eventually into a bitter and vituperative dispute culminating in Bihbahānī's declaration that the Akhbārīs were infidels (*Kuffār*).

At first, the Akhbārīs predominated at the shrine cities of Iraq but it was Bihbahānī who, at the end of the 18th century, reversed this and, indeed, completely routed the Akhbārīs at Karbalā and Najaf. South Iraq, Bahrain and a few cities in Iran such as Kirmān remained Akhbārī strongholds for a few more decades but eventually the Uṣūlī triumph was complete and only a handful of Shiʻi ulama have remained Akhbārī to the present day.

The results of Bihbahānī's victory for Twelver Shiʻism were to be far-reaching. By his *takfīr* (declaration of infidelity) against the Akhbārīs,

Bihbahānī continued the work of Majlisī in narrowing the field of orthodoxy in Twelver Shi'ism. But where Majlisī had acted to exclude Sufism and philosophy which were at the periphery of the concerns of most of the ulama, Bihbahānī brought the threat of *takfīr* into the central field of theology and jurisprudence, where previously only *ikhtilāf* (agreement to hold differing opinions) had existed. Bihbahānī was now to exclude by *takfīr* all who disagreed with the principles of reasoning (*'aql*) and *ijtihād* as sources of law. This paved the way for a great increase in the power and influence of the mujtahids in Qājār times and for the evolution of the concept of the *marja' at-taqlīd* (see p. 204). Bihbahānī's importance was acknowledged by later generations of Shi'i ulama who referred to him as *Mu'assis* (founder of the Uṣūlī School), *Ustād-i Kull* (Universal Teacher), *Murawwij* (Propagator) and the *Mujaddid* (Renewer) of the 13th Islamic century. His achievement was to set the tone and direction of Shi'i development up to the present time.

Another development which characterised Bihbahānī's period of primacy among the ulama was his insistence on the right of enforcing his own judgements. Previously, the ulama had been dependent on the secular authorities for carrying out their judgements. Bihbahānī, however, surrounded himself with a corps of *mīrghaḍabs*, servants who would carry out either corporal or capital punishment, and had his judgements carried out immediately and usually in his presence.

During the eighteenth century there was a return to Iran of some of the Sufi groups who had been driven to India by Majlisī in the previous century. They again began to pose a threat to the ulama's dominance in the religious sphere. At Kirmān it is reported that thousands flocked to the meetings of Nūr 'Alī Shāh and Mushtāq 'Alī Shāh, two Sufi Shaykhs of the Ni'matu'llāhī order. The people appeared to prefer the ecstatic esotericism of the Sufis to the intellectual hair-splitting of the ulama. Against this threat, the ulama, with Bihbahānī at their head, acted vigorously, writing anti-Sufi tracts rejecting the claim that Sufism is compatible with Shi'ism. In 1792 Mullā 'Abdu'llāh, a mujtahid of Kirmān, had Mushtāq 'Alī Shāh put to death and forced Nūr 'Alī Shāh to flee, thus breaking up the Kirmān Sufi group.

Shi'ism in other lands

During much of the eighteenth century the Shi'i overlords of Ba'ālbakk, the Ḥarfūsh family, were overshadowed by the Druse. The Shī'ī Ḥamāda family were driven out of the western side of Mount Lebanon by the Maronites in 1773 and retreated to Hirmal in the Biqā' Valley where they have remained an influential family to the present day. Further south in the Jabal 'Āmil, the 'Alī aṣ-Ṣaghīr family, who had been local chiefs of the Bishāra (the area south of the Liṭānī River) since about the 14th century, rose in the 18th century to become overlords of the whole area and had control of Tyre for a time. But their chief, Nāṣīf an-Naṣṣār was defeated and killed by Aḥmad al-Jazzār, Pāshā of 'Akkā, in 1781.

Bahrain and al-Aḥsā during this period were overshadowed by the growing power of the puritanical Sunni Wahhābīs in central Arabia. The first Wahhābī attack on al-Aḥsā was in 1788. A further attack in 1789 overthrew the ruling Shi'i Banū Khālid tribe and in 1792 al-Aḥsā submitted, leading to a ruthless suppression of Shi'ism and the destruction of Shi'i shrines. A revolt of the people of Hufūf in 1793 was crushed and the province laid waste.

Iran had conquered Bahrain during the Safavid period, but in 1717 it was attacked by the Imam of Masqat and, in 1736, the local ruler, Shaykh Jabbāra, refused to acknowledge Nādir Shāh's sovereignty over the island. Nādir Shāh sent an expedition which re-established his control, but in 1782 it was conquered by the Sunni al-Khalīfa tribe from Qaṭar. This tribe has remained in power to this day although they were defeated on several occasions by the Imam of Masqat and the Wahhābīs.

With the deteriorating conditions, many of the Shi'i ulama of Bahrain and al-Aḥsā fled to Iraq and Iran and consolidated the importance of Karbalā and Najaf as the centres of Shi'i scholarship in this period.

In India the suppression of the Shi'i kingdoms in the south by the Mogul Empire towards the end of the 17th century was followed by the setting up of the Shi'i kingdom of Oudh (Awadh) with its capital in Lucknow, early in the 18th century.

Mīr Muḥammad Amīn Mūsawī (d. 1145/1732) was descended from the Seventh Imam Mūsā and was given the governorship of Oudh in 1722 by the Mogul Emperor, Muḥammad Shāh. He became known as Sa'ādat Khān and was an intermediary between Nādir Shāh and Muḥammad Shāh when the former invaded India in 1738. Sa'ādat Khān's three successors, Ṣafdār Jang (d. 1152/1739), Shujā'u'd-Dawla (d. 1166/1753) and Āṣafu'd-Dawla (d. 1212/1797), each held the post of minister (*Wazīr*) to the Mogul Emperor as well as being initially *Subahdārs* and then Nawwabs of Oudh. During this period the Mogul court was split into a Shi'i 'Īrānī' faction headed by the Nawwabs of Oudh and a Sunni 'Tūrānī' faction. Ṣafdār Jang built a new capital at Fyzabad but Āṣafu'd-Dawla returned the capital to Lucknow. Both at Fyzabad and Lucknow a large number of magnificent buildings were erected during this period, many of them for religious purposes. These include several *Imāmbāras* (buildings where mourning assemblies for the Imam Husayn were held).

In summary, then, the period between the fall of the Safavids and the rise of the Qājārs saw some important developments:

a. The fall of the Safavids brought about a cutting of the ties between the ulama and the state (especially during the reign of Nādir Shāh). This allowed the ulama (in a period of great uncertainty and confusion) to increase their power and independence; features that would come into the fore in the Qājār era.

b. It was probably also the period of uncertainty and weak government during this time that increased the attractiveness of the Uṣūlī School with its stronger claims of leadership and authority for the ulama and thus brought about the Uṣūlī victory over the Akhbārīs.

c. The main centre of Shi'i scholarship moved from Iran to the shrine cities of Iraq, where it was effectively removed from the control of the Iranian government – another development that was to have important consequences in the Qājār era.

The Nineteenth Century

Political Developments under Fatḥ 'Alī Shāh and Muḥammad Shāh

The Qājārs were one of the Turkoman tribes who supported Ismā'īl, the first Safavid monarch, in his conquest of Iran. They were rewarded by being given extensive fiefdoms and, on this basis, became one of the most important elements in Iran until, in 1794, Āghā Muḥammad defeated the last of the Zand dynasty and two years later was crowned as Shāh. His reign was only to last for one further year before he was assassinated by two of his servants whom he had condemned to death on the following day. He had by that time, however, consolidated his rule over all Iran and had recaptured Georgia. The reign of his nephew and successor, Fatḥ 'Alī Shāh (d. 1834), was marked by two disastrous campaigns against Russia in 1804–13 and 1826–8 in which Iran lost all its Caucasian provinces. Apart from Russia, Iran also came into close contact during this period with other European powers such as England and France.

Fatḥ 'Alī Shah deferred greatly to the Shi'i ulama. This was probably partly due to genuine piety and partly due to the Qājār dynasty's need to establish its own legitimacy (see p. 194). Fatḥ 'Alī Shāh, apart from numerous pilgrimages to Qumm and Mashhad, spent much money on the repair and embellishment of these shrines as well as those in Iraq. As well as making large disbursements to the ulama, he built a number of mosques and religious colleges (*madrasas*) and, in particular, he rebuilt the Madrasa Fayḍiyya, the foremost college at Qumm. The Qājārs had made Tehran their capital and Fatḥ 'Alī Shāh tried to induce some of the prominent ulama to come and take up residence there in order to give the new capital prestige. However, Tehran never became an important religious centre in the way that Isfahan had been in Safavid times. This fact is probably a reflection of the changed relationship between the government and the ulama (see below).

Fatḥ 'Alī Shāh, the progenitor of a record number of offspring, was succeeded by his grandson, Muḥammad Shāh (reigned 1834–1848). After suppressing a number of contenders for the throne, Muḥammad Shāh had an unremarkable reign during which he was dominated by his Prime Minister, Ḥājjī Mīrzā Āqāsī. Muḥammad Shāh was much attracted to Sufism and Ḥājjī Mīrzā Āqāsī was his Sufi guide. There was a sharp reversal of policy during this reign in that Muḥammad Shāh favoured Sufis and expended money on their shrines, neglecting the ulama.

The Ulama during the Reigns of Fatḥ 'Alī Shāh and Muḥammad Shāh

The ulama of the early Qājār period were dominated by the pupils of Vaḥīd Bihbahānī. The most prominent of these was Sayyid Muḥammad Mahdī Ṭabāṭabā'ī Burūjirdī, known as Baḥru'l-'Ulūm (d. 1212/1797). This man was held in extraordinary awe and deference by his contemporaries and many miracles are related of him. Indeed, one may even surmise that some of his contemporaries regarded him to be the Hidden Imam himself in the state of occultation. Thus, for example, in one of the biographical works, it is written that one of his contemporaries stated that had he claimed infallibility (*'isma*, an attribute particular to the Prophets and Imams only), none would have been able to refute it.[17] Baḥru'l-'Ulūm had been born in Karbalā and had studied under Vaḥīd Bihbahānī and the other prominent ulama there but had transferred his residence to Najaf. Thus when Bihbahānī died and leadership among the ulama fell to Baḥru'l-'Ulūm, the centre of Shi'i scholarship shifted from Karbalā to Najaf, where it was to remain until the twentieth century.

The consolidation of Najaf as the centre of Shi'i scholarship was achieved by Baḥru'l-'Ulūm's successor, Shaykh Ja'far ibn Khiḍr an-Najafī (d. 1227/1812), known as Kāshifu'l-Ghiṭā on account of his authorship of the *Kashf al-Ghiṭā*, a popular legal work.

After the death of Kāshifu'l-Ghiṭā there was no clear successor to pre-eminence among the ulama. Among the contenders were: Mīrzā Abu'l-Qāsim ibn Muḥammad Ḥasan, known as Mīrzā-yi Qummī or Fāḍil-i Qummī (d. 1231/1816) at Qumm; Mullā Aḥmad ibn Mahdī Narāqī (d. 1245/1829) at Kāshān; Shaykh Mūsā, son of Kāshifu'l-Ghiṭā, (d. 1243/1827) and Shaykh Muḥammad Ḥasan ibn Bāqir an-Najafī (d. 1266/1850)

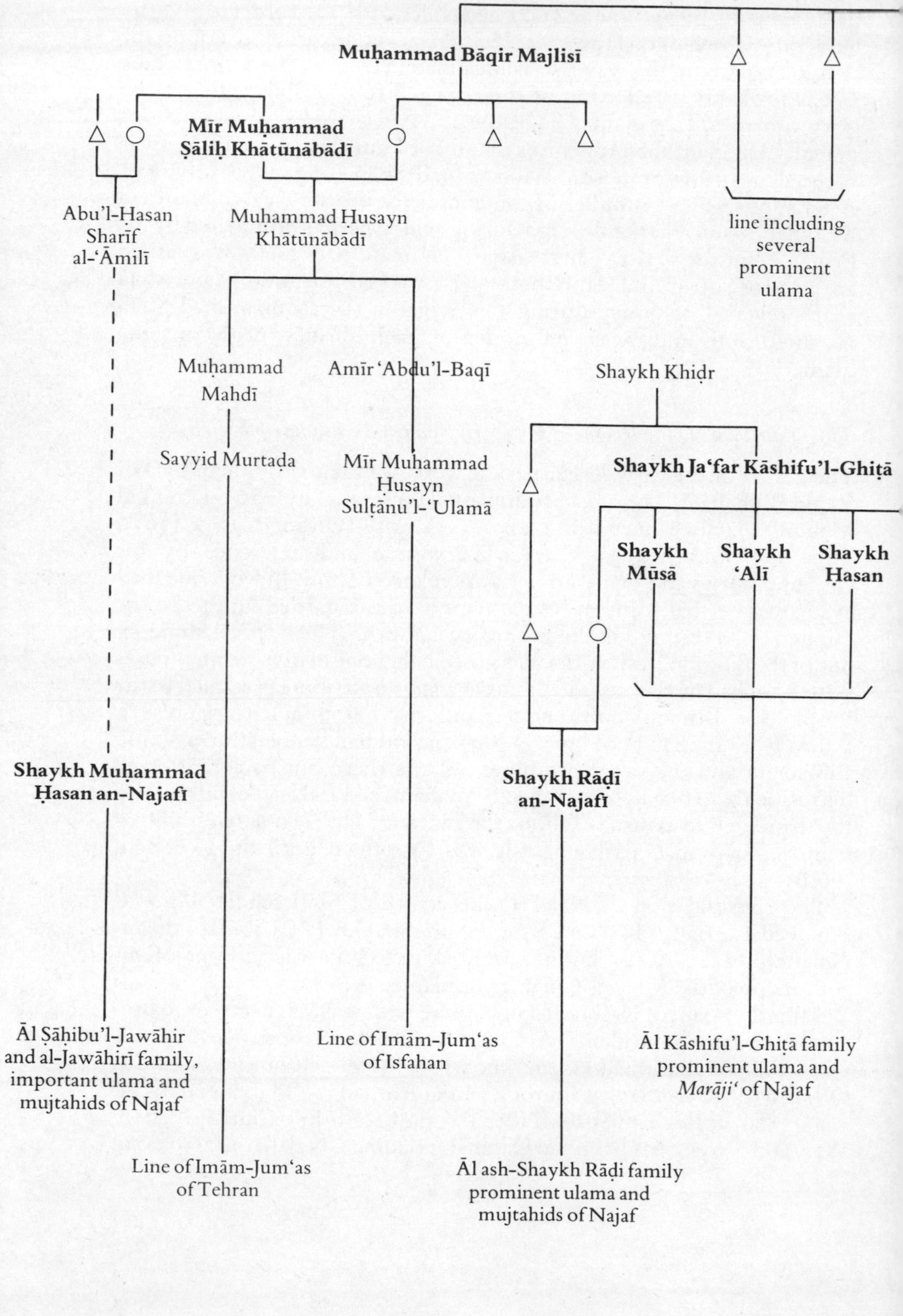
Muḥammad Bāqir Majlisī
Mīr Muḥammad Ṣāliḥ Khātūnābādī
Abu'l-Ḥasan Sharīf al-ʿĀmilī
Muḥammad Ḥusayn Khātūnābādī
line including several prominent ulama
Muḥammad Mahdī
Amīr ʿAbdu'l-Baqī
Shaykh Khiḍr
Sayyid Murtaḍa
Mīr Muḥammad Ḥusayn Sulṭānu'l-ʿUlamā
Shaykh Jaʿfar Kāshifu'l-Ghiṭā
Shaykh Mūsā
Shaykh ʿAlī
Shaykh Ḥasan
Shaykh Muḥammad Ḥasan an-Najafī
Shaykh Rāḍī an-Najafī
Āl Ṣāḥibu'l-Jawāhir and al-Jawāhirī family, important ulama and mujtahids of Najaf
Line of Imām-Jumʿas of Isfahan
Āl Kāshifu'l-Ghiṭā family prominent ulama and *Marājiʿ* of Najaf
Line of Imām-Jumʿas of Tehran
Āl ash-Shaykh Rāḍi family prominent ulama and mujtahids of Najaf

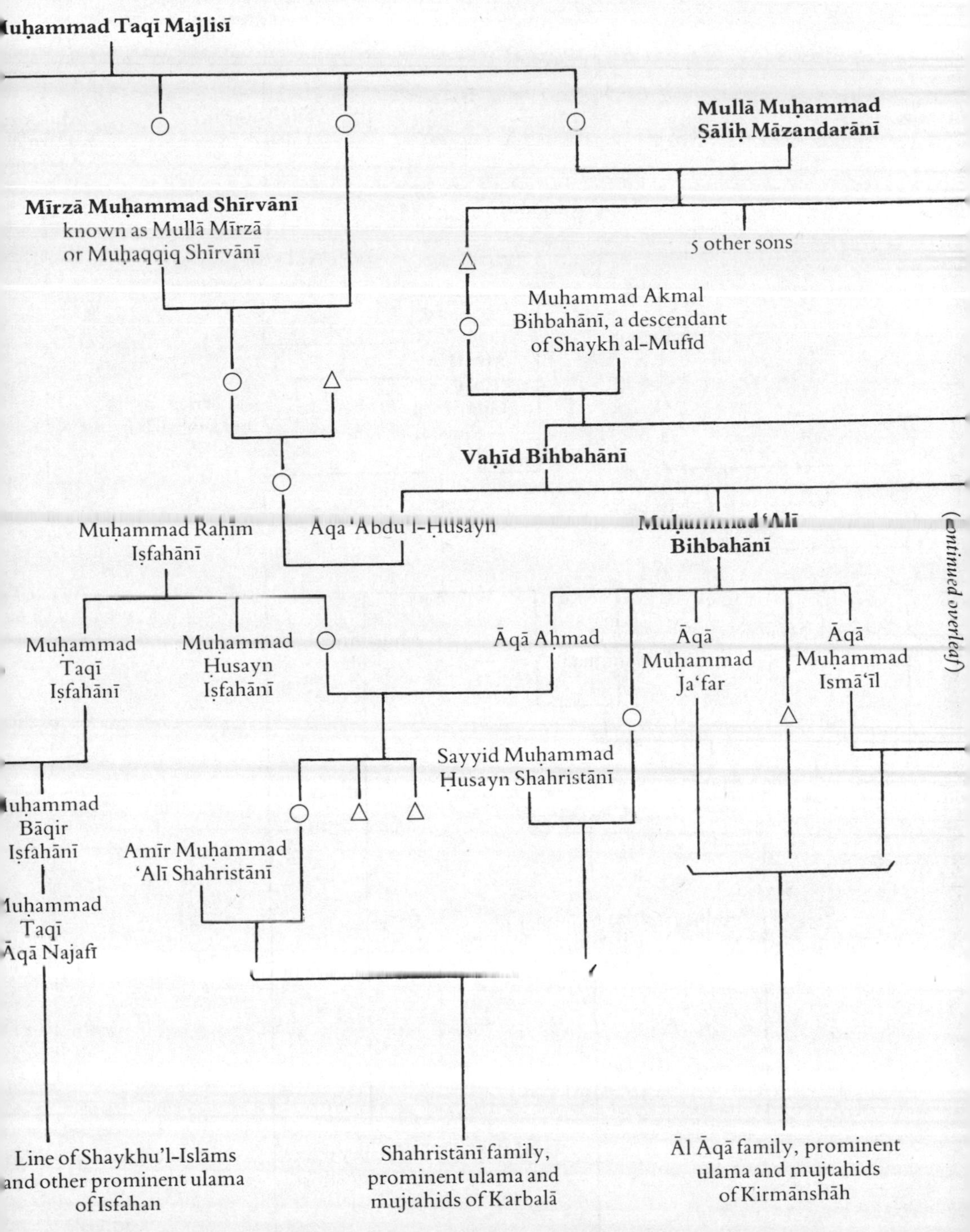

Chart 2, showing inter-marriage and relationships of the leading ulama from the late 17th to the early 19th centuries (All ulama named were of some importance, but ulama shown in bold were of the first rank. Descent to prominent families of the present day is shown along the bottom.)

key: △ = male, ○ = female

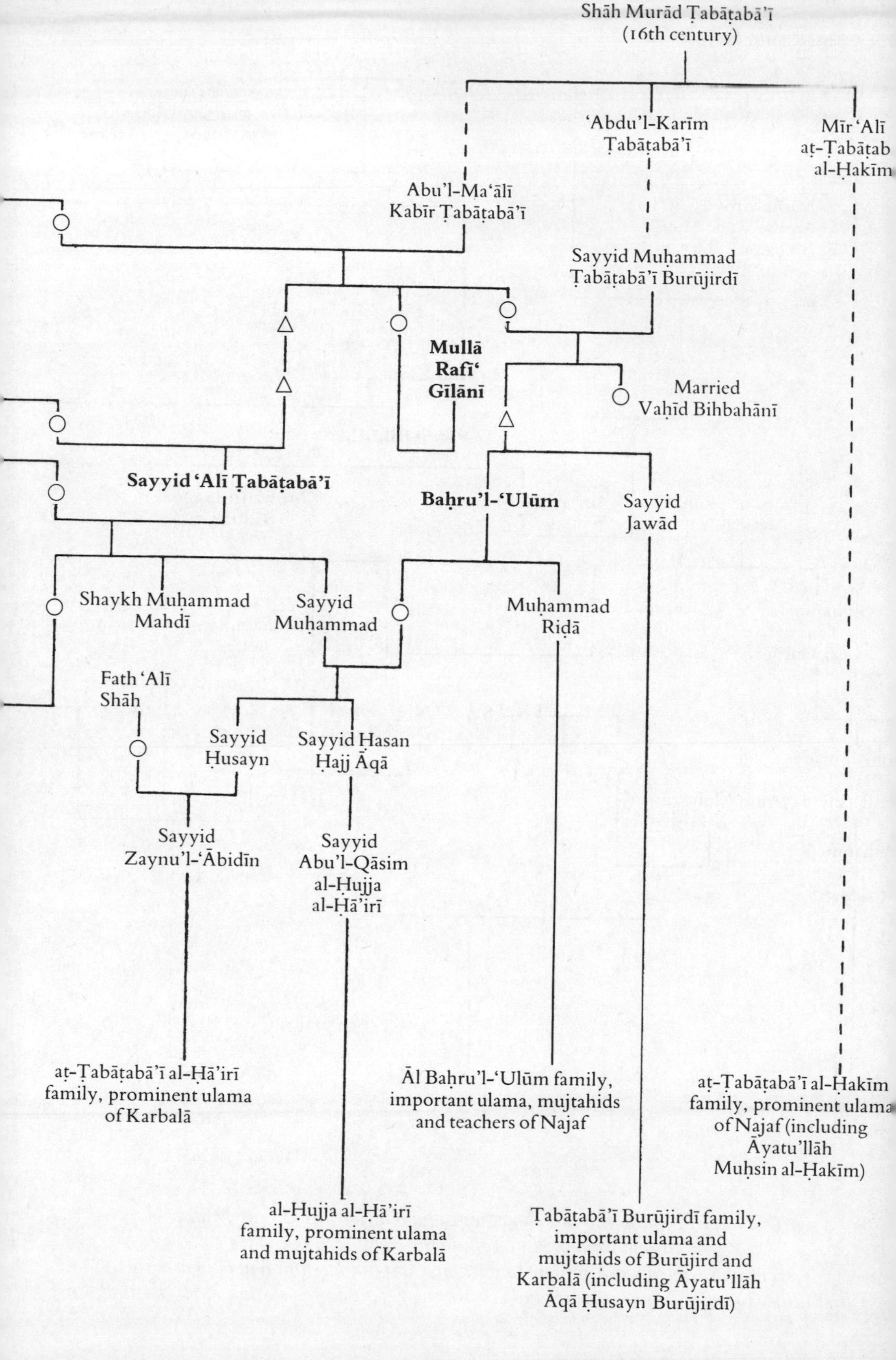
Shāh Murād Ṭabāṭabā'ī
(16th century)
'Abdu'l-Karīm
Ṭabāṭabā'ī
Mīr 'Alī
aṭ-Ṭabāṭab
al-Ḥakīm
Abu'l-Ma'ālī
Kabīr Ṭabāṭabā'ī
Sayyid Muḥammad
Ṭabāṭabā'ī Burūjirdī
Mullā
Rafī'
Gīlānī
Married
Vaḥīd Bihbahānī
Sayyid 'Alī Ṭabāṭabā'ī
Baḥru'l-'Ulūm
Sayyid
Jawād
Shaykh Muḥammad
Mahdī
Sayyid
Muḥammad
Muḥammad
Riḍā
Fath 'Alī
Shāh
Sayyid
Ḥusayn
Sayyid Ḥasan
Ḥajj Āqā
Sayyid
Zaynu'l-'Ābidīn
Sayyid
Abu'l-Qāsim
al-Ḥujja
al-Ḥā'irī
aṭ-Ṭabāṭabā'ī al-Ḥā'irī
family, prominent ulama
of Karbalā
Āl Baḥru'l-'Ulūm family,
important ulama, mujtahids
and teachers of Najaf
aṭ-Ṭabāṭabā'ī al-Ḥakīm
family, prominent ulama
of Najaf (including
Āyatu'llāh
Muḥsin al-Ḥakīm)
al-Ḥujja al-Ḥā'irī
family, prominent ulama
and mujtahids of Karbalā
Ṭabāṭabā'ī Burūjirdī family,
important ulama and
mujtahids of Burūjird and
Karbalā (including Āyatu'llāh
Āqā Ḥusayn Burūjirdī)

at Najaf; Sayyid 'Alī ibn Muḥammad 'Alī Ṭabāṭabā'ī (d. 1231/1815) and Sayyid Ibrāhīm ibn Muḥammad Bāqir Qazvīnī (d. 1262/1846) in Karbalā; while Isfahan made, during this period, a strong bid to regain its pre-eminence as the centre of Shi'i scholarship with the presence there of Mullā 'Alī ibn Jamshīd Nūrī (d. 1246/1830–1), Ḥājjī Muḥammad Ibrāhīm ibn Muḥammad Ḥasan Kalbāsī (or Karbāsī, d. 1261/1845) and Ḥājjī Sayyid Muḥammad Bāqir ibn Muḥammad Taqī Shaftī Rashtī, known as Ḥujjatu'l-Islām (d. 1260/1844) who was *Shaykh al-Islām* of Isfahan. The last two, in particular, had extensive influence over a wide area of Iran, Iraq and India and in their prestige appears to be the beginnings of the emergence of *marāji' at-taqlīd* with influence over a wide area. However, this brief resurgence of Isfahan as the centre of Shi'i scholarship was not to last and, following the death of Kalbāsī, Najaf regained its primacy although Isfahan remained the most important Iranian centre until the rise of Qumm in the twentieth century. At Najaf, Shaykh Muḥammad Ḥasan ibn Bāqir Najafī, the author of an important work in Shi'i law, the *Jawahir al-Kalam*, carried forward the process of consolidating the authority of *marja' at-taqlīd* within one individual. Indeed, with the death of both Kalbāsī and Shaykh Ḥasan, the son of Kāshifu'l-Ghiṭā, in 1846, he may have succeeded in doing this for the last four years of his life. In some sources he is called *Ra'īsu'l-'ulamā* (leader of the ulama) and even *Nā'ib-i Imām* (deputy of the Imam). One feature of the ulama of the 18th century down to the present day is the degree to which they are inter-related (see chart).

The major concerns of the ulama during this period were the conclusion of the Uṣūlī-Akhbārī conflict, the appearance of the Shaykhī and Bābī movements, a renewed conflict with the Sufis and the emergence of the ulama into the political arena.

Although the Akhbārīs had been decisively defeated in the time of Vaḥīd Bihbahānī, they were not as yet finished, and, during the reign of Fatḥ 'Alī Shāh, the 'episode of the inspector's head' brought them a temporary surge of fame and prestige. Mīrzā Muḥammad Nishāpurī Akhbārī promised Fatḥ 'Alī Shāh the death by supernatural means of Tsitianov, the Russian General then besieging Baku, in return for the Akhbārī doctrine being made the official creed of Iran. After forty days, Tsitianov's head was presented to Fatḥ 'Alī Shāh. But the Shāh realised that it was beyond his ability to reverse the Uṣūlī triumph and did not keep his end of the bargain. Fearing that Mīrzā Muḥammad's extraordinary powers would be turned against him, Fatḥ 'Alī Shāh exiled him to Iraq where he was set upon by Uṣūlīs in Kāẓimayn in 1816, killed, and so bitter had become the animosity between the two parties that his body was fed to the dogs. After this Akhbārī doctrine never again achieved any prominence.

Much more important during the Qājār era was the emergence of the Shaykhī movement. Shaykh Aḥmad ibn Zaynu'd-Dīn al-Aḥsā'ī (1753–1826), the founder of the Shaykhī movement, was a prominent Shi'i scholar of al-Aḥsā, who had studied under Baḥru'l-'Ulūm, Kāshifu'l-Ghiṭā and the other prominent ulama of Iraq. In the second decade of the 19th century, Shaykh Aḥmad looked set to become the leading Shi'i scholar of his generation, and as he travelled around Iran he was accorded the highest honours by princes, ulama and even the Shāh.

Shaykh Aḥmad, however, had a number of views which were considered heterodox by some of the ulama. A fuller description of Shaykhī doctrine is given elsewhere in this book (see pp. 225ff.), but for the purposes of this chapter it will suffice to describe Shaykh Aḥmad's views as being in the tradition of the *Hikmat-i Ilāhi* of the School of Isfahan (see pp. 217–19). Had Shaykh Aḥmad lived two centuries earlier, his ideas would have been included in the corpus of that school and no movement separate from the main body of Twelver Shi'ism would have resulted. However, in the intervening period, figures such as Majlisī and Bihbahānī had considerably narrowed the field of Shi'i orthodoxy. And so, when Shaykh Aḥmad came into conflict with some of the ulama, they responded as Bihbahānī had done with the Akhbārīs, by pronouncing *takfīr* (declaration of being an unbeliever) against him. This *takfīr* was first pronounced in 1822 by Mullā Muḥammad Taqī Baraghānī of Qazvīn (he was later killed by a Shaykhī in 1847). After this other ulama confirmed the pronouncement but it is interesting to note that none of the contemporary ulama of the first rank such as Mullā Aḥmad Narāqī, Shaykh Mūsā the son of Kāshifu'l-Ghiṭā, Mullā 'Alī Nūrī, Ḥājjī Muḥammad Ibrāhīm Kalbāsī and Ḥājjī Sayyid Muḥammad Bāqir Shaftī supported the *takfīr*.[18] Indeed, it was not until after Shaykh Aḥmad's death in 1826, under his successor, Sayyid Kāẓim ibn Qāsim Rashtī (d. 1259/1843), that any real separation can be said to have occurred between the Shaykhīs and the main body of Twelver Shi'is. Certainly it was not the wish of Shaykh Aḥmad or Sayyid Kāẓim to create a separate movement, but Twelver Shi'ism was no longer a sufficiently broad church to retain them. Indeed, the ulama used the Shaykhī controversy to further refine and narrow the orthodox position.

The reign of Muḥammad Shāh saw the start of the Bābī movement. In 1844 Sayyid 'Alī Muḥammad of Shīrāz, who took the title of Bāb (Gate, 1819–1850), began to put forward his claims (see p. 231). At first he commanded his followers to observe the Muslim *Sharī'a* and there was little conflict with orthodox Islam. But in 1848, shortly before Muḥammad Shāh's death, the Bāb declared that the Qur'an and Muslim *Sharī'a* were abrogated and a new religious dispensation with a new holy book and a new *Sharī'a* had begun. This was to result in conflict between his followers and the ulama and government during the next reign.

Throughout the course of the 18th century, Sufism had reasserted itself in Iran and remained a major preoccupation of the ulama for the first few decades of the 19th century. The thrust against Sufism begun by Bihbahānī at the close of the 18th century was continued vigorously. Bihbahānī's son, Āqā Muḥammad 'Alī, even became known as *Ṣūfī-kush* (Sufi-slayer) on account of the number of Sufis he caused to be killed; these included Ma'sum 'Alī Shāh and Muẓaffar 'Alī Shāh, two of the leading Ni'matu'llāhī Sufi Shaykhs.

There was a marked change in the relations between the ulama and the state during the reign of Muḥammad Shāh who, as noted above, had a predilection for Sufism. Indeed, the revolt of Ḥusayn 'Alī Mīrzā, Farmān-Farmā, in Isfahan at the start of this reign received the support of Ḥājjī Sayyid Muḥammad Bāqir Shaftī, probably because Farmān-Farmā had no such pro-Sufi proclivities and supported the ulama.[19] During this reign, it was no longer possible for the ulama to persecute the Sufis as they had during the previous reign. But although Sufism made progress among the royal family and government circles, it failed to make any significant headway among the people.

The most important development of this period was, however, the emergence of the ulama into the political sphere. Although prominent members of the ulama had been influential at the local level since Safavid times and had, on occasions, even caused the dismissal of a Governor, and although the ulama of the late Safavid period exercised a remarkable degree of independence and even defiance of the government, it was not until the reign of Fatḥ 'Alī Shāh that the ulama entered the field of politics at the national level. Fatḥ 'Alī Shāh's marked deference to the ulama and his need of them to underpin the legitimacy of his dynasty no doubt contributed to this.

There was a marked change in the relations between the state and the ulama in the Qājār period compared with the Safavid era. The Safavids had claimed authority on the basis of being both the 'Shadow of God on Earth' (the ancient Iranian concept of kingship, i.e. temporal authority) and the 'representative of the Hidden Imam' (i.e. spiritual authority), while the leading ulama of the Safavid period had all been incorporated into the state apparatus. The Qājārs, however, only claimed the title of 'Shadow of God on Earth' and left the claim of being the 'representative of the Hidden Imam' to the ulama. The major ulama of this period were not only outside the state apparatus, but also most of them resided in Iraq outside the state's jurisdiction. Even when the ulama were appointed to state positions, such as Ḥājjī Sayyid Muḥammad Bāqir Shaftī who was *Shaykh al-Islām* of Isfahan, they acted independently and often in defiance of the government.

The most marked instance of the political involvement of the ulama during this period was in the case of the Russo-Iranian Wars. During the first war, 1804–13, Mīrzā Buzurg, Qā'im-Maqām, the Minister of 'Abbās Mīrzā, the Crown Prince, who was conducting the war, wrote to the ulama of Iraq and Isfahan to obtain *fatwās* declaring the war against Russia to be *jihād* (holy war). Many of the prominent ulama, such as Shaykh Ja'far Kāshifu'l-Ghiṭā and Mullā Aḥmad Narāqī, responded to this request and issued such *fatwās*. This first Russo-Iranian War ended in defeat for Iran and the Treaty of Gulistān in 1813 stripped her of all her Caucasian provinces.

In the years after the war, reports began to reach the ulama of ill-treatment by the Russians of their newly-conquered Muslim subjects. The ulama began to agitate for a *jihād*. Fatḥ 'Alī Shāh was reluctant but when, in 1826, he set out for his summer residence in Sulṭāniyya, he was followed there by Āqā Sayyid Muḥammad Ṭabāṭabā'ī of Karbalā (a son of Sayyid 'Alī Ṭabāṭabā'ī), Mullā Aḥmad Narāqī, Mullā Muḥammad Taqī Baraghānī of Qazvīn and a number of other prominent ulama, who demanded that Fatḥ 'Alī Shāh declare war on Russia. The ulama were in fact threatening to take control of the affairs of government and launch the *jihād* themselves if Fatḥ 'Alī Shāh would not do this. They issued *fatwās* declaring the *jihād* to be obligatory and opposition to it a sign of unbelief (*kufr*). Fatḥ 'Alī Shāh was pressured into acquiescing. The outcome of the second Russo-Iranian War was as disastrous as the first. Although the ulama supported the troops in battle initially, after the first reverses they withdrew and it was indeed one of their number, Mīr Fattāḥ, who betrayed Tabrīz into the hands of the Russians.[20] As the result of the treaty of Turkomanchay, 1828, further territory and a large indemnity were ceded by Iran.

The importance of the second Russo-Iranian War from the point of view of the ulama, however, was their emergence as a force capable of shaping national policy. This was, indeed, the first of a chain of episodes where the ulama were to have a marked influence on the course of Iranian history. The subsequent links in this chain were to include agitation against Ḥusayn Khān Sipahsalār in 1873, the opposition to the Tobacco Regie in 1891–2, the involvement of the ulama in the Constitutional Movement 1905–9, and culminating in the Iranian Revolution of 1979.

Political Developments under Nāṣiru'd-Dīn and Muẓaffaru'd-Dīn Shāhs

The long reign of Nāṣiru'd-Dīn Shāh, from 1848 to 1896, was marked by several important events. It began with a bloody suppression of the Bābī movement in the years 1848–52 under Nāṣiru'd-Dīn Shāh's first Prime

Minister, Mīrzā Taqī Khān (executed 1852). There were a number of attempts at reforming and modernising Iran, the most notable of which were undertaken by Mirza Taqi Khan until his downfall in 1851 and Ḥusayn Khān Sipahsalār in 1871–3. Hand-in-hand with modernisation came increasing penetration of Iran by Europeans. The Shāh, desperate for revenue, farmed out many of the resources of the country in the form of concessions to European consortiums. The most extensive of these was the Reuter concession of 1872 which granted the monopoly of the working of the nation's mines, construction of railways and the national bank to Julius de Reuter, a naturalised British subject. This concession, which became an embarrassment to the British government, was eventually annulled over a minor technicality, but another concession, the monopoly of tobacco production and sale in 1890–92, aroused great public indignation and will be dealt with later in this chapter. The last years of Nāṣiru'd-Dīn Shāh's reign saw an increasing political ferment among Iranians with many issues such as nationalism, Pan-Islamism and modernisation being the focus of attention. It was an adherent of Sayyid Jamālu'd-Dīn Afghānī's Pan-Islamism who ended Nāṣiru'd-Dīn Shāh's reign with an assassin's bullet in 1896.

Nāṣiru'd-Dīn Shāh does not appear to have inherited his father's Sufi proclivities and showed himself to be religiously devout in an orthodox way although somewhat fond of an excessive display of ceremony and ostentation in respect to religious occasions, which was frowned upon by the ulama. He went on pilgrimages to Mashhad and the shrines in Iraq and paid for the gilding of the domes of the shrines at Qumm, Shāh 'Abdu'l-'Aẓīm, Karbalā and Sāmarrā. He was not, however, subservient to the ulama in the way Fatḥ 'Alī Shāh had been but rather pursued an independent line that on occasions brought him into conflict with the ulama.

Nāṣiru'd-Dīn Shāh was succeeded by his son, the mild and inoffensive Muẓaffaru'd-Dīn Shāh. Muẓaffaru'd-Dīn, while Crown Prince in Tabrīz, had been suspected of being under the influence of the Shaykhīs but once on the throne he does not appear to have shown any outward heterodoxy. The principal event of his reign was the build-up of increasing pressure for a constitutional government. The ulama became leading voices in this movement.

The Ulama during the Reigns of Nāṣiru'd-Dīn and Muẓaffaru'd-Dīn Shāhs

The years of Nāṣiru'd-Dīn Shāh's reign saw important hierarchical developments among the ulama. Najaf remained at first the undisputed centre of the Shi'i world and it has already been noted that Shaykh Muḥammad Ḥasan Najafī had almost succeeded before his death in 1850 in concentrating in himself the authority of *marja' at-taqlīd* for the entire Shi'i world.

After the death of Shaykh Muḥammad Ḥasan, a number of prominent mujtahids were recognized as *marāji'* until, by the mid 1850s, with the death of other contenders Shaykh Murtaḍā ibn Muḥammad Amīn Anṣārī, originally of Dizfūl in south-west Iran but resident in Najaf, emerged as the sole *marja' at-taqlīd*.[21] Interestingly, Shaykh Muḥammad Ḥasan had tried to determine the succession by specifically appointing Anṣārī on his death-bed; this attempt to institutionalize the succession was not, however, continued by later *marāji'*.

This emergence of a sole *marja' at-taqlīd* in the Shi'i world and the frequent references to him as the *Nā'ib al-Imām* (deputy of the Imam) concentrated enormous power and, since the *zakāt* and *khums* were also paid to him by all Shi'is, enormous wealth in the hands of one person.

Shaykh Murtaḍā was responsible for important developments in the field of jurisprudence (see pp. 186–7). He steadfastly refrained, however, despite his extensive influence, from any political involvement. His biographers present him as an extremely pious, austere man who was so obsessed with the fear of displeasing God that he refrained from issuing judgements and *ijāzas* until he was convinced of there being no possibility of having made an error.

Shaykh Murtaḍā Anṣārī died in 1864 and by about 1872 his pupil Ḥājjī Mīrzā Sayyid Muḥammad Ḥasan ibn Maḥmūd, known as Mīrzā-yi Shīrāzī, had become acknowledged as sole *marja'*.[22] In 1874 he transferred his residence from Najaf to Sāmarrā, where the Shrines of the Tenth and Eleventh Imams are situated and where the Twelfth Imam is said to have gone into occultation. He built a *madrasa* and other buildings and attracted a large number of students there, so that this town became for a short while the centre of Shi'i scholarship. He died in 1895 and leadership of the Shi'i world passed to a group of mujtahids in Najaf.

It was also during this period that a number of the ulama of Iran became extremely wealthy. Apart from their income from donations and pious benefactions, some of these ulama were not averse to such practices as hoarding grain during famines and then selling them at vastly inflated prices to a starving populace. In these ways, such figures as Mullā 'Alī Kanī of Tehran and Aqā Najafī of Isfahan became very rich.[23]

The second half of the 19th century saw the ulama coming more and more into political issues. Their principal concerns now became identified with national issues. These included the response to the Bābī movements and Shaykhism, increasing involvement in criticising the running of the government, increasing concern with the penetration of Iran by Europeans, and the issues of Pan-Islamism, modernisation and the Constitutional Movement.

Although both Shaykhism and the Bābī movement began in previous reigns, the most violent opposition to these movements began in Nāṣiru'd-Dīn Shāh's reign and continued on into the 20th century. It was the ulama who took the lead in condemning the Bāb and his followers. In Baghdad in 1845 the Governor, Najīb Pāshā, convened a court of some of the most prominent Sunni and Shi'i ulama who issued a joint *fatwā* declaring the Bāb's writings to constitute unbelief (*kufr*). In Kirmān, Ḥājjī Muḥammad Karīm Khān Kirmānī, the Shaykhī leader, was one of the first to voice his opposition to the Bāb and, in Qazvīn, Mullā Muḥammad Taqī Baraghānī, who had been the first to condemn the Shaykhīs, now also preached against the Bābīs.

In two of the major armed conflicts between Bābīs and the government troops (at Shaykh Ṭabarsī in Māzandarān in 1848–9 and at Zanjān in 1850), it was the ulama who initiated the conflict by preaching against the Bābīs and rousing the population against them. However, it was the government who undertook the responsibility of carrying out the attempt to suppress the new religion. Following an attempted assassination of the Shāh in 1852 there was a particularly brutal suppression of the Bābīs. The movement was driven underground but was to re-emerge decades later as the Bahā'ī religion under the leadership of Bahā'u'llāh (1817–92). Throughout the rest of the 19th century the ulama, in particular, initiated sporadic outbursts of persecution against the Bahā'īs. Particularly active in this respect were Shaykh Muḥammad Bāqir, a mujtahid of Isfahan (d. 1883) and his son Shaykh Muḥammad Taqī, known as Āqā Najafī (d. 1914). Thus in Isfahan between 1864 and 1914 there were thirteen violent episodes of persecution. Ādharbāyjān, Tehran, Khurāsān, Fārs and Yazd saw other major persecutions against the Bahā'īs. It was principally due to Āqā Najafī, but instigated by the Imām-Jum'a of Yazd, that a particularly violent outbreak of persecution of the Bahā'īs occurred in Yazd in 1903, leaving over a hundred Bahā'īs dead. These persecutions continued into the 20th century and have intensified since the 1979 Revolution.

The Shaykhīs too were subjected to persecution at the instigation of the ulama during this period. The major disturbances occurred in Kirmān in 1878 and 1904–5, in Hamadān in 1897 and in Tabrīz in 1848, 1868 and 1903.

Nāṣiru'd-Dīn Shāh's first Prime Minister, Mīrzā Taqī Khān, was too strong and single-minded to allow the ulama to interfere too much in the processes of government, but under his successors the ulama resumed their gradual encroachment onto the field of national politics. In 1873 the ulama played a leading role in overthrowing the Prime Minister, Mīrzā Ḥusayn Khān, whose European-inspired modernisation they both feared and resented.

The most important example of the ulama's involvement in the political sphere during Nāṣiru'd-Dīn's reign was in the agitation leading up to the repeal of the Tobacco Concession in 1891. Whereas in previous confrontations between the ulama and the state, the nation as a whole had been largely uninvolved, in this episode the ulama became the leaders of the people in a protest that involved the entire nation. A tobacco monopoly concession was granted to a British syndicate in 1890 and the company began its work in 1891. Almost immediately there was an outcry against the company. The ulama led the protests but the people themselves bitterly resented the concession and rioted in support of the ulama's demands for its abrogation. Then in December 1891 a *fatwā* was distributed purporting to be from Mīrzā-yi Shīrāzī, the *marja' at-taqlīd* of the entire Shi'i world. This *fatwā* forbade the use of tobacco and was universally obeyed throughout the country. The concession thus became valueless and was eventually withdrawn by the Shāh in order to quell the general agitation. The ulama had won this major confrontation with the Shāh and now realized the full extent of their political power. The episode itself was to be but a prelude to the ulama's involvement in the Constitutional Revolution of 1905–9.

One other political issue that concerned the ulama during this period was the Pan-Islamic Movement. This was the proposal put forward most vigorously by Sayyid Jamālu'd-Dīn Afghānī (Asadābādī, 1838–97) that the entire Muslim world unite under the Caliphate of the Ottoman Sulṭān and thus resist more effectively the encroachment of the West. Although this proposal occasioned lively debate, Afghānī does not appear to have been successful in obtaining the support of any of the prominent Shi'i ulama and the whole question gradually subsided following Afghānī's own death in 1897.

With the increasing contacts with Europe during this period, the ulama became very concerned at the rate and degree to which Western ideas and technology were being introduced into Iran. Some of these ideas, such as the notion of a constitutional government, were in parallel with the ulama's aims and were pronounced to be compatible with (and even derived from) Islam. Even some of the new technology such as the telegraph which gave better access to the mujtahids in the shrine cities to Iraq, came to be accepted. But, for the most part, the ulama were against change and particularly Western ideas and technology. They resisted and resented the increasing European penetration of the country with respect to trade and with respect even to the administration of the country. They attributed this to the corruption and venality of the Qājārs and therefore put their influence behind the movement to limit the Shāh's authority by means of a constitution.

The Popular Religion

The 19th century saw important changes in the popular religion for the generality of the Shi'a. It saw the ulama and particularly the mujtahids pushing their way more forcefully into the lives of the ordinary Shi'i through the doctrine of *taqlīd* and the rise of the *marja' at-taqlīd*. From being at the periphery of the life of the believer and only involved in such social transactions as marriage, death and inheritance, the ulama were able to thrust themselves into the centre of the life of the believer, insisting that even in the ordinary actions of everyday life it is necessary for a devout believer to turn to the *marja' at-taqlīd* for advice and guidance and as a model to be imitated.

In parallel with this development, the people began increasingly to look to the ulama as their leaders and their voice *vis-à-vis* the government. This role of the ulama, which had begun during the Safavid period, was greatly expanded in the Qājār era. The home of the mujtahid became a frequent place of sanctuary (*bast*) for persons being pursued by the authorities. When the populace wished to protest against an oppressive Governor or an unpopular government policy, it was to the ulama that they turned to voice their dissatisfaction. The ulama, being financially independent of the government and relatively immune from its pressure, were able to criticise it with impunity. This role of the ulama reached its climax in the opening years of the 20th century in the Constitutional Revolution.

The religious fervour of the masses was fanned by the increasing use of *Rawḍa-khānī*, the recital of Husayn's sufferings, and by the introduction of the *ta'ziya*, a highly-stylised enactment of the Karbalā tragedy. The Qājārs encouraged this development by the erection of buildings (*takiyyas*) for the performance of these plays which were put on during Muḥarram (see pp. 240–42). Several of the Shi'i Holy Days such as the birth of the Imam 'Ali, Imam Husayn and the Twelfth Imam as well as the commemoration of the day of Ghadīr were declared as public holidays by Nāṣiru'd-Din Shah.

Shi'ism in Arab Lands

For the Shi'is of Iraq the start of the 19th century saw the emergence of a frightening spectre from the south in the shape of the Wahhābīs, whose attack on the Shi'is of al-Aḥsā has already been mentioned. In 1801 they sacked Karbalā. The Wahhābī creed held all shrines to be contrary to the monotheistic teachings of Islam and so the Shrines of the Imam Husayn and 'Abbās, his brother, at Karbalā, were stripped of all their gold and precious ornaments. In 1803 and 1806 they attacked Najaf but were repulsed. Up to about 1811 there were regular Wahhābī raids upon the

Shi'i tribes and villages in southern Iraq but after this the Wahhābīs, under attack from the Egyptians in the west of their territories, became less of a threat to Iraq.

The line of semi-independent Mamluk Pāshās that had ruled Iraq from 1747 ended in 1831 with the Ottoman government reasserting its authority over that province. There now came a series of Governors appointed by the Ottoman government. It was one of these, Najīb Pāshā, who decided to end the semi-autonomous state that had prevailed in Karbalā and Najaf for a number of years due to the activities of gangs of ruffians. Several previous Governors had been refused permission to enter and no taxes were forthcoming. In 1843 Najīb Pāshā invested Karbalā and after negotiations had failed stormed it, causing great loss of life. The killing even occurred in the Shrine of 'Abbās and the two Shrines of Husayn and 'Abbās were desecrated by being used as stables. In 1852 Najaf suffered a similar, if less severe, fate at the hands of another Governor, Nāmiq Pāshā. But from this date onwards, the shrine cities of Iraq were left in peace. The extension of the telegraph to Najaf and Karbalā in the 1860s allowed the great mujtahids of Iraq even closer contact with the ulama of Iran and other parts of the Muslim world and strengthened the position of the *marja' at-taqlīd*.

The period from 1788 to 1840 saw Lebanon comparatively peaceful and prosperous under its semi-independent Amir Bashīr II. There was then a period of twenty years of intense fighting between the Christians and Druse until 1860 when, under foreign pressure, a new administration was set up for the Christian areas under a Christian Pāshā who was directly responsible to Istanbul. Under the new system the area prospered greatly although, despite this, great numbers emigrated to Egypt and the Americas. Politically, the region became dominated by the Christian Maronites and Druse. The Twelver Shi'is, in the main, remained apart from the factional fighting, nor did they participate as much in the emigration as the Christians of Mount Lebanon. The community turned very much in upon itself, practically its only outside contacts being the ulama who were sent for the final stages of their education to the shrine cities of Iraq.

For much of the late 18th and the 19th centuries there was a process of migration whereby the Shi'is on the west side of Mount Lebanon moved to the Biqā' Valley and Maronites moved in the opposite direction. The Shi'i Ḥarfūsh family which had controlled the Ba'ālbakk area was overthrown in 1282/1865. In the other main Shi'i area of Lebanon, the Jabal 'Āmil, the 'Alī aṣ-Ṣaghīr family was finally overthrown in 1865. The Shi'i residents in Jizzīn came under intense pressure during this period and left this town which had formerly been an important Shi'i centre.

In Bahrain, the rule of the Sunni al-Khalīfa tribe resulted in a gradual attrition in the position of the Shi'i community. Sunni Arabs were brought in from other parts of Arabia and soon formed the urban population including the ruling class, the military and many of the traders. The Shi'is were relegated to the villages. There they gradually lost ownership of the land through a system of heavy taxes and other extortions and were reduced to cultivating the palm groves as feudal peasants of their Sunni overlords.

The beginning of the 19th century saw the Shi'is of al-Aḥsā suffering under the fiercely anti-Shi'i Wahhābīs. In 1871, however, after a split in the Sa'ūdī dynasty the Ottoman Governor of Iraq, Midḥat Pāshā, was able to annexe al-Aḥsā and this gave some relief to the Shi'a there.

Shi'ism in India

In India the principal Shi'i power continued to be the Nawwābs of Oudh. In 1819 Ghāziyu'd-Dīn Ḥaydar (d. 1827) had himself crowned King of Oudh, thus effectively throwing off the Mogul suzerainty. The next King, Nāṣiru'd-Dīn (d. 1837), had coins struck with the inscription: 'the Nā'ib of the Mahdī, Nāṣiru'd-Dīn Ḥaydar, the King'. He was succeeded by his uncle, Muḥammad 'Alī Shāh (d. 1842). During the reign of the next sovereign 'Amjad 'Alī Shāh (d. 1847), the law of the kingdom which had been Sunni (in accordance with the custom of the Mogul Empire) was changed to Shi'i law and a Shi'i mufti appointed. The last King of Oudh was Wājid 'Alī Shāh who was forced by the British to abdicate in 1856.

Ghāziyu'd-Dīn Ḥaydar left a very considerable sum of money as a pious bequest. The income from this endowment was at first sent to the leading mujtahids in each of the cities of Najaf and Karbalā. Later, after the British annexation, the British government became responsible for the dispersement of the money and in 1900 it was decided to increase the number of recipients of the bequest to ten mujtahids in Najaf and Karbalā. The British attempted to use the bequest to influence the mujtahids politically but with only limited success.

One of the most important figures of this period is Sayyid Dildār 'Alī ibn Muḥammad Mu'ayyan Naṣīrābādī (1166/1752–1235/1820). In 1200/1785 he became the first Indian to return to India as a recognised mujtahid, having studied under Bihbahānī in Karbalā. He was instrumental in establishing the Uṣūlī School in Oudh and also for a campaign against Sufism.

In western India the Khoja community had consisted of a mixture of Ismā'īlīs and Twelvers. When, however, in 1842, the Agha Khan fled Iran and settled in India, he enforced a separation between the two religious groups. Some Isma'ili Khojas became Twelvers in 1901 in protest at the leadership of the third Agha Khan. In the 1870s the Twelvers petitioned Shaykh Zaynu'l-'Ābidīn Māzandarānī of Karbalā (d. 1892) whom they regarded as their spiritual leader to send them someone who could instruct them in religious matters. In 1873 Mullā Qādir Ḥusayn was sent and he remained in Bombay until 1900 instructing the Twelver Khojas and establishing the community there on an independent footing.

Twelver Shi'ism was spread during this period by Indians and Iranians, mainly as a result of settlement for trading purposes, into Nepal, Tibet, Burma, Thailand, Java and East Africa.

7
The Imamate

The Sunni concept of leadership of the Muslim community after the death of the Prophet, the Caliphate, is essentially a temporal leadership. The Caliph is a first among equals, elected ideally by consensus, although later the hereditary principle became the norm. To others, the theologians and experts in jurisprudence, is given the task of expounding upon religious questions.

To the Shi'is, however, the succession to the Prophet is a matter of the designation by the Prophet of an individual ('Ali) as Imam. Each Imam designates his successor during his lifetime. The authority of the Imam derives from his designation by his predecessor to a spiritual station and is independent of his temporal standing, i.e. it makes no difference to the Imam's station whether he is acknowledged by the generality of Muslims or not, whereas this quite clearly does not apply to a Sunni Caliph whose station is totally dependent on such acknowledgement.

The Sunnis and Shi'is are basically in agreement with each other over the nature and function of prophethood. The two main functions of the Prophet are to reveal God's law to men and to guide men towards God. Of these two functions, the Sunnis believe that both ended with the death of Muhammad, while the Shi'is believe that whereas legislation ended, the function of guiding men and preserving and explaining the Divine Law continued through the line of Imams.

The Continuity of the Imamate

As can be seen from the above, the Imamate, as conceived in Shi'i theology, is not an institution confined to Islam. From the time of the first prophet Adam, there has been a continuous succession of Imams. Some figures, such as Noah, Abraham, Moses, Jesus and Muhammad have combined in themselves the function of prophethood and the Imamate but at no time is the earth left without an Imam who is the Guide (*Hādī*) and Proof (*Ḥujja*) of God. Thus the Fifth Imam, Muḥammad al-Bāqir, is reported as having said: 'By God! God has not left the earth, since the death of Adam, without there being on it an Imam guiding (the people) to God. He is the Proof of God to His servants and the earth will not remain without the Proof of God to his servants.'[1] The Sixth Imam, Ja'far aṣ-Ṣādiq, is reported as having said: 'Were there to remain on the earth but two men, one of them would be the Proof of God.'[2]

A much longer saying attributed to the Fifth Imam, Muḥammad al-Bāqir, states that Jābir asked him: 'Why is the Prophet and the Imam necessary?' He answered:

So that the World may remain in righteousness. Thus God withholds chastisement from the World while a Prophet or Imam is upon it, for God has said: 'God will not chastise them while you are among them' (Qur'an 8:33) and the Prophet has said: 'The stars are safety for the people of heaven and the members of my family are safety for the people of the earth. If the stars went, there would come to the people of heaven, something hateful to them. And if the members of my family went, there would come to the people of earth, something hateful to them.' By 'members of my family' is meant the Imams. And God has linked obedience to them to obedience to Him and He has said 'O believers, obey God and the Apostle and those possessed of authority among you' (Qur'an 4:59). And they are the sinless, the pure ones who do no wrong and do not rebel and they are the ones who give help and success and right guidance. Through them God gives sustenance (*rizq*) to his servants and through them his lands prosper, and the rain falls from heaven and the earth gives out its blessing and the rebellious people are granted a respite and their penalty and chastisement does not speedily come to them. The Holy Spirit does not leave them (the Imams) and they do not leave it, nor does the Qur'an leave them and they do not leave it. May the blessing of God be upon them all.[3]

Some Shi'i Traditions even give the names of all the Imams going back from Muhammad to Adam.[4]

The Station of the Imams

Muhammad, Fāṭima and the Imams are conceived in their mystical dimension as being a light that God created before the creation of the material world. This light then became the cause and instrument of all the rest of creation. The following Tradition is attributed to the Prophet: 'God created 'Ali and me from one light before the creation of Adam . . . then He split (the light) into two halves, then He created (all) things from my light and 'Ali's light.'[5]

The First Imam, 'Ali, is reported to have said: 'God is one; He was alone in His singleness and so He spoke one word and it became a light and He created from that light Muhammad and He created me and my descendants (i.e. the other Imams), then He spoke another word and it became a Spirit and He caused it to settle upon that light and He caused it to settle on our bodies. And so we are the Spirit of God and His Word . . .

and this was before He created the Creation.'[6]

And the Sixth Imam, Ja'far aṣ-Ṣādiq, is reported to have said: 'Our light separates from our Lord like the rays of the sun from the sun.'[7]

In the *Khuṭba aṭ-Ṭūtunjiyya,* 'Ali is reported to have said: 'I am the First and I am the Last; I am the Hidden and I am the Manifest; I was with the Universal Cycle before it began; I was with the Pen and the Tablet before they were created; I am the Lord of Pre-eternity.'[8]

This light, created by God, which is the inner essence of the Imams, descended in turn upon Adam and then upon each of the Prophets and Imams until it became embodied in Muhammad, Fāṭima and the twelve Imams.

Muhammad, Fāṭima and the Imams are created out of the substance of 'Illiyyūn.[9] There is some difference of opinion among the commentators as to what exactly is meant by 'Illiyyūn (see Qur'an 83:19) but Shi'is generally consider that it is a synonym for an elevated station, the Seventh Heaven, or the Farthest Tree (*Sadrat al-Muntahā*).[10] The word itself is almost certainly derived from the Hebrew *'elyōn* meaning the highest.

The Imams are assisted by God through the Holy Spirit. The Third Imam, Husayn, was asked: 'From what stems your authority?' He replied: 'We rule by the authority of the House of David, and if we lack anything then the Holy Spirit sends it to us.'[11]

Although the consensus of the Shi'is is that the full prophetic revelation (*waḥy*) that came to Muhammad and the other apostles of God (such as Moses and Jesus) did not come to the Imams, nevertheless some of the Shi'i scholars have allowed that a lesser form of *waḥy* did come to the Imams. This type of *waḥy* is explained in a Tradition ascribed to Muḥammad al-Bāqir, the Fifth Imam: 'It is not the *waḥy* of prophethood but, rather, like that which came to Mary, daughter of 'Imrān (see Qur'an 3:45) and to the mother of Moses (Qur'an 28:7) and to the bee' (Qur'an 16:68).[12] In any case, if there is disagreement among the Shi'i scholars on the question of *waḥy*, there is no disagreement on the fact that the Imam received inspiration (*ilḥam*) from God. The following is attributed to Muḥammad al-Bāqir, the Fifth Imam: "Ali used to act in accordance with the book of God, i.e. the Qur'an, and the Sunna [example or Tradition] of His Apostle [i.e. Muhammad] and if something came to him and it was new and without precedent in the book or the Sunna, God would inspire him.'[13]

In some of the Traditions the link between God and the Imams is visualised as being a pillar of light descending from heaven upon the Imam.

The difference between the apostles,* the prophets and the Imams is

* Apostle (*Rasūl*) is here used to mean Messenger of God or major prophet. This should not be confused with its Christian usage.

summarised thus in a saying attributed to the Sixth Imam, Ja'far aṣ-Ṣādiq:

An apostle is one who sees the Angel who comes to him with the message from his Lord. He speaks with him just as one of you would speak with your companion. And the prophet does not see the Angel but revelation (*waḥy*) descends upon him and he sees (the Angel) in a vision . . . and the speaker (*al-muḥaddith*, i.e. the Imam[14]) hears the voice but does not see anything.[15]

The Imam is the Proof of God (*Ḥujjat Allāh*) to mankind and the Sign of God (*Āyat Allāh*) on Earth. Indeed, 'Ali is reported to have said: 'God has no greater sign than me.'[16] The Imam is the successor of the Prophet and the Vicar of God on Earth. All political authority and sovereignty is his. Obedience to him is obligatory to all on Earth. The Sixth Imam, Ja'far aṣ-Ṣādiq, is reported to have said:

We are the ones to whom God has made obedience obligatory. The people will not prosper unless they recognise us and the people will not be excused if they are ignorant of us. He who has recognised us is a believer (*mu'min*) and he who has denied us is an unbeliever (*kāfir*) and he who has neither recognised nor denied us is in error unless he returns to the right guidance which God has made obligatory for him. And if he dies in a state of error, God will do with him what He wishes.[17]

• The Imam has, according to tradition, certain books in his possession. These include certain books of the Prophet: *Al-Jafr* (The Divination), *As-Saḥīfa* (The Book); *Al-Jāmi'* (The Compilation); another is the Book of Fāṭima (*Maṣḥaf Fāṭima*), a book revealed by Gabriel to Fāṭima to console her on the death of her father, the Prophet. Also with the Imams is a copy of the Qur'an written by 'Ali and containing 'Ali's commentary.

The Imam has knowledge of one of the great mysteries in Islam, the Greatest Name of God. Indeed, it is through his knowledge of this that he has been given his powers:

Our Lord has given to us knowledge of the Greatest Name, through which, were we to want to, we would rend asunder the heavens and the earth and paradise and hell; through it we ascend to heaven and descend to earth and we travel to the east and to the west until we reach the Throne (of God) and sit upon it before God and He gives us all things, even the heavens, the earth, the sun, moon and stars, the mountains, the trees, the paths, the seas, heaven and hell.[18]

There was no straightforward statement in the Qur'an designating 'Ali and his descendants as Imams. However, the Qur'an is divided by scholars into clear verses (i.e. those whose meaning is clear) and ambiguous verses (see Qur'an 3:7). Since Imams are the sole authorised interpreters of the Qur'an, they are the ones to whom it is obligatory to turn in the case of the ambiguous verses. In carrying out this function, Imams have interpreted many of these verses as referring to the Imamate and its station. Indeed, 'Ali is reported to have said that one quarter of the Qur'an is about the Imams.[19] Among the verses of the Qur'an which are interpreted in this way are the following:

1. The Signs of God: 'Only the unbelievers would deny our signs' (Qur'an 29:49). The Imams are the Signs of God (*Āyāt Allāh*) on Earth. Many other references to 'sign' or 'signs' are also references to the Imams (e.g. 7:9; 10:7 and 101; 22:57; 38:29).[20]
2. The Straight Path. 'Guide us to the Straight Path' (1:6). The Imams are the 'Straight Path' (*as-Ṣirāṭ al-Mustaqīm*) referred to in this opening chapter of Qur'an (and also in 6:153; 15:41; 16:76; 20:135; 43:42).[21]
3. The Way. The Imams are the Way (*as-Sabīl*) referred to in several verses (25:8,27; 6:153; 29:69; 31:15).[22]
4. The Bounty of God. 'Do you not see those who exchange the Bounty of God for disbelief' (14:28,29). The Imams are the Bounty of God and the people referred to in this verse are their opponents and especially the Umayyads (see also 16:83).[23] The Imams are also 'the favours of God' (7:69; 55:13).[24]
5. The Firmest Handle. 'He who disbelieves in idols and believes in God has grasped hold of the firmest handle (*al-'Urwa al-Wuthqā*) which will not break' (2:256). The 'firmest handle' is love for the house of the Prophet, i.e. the Imams.[25]
6. The Cord of God. 'Hold fast to the cord of God (*Ḥabl Allāh*)' (3:102). The (cord) or rope of God can mean the Qur'an or the religion of Islam, but it is also interpreted as referring to the Imamate.[26]
7. The Light of God. 'Therefore believe in God and His Apostle and the Light which we have sent down' (64:8). The light of God is within the Imams (see p. 148). Several other verses mentioning light are stated to refer to this light (e.g. 4:174; 6:122; 7:157; 9:32; 24:36; 57:28; 66:8).[27]
8. The Trust. 'We offered the Trust to the Heavens and to the Earth and to the mountains, but they refused to undertake it and were afraid of it; but man undertook it; surely he is sinful and ignorant' (33.72). The trust referred to is stated to be the *Walāya* or Imamate of 'Ali and the sinful and ignorant men are those who took the rightful place of the Imams.[28]

'God has ordered you to make over the trusts to those who are entitled to them' (4:58). This is stated to refer to the designation by each Imam of the one who is to follow him.[29]

9. The Guides of Men. 'Among those whom We have created are a people who guide (men) to the truth and through it they act with justice' (7:181). These are, of course, the Imams.[30]
10. The Possessors of Knowledge. 'No-one knows the interpretation of it (the Qur'an) except God and those who are deeply rooted in

knowledge' (3:7). 'Those who are deeply rooted in knowledge' is held to refer to the family of Muhammad (i.e. the Imams).[31]

'God is sufficient as a witness between you and me and so also are those who possess knowledge of the book' (13:43). 'Those who possess knowledge of the book' refers to the Imams.[32] This phrase occurs in several other places (e.g. 16:27; 29:49; 34:6).[33]

11. The Inheritors of the Book. 'We have caused those of our servants whom We chose to inherit the Book . . .' (35:32). This is stated to refer to the Imams, although there is some difference of opinion as to whom the rest of the verse is referring.[34]

'Those to whom We have given this book and who recite it as it should be recited, they believe in it' (2:121). This whole passage refers to the Imams.[35]

12. The Possessors of Authority. 'O believers! Obey God and obey the Apostle and those who have been given authority among you' (4:59). 'Those who have been given authority' are the Imams and thus this verse makes obeying them obligatory.[36]

13. The Truthful Ones. 'O ye who believe! Fear God and be with the truthful ones' (9:119). The Imams are the 'truthful ones'. But the phrase 'truthful ones' is also held to refer to Hamza, Muhammad's uncle and Ja'far, 'Ali's brother (see also 33:23).[37]

14. The Family of Yā Sīn. 'Peace be upon the family of Yā Sīn' (37:130). Yā Sīn is interpreted as Muhammad and thus his family refers to Imams.[38]

15. The People of the Remembrance. 'Then question the people (or family) of the Remembrance if you do not know' (16:43–4). The Remembrance is held to be Muhammad and thus his family refers to the Imams whom it is obligatory to question regarding any points in the Qur'an that are not understood.[39]

16. The Family of Abraham. 'God has chosen . . . the family of Abraham' (3:33). This is stated to refer to the family of Muhammad (i.e. the Imams, but see also page 172).[40] In other places the seed of Abraham is stated to refer to the Imams (e.g. 19:58; 14:38).

17. The Family of the Prophet. 'Say: I ask of you no recompense for it except love among kindred' (42:23). Shi'i commentators have interpreted the last phrase as 'love for my kindred' (i.e. the Imams),[41] and even Sunni commentators like Bayḍāwī and Rāzī agree that this phrase refers to 'Ali and Fāṭima and their sons.[42]

'And the blood relatives (of the Prophet), some of them are nearer to one another in the book of God than the believers and the emigrants' (33:6). This is held to refer to the authority vested in the Imams.[43]

18. The People of the Right Hand. Concerning the time of the End, the 'people of the right hand' who are to be greeted in Heaven are the Shi'is

and the 'people of the left hand' who are to go to Hell are their enemies. The 'predecessors' who are 'the near ones' refers to Muhammad, Fāṭima and the Imams (56:8–11, 88–91).[44]

19. The Sun and Moon. 'By the Sun and its brightness and the moon when it follows it and the day when it reveals its glory and the night when it covers it' (91:1–4). The Prophet is the sun and the moon is 'Ali. The day is the Imam (or in some Traditions, specifically the Imam Mahdī) and the night represents the enemies of the Imams and in particular Abū Bakr whose caliphate 'covered' 'Ali.[45]

20. The Two Seas. 'He has set the two seas in motion that they may meet one another, and between them is a barrier that they overpass not, . . . and from the two of them come forth pearls and coral' (55:19–22). The 'two seas' are 'Ali and Fāṭima, neither of whom is superior to the other and the Imams Hasan and Husayn are the 'pearls and coral' that come out of the two seas.[46]

21. The Party of God. 'Those who take God and his Apostle as their masters and those who believe, surely the Party of God will triumph' (5:56). The Imams and the Shi'is are the Party of God.[47]

22. The Servants of the All-Merciful. The whole of the lengthy passage that begins: 'The servants of the all-merciful are those who walk upon the Earth with humility . . .' (25:63) refers to the Imams.[48]

23. The Men on the Battlements (*al-A'rāf*). Regarding entry to Heaven or Hell, it is written: 'And on the battlements are men who recognise all by their signs . . .' (7:46). The men on the battlements are the Imams who, on the Day of Judgement, decide who will enter Heaven and who will enter Hell.[49]

There are many other verses of the Qur'an that are similarly interpreted but the above is sufficient to give the reader some idea of the manner of Shi'i commentary upon the Qur'an on this subject.

Necessary Attributes of the Imams

There are several attributes considered by Shi'is to be necessary for the Imams and these conditions are held to be proved both by Traditions and by logical necessity. Thus the Imams are considered to be *manṣūṣ* (designated), *ma'ṣūm* (sinless or infallible) and *afḍal an-nās* (the best of the people).

A. The Conferment of the Imamate by Designation or Covenant

One of the important principles of Shi'i Islam is that the Imamate can only be passed on from one Imam to the next by divinely-inspired designation (*naṣṣ*). This process is sometimes referred to as a covenant (*'ahd*) from one to the next. The following Tradition is from the Sixth Imam, Ja'far aṣ-Ṣādiq: 'Each Imam knows the Imam who is to come after him and so he appoints him as his successor.'[50]

This succession is not a matter of the personal choice of the Imam, as these two Traditions from the same Imam show:

Do you imagine that we place this Cause of ours (i.e. the Imamate) with whomsoever we wish? No! Not at all! By God! It is a covenant of the Apostle of God with 'Ali, the son of Abū Ṭālib, and then one man after another until finally it comes to the Lord of this Cause (i.e. the Mahdī).[51]

And

None of us (the Imams) die until God has informed us of the one who is to succeed us.[52]

At any one time there is only one Imam, but his successor, if alive, is called the Silent Imam (*al-Imām aṣ-Ṣāmit*). The following Tradition from the Sixth Imam illustrates this point:

The Sixth Imam said: "Ali, the son of Abū Ṭālib, was the possessor of knowledge in this community, and his knowledge became an inheritance, and not one of us die until he has passed on the knowledge that he learned from his father. And the earth will not remain one day without an Imam from us with whom the community can take refuge.' And I asked him: 'May there be two Imams?' He said: 'No! Unless one of them be the Silent one who does not speak until the first one has died.'[53]

Thus each prophet sets up two covenants, one regarding the next prophet who will eventually come and one regarding his immediate successor, the Imam. This is most clearly expressed in a Tradition attributed to the Sixth Imam, Ja'far aṣ-Ṣādiq:

Noah lived for five hundred years after his disembarkation from the Ark. Then Gabriel came to him and said: 'The period of your prophethood has ended, O Noah! And the days of your life are drawing to a close and God says: 'Pass on the inheritance of your knowledge and the signs of your prophethood to your son, Sām. For I do not leave the earth without there being on it someone who knows obedience to Me and is a source of salvation between the death of one prophet and the sending out of the next. And I do not leave the people without a Proof and someone who will summon them to Me, and guide them to My path, someone who knows My Cause. And I have decreed that I will place for each people a Guide who will guide fortunate ones and who will be a Proof to the wretched ones.' And so Noah handed all this over to his son, Sām [who thus became the Imam]. And as for Hām and Yāfith, they did not have a knowledge which would benefit them. And Noah also gave the good news of the coming of Hūd [i.e. the next prophet] and ordered them to follow him.[54]

The conferment of the Imamate by designation is also considered a logical necessity since the Imam must be immune from sin and error (see next section) and only God can know who is thus immune and can therefore designate the Imam. This designation can similarly only be conveyed to mankind by one who is himself immune from error, the previous prophet or Imam.

B. Immunity from Sin and Error

'Isma (sinlessness and infallibility) is considered a necessary precondition for the Imamate. This is proved from logic by Shi'i writers in that, since God has commanded obedience to the Imam, the Imam can only order what is right, or otherwise God would be commanding man to follow the pathway of error and this would be contrary to God's justice.

The sinlessness of Muhammad, Fāṭima and the twelve Imams is also considered proven by Tradition. According to the Qur'an (33:33): 'God desires to remove all uncleanliness from you, O members of his family, and to purify you completely.' Shi'i Traditions relate this verse to the Imam. One Tradition reports the Prophet as saying: 'I, 'Alī, Hasan, Husayn and nine of the descendants of Husayn are pure and sinless.'[55]

The concept of *'Isma* includes sinlessness or impeccability and also, because of being protected from error, infallibility. The Sixth Imam, Ja'far aṣ-Ṣādiq, is reported as having said.

> The one who is sinless (*ma'ṣūm*) is the one who is prevented by God from doing anything that God has forbidden. For God has said: 'He who cleaves to God is guided to the Straight Path.'[56]

C. He is the Best of Men

The Imam is the most excellent of men in all attributes vital in religion. This is considered to be a logical necessity of the fact that he is immune from sin. Also it is considered that if there were any man better than he, God would choose that man to be His Proof on Earth and His Guide to the people.

Other Attributes of the Imams

Apart from the above necessary attributes of the Imams, there are a large number of other qualities attributed to them. These include:

A. Knowledge ('Ilm)

This refers to both general and religious knowledge. Religious knowledge may also be divided into knowledge concerning the externals of the religion (such as the Qur'an, *ḥadīth*, principles of jurisprudence, etc.) and esoteric knowledge which includes the allegorical interpretation of the Qur'an and mystical knowledge. The following Tradition illustrates this point:

> I was with Abu'l-Ḥasan in Mecca when a man said to him: 'You are commenting from the Book of God some matters which you did not hear.' And he said: 'It was revealed to us before it was revealed to the people and we commented upon it before it was commented upon by others. We know what is permitted and forbidden in it, we know which verse abrogates and which verse is abrogated in it, and how many verses were revealed on which night, and concerning what and whom they were revealed. We are the judges of God on His Earth and His witnesses for His creation.'[57]

And concerning the Qur'anic verse: 'He is it who has sent down the Book . . . and none know its explanation except God and those who are deeply-rooted in knowledge' (3:7), the Imam Ja'far aṣ-Ṣādiq said: 'We are the ones who are deeply-rooted in knowledge and we know its explanation.'[58]

The channel by which the knowledge reaches the Imams is a Spirit from God. Thus in the following Tradition Ja'far aṣ-Ṣādiq is questioned:

> 'Inform me about the knowledge that you have. Is it something that you learnt from the mouths of men . . . or something written that you possess from the Apostle of God?' And he said: 'The matter is greater than that. Have you not heard the words of God in His Book: "Thus we have revealed to you a Spirit by Our command. You did not know what the Book was nor Belief." and when God gives this Spirit, knowledge is with it. And thus when it comes to a servant (of God), knowledge and understanding are with it.'[59]

There is also the following Tradition, attributed to the same Imam, that defines two types of knowledge and indicates that the Imam's knowledge is co-extensive with that of the prophets and apostles:

> God has two types of knowledge: A knowledge that He manifests to His angels, prophets and apostles and what he has manifested to these, we also know; and a knowledge which is confined to Himself. And when He spread some of this [second type of knowledge], he caused us to learn it and he showed it to those Imams who were before us.[60]

However, the exact extent of the knowledge of the Imams has been a subject of some controversy among the Shi'is. Most Shi'i theologians have agreed, however, that the Imams do not inherently possess knowledge of the unseen (*'ilm al-ghayb*), that is to say what is in the future and what is in men's minds, although glimpses of this knowledge are occasionally given to them by God out of His bounty.[61]

Thus the Imam as a result of his knowledge is perfectly able to give judgement on all matters of religious law and his judgement is always legally correct. He is the Guardian of the Law. The Imam is also a supreme educator of mankind.

Concerning the time and manner of the transfer of this knowledge from Imam to Imam there is some disagreement. For with respect to 'Ali, there are numerous Traditions attesting to how assiduous 'Ali was in collecting knowledge concerning the Revelation and how he would not go to sleep each evening until he had ascertained what Revelations had been vouchsafed to Muhammad that day and the circumstances of the Revelation. However, with respect to some of the later Imams, and in particular the Ninth and Tenth Imams, Muḥammad at-Taqī and 'Alī al-Hādī, who became Imams while they were mere children, the emphasis is on a miraculous transfer of knowledge at the moment of death of the previous Imam.[62]

B. Spiritual Guidance (Walāya)

The concept of *Walāya* or *Wilāya* is one of the most difficult Islamic terms to translate, particularly since in different contexts its meaning varies. The word is derived from the same root as *walī* which has already been discussed, and can mean master or friend (see p. 17). The Imam is seen as the spiritual friend or supporter who guides and initiates mankind into the mystical or inner truth of religion. It is through him that God's grace reaches the Earth. As the apostles or prophets are concerned with the external aspects of the religion, in particular with the legislation of religious laws and ordinances, the Imam (and this also, of course, applies to the apostle in his function as an Imam) is concerned primarily with the inner or esoteric aspects of religion, guiding mankind onto the path of spiritual enlightenment and progress. The Imam is therefore, at one and the same time, master and friend in the journey of the spirit. This theme is, of course, very close to the Sufi idea of the *Wilāya* possessed by a Sufi Shaykh (see p. 208).

The Necessity of Recognising the Imam

God and the Prophet have made a covenant (*mīthāq*) with the whole of creation regarding the Imams. Thus the Sixth Imam, Ja'far aṣ-Ṣādiq, relates the following words of 'Ali:

> The Apostle of God said: 'God does not cause a prophet to die until he has ordered him to appoint a successor someone from his close family', and He ordered me to appoint a successor. And so I asked Him: 'Who? O Lord.' And He replied: 'Appoint your cousin 'Ali, the son of Abū Ṭālib, as your successor, O Muhammad! For I have established this in the former books and have written that he is your successor and have made a covenant with all created things and with My prophets and apostles. I have made covenants with them all concerning My Lordship and your prophethood, O Muhammad, and the successorship of 'Ali, the son of Abū Ṭālib.'[63]

Thus it is necessary for everyone to recognise and obey the Imam. One of the most famous sayings attributed to the Apostle is as follows: 'He who dies not knowing his Imam dies the death of the Jāhiliyya [the period of ignorance before Islam arose].'[64] 'By the death of the Jāhiliyya is meant in the condition of idol-worship and ignorance of the principles of Islam, the condition of the people before Islam came.'[65]

Thus knowledge of the Imam of his age is an essential part of Islam for every believer. The Sixth Imam, Ja'far aṣ-Ṣādiq, is reported as having said:

Husayn, the son of 'Ali, came one day to his companion and, after praising God and wishing peace upon the Apostle of God, he said: 'By God! God created mankind in order that they might know Him and in knowing Him they might worship Him, and, in worshipping Him, might free themselves from the worship of anything other than Him.' And a man said to him: 'O descendant of the Apostle of God! What is knowing God?' He replied: 'It is that the people of each age know their Imam, for obedience to him is obligatory for them.'[66]

And concerning one who opposes the Imam, when the Prophet was asked: 'Who is the Imam?' he is reported to have replied:

They are my successors. Whosoever of my community dies and does not have an Imam from among them, has died the death of the Jāhiliyya. If he has not recognised him [i.e. the Imam] and has been at enmity with him, he is a polytheist (*mushrik*) and if he has not recognised him but has not been an enemy nor assisted his enemies, then he is merely accounted as being of the ignorant and is not a polytheist.[67]

The judgement of the Fifth Imam, Muḥammad al-Bāqir, is equally severe:

He who has repudiated an Imam from God and has cut himself off from him and his religion is an unbeliever, an apostate from Islam. For the Imam is from God and his religion is the religion of God and he who cuts himself off from the religion of God, his blood, while he is in this state, may be spilt with impunity, unless he returns and repents to God all that he has said.[68]

Moreover, it is necessary for the believer to recognise the living Imam of his age. It is not enough to have recognised past Imams. When asked: 'Is one who has recognised the Imams, but does not recognise the Imam of his age, a believer (*mu'min*)?', Ja'far aṣ-Ṣādiq replied: 'No!' When then asked: 'Is he a Muslim?', he replied: 'Yes!'[69] The Shi'i scholar, Ibn Bābūya, has explained the difference between one who has Islam (a Muslim) and one who has *Īmān* (belief, i.e. a *mu'min*):

Islam is acknowledgement of the *Shahādatayn* [the declaration that there is no God but God and that Muhammad is His Apostle], and whoever does this may retain his life and possessions. But recompense is for belief (*Īmān*).[70]

The Eighth Imam, 'Alī ar-Riḍā, is reported to have said that the Prophet told 'Ali:

You and the Imam from among your descendants, O 'Ali, are the Proof of God to His creation after me, and the people of knowledge among His creation. He who denies any one of you, has denied me; he who has opposed any one of you, has opposed me; he who has treated any one of you harshly, has treated me harshly; he who has reached you, has reached me; he who has obeyed you, has obeyed me; he who has befriended you, has befriended me; and he who is an enemy to you, is an enemy to me. For you are of me, you are created of my substance, and I am of you.[71]

Moreover, there is no entry to Heaven without acknowledgement of the Imam. The Apostle is reported to have said:

O 'Ali! When the Day of Judgement comes, we will be seated on the Path, you, Gabriel and I, and we will not permit anyone to pass who does not possess a writ of being guiltless with respect to your authority.[72]

Rational Proofs for the Imamate

In the eyes of the Shi'i ulama, the rational proofs of the necessity of the Imamate are equally as if not more important than the proofs derived from the Traditions. Since these rational proofs are so important in Shi'i eyes, a brief *résumé* of the main lines of reasoning used are given here:

i. Since there are verses in the Qur'an that are not clear and guidance is needed to understand these passages, God could not have caused the Qur'an to be revealed without also providing someone to explain it.

ii. Since there are many possible interpretations of the sacred law (the *Sharī'a*), the Imam is needed to give authoritative guidance on the application of the law. Otherwise the people would err in applying the sacred law and a just God could not hold a people responsible for their breaking the law if they had not been properly guided in it.

iii. Since a perfectly just ruler is necessary to maintain order in the world, God, who is beneficent and does not wish to see tyranny and anarchy in the world, must of necessity provide such a ruler – the Imam. The analogy is made with the human body: the mind is needed to control and co-ordinate the body as well as to make sense of the incoming sensory data. In human society, the Imam fulfils the same role.

iv. It is proved from the above that a leader is needed for the Muslims to rule and guide them. If God had left it to the choice of the people, then they might have chosen someone who was not adequate for the task and this would have made God's favour to mankind incomplete. Since the best course then is for God to choose and designate the leader, and since God is beneficent and all-wise and would always choose the best and most expedient course, this must result in God's provision of an Imam.

Many of the most important Shi'i books of the early and medieval period (and particularly from the 10th to the 13th Christian centuries) contain both rational proofs (from Mu'tazili-based *kalām*) and traditional proofs (from the Traditions of the Prophet and the Imams) on the Imamate as well as on a mixture of other subjects such as the legitimacy of 'Ali's succession to the Prophet, the lives and miracles of the Imams and the Occultation of the Twelfth Imam. This admixture often makes it difficult to assign a classification of subject matter to these books. They were usually written to counter Sunni polemics. The following is a list of the most important of such works, indicating the main subjects that they deal with (the following abbreviations are used: I – the Imamate; AS – 'Ali's succession; LI – Lives of the Imams; O – Occultation of the Twelfth Imam):

Muḥammad an-Nu'mānī, *Kitāb al-Ghayba* (Book of the Occultation; composed 342/953) – O

Ibn Bābūya, *al-Amālī* (Dictated Notes) – AS, LI

Ibn Bābūya, *Kamāl ad-Dīn wa Tamām an-Ni'ma* (The Completion of Religion and the Perfection of Beneficence) – I, O

Shaykh al-Mufīd, *al-Ikhtiṣāṣ* (Distinction) – I, LI, O

Shaykh al-Mufīd, *Kitāb al-Irshād* (Book of Guidance) – LI

Shaykh al-Mufīd, *Awā'il al-Maqālāt* (The Foremost of Treatises) – I

Shaykhu'ṭ-Ṭā'ifā aṭ-Ṭūsī, *Kitāb al-Ghayba* (Book of Occultation) – O

Shaykhu'ṭ-Ṭā'ifa, *as-Shāfī fi'l-Imāma* (The Salutory Book about the Imamate) – I

al-Faḍl ibn Ḥasan aṭ-Ṭabarsī, *al-Iḥtijāj* (Argumentation) – I, AS

Ibn Shahrāshūb, *Manāqib Āl-Abī Ṭālib* (The Virtuous Deeds of the Family of Abū Ṭālib, i.e. the 'Alids) – I, LI

'Alī ibn Mūsā, Ibn Tāwus, *al-Yaqīn fi Imāra Amīr al-Mu'minīn* (Certainty regarding the Authority of the Commander of the Faithful) – I, AS

'Alī ibn 'Īsā al-Irbilī, *Kashf al-Ghumma fi ma'arifat al-A'imma* (The Disclosure of Affliction; concerning knowledge of the Imams) – I, LI, O

8

The Twelfth Imam, His Occultation and Return

Perhaps no aspect of the history of Shi'i Islam is as confused as the stories relating to the Twelfth Imam and this is not surprising as this is the point in Shi'i history where the events related become of a miraculous, extraordinary nature and the non-believer may be unwilling to go along with the facts as related by Shi'is. But even for the committed believer, it is difficult to decide which of the many and often contradictory versions presented in the Traditions to follow. The following version is the one that is usually presented in the books published for popular reading.

The mother of the Twelfth Imam was a Byzantine slave-girl named Narjis Khatun (or Ṣaqil or Sawsan or Rayḥana). In the more fully elaborated versions of the story she becomes the Byzantine Emperor's daughter who was informed in a vision that she would be the mother of the Mahdī. She was bought by the Tenth Imam, 'Alī al-Hādī, for his son the Eleventh Imam, Ḥasan al-'Askarī.

The Twelfth Imam was born in 255/868 (some sources vary by as much as five years from this date) in Sāmarrā. He was given the same name as the Prophet, Abu'l-Qāsim Muḥammad.

The usual miraculous accounts of his talking from the womb, etc. (see p. 23) may be passed over to the only occasion on which he is said to have made a public appearance. This was in 260/874 when the Eleventh Imam died. It appears that none of the Shi'i notables knew of the birth of Muḥammad and so they went to the Eleventh Imam's brother, Ja'far, assuming that he was now the Imam. Ja'far seemed prepared to take on this mantle and entered the house of the deceased Imam in order to lead the funeral prayers. At this juncture a young boy came forward and said: 'Uncle, stand back! For it is more fitting for me to lead the prayers for my father than for you.' After the funeral, Ja'far was asked about the boy and said that he did not know who the boy was. For this reason, Ja'far has been vilified by generations of Shi'is as *Kadhdhāb*, the liar.

The boy was seen no more and Shi'i tradition states that from that year he went into occultation. At Sāmarrā, beside the gold-domed Shrine of the Imāms 'Alī al-Hādī and Ḥasan al-'Askarī is a mosque under which there is a cave. The end of one of the rooms of the cave is partitioned off by a gate which is called Bāb al-Ghayba (Gate of the Occultation) and was built on the instructions of the Caliph an-Nāṣir in 606/1209. The area behind the gate is called Ḥujrat al-Ghayba (Chamber of the Occultation) and in the corner of this is a well, the Bi'r al-Ghayba (Well of the Occultation) down which the Imam Mahdī is said to have disappeared. Shi'is gather in the rooms of the cave and pray for his return.

The Lesser Occultation

Those Shi'is who followed the line of the Imams were thrown into confusion by the death of Ḥasan al-'Askarī. Ja'far remained unshakeable in his assertion that his brother had no progeny and some gathered around him as the Imam. Others asserted that the Twelfth Imam had not yet been born but would be born in the Last Days just before the Day of Judgement. Others asserted that it was the Eleventh Imam, Ḥasan al-'Askarī, who had gone into occultation. Thus the Shi'a were fragmented into several factions (for a fuller account of these sects see pp. 59–60). It is difficult to assess at this distance in history and with the bias of the sources available what proportion of the Twelver Shi'is of the time accepted the position of 'Uthmān al-'Amrī which was to become the orthodox Twelver position. Al-'Amrī claimed that Muḥammad, the son of Ḥasan al-'Askarī, did exist and was in occultation and that he, 'Uthmān, was the intermediary between the Hidden Imam and the Shi'a.

But it should not necessarily be assumed that 'Uthmān al-'Amrī's assertion was perceived by the Shi'is of the time as being a radical change. For, after all, the Tenth and Eleventh Imams, as far as the generality of their followers were concerned, had also been in effective occultation. Because of the vigilant and hostile surveillance of the 'Abbasids, they had rarely showed themselves to their followers and are even said to have spoken to some of those who met them from behind a curtain. Their contact with their followers was through a network of Shi'i agents called the *Wikāla* which had been responsible for communicating the messages of the Imams and collecting the monies offered by the Shi'a. This network of agents was in contact with one or two special agents of the Tenth and Eleventh Imam who in turn were in direct contact with the Imam. 'Uthmān al-'Amrī had been the secretary and special agent of the Tenth and Eleventh Imams and thus effectively controlled the *Wikāla*. With the death of the Eleventh Imam, all that al-'Amrī was saying was that the Twelfth Imam was also in hiding due to the threat against his life from the 'Abbasids and that he, 'Uthmān, had been appointed to continue the position that he had held under the previous Imams. For the majority of the Shi'a it must have seemed that nothing much had changed. It is probably only after about seventy years (i.e. the normal life-span of a man) had passed that the question of the Occultation became problematical (see pp. 74–5) and began to require doctrinal exposition. Thus al-Kulaynī, who completed his book (see p. 174) less than seventy years after the start of the Occultation has little or no discussion of the Occultation itself or of the position of al-'Amrī and his successors as intermediaries and neither do any of the extant Shi'i books preceding it. A few decades later, however, it is a topic of major importance to most Shi'i writers and whole books are devoted to the issue.

'Uthmān nominated his son, Abū Ja'far Muḥammad ibn 'Uthmān, as his successor. For forty-five years these two laid claim to the position of being the agents of the Hidden Imam. They would take messages and questions from the Shi'a to the Hidden Imam and would return with answers, usually verbal but sometimes written. They would also receive the monies offered by the Shi'a to the Imam as *khums* and *zakāt* (see p. 179). They were involved in bitter disputes with Ja'far and his followers who denied the existence of the Eleventh Imam's son and laid claim to his brother's estate – a legal battle that took seven years and was finally decided by the Caliph al-Mu'tamid. Narjis, the supposed mother of the Twelfth Imam, was also the subject of much wrangling that went on over twenty years.

The third person to be nominated as the agent of the Hidden Imam was Abu'l-Qāsim Ḥusayn ibn Rūḥ an-Nawbakhtī. He came to this position in 305/917, after the death of Muḥammad al-'Amrī. Conditions had changed considerably by this time. The Caliph Muqtadir (reigned AD 907–932) was favourable to the Shi'a and the Nawbakhtī family, who were Shi'is, wielded considerable power at his court as ministers. However, even at this late date there were disputes among the Shi'a over the question of the Occultation. Abū Ja'far Muḥammad ibn 'Alī ash-Shalmaghānī (executed in 322/933), who had been a close confidant of Ḥusayn ibn Rūḥ and his agent in Baghdad, suddenly turned against the latter and at first laid claim to the position of being the rightful agent of the Imam and later denounced the whole concept of the Occultation as a lie. Another who fell out with what was rapidly by now becoming the Twelver Shi'i orthodoxy was Ḥusayn ibn Manṣūr al-Ḥallāj (*c.* 244/858 – executed 309/922). Exactly what it was that Shalmaghānī and Ḥallāj said or did which brought upon them the anger of the Shi'is and eventually, through the power of the Nawbakhtī family, death at the hands of the state cannot now easily be discerned among the mass of gratuitous accusations and disinformation piled upon them by later writers. It has been suggested, however, that their open avocation of extremist claims (*ghuluww*) was threatening the delicate balance which allowed Shi'i families such as the Nawbakhtīs and the Āl al-Furāt to hold power and authority in a Sunni state and thus allowed Shi'is to enjoy unprecedented freedom. It is clear that whatever differences there may have been among the Shi'a following the death of the Eleventh Imam in 874, by the third and fourth decades of the 10th century (i.e. the closing years of the Lesser Occultation), the majority of the Shi'is were agreed about the line of Twelve Imams. There was still confusion and doubt over the question of the Occultation and this was to continue for a further hundred years. It was also during this period that the first of the four 'canonical' collections of *ḥadīth*, *al-Kāfī fī 'Ilm ad-Dīn*, was being completed by al-Kulaynī thus helping to bring about a convergence and consolidation of views among the Twelver Shi'is.

The fourth and last agent of the Hidden Imam was Abu'l-Ḥusayn 'Alī ibn Muḥammad as-Samarrī. He held office for only three years and died in 329/941. These four successive agents of the Hidden Imam are each called by the Shi'is the *Bāb* (Gate, plural *Abwāb*), the *Safīr* (Ambassador, plural *Sufarā*) or *Nā'ib* (Deputy, plural *Nuwwāb*) of the Twelfth Imam.

At the time of his death, as-Samarrī brought the following written message from the Hidden Imam:

> In the name of God the Merciful, the Compassionate! O 'Alī ibn Muḥammad as-Samarrī, may God magnify the reward of your brethren upon you! There are but six days separating you from death. So therefore arrange your affairs but do not appoint anyone to your position after you. For the second occultation has come and there will not now be a manifestation except by the permission of God and that after a long time has passed, and hearts have hardened and the earth become filled with tyranny. And there will come to my Shi'a those who claim to have seen me, but he who claims to have seen me before the emergence of the Sufyānī and the Cry (from the heavens) is assuredly a lying imposter. And there is no power nor strength save in God the Almighty, the All-High.[1]

And so the Shi'is passed, in 329/941, into what is known as the Greater Occultation, the period of time when there is no agent of the Hidden Imam on earth.

One final historical point is that although the history of the four agents of the Hidden Imam has been given above as it is to be found in the Shi'i histories, there is some considerable evidence that this was a later superimposition of interpretation on the facts of history. In the early works there is no indication that the number of agents was limited to four and several others are mentioned.[2] It seems likely, then, that after the death of the Eleventh Imam, for the duration of a natural lifespan (i.e. seventy years), the former system of the *Wikāla* had continued to operate. But then the Shi'is began to be thrown into confusion and doubt over the matter of the Occultation.[3] And so the scholars of the early Buyid period spent a great deal of time in writing books explaining and proving the doctrine of the Occultation of the Twelfth Imam. It was probably also at about the end of the Lesser Occultation that the Twelfth Imam came to be identified with the figure of the Mahdī.

The Doctrine of Occultation

In its simplest form, the doctrine of the Occultation (*Ghayba*) declares that Muḥammad ibn Ḥasan, the Twelfth Imam, did not die but has been concealed by God from the eyes of men. His life has been miraculously prolonged until the day when he will manifest himself again by God's permission. During his Lesser Occultation, he remained in contact with his followers through the four *Bābs* (*al-Abwāb al-Arba'a*). During the Greater Occultation, which extends to the present day, he is still in control of the affairs of men and is the Lord of the Age (*Ṣāḥib az-Zamān*) but there is no longer a direct route of communication. However, it is popularly believed that the Hidden Imam does still occasionally manifest himself to the pious either when awake or more commonly in dreams and visions. It is believed that written messages left at the tombs of the Imams can reach him. The Hidden Imam was popularly supposed to be resident in the far-off cities of Jābulsā and Jābulqā and in former times books were written about persons who had succeeded in travelling to these places. Less has been made of this particular tradition in recent times when modern geographical knowledge permeated the Shi'i masses and it became generally realised that no such places existed. There are also accounts of persons who have seen the Imam in person, in visions or dreams.[4]

The occurrence of the Occultation is considered to have been due to the hostility of the Imam's enemies and the danger to his life. He remains in occultation because of the continuance of this threat. The severance of communication with the Hidden Imam is not considered to contradict the dictum that 'the earth is not left without an Imam', for, say the Shi'i writers, the sun still gives light and warmth to the earth even when hidden behind a cloud.

The Hidden Imam has a large number of titles including the following: Ṣāḥib az-Zamān (Lord of the Age), Ṣāḥib al-Amr (Lord of Command), al-Mahdī (the Rightly-Guided One), al-Qā'im (He who will arise), al-Imām al-Muntaẓar (the Awaited Imam) and the Baqiyyat Allāh (Remnant of God).

The Doctrine of Return (Raj'a)

The Hidden Imam, the Imam Mahdī, is in occultation awaiting the time that God has decreed for his return. This return is envisaged as occurring shortly before the final Day of Judgement. The Hidden Imam will then return as the Mahdī with a company of his chosen ones and there will also return his enemies led by the one-eyed Dajjāl and the Sufyānī. The Imam Mahdī will lead the forces of righteousness against the forces of evil in one final apocalyptic battle in which the enemies of the Imam will be defeated.

The Imam Mahdī will rule for a number of years and after him will come the return of Christ, the Imam Husayn and also the other Imams, prophets and saints. Strictly speaking, the term *raj'a* only applies to the return to life of figures who have died such as the Imam Husayn. It is more correct to refer to the *ẓuhūr* (appearance) or *qiyām* (arising) of the Twelfth Imam who did not die and is in occultation. Return is envisaged by Shi'is as involving only the Imams, their supporters and their enemies. Those who were neutral in or unaffected by the struggle will remain in their graves until the Day of Resurrection.[5]

Signs of the Return of the Imam Mahdī

Eschatological expectation in relation to the Twelfth Imam plays a very important part in the popular religion of Twelver Shi'is. In the Traditions relating to the advent of the Mahdī, there are numerous signs that are held to herald his advent. Some of these are related to the general condition of the world when the Mahdī will appear while others give specific signs of his return.

Perhaps the best known of the general signs, a Tradition that is related in both Shi'i and Sunni sources, states that the Mahdī will fill the earth with justice after it has been filled with injustice and tyranny.[6]

Some modern Shi'is, such as the scholar az-Zanjānī, claim that some of the conditions of the world that have been related as accompanying the advent of the Mahdī appear to have been fulfilled by modern scientific inventions. Thus one of these Traditions seems to be referring to television:

> 'I heard Abū 'Abdu'llāh [the Sixth Imam] saying: the believer, in the time of the Qā'im, while in the east, will be able to see his brother in the west and he who is in the west will be able to see his brother in the east.'[7]

Other prophecies are seen as referring to the radio and aeroplane.[8] The following is a lengthy Tradition quoted from the Sixth Imam, Ja'far aṣ-Ṣādiq, by Kulaynī which describes the moral degradation at the time of the coming of the Mahdī and is seen as referring to several modern phenomena such as the secularisation of society, the appearance of women in national parliaments and other consultative assemblies and the advent of the 'permissive society':

When you see that truth has died and people of truth have disappeared, and you see that injustice prevails through the land; and the Qur'an has become despised and things are introduced into it that are not in it and it is turned towards men's desires; and you see the people of error having mastery over the people of truth; and you see evil out in the open and the doers of evil are not prevented nor do they excuse themselves; and you see moral depravity openly manifest and men being content with men and women satisfied by women; and you see the believer silent, his word not being accepted; and you see the sinful lying and he is not refuted nor does his deceit redound upon him; and you see the lowly despising the great; and you see the wombs cut open; and you see he who boasts of moral depravity is laughed at and is not spurned; and you see young men being handed over like women and women co-habiting with women and their numbers increasing; and you see men spending their wealth on things other than pious deeds and no-one opposes or hinders them; and you see the onlooker turn his back on the efforts of the believer; and you see one person molesting his neighbour and no-one prevents it; and you see the unbeliever joyful because he does not see gladness in the believer when he sees corruption in the world; and you see alcoholic drinks being drunk openly . . . and you see women occupying places in the assemblies just as men do and usury is carried out openly and adultery is praised . . . and you see the forbidden thing made legal and the legal thing forbidden; and you see that religion becomes a matter of opinion and the Book and its laws fall into disuse; and you see the leaders drawing close to the unbelievers and away from good people; and you see the leaders corrupt in their rule; . . . and you see men eating what their wives have obtained as a result of their immorality and knowing this and persisting in it; . . . and you see places of entertainment appearing which no-one who passes them forbids them and no-one is bold enough to put an end to them; and you see a worshipper only praying in order that the people may see him; and you see the experts in religious law devoting themselves to things other than religion, seeking the world and leadership; and you see the people living together like animals; and you see the pulpit from which fear of God is enjoined but the speaker does not act in the manner he has enjoined others to act; . . . and when you see the tokens of truth that I have taught, then be aware [of the advent of the Mahdī] and seek salvation from God.[9]

There are several similar prophecies such as the following Tradition from the Imam 'Ali concerning the coming of the Imam Mahdī:

I do not know when it will be any more than you do but some signs and conditions will follow one another, and the signs are these: When the people allow the saying of prayers to die out; and they destroy trust; and they regard lying as permissible; and they take usurious interest; and they sell religion in exchange for the world; and they employ fools; and they consult women; and they cut open the wombs; and they follow their lusts; and they take the spilling of blood lightly; and their discernment is weak; and tyranny becomes a source of pride; and the leaders become profligate, the ministers oppressors, the ulama faithless and the poor depraved; and false testimony is made; immorality, lies, crime, and repression are carried out openly; and books are embellished, the mosques adorned and the minarets made tall; . . . and women assist their husbands in trade out of greed for the things of this world; and sinners are extolled and listened to; and the leader of the people is the most despicable of them and he is wary of the libertine, fearing his evil, and he gives credence to the liar and has faith in the traitor, and he imitates young girls; and men appear like women and women appear like men; . . . the best place to live on that day will be Jerusalem, for there will certainly come a day for the people when each of them will eagerly desire to be one of its inhabitants.[10]

Islam itself will be in a degraded state at the time of the advent of the Mahdī:

The Apostle of God said: 'There will come a time for my people when there will remain nothing of the Qur'an except its outward form and nothing of Islam except its name and they will call themselves by this name even though they are the people furthest from it. Their mosques will be full of people but they will be empty of right guidance. The religious leaders (*fuqahā*) of that day will be the most evil religious leaders under the heavens; sedition and dissension will go out from them and to them will it return.'[11]

With respect to specific signs of the coming of the Mahdī, there are some signs that the Sunnis and Shi'is are agreed upon (for Shi'is, of course, the Mahdī is the Twelfth Imam):

1. That the Mahdī will be a descendant of the Prophet Muhammad of the line of Fāṭima.[12]
2. That he will bear the name Muḥammad.[13]
3. He will rule for either seven, nine or nineteen years.[14]
4. His coming will be accompanied by the raising of a Black Standard in Khurāsān. These Traditions state: 'If you see it [the Black Standard] then go to it even if you have to crawl over the snow, for with it is the Mahdī, the vicegerent of God.'[15]
5. His coming will be accompanied by the appearance of Dajjāl (the Anti-Christ) in the East.[16]

The Shi'i sources are very prolific in their descriptions of what will occur at the time of the coming of the Mahdī. Among these numerous, sometimes contradictory, Traditions, the following are the most commonly reported regarding the specific signs presaging the advent of the Mahdī:[17]

1. Before his coming will come the red death and the white death. The red death is the sword and the white death is the plague.[18]
2. Several figures will appear: the one-eyed Dajjāl, the Sufyānī and the Yamanī. Another figure, the Pure Soul (an-Nafs az-Zakiyya), will be assassinated.
3. The sun will rise from the West and a star will appear in the East giving out as much light as the moon.[19]
4. The Arabs will throw off the reins and take possession of their land, throwing out the authority of the foreigners.[20]

5. A caller will call out from heaven.[21]
6. There will be a great conflict in the land of Syria until it is destroyed.[22]
7. Death and fear will afflict the people of Baghdad and Iraq. A fire will appear in the sky and a redness will cover them.[23]

About the Mahdī himself, the following Traditions are recorded:

1. He will not come in an odd year.[24]
2. He will announce himself in Mecca between the Corner (of the Ka'ba) and the Station (of Abraham) and will summon the people to pay allegiance to him.[25]
3. He will go from Mecca to Kūfa.[26]
4. As for his appearance, he is a young man of medium stature with a handsome face and beautiful hair which flows onto his shoulders. A light dawns from his face. Black is the colour of the hair of his beard and of his head. He is the son of the best of mothers.[27]
5. The Mahdī will do what the Prophet did. He will demolish whatever precedes him just as the Prophet demolished the structure of the Time of Ignorance (*al-Jāhiliyya* – the period before Islam).[28]
6. He will come with a new Cause – just as Muhammad, at the beginning of Islam, summoned the people to a new Cause – and with a new book and a new religious law (*Sharī'a*), which will be a severe test for the Arabs.[29]
7. Between the Mahdī and the Arabs (the Quraysh), there will only be the sword.[30]
8. The Qā'im when he arises will experience as a result of the ignorance of the people worse than what the Apostle of God experienced at the hands of the ignorant people of the Time of Ignorance because the Apostle of God came to a people who worshipped stones and wood but the Qā'im will come to a people who will interpret the Book of God against him and will bring forward proofs from it against him. When the flag of the Qā'im is raised, the people of both East and West will curse it.[31]
9. When the Qā'im arises, he will rule with justice and will remove injustice in his days. The roads will be safe and the earth will show forth its bounties. Everything due will be returned to its rightful owner. And no people of religion will remain who do not show forth submission (Islām) and acknowledge belief (Īmān), . . . And he will judge among the people with the judgement of David and of Muhammad . . . At that time men will not find anywhere to give their alms or to be generous because riches will encompass all.[32]
10. All knowledge is encompassed in 27 letters and all that the messengers of God have brought is two of these letters, and so the people only know these two letters. But when the Qā'im will arise, he will bring forth the other 25 letters and will spread them among the people.[33]

With the coming of the Mahdī, there will occur the return (*raj'a*) of other figures of the past:

1. The first to return will be the Imam Husayn who will come with the 72 companions that were killed with him at Karbalā.[34]
2. There will also occur the return of Jesus which is also anticipated in the Sunni traditions.[35]
3. The 313 who fought with the Prophet at the Battle of Badr will also return.[36]
4. The other Imams and prophets of former ages will also return.[37]

Consequences of the Occultation of the Twelfth Imam

The Occultation of the Twelfth Imam left a considerable gap in Shi'i theory. The Imam was both the spiritual and political head of the community. He interpreted the law and was theoretically responsible for its execution. The Lesser Occultation in which the four agents each successively claimed to be the mouthpiece of the Hidden Imam was followed by the Greater Occultation in which there was no communication. And yet the Imam had left no specific instructions as to how the community was to be organised in his absence. In particular, the Imam's role as the head of the community was left vacant and a number of functions invested in him as head of the community thus theoretically lapsed. Initially this did not matter too much since the Shi'is had no political power and therefore such theoretical functions of the Imam as leading the *jihād* and the Friday prayer could easily be dispensed with.

In later centuries, however, as Shi'i states arose, a tension arose between the theoretical consequences of the Occultation and political realities. Since the Twelfth Imam, though hidden, still lives and is the Lord of the Age and the leader of the community, there can be no theoretical justification for taking his place. And yet the political reality was that the Shi'i states that arose in later centuries had at their head either a king or an amir who had arrogated to himself some of the functions of the Hidden Imam.

The political consequences of this divergence between theoretical consideration and political realities have caused continuing tension between government and religion throughout the ages. No-one has seriously questioned the ulama's arrogation of certain functions of the Hidden Imam (see Chapter 10 for a fuller description of the ulama's gradual assumption of these functions). But the ulama have often expressed doubt and antagonism to the assumption of political power by temporal rulers on the grounds that this was usurpation of the prerogatives of the Hidden Imam. Over the years, whenever the temporal rulers were strong and acted with justice, many of the ulama would co-operate with the government and in their writings find justifications for the temporal state while others would be muted in their opposition or more commonly indifferent to political matters. But when rulers became weak or tyrannical, the ulama would re-emerge with their claim to represent the Hidden Imam and would voice their opposition to the temporal authorities. This was to be the pattern of historical events, particularly in Iran after the emergence of the Safavid dynasty.

9

Doctrines, Ritual Practices and Social Transactions

The main sources for all rituals and legal practices in Islam are the Qur'an and the Traditions (*ḥadīth*). In the matter of basic theological principles, however, Shi'is hold that reason is the primary source.

The Qur'an

The Qur'an is considered to be the Word of God revealed through Muhammad acting as God's mouthpiece. The text of the Qur'an in the recension compiled under the direction of the third Caliph, 'Uthmān, is accepted by both Sunnis and Shi'is.

There is, however, considerable evidence that the early Shi'a did not accept the standard text of the Qur'an. Even as late as the time of Shaykh al-Mufīd, there was considerable discussion among the Shi'a as to what had been omitted from the Qur'an by the enemies of 'Ali, although by that time there was a consensus that nothing had been added. In other words, it was felt that although the standard text of the Qur'an represented God's word with no human additions, part of the text extolling 'Ali and pointing to his Imamate had been excised by his enemies.

Although most Shi'is eventually took the view that nothing had been omitted or added to the Qur'an, traces of the earlier view are enshrined among some of the *ḥadīth* and are even reproduced in some of the later books. The following are some examples taken from the *Biḥār al-Anwār*, the important collection of *ḥadīth* made by the seventeenth-century scholar, Muḥammad Bāqir Majlisī:

1. In the verse: 'God has chosen Adam, Noah, the family of Abraham and the family of 'Imrān above all beings' (Qur'an 3:33), the phrase 'and the family of Muhammad' is considered to have originally been present after the phrase 'family of 'Imrān'.[1]
2. In commentary upon the verse: 'O would that I had not chosen such-

and-such as a friend' (Qur'an 25:28), the Sixth Imam, Ja'far aṣ-Ṣādiq, said: 'In 'Ali's copy is: "O would that I have not chosen the second as a friend," and this will appear one day.'[2] This is a clear reference to Abū Bakr who is known as *ath-Thānī* (the second) because he was the second in the cave during Muhammad's flight from Mecca.

3. The phrase: 'You are the best of people' (*khayr al-umma*, Qur'an 3:110), should read: 'You are the best of Imams' (*khayr al-a'imma*).[3]
4. The Qur'an has been altered so that it has dropped the names of the successors (*awṣiyā*, i.e. the Imams) and the hypocrites (*munāfiqun*, i.e. the enemies of the Imams).[4]

A small minority of Shi'is have attempted to get much larger passages (and even whole *sūras*) accepted as being missing portions of the Qur'an but without success.[5]

Commentary (*tafsīr*) on the Qur'an has become an important branch of the religious sciences in Shi'ism as in Sunnism. Shi'is, however, have tended to emphasise the esoteric interpretation (*ta'wīl*) of the Qur'anic verses by the Imams. An example of Shi'i commentary can be found in the interpretations of verses in relation to the Imamate in Chapter 7.

The best known of the Shi'i commentaries on the Qur'an are two very early *tafsīrs* by 'Alī ibn Ibrāhīm al-Qummī and Muḥammad al-'Ayyāshī and two later works, *At-Tibyān* (The Exposition) by Shaykhu't-Ṭā'ifa Muḥammad aṭ-Ṭūsī and the *Majma' al-Bayān* (Collection of Elucidation) by al-Faḍl ibn al-Ḥasan aṭ-Ṭabarsī. A recent work, *al-Mīzān* (The Balance) by 'Allāma Muḥammad Ḥusayn Ṭabāṭabā'ī, may well come to be regarded as the equal of these in importance.

The Traditions (Ḥadīth)

Since the Prophet and, for Shi'is, the Imams were sinless and infallible, their words and deeds are a guide and model for all to follow. These were eventually written down after being transmitted orally for several generations. Thus each *ḥadīth* consists of the names of the chain of transmitters (*isnād*) followed by the text (*matn*) of the Tradition being transmitted. The *ḥadīth* constitute the *Sunna* (practice) of the Prophet and Imams. They are also frequently called *khabar* (information, plural *akhbār*) by Shi'is.

In Sunni Islam there are six collections of Traditions relating to the Prophet and passed on by his companions which are regarded as canonical. In Shi'i Islam, however, the majority of the companions, in accepting the Caliphate of Abū Bakr, 'Umar and 'Uthmān in preference to 'Ali, are considered to have erred and, therefore, cannot be regarded as reliable transmitters of Traditions. The Shi'i Traditions usually rely on the words or actions of one of the Imams and even those that go back to the Prophet are usually transmitted through one of the Imams. It was clear to Muslim scholars that large-scale forgery of Traditions was occurring in order to support factional and political opinions. The Muslim answer to this problem was to develop a whole branch of the religious sciences which consisted of examining the chains of transmitters in order to assess the reliability of Traditions. These were then classed according to their reliability into one of four categories: *ṣaḥīḥ* (correct), *ḥasan* (good), *muwaththaq* (trustworthy) and *ḍa'īf* (weak). The exact definitions of these categories are not, however, very clear and different authorities will place the same Tradition in different categories. In addition, the Traditions were classified as *mutawātir* (successive) meaning Traditions handed down through several chains of reliable authorities and considered as genuine in every generation from the time of Muhammad and the Imams; and *khabar al-wāḥid* (plural *āḥād*) meaning Traditions which are only known through one chain of transmitters. The former are regarded as binding while the latter may be used as a guide.

There are four early collections of the *ḥadīth* that have become regarded by Shi'is as canonical. These were written by three authors who are known as the 'Three Muḥammads':

a. *Al-Kāfī fī 'Ilm ad-Dīn* (The Sufficient in the Science of Religion) by Muḥammad al-Kulaynī (d. 328/939). This is the only one of these four to contain a section on the fundamentals of the religion (*uṣūl ad-dīn*, see below in this chapter).

b. *Man la yaḥduruhu al-Faqīh* (He who has no Jurist present) by Muḥammad ibn Bābūya (d. 381/991).

c. *Tahdhīb al-Aḥkām* (The Rectification of Judgements) by Shaykh Muḥammad aṭ-Ṭusī, Shaykhu'ṭ-Ṭā'ifa (d. 460/1067).

d. *Al-Istibṣār* (The Perspicacious) by the same author.

In addition to these four, there are three other books which belong to more modern times and which are highly regarded in this field. Their authors have also been named as a modern 'Three Muḥammads'.

a. *Al-Wāfī* (The Complete) by Muḥammad ibn Murtaḍā, known as Mullā Muḥsin-i Fayḍ (d. 1091/1680).

b. *Wasā'il ash-Shī'a* (The Means of the Shi'a) by Muḥammad ibn Ḥasan, known as al-Ḥurr al-'Āmilī (d. 1104/1692).

c. *Biḥār al-Anwār* (Oceans of Lights) by Muḥammad Bāqir Majlisī (d. 1110/1699).

Even more modern is the collection *Mustadrak al-Wasā'il* (The Rectification of *al-Wasā'il*) by Ḥusayn an-Nuri aṭ-Ṭabarsī (d. 1320/1902).

The need for information regarding the transmitters of the Traditions in order to be able to assess their reliability led to a large number of biographical dictionaries. The most important of these are the three on *Rijāl* by Aḥmad ibn 'Alī an-Najāshī, Muḥammad ibn 'Umar al-Kashshī and Shaykhu'ṭ-Ṭā'ifa, and the bio-bibliographical work, the *Fihrist*, also by Shaykhu'ṭ-Ṭā'ifa.

Each generation of the ulama is regarded as transmitters of the Traditions and so biographical works on the later ulama are also an important part of the Shi'i literature. Among the most well-known of these are:

a. *Ma'ālim al-'Ulamā* (Guide-posts of the Ulama) by Ibn Shahrāshūb
b. *Amal al-'Āmil* (The Hope of the [Jabal] 'Āmil) by al-Ḥurr al-'Āmilī
c. *Lu'lu'āt al-Baḥrayn* (The Pearls of Bahrain) by Yūsuf al-Baḥrānī
d. *Nujūm as-Samā* (The Stars of the Firmament) by Muḥammad 'Alī Kashmīrī
e. *Rawḍat al-Jannāt* (The Garden of Paradise) by Muḥammad Bāqir al-Khwānsārī
f. *Qiṣaṣ al 'Ulamā* (Stories of the Ulama) by Muḥammad Tunukābunī
g. *Ṭabaqāt A'lām ash-Shī'a* (The Generations of the Eminent Persons of the Shi'a) by Āghā Buzurg Ṭihrānī
h. *A'yān ash-Shī'a* (The Notables of the Shi'a) by Muḥsin al-Amīn

Independent Investigation and Blind Imitation

There are several verses in the Qur'an which forbid the blind imitation (*taqlīd*) of others in matters of religion (Qur'an 5:104–5; 17:36; 21:52–4; 43:22–4). However, this prohibition is interpreted to refer only to the fundamentals of religion (*uṣūl ad-dīn*). As far as the details of law and ritual practices are concerned, knowledge of these, although incumbent upon the believers, is what is called *wājib kifā'ī*. This means an obligation which if undertaken by a sufficient number of the community need not be undertaken by the rest. In other words, provided a sufficient number of persons undertake the detailed study of religious law and ritual (i.e. the ulama and, especially, the mujtahids or *fuqaha*), it is not obligatory for the ordinary believer. It is obligatory, however, for all to follow the provisions of the religious law, the *Sharī'a*. Therefore it is necessary for every believer who has not made a special study of the *Sharī'a* to seek out the person who is known to him as the most learned in the religious law and to follow that person. This following of a mujtahid is called *taqlīd* (imitation) and the person doing it is called a *muqallid* while the mujtahid becomes *marja' at-taqlīd* (reference point for imitation).

Thus, in summary, belief in the fundamentals of the religion must be the result of each individual's own independent investigation and must not be the result of merely following one's parents or religious leaders. However, with respect to the subsidiary elements of the religion (*furū' ad-dīn*), religious law and rituals, these can only be learned through extensive study and anyone who has not carried out this study follows the guidance of those who have.

The Fundamental Elements of the Religion (Ūṣūl ad-Dīn)

Both Sunni and Shi'i Islam agree on three fundamental elements of religion: *Tawḥīd* (the unity of God), *Nubuwwa* (prophethood) and *Ma'ād* (the resurrection). However, to this the Shi'is add two further fundamentals: *Imāma* (the Imamate) and *'Adl* (Justice of God).

1. *Tawḥīd (Divine Unity)*

At its simplest level, this is the assertion in the first half of the *Shahāda* (declaration of faith) which says: 'There is no god but God' (*lā ilāhā ila Allāh*). Over the centuries, Sunnis have accused Shi'is of violating this fundamental doctrine by elevating the station of the Imams and venerating them to a point where they become partners with God in the people's hearts. Shi'is, of course, reject this accusation, stating that it has originated from the early heresiographers lumping the Twelver Shi'a with the *ghulāt* or extremists.

In the dispute between the Mu'tazilī and Ash'arī theological positions that concerned Islam a great deal in its early days, Shi'is took the Mu'tazilī viewpoint. One consequence of this is that they hold the names and attributes of God to have no independent or hypostatic existence apart from the Being and Essence of God. Any suggestion of these names and attributes being conceived of as separate is thought to entail polytheism. It would even be incorrect, for example, to say that God knows by His Knowledge which is in His Essence. The correct statement is: God knows by His Knowledge which is His Essence. Similarly the viewpoint held by Sunni theologians, that the Qur'an is the uncreated, eternal Word of God, is considered to set up two eternal entities (God and the Qur'an) which is polytheism. Thus the Shi'is consider the Qur'an to have been created in time.

Also related to the Mu'tazilī position adopted by Shi'ism is the assertion that God has no physical form and that such Qur'anic verses as seem to imply that the believer shall achieve a beatific vision of God should be understood metaphorically and not literally as should those verses that appear to attribute to God physical organs such as a face or hands, etc.

More philosophically-minded Shi'i writers have expanded the concept of *tawḥīd* to include such concepts as the unity of the heart and mind and the integration of the individual in society. This sort of interpretation of *tawḥīd* is particularly prominent in the writings of 'Alī Sharī'atī (see pp. 258–9).

2. *Nabuwwa (Prophethood)*

Each prophet is an intermediary between God and man. The mission of the prophet is to bring God's revelation in its pure form to man. This revelation, the word of God, is in the form of teachings and laws to guide mankind. In addition, the prophet also leads mankind and interprets the word of God. In order to carry out his mission, God bestows sinlessness or infallibility upon the prophet and thus the prophet is also the perfect model of the teaching that he brings.

Throughout the ages God has sent many prophets to mankind in different parts of the world. According to the Traditions these have numbered 124,000 or 144,000. Certain of the more important prophets are called *Ulū al-'azm*, prophets endowed with constancy. These are those prophets that brought a book and a new religious law and in the Qur'an they are also called *rusul*, apostles (from God). Among those recognised to be such prophets are Noah, Abraham, Moses, Jesus, until in the succession of the prophets, Muhammad is reached.

Muhammad is not considered to be just a prophet for the Arabs or for the limited area in which he lived, but a prophet with teachings from God for the whole world.

3. *Ma'ād (the Resurrection)*

In the Qur'an there are numerous verses about the Day of Resurrection and the Day of Judgement. Indeed, most of those *sūras* revealed during the Meccan period of the Prophet's life have a large eschatological content. The occurrence of the resurrection is considered a logical necessity of divine justice, since only with the resurrection can each man's full reward and punishment be given.

4. *Imāma (The Imamate)*

This subject, which is distinctive to Shi'ism as compared to Sunnism, is fully discussed in Chapter 7.

5. *'Adl (Divine Justice)*

It may, at first sight, seem strange that just one of God's attributes, His justice, has been picked out by Shi'is as one of the fundamental elements of their faith. But in fact this is another historical remnant of the Mu'tazilī-Ash'arī debate in the period when Shi'i doctrine was being crystallised in the 4th–5th/10th–11th centuries. The Mu'tazilī position, which was eventually adopted by Shi'is, stressed the individual's own responsibility for his own action and God's subsequent judgement of these actions according to His justice. Ash'arism, which was adopted by many of the Sunnis, stressed much more that God created man's acts and thus there is little room for a man's own volition in this doctrine. It was because of the fierce debate that raged at this time that the Mu'tazilī concept of divine justice became enshrined as one of the fundamental principles of Shi'ism.

Ritual Practice ('Ibādāt)

Ritual practices are traditionally divided into eight elements. One factor that has been given a great deal of importance in the works of some Shi'i writers is the intention (*niyya*) in the mind of the believer when performing the ritual. The intention must be pure; the ritual is performed for the love of God – not for the sake of social standing or even the reward of paradise. In the following sections, the various ritual practices will not be described in detail as this would take a great deal of space but rather the differences from Sunni practice will be briefly described:

1. *Obligatory Prayer (Ṣalāt or Namāz)*

The word *ṣalāt*, or in Persian *namāz*, has been translated as obligatory prayer to distinguish it from other forms of prayer which are dealt with later in this chapter. The obligatory prayers are to be said five times a day by all Muslims; sunrise, noon, afternoon, evening and night. However, Shi'is consider it permissible to run together the noon and afternoon and the evening and night prayers so that the prayers are only said on three separate occasions during the day. The Prophet is said to have considered this an allowable practice and there is some support for this view even in the Sunni collections of *ḥadīth*.[6]

The call to prayer (*adhān*) has three slight differences in Shi'ism as compared to Sunnism. The phrase 'Come to the best of actions' is added. It is considered that this phrase was in the original *adhān* but was omitted on the orders of the Caliph 'Umar. 'Umar is also considered to have added the phrase 'Prayer is better than sleep' to the dawn *adhān* and so this is omitted by Shi'is. The addition of the phrase 'I bear witness that 'Ali is the *Walī Allāh*' (literally: the friend of God, but here meaning the guardian of the religion of God) after the declaration that Muhammad is the Apostle of God is considered to be commendable but not obligatory.

Preparatory to the prayers themselves are the ablutions (*wuḍū*). Here again there are minor differences between Sunni and Shi'i practice. In Shi'ism, for example, the water is allowed to run from the elbow to the palm, while Sunnism decrees the opposite direction.

The content of the obligatory prayer itself contains no more variations from the Sunni formula than the variation among the four Sunni schools themselves. The only distinctively Shi'i feature is the insistence that the forehead be placed on dust or the earth (and preferably a block of baked mud from the earth of Karbalā) during the prostration phase of the prayers, whereas the Sunnis place their foreheads directly onto their prayer-mats.

2. *Fasting (Ṣiyām, Ṣawm)*

During the whole of the month of Ramaḍān, food, drink, smoking and sexual intercourse are forbidden from dawn to sunset. The physical abstentions are only symbolic of an inner purification of the character. The fast of the Shi'is is a little longer than the Sunni fast in that they wait until the sun has completely set.

3. *Alms (Zakāt)*

The alms or poor-rate is levied on crops, livestock, gold, silver and cash. It is not payable by anyone whose debts exceed his assets. The formula for deriving how much is levied is complicated in the case of livestock and grain. With respect to gold, silver and cash, it is approximately two and one half percent once a minimum threshold of assets is exceeded.

This tax is, according to the text of the Qur'an (9:60), intended to assist the poor and needy, those in debt and travellers. It is also used for ransoming captives of war and the expenses of collecting and administering the tax.

The principal difference between Shi'ism and Sunnism is that whereas in Sunnism this tax is paid to the state which is responsible for supervising its disbursement according to the provisions of the Qur'an, in Shi'ism it is paid by the believers to their *marja' at-taqlīd* for disbursement (see pp. 206–7).

4. *The One-Fifth Tax (Khums)*

Also in the Qur'an (8:41) is a provision for an annual tax of one-fifth. This is levied by Shi'is on net income (after paying all expenses), net increase in land holdings, stored gold, silver and jewellery, mined products, items taken from the sea and war booty. This tax is to be spent on the Prophet, his family, orphans, the needy and travellers.

Among Shi'is, half of the *khums* (i.e. a one-tenth tax or a tithe) is considered to be the share of the Imam (*sahm al-Imām*), being the Imam's inheritance from the Prophet. This share of the Imam is paid by the believers to their *marja' at-taqlīd* in his capacity as the representative (*nā'ib al-'āmm*) of the Imam.

5. *Pilgrimage (Ḥajj)*

Once in a lifetime, pilgrimage to Mecca is enjoined for those who can afford it. There is an extensive ritual for the performance of the pilgrimage covering every aspect of the five key days, the sixth to the tenth days of the month of Dhu'l-Ḥijja. The details of this are much the same for Sunnis and Shi'is. Shi'is are highly recommended to complete their pilgrimage by travelling to Medina and visiting the tomb of the Prophet and of Fāṭima and the Second, Fourth, Fifth and Sixth Imams at al-Baqī' cemetery.

6. *Religious War (Jihād)*

Participation in the *jihād* is obligatory for all able-bodied male Muslims. However, since it is only the Imam who can call for offensive *jihād* against the non-Muslim world, this obligation has effectively lapsed with the occultation of the Imam though defensive *jihād* is still obligatory. However, *jihād* in its metaphorical meaning, the war against one's own corrupt desires and inclinations, is an ever-present battle. Some forms of missionary endeavour in the non-Muslim world have also been referred to as *jihād*.

7. *Enjoining to Do Good (Amr bi'l-Ma'rūf)*

This is an injunction that every Muslim should lead a virtuous life, perform all the religious obligations and act in accordance with the religious law (*Sharī'a*). In addition, he should enjoin all other Muslims to do the same (see Qur'an 16:125).

8. *Exhortation to Desist from Evil (Nahy 'an al-Munkar)*

It is obligatory for every Muslim to avoid all vices and other evil actions prohibited in religious law. It is also obligatory to enjoin this on others and to act to prevent evil being committed (see Qur'an 3:103, 109).

These last two injunctions have become the focus of a great deal of debate in the writings of 'Alī Sharī'atī and in post-revolutionary Iran.

Doctrines and Practices Specific to Shi'ism

In the field of doctrines, Shi'is have placed doctrines specific to themselves in parallel with those accepted by Sunnism.

The field of jurisprudence may be divided into ritual observances (*'ibādāt*) and social transactions (*mu'āmalāt*). As far as the former are concerned, Shi'ism does not differ much from the four schools of Sunnism. But with respect to social transactions (e.g. marriage, inheritance, etc.) there are more marked divergences. Shi'is have, however, tended to highlight their differences from Sunnis, even in the field of ritual observances, by emphasising parallel rituals that are specific to Shi'ism.

1. *Shi'i Doctrines*

In the matter of doctrines, as has already been demonstrated, Shi'is place alongside the unity of God, God's justice which they define in such a way as to set it apart from the same Sunni concept. Parallel to the doctrine of prophethood, Shi'is place the Imamate, while even with such a powerful concept as the Day of Resurrection, Shi'is displace its importance by emphasising the Return of the Twelfth Imam and focusing the attention of the believers on this event (see Chapter 8).

2. *Prayers*

The Friday prayer has never held the same importance among Shi'is as it has among Sunnis. With the Occultation of the Twelfth Imam who is the true leader of the Friday prayer, the significance of this observance is diminished. In most Shi'i centres, although the Friday prayer is performed, it does not attract the large numbers seen in other Muslim communities. But this situation has changed in Iran since the 1979 Revolution (see p. 298).

In addition to the obligatory prayers, Shi'is have a large number of prayers, revealed by the Imams, which are for use either on special occasions such as the Ramaḍān fast or are purely devotional in nature. This type of prayer is known as *du'ā* or *munājāt*.

3. *Visiting Shi'i Shrines (Ziyārat)*

The pilgrimage to Mecca was, until recent times, beyond the means of the majority of Shi'is resident in Iran and Iraq. It was an expensive and often hazardous journey. Therefore, the custom of visiting the shrines of the Imams was built up as an alternative parallel activity given an importance which in the eyes of the ordinary believer often appeared to exceed that of the pilgrimage to Mecca. Visiting the Shrines of 'Ali at Najaf, Husayn at Karbalā, the Seventh and Ninth Imams at Kāẓimayn, of Imām Riḍā at Mashhad and of Fāṭima Ma'sūma, the sister of the Imām Riḍā, at Qumm, became an important activity in Shi'i religious life and one in which comparatively humble persons could participate. In the 19th century (and to a lesser extent among the older generation today), it became customary to designate persons who had visited the Shrines at Karbalā and Mashhad by such prefixed titles as Karbalā'ī and Mashhadī, in parallel to the designation of Ḥājjī given to those who had performed the pilgrimage to Mecca (the *Ḥajj*). The conferring of these designations appears to vary from area to area depending on the distance to the shrines. Among the Shi'is of southern Iraq, for example, there is no particular designation for visiting the shrines at nearby Karbalā and Najaf but a visit to distant Mashhad confers upon the pilgrim the designation *Zā'ir* (visitor). Similarly, in Khurāsān and Afghanistan, visiting Mashhad does not confer a title, but the visitor to Karbalā becomes Karbalā'ī.

Elaborate rituals were drawn up for the performance of the visitation of the shrines, again in parallel to the ritual of the pilgrimage to Mecca. Part of this ritual includes recitation of the prayer of visitation (*Ziyārat-Nāma*). Popular manuals, in particular those written by Muḥammad Bāqir Majlisī, helped to spread this practice among the people.

Visiting the shrines of minor Shi'i saints and, in particular, the descendants of the Imams, also became an important activity with each shrine having its own prayer of visitation. These shrines (called *Imāmzādas*) are to be found in large numbers in Iran, especially in the areas around Qumm, Tehran, Kāshān and Māzandarān which have been Shi'i from the earliest times and therefore tended to be a refuge for 'Alids who were often being persecuted in other parts of the Muslim world. Visiting these minor shrines has become an activity for a day out.

4. *Temporary Marriage (Mut'a)*

Marriage for a fixed term and usually for a pre-determined financial arrangement is considered allowable by Shi'is. The marriage may be for any length of time, even for a matter of hours. There is also a period of time after the marriage during which the woman is not supposed to marry again, although there are ways of getting around this latter law. Sunnis do not hold temporary marriage to be allowable and indeed consider it to be mere prostitution but Shi'is maintain it was a practice that was allowed during the Prophet's lifetime and only later prohibited by the second Caliph, 'Umar. There are indeed some *ḥadīth* in the Sunni literature that tend to confirm this.[7] In Persian, this practice is called *sīgha* and it is also sometimes called *nikāḥ al-muwaqqat* (temporary marriage). Shi'is consider that the Qur'an refers to this practice (see Qur'an 4:24).

5. *Religious Dissimulation (Taqiyya)*

Religious dissimulation while maintaining mental reservation is considered lawful in Shi'ism in situations where there is overwhelming danger of loss of life or property and where no danger to religion would occur thereby. The following Qur'anic verse (16:106) is held to justify this belief: 'Whoever disbelieves in God after believing – *except for those who are compelled while their hearts are firm in faith* – and then finds ease in his disbelief, upon him will be the wrath of God.' (The section of this verse in italics is held to refer to *taqiyya*.) Living as a minority among a frequently-hostile Sunni majority, the condition of most Shi'is until the rise of the Safavid dynasty, made such a doctrine important to Shi'is.

6. *Divorce (Ṭalāq)*

In general terms, divorce is made more difficult under Shi'i law than under Sunni. Only the stricter divorce according to the Sunna (*ṭalāq as-sunna*) and not the easier innovated divorce (*ṭalāq al-bida'*) is allowed. As distinct from the Sunni schools, Shi'i law holds that the statement of the divorce formula must be made explicitly, in the presence of two witnesses and is not allowable if made in the state of intoxication or rage. Both Shi'is and Sunnis agree that if a man divorces his wife three times, he cannot marry her again unless she is first married to another. Shi'is, however, do not allow the three statements of divorce to be made on one occasion.

7. *Inheritance*

Under Sunni law, where there are males and females equally close in kinship to the deceased, then the inheritance passes to the male in preference to the female. In Shi'i law, however, the presence of male heirs does not exclude the female, although the share of the male is, in accordance with a Qur'anic rule, double that of the female.

The more accommodating attitude to women expressed in Shi'i law over divorce and inheritance has been attributed to the important position held by Fāṭima among Shi'is. Fāṭima's position is crucial for the line of Imams after 'Ali since it is through her that they inherit their link with the Prophet. But for a further analysis of why Shi'i law differs from Sunni law, see p. 184.

10

Shi'i Jurisprudence and the Religious Hierarchy

Shi'i Islam can be said to have three facets in its religious expression: the popular religion of the masses, the mystical religion of the Sufis and the scholarly legalistic religion of the clerical classes (the ulama). Of these three, it is undoubtedly the last which has dominated the others in terms of the respect and influence it enjoys. Although there are other schools of jurisprudence in Shi'i Islam (see Chapter 12), it is the Uṣūlī School which predominates and which will be considered in this chapter.

When Twelver Shi'i Islam first emerged as a distinct entity separate from other Shi'i groups at the turn of the 2nd-3rd Islamic centuries (8th/9th centuries AD), it was principally the ulama who took the lead in defining its doctrines and evolving its polemics. In Sunni Islam the Caliph was looked upon as the symbolic head of the community even when he had ceased to exercise any political power. But in Shi'i Islam, during the Occultation of the Imam, the Shi'is tended to look to the most learned of their ulama, such figures as Shaykh al-Mufīd and Shaykhu'ṭ-Ṭā'ifa, as the heads of the community.

In most of its legal and juristic forms and practices, Twelver Shi'ism was two centuries or more behind Sunni Islam and tended to follow the latter very closely. Thus the canonical books of Traditions (*ḥadīth*) were written towards the end of the 4th/10th and during the 5th/11th centuries by Kulaynī, Ibn Bābūya and Shaykhu'ṭ-Ṭā'ifa (see p. 174) and it was not until the 8th/14th century that 'Allāma al-Ḥillī systematised the methods for organising and evaluating the *ḥadīth* literature.

It used to be stated that Shi'i Islam came to follow Sunni Islam so closely in legal matters that its jurisprudence does not differ more from the four schools of Sunni jurisprudence than they differ among themselves. But a recent writer has postulated that, although they use the same methods and terminology, Sunni and Shi'i law are fundamentally different in that Sunni law is based on the assumption that the Islamic revelation only modified the existing customary tribal law while Shi'i law assumes that Islam represents a fundamental break and a new legal system based on the 'nuclear family'.[1]

The Development of the Principles of Jurisprudence (Uṣūl al-Fiqh)

The mainstream of Twelver Shi'i Islam is called the Uṣūlī School because it adheres to certain principles (*uṣūl*) of jurisprudence (see pp. 223–4). Historically, it would appear that among the earliest Shi'i ulama, such as Kulaynī and Ibn Bābūya, the most important activity was transmission of *ḥadīth*. Thus the Traditions related by these scholars often praised the transmitters of *ḥadīth* (see the Maqbūla of Ibn Ḥanẓala and other Traditions cited in the section 'The Theoretical Basis to the Ulama's Authority' later in this chapter). The proud boast of the Shi'a at this time was that whilst Sunni law had to rely on such fallible methods as *qiyās* (analogical reasoning) and *ijtihād* (innovative exegesis using independent judgement), Shi'is were able to obtain knowledge directly from the Traditions of the Imams.

However, as time progressed and the complexities of life threw up problems that could not be solved in such a simple manner, the discipline of *fiqh* or jurisprudence grew up to cover that part of the *Sharī'a* (religious law) for which there were no certain answers. Simultaneously as the Mu'tazilite School began to influence Shi'ism during the lifetime of Shaykh al-Mufīd and his successors and the use of reason became increasingly important in the development of theology, so this had an effect in the sphere of jurisprudence. The use of deductive reasoning based on the Qur'an and the Traditions became increasingly important. Eventually Shi'i jurisprudence came to be based on four pillars; the Qur'an, the *ḥadīth*, *ijma'* (consensus) and *'aql* (reasoning or intelligence).

As for the *ḥadīth*, initially the Shi'is collected all Traditions uncritically. It was 'Allāma al-Ḥillī who established the methodology and terminology of the critical study of the *ḥadīth* literature (*dirāya*) closely modelled on the Sunni methods. It is interesting to note that the two Shi'i scholars who made the greatest contribution to starting the systematic study of *ḥadīth* in Shi'ism, 'Allāma al-Ḥillī and Shahīd ath-Thānī, were also almost the only two ulama of this period who are specifically recorded as having studied under Sunni as well as Shi'i teachers.[2] Further confirmation that there was no real analytical study of the *ḥadīth* in Shi'ism prior to this time comes from the statement that Shaykh 'Alī ibn Sulaymān al-Baḥrānī (d. 1064/1653), a contemporary of Shahīd ath-Thānī, was the first to introduce the study of the *ḥadīth* in Bahrain.[3]

Having demonstrated the unreliability and uncertainty of much of the *ḥadīth*,[4] 'Allāma al-Ḥillī reorganised Shi'i jurisprudence so as to make reasoning (*'aql*) its central feature. Thus the Shi'i jurist uses *'aql*, usually supported by the other three sources of law (the Qur'an, the *ḥadīth* and consensus), to arrive at legal decisions and this process is called *ijtihād*. Thus *ijtihād* may be defined as the process of arriving at judgements on points of religious law using reason and the principles of jurisprudence (*uṣūl al-fiqh*). The aim of *ijtihād* may be thought of as uncovering (through knowing transmitted sources as well as through rational processes) knowledge of what the Imams would have decided in any particular legal case. Although theoretically the process of *ijtihād* may appear to give mujtahids a great deal of latitude for innovative thinking, in practice the concurrent attitude of *iḥtiyāṭ* (prudence and caution, lest one stray from the path of the Imams) has severely limited any initiatives outside traditional avenues of thought and practice.

The question of differences of opinion (*ikhtilāf*) among the ulama poses something of a problem since it would obviously be difficult for the ulama to be impugning the views of each other and still consider themselves to be collectively the *Nā'ib al-'Āmm* (see next section of this chapter) of the Hidden Imam and the purveyors of the Imams' traditions. This difficulty was overcome by arguing that if the truth lay in only one of two opposing views and this could not be discerned through the techniques of *uṣūl al-fiqh,* then it would be obligatory for the Hidden Imam to manifest himself and give a decision. If he does not manifest himself, the truth must lie with both parties and, indeed, as long as the Hidden Imam remains in occultation, the Shi'i community can be sure it has produced no ruling that is in error.

In addition, any decision agreed upon by a consensus (*ijma'*) of the whole community must include the opinion of the Hidden Imam and thus also be correct. Thus for any major point of law or doctrine, individual Shi'i mujtahids come to various differing opinions (*ikhtilāf*) through use of *ijtihād*. From considering these varying opinions, the community finally arrives at a consensus (*ijma'*) which is the truth.

Although much of the theoretical basis of Shi'i jurisprudence had been laid by such figures as 'Allāma al-Ḥillī, Shahīd al-Awwal and Shahīd ath-Thānī in the 14th–16th centuries AD there was then a hiatus while the Uṣūlī-Akhbārī controversy was debated. It was not until Bihbahānī, at the end of the 18th century, completed the Uṣūlī victory that much of this theory was put into practice. It was from this time on that the term mujtahid, one who exercises *ijtihād*, became synonymous with the term *faqīh*, one who is an expert in jurisprudence, and the importance of the *Sharī'a* (religious) courts began to increase greatly at the expense of the *Urfī* (common law) courts. Indeed, Bihbahānī has been named in some sources as the founder (*mu'assis*) of the Uṣūlī School.

The next major development in the principles of jurisprudence was brought about by Shaykh Murtaḍā Anṣārī and this also represents the formulation of this branch of the religious sciences that remains current to the present day. Shaykh Murtaḍā Anṣārī's most important contribution was in deriving a set of principles to be used in formulating decisions in cases where there was doubt. Shaykh Murtaḍā Anṣārī and his successors who developed this school of law divided legal decisions into four categories:

a. *Certainty (qaṭ')*. This represents cases where clear decisions can be obtained unambiguously from the Qur'an or reliable Traditions and there is no need to involve reasoning (although, since the laws embodied in the Qur'an and reliable *ḥadīth* are derivable from reason, this method could be used).

b. *Valid Conjecture (ẓann)*. This represents cases where the probability of correctness can be created by using certain rational principles to arrive at individual binding norms.

c. *Doubt (shakk)*. This refers to cases where there is no guidance obtainable from the sources and nothing to indicate the probability of what is the correct answer. It is in relation to these cases that Shaykh Murtaḍā Anṣārī formulated four guiding principles which he called *uṣūl al-'amaliyya* (practical principles); most of Shaykh Murtaḍā's important work *ar-Rasā'il* is taken up with expounding these. They consist of: *al-barā'a* (allowing the maximum possible freedom of action); *at-takhyīr* (freedom to select the opinions of other jurists or even other schools of law if these seem more suitable); *al-istiṣḥāb* (the continuation of any state of affairs in existence or legal decisions already accepted unless the contrary can be proved); and *al-iḥtiyāṭ* (prudent caution whenever in doubt).

d. *Erroneous Conjecture (wahm)*. This refers to decisions where there is a probability of error; such decisions are of no legal standing.

The effect of the development instituted by Shaykh Murtaḍā al-Anṣārī was far-reaching. Whereas previously the mujtahids had restricted themselves to ruling on points where there was the probability or certainty of being in accordance with the guidance of the Imams, the rules developed by Anṣārī allowed them to extend the area of their jurisdiction to any matter where there was even a possibility of being in accordance with the Imam's guidance. This effectively meant that they could issue edicts on virtually any subject. Anṣārī's own strict exercise of *iḥtiyāṭ* (prudent caution) severely restricted this freedom but other mujtahids allowed themselves a freer hand.

Thus, in summary, although God is, of course, the ultimate source of law, he has created reason (*'aql*) as the means of divining the law. The authority of the *Sharī'a* derives from its consistency with *'aql*. Only decisions that are in conformity with *'aql*, as derived through the process of *ijtihād*, are legally valid. Once an individual mujtahid has arrived at a conclusion, he must act according to his own conviction even if other mujtahids have reached different conclusions about the same problem. Therefore, originally it was considered theoretically not permissible for one mujtahid to follow the opinions of another whether living or dead (i.e. *taqlīd* between mujtahids was not permissible). But during the 18th and 19th centuries it became increasingly common for mujtahids to defer to the decision of whomever was considered the most knowledgeable among them and so the concept of the *marja' at-taqlīd* evolved.

It should be kept in mind, however, that despite very considerable differences in the principles of jurisprudence between Shi'ism and all four of the Sunni schools of law, there are fewer differences in the practical application of jurisprudence to ritual observances and social transactions.

Each age has had its own important works on *fiqh* (jurisprudence) and *uṣūl al-fiqh* (principles of jurisprudence). The following is a list of a selection of the most important works from each period of history:

Period	*Fiqh (jurisprudence)*	*Uṣūl al-Fiqh (principles of jurisprudence)*
Buyid and Seljuq	Shaykhu'ṭ-Ṭā'ifa, *an-Nihāya* (The Conclusion)	Shaykhu'ṭ-Ṭā'ifa, *'Uddat al-Uṣūl* (The Instrument of Uṣūl)
Mongol and Timurid	Muḥaqqiq al-Ḥillī, *Sharā'i' al-Islām* (The Laws of Islam); Shahīd al-Awwal, *al-Lum'a ad-Dimashqiyya* (The Gleam from Damascus)	'Allāma al-Ḥillī, *Tahdhīb al-Wuṣūl* (The Rectification of Attainment)
Safavid	Shahīd ath-Thānī, *Rawḍat al-Bahiyya* (The Glorious Paradise); Muḥaqqiq al-Karakī, *Jāmi' al-Maqāsid* (The Compilation of Intentions); Shaykh Bahā'ī, *al-Jāmi' al-'Abbāsī* (The Compilation of [Shāh] Abbās)	Shaykh Ḥasan Ṣāḥibu'l-Ma'ālim *al-Ma'ālim fi'l Uṣūl* (The Guideposts on Uṣūl)
Qājār	Shaykh Muḥammad Ḥasan an-Najafī, *Jawāhir al-Kalām* (The	Mīrzā-yi Qummī, *Qawānīn al-Uṣūl* (Rules of Uṣūl); Shaykh Murtaḍā al-Anṣārī, *ar-Rasā'il*

	Jewels of Utterance); Shaykh Murtaḍā al-Anṣārī, *al-Makāsib* (Profit)	(The Epistles), Ākhūnd Khurāsānī, *al-Kifāya fi'l Uṣūl* (The Sufficiency of Uṣūl)
Twentieth Century	Sayyid Muḥammad Kāẓim Yazdī, *'Urwa al-Wuthqā* (The Firmest Handle)	Shaykh Muḥammad Ḥusayn Nā'īnī, *Taqrīrāt* (The Stipulations); Āyatu'llāh Khū'ī, *Ajwad at-Taqrīrāt* (The Best of Stipulations)

The Evolution of the Role of the Ulama

Initially during the Buyid period it was considered by the Twelver ulama that since the Imam had gone into occultation and there was no longer present his special representative (*Nā'ib al-Khāṣṣ*), the four *Bābs* during the Lesser Occultation (see p. 164), all the functions invested in the Imam had lapsed (*sāqiṭ*). The principal functions of the Imam were considered to be:

a. Leading the Holy War (*jihād*)
b. Division of the booty (*qismat al-fay*)
c. Leading the Friday Prayer (*ṣalāt al-jum'a*)
d. Putting judicial decisions into effect (*tanfīdh al-aḥkām*)
e. Imposing legal penalties (*iqāmat al-ḥudūd*)
f. Receiving the religious taxes of *zakāt* and *khums*.

This doctrine of lapse of the functions of the occulted Imam was almost certainly very convenient politically at first, since it established the Twelvers as being non-revolutionary in sharp contrast with the Ismā'īlīs who, with their Imam-Caliph present in Cairo and their active propaganda, were threatening to destabilise and overthrow the Buyids. Indeed, this consideration may have been one of the principal reasons for the evolution of the doctrine of *Ghayba*, the Occultation of the Twelfth Imam.[5]

However, it soon became apparent that the situation caused by the concept of the lapse of functions of the Hidden Imam was extremely impractical and left the Twelver community at a great disadvantage with no leadership, no organisation and no financial structure. Therefore, as early as the 5th/11th century, Shaykhu'ṭ-Ṭā'ifa was reinterpreting the doctrine so as to allow delegation of the Imam's judicial authority to those who had studied *fiqh* (jurisprudence, these are called the *fuqahā*), although he implies in his writings that this function should only be undertaken by the ulama if there is no-one else to do it (i.e. that it was a somewhat distasteful task). Shaykhu'ṭ-Ṭā'ifa considered the ulama as the best people to act as agents of the donor in distributing the religious taxes since they knew to whom it should be distributed; but nevertheless individuals were free to do this themselves if they wished. He allowed the *fuqahā* to organise the Friday prayers in the absence of the Imam or his special representative.[6] This last point remained controversial with such figures as 'Alamu'l-Hudā, Ibn Idrīs and 'Allāma al-Ḥillī disagreeing.

By the 7th/13th century, Muḥaqqiq al-Ḥillī (d. 676/1277) was able to advance these concepts very considerably. He extended the judicial role of the ulama to *iqāmat al-ḥudūd* (the imposition of penalties, i.e. by the ulama themselves rather than the temporal authorities). In his writings it is possible to see the evolution in his thinking whereby the *fuqahā* develop from being deputies of the donor for the distribution of religious taxes in his early writings to being the deputies of the Hidden Imam for the collection and distribution of the taxes in his later works.[7]

Muḥaqqiq al-Karakī (d. 940/1533) was the first to suggest, arguing from the *ḥadīth* of 'Umar ibn Ḥanẓala (see below), that the ulama were the *Nā'ib al-'Āmm* (general representative – as distinct from the four *Bābs* who were each the *Nā'ib al-Khāṣṣ*, the special representative) of the Hidden Imam. But he restricted his application of this argument to the assumption of the duty of leading Friday prayers.[8]

It was Shahīd ath-Thānī (d. 966/1558) who took the concept of *Nā'ib al-'Amm* to its logical conclusion in the religious sphere and applied it to all of the religious functions and prerogatives of the Hidden Imam. Thus the judicial authority of the ulama now became a direct reflection of the authority of the Imam himself. It was now obligatory to pay the religious taxes directly to the ulama as the trustees of the Imam for distribution, and the donor who distributed these himself was considered to obtain no reward. Furthermore, Shahīd ath-Thānī extended the range of those eligible to receive money from the *zakāt* (poor tax) to include the *ṭullāb* (religious students) and the ulama themselves, who thus became the recipients of the money as trustees and were also able to expend the money on themselves and their circle of students. Even in the field of defensive *jihād* (defending the realms of Islam against attack by an infidel), Shahīd ath-Thānī identified a role for the ulama. Only in the field of offensive *jihād* did he allow that the role of Hidden Imam had lapsed pending his return.[9]

Thus up to the time of Shahīd ath-Thānī, the ulama were gradually evolving the theoretical basis of their authority. But the Safavids were too strong and maintained too close a control over the ulama to enable them to put much of this into practice. It was left to the Qājār period, after the victory of the Uṣūlīs over the Akhbārīs (see p. 127), before the ulama were able to bring most of these theoretical functions into practice.

The end of the Safavid dynasty brought about the weakening of the state system of courts with government-appointed judges (*qāḍīs*) and the mujtahids were able to replace these with *Sharī'a* courts of their own to which people came in increasing numbers, thus enabling the ulama to assert their judicial authority.

During the first Russo-Iranian War (1804–13), Fatḥ 'Alī Shāh's son and heir, 'Abbās Mīrzā, who was conducting the campaign, turned to the ulama and obtained from Shaykh Ja'far Kashifu'l-Ghiṭā (d. 1227/1812) and other eminent clerics in Najaf and Isfahan a declaration of *jihād* against the Russians, thus implicitly recognising their authority to issue such a declaration – one of the functions of the Hidden Imam. Furthermore, Kāshifu'l-Ghiṭā used the opportunity to extract from the state acknowledgement of the ulama's right to collect the religious tax of *khums*.[10]

During the same period, another eminent mujtahid, Sayyid Muḥammad Bāqir Shaftī (d. 1260/1844), was asserting the right of carrying out the penalties imposed in his religious court (*iqāmat al-ḥudūd*). He is said to have executed some seventy persons.[11]

Thus, one by one, the lapsed functions of the Hidden Imam were being taken over by the ulama. However, there was as yet no claim by the ulama to political authority.

In summary, it may be said that over some nine centuries, by a process of exegesis and innovative interpretation, the ulama were able to effect a very considerable theoretical consolidation of their authority but in such small stages as to make the process scarcely discernible to each generation and thus to give the impression of there having occurred no change at all. This is not meant to imply, however, that this was a conscious process among the ulama. They were merely responding to social and economic pressure and particularly the advent of the Shi'i Safavid and Qājār states, in such a manner as to maximise both the benefit to themselves and the consolidation of their authority, while at the same time justifying and explaining the social and political realities around them.

The Ulama's Attitude Towards Political Authority

Sunni Islam developed its constitutional theory in the presence of a Sunni state. Thus the political sphere was incorporated into the doctrine of the religious sphere and religion became one of the main supports of the state. Obedience to the ruler became a religious obligation even if the ruler were unjust, for that was preferable to anarchy. Conversely the judgement of one of the ulama appointed as judge (*qāḍī*) would be considered competent only because of his appointment by the government and regardless of his ability, knowledge or sense of justice.

The development of Shi'i Islam, on the other hand, took place for much of the time with the Shi'is a persecuted minority in a Sunni state. Thus the Shi'is, during their early period, had no need of someone like Māwardī, who in Sunnism integrated the political sphere into the religious sphere.

One of the key statements in the Qur'an around which much of the exegesis on this issue has revolved is the verse: 'O believers! Obey God and obey the Apostle and those who have been given authority [*ūlā al-amr*] among you' (Qur'an 4:59). For Sunnis, *ūlā al-amr* (those who have been given authority) are the rulers (Caliphs and kings) but for Shi'is this expression refers to the Imams.

All political authority for Shi'is is theoretically vested in the Imam. However, the Imam of the age is occulted and thus his political authority has lapsed. This tendency to depoliticise the Imamate, which was important for the Shi'is in the 4th/10th century, was reinforced during the Ilkhanid and Timurid period when, under the influence of Ismā'īlī and Sufi thought, the Imam became seen more in terms of a religious saviour, interceding in Heaven with God for men, rather than as a veiled earthly figure. Thus the concept of the Imamate became removed from consideration in the sphere of political authority and became a theological concept. As a result of this, Shi'i Islam did not at this stage evolve any real political theory and the ulama came to regard politics as outside their realm of concern.

Since legitimacy could not be given nor withheld from any government, temporal authorities came to rely on the pre-Islamic Sassanian Iranian concept of kingship as the basis of their authority and the title 'Shadow of God on Earth' which was adopted by the kings is an expression of that.

The Shi'is saw themselves as an 'elect' (*al-khāṣṣa*) living among the generality (*al-'āmma*) of the Muslims. The Sunnis were and still are acknowledged as Muslims but only Twelver Shi'ism confers true belief (*Īmān*) and makes one a true believer (*mu'min*). For Shi'is, the sacred community consisted of the believers with the ulama at their head guiding and directing their actions. All political, administrative and economic matters not directly concerned with the *Sharī'a* and therefore, not under the control of the ulama, were outside the concern of the sacred community.

Thus, whereas Sunnis lived their lives in a system where political affairs were integrated into the sacred community, Shi'is lived simultaneously in two different systems, the sacred community and the profane community. Since the ulama and the political leaders of the community were in fact rivals for the leadership of the people, this not infrequently meant that Shi'is were living in two communities between which there was rivalry and tension.

For the ulama there were three possible ways of relating to the state. All three are, of course, justified by their proponents through exegesis from the Qur'an and *ḥadīth*:

1. *Political Co-operation*. The ulama can co-operate with the state and provide it with recognition. They can accept appointment to official positions in the state. This can be justified by the contention that the state is preventing anarchy and only where there is order can the provisions of the *Sharī'a* be fully implemented. It is permissible to co-operate with a state that is enforcing the Shi'i *Sharī'a* and the ruler of which is just. Co-operation with a non-Shi'i or unjust government is only permissible under compulsion on the pain of death or grave loss when the provisions of *taqiyya* (religious dissimulation, see p. 183) come into play.

Theoretically, even when they accept a state's appointment (as judge or some other post), this is not the sole source of the Shi'i ulama's authority. Their authority derives also by virtue of the concept of their being the *Nā'ib al-'Āmm* (general representative) of the Hidden Imam.

Many of the leading ulama of the Safavid period took this view, but, in later periods, ulama who took posts identified with the government were looked upon with some disdain by their colleagues.

2. *Political Activism*. The ulama can actively involve themselves in politics, seeking to bring the temporal authorities into line with the *Sharī'a*. Thus if the government complies with them they dominate it (as happened during parts of the Safavid period and also in present-day Iran). Or else they oppose the government. This attitude can be justified since all government is usurping (*jā'ir*) the authority of the Hidden Imam and the ulama as the *Nā'ib al-'Āmm* of the Hidden Imam and as experts in the *Sharī'a* are the best persons to guide the government. Western scholars have tended to make a great deal out of this political option (even to the extent of disregarding the others), and it cannot be denied that there have been a few dramatic occasions, such as the agitation against the Tobacco Regie in 1891–2, the Constitutional movement in 1905–9 and the 1979 Revolution in Iran, when this option has been taken up by the majority of the ulama with dramatic political effect. But this should not obscure the fact that this has not been the attitude of the majority of the ulama for most of the time. For example, Mīrzā Muḥammad Ḥasan, Mīrzā-yi Shīrāzī, the foremost Shi'i mujtahid of the late 19th century, spent most of his life politically aloof. However, for a very short period of time he chose to take a political initiative and opposed the state over the question of the Tobacco Regie.

3. *Political Aloofness*. The ulama can remain totally aloof from all political matters. This has always traditionally been the attitude of the majority of the ulama. Indeed, it has usually been considered that only

ulama who have remained aloof from all other activity and concentrated on furthering the *Sharī'a* can rise to the highest ranks (this did not apply, however, during Safavid times nor does it in present-day Iran).

The writings of Shi'i ulama through the ages have shown elements of all three of these attitudes and thus it cannot be said that any coherent Shi'i theory of political legitimacy or any unified stance by the ulama towards the state has existed. Even individual ulama have changed their attitude at different periods in their lives according to circumstances, as the above example of Mīrzā-yi Shīrāzī shows.

Up to the time of the Safavids, the question of a political theory in Shi'i Islam did not arise, for up to that time the ulama had existed in the milieu of a strongly Sunni state (or, as in the case of the Buyids, a Shi'i state that made no concessions to the ulama).

The early Safavid monarchs rested their power base on a Shi'i claim that was closer to the ideas of the 'extremists' (*ghulāt*) than of Twelver Shi'is. They were venerated as divine figures by their troops. The late Safavids emphasised their claimed descent from the Seventh Imam, Mūsā al-Kāẓim, as the source of charismatic religious authority. Although they gave the ulama a free hand in teaching Twelver doctrines to the people, they were sufficiently dominant to inhibit the ulama from trespassing into the field of political theory. The ulama, however, did come to regard themselves as guardians of public morals and towards the end of the Safavid period did not hesitate to speak out if they felt that the king was straying from the path of the *Sharī'a*. The Safavid dynasty can thus be seen as a period which saw a certain degree of separation between church and state but with the state exercising a degree of authority over the religious field through its pseudo-religious charismatic claims and its political control.

The Qājār dynasty claimed no hereditary charisma in the same way as the Safavids did and so it turned to the ulama for justification of its rule. The ulama were prepared to grant this but used the opportunity to consolidate their position and affirm their independence. For example, Shaykh Ja'far Kāshifu'l-Ghiṭā, as already mentioned, gave a *fatwā* (legal decision) declaring *jihād* on the Russians and authorising Fatḥ 'Alī Shāh to fight them. This gave some derived *de jure* legitimacy to the Qājār government.

It was ulama like Mīrzā Abu'l-Qāsim Qummī (d. 1231/1816) and, more particularly, Sayyid Ja'far Kashfī (d. 1267/1850), who produced a fully-developed Shi'i political theory which justified the Qājār dynasty. Sayyid Ja'far considered that the Imam held both the religious and political leadership in the community. With the Occultation of the Twelfth Imam, however, his functions have been divided and devolve upon two groups, who are the *Nā'ibs* (representatives or vicegerents) of

Figure 1 Painting. Muhammad and ʻAli destroying idols in the Kaʻba. When Muhammad entered Mecca in triumph following the surrender of the Meccans, he went into the Kaʻba and placing ʻAli upon his shoulders instructed the latter to destroy the idols there. From a Safavid manuscript of Mīr Khwānd, *Rawḍat aṣ-Ṣafā*. According to the tradition in many schools of Islamic painting, the face of the Prophet (and in this case ʻAli) is not shown but his head is surrounded by flames.

Figure 2 Painting: Muhammad appoints ʻAli as his successor at Ghadīr Khumm. On the farewell pilgrimage, at Ghadīr Khumm, Muhammad ascended a makeshift pulpit of saddles and addressed his followers, appointing ʻAli as their Master (see p. 15). From a Safavid manuscript of Mīr Khwānd's *Rawḍat aṣ-Ṣafā*.

Figure 3 Najaf: Shrine of the First Imam, 'Ali. From an aerial view taken in 1927.

Figure 4 Karbalā: panoramic view. The dome on the right is the Shrine of Imam Husayn, the dome on the left the Shrine of his half-brother 'Abbās; from a photograph by Dieulafoy taken in 1881.

Figure 5 Karbalā: Sarcophagus of Imam Husayn.

Figure 6 Panorama of Qumm: drawn by Sir John Chardin who visited Iran during the Safavid era in 1666 and 1672.

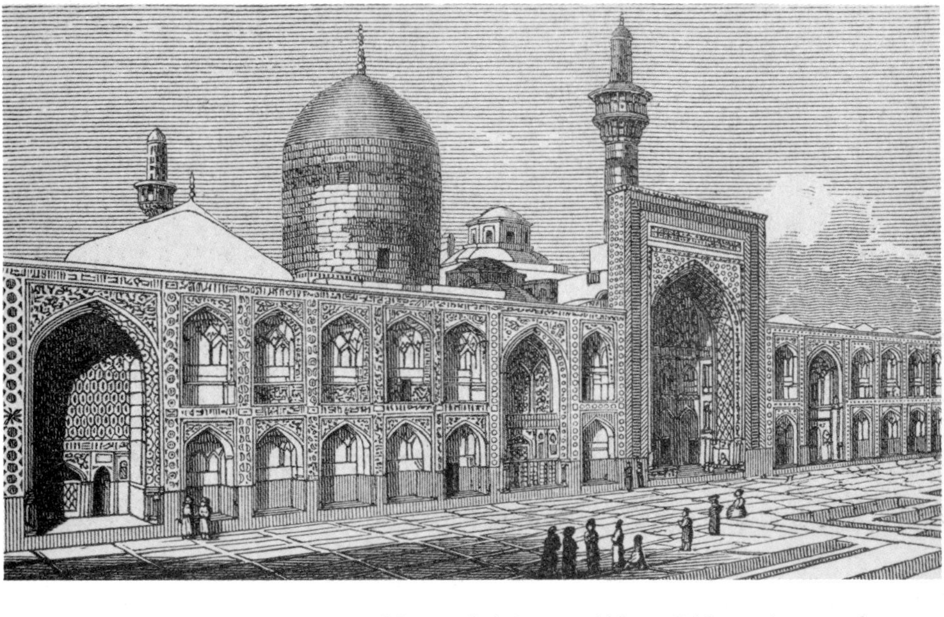

Figure 7 Mashhad: Shrine of the Eighth Imam, 'Alī ar-Riḍā, a nineteenth-century print.

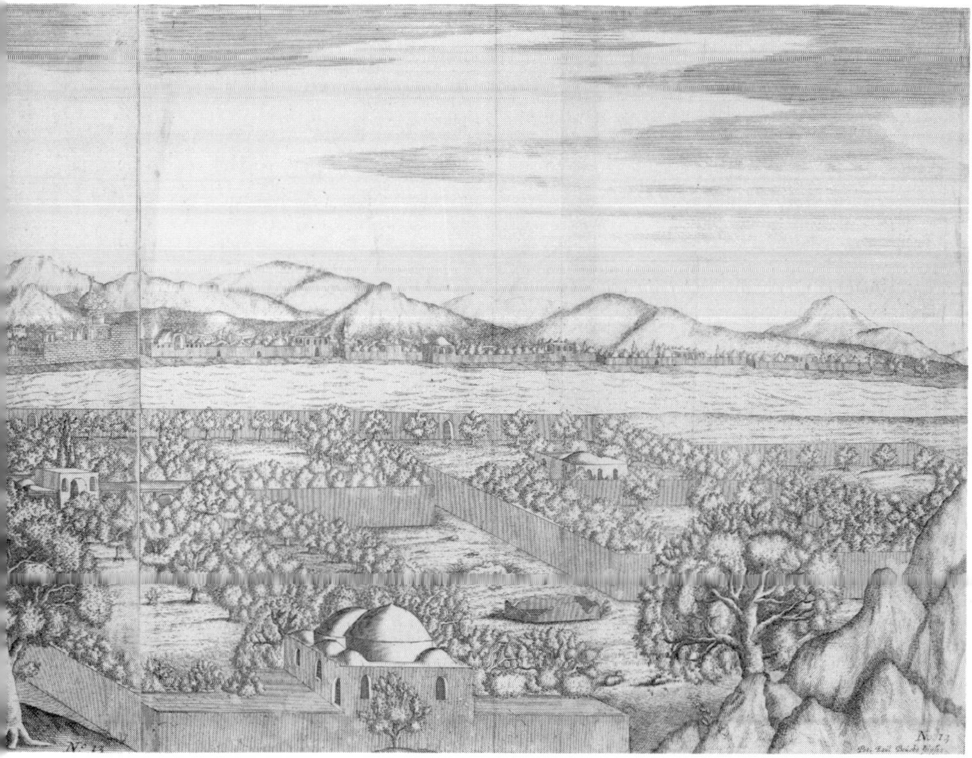

Figure 8 Sāmarrā: in the foreground is the gold-domed shrine of the Tenth Imam, 'Alī al-Hādī, and the Eleventh Imam, Ḥasan al-'Askarī. Behind this is the Mosque of the Occultation beneath which is the underground chamber in which the Twelfth Imam is said to have disappeared (see p. 162). From an aerial view taken in 1927.

Figure 9 Karbalā: Shrine of the Third Imam, Husayn.

Figure 10 Kāẓimayn: Shrine of Imams Mūsā al-Kāẓim and Muḥammad at-Taqī, the Seventh and Ninth Imams. This was originally the site of the Quraysh cemetery outside Baghdad. It is now a suburb of Baghdad. (aerial photograph of early 1920s.)

Figure 11 Qumm: Shrine of Fāṭima, the sister of the Eighth Imam. This picture shows the shrine from the New or Atabegi Court; in the foreground, the women are gathering for prayer and a little further back to the left of the pond, the men are gathering. Around the periphery of the courtyard are cloisters behind which are the tombs of statesmen from the Qājār period. The tomb of Fāṭima is under the gold dome in the centre. The dome to the left is called the Masjid-i-Bālā-Sar and is relatively new.

Figure 12 Sulṭāniyya: Tomb of Oljeitu (Khudābanda). Tomb of the Ilkhanid ruler Oljeitu who converted to Islam and later to Shiʿism and took the name Khudābanda. 'One of the world's great buildings'; Arthur Pope, *A Survey of Persian Art*.

Figure 13 Aleppo: capital of the Hamdanid and Mirdasid dynasties and centre of Shiʻi scholarship for the last half of the twelfth century AD.

Figure 14 Ḥilla: built in 1101 as the Mazyadid capital by Sayfu'd-Dawla. For two hundred and fifty years from about 1200 to 1450, it was the centre of Shiʻi scholarship. From an aerial view taken in 1927.

Figure 15 Ardibīl: Shrine of Shaykh Ṣafī, the founder of the Safavid Sufi order which went on to produce the Safavid dynasty.

Figure 16 Isfahan: Madrasa Chahār Bāgh, one of the religious colleges of the city. Also known as Madrasa Shāh Sulṭān-Ḥusayn or Madrasa Mādar-i Shāh (College of the Mother of the Shāh). Built in 1710.

Figure 17 Isfahan: Maydān-i Shāh. The magnificent square built by Shāh 'Abbās I at the centre of his capital. This view was drawn by Cornelius le Bruyn in 1704 and shows: on the right, the Mosque of Shaykh Luṭfu'llāh; and on the left, the 'Ālī Qāpū, the royal pavilion which stood at the gateway to the royal palace. From this picture it would appear that the square was used as a market at this time.

Figure 18 Isfahan: Maydān-i Shāh, after a photograph taken by Dieulafoy in 1881.

Figure 19 Shah 'Abbās I.

Figure 20 Mullā Muḥammad Bāqir Majlisī, the most powerful religious figure of the Safavid period.

Figure 21 Tehran: the Qājārs moved the capital of Iran to Tehran. This view was drawn by Morier in 1809.

Figure 22 Nādir Shāh.

Figure 23 Fatḥ 'Alī Shāh.

Figure 24 Lucknow, India: view of Lucknow in the nineteenth century. In the foreground is the gateway called the Rūmī Darwāza. To the far right, the rectangular building is the Great Imāmbārā and next to this is the Mosque of the Great Imāmbārā. These three structures were begun by Āṣafu'd-Dawla in 1784 as a famine relief measure.

Figure 25 Juba‘: an important Shi‘i village of the Jabal ‘Āmil. Several of the important ulama of the fifteenth to seventeenth centuries came from this village: Shahīd ath-Thānī, Shaykh Ḥasan Ṣāḥibu'l-Ma‘ālim and Shaykh Bahā'ī. A print dated 1857.

Figure 26 Isfahan: Masjid-i Shāh. Begun by Shāh 'Abbās I in 1612 but not completed by the time of his death.

Figure 27 Isfahan: Madrasa Chahār Bāgh. A group of mullās holding a discussion in one of the religious colleges of Isfahan.

Figure 28 The Bastinado: a frequent form of punishment meted out by both civil and religious courts especially in the Qājār era.

Figure 29 Shaykh Murtaḍā Anṣārī, who from about 1855 until his death in 1864 was the sole *marja' at-taqlīd* for the Shīʿī world.

Figure 30 A mujtahid and several mullas: after a photograph taken by Dieulafoy in Tabrīz in 1881.

Figure 31 Mulla preaching to a crowd in a mosque during Muḥarram. Photograph taken in Tehran in early 1900s.

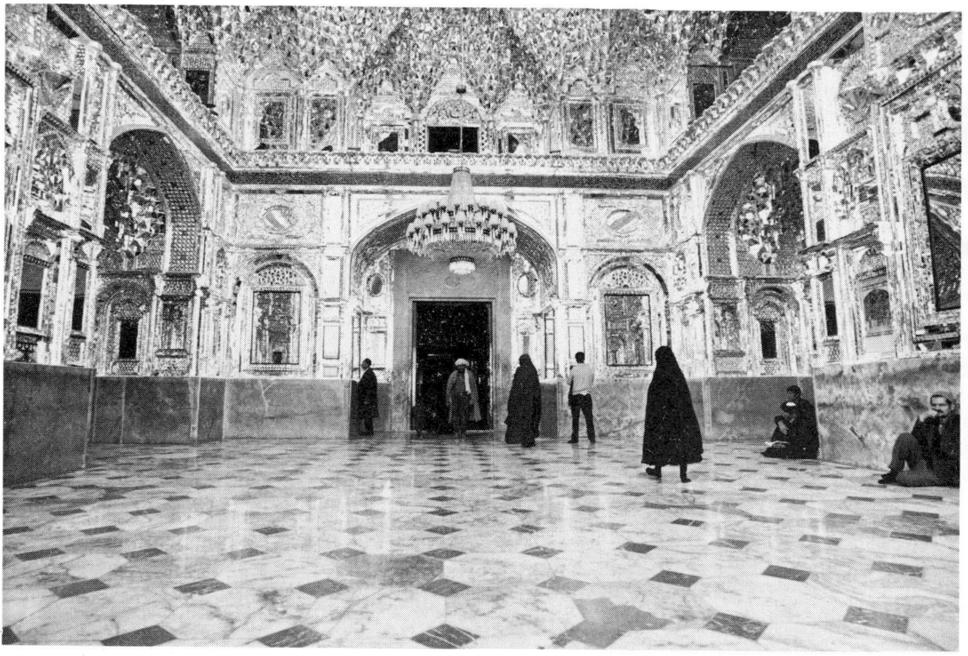

Figure 32 Qumm: interior of the Shrine of Fāṭima, showing decorative mirror-work.

Figure 33 Shaykh Aḥmad Aḥsā'ī, founder of the Shaykhī School.

Figure 34 Sayyid Kāẓim Rashtī, second leader of the Shaykhī School.

Figure 35 ʿAllāma Sayyid Muḥammad Ḥusayn Ṭabāṭabāʾī, one of the foremost philosophers and scholars among contemporary Shiʿi ulama

Figure 36 Mahān, near Kirmān: Shrine of Shāh Niʿmatu'llāh Walī, the founder of the Niʿmatu'llāhī order.

Figure 37 Kāẓimayn: Shrine of Imams Mūsā al-Kāẓim and Muḥammad at-Taqī, detail.

Figure 38 Isfahan: interior of Shaykh Luṭfu'llāh Mosque, showing intricate tile work.

Figure 39 Banner depicting scenes from the life of the Imam Husayn: a local variation of the Muḥarram commemorations. A large banner with scenes from the life of Husayn is spread in a public place and the story of Husayn is recited in front of it (*pardih-dārī*). This picture was taken in Shīrāz and the shadow of some branches overhangs the centre of the banner. In the centre is Husayn slaying one of his enemies; the top left shows him with his dying son ʻAlī Akbar; the bottom left shows ʻUbaydullāh striking the decapitated head of Husayn; and to the right of that, the head brought before Yazīd; the bottom right shows the marriage of Qāsim Husayn's nephew, just before the final battle; the right may depict the captured women at the court of Yazīd; the top centre shows Husayn holding his infant son ʻAlī Aṣghar who has been struck by an arrow. As can be seen in popular art forms there is no compunction about depicting the face of the Imam (or of the Prophet) as there is in more formal art (Compare this fig. and fig. 42 with figs. 1 and 2).

Figure 40 *Ta'ziya*: dramatic representation of the martyrdom of Husayn. This picture depicts a *ta'ziya* seen by Dieulafoy in Qazvīn in 1881. It is obviously a small local affair, much less grand than the ones put on by the King or one of the Prince-Governors.

Figure 41 *Rawḍa-Khānī*: recital of the sufferings and martyrdoms of the Imams, in particular the Imam Husayn. The *rawḍa-khān* (reciter) can be seen on the left of the picture. Although the women are shown in the same room veiled, it would be more usual for them to be in another room with the door open or in a curtained-off portion of the room. From a nineteenth- century painting.

Figure 42 Painting over entrance to Ḥusayniyya: this painting over the Ḥusayniyya Mushīr in Shīrāz is a good example of popular religious art. It shows, along the bottom from left to right: the Umayyad troops advancing, led by Ibn Sa'd; Husayn in combat against the Umayyad troops; possibly Husayn on his way to Karbalā; Husayn with his slain infant son, 'Alī Aṣghar; Husayn with his dying eldest son, 'Alī Akbar; Husayn speaking to his sister Zaynab and the women-folk. The top part represents: on the right, possibly the martyrs and the family of Husayn in Heaven standing before Muhammad and 'Ali, the women carrying the head of Husayn, the body of the infant 'Alī Aṣghar and the arm of Husayn's brother 'Abbās which was cut off as he tried to obtain water for the holy family; on the left are the enemies of Husayn in Hell.

Figure 43 Muḥarram processions, accoutrements: traditional items carried in the Muḥarram processions. The pole has a hand at the tip (signifying the five members of the holy family – Muhammad, ʻAli, Fāṭima, Hasan, Husayn). The other object is called a *ḍarīḥ* or *naql* and represents the tomb of Husayn.

Figure 44 Muḥarram processions in Tehran in early 1900s. In the procession can be seen models of the Shrine of Husayn (*naql*) and poles with a hand at the top (see fig. 43).

Figure 45 Muḥarram processions: group carrying a model of the Shrine of Husayn at Karbalā. In India this is called a *ta'ziya* and elsewhere a *ḍarīḥ* or *naq*. Photograph taken in Karachi in 1982.

Figure 46 Muḥarram processions with flagellants: self-flagellation with chains *(zanjīr-zanī)* as a sign of grief and mourning for the martyred Imam Husayn is a common feature of these processions in every part of the Shi'i world. The chains often include, as in this case, metal blades to increase the injury. Photograph taken in Karachi in 1982.

Figure 47 Muḥarram processions, self-mutilation: the practice of cutting open the forehead with a sword (*qumma-zanī*) is not uncommon during the day of ʿĀshūra. This photograph was taken in Tehran in the early 1900s.

Figure 48 Muḥarram processions with flagellants: photograph taken in Karachi in 1982.

Figure 49 Muḥarram processions: in the foreground is a flagellant. In the background is a caparisoned horse which represents the horse of the Imam Husayn. Photograph taken in Karachi in 1982.

Figure 50 Muḥarram processions: beating of the chest. A common feature of the Muḥarram processions in most parts of the Shiʿi world is the rhythmic beating of chests in unison (*sīna-zanī*). Photograph taken in Karachi in 1982.

Figure 51 An *Imāmzāda*: this one is the Imāmzāda Ḥusayn in Qazvīn, from a photograph taken by Dieulafoy in 1881.

Figure 52 Mashhad: Sarcophagus of Imam ʿAlī ar-Riḍā, showing the crush of pilgrims each seeking to obtain blessings (*baraka*) by touching the sarcophagus.

Figure 53 Carriage of corpses to Karbalā. When prominent citizens died, it was customary to carry their corpses to a shrine for burial. The favourite site for this was Karbalā as it was believed that the Mahdī would appear there and those buried there would be resurrected as part of his army.

Figure 54 Imām Rūḥu'llāh Khumaynī.

Figure 55 Three mujtahids of Najaf who supported the Constitutional Revolution. From left to right: Ākhūnd Khurāsānī (Mullā Muḥammad Kāẓim), Mīrzā Ḥusayn ibn Khalīl (Khalīlī) Ṭihrānī and Mullā ʿAbdu'llāh Māzandarānī.

Figure 56 Cartoon: finding reasons for the Constitution in the Qur'ān. From the Iranian magazine *Mullā Naṣru'd-Dīn* which appeared during the Constitutional period.

Figure 57 Shaykh Faḍlu'llāh Nūrī, one of the main clerical opponents of the Constitutional Movement of 1906. Executed in 1909.

Figure 58 Shaykh Ḥasan Mudarris, a leading clerical opponent of the religious policy of Riḍā Shāh.

Figure 59 Isfahan: Shaykh Luṭfu'llāh Mosque, built by Shāh 'Abbās I. It is considered one of the most beautiful buildings in Iran.

Figure 60 Bahā'ī national headquarters in Tehran being demolished in 1955: Mullā Muḥammad Taqī Falsafī, as personal representative of Āyatu'llāh Burūjirdī, looks on as workmen demolish the dome.

Figure 61 Isfahan: Maydān-i Shāh, now renamed Maydān-i Imām Khumaynī.

Figure 62 Sayyid Abu'l-Qāsim Kāshānī. A poster from post-revolutionary Iran.

Figure 63 Āyatu'llāh Sayyid Kāẓim Sharī'atmadārī.

Figure 64 Āyatu'llāh Muḥammad Riḍā Gulpāygānī.

Figure 65 Āyatu'llāh Shihābu'd-Dīn Mar'ashī-Najafī.

Figure 66 Āyatu'llāh Ḥasan 'Alī Muntaẓirī.

The innocent martyr Ayatollah Doctor Beheshti
Beheshti lived and died innocently. He was a thorn in the eyes of the enemies of Islam
Imam Khomeini

Figure 67 Āyatu'llāh Muḥammad Ḥusaynī Bihishtī (1928–1981), a leading figure of the Iranian Revolution until his assassination. A poster from post-revolutionary Iran.

Figure 68 Mashhad: Gawhar-Shād Mosque, built by the wife of the Timurid ruler, Shāh-Rukh. With its blue dome, it

the Hidden Imam: the ulama who are charged with the religious vicegerency and the rulers who have political vicegerency. If these two co-operate then the affairs of the community run smoothly since the ulama cannot apply the *Sharī'a* unless the ruler establishes order, while the ruler needs the ulama without whose guidance he will stray towards injustice and tyranny.[12]

Through this means, Sayyid Ja'far not only satisfied the Qājār dynasty's need for justification but also obtained from the Qājārs their recognition of the ulama's claim. It was work such as this that created the theoretical framework which was to remain the norm in Iran until the 1979 Revolution. Within this framework those ulama who wished to could collaborate with the state and those who wished to could remain aloof.

In the period immediately preceding the 1979 Revolution, groups of ulama can be identified who clearly fall into the three patterns of response to government delineated above:

i. Ulama who co-operated with the state; this group included the Imām-Jum'a of Tehran, Dr Ḥasan Imāmī, 'Allāma Vaḥīdī and others.

ii. The activist ulama who sought to reform the temporal authorities; this group was represented by Āyatu'llāhs Khumaynī, Muntaẓirī and Maḥallātī-Shīrāzī.

iii. Ulama who avoided any interference with political matters; this group included most of the religiously-important ulama and especially the *marāji' at-taqlīd*, Āyatu'llāh Burūjirdī and his successors, Āyatu'llāhs Sharī'atmadārī, Gulpāygānī and Mar'ashī-Najafī.

Although the ulama had, since the Safavid and Qājār periods, claimed to be the *Nā'ib al-'Amm* of the Hidden Imam, they had refrained from the obvious next step of claiming the political authority and temporal rule implicit in their vicegerency. Indeed, Sayyid Ja'far Kashfī and others had specifically denied the ulama such a role. Initially, Āyatu'llāh Khumaynī went along with this view. In his earlier writings such as the *Kashf al-Asrār* he attacked the Shāh's government on the grounds of its injustice and tyranny and because of its secularisation programme. But at this stage Khumaynī's aim was only to exert pressure on the Shāh and government to reform itself. He still allowed the legitimacy of the temporal authorities provided they acted justly, which is defined as acting in accordance with the *Sharī'a*. Khumaynī's view, at this time, was that monarchy is a divine privilege entrusted to the king by the people. Thus it is necessary for every king to obtain his mandate from the people.

In 1963 Khumaynī was exiled following his opposition to the Shāh's reforms. After this, in his addresses to the religious students at Najaf, he began to take a new line. His addresses were published in 1971 in a book entitled *Ḥukūmat-i Islāmī* (Islamic Government). In this book

Khumaynī argues that Islam is not just an ethical religion but has all the laws and principles necessary for government and social administration. Therefore, true Islamic government is a constitutional government with the Qur'an and the Traditions as its constitution. Although there is no specific provision in the Qur'an or the Traditions for designating a ruler during the Occultation, social order is necessary for the *Sharī'a* to be enforced. The Islamic ruler needs to be just (which, as mentioned above, means acting in accordance with the *Sharī'a*) and therefore needs to have an extensive knowledge of the *Sharī'a* in order that his actions may be determined by it. These conditions are fulfilled only by the *faqīh*, the expert in Islamic jurisprudence. Therefore, he is the person most fitted to rule an Islamic society – the *Vilāyat-i Faqīh*, governance by the jurisprudent. The *faqīh* as ruler has the same authority and can carry out the same functions as the Imam, although he is not of course equal to the Imam in station. In all this there is no place for kings or other temporal rulers. These Khumaynī now regards as historical aberrations who, since the death of the Imam 'Ali, have by their very existence blocked the way to the emergence of the true Islamic government.

It is interesting to note that Khumaynī cites Mullā Aḥmad Narāqī (d. 1245/1829) and Shaykh Muḥammad Ḥusayn Nā'īnī (d. 1936) as two previous authorities who held a similar view to himself regarding the political prerogatives of the ulama. These two clerics, even if they did hint at this in their writings, did not make it the central theme of their political theory as Khumaynī does. The most that previous Shi'i writers have claimed is that kings and rulers should be guided in their actions and policies by the Shi'i *faqīh* (a concept embodied in the 1906 Constitution of Iran). Khumaynī, on the other hand, asserts that the *faqīh* should supplant the ruler and rule in his place. Where highly technical matters may need to be dealt with which are beyond the knowledge of the *faqīh*, these tasks may be delegated to those with that type of knowledge, but superintendency of all social and political matters must remain in the hands of a just *faqīh*.

Khumaynī decries those of the ulama who refuse to involve themselves in social and political matters. He considers that these have betrayed the trust and the mission delegated to them by the Imams. Even worse than these, however, are the 'ulama of the court' (*Akhund-hā-yi Darbārī*, i.e. those who have sided with the Shāh and accepted posts under the government). These are the enemies of Islam and must be expelled from their posts.

In summary, Khumaynī has taken the *Nā'ib al-'Āmm* concept to its logical conclusion by asserting the right of the *faqīh* as the deputy of the Imam to superintend all religious, social and political affairs – the *Vilāyat-i Faqīh*.

The Theoretical Basis to the Ulama's Authority

Since the concept of the ulama being the general representative (*Nā'ib al-'Āmm*) of the Hidden Imam became the basis of their authority and influence, the theoretical basis of this concept, and the concept of *Vilāyat-i Faqīh* which is related to and dependent on it, is of some interest.

In fact, there is not a very strong or clear basis in the Shi'i Traditions for the *Nā'ib al-'Āmm* concept. Indeed, had there been such a basis, the whole Akhbārī-Uṣūlī controversy would never have occurred. Most of the Traditions on this subject are called by the technical term 'weak' (*ḍa'īf*), which means that they are transmitted by persons considered unreliable or have other flaws.

The only Tradition relating to this concept that is accepted as reliable by Shi'i scholars is called the Maqbūla of 'Umar ibn Ḥanẓala (the term Maqbūla meaning a Tradition which is accepted as reliable). This Tradition, which is cited on the authority of 'Umar ibn Ḥanẓala, states:

> I asked Abū 'Abdu'llāh (Imam Ja'far aṣ-Ṣādiq) for his opinion concerning two of our companions between whom there was a dispute concerning matters of debt and inheritance and they took the case before the temporal ruler and the courts. He said: 'Whoever has sought their arbitration, whether he be in the right or in the wrong, has sought the arbitration of a false god (*Ṭāghūt*) and whatever is judged his (in this manner), he will have taken illegally, even if it is established that he is right, for he will have taken it by the ruling of a false god. For that is an action that God has decreed should be disallowed when He has said: "They wish to seek the judgement of a false god when they have been ordered to disavow it."' I said: 'And so what should they do?' He said: 'They should look for someone from among them who has transmitted our Traditions and has examined what is permitted by us and what is forbidden and has learned our laws . . . then let them agree to having him give judgement for I have made such a person judge (*ḥākim*) over you.'[13]

There is some ambiguity in the last phrase of this Tradition since the word *ḥākim* can be translated both as judge and ruler. On the face of it, this Tradition sets out the procedure for solving disputes. It forbids taking the case to the law courts of the land but rather enjoins recourse to one of the Shi'i ulama that is acceptable to both parties. However, such Shi'i writers as Muḥaqqiq al-Karakī and Shahīd ath-Thānī argued from this Tradition, and particularly from the last phrase in it: 'I have made such a person judge/ruler over you', that this in fact represented the Imam Ja'far's delegation of authority to them, the *Nā'ib al-'Āmm* concept, while Khumaynī has taken the same argument to its logical extension and stated that only government by a *faqīh* is permissible, the *Vilāyat-i Faqīh*.

Khumaynī has cited a number of other Traditions in connection with his concept of *Vilāyat-i Faqīh* but with these there is either a potential ambiguity which makes the meaning controversial or the Tradition is considered 'weak' by virtue of its transmitters:

i. The Prophet when asked 'Who are your successors (*khulafā*)?' replied: 'Those who come after me, transmit my *ḥadīth* and *sunna* and teach it to the people after me.'[14] However, this can be held to refer to the Imams, who are often referred to in the Traditions as the *khulafā* of the Prophet. Another problem with this *ḥadīth* is that although it is found in several sources through different chains of transmitters, in those sources which are considered most reliable the last phrase 'and teach it to the people after me' is omitted. On the face of it this may not appear an important difference but, to Khumaynī, it is of vital importance since he is concerned to establish that the vicegerency (*niyābat*) of the Hidden Imam rests not just with the ulama who undertake the socially-passive activity of transmitting Traditions but rather with the more socially-active role implied in the phrase 'and teach it to the people after me'. Thus Khumaynī writes at length to establish the case that the correct form of this Tradition includes the last phrase.[15]

ii. The Seventh Imam, Mūsā al-Kāẓim, stated: 'The *fuqahā* (jurists) who are believers (*mu'min*, i.e. Shi'i) are the citadels of Islam.'[16] Khumaynī interprets this Tradition as meaning that the *fuqahā* are entrusted with preserving Islam which in turn means, for Khumaynī, an active social role for the ulama. This Tradition, although entrusting the ulama with a mission, cannot be said to delegate authority to them.

iii. The Prophet is reported as having said: 'The *fuqahā* are the trustees of the prophets . . . as long as they do not . . . follow the Sulṭān . . . '[17] Khumaynī interprets this Tradition as meaning that the *fuqahā* are entrusted with all the authority that the prophets themselves had.

iv. The Sixth Imam, Ja'far aṣ-Ṣādiq, said: 'Beware the government! For government belongs to an Imam who is knowledgeable in the just administration of the law among the Muslims, to a prophet or a prophet's trustee.'[18] This Tradition appears to refer to the Imam but Khumaynī argues that since it clearly states that only someone knowledgeable in Islamic law and just is authorised to govern, in the situation of the Occultation of the Imam this condition is best filled by the *fuqahā*.

v. The Hidden Imam, in answer to a question posed to him through the second of the four agents of the Lesser Occultation, Muḥammad ibn 'Uthmān al-'Amrī, is reported to have replied: 'And as for events that occur, refer them to those who transmit our Traditions, for they are my proof to you and I am God's proof.'[19] Khumaynī interprets this Tradition as making the ulama the point of reference for contemporary social problems as well as points of law.

vi. The Sixth Imam, Ja'far aṣ-Ṣādiq said: 'The ulama are the heirs of the prophets. The prophets did not leave a single dinar or dirham for an inheritance. Rather they left knowledge as an inheritance and whosoever takes from it, has taken an abundant share.'[20] Khumaynī argues that this Tradition does not merely mean that the ulama are the inheritors of the knowledge left by the prophets, but also they inherit the Prophet's authority and rule.

Other Sources of the Ulama's Authority and Social Prestige

The Hidden Imam is thought to be among the body of the Shi'is incognito. Since he must undoubtedly be accounted as one of the learned, there is always the possibility that one of the ulama may indeed be the Hidden Imam. In addition, numerous stories exist of the Hidden Imam manifesting himself to prominent members of the ulama. This feeling that the ulama, and particularly the great mujtahids, are in close contact with the Hidden Imam undoubtedly contributes greatly to their prestige and authority among the ordinary people. Their standing is further bolstered by the attribution to them of miracles (*karamāt*).

During the Qājār period it became normal for the prominent ulama in any town to surround themselves with a band of the town's ruffians, known as *lūṭīs*, to their mutual benefit. The ulama had a ready band who would take to the street and create agitation when it suited the ulama to call them out, and many a governor in nineteenth-century Iran was withdrawn because of such agitation. The *lūṭīs*, in turn, had a protector with whom they could take refuge if the government moved against them. The *ṭullāb* (religious students) attached to the religious colleges were used by the ulama in much the same way in the larger towns. This type of behaviour came to the fore once more in the 1979 Revolution in Iran. Since the Revolution, essentially the same group of persons, now called *Ḥizbu'llāhīs* (the Party of God) are providing support for the radical ulama at the street level. Some of these elements have been incorporated into the Revolutionary Guards.

Also closely involved in the power structure of the religious classes are the Sayyids. These are persons who claim descent from the Prophet through Fāṭima and the Imams. Their prestige in the community is based solely on this heredity. As a class they lay no claim to religious learning (although as individuals many of them do undertake religious education and become ulama as well) but, according to the religious law, they are entitled to part of the *khums* religious tax (see p. 179) and they are highly regarded by the ordinary people. Thus this group are often asked to bless a newborn child and a marriage into a Sayyid family is regarded as highly advantageous. The Sayyids and the ulama are often closely inter-related by marriage and are mutually supportive socially.

Two social groups that usually provide the ulama with support are: the Bazaar (the complex net of merchants, bankers and craftsmen who make up the heart of the traditional Islamic city) an element which has a tradition of being conservative and 'religious';[21] and the *Zūr-Khānas* which are combined gymnasia and wrestling schools (historically these are evolved from the *futuwwa*, see p. 90, and are linked to the *lūṭīs* mentioned above).

Education of the Ulama

Prior to the establishment of a modern school system in Iran, elementary education was provided in the villages and towns by the *maktab*, a school which was usually run by a minor member of the ulama. These gave their pupils a basic literacy but concentrated on memorising passages of the Qur'an (which being in Arabic was unintelligible to the pupils), teaching religious duties (such as obligatory prayers, etc.) and usually also some Persian poetry (Sa'dī, Hāfiẓ, Rūmī, etc.). From the *maktab* students would go on to a *madrasa* (religious college) which would be situated in the larger towns. In the present day, at about the age of fifteen those aiming to become top-ranking ulama will head for the most important centres of religious learning which are, at present, Qumm, Mashhad and Najaf, and will enrol in the *madrasas* there.

The course at a *madrasa* is composed of three levels, and as each level is completed the student (*ṭālib*, plural *ṭullāb*) goes on to the next level. Table 6 shows the subjects taken and books studied at each level.

a. *Muqaddamāt (the preliminary level)*. At this level the emphasis is on obtaining a good grasp of Arabic, which is vital to all further studies. Usually, groups of students will gather around a teacher who will go through the texts with them in lessons lasting between one-and-a-half and two hours. Teachers at this level are usually senior students or assistants of the principal mujtahids.

b. *As-Suṭūḥ (the externals)*. At this level the teachers are usually mujtahids who have only recently obtained their authority of *ijtihād* and are seeking to build up their reputations. A number of these will announce lectures based on the main texts and the students are free to choose which lectures to attend. Students can at the same time develop a special interest by attending lectures in one of the optional subjects but their progress to the next level is dependent on their obtaining a thorough grasp of the main texts in the two principal subjects, *fiqh* and *uṣūl al-fiqh*.

c. *Dars al-Khārij (or Baḥth al-Khārij, graduation classes)*. It will usually have taken students about ten years to reach this stage and thus most will

Table 6: Subjects taken and books studied at each level of studies

Subjects	*Books*	*Authors*
A. MUQADDAMĀT (PRELIMINARY STUDIES)		
Naḥw (Syntax)	*al-'Awāmil*	Mullā Muḥsin al-Qazwīnī
	Ibn Mālik's Alfiyya	Commentary by Suyūṭī
	Sharḥ Qaṭr an-Nada	Ibn Hishām
	Mughnī al-Labīb	Ibn Hishām
	Hidāya	Zamakhsharī
Ṣarf (Grammatical Inflections)	*Ṣarf-i Mīr*	Mir Sayyid Sharīf Jurjānī
	Sharḥ-i Taṣrīf	Taftazānī
	Sharḥ an-Niẓām	Nīshābūrī
Manṭiq (Logic)	*Hāshiya*	Mullā 'Abdu'llāh
	Sharḥ ash-Shamsiyya	Quṭbu'd-Dīn Rāzī
Balagha (Rhetoric)	*al-Mutawwal*	Taftazānī

Optional Subjects include: Literature, Mathematics, Astronomy and often some introductory *fiqh* working from one of the *Risāla Amaliyya* (Tracts on Practice) of one of the contemporary *marāji' at-taqlīd*

B. SUṬŪḤ (EXTERNALS)		
Uṣūl al-Fiqh (Principles of Jurisprudence)	*Ma'ālim fi'l-Uṣūl*	Shaykh Ḥasan Ṣāḥibu'l-Ma'ālim
	Qawānīn al-Uṣūl	Mīrzā-yi Qummī
	Rasā'il	Shaykh Murtaḍā Anṣārī
	Kifāyat al Uṣūl	Ākhūnd Khurāsānī
	Uṣūl al-Fiqh	Muḥammad Ḥusayn Muẓẓafar
	(The last has replaced the first two at Najaf)	
Fiqh (Jurisprudence)	*Sharḥ al-Lum'a*	Shahīd ath-Thānī
	Sharā'i' al-Islām	Muḥaqqiq al-Ḥillī
	al-Makāsib	Shaykh Murtaḍā Anṣārī
	al-'Urwa al-Wuthqā	Sayyid Muhammad Kāẓim Yazdī

Optional Subjects include: *Tafsīr* (Qur'an Commentary or Exegesis), *Dirāya* (Critical study of the *Ḥadīth*), *Rijāl* (Biography of transmitters of *Ḥadīth*), *Kalām* (Theology), *Falsafa* (Philosophy), *Ḥikma* (Theosophy), *'Irfān* (Gnosis), *Ta'rīkh* (History) and *Akhlāq* (Ethics).

C. DARS AL-KHĀRIJ (OR BAḤTH AL-KHĀRIJ, GRADUATION CLASSES)

There are no set books at this level; the student refers to whichever books he needs either in following up lectures and debates or in writing his treatise.

be in their mid-twenties. At this level the teaching is done by the principal mujtahids themselves. Each mujtahid will announce a time and place for his teaching session and the students are free to pick and choose whose lectures they will attend. The subjects are usually *fiqh* and *uṣūl al-fiqh*. If a popular or very eminent mujtahid is giving a session, several hundred students (and even other mujtahids) may be gathered around him. Each mujtahid's method of teaching is of course different, but in general there is a tendency to a dialectical involvement of the audience. One favourite style of teaching is known as *mas'ala-sāzī* (constructing hypothetical examples) and is said to have been introduced by Shaykh Murtaḍā Anṣārī in the 19th century. This consists of posing a hypothetical legal problem and then discussing all the possible ramifications and resolutions of the problem. At the teaching sessions the more senior students are encouraged to argue points with the teacher and thus most students, by the time they complete their studies, are skilled in the art of abstract discursive argumentation.

The culmination of the student's endeavours is the receipt of an *ijāza* (permission or authorisation) from a recognised mujtahid. The student usually prepares a treatise on *fiqh* or *uṣūl al-fiqh* and presents it to the mujtahid. If the mujtahid considers the student himself and the work worthy of it, he issues an *ijāza* which in effect states that the recipient is, in his opinion, capable of exercising *ijtihād* and thus can be called a mujtahid. The more eminent the mujtahid, the more prestigious is the *ijāza* that he signs and any student wanting to achieve recognition will usually try and obtain *ijāzas* from all of the most eminent mujtahids at his centre of learning. It is uncommon to obtain an *ijāza* before the age of thirty and not uncommon for forty- and fifty-year-olds to be still students.

The formal preconditions for being considered to be able to give legal opinions (*iftā*) and thus to be a mujtahid are:

a. Maturity.
b. Being of the male sex (this is the subject of some controversy).[22]
c. Being of legitimate birth.
d. Faith.
e. Intelligence.
f. Justice (integrity).

The concept of justice is not, however, the usual Western view of that word but rather it implies one whose words and deeds are strictly controlled by the *Sharī'a*, refraining from all its prohibitions and performing all of its obligations.

There are no fees for studying at the *madrasas* and indeed the students are given their room and an allowance for their essential needs. This allowance is almost always just enough for subsistence and those students from a poor background who receive no additional funds from home usually lead a very harsh, spartan existence.[23]

The Hierarchy of the Ulama

The clerical class constitutes a fairly distinctive entity in Iran and to a lesser extent in other Shi'i communities. The terms most usually used for a member of this class in Iran is *mullā* or *ākhūnd*. But since these two expressions have acquired a somewhat pejorative connotation, in recent years a third term, *rūḥānī* (spiritual) has been promoted especially by the clerical class itself.

Only a small percentage of those who enter a *madrasa* succeed in obtaining an *ijāza*. Most students leave at some stage before this either out of financial or personal considerations or because they do not have the intellect and perseverance to last the course. Most of those that leave the *madrasa* at an early stage consider themselves members of the ulama, although many will go to other occupations such as merchants, tradesmen and craftsmen. Often a village or town will petition one of the mujtahids to send them a teacher for the *maktab* or a *pīshnamāz* (a prayer-leader), or a position as a *mutawallī* (custodian) of a shrine or endowment will become vacant and the mujtahid will appoint one of his students who obviously does not have the capacity to complete the course to this position. Others will leave the *madrasa* with the intention of becoming a *wā'iẓ* (travelling preacher) or *rawḍa-khān* (narrators of the Karbalā tragedy), although these latter need not have attended a *madrasa* at all.

The obtaining of an *ijāza*, although a considerable achievement and entailing a degree of prestige, does not automatically result in recognition as a mujtahid. For the status of mujtahid can only be achieved by public recognition. In other words, the possessor of an *ijāza*, although considered by his teacher to be worthy of being a mujtahid, does not in fact become one until he gathers among the public a following who are prepared to acknowledge him as such and refer to him on legal matters. The patronage of one of the eminent mujtahids obviously assists greatly in achieving recognition as a mujtahid, but prestige among one's fellow students, family connections and the ability to preach and communicate with the people are also important. There are many who having obtained an *ijāza* fail to achieve recognition as mujtahids and these are sometimes referred to as *mujtahid muḥtaṭ* (mujtahid in abeyance).

Once recognition as a mujtahid has been achieved, movement upwards towards pre-eminence among one's fellow mujtahids is once again dependent on public acclaim of one's piety and learning and also, to a certain extent, the natural result of the death of more prominent mujtahids.

There is no formal organisation or hierarchy among the ulama. Rather the situation has been described as a hierarchy of deference.[24] The lowest ranks of the ulama, the village *mullā*, the *rawḍa-khān*, the *pīshnamāz* of a small mosque, will defer to one or all of the locally-prominent mujtahids, and these in turn will defer to the eminent mujtahids at the main centres of Najaf, Qumm and Mashhad. But since every mujtahid has the obligation and right to exercise independent judgement, this acts to counter any building up of a hierarchy and limits the degree of cohesion and hierocratic order that can be achieved.

Historically, the ulama initially had no hierarchical structure. Members of the ulama would choose to specialise in different fields such as philosophy or theology and would not suffer any loss of prestige thereby, although by far the greatest number studied jurisprudence (*fiqh*) since this was the field for which there was the greatest need in the towns and villages of the Shi'i world.

However, in the late 18th and early 19th centuries this situation changed radically. One of the consequences of the Uṣūlī triumph over the Akhbārīs (see p. 127) was the consolidation of the concept of *ijtihād* and the rise in the importance of the position of the mujtahid. Following on from this it was argued that since only someone who has expended the time and effort to become a mujtahid could possibly know all the details of religious observances and law, it was obligatory for anyone who was not himself a mujtahid to follow the rulings of a mujtahid (otherwise they were liable to err). The Shi'i world was thereby divided into mujtahid (those who could follow their own independent judgement) and *muqallid* (those who had to follow the rulings of a mujtahid).[25]

One result of this division was that those ulama who had not concentrated on jurisprudence in their studies and were thus not considered eligible to be mujtahids fell sharply in the hierarchy of deference and henceforth only mujtahids could aspire to the highest ranks of the ulama.

The practice of following or emulating a mujtahid is called *taqlīd* and thus the mujtahid became the *marja' at-taqlīd* (reference point for emulation).

Up to the middle of the 19th century there were very few mujtahids (three or four) anywhere at any one time. Probably due to the new emphasis on the position of mujtahids there was, after this, a sudden explosion in the numbers of mujtahids so that several hundred existed by the end of the 19th century.

At all times it was considered obligatory to seek the most knowledgeable person available to give legal opinions. During the 19th century, improving communications made it increasingly easy for important or controversial questions to be referred to the eminent mujtahids at Najaf both by ordinary Shi'is and local mujtahids. In this way a small number of eminent mujtahids in Najaf became regarded as being the *marja' at-taqlīd* for a particular area. Shaykh Muḥammad Ḥasan Najafī almost succeeded in consolidating the function *marja' at-taqlīd* in himself but there seems general agreement that either Shaykh Murtaḍā Anṣarı towards the end of his life or Mīrzā-yi Shīrāzī were the first to become sole *marja' at-taqlīd (marja' at-taqlīd al-muṭlaq)* for the entire Shi'i world. After Mīrzā-yi Shīrāzī there developed a pattern whereby on the death of each *marja' at-taqlīd*, there would either be an obvious successor or there would be a small group of mujtahids of equal renown. In the latter case, the group would share the leadership until, as one after another died, only one would be left and he would become the sole *marja' at-taqlīd*. The situation continued until the death of Āyatu'llāh Burūjirdī in 1961 (for developments after this see p. 248).

In recent years several lists of *marāji' at-taqlīd* going back to the time of Kulaynī at the start of the Greater Occultation have been produced.[26] But this is a practice of dubious historical authenticity since the concept of *marja' at-taqlīd* originated in the 18th century, possibly with Bihbahānī.

In addition there has been a tradition in Islam that at the beginning of each Islamic century there would arise a great figure who would revitalise the religion. This figure is called the *Mujaddid* (Renewer). Although there is general consensus for who this figure was in some centuries, there is not for others. Table 7 shows a provisional list.

The local mullas and the great mujtahids are mutually interdependent. The local mullas are the main means of spreading public recognition of a mujtahid's piety and learning since the common people are not considered able to discern such things (piety being a question of how closely one's actions conform to the norms laid down by the *Sharī'a*; this, naturally, can only be assessed by a member of the ulama). Thus the great mujtahids need the local mullas for recognition and the income that that ultimately entails. Local mullas need the great mujtahids since they tend to bask in the reflected glory of the mujtahid that they follow.

Prefixed designations such as 'Āyatu'llāh' are a relatively new phenomenon. In the 19th century a number of the most prominent mujtahids such as Sayyid Muḥammad Bāqir Shaftī and Mīrzā-yi Shīrāzī were referred to as 'Ḥujjatu'l-Islām' (the proof of Islam). Then in the 20th century, the title 'Āyatu'llāh' (the sign of God) became customary for designating a *marja' at-taqlīd*.[27] In recent years, and particularly after the 1979 Revolution, there was a vast proliferation of individuals calling

Table 7: Shi'i Mujaddids of each Islamic century

Century	*began* AD	*Mujaddid (Renewer)*
1	622	(Muhammad, as founder, cannot strictly be considered as Renewer of the religion)
2	718	Imām Muḥammad al-Bāqir or Ja'far aṣ-Ṣādiq
3	815	Imam 'Alī ar-Riḍā
4	912	Muḥammad al-Kulaynī
5	1009	Shaykh al-Mufīd or 'Alamu'l-Hudā
6	1106	?
7	1203	?
8	1300	Ḥasan, 'Allāma al-Ḥillī
9	1397	?
10	1494	'Alī, Muḥaqqiq al-Karakī
11	1591	Muḥammad, Shaykh-i Bahā'ī
12	1688	Muḥammad Bāqir Majlisī
13	1785	Muḥammad Bāqir, Vaḥīd Bihbahānī
14	1882	Muḥammad Ḥasan, Mīrzā-yi Shīrāzī
15	1979	?Ruḥu'llāh Khumaynī

themselves 'Āyatu'llāh', thus effectively degrading the title. At present three levels of prefixed designations appear to be in use: 'Āyatu'llāh al-'Uẓmā' (the greatest sign of God), designates a *marja' at-taqlīd*; 'Āyatu'llāh', used for any established mujtahid; and 'Ḥujjatu'l-Islām' for aspiring mujtahids.[28]

The Finances of the Ulama

In Sunni Islam the *khums* (fifth) is generally confined to a portion of war booty that was reserved for the Prophet and, after him, the Caliphs. The *zakāt*, a tax for the benefit of the poor and the traveller, was rationalised as part of the taxes raised by the state. Shi'i Islam, however, does not acknowledge the right of the temporal government to collect this tax. After the Prophet, the Imams were the legitimate recipients of the *zakāt* and of the *khums*.

Initially after the Occultation of the Twelfth Imam it was considered that half of the *khums* being the personal share of the Imam (the *sahm-i Imām*) had lapsed or else should be hidden in the ground pending the emergence of the Hidden Imam, while the individual had the responsibility of distributing the *zakāt*. Gradually the ulama, as has been described in a previous section of this chapter, through the concept of

Nā'ib al 'Āmm came to assert their right to receipt of this money which represents a considerable income and gave the ulama financial independence from the government. With the development of the *marja' at-taqlīd* concept, financial power was concentrated in the hands of one man or a small group of men, to be distributed more or less as they saw fit. In addition, the ulama were the natural choice to be administrators of properties made over as religious endowments (*waqf*) and this made further considerable funds available to the leading mujtahids. A third source of income for the ulama is fees for certification of land transactions, marriages, etc.

Although the ulama have given themselves the right to collect these religious taxes (*khums* and *zakāt*), their actual ability to do so has varied during each period of history and among the differing segments of the population. The craftsmen and tradesmen of the Bazaar have always strongly supported (and intermarried with) the ulama and so income from this source has always been readily available, but the income from villages has depended to a large extent on the influence of local mullas. In addition, the amount of money coming to the ulama has depended on how much is being taken by the government and thus the ulama have always had more reason than one for opposing tyrannical governors and governments.

From these funds, the mujtahids run *madrasas* including supporting the students at the *madrasa*; they have a responsibility to support needy Sayyids (descendants of the Prophet); in addition, they provide various social benefits such as giving financial assistance to the poorest families and setting up medical clinics.

Although the religious taxes of *khums* and *zakāt* give the ulama an independence from the state not enjoyed by Sunni ulama, there is a price to pay for this independence. In some parts of the Shi'i world most of the ulama's income derives from the Bazaar. Since the ulama have no way of enforcing payment of these religious taxes, the payers of the tax can, to a certain extent, express their approval or disapproval of the actions of a particular Āyatu'llah by their readiness to pay and the amounts they pay. In other parts of the Shi'i world, the ulama are closely identified with landed interests (either themselves owning land or being closely allied to landowners). Both the Bazaar and landed interests tend to influence the ulama in a conservative direction. Thus the theoretical freedom of innovative exegesis given to the ulama by the concept of *ijtihād* is, in practice, negated by the restrictions imposed by their financial basis.

The finances of the ulama in Iran have of course been radically altered by the 1979 Revolution. As one popular song has a mulla saying: 'My poor old mule died last week; so to replace him I bought a Mercedes Benz.'

11

Sufism, 'Irfān and Ḥikma

Sufism

In Sunni Islam, Sufism has, through the Sufi Shaykhs, a major hold on the religious devotion of the masses. But in Shi'ism it has become largely a side-issue, a minority interest. It is the orthodox ulama who hold the religious leadership of the Shi'i community and few of them will have anything to do with Sufism. It is not possible in a work of this nature to undertake a systematic treatment of the mystical and metaphysical ideas of Sufism. And so in this chapter only Sufism in its relationship to Shi'ism and the history of the Shi'i Sufi orders will be considered.

Although most histories of Sufism go back to individual ascetics such as Ḥasan al-Baṣrī and Rābi'a al-'Adawiyya who lived in the centuries immediately after the Prophet, Sufism as it is known today, with its organised orders and their hierarchies and rituals, dates from the 12th and 13th centuries AD.

The roots of this organised Sufism have a complex inter-relationship with the Shi'ism of the 12th to 14th centuries AD. Shi'ism achieved political power over almost all of the Islamic world in the 10th and 11th centuries. Then in the middle of the 11th century the Seljuqs came to power and severely repressed Shi'ism. It has been suggested that Sufism, in its organised form, arose at about this time to fill the vacuum left by the suppression of Shi'ism.[1] Certainly there is a great deal of similarity between Shi'ism and many aspects of Sufism which would tend to support this thesis.

One of the most important doctrines of Sufism is the concept of the Perfect Man (*al-Insān al-Kāmil*). This doctrine states that there always must exist upon the earth a man who is the perfect channel of grace from God to man. This man who is called the *Quṭb* (Pole or Axis, of the Universe) is considered to be in a state of *wilāya* (sanctity, being under the protection of God). It can already be seen that there are great similarities between the concept of the *Quṭb* in Sufism and the Shi'i Imam. Indeed, many of the Traditions referring to the Imam (see

Chapter 7) are also to be found among Sufis in relation to the *Quṭb*: there can only be one *Quṭb* on the earth at any one time; anyone who dies without recognising the *Quṭb* of his time has died the death of the Jāhiliyya; only recognition of the *Quṭb* confers true belief, etc.[2]

The authority to teach the Sufi path has been handed down from master (*Quṭb, Shaykh, Murshid* or *Pīr*) to pupil (*Murīd, Ṭālib, Sālik*) through the generations. Most of these 'chains' of authority (*silsila*) traditionally go back through various intermediaries to 'Ali who among Sufis is considered to have received initiation into mystical truth from Muhammad. Thus among certain Sufi orders there has been a tendency to glorify 'Ali. This tendency (as has been noted in Chapters 5 and 6) may well have helped to prepare the people of Iran during the 14th and 15th centuries for accepting Shi'ism under the Safavids.

However, it is precisely this closeness in certain areas between Shi'ism and Sufism that has led to antagonism among Shi'i ulama towards Sufism. The concept of the *Quṭb* (who for most Sufi orders is the head of the order) as the purveyor of spiritual guidance and of God's grace to mankind is in direct conflict with the concept of the Imam who in Shi'ism fulfils this role. The vow of obedience to the *Shaykh* or *Quṭb* which is taken by Sufis is considered incompatible with devotion to the Imam. Indeed, for Shi'is, the Twelfth Imam, who is alive and only in occultation, is the living *Quṭb* and there can only ever be one *Quṭb* upon the earth at any one time.

There are several other reasons for the antagonism of the ulama towards Sufism: the doctrine of *waḥdat al-wujūd* (existential monism) is considered to be blasphemous; the chains of authority of even the Shi'i Sufi orders do not include all twelve of the Shi'i Imams, rather they progress through the first eight Imams, but after 'Alī ar-Riḍā they diverge through Ma'rūf al-Karkhī to other individuals; the *zakāt* is paid by members of the order to the head of the order and not to the ulama.

The Shi'i Sufi orders have sought to bring their ideas more closely into line with orthodox Shi'i opinion. Thus, for example, the head of the order is often referred to as the *Nā'ib-i Imām* (deputy of the Hidden Imam). But even this modification is not acceptable to the orthodox who regard themselves as the *Nā'ib-i 'Āmm* (general deputy) of the Twelfth Imam while no *Nā'ib-i Khāṣṣ* is permissible during the Greater Occultation (see p. 165).

Historically (as has been shown in Chapter 5) several Sufi orders became increasingly oriented towards Shi'sm during the 15th century but it was not until the Safavid order became Shi'i and conquered Iran that several orders such as the Nūrbakhshī, Dhahabī and Ni'matu'llāhī became openly Shi'i.

The Nūrbakhshī and Dhahabī orders have a common origin. Khwāja

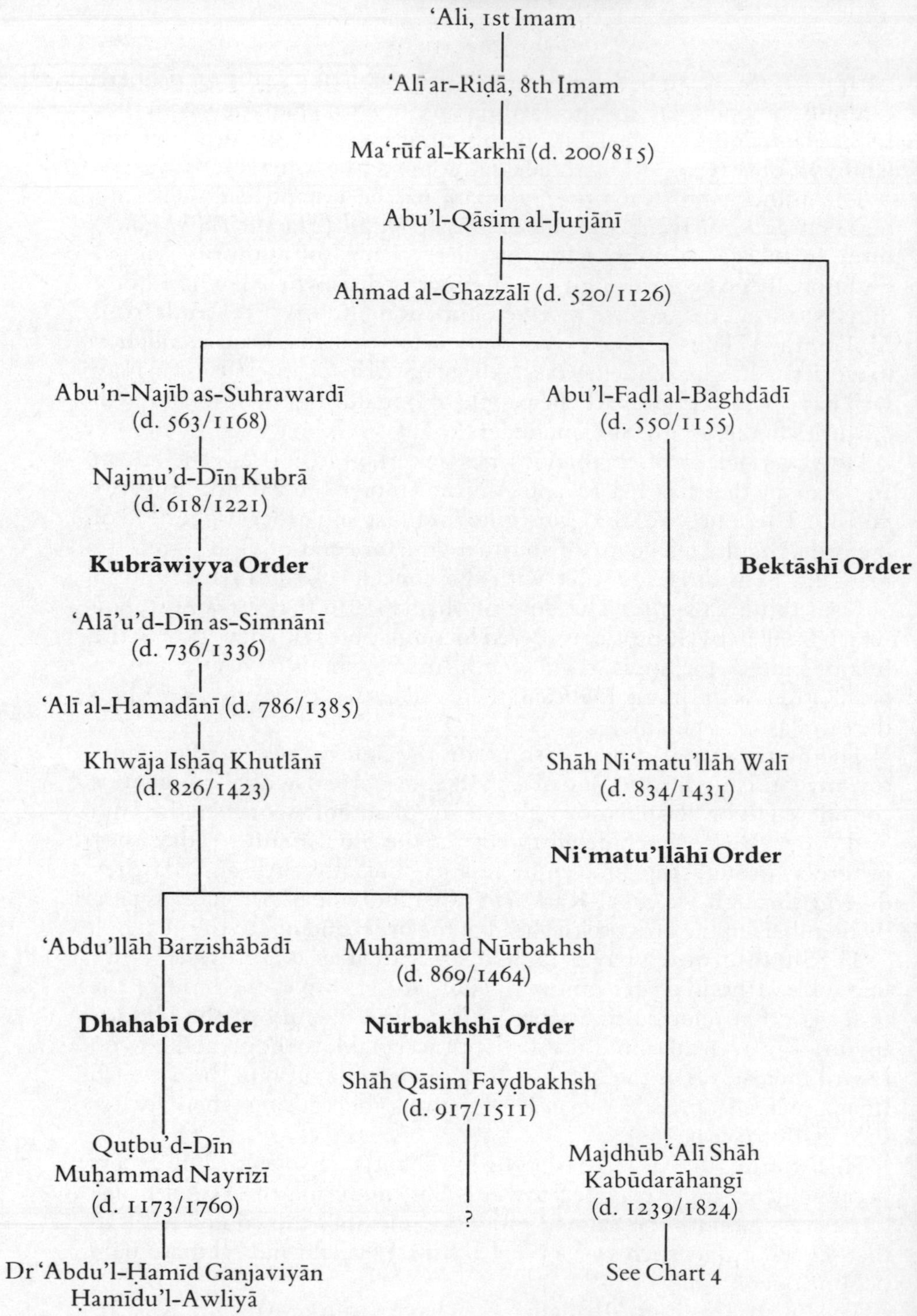

Chart 3, demonstrating relationships of the various Shi'i Ṣūfī Orders

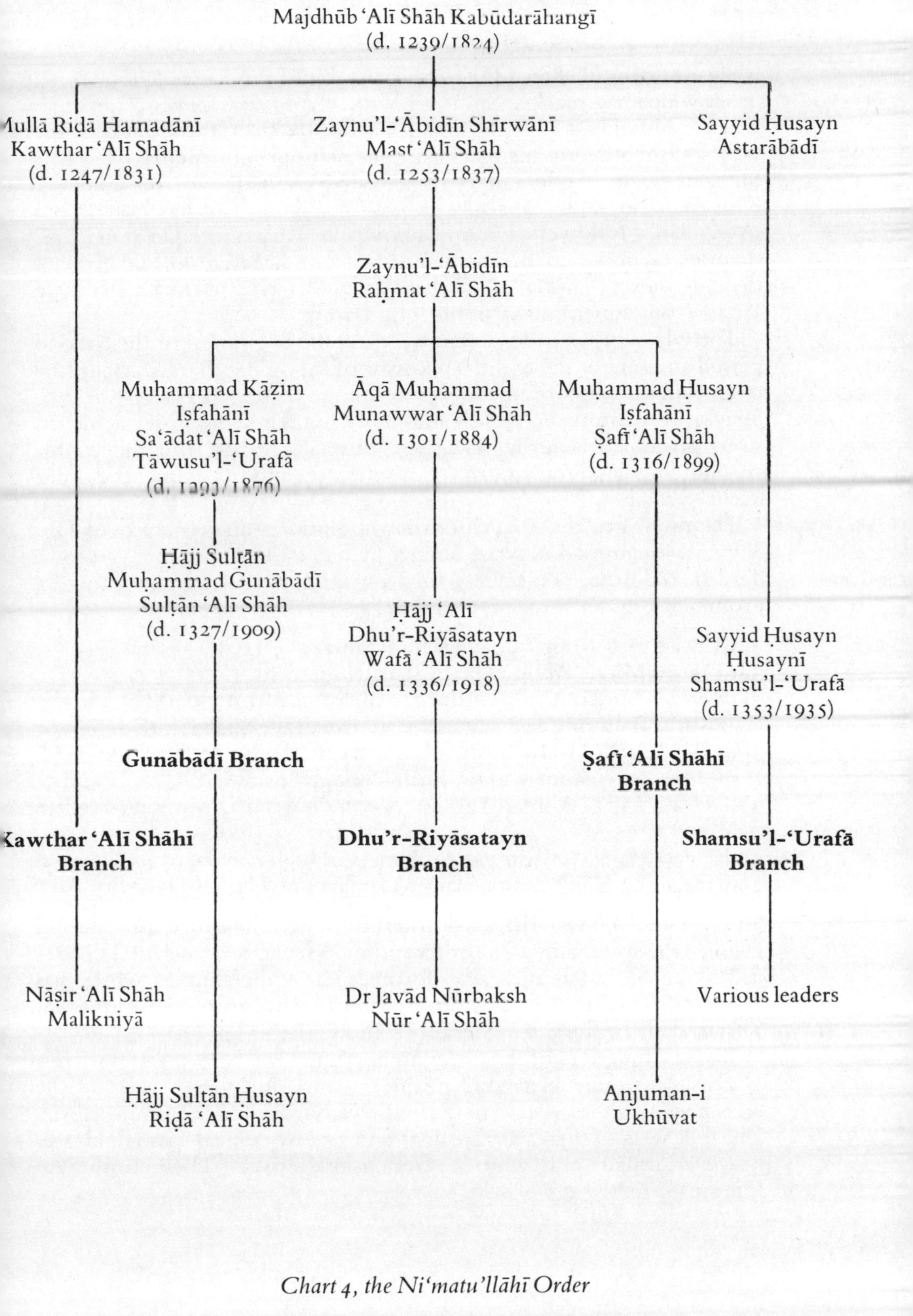
Majdhūb ‘Alī Shāh Kabūdarāhangī
(d. 1239/1824)
Mullā Riḍā Hamadānī
Kawthar ‘Alī Shāh
(d. 1247/1831)
Zaynu’l-‘Ābidīn Shīrwānī
Mast ‘Alī Shāh
(d. 1253/1837)
Sayyid Ḥusayn
Astarābādī
Zaynu’l-‘Ābidīn
Raḥmat ‘Alī Shāh
Muḥammad Kāẓim
Iṣfahānī
Sa‘ādat ‘Alī Shāh
Ṭāwusu’l-‘Urafā
(d. 1293/1876)
Āqā Muḥammad
Munawwar ‘Alī Shāh
(d. 1301/1884)
Muḥammad Ḥusayn
Iṣfahānī
Ṣafī ‘Alī Shāh
(d. 1316/1899)
Ḥājj Sulṭān
Muḥammad Gunābādī
Sulṭān ‘Alī Shāh
(d. 1327/1909)
Ḥājj ‘Alī
Dhu’r-Riyāsatayn
Wafā ‘Alī Shāh
(d. 1336/1918)
Sayyid Ḥusayn
Ḥusaynī
Shamsu’l-‘Urafā
(d. 1353/1935)
Gunābādī Branch
Ṣafī ‘Alī Shāhī
Branch
Kawthar ‘Alī Shāhī
Branch
Dhu’r-Riyāsatayn
Branch
Shamsu’l-‘Urafā
Branch
Nāṣir ‘Alī Shāh
Malikniyā
Dr Javād Nūrbaksh
Nūr ‘Alī Shāh
Various leaders
Ḥājj Sulṭān Ḥusayn
Riḍā ‘Alī Shāh
Anjuman-i
Ukhūvat

Chart 4, the Ni‘matu’llāhī Order

Isḥaq Khutlānī (d. 826/1423) was a Shaykh of the Sunni Kubrāwiyya order which had marked Shi'i sympathies. A hostile report claims that when he appointed Sayyid Muḥammad Nūrbakhsh, the founder of the Nūrbakhshī order, as his successor, one of his prominent disciples, Mīr Shihābu'd-Dīn 'Abdu'llāh Barzishābādī Mashhadī, got up and left. Khwāja Isḥāq said: 'Dhahaba 'Abdu'llāh ('Abdu'llāh has gone)' and 'Abdu'llāh's followers became known as Dhahabīs. The Dhahabīs themselves, however, derive their name from *dhahab*, gold, and speak of their affiliation as *silsilat adh-dhahab*, the golden chain. The Dhahabiyya are also sometimes known as the Ightishāshiyya.

The Dhahabiyya order became Shi'i at the beginning of the Safavid period and, under the eighth successor of 'Abdu'llāh Barzishābādī (the twenty-ninth head of the order counting from Ma'rūf al-Karkhī), Shaykh Muḥammad 'Alī Mu'adhdhin Khurāsānī, the order achieved some prominence during the reign of Shāh 'Abbās. But then, after encountering antagonism from both the state and the ulama, the order declined again.

The revival of the Dhahabī order in Shīrāz is due to Quṭbu'd-Dīn Sayyid Muḥammad Nayrīzī Shīrāzī (d. 1173/1760), the thirty-second head of the order. Following on from him, the order continued its prominence under successive leaders:

33rd Head, Āqā Muḥammad Hāshim Shīrāzī (d. 1199/1785)
34th Head, Mīrzā 'Abdu'n-Nabī Sharīfī Shīrāzī (d. 1231/1815)
35th Head, Mīrzā 'Abu'l-Qāsim Sharīfī Shīrāzī (d. 1286/1869), known as Mīrzā Bābā or Rāz-i Shīrāzī, custodian of the Shāh Chirāgh Shrine
36th Head, Jalālu'd-Dīn Muḥammad Sharīfī Majdu'l-Ashraf Shīrāzī (d. 1331/1913), custodian of the Shāh Chirāgh Shrine
37th Head, Mīrzā Aḥmad Tabrīzī, Nāyibu'l-Wilāya, Waḥīdu'l-Awliyā (d. 1375/1955)
38th Head, Ḥājjī Muḥammad 'Alī Ardibīlī, Ḥubb Ḥaydar (d. 1382/1962)
39th Head, Dr Ḥājj 'Abdu'l-Ḥamīd Ganjaviyān, Ḥamīdu'l-Awliyā

After Jalālu'd-Dīn Sharīfī, his brother, Sayyid Muḥammad Riḍā Sharīfī, claimed the leadership of the order and and a separate branch of the order called the Sharīfī branch was formed, the leadership of which has remained hereditary in this family. Custodianship of the important Shrine of Shāh Chirāgh in Shīraž remains with this line.

The headquarters of the order are in Shīrāz and they possess there a *khānagāh* (meeting-place and hospice) which includes shrines of the recent heads of the order. There are also *khānagāhs* in Tehran and Tabrīz. The followers of this order are distinguished by conical hats which are, however, usually only worn at meetings of the order. Their numbers in Iran are estimated at 3,000.[3]

The Nūrbakhshī order originated with 'Alā'u'd-Dīn Sayyid Muḥammad Nūrbakhsh (d. 869/1464) who was a Sunni with strong Shi'i proclivities. His son and successor, Shāh Sayyid Qāsim Fayḍbakhsh (d. 917/1511), was still alive when the Safavids came to power. At this time the order became Shi'i and achieved considerable prominence. Many of the eminent Shi'i ulama of the early and middle Safavid period were affiliated to this order: Shaykh Bahā'ī, Mullā Muḥsin-i Fayḍ and Qāḍī Nūru'llāh Shustarī. Certainly the Nūrbakhshī order was a significant influence upon the evolution of the *Ḥikmat-i Ilāhī* of the School of Isfahan (see later in this chapter). It was also important in the spread of Shi'ism in India and Kashmir.

As with all other Sufi orders, it was suppressed in Iran towards the end of the Safavid period although it retained a presence in India where it was instrumental in bringing Shi'ism to Kashmir. It has never re-established itself in Iran as an organised order, although individual prominent Sufis such as Mīrzā 'Abdu'l-Wahhāb Nā'īnī (d. 1212/1797) and Mīrzā Abu'l-Qasim Sukut-i Shīrāzī (d. 1239/1823) have been said to be of this order.[4]

The Ni'matu'llāhī is the largest and most influential of the Sufi orders in Iran. The relationship of the Ni'matu'llāhī order to the other Shi'i orders in terms of the chains of authority is shown in the diagram (Chart 3).

The founder of the order, Shāh Ni'matu'llāh Walī (d. 834/1431) was Sunni but sympathetic to Shi'ism. He died in Mahān near Kirmān where his grave is still an important centre for this order. His successors moved to Hyderabad in the Deccan, India, where they were enthusiastically received by the Bahmānī rulers. But the order maintained a presence in Iran and there was a network of local Shaykhs. When the Safavids came to power, the order closely identified itself with them and became Shi'i. One of the local Shaykhs of the order, Mīr Niẓāmu'd-Dīn 'Abdu'l-Baqī, was appointed by Shāh Ismā'īl to the position of *Ṣadr* in 917/1511. From about the time of Shāh 'Abbās, however, the influence of the order in Iran declined under attack from both state and ulama.

The revival of the Ni'matu'llāhīs in Iran dates from 1190/1776 when Riḍā 'Alī Shāh Dakanī, (d. 1214/1799), the thirteenth successor of Shāh Ni'matu'llāh, sent his disciple and successor, Ma'sūm 'Alī Shāh Dakanī, from India to Iran. The latter was very successful and large crowds gathered everywhere that he went. For example, he is said to have had 30,000 disciples in Shīrāz where Karīm Khān Zand held court. This aroused the wrath of the ulama, and Ma'sūm 'Alī Shāh was eventually killed in Kirmānshāh at the instigation of Mullā Muḥammad 'Alī Bihbahānī in 1212/1797.[5] The next Shaykh of the order was an Iranian, Mīrzā Muḥammad 'Alī Ṭabasī Iṣfahānī, Nūr 'Alī Shāh (d. 1212/1797) and from this time onwards the Shaykhs of the order have been Iranians and the centre of the order in Iran.

Majdhūb 'Alī Shāh Kabūdarāhangī (d. 1239/1823), the seventeenth successor of Shāh Ni'matu'llāh, did not clearly appoint a successor and so there was a dispute over the succession after him. Mullā Muḥammad Shāh Hamadānī, Kawthar 'Alī Shāh (d. 1247/1831), split off from the main body of the order and formed a branch known as Kawthar 'Alī Shāhī which has survived to the present day under a succession of leaders and is centred in Hamadān, Marāgha and Tehran. Its present leader is Nāṣir 'Alī Shāh Malikniyā who resides at the order's *khānagāh* in Tehran.

A second branch which split off at the death of Majdhūb 'Alī Shāh was founded by Sayyid Ḥusayn Astarābādī. Its most famous Shaykh was Sayyid Ḥusayn Ḥusaynī Ṭihrānī, Shamsu'l-'Urafā (d. 1353/1935), and so this line is called the Shamsu'l-'Urafā or Shamsiyya line. Shamsu'l-'Urafā's successors included Ḥajj Mīr Sayyid 'Alī Burqu'ī, a well-known mujtahid who was responsible for the religious training of Muḥammad Riḍā Shāh Pahlavī. This group have a *khānagāh* in Tehran.

The main line of the Ni'matu'llāhīs continued after Majdhūb 'Alī Shāh under Zaynu'l-'Ābidīn Shīrvānī, Mast 'Alī Shāh (d. 1253/1837). He was succeeded by Raḥmat 'Alī Shāh (d. 1278/1861) who was known as Nāyibu's-Ṣadr, but after this there was a further split in the order. This split was a much more serious affair and the order has remained divided into three groups ever since.

The uncle of Raḥmat 'Alī Shāh, Āqā Muḥammad, Munavvar 'Alī Shāh (d. 1301/1884), was one claimant to the succession. His son, Ḥājj 'Alī Dhu'r-Riyāsatayn, Wafā 'Alī Shāh (d. 1336/1918), succeeded him and the line is usually known as the Dhu'r-Riyāsatayn branch (or occasionally as the Mu'nis 'Alī Shāhī branch after a later leader). Wafā 'Alī Shāh was succeeded by Sayyid Ismā'īl Ujāq, Ṣādiq 'Alī Shāh (d. 1340/1922) and then by Ḥājj 'Abdu'l-Ḥusayn Dhu'r-Riyāsatayn, Mu'nis 'Alī Shāh (d. 1373/1953). After the last-named, there was some dispute over the succession with several of the local Shaykhs of the order claiming successorship. However, one of these, Dr Javād Nūrbakhsh Kirmānī, Nūr 'Alī Shāh, who had been Shaykh in Tehran, succeeded in consolidating his authority over most of this branch of the order. Under Dr Nūrbakhsh, this branch of the order has undergone a vigorous expansion with several new *khānagāhs* built in Iran and, taking advantage of the interest in Sufism in the West, an expansion of the order to England and the USA.

Another claimant to Raḥmat 'Alī Shāh's successorship was Ḥājj Muḥammad Ḥasan Iṣfahānī, Ṣafī 'Alī Shāh (d. 1316/1899). After various travels, Ṣafī 'Alī Shāh settled in Tehran and succeeded in attracting several notables of the Qājār court as disciples. The next Shaykh of this line was Mīrzā 'Alī Khān, Ẓahīru'd-Dawla, Ṣafā 'Alī Shāh, a Qājār prince (d. 1342/1923). Ṣafī 'Alī Shāh had formed his followers into a society called the Anjuman-i Ukhūvat (Society of Brotherhood) and after the death of Ẓahīru'd-Dawla most of the members of the order came under the leadership of the eleven-man council of this society. This branch of the Ni'matu'llāhī order is called the Ṣafī 'Alī Shāhī branch and is spread through most of Iran with some ten or more *khānagāhs*.

The third branch of the order to arise after Raḥmat 'Alī Shāh was founded by Ḥājj Muḥammad Kāẓim Iṣfahānī, Sa'ādat 'Alī Shāh (d. 1293/1876), known as Tāwusu'l-'Urafā. He was succeeded by Ḥājj Sulṭān Muḥammad Gunābādī, Sulṭān 'Alī Shāh (murdered 1327/1909), who used to teach a circle of disciples in the village of Bīdukht in the Gunābād area near Mashhad in Khurāsān. Thus this important branch became known as Gunābādī. After him, the leadership of this branch passed to his son Ḥājj Mullā 'Alī, Nūr 'Alī Shāh (murdered 1337/1918), and grandson, Ḥājj Shaykh Muḥammad Ḥasan, Ṣālih 'Alī Shāh (d. 1386/1966). The present leader of this branch is the son of Ṣālih 'Alī Shāh, Ḥājj Sulṭān Ḥusayn, Riḍā 'Alī Shāh Tābanda. In Bīdukht, Gunābād, there is an extensive array of buildings which are the headquarters of the order.

The Sufi orders in Iran have very little following among the lower classes. The branches of the Ni'matullāhī order have, however, had a considerable following among government officials and the nobility during the last 150 years. Perhaps because of this and the way that Sufis attempt to help their fellow-Sufis, the order has had attractions for young men entering government service. A recent estimate put the number of Ni'matu'llāhīs in Iran at between 50,000 and 350,000 with Gunābādīs 30–50%, Dhu'r-Riyāsatayn 20–45%, Ṣafī 'Alī Shāhī 15–30% and other splinter groups at less than 5%.[6]

The third major Sufi order extant in Iran, apart from the Dhahabī and Ni'matullāhī, is the Khāksār order. The originator of this order is said to be one Jalālu'd-Dīn or Quṭbu'd-Dīn Ḥaydar in the 8th/13th century. The exact identity of this figure remains unclear pending further research. It has been suggested that he is identical with the Suhrawardī Shaykh, Jalālu'd-Dīn Bukhārī (d. 690/1291). It is said that his tomb is at Turbat-i Ḥaydarī in Khurāsān and it is his name that was given to the faction in each major Iranian town which, during Safavid and Qājār times, was opposed by the Ni'matī faction (said to be named after Shāh Ni'matu'llāh Walī) leading to frequent faction-fighting and rioting especially on public holidays such as Naw-Rūz.

There appear to be historical links between this order and the Safavid order before its conquest of Iran. There is also a complex interrelationship with the Ahl-i Ḥaqq ('Aliyu'llāhīs). Indeed, many regard the Ahl-i Ḥaqq as a Sufi order linked to the Khāksār rather than a Shi'i sect.

There appears to be little organisation in the Khāksār order, with many individuals claiming to be Shaykhs. The wandering dervishes or Qalandars are often said to be of this order. Several different branches of the order exist, such as the Jalālī Ghulām 'Alī Shāhī and the Dawda Ma'sūm 'Alī Shāhī. The order has *khānagāhs* in several cities and possibly has as many as 3,000 members. There are also some adherents of this order in Iraq.[7]

Philosophy, Ḥikma and 'Irfān

The goal of philosophy is considered to be the achievement of wisdom (*ḥikma*). Philosophers (*ḥukamā*) have traditionally been divided into two groups: the Mashā'iyūn (peripatetic philosophers) who consider that wisdom is to be achieved by intellectual effort and rational processes; and the Ishrāqiyūn (illuminationist philosophers) who consider that true wisdom is best gained through spiritual discipline, the cleansing of the soul from all defilement and the acquisition of virtues.

Also closely associated with *ḥikma* is *'irfān* (gnosis or mystical knowledge). Although the Shi'i ulama have been opposed to Sufism for the reasons stated above, *'irfān* is much more acceptable. It includes many of the ideas and much of the technical vocabulary of Sufism but divests itself of the features which the ulama find most objectionable: the formal structure of the orders, initiation, the *murshid-murīd* (i.e. spiritual master to pupil) relationship, *dhikr* (repetitive recitations), concepts such as *waḥdat al-wujūd* (existential monism), etc.

Typical works in the field of *'irfān* deal with bringing out the inner, esoteric meaning of the Qur'an based on the process of *ta'wīl* (bringing out of the spiritual meaning) rather than *tafsīr* (technical commentary) of the verses. It is thus a very intellectual activity and can perhaps be better described as esotericism in contrast to the ecstatic mysticism of the Sufis.

In this form mysticism has managed to retain a foothold within the curriculum of teaching in the Shi'i religious colleges but very much on the periphery. Interestingly, Āyatu'llāh Khumaynī taught *'irfān* in Qumm prior to his expulsion in 1963.

A movement that has had a great deal of influence on Shi'i thought is what is called *Ḥikmat-i Ilāhī*. It can be thought of as the philosophical analysis and description of the mystical path. The name itself, *Ḥikmat-i Ilāhī*, can be translated as Divine Wisdom, Divine Philosophy or Theosophy. It has also gone under the name of *Ḥikmat-i Muta'āliyya* which can be translated as Transcendent Theosophy.

The school of philosophy called *Ḥikmat-i Ilāhī* represents the culmination of the endeavour to bring together and harmonise the three major sources of spiritual knowledge in the Islamic experience: the revealed and transmitted sources which revolve around the Qu'ran and Traditions; the conclusions drawn from the rational analysis of religion; and intuitive and ecstatic spiritual illumination. The roots of this movement go back to the earliest period of Islam and extend beyond Shi'ism itself. Its culmination and flowering was in the School of Isfahan (see pp. 112–13).

Foremost among the influences on this movement was, of course, the Qur'an itself and in particular the *ta'wīl* (esoteric interpretation or spiritual hermeneutics) of the Qur'an that is to be found in the corpus of the Traditions ascribed to the Shi'i Imams. Indeed, some of the most important works of the philosophers of this school consist of commentaries upon the Traditions of the Imams.

The field of speculative theology (*kalām*) had, in previous centuries, been a major area of intellectual activity and the writers of the School of Isfahan were influenced not only by Shi'i *kalām* which had found its fullest expression in the works of Khwāja Naṣīru'd-Dīn Ṭūsī but also by the Mu'tazilī *kalām* upon which earlier Shi'i theology had been based, as well as the Ash'arī *kalām* of Sunnism which had reached its culmination in the works of such figures as al-Ghazālī, Fakhru'd-Dīn Rāzī and Sa'du'd-Dīn Taftazānī.

One of the most important influences on the *Ḥikmat-i Ilāhī* movement was Shaykhu'l-Ishrāq Shihābu'd-Dīn Suhrawardī (executed in Aleppo in 587/1191). His work in turn drew upon several inter-related strands: the revival of Zoroastrian angelology, Neo-Platonic cosmology, and in particular the metaphysical works of Ibn Sīnā (Avicenna). From these sources and from direct spiritual experiences, Suhrawardī created the Ishrāqī philosophy or the philosophy of oriental (in its metaphysical sense) illumination, a description of ecstatic and mystical experience in the context of philosophical concepts.

A similarly important source of influence upon the School of Isfahan was the gnostic mysticism of Muḥiyu'd-Dīn, Ibn al-'Arabī, Shaykh al-Akbar (560/1165–638/1240). His metaphysical doctrines, which were to evolve within his school into such concepts as the Perfect Man (*al-Insān al-Kāmil*) and existential monism (*waḥdat al-wujūd*), exercised a great influence on all aspects of Islamic mysticism.

Sufism itself was one of the most important sources of inspiration for *Ḥikmat-i Ilāhī*. Not only were several individual philosophers of this school themselves members of Sufi orders (and in particular the Nūrbakhshī order), but there is frequent quotation in the writings of these philosophers from the great Iranian Sufi poets such as Jalālu'd-Dīn Rūmī and 'Abdu'r-Raḥmān Jāmī.

The *Ḥikmat-i Ilāhī* philosophers were, of course, familiar with the philosophy of both the Aristotelian and Neo-Platonic traditions found in the writings of the Greek philosophers as well as the early Muslim philosophers such as Ibn Sīnā (Avicenna) and al-Fārābī.

The full flowering of *Ḥikmat-i Ilāhī* in the School of Isfahan in the 17th century was preceded by a number of similar preliminary works. Mention has been made elsewhere in this book of the work of Sayyid Ḥaydar Āmulī in bringing together Shi'ism and Sufism. There is also the important work of Ibn Abī Jumhūr who attempted an integration of philosophy, *kalām* and Sufi concepts into Shi'ism thereby laying an important foundation for the School of Isfahan. As a further example there is the work of Ṣā'inu'd-Dīn, Ibn Turka Iṣfahānī (d. 835/1431 or 836/1432) who integrated many of the themes of Suhrawardī and Ibn al-'Arabī into his writings.

The names of the key figures in the School of Isfahan are given elsewhere (see p. 113). After being vigorously attacked by the orthodox ulama during the course of the 18th century, it began to re-emerge in the course of the 19th century. The Shaykhī School may be considered as derived from this movement (although Shaykh Aḥmad himself strongly disagreed with Mullā Ṣadrā and Mullā Muḥsin-i Fayḍ on some issues) and the outlines of the Shaykhī teachings (given on pp. 226–8) can also serve to give an idea of some of the main themes of the School of Isfahan. Also during the 19th century, Mullā Hādī Sabzivārī (d. 1878) revived the teaching of philosophy and himself wrote commentaries on works of Mullā Ṣadrā.

In the years after the Second World War, 'Allāma Muḥammad Ḥusayn Ṭabāṭabā'ī succeeded in having the subject introduced into the syllabus of studies at Qumm. Since then, he, Sayyid Jalālu'd-Dīn Āshtiyānī and Sayyid Ḥusayn Naṣr, ably assisted by the French orientalist Henri Corbin, have written extensively on the subject so that its themes and ideas have become almost as well-known in the West as in the East.

It is not possible to give an adequate descriptive survey of the breadth of *Ḥikmat-i Ilāhī* in an introductory work such as this. Briefly, however, some of the characteristic concepts of the school, and of the writings of Mullā Ṣadrā in particular, are:

a. The integration of the Fourteen Pure Souls (Muhammad, Fāṭima, and the Twelve Imams) into Avicennan cosmology where they, in effect, replace the Active Intelligences as the ontological causes of existence.

b. The belief in the reality of an independent world of images (the *'ālam al-mithāl*) between the intelligible world and the sensible world.

c. The replacement of the principle of the fundamentality of quiddity as the basic of metaphysics by the fundamentality of being (*aṣālat al-wujūd*). In this respect, Mullā Ṣadrā disagreed with his teacher Mīr Dāmād and with Suhrawardī.

d. The doctrine of the substantial motion (*al-ḥaraka al-jawhariyya*) of being. This doctrine asserts that the being of anything that exists is susceptible to change, intensification and perfection.

e. The essence of individuality is the soul. It is this that is eternal and which experiences the resurrection.

As an example of the metaphysical system of this school and to demonstrate its links with other avenues of Islamic thought, the following is a brief analysis of the four journeys described by Mullā Ṣadrā in *Al-Ḥikmat al-muta'āliyya fi'l-asfār al-'aqliyya al-arba'a* (The Transcendental Theosophy concerning the Four Journeys of the Rational Soul). This work concerns the four journeys: from the creatures to the True One; from the True One to the True One; from the True One to the creatures; and from the creatures to the creatures.

The first journey is described as being the path whereby man detaches himself from the physical world and his carnal self (*nafs*) and rending the veils that intervene between him and the Divine Beauty reaches the station of Annihilation in the Divine. In this 'journey' Mullā Ṣadrā gives an exposition of metaphysics and ontology dealing with several philosophical issues.

The second journey is described as being the path along which the traveller contemplates and comes to know and understand the Divine Names and Attributes. This is the station of sainthood in which the traveller comes to hear with His hearing, sees with His sight and is thus totally annihilated in the Divine Essence, Actions and Attributes. In this 'journey', Mullā Ṣadrā discusses a number of philosophical questions such as creation *ex nihilo*, substance, quantity, quality and the receptivity of things to the Divine Grace.

The third journey involves the termination of Annihilation (*fanā*) and the start of Subsistence (*baqā*) in God. This is the state of the prophets (but not those prophets that bring laws). In this state, the traveller is able to travel through all the worlds of creation and to see all these worlds in their essence and exigencies. In this 'journey', our author deals with God in His Essence, His Names and Attributes, discussing such subjects as divine will, fate, evil and God's knowledge.

The fourth journey is among the creatures but now the traveller, who is in the station of a prophet who brings laws, sees all beings in their essence and knows of the manner of their return to God and so is able to give them guidance. In describing this 'journey', Mullā Ṣadrā deals with the soul and its development and with the question of the resurrection and other eschatological matters.[8]

12

Schools within Twelver Shi'ism

In Chapter 3 the traditional account of the formation of the various Shi'i sects has been given. But in historical terms, it is extremely difficult to determine when exactly each group can be considered to have become a separate sect. There were two main periods of time when there was intensive religious speculation and a rapid evolution of groups and sects.

The first of these two periods was from about AD 750 to 950 in Iraq and in particular in Kūfa and Baghdad. Something of the nature of the speculations of this period can be discerned from the accounts already given in Chapter 3. It would appear that during this two-hundred-year period, the main body of Shi'a began to break up into a number of groups. At first the boundaries of these groups were ill-defined, but as time went by their distinctive differences became sharper and many died out. In general terms it can be said that the Shi'a broke into three broad groups: those who advocated political action, the political quietists and those attracted to esoteric and gnostic ideas. These became the Zaydī, Ithnā-'Asharī (Twelver) and Ghulāt/Ismā'īlī groups respectively.

The second period of intense religious speculation and rapid sectarian development occurred in the 15th century. During this time, in a broad crescent stretching from south-west Iran and eastern Iraq into north-west Iran and eastern Anatolia and across into northern Syria, there was a ferment of religious activity most of which would be described by orthodox Shi'is as 'extremist' (*ghuluww*) because of the exaggerated position given to 'Ali. But most groups honoured all of the Imams of the Twelvers. Included within the orbit of this religious activity was the Musha'sha' state in south-west Iran, the religious speculation of the Qara-Quyūnlū, the rising Safavid order in Ardibīl, the Bektāshī order in eastern Anatolia and the 'Alawīs (Nuṣayrīs) in north Syria. Some of these movements (the Musha'sha' and the Safavids) were absorbed into orthodox Twelver Shi'ism and influenced it. But others divided off into separate religious movements: the 'Alawīs (Nuṣayrīs), the Ahl-i Ḥaqq groups and the Bektāshīs.

The evolution of the Shi'i sects and schools may be represented thus

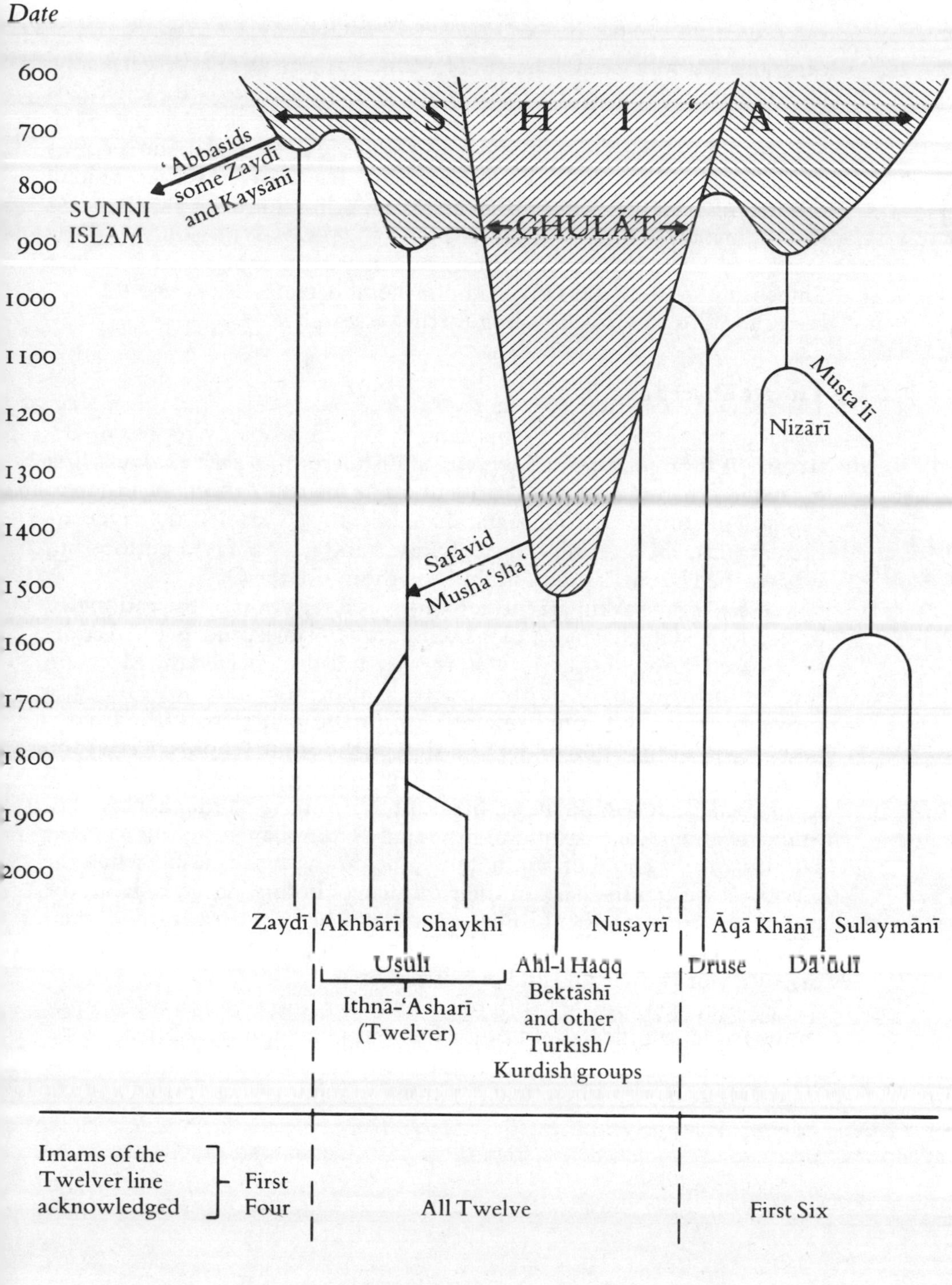

Chart 5, a diagrammatic representation of the emergence and evolution of Shiʻi sects

diagrammatically (see Chart 5). The Ithnā-'Ashariyya (Twelver) is the largest group of the Shi'a in the world today and the one with which this book is concerned. The vast majority of Twelvers belong to the Uṣūlī School and it is the tenets of this school that are described in the sections of this book and particularly in Chapter 10. There are, however, a small number of Twelvers who subscribe to the Akhbārī and Shaykhī Schools (for the history of these schools see pp. 117–18, 127–8, 135–6). Very little research has been done on these two minority schools in Twelver Shi'ism and so the details given about their doctrines below should only be regarded as tentative pending further research.

The Akhbārī School

As described in Chapter 6, this school, which probably represented a stream of thought within Twelver Shi'ism from its earliest days, first crystallised out as a separate movement in the wake of the writings of Mullā Muḥammad Amīn Astarābādī (d. 1033/1623). It achieved its greatest influence during the late Safavid and post-Safavid periods but was crushed by the Uṣūlī mujtahids on the eve of the Qājār era.

In essence, the Akhbārī movement was a rejection of the rationalist principles on which *ijtihād* and the whole of Shi'i jurisprudence had come to be based. Some Akhbārīs went further and also rejected the Mu'tazilī (i.e. rationalistic) basis of Shi'i doctrine also. In practice this meant a move towards the Sunni principles of jurisprudence (with the Imams taking over the position of the founders of the Sunni schools of law) and an almost-Ash'arī (i.e. Sunni) position in theology. In other words, had it succeeded, it would have brought Shi'ism very much closer to Sunnism and it is interesting to note that Nādir Shāh's attempt to make Shi'ism a fifth school of Sunni law coincides with the period when the Akhbārīs were at the peak of their influence. In turning away from the rationalist basis of the Uṣūlīs, many of the Akhbārīs turned their attention to 'non-rational' avenues of knowledge such as *kashf* (intuitive discovery of knowledge) and occult sciences.

The principal areas of difference between the two schools can be summarised as follows (although it should be appreciated that, at the start, there were not many differences between the two groups and the following represents their final positions which are much further apart):[1]

A. *On the Sources of Doctrine and Law*

UṢŪLĪ SCHOOL	AKHBĀRĪ SCHOOL
1. The Uṣūlīs accept four sources of authority in matters of doctrine and law: the Qur'an, the Sunna, consensus (*ijma'*) and the intellect (*'aql*);	The Akhbārīs only accept the first two and some of them only the second (since the Qur'an can only be understood with the help of the Traditions);
2. accept and use the literal meaning of the Qur'an and the Traditions claiming that it is possible to know the meaning of these through the use of the intellect (*'aql*);	consider that the Qur'an and Traditions can only be understood where their meaning has been made explicit by the commentary (*tafsīr* and *ta'wīl*) of the Imams;
3. consider the four 'canonical' books of Traditions (see p. 174) to contain many unreliable Traditions;	consider the four books to be reliable;
4. accept as authoritative only Traditions from the Imams transmitted through reliable Shi'is;	allow a much wider search to be made for Traditions bearing on a particular problem, allowing Traditions from Sunni or other sources (provided the transmission is 'protected from fabrication') and even from an unknown source if there is good evidence supporting it.
5. divide the Traditions into four categories: *saḥīḥ*, *ḥasan*, *mutawātir* and *ḍa'īf* (see p. 174); and	recognise only two categories: *saḥiḥ* and *ḍa'īf*; and
6. consider that doctrines or legal decisions derived from transmitted (*naqlī*) sources (i.e. the Qur'an and Traditions) cannot contradict what is derived from rational principles.	consider that what is derived from *naqlī* sources always has precedence over what is derived from the use of reason.

B. *On the Principles of Jurisprudence*

UṢŪLĪ SCHOOL	AKHBĀRĪ SCHOOL
1. The Uṣūlīs accept *ijtihād*;	The Akhbārīs reject *ijtihād*;
2. consider that decisions can be given on the basis of *ẓann* (valid	consider that decisions can only be given where there is certain

UṢŪLĪ SCHOOL	AKHBĀRĪ SCHOOL
conjecture) achieved through *ijtihād*, in cases where certain knowledge (*'ilm*) from an explicit text in the Qur'an or Traditions is not available;	knowledge through a relevant Tradition from the Imam;
3. consider that knowledge was only obtainable directly from the Imams by those who were in their presence (i.e. that the legal decisions of the Imams may have been affected by individual circumstances and do not necessarily have general applicability) and so, during the Occultation, it is necessary to resort to *ijtihād*, and *fatwās* (legal decisions) can only be issued through use of this;	consider it obligatory to refer to the Imams even if through an intermediary (i.e. a transmitted Tradition) and that these have general applicability and that *fatwās* can only be issued on the basis of a relevant Tradition;
4. consider that through the use of *ijtihād*, the Traditions can be examined, one Tradition can be preferred over another contradictory one and practices can be derived from unclear and ambiguous texts; and	use only explicit texts from the Imams; and
5. act on the basis of freedom and the permissibility of all actions if there is no clear text against it.	consider that in cases where there is no clear text, caution must be exercised.

C. *On the Position of the Faqīh (jurist)*

1. The Uṣūlīs divide men into two groups: mujtahid and *muqallid* (see p. 175);	The Akhbārīs hold that all men are *muqallid* to the Imam and it is not permissible to turn to a mujtahid;
2. consider that the unrestricted (i.e. fully competent) mujtahid is learned in all of the ordinances of the religion since the condition for issuing legal decisions is knowledge of a large number of	consider that only the Imam is informed of all of the ordinances of the religion and that the only condition for issuing legal decisions is a knowledge of the terms used by the Imams and

UṢŪLĪ SCHOOL	AKHBĀRĪ SCHOOL
sciences, the most important of which is *uṣūl al-fiqh* (principles of jurisprudence);	knowing of a Tradition confirming the matter;
3. forbid following (*taqlīd*) a dead *marja'*;	allow use of the decisions of a dead jurist;
4. consider it obligatory to obey a mujtahid as much as it is to obey the Imam; and	reject this; and
5. consider that the use of *ijtihād* will result in a (heavenly) reward even if the decision is incorrect.	consider that the issuing of a decree except on the basis of a reliable and explicit Tradition is blameworthy.

It can be seen from the above that had the Akhbārīs been successful, the ulama would have been restricted in the field of jurisprudence to only those areas in which there is an explicit Tradition (all other cases would have to go to secular courts). But the Uṣūlīs, through the use of *ijtihād*, can give a judgement on virtually any subject. The Akhbārī position also severely restricted the authority and prerogatives of the ulama and effectively negated the *Nā'ib al-'Āmm* concept (see p. 190). It is not surprising that it was, in the end, decisively rejected by the ulama.

Today, Akhbārism survives in pockets throughout the Shi'i world. It is perhaps strongest in Bahrain where a considerable proportion of the island's Shi'is follow ulama of this school. There is also a band of territory stretching from the lands of the tribes at the western end of Lake al-Hammar (i.e. around Sūq ash-Shuyūkh) in southern Iraq to the Khurramshahr (Muḥammara) region of Iran where Akhbārism survives and there are one or two small Akhbārī religious schools (*madrasas*). The main centre of this area is the city of Baṣra and here the descendants of Mīrzā Muḥammad Akhbārī (see p. 135) continue to live and to lead the Akhbārīs of the area. There are also a few Akhbārīs in India. It has, however, continued to influence the mainstream of Twelver Shi'ism and not a few Uṣūlī ulama have questioned the extent to which *ijtihād* should be allowed. Even the late Āyatu'llāh Burūjirdī was said to have had doubts regarding the Uṣūlī position.[2]

The Shaykhī School

Whereas the Akhbārī School differed from the Uṣūlīs principally in the field of jurisprudence or the *furū'* (peripheral elements) of the religion, the Shaykhī School, founded by Shaykh Aḥmad ibn Zaynu'd-Dīn al-

Aḥsā'ī (1166/1753–1241/1826) differed principally in the field of doctrines and the *uṣūl* (fundamental principles) of the religion. Although Shaykh Aḥmad disagreed with Mullā Muḥsin-i Fayḍ on a number of points, the Shaykhī School may be regarded, on the simplest level of analysis, as a further development of the *Ḥikmat-i Ilāhī* of the School of Isfahan (see pp. 216–19). The doctrines of Shaykhism require a great deal more research but, pending that, the following is a brief outline of the major themes, emphasising those aspects where Shaykhism differs from the orthodox position:

A. *On God*: In order to have knowledge of something, there must be some similarity between the knower and the known. Since there is no similarity whatsoever between God and man, man can never know God's Essence. Any knowledge that man has of God is only a creation of his own imagination. At most it relates to an image or reflection of God but can never attain His reality. From God issues forth His Will and it is this which is the cause of creation. This view of God essentially negated the Sufi concept of *waḥdat al-wujūd* (existential unity) and the mystical union with God.

One aspect of Shaykh Aḥmad's views about God which brought him into conflict with the mainstream of Twelver Shi'i thought was his view regarding the knowledge of God. Shaykh Aḥmad considered that God had two types of knowledge, an essential (*dhātī*) knowledge which is inseparable from His Essence; and a created (*muḥdath*) knowledge which comes into being when God acts within creation. This same division may be applied to all of the attributes of God.

B. *On the Prophets*: The prophet stands as an intermediary between man and God. There is no similarity between God and the prophet nor between man and the prophet. The prophet is not merely a man whom God has chosen to become the recipient of his revelation but is unique and possessed of capabilities and attributes beyond the reach of even the most perfect man. In this, Shaykh Aḥmad is denying the Sufi idea that man can by purifying himself achieve the station of prophethood.

C. *On the Imams*: Shaykh Aḥmad considered that the first creation issuing forth from God's will was the light of Muhammad (*an-Nūr al-Muḥammadiyya*). From this light the light of the Imams came into being. From the light of the Imams the light of the believers came into being, and so on. Thus the Imams are the instruments of the creation of the world. They are also the ultimate cause of creation since God has created the world for their sake. They are the intermediaries through which man can obtain some comprehension of God and God's bounties can reach man.

It was Shaykh Aḥmad's conception of the Imams that drew from the orthodox camp the accusation of *tafwīḍ* (attributing God's attributes to someone other than God).

Another result of Shaykh Aḥmad's extreme veneration of the Imams was that, when visiting the shrines of the Imams, who were buried as is Muslim custom with their heads pointing towards Mecca, Shaykh Aḥmad would pay his respects at the foot of the Imam and never approached the head because he considered it disrespectful and because he did not wish, when the time for prayers came, to have to turn his back on the Imam, when he turned towards Mecca. This way of visiting the shrines of the Imams became characteristic of the followers of the Shaykh who became known as *Pusht-i Sarīs* (behind-the-headers) while the orthodox Shi'is were *Bālā-Sarīs* (above-the-headers). In the conflict between the Shaykhīs and their orthodox opponents that occurred from time to time, the two sides were often referred to as Shaykhīs and Bālā-Sarīs.

D. *On the Nature of the World*: Between the physical world and the spiritual world, there exists an intermediary world, the world of Hūrqalyā (or Huvarqalyā – variously stated to be Hebrew, Greek or Syriac in origin) or the world of archetypal images (*'Ālam al-mithāl*). This is identified as the *barzakh* (isthmus or purgatory) of orthodox Islamic eschatology.[3] Everything in the physical world has its counterpart in the world of Hūrqalyā. Each individual human being has two bodies, one of which exists in the physical world and one in Hūrqalyā. The occulted but living Twelfth Imam and the cities of Jābulsā and Jābulqā, where he is supposed to live, all exist in the realm of Hūrqalyā.

E. *Eschatology*: It was the consequences of Hūrqalyā, more than anything else, that led to Shaykh Aḥmad's conflict with the orthodox ulama. For the Shaykh's chief endeavour was to harmonise reason and religion and he used the concept of Hūrqalyā to explain some of the doctrines of Islam that appeared contrary to reason.

For Shaykh Aḥmad, the Occultation of the Twelfth Imam did not mean that a living physical Imam was in hiding somewhere on earth but rather that, although direct physical contact with the Imam was no longer possible, the Imam lived on in the world of archetypal images, the realm of Hūrqalyā, and, for those who strive to reach him in that world, he is still able to perform the key function of the Imam, that of initiating the seeker into the divine mysteries (*walāya*).

With regard to the phenomenon of resurrection, Shaykh Aḥmad also regarded this as an event that occurs to man's subtle body in the world of Hūrqalyā. Similarly, heaven and hell are the results of men's actions which create the situation of either heaven or hell in each individual's personal life in Hūrqalyā.

F. *The Night Ascent of Muhammad (Mi'rāj)*. One of the key events in the life of the Prophet was the night that, according to orthodox Muslim belief, he was transported bodily to a place near Jerusalem and then ascended to heaven. Shaykh Aḥmad asserted that the Mi'rāj took place with Muhammad's subtle body and not with his physical.

G. *The Fourth Support*: This key doctrine of the Shaykhīs was developed not so much by Shaykh Aḥmad himself as by his successors. Orthodox Shi'is believe in five supports or principles of the religion (*uṣūl ad-dīn*, see pp. 176–7). Shaykh Aḥmad considered that two of these, the unity of God and the justice of God could be put together as one, knowledge of God. Also, the resurrection, as part of the prophetic teaching, could be put under that heading and did not need to exist by itself. This left three supports to which a fourth was added. In the time of Sayyid Kāẓim and among the early writings of Karīm Khān Kirmānī, the Fourth Support (*ar-Rukn ar-Rābi'*) appears to mean the continuing presence in the physical world of a Perfect Shi'i (*ash-Shī'ī al-Kāmil*, cf. the Sufi concept of the Perfect Man) who is able to act as the intermediary between the Hidden Imam and the world. The Hidden Imam inspires this intermediary who thus comes to represent the will of the Hidden Imam. This Perfect Shi'i stands at the head of a hierarchy of figures, *nujabā* and *nuqabā*, who are each able to impart some of the Imam's knowledge and authority. The term *ar-Rukn ar-Rābi'* (or in its Persianised form *Rukn-i Rābi'*) is sometimes applied to the Perfect Shi'i alone and sometimes to the whole hierarchy. It is reasonably clear that the early Shaykhīs regarded Shaykh Aḥmad and Sayyid Kāẓim as each being successively the Perfect Shi'i, the Fourth Support, the gate to the Hidden Imam.[4] At a later stage in the evolution of Shaykhī doctrine, when the Shaykhīs were trying to be less controversial doctrinally, the term *ar-Rukn ar-Rābi'* came to be applied to the body of the ulama as a whole and indeed came to resemble the *Nā'ib al-'Āmm* concept.

However, underlying the bitter opposition of many mujtahids to the Shaykh's doctrines was undoubtedly a fear that the Shaykh's preference for intuitive knowledge, which he claimed to obtain directly by inspiration from the Imams, would seriously undermine the authority of their position which was based on knowledge derived by the rational processes of *ijtihād*. Shaykh Aḥmad's preference for the intuitive uncovering of knowledge (*kashf*) led his school to be called Kashfī by some.

In matters of jurisprudence Shaykh Aḥmad appears to have taken an intermediate position between the Uṣūlīs and the Akhbārīs. He did not deny the validity of *ijtihād* but considered it desirable to remain within the area demarcated by the Traditions of the Imams.

These doctrines of Shaykh Aḥmad inevitably brought him into conflict with the more fundamentalist ulama. The first matters that became the subject of conflict were the questions of the night ascent of Muhammad and the resurrection which the Shaykh's opponents considered to have occurred or were to occur with the physical body. There was also the question of *tafwīḍ* (see above) and of the knowledge of God.[5] Later numerous other points were added to the list of differences.

Shaykh Aḥmad, during his lifetime, had appointed Sayyid Kāẓim as his trustee and successor. During Sayyid Kāẓim's time, the conflict with orthodoxy intensified. At his death in 1259/1843, Sayyid Kāẓim failed to appoint a successor and the Shaykhīs, apart from those that went on to become Bābīs (see next section), split into three main factions: one led by Mīrzā Ḥasan Gawhar in Karbalā, one led by Ḥājjī Mīrzā Shafī', Thiqatu'l-Islām and Mullā Muḥammad Mamaqānī Ḥujjatu'l-Islām in Tabrīz and one led by Ḥājjī Muḥammad Karīm Khān Kirmānī in Kirmān.

At Karbala many of the Shaykhīs followed Mīrzā Ḥasan Gawhar (Mullā Muḥammad Ḥasan Qarāchadāghī) although two other figures, Mīrzā Muḥammad Ḥusayn Muḥīṭ Kirmānī and Sayyid Kāẓim's son, Aḥmad (killed 1878), had considerable influence. Leadership of this group was assumed after Gawhar's death by Mullā Muḥammad Bāqir Uskū'ī (d. 1301/1883). After him leadership passed to his son, Mīrzā Mūsā, and now rests with his grandson, Mīrzā 'Alī Ḥā'irī, who is resident in Kuwait. They are known as Uskū'īs.

The Tabrīz Shaykhīs quickly suppressed all external evidence of heterodoxy. Thus, for example, in the field of jurisprudence, they unreservedly adopted the Uṣūlī School. This did not, however, save them from the animosity of the populace. During the last half of the 19th century there were frequent anti-Shaykhī riots and, indeed, the splitting of the city into Shaykhī and Bālā-Sarī quarters came to replace the Ni'matī-Ḥaydarī division of other Iranian cities (see p. 215). Leadership among the Tabrīz Shaykhīs came to lie in two families. At first it was the Ḥujjatu'l-Islām family that was predominant. Mullā Muḥammad Mamaqānī Ḥujjatu'l-Islām (d. 1269/1852) led the prayers in the Ḥujjatu'l-Islām Mosque and became one of the prominent religious leaders of Ādharbāyjān. His three sons, Mullā Muḥammad Ḥusayn (d. 1303/1885), Mullā Muḥammad Taqī (d. 1312/1894) and Mīrzā Isma'īl (d. 1317/1899) and Mullā Muḥammad Ḥusayn's son, Mīrzā Abu'l-Qāsim (d. 1362/1943) each in turn took the title Ḥujjatu'l-Islām and became the leader of prayers in the Ḥujjatu'l-Islām Mosque. After the last-named, however, the family died out. The second family was the Thiqatu'l-Islām family. Ḥājj Mīrzā Shafī' Thiqatu'l-Islām (d. 1301/1884) was, like Mullā Muḥammad Mamaqānī, a student of Shaykh

Aḥmad and Sayyid Kāẓim. He was succeeded in turn by his son Shaykh Mūsā (d. 1319/1901) and grandson Mīrzā 'Alī, each of whom successively took the title Thiqatu'l-Islām. During the lifetime of Mīrzā 'Alī, the Thiqatu'l-Islām family overtook the Ḥujjatu'l-Islām family in importance and became the leader of the majority of the Tabrīz Shaykhīs. Mīrzā 'Alī became a national hero when he was hanged by the Russians in 1912 for resisting the occupation of Tabrīz. A large number of the writings of Shaykh Aḥmad were lithographed in Tabrīz during the 19th century. (Tabrīz also had a group of Shaykhīs who followed Muḥammad Karīm Khān Kirmānī and these were centred on the Kāẓimī Mosque.)

The most important group of Shaykhīs, however, was that led by Ḥājjī Muḥammad Karīm Khān Kirmānī (1810–71) who was a member of the ruling Qājār family (his mother was Nāṣiru'd-Dīn's great-aunt and he was the maternal uncle of the mother of Muẓaffaru'd-Dīn Shāh). After his death leadership of this group of Shaykhīs went successively to members of his family who were each known by the title 'Sarkār Āqā' (His Lordship). For a while there was a dispute over the leadership between Muḥammad Karīm Khān's two sons, Ḥājjī Muḥammad Raḥīm Khān and Ḥājjī Muḥammad Khān. Then in 1878 there was a violent Shaykhī-Bālā-Sarī conflict in Kirmān which lasted for over a year. At the end of this time Muḥammad Raḥīm Khān was expelled by the Governor and the leadership crisis was thus resolved in favour of Ḥājjī Muḥammad Khān. Most of the followers of Muḥammad Raḥīm Khān rejoined the main group after a while. A more serious split was caused by Ḥājjī Mīrzā Muḥammad Bāqir Hamadānī (d. 1901) who objected to the leadership becoming hereditary and considered himself more learned than Ḥājjī Muḥammad Khān. His residence was in Hamadān until 1897 when a Shaykhī-Bālā-Sarī riot forced him to move to Nā'īn. His followers, known as Bāqirīs, are most numerous in Hamadān, Nā'īn and Isfahan. Muḥammad Khān's followers were known as Nāṭiqīs or Nawāṭiq.

Ḥājjī Muḥammad Khān died in 1906 and was succeeded by his brother Ḥājjī Zaynu'l-'Ābidīn Khān (d. 1941) who in turn was succeeded by his son Ḥājjī Abu'l-Qāsim Khān Ibrāhīmī (d. 1969) and grandson Ḥājjī 'Abdu'r-Riḍā Khān Ibrāhīmī. The latter was killed during the disturbances following the Iranian Revolution on 26 December 1979 in Kirmān. After this leadership of the movement went out of the Ibrāhīmī family and the new leader is Sayyid 'Alī Mūsawī who is resident in Baṣra in Iraq.

Under Muḥammad Karīm Khān and his successors Shaykhism underwent a phenomenon that might be called doctrinal drift. By this is meant that each successive Shaykhī leader expounded the doctrines of the school in such a way as to bring them more and more closely into line with orthodoxy. The culmination of this process occurred in 1950 when Āqā Muḥammad Taqī Falsafī (acting on behalf of Āyatu'llāh Burūjirdī) put twenty-five questions to Ḥājjī Abu'l-Qāsim Khān Ibrāhīmī on matters of doctrine. These were answered (in the *Risāla-yi Falsafiyya*) in so completely orthodox a manner that Falsafī was left wondering why the Shaykhīs chose to call themselves by a separate name.

Shaykhīs have remained a small minority in the Shi'i world, numbering perhaps 200,000 in Iran and 300,000 in Iraq and the Gulf. They are to be found in most cities but are most numerous in Kirmān, Tabrīz, Khurramshahr, Ābādān, Tehran, Ābāda, Marvdasht, Rafsanjān, Shīrāz and Zunūz as well as in Baṣra in Iraq. At Kirmān the Shaykhīs have a small religious college, the Madrasa Ibrahimiyya, with some 30 or 40 students, and a publishing house and press. There is also a religious college in Baṣra.

The Bābī Movement and the Bahā'ī Religion

The approach of the Muslim year 1260 (1844) was accompanied by a general rise in expectancy of the return of the Hidden Imam. This was because that year marked the one thousandth anniversary of the disappearance of the Twelfth Imam and the beginning of the period of Occultation. There were several indications in the Qur'an and the Traditions that the dispensation of Muhammad would be one thousand years long[6] and thus the year 1260 was greatly anticipated throughout the Shi'i world.[7]

Sayyid 'Alī Muḥammad Shīrāzī (1819–50), who took the title the Bāb (the Gate), was, until the death of Sayyid Kāẓim Rashtī in 1843, closely associated with the Shaykhī School. Then, in 1844, he put forward a claim and gained many adherents, initially mostly from among the Shaykhī School. At first the Bāb only appeared to be claiming to be the Gate to the Hidden Imam and his followers kept to the Islamic *Sharī'a*. But in 1848 he advanced the claim of being the returned Twelfth Imam himself who had come to abrogate the Islamic dispensation and inaugurate a new prophetic cycle.

Developing the argument of the Shaykhī School, from the Bābī viewpoint, just as the Hidden Imam existed in the world of Hūrqalyā, the realm of archetypal images, so the return of the Twelfth Imam was not the return of the self-same physical body of the Imam but rather the advent of a man who in the realm of Hūrqalyā is the archetypal figure of the Imam. Thus it was that the Shaykhī teachings paved the way for the Bāb and it is doubtful if the Bāb would have attracted so many adherents if it had not been for the Shaykhī doctrines.

The Bāb was put to death by a firing squad in Tabrīz in 1850. He had appointed as his successor Mīrzā Yaḥyā, Subḥ-i Azal, and had prophesied the advent of another messianic figure whom he called 'Him whom God shall make manifest'. Privately in 1863 and publicly in 1866, Mīrzā Ḥusayn 'Alī (1817–1892), who took the title Bahā'u'llāh (Glory of God), claimed to be this messianic figure foretold by the Bāb. The majority of Bābīs became Bahā'īs. Bahā'u'llāh considerably expanded the scope of his appeal beyond the confines of Shi'i Iran by claiming to be the fulfilment of the messianic expectations of other religions such as Judaism, Christianity and Zoroastrianism.

Bahā'u'llāh was succeeded by his son 'Abbās Effendi (1844–1921), who took the title 'Abdu'l-Bahā (Servant of the Glory). He was given the position of authorised interpreter of Bahā'u'llāh's teachings. He appointed his grandson, Shoghi Effendi (d. 1957), as Guardian of the Bahā'ī Faith. Since 1963 the religion has been administered by an elected body, the Universal House of Justice.

The Bahā'ī Faith, during the time of 'Abdu'l-Bahā, spread to Europe and North America. In the last few decades, it has gained large numbers of adherents in India, Africa, South America and Australasia such that it has outstripped its Islamic heritage and Iran is no longer even the largest national Bahā'ī community. Thus the Bahā'ī Faith is now an independent religion separate from Islam. It has its own holy books, its own teachings and laws and considers its prophets, the Bāb and Bahā'u'llāh, to be independent prophets of God equal in station to Muhammad and bearers of a new revelation from God abrogating the Islamic dispensation. It would therefore be inappropriate to consider it any further in a book on Twelver Shi'ism.

13

The Popular Religion

In Chapter 10 Shi'i Islam was viewed from the aspect of the ulama. In this chapter we will try to give an impression of what the religion means to the Shi'i masses and how it affects their lives.

In Sunni Islam it has tended to be the Sufi Shaykhs and their mysticism that have held sway over a large part of the population. Shi'is, however, look to the ulama for guidance in religious matters. And therefore Islam for the Shi'is is, even more than for Sunnis, a religion of rituals, obligations and prohibitions.

The Personal Religious Outlook

Life for a devout Shi'i is perceived very much as having an account with God. This account is credited and debited during one's life. At death, for those with a sufficiently large positive balance in their account there is heaven; for those with a large negative balance there is hell; and for those in between there is the in-between world of *barzakh* (purgatory) where they are punished for their sins sufficiently to make them eventually worthy of heaven.

In order to avoid debits to one's account, one must live one's life within the bounds of what is permitted (*ḥalāl*) but, in addition, one can credit one's account by living one's life as closely as possible to the ideal pattern laid down in the *Sunna* (pattern of words and deeds as conveyed in the Traditions) of the Prophet and the Imams. This involves performance of the various ritual observances which occur on a daily basis (e.g. the obligatory prayers), a weekly basis (e.g. the Friday prayer) or a yearly basis (e.g. the fast in Ramaḍān). All of these must be observed with a rigorous attention to detail, for the slightest error may result in a state of ritual impurity thus negating all benefit from the performance of the ritual.

In addition to this, one's account can be credited by the performance of specific deeds which are not in themselves obligatory. These include such things as performing a visitation to a shrine or hosting a gathering for the recital of the sufferings of the Imams. Charitable deeds such as donating money for hospitals or helping someone who is in trouble will also credit one's account.

Any meritorious action which will credit one's account is called a *thawāb* and each action has its own scale of recompense, thus one can have big *thawābs* and little *thawābs*.

On the debit side of one's account go failure to perform rituals when one is able to perform them; committing acts that are forbidden (*ḥarām*); and failing to live up to one's social obligations.

Every action performed by an individual may be classified into one of five categories and these, with their credit and debit resulting from their commission or omission, are listed below:

Action	*Commission of that Action*	*Omission of that Action*
Obligatory (*wājib*)	+	–
Desirable (*mustaḥabb*)	+	0
Neutral (*mubāḥ*)	0	0
Undesirable (*makrūh*)	0	+
Forbidden (*ḥarām*)	–	+

\+ = credit to account
– = debit to account
0 = no change in account

The result of this concentration on the externals of the religion is that in tight-knit social groups such as the Bazaar, one's piety and religious merit are judged by others not on the basis of one's beliefs (which are indeed seldom discussed) but on the basis of being observed to be performing the required rituals (i.e. orthopraxy rather than orthodoxy is the standard by which one is assessed).

The ulama are of course necessary as a guide to the complex details of what is and what is not permissible. Although individual mullas may be regarded as charlatans or hypocrites, the ulama as a class are highly regarded both because of their guidance in traversing the snakes-and-ladders world of obligations and prohibitions and also because the local mulla is regarded as an intermediary between the ordinary Shi'i and the great *mujtahids* who are the *marāji' at-taqlīd*. At the village level the mulla is often the only literate person and serves an important role in communications and in social and business transactions.

There is a great deal of genuine popular esteem for the *marāji' at-taqlīd*. This is partly because of their perceived piety and sanctity and partly because of their role as the deputies of the Hidden Imam, the latter being the focus of the eschatological and soteriological aspirations of the masses. This image of the *marja'* is carefully fostered by stories told of miracles attributed to them. These miracles are called by the term *karāmāt* (so as not to compare them to the miracles, *mu'jizāt*, which are one of the proofs of the prophets and Imams).

Whereas in Sunni Islam there is a direct relationship between the believer and God as revealed in the religion of Islam, in Shi'i Islam there is something of a triangular relationship. While for some things, such as the daily obligatory prayers, the individual is in direct relationship to God, in other matters he looks (usually through the mediation of the local mulla) to the *marja' at-taqlīd* who is regarded as being in a more direct relationship with God. Indeed, in the minds of many of the less educated, the ulama and the *marja'* are intermediaries between them and God and the relationship is not so much triangular as hierarchical (see Chart 6 on p. 243).

Another group who have a popularly perceived sanctity are the *Sayyids* (those who claim descent from Muhammad through 'Ali and Fāṭima). Marriage into such a family is considered a great honour and *Sayyids* are often asked to bless a marriage or a new-born child.

The emphasis on the observation of the externals of the religion does not mean, however, that there is no room for individual piety. Apart from the obligatory prayer (*ṣalat*) which is said in Arabic, one can say personal prayer (*du'ā*) and communions with God (*munājāt*) in one's own language, addressing God in relation to the events of one's daily life.

It is, however, upon the Fourteen Pure Ones (Muhammad, Fāṭima and the Twelve Imams) that the religious fervour of the individual is concentrated. Not only can addressing them in prayer and visiting their shrines induce them to act as intercessors with God for the pardoning of sins, but, through the recital of the details of their lives and struggles (especially at gatherings commemorating their births and deaths), they become models for and guides to the daily existence of the individual. In particular it is the Holy Family (consisting of Muhammad as a grandfather figure, 'Ali and Fāṭima, their sons Hasan and Husayn, and to a lesser extent their daughter, Zaynab) which is looked to as the model family for all Shi'is to follow in their family inter-relationships. Fāṭima (and to a lesser extent Zaynab) has become the model of ideal womanhood, while 'Ali or Husayn serve that role for men.

The Holy Family are connected with a large range of religious symbolism. Muhammad is, of course, the recipient of the revelation, the link with God; he is, however, so exalted as to be only approachable through one of the other members of the family; 'Ali represents the intellectual, esoteric side of religion (the way to obtain the true meaning of the revelation) and its legalistic aspect ('Ali had complete knowledge of the religious law and was the perfect judge); Fāṭima is the Mother-

Creator figure, not very different from the image of Mary in Roman Catholicism, she is even referred to as 'virgin' (*batūl*); Husayn represents atonement, his redemptive martyrdom gives to all the possibility of salvation; the Twelfth Imam is the focus of eschatological hopes of triumph over tyranny and injustice and final salvation. While the ulama look to the image of 'Ali, the image of the intellectual, esoteric yet legalistic attitude towards religion, it is undoubtedly Husayn and his representation of redemption through sacrifice and martyrdom that has caught the imagination and devotion of the Shi'i masses.

The theme of martyrdom and patient suffering is one that is very strong in Shi'ism. This is perhaps not surprising in a sect that has for much of its existence been a persecuted minority. This theme is embodied in the lives of the Imams themselves who are each regarded as having suffered intense persecution, in some cases imprisonment and physical punishment and who are all popularly considered to have been martyred (except of course the Twelfth Imam, but see Chapter 3 regarding the historicity of this claim). The essence of this Shi'i attitude is summed up in the word *maẓlūmiyyat* which means the patient endurance of suffering caused by the tyrannical actions of those who have power over you. All the Imams are considered to have displayed this virtue and, at each of their anniversaries, their lives are recounted emphasising in particular the wrongs that they suffered at the hands of the Umayyad and 'Abbasid governments.

There is thus a strange paradox in Shi'i Islam in that two apparently contradictory attitudes are both equally praised and commended. The Imams are praised for their patient endurance of suffering at the hands of those with political power; they are commended for their use of *taqiyya* (religious dissimulation) in the face of overwhelming odds. And yet the greatest Shi'i hero, the Imam Husayn, is praised and commended for not submitting to tyranny and rising up (*qiyāmat*) and fighting even in the face of overwhelming odds and the certainty of martyrdom.

This paradox has indeed given Shi'is religious justification for an extraordinary political versatility. Those who wish to lead the Shi'i masses can, if the opposition seems overwhelmingly superior or it is expedient to do so, enjoin upon the Shi'is the patient endurance (*maẓlūmiyyat*) of the Imams. And yet when the opportunity seems right, the Shi'i masses can be whipped up to the frenzy of revolution by appeal to the spirit of uprising (*qiyām*) of Husayn. In this state, as was seen in Iran in 1979, the Shi'is are prepared to go into the streets unarmed in eager anticipation of martyrdom. Indeed, it is this (rather than, as has been stated by many Western orientalists, any theoretical illegitimacy of temporal power during the Occultation of the Twelfth Imam) that is the source of the revolutionary fervour latent within Shi'i Islam.[1]

One further feature of the Shi'i world-view, which is also a feature of many centuries of being a persecuted minority, is the need for a scapegoat. Although it is centuries since Shi'ism was made the official religion of Iran, this world-view is still strong among Iranian Shi'is. Thaiss has described it thus:

> The environment (in the broadest sense) to an Iranian Shi'a is seen as threatening, a perception in which the directionality involved is *from* the environment toward the person, so that he is viewed as an effect, and various external factors as cause. A person in such a cultural situation would not likely hold himself accountable when things go wrong and would generally react by turning anger and hostility outward toward others – perceived Sunni oppressors, an arbitrary and unjust government, imperialists, agents of change and modernization, minority groups such as Jews, Baha'i etc.[2]

This world-view is as much present among the ulama as among the ordinary people and usually it has been the ulama who, as the natural leaders of the community, have directed the people as to the identity of the scapegoat. While Shi'ism was a minority, the Sunni majority were, of course, the scapegoats and for a while under the Safavids they remained in this role. Later, when the threat from the Ottoman Empire receded, internal scapegoats were found, especially among those who challenged the authority of the ulama. At first it was the Akhbārīs, then successively the Shaykhīs, the Bābīs and then the Bahā'īs. From time to time, the government or the Jews have also been cast in this role. The motif was very strong in the period immediately before the overthrow of the Shāh in 1979, with the Shāh being openly identified with Mu'āwiya, the enemy of the Imam Husayn. Since the Revolution, the Iraqi government, American imperialism and the international Zionist conspiracy have become the major external scapegoats, while the Bahā'īs have resumed their role as internal scapegoats.

The Pattern of Religious Life

The pattern of life for the religiously devout is punctuated by the rituals of the religion. These rituals may be classified according to whether they occur on a daily, weekly, yearly or irregular basis. These rituals are described elsewhere in this book (see Chapter 9) and are only briefly listed here to demonstrate their pattern of occurrence.

Daily:	Between dawn and sunrise Between noon and late afternoon Between sunset and midnight	Call to prayer (*adhān*) Ablutions (*wuḍū*) Prayer (*ṣalāt*)
Weekly:	Friday	Friday prayer (*ṣalāt al-jum'a*)

Yearly:	Month of Ramaḍān	Fast (*sawm, siyām*)
	Various commemorations on particular days (see Table 8): Births of Imams by joyous feasts (*'Īds*, Persian *'Ayds*) and Deaths of Imams by mourning ceremonies (*'azā-dārī*)	
Irregular:	Month of Dhu'l-Ḥijja	Pilgrimage to Mecca (*Ḥajj*)
	Anytime	Pilgrimage to shrines of Imams, descendants of Imams (*Imāmzādas*) and other saints (*Ziyārat*)

The yearly cycle is punctuated by a large number of events of religious significance. Several of these, such as the month-long fast during Ramaḍān, the feast of *Qurbān* (Sacrifice, commemorating Abraham's intended sacrifice of Ishmael) and the death of Muhammad are shared with the Sunnis. In addition, however, the births and deaths of each of the Imams are commemorated by festive gatherings or mourning ceremonies as appropriate. A full list may be found in Table 8.

The most important of these commemorations is that of the martyrdom of the Imam Husayn. The commemorations of this are detailed later in this chapter. It is traditional to keep an all-night vigil of mourning for the three days that commemorate the interval between the stabbing and death of the Imam 'Ali (19 to 21 Ramaḍān).

Of the religious events that occur sporadically in the life of an individual, the pilgrimage to Mecca (*ḥajj*) is of course a high point and is undertaken by all who can afford it. However, all of the important events of life such as marriage, birth and death are commemorated by religious gatherings both in the home and in the mosque. Indeed, for the less devout these may be their only contact with religion.

Religious Gatherings

It has been customary in Iran for the devout to gather together in informal groups, usually on a neighbourhood basis, for the purpose of religious instruction and the commemoration of the events of the religious calendar. These groups, which are called *hay'ats*, are not organised by the ulama and the gatherings usually rotate among the houses of the members of the group. A member of the ulama will, however, often be asked to attend either to preach or to assist in the study of the Qur'an.

The most conservative and traditionally-devout section of Iranian society has always been the Bazaar. Many of the Bazaaris form *hay'ats* on the basis of their guilds (i.e. on the basis of occupation). Other *hay'ats* may be formed on the basis of ethnic affiliation (e.g. Turkish-speaking

Table 8: Calendar of Religious Commemorations

Muḥarram	1–10	Martyrdom of the third Imam, Husayn at Karbalā
	9*, 10*	Tāsū'ā and 'Āshūrā, culmination of Karbalā commemorations
	11†	Death of fourth Imam, Zaynu'l-'Ābidīn
Ṣafar	3†	Birth of fifth Imam, Muḥammad al-Bāqir
	7	Birth of seventh Imam, Mūsā al-Kāẓim
	20	Arba'īn (fortieth day after death of Husayn)
	28*	Death of the Prophet Muhammad and second Imam, Hasan
	30†	Death of eighth Imam, 'Alī ar-Riḍā
Rabī' I	8	Death of eleventh Imam, Ḥasan al-'Askarī
	9	Death of 'Umar the second Caliph (a joyful occasion for Shi'is)
	17*	Birth of Muhammad (Sunnis celebrate this on 12th) and of sixth Imam, Ja'far aṣ-Ṣādiq
Rabi' II	8†	Birth of eleventh Imam, Ḥasan al-'Askarī
Jamādī I	5	Birth of Zaynab, sister of Imam Husayn
	13†	Death of Fāṭima
Jamādī II	20*†	Birth of Fāṭima
Rajab	3	Death of tenth Imam, 'Alī al-Hādī
	10†	Birth of ninth Imam, Muḥammad at-Taqī
	13*	Birth of first Imam, 'Ali
	15	Death of Zaynab, sister of Imam Husayn
	25	Death of seventh Imam, Mūsā al-Kāẓim
	27*	'Īd al-Maba'th (commemoration of the start of the Prophet's mission)
Sha'bān	3†	Birth of third Imam, Husayn
	5†	Birth of fourth Imam, Zaynu'l-'Ābidīn
	8†	Occultation of twelfth Imam, al-Mahdī
	15*	Birth of twelfth Imam, al-Mahdī
Ramaḍān	Whole month	Month of fast – frequent religious gatherings
	15	Birth of second Imam, Hasan
	19	Stabbing of first Imam, 'Ali
	21*	Death of first Imam, 'Ali
Shawwāl	1*	'Īd al-Fiṭr (commemorates end of fast)
	25*	Death of sixth Imam, Ja'far aṣ-Ṣādiq
Dhu'l Qad'a	11*	Birth of eighth Imam, 'Alī ar-Riḍā
	29	Death of ninth Imam, Muḥammad at-Taqī
Dhu'l-Ḥijja	7	Death of fifth Imam, Muḥammad al-Bāqir
	10*	'Īd al-Qurbān (Feast of Sacrifice)
	15	Birth of tenth Imam, 'Alī al-Hādī
	18*	'Īd al-Ghadīr (celebrates Muhammad's designation of 'Ali as his successor at Ghadīr Khumm, see p. 15)

* These more important commemorations are public holidays in Iran.

† These dates are variable from one Shi'i community to another; the dates given in this table are the ones generally used in Iran.

Ādharbāyjānīs) or just on friendship. Women, too, may have their own *hay'ats* or participate in the neighbourhood ones.

In the decades preceding the 1979 Revolution in Iran, some religious groupings took on a more political aspect and became foci of anti-government sentiment. In these groups, names such as Mu'āwiya and Umayyad became code-names for the Shāh and the government respectively and whole orations could be given in such a mutually-understood code. Some of these groups such as the Fidā'iyān and Mujāhidīn translated the rhetoric of Husayn's rising against a tyrannical government into action by forming themselves into terrorist groups.

Apart from the gatherings of the *hay'ats* and other religious groups, individual Shi'is will frequently convene other religious gatherings, often in fulfilment of a vow taken to hold such a meeting in return for recovery from an illness or similar crisis.

The commonest of these meetings is the *rawḍa-khānī*, recital of the sufferings and martyrdom of the Imam Husayn (or sometimes the other Imams also). The host for the gathering will send invitations to a number of friends and colleagues at work, will invite the *rawḍa-khān* (reciter of the *rawḍa*), and provide refreshments, usually in the form of tea and sweet-meats. The *rawḍa-khān* is considered a good one if he is able to raise the emotions of his audience to the point of weeping and lamentation. At some meetings, some men will start to beat themselves on the chest as the narration reaches its climax while others call out to Husayn and weep.

Rawḍa-khānī is held throughout the year but, in particular, in the month of Muḥarram during which the martyrdom of Husayn is commemorated. On 10 Muḥarram, the day of 'Āshūrā, when the martyrdom itself occurred, most of the people attend a *rawḍa*, either in a private house, or in a mosque, or in another building called a *Ḥusayniyya*, which has been specially built or converted for such use. Another aspect of the Muḥarram commemorations are street processions. These processions often carry a simulated body or a replica sarcophagus (*naql*) and are, in effect, ritualised funeral processions for the Imam Husayn. The procession goes through the streets and the bazaar chanting eulogies and threnodies to the martyred Imam while rows of men (*dastas*) beat themselves rhythmically with sticks, chains and swords until the blood flows from their backs or foreheads. This self-flagellation can be seen in all parts of the Shi'i world (see Figs. 46–9). In India the procession forms around a replica of the tomb of Husayn in Karbalā and the ceremony ends with the burial of the replica tomb.

A third feature of the Muḥarram commemorations is the *ta'ziya*. This is a highly stylised theatrical presentation of the Karbalā tragedy. It evolved in Iran during the late Safavid and Qājār periods[3] and spread to

Iraq and south Lebanon but does not appear to be popular in other Shi'i communities. It had almost died out in Iran in recent years but has been revived since the 1979 Revolution. It has been called the Shi'i equivalent of the Christian Passion Play.

The following is an account of a *ta'ziya* as witnessed by J. M. Tancoigne at Tehran. Although this account relates to the 19th century, it remains a remarkably good portrayal of such events even to the present day:

But the most curious and extraordinary of all those we have hitherto seen, is the Tazies, or desolations, a kind of funeral games, instituted in memory of the martyrdom of the Imans, Hassan and Hussein, sons of Ali. It is very difficult to give an exact description of such a spectacle, even after having seen it; I shall, however, attempt to give you an idea of the scene. We were invited by the king to be present at their celebration, and being placed conveniently in the shade of a tent raised on one of the terraces of the palace, it enabled us to enjoy a good sight of the whole at one view.

The object of the Tazies is to remind the people of these memorable events, and to preserve their hatred and resentment against the Sunnis. The festival commences on the first of Mouharrem, and lasts until the 11th of the same month.

During those days of mourning, all the mosques are hung in black, the public squares and crossways are covered with large awnings, and at regular distances are placed stands, ornamented with vases of flowers, small bells, and arms of every kind. The Mollahs stationed in pulpits sing in a mournful voice sacred hymns and lamentations, and the whole auditory respond to them with tears and deep sighs. Men almost naked run through the city, striking their breasts rapidly; others piercing their arms and legs with knives, fastening padlocks in the flesh under their breasts, or making wide gashes in their heads, invoke their saints with frightful howlings, shouting out Hassan! Hussein!

It is in the great court of the king's palace that the five last representations take place. They might be, in some respects, compared to those ancient spectacles, in which the miseries of the passion were acted. The vizirs pay the expences of the first day, and the city of Teheran, which is divided into four districts, pays those of the remaining four.

On a theatre erected opposite the king's kiosk, is to be seen the family of Hussein, represented by men in women's dresses. They are in great agitation, seem to have a foreboding of the dismal fate which that Iman must experience in the plain of Kerbela, and make the air resound with shrieks and dreadful groans. Horsemen soon arrive, load them with chains and carry them off. The two armies of the Iman Hussein and the caliph Yezid then appear in the square: the battle commences; Hussein soon falls from his horse covered with wounds, and Yezid orders his head to be cut off. At that moment the sobbings and lamentations of all the assembly are redoubled; the spectators strike their breasts, and tears stream from every eye!

On the following days, the representation of this tragedy is continued; Yezid successively destroys Hassan* and the two children of Hussein, who had fallen into his power, and a general procession terminates the fifth day.

* This is evidently a mistake as the Imam Hasan had died previously. However, these *ta'ziya* did often include representations of the deaths of 'Ali and Hasan.

The march was opened by a crowd of men of the lower orders, carrying flags surmounted with a hand of steel, and banners of Cachemire shawls, the richness of which formed a singular contrast with the poverty of their own dresses. Then came led horses magnificently caparisoned, their trappings shining with gold and jewels; litters ornamented with foliage and verdure; figures of dead bodies covered with blood, and pierced with daggers, round which aquatic birds moved. Naked and bleeding men marched behind; some of them had a large scimetar stuck into a false skull half open, fitted on their heads, or arrows which seemed to pierce through their breasts. They were followed by a long train of camels mounted by men dressed in black, as were the female mourners, and an infinity of persons of that sort, who threw ashes and chopped straw on their heads in token of mourning.

A more pompous and imposing spectacle suddenly came to variegate these hideous scenes. There appeared two great mosques of gilt wood, carried by more than three hundred men: both were inlaid with mirrors, and surmounted with little minarets: children placed in the galleries sang sacred hymns, the soft harmony of which agreeably recompensed the spectators for the frightful shoutings they had heard just before. Several Mollahs, magnificently dressed, prayed in the interior, at the tomb of the two Imans. The representation of the Kaaba, or house of Abraham, at Mecca, appeared immediately after the two mosques, and was not inferior to them in richness of ornament. It was followed by Hussein's war horse, pierced all over with arrows, and led at large by his faithful slave, naked and armed with a battleaxe. A great number of children with wings of painted pasteboard, figured as angels or genii, marched in the rear.

The procession was closed by two or three hundred of the common people in tatters, who struck their breasts, and drove two round pieces of wood with violence against each other, crying 'Hassan, Hossein! Ali!' lastly, by Mollahs, each carrying a large torch of yellow wax in a candlestick. The latter stopped a moment under the windows of the kiosk, where the king was; and the Cheik ul Islam addressed, according to custom, praises to his majesty.

We did not receive an invitation for the last day of the festival: the king wishing to spare the legation from witnessing the assassination of a Greek ambassador, who Yezid caused to be put to death, for having interceded with him for the pardon of Hussein's brother. The Persians, from what motive I know not, produce this ambassador in the modern European dress.

All these ceremonies are also repeated in the houses of the nobility. I give you only an imperfect idea of them, for it would be impossible for me to recollect the numerous peculiarities of the representation: yet I can assure you of the exactness of those I have related.[4]

There appears to be a good deal of variation in different parts of the Shi'i world for the terms associated with mourning for the Imam Husayn. The terminology used above is that which is prevalent in Iran. The word *ta'ziya* in India denotes the model of Husayn's tomb carried in the processions (also called *ḍarīḥ*); in Iran, as noted above, it means the 'Passion Play'; in Lebanon it denotes the *rawḍa* gathering; while in southern Iraq and Bahrain it is the name given to the ceremonial processions (these latter are called *jalūs* in India). The *rawḍa* in India is called a *majlis* and in southern Iraq a *qirāya*. The *ta'ziya* or 'Passion Play' is sometimes in Iran and usually in Iraq called a *shabīh*; in Lebanon it is called *shabīh* or *tamthīl al-Ḥusayn*. The building used for *rawḍas* is called a *Ḥusayniyya* in Iran, Iraq and Lebanon, an *Imāmbāṛa* in India and a *Ma'tam* in Bahrain (see Table 9).

Although women also participate in *rawḍa-khānīs* and may host such events exclusively for women, there is another type of religious meeting particular to women. This is called the *sufra* (literally tablecloth) and consists of an invitation by the hostess to a number of other women to join her for a meal which is usually preceded or followed by a discourse by a mulla (often female) on a religious theme. *Sufras* are often held in the name of one of the members of the Holy Family (who then becomes the theme of the sermon for the mulla) and are often in fulfilment of a vow.

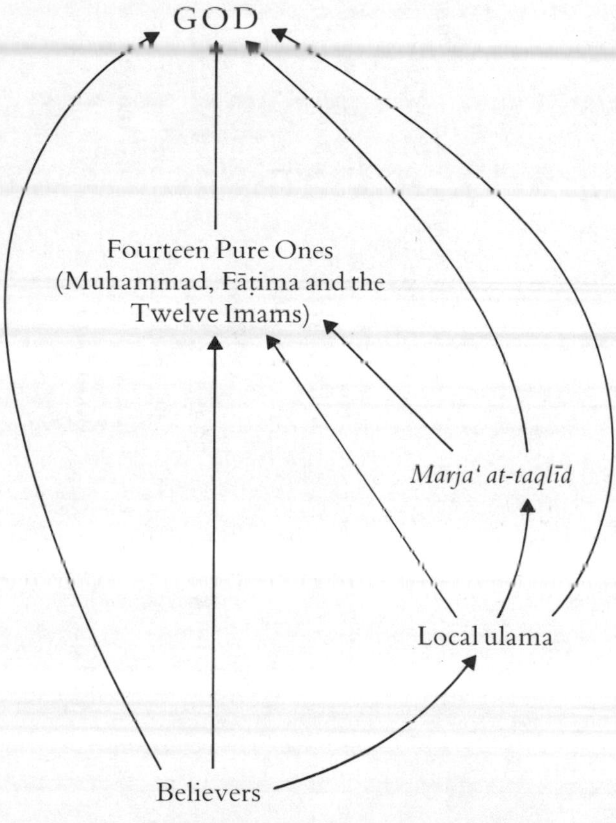

Chart 6. Diagram illustrating religious relationships as perceived by the ordinary believer (see p. 235)

Table 9: Names associated with mourning for the Imam Husayn in different Shi'i communities

Country	*Oration mourning Imam Husayn*	*Place where such orations held*	*Theatrical performances of the Karbalā tragedy*	*Ceremonial Processions*
Iran	Rawḍa	Ḥusayniyya	Ta'ziya or Shabīh	No particular name
Iraq	Qirāya	Ḥusayniyya	Shabīh	Ta'ziya, Mawkib
Bahrain	'Āshūrā	Ma'tam	Not performed	Ta'ziya
Lebanon	Ta'ziya or Dhikrā	Held in private houses	Shabīh or Tamthīl al-Ḥusayn	No particular name
India	Majlis	Imāmbāra	Not often performed	Jalūs

The Role and Position of Women

The role and position of women is, throughout the Shi'i world, more a matter of cultural than religious determination. Although it is true that in most parts of the Middle East women play a subordinate role in the society, yet one can find examples, especially in tribal and village societies, where women work alongside men unveiled and with much greater social freedom.

The most conservative and traditional sections of Shi'i society, supported by the majority of the ulama, view the role of women as being essentially to remain within the house as domestic supervisor, to provide their husbands with sexual pleasure, to bring up children and to keep away from men other than close relatives. Women are regarded as not worth any substantial education, too emotional to be trusted with any important decisions and liable, if unveiled, to lead men astray by arousing sexual desires. A woman is considered incapable of becoming a mujtahid and giving legal decisions.[3]

It is true that a woman has substantial but strictly defined rights under Islamic law: the right to inherit, to possess property independently of her husband, to choose her husband, to work and to initiate divorce. Few women, however, are in practice able to exercise these rights effectively in a male-dominated religion. There is no mechanism whereby women can act in society independently of men. Thus only an independently wealthy woman, who can buy the services of a male agent, or a woman who is fortunate enough to obtain the full backing of the male members of her family has any hope of bringing a legal action against another person.

Modern Shi'i writers have attacked the image of the Western, 'liberated' woman which has penetrated Shi'i society. They regard women in the West as being manipulated by society to become sex objects, consumers of cosmetics and other products of the Western economy. This degradation of women has led, they maintain, to promiscuity, adultery, divorce and the break-down of the family unit in the West. Thus they vigorously reject all movement towards importing any Western ideas of female emancipation. Any movement that had been made in that direction in Iran in the last few decades has been more than reversed since the 1979 Revolution.

14

Contemporary Shi'ism

The 20th century has seen great changes in all the Shi'i communities of the world. The principal change has been in the political sphere where the Shi'i communities have become more assertive, particularly in countries such as Iraq, Lebanon and Bahrain where they form a significant proportion of the population but wield little political power. This process will undoubtedly be accelerated by the 1979 Revolution in Iran but the full effect of this remains to be seen.

The Religious Leadership

After the death of Mīrzā-yi Shīrāzī in 1895 there was a period when leadership was shared among a group of prominent mujtahids in Najaf. This group included Mullā Muḥammad known as Fāḍil Sharabiyānī (1245/1829–1322/1904), Shaykh Muḥammad Ḥasan ibn 'Abdu'llāh Mamaqānī (1238/1822–1323/1905), Mīrzā Ḥusayn ibn Mīrzā Khalīl (Khalīlī) Ṭihrānī (d. 1326/1908) and Mullā Muḥammad Kāẓim known as Ākhūnd Khurāsānī (1255/1839–1329/1911). With the death of the other members of this group, the last-named was for a time the sole *marja' at-taqlīd*.

During this period the leading mujtahids at Najaf were strongly in favour of the Constitutional Movement in Iran. In 1909, in protest at the actions of Muḥammad Shāh and the continued presence of Russian troops in Iran, the leading mujtahids of Najaf left the town and retired to Karbalā, but the success of the Constitutionalist forces in taking Tehran caused them to return. Again in 1911 after the Russian occupation of several Iranian towns and the threat of Muḥammad 'Alī Shāh's restoration, the mujtahids planned to leave Najaf and return to Iran to lead the people. The sudden death of Ākhūnd Khurāsānī delayed their departure but in January 1912 they reached Kāẓimayn. By that time negotiations between the Russians and the Iranian government were at an advanced stage and so the mujtahids returned to Najaf.

There was also, during the Constitutional Revolution, some

resurgence of interest among the Shi'i ulama in Pan-Islamism. The mujtahids of Najaf addressed several telegrams to the Ottoman Sulṭān addressing him as Caliph of the Muslims and asking him to intervene in Iran against Muḥammad 'Alī Shāh and the Russians. But that was a short-lived revival and faded soon after the Constitutionalist triumph.

After Khurāsānī, Sayyid Muḥammad Kāẓim Yazdī (d. 1918) became sole *marja'*. He was different in many ways from the *marāji'* who preceded and succeeded him. He had been opposed to the Constitutional Movement in Iran and, unlike the other mujtahids, was friendly towards the British after their occupation of Iraq. Under his leadership the ulama as a whole became much less enthusiastic about the Constitution, particularly as they observed the resulting secularisation of many aspects of life such as education.

Yazdī's successor was Mīrzā Muḥammad Taqī Shīrāzī (d. 1920), a resident of Karbalā, who was an implacable opponent of the British in Iraq and even issued a decree calling for a *jihād* against them. The next *marja' at-taqlīd*, Shaykh Fatḥu'llāh Iṣfahānī, known as Shaykhu'sh-Sharī'a (d. 1920), survived his predecessor by only four months.

In 1920 an event took place in Qumm that was to have far-reaching consequences. For a number of years prior to this date, a group of ulama had been busy refurbishing the *madrasas* of Qumm which had fallen into disuse and disrepair for a century. Then in 1920 Shaykh 'Abdu'l-Karīm Ḥā'irī-Yazdī (d. 1937) was invited to come from Sulṭānābād (Arāk), where he had been teaching, to Qumm. This event marked the beginning of the renaissance of Qumm.

From 1920 onwards there was a period similar to the years after the death of Mīrzā-yi Shīrāzī when several of the leading mujtahids were all regarded as being *marāji' at-taqlīd*. These were Shaykh 'Abdu'l-Karīm Ḥā'irī-Yazdī (d. 1937) in Qumm, and Shaykh 'Abdu'llāh Mamaqānī (d. 1933), Shaykh Muḥammad Ḥusayn Nā'īnī (d. 1936), Shaykh Ḍiyā'u'd-Dīn 'Irāqī (d. 1942) and Sayyid Abu'l-Ḥasan Iṣfahānī (d. 1946) in Najaf. After the death of the others, the last-named became sole *marja'*. His successor, Sayyid Āqā Ḥusayn ibn Muḥammad Ṭabāṭabā'ī known as Āyatu'llāh Qummī, a resident of Karbalā, survived him by only three months, dying in February 1947.

After the death of Ḥā'irī-Yazdī in 1937, the centre of learning (*hawza-yi 'ilmī*) at Qumm continued to increase in importance. At first Ḥā'irī-Yazdī's work was continued by Āyatu'llāhs Sayyid Muḥammad Taqī Khwānsārī (d. 1952), Sayyid 'Alī Ḥujjat (d. 1953), and Sayyid Ṣadru'd-Dīn Ṣadr (d. 1954). Then in Muḥarram 1364 (December 1944–January 1945), Āyatu'llāh Burūjirdī came to Qumm from Burūjird and began teaching there. After this Qumm increased even more in importance until it rivalled Najaf.

On the death of Āyatu'llāh Qummī in 1947 there was agreement among the ulama that his successor should be Āyatu'llāh Burūjirdī of Qumm. Thus at this point in time, with the residence there of the sole *marja' at-taqlīd*, Qumm took over as the leading centre of Shi'i scholarship. Najaf, however, continued to contest this leadership and many students, especially from the Arab countries and the Indian subcontinent, continued to go there. But for Iranian students Qumm now superseded Najaf.

Burūjirdī himself played a very quietist role politically but towards the end of his life was moved to speak out against the Bahā'īs in 1955 and against the land reform proposals of the Shāh in 1960. He died in March 1961.[1]

After Āyatu'llāh Burūjirdī there was no-one who could claim to be outstandingly superior to the other mujtahids in his knowledge. At Qumm there were Āyatu'llāhs Sharī'atmadārī, Gulpāygānī and Mar'ashī-Najafī; at Mashhad, Āyatu'llāh Muḥammad Hādī Mīlānī; in Tehran, Āyatu'llāh Aḥmād Khwānsārī; and in Najaf, Āyatu'llāhs Khū'ī, 'Abdu'l-Hādī Shīrāzī (d. 1381/1961), Āl Kāshifu'l-Ghiṭā and Muḥṣin al-Ḥakīm (d. 1970).[2] The last-named received the broadest support but was unable to consolidate his position sufficiently, especially among the ulama of Qumm, to become regarded as the sole *marja'*.

At the same time, there was a great deal of discussion regarding the whole concept of *marja' at-taqlīd*. In the book *Baḥthī dar bāra-yi Marja'iyyat wa Rūḥāniyyat* (Discussion regarding the *marja'* and the Religious Classes, see p. 258), a number of ulama as well as some leading laymen discussed the question of the leadership of the ulama and some of the political problems confronting Iranian Shi'ism. One view which was discussed by several writers in this book and which had been favoured by Shaykh 'Abdu'l-Karīm Ḥā'irī-Yazdī was that the concept of a sole *marja' at-taqlīd* be abandoned in favour of each mujtahid specialising in a particular field and being followed in that field. Parallel with this view was the idea of a council of mujtahids sharing leadership. It was argued that problems were now too complex for any individual mujtahid to have universal competence.

For a time Mashhad seriously rivalled Qumm in importance with the presence there of Āyatu'llāhs Kafā'ī-Khurāsānī and Mīlānī, but with the death of the first in 1971 and of the second in 1975, together with the destruction of Mīlānī's theological college in the course of municipal improvements, there was a relative decline in Mashhad's importance although it remains one of only three centres (the others being Qumm and Najaf) from which universally-recognised mujtahids can graduate.[3]

The events of 1963 (see p. 254) catapulted Āyatu'llāh Khumaynī into prominence as a *marja' at-taqlīd* and so after the death of Mīlānī in 1975 there remained six top-ranking *marāji' at-taqlīd*: in Najaf, Āyatu'llāhs Khū'ī and Khumaynī; in Qumm, Āyātu'llāhs Sharī'atmadārī, Gulpāygānī and Mar'ashī-Najafī; and in Tehran, Āyatu'llāh Khwānsārī.

At present the leading *marāji' at-taqlīd* appear to be: Āyatu'llah Khumaynī at Jamarān, near Tehran; Āyatu'llahs Muḥammad Riḍā Gulpāygānī, Shihābu'd-Dīn Mar'ashī-Najafī and Aḥmad Khwānsārī* at Qumm; Āyatu'llah Abu'l-Qāsim Musavī Khū'ī in Najaf; and Āyatu'llāhs Ḥasan Qummī and 'Abdu'llāh Shīrāzī* at Mashhad. It remains to be seen whether the announcement of Āyatu'llāh Kāẓim Sharī'atmadārī's deposition as a *marja'* will be taken notice of by his supporters or not. Early indications are that Sharī'atmadārī still has considerable support in Ādharbāyjān.

Iran

The Constitutional Movement

The first decade of the 20th century saw the ulama of Iran and Iraq much involved in the Constitutional Movement. The leading mujtahids of the Shi'i world, who were resident in Najaf and therefore relatively immune from the political power of the Shāh, threw their weight behind the Constitutionalists. Three of them in particular, Mīrzā Ḥusayn ibn Khalīl Tihrānī, Mullā Muḥammad Kāẓim Khurāsānī and Mullā 'Abdu'llāh Māzandarānī, showed constant support for the movement by letters, telegrams and *fatwās*. Some of the ulama were, however, against the Constitutionalists. These included Shaykh Muḥammad Kāẓim Yazdī at Najaf, Ḥājjī Mīrzā Ḥasan at Tabrīz and most notably Shaykh Faḍlu'llāh Nūrī. The latter held that the reforms advocated by the Constitutionalists would weaken the *Sharī'a* and increase European penetration of Iran. He felt that the laws of the nation should be dictated by the *Sharī'a* and not by parliamentary assembly.

The Constitution was finally granted, after much public agitation, by Muẓaffaru'd-Dīn Shāh in August 1906 and signed one week before his death on 8th January 1907. His successor, Muḥammad 'Alī Shāh, lost no time in trying to cancel out its effects and finally, in June 1908, staged a *coup d'état* and overturned the Constitution. At first it appeared that the king would have his way but, slowly, the forces of the Constitutionalists gathered and in the spring and summer of 1909 they advanced on Tehran, eventually forcing Muḥammad 'Alī Shāh's abdication on 16 July 1909.

* As this book was being prepared for publication, news was received of the death of Āyatu'llāh Shīrāzī in Mashhad on 27 September 1984 and of Āyatu'llāh Aḥmad Khwānsārī in Tehran on 19 January 1985.

Among those executed by the triumphant Constitutionalist forces was Shaykh Faḍlu'llāh Nūrī. His memory was generally execrated by Iranians because of his anti-Constitution stand until the 1979 Revolution, since when he has been rehabilitated as a great champion of the *Sharī'a*.

The Constitution recognised Twelver Shi'ism as the official religion and provided for a committee of five mujtahids who would vet all the legislation of the National Assembly and reject anything that was not in accordance with the *Sharī'a*. This last provision was, however, never activated.

In 1911, when the Russians occupied Tabrīz and threatened to restore Muḥammad 'Alī Shāh, it was the turn of a Constitutionalist religious leader, Mīrzā 'Alī Thiqatu'l-Islām, to be executed. After the First World War the mujtahids continued to play a political role although it was increasingly the Nationalist politicians who were in the foreground.

Riḍā Shāh Pahlavī

When in 1923 Riḍā Khān came to power and forced Aḥmad Shāh to leave the country, all the talk was of declaring a republic. But the ulama, seeing the markedly secular direction of the newly-formed Turkish republic under Ataturk, took fright and began to call for a rejection of republicanism. Riḍā Khān, who at this time needed the support of the ulama, fell into line with their wishes and in 1925 had himself proclaimed Shāh, thus starting the Pahlavī dynasty.

No sooner was Riḍā Shāh firmly in power, however, than he began to take measures to curtail the power and influence of the ulama. Between 1925 and 1928 a secular commercial, criminal and civil code of law was introduced beginning the erosion of the influence of the *Shar'* (religious) courts. In 1928 a law was passed making the abandonment of traditional dress in favour of Western attire compulsory. Although the ulama were exempt from this, the law stated that they had to prove their status by examination (except for recognised mujtahids), thus giving the government the *de facto* power of deciding who was and who was not a member of the ulama. In 1929 government examinations were decreed for the teachers and the *ṭullāb* (students) at the religious colleges and in 1934 the Ministry of Education announced a curriculum for these colleges, while the foundation of the University of Tehran with a Faculty of Theology (established in 1934) provided, for the first time, an alternative means of acquiring a religious education. Thus the government was giving itself the right to determine who was a member of the ulama and who could enter this class, whereas previously there had been no restriction on this. The rapid expansion of the state school system replacing the old *maktabs* (see p. 200) resulted in a secularisation of general education. The powers of the ulama were further curtailed in 1931 when strict limits were placed on the *Shar'* courts. Thenceforward, these could only deal with matters of personal status (marriage, divorce, inheritance, etc.). The referral of other cases to these courts had to be by approval of the civil courts or the Attorney-General and then they had only power to determine guilt, not to pass sentence. In 1932 the power of registering documents and property titles was also removed from the *Shar'* courts. The final stage of Riḍā Shāh's attack on the ulama was the Law on Religious Endowments (*Awqāf*) of 1934. This law provided for all religious endowments where the administrator of the endowment was unknown, was incompetent or was diverting the endowment to private gain to be taken over and administered by a government Department of Endowments (which meant, of course, that the government determined how the income was to be spent).

Apart from his direct attack on the ulama, Riḍā Shāh also carried out a number of other measures that were seen as an attack on religion. The use of the veil by women was prohibited in 1936, an attempt was made to suppress *ta'ziyas* and *rawḍa-khānīs* in 1932, the Muslim lunar calendar was replaced by a solar calendar and even the pilgrimage to Mecca was prohibited for a time. The state also took over a number of social functions such as the provision of hospitals, public baths and orphanages, which had usually been the domain of the ulama.

By the end of Riḍā Shāh's reign the ulama had been greatly subdued. In contrast to the early decades of the 20th century, there was little political activity among them. The numbers at the religious colleges were declining.

The most important religious thinker of the period of Riḍā Shāh was probably Mīrzā Riḍā Qulī Sharī'at-Sanglajī. He made a plea to the ulama to abandon their reactionary and superstitious attitudes and to use the tool of *ijtihād* to reinterpret and modernise Islam. Another important religious figure of this period was Sayyid Ḥasan Muddaris who led the religious opposition to the Shāh's secularisation programme in the Majlis (Parliament). He was imprisoned in 1929 and killed on 14 December 1937 (see Fig. 58).

Muḥammad Riḍā Shāh

After the abdication of Riḍā Shāh in 1941 the ulama pressed for and obtained the reversal of several measures which had been considered anti-religious. These included the repeal on the ban on *ta'ziyas* and *rawḍa-khānīs*, and the observance of Ramaḍān by government offices. Even the veil made a reappearance on the streets. The British, who had spearheaded the Allied occupation of Iran which forced Riḍā Shāh's abdication during the war, also encouraged this resurgence of the ulama as a bulwark against communists who had occupied parts of northern Iran.

Up to 1953 the new Shāh, Muḥammad Riḍā, was unable to exert any authority and became increasingly eclipsed by political figures such as Aḥmad Qavām and Muṣaddiq.

Parallel to the rising importance of the ulama themselves was the emergence of powerful and active religious groups. The first of these, the Fidā'iyān Islām, led by Navvāb Ṣafavī, was formed in 1945. It was a right-wing fundamentalist Islamic movement with much support among the lower classes and the Bazaar elements. It was not, however, a supporter of the ulama and they were not sympathetic to it. It was responsible for several assassinations between 1946 and 1951.

Closely linked with the Fidā'iyān was a politically-active member of the ulama, Āyatu'llāh Kāshānī (d. 1962), and his group of religious delegates in the National Assembly who were called Mujāhidīn-i Islām. Kāshānī was popular among the lower-ranking ulama and the middle classes. Kāshānī's expressed aims were to make the *Sharī'a* the law of the land and to have the ulama as the principal element administering and guiding the community. In all this he appears to have been a forerunner of Khumaynī. Kāshānī was a supporter of Pan-Islamism but above all else he was anti-British. He came to act as a link in an alliance of Fidā'iyān, ulama and the National Front party which brought Muṣaddiq to power in 1951 with a programme to eliminate Western influence in the country and nationalise the oil company. However, immediately Muṣaddiq came to power the coalition fell apart. First the Fidā'iyān were refused a part in the government. Then Kāshānī also fell out with Muṣaddiq when the latter tried to assume extraordinary powers. The increasing infiltration of the National Front by the communist Tūdih Party had made Kāshānī and the rest of the ulama antagonistic towards Muṣaddiq's government. Thus when the Shāh staged his dramatic return to Iran in August 1953, almost the entirety of the ulama from Kāshānī to the leading religious figure in Tehran, Āyatu'llāh Bihbahānī, enthusiastically welcomed him back and were active in mobilising the crowds that took to the streets and overthrew Muṣaddiq.

After Muṣaddiq, the Shāh, with strong British and American support, became increasingly dictatorial and soon all elements of democracy were gradually eradicated or negated. The Fidā'iyān-i Islam were ruthlessly crushed and their leader Navvāb Ṣafavī executed on 18 January 1956.

The ulama during this period after the fall of Muṣaddiq withdrew from active involvement in politics to a large extent but gave the Shāh much-needed support in the early days of his efforts to re-establish his authority. In return, the Shāh maintained an outward show of deference to the ulama and even accommodated some of the requests of the ulama such as for more Islamic instruction in the schools. Part of this accommodation between the ulama and the Shāh was the leeway given to the ulama to raise a violent anti-Bahā'ī campaign.

The Bahā'īs had, for over a century, been a convenient scapegoat for both the ulama and the government of Iran principally because persecution of this religious minority was less likely to cause international repercussions than persecutions of Christians or Jews. Also the Bahā'īs had been successful in making converts from the Muslim population thus, in effect, threatening the position of the ulama in a way that the other religious minorities did not. During the month of Ramaḍān (May-June) in 1955, the popular preacher Shaykh Muḥammad Taqī Falsafī was allowed to broadcast, over the government-controlled radio, several very inflammatory attacks on the Bahā'īs. Ayatu'llāh Burūjirdī gave his support to Falsafī and soon Bahā'īs and Bahā'ī properties in all parts of the country were under attack. Beatings, killings, looting and raping went on for several weeks, usually incited by the ulama in each locality. The Shāh appeared, at first, to countenance these disturbances which probably acted as a useful smoke-screen to hide the fact that he was in the midst of signing the Baghdad Pact (CENTO) allying himself formally with the much-distrusted British and Americans. It may even have been that the Shāh had negotiated a secret deal whereby the clergy agreed not to agitate against such issues in return for being allowed a free hand against the Bahā'īs. Eventually, however, international pressure forced the Shāh's government to restore order.

Following the anti-Bahā'ī persecution of 1955 there followed a period of relative calm, during which the Shāh drew up his plans for modernising Iran, plans that would inevitably bring him into conflict with the conservative ulama. The comparatively good relations between the state and the ulama came to an end in 1960 when Āyatu'llāh Burūjirdī, who had previously studiously avoided political involvement, began to speak out against the Land Reform Bill that had been drafted. Although the ulama, as controllers of large religious land endowments, were obviously concerned at any measures involving the land, and although they were acting to an extent on behalf of the landowners who were one of their main benefactors, it is likely that the land issue was merely the 'last straw' in a series of measures which the ulama had perceived as threatening and had thus become the focal point around which these resentments burst out. This is shown by the fact that immediately afterwards, a number of other issues were joined to the land question as being policies that the ulama objected to. These issues included: the question of women's rights and enfranchisement; the regime's foreign policy and, in particular, the close links with Israel; the growing Western cultural penetration of the country which the Shāh's regime appeared to be actively encouraging; and the increasingly totalitarian nature as well as the corruption of the regime.

Interestingly, at this juncture, as in previous times when relations between the ulama and the state were deteriorating, the idea of Pan-Islamism re-emerged strongly. One sign of this was the issuing, in 1959, by Shaykh Maḥmūd Shaltūt, the Rector of al-Azhar in Cairo, the leading theological institution of the Sunni world, of a *fatwā* recognising Ja'farī (i.e. Twelver) Shi'ism as a legitimate Islamic school of law. This was matched by increased interest in Pan-Islamism among the Shi'i ulama.

In March 1961 Āyatu'llāh Burūjirdī died and there was no single figure prominent enough to succeed him as sole *marja' at-taqlīd*. The Shāh used this opportunity of disarray among the ulama to push forward with his plans. In May 1961 he dissolved the National Assembly and, in effect, suspended the Constitution by not allowing further elections. He then pressed ahead with land reform decrees and in 1963 announced and won approval by referendum for his 'White Revolution'.

Paradoxically, however, the lack of a clear successor to Burūjirdī had, by giving increased independence to local religious leaders, strengthened the political effectiveness of the ulama. The increasing dissatisfaction of the ulama now boiled over into attacks upon the government. By 1962 the ulama were organising demonstrations and riots. On 22 January 1963, four days before the referendum on the 'White Revolution', the ulama, acting in concert with their traditional supporters in the Bazaar, staged violent demonstrations and closed the Bazaar. The disorder reached such a pitch that the Shāh went to the previously undreamt-of lengths of detaining a leading *marja' at-taqlīd*, Āyatu'llāh Sharī'atmadārī, together with Āyatu'llāhs Khumaynī, Maḥallātī-Shīrāzī, Qummī and Ṭālaqānī.

It was Āyatu'llāh Ruḥu'llāh Musavī Khumaynī (b. 1902) who came into prominence this year. He was the most outspoken of the ulama in his criticism of the regime; his pictures suddenly appeared everywhere as symbols of anti-government feeling. It was his arrest at 2.00 a.m. on 5 June 1963 that sparked off the worst of the rioting that year during the Muḥarram mourning period. Khumaynī remained in prison until August 1963. He was tried and sentenced to death by a military court. However, at the instigation of Āyatu'llāhs Sharī'atmadārī and Mīlānī, the combined Iranian Āyatu'llāhs proclaimed Khumaynī to be elevated to the rank of *Āyatu'llāh al-'Uzmā* and thus saved him.[4] Although released from prison, Khumaynī continued his criticism of the government and was eventually exiled to Turkey in November 1964 where he remained until October 1965 when he moved to Najaf.

Khumaynī's rise to prominence at this time is probably unique in Shi'i history. The usual way in which a mujtahid rises to become a top-ranking *marja' at-taqlīd* is through being recognised by other ulama and by the *ṭullāb* as being pre-eminent in scholarship (in the traditional fields of jurisprudence and principles of jurisprudence) and piety. However, Khumaynī (who had not specialised in jurisprudence and principles of jurisprudence) projected himself into the top-ranking echelon of *marāji' at-taqlīd* by his political appeal to the masses.

The ulama and all other opposition groups were effectively crushed by the Shāh in 1963 and the next fourteen years saw a period of what appeared to be relative political calm. The ulama were kept under firm government control and were thus forced into political quietism. Censorship ensured that only religious works on non-controversial topics could be published and the few ulama who did venture to speak out against the regime such as Āyatu'llah Sayyid Maḥmud Ṭālaqānī and Āyatu'llāh Muḥammad Riḍā Sa'īdī were immediately dealt with (the latter was tortured to death in 1970). The Shāh's secret police, SAVAK, infiltrated religious groups and dealt harshly with any protests.

Religious Developments in the 1960s and 1970s

However, under this surface calm there were some very important religious developments going on. These developments during the 1960s and 1970s can best be considered under four headings: the attempt by the Shāh to create a religious system independent of the ulama and controlled by the government; the discussions within the ranks of the religious classes aimed at reform of the ulama; the rethinking of Shi'i concepts in order to bring them up to date and thus counter more effectively the increasing pervasion of Iranian society by materialistic Western culture; and the continuing underground opposition of some of the ulama to the Shāh's regime.

Having effectively muzzled the ulama, the Shāh, recognising that the innate religiosity of the masses would always give the ulama a power base within the country, set about constructing an alternative religious system. The groundwork for this had been laid by Riḍā Shāh when he had begun the process of taking over control of some of the religious endowments. Religious endowments formed a large proportion of the income of the ulama and, although the government Department of Religious Endowments continued to use the income from the endowments for religious, charitable and educational purposes, it was now the government that was increasingly in control of the uses to which the money was put. Also, as mentioned before, the establishment of the Faculty of Theology at Tehran University during Riḍā Shāh's reign provided an alternative means, under government control, of acquiring a religious education.

The first stage of Muḥammad Riḍā Shāh's plan to set up a religious structure to rival the ulama was the creation under the White Revolution of a Literacy Corps (*Sipāh-i Dānish*) which was to bring literacy and education to the villages. Since the Corpsmen also taught the Qur'an and religious education as part of their programme in each village, they became, in effect, rivals of the village mullas. Following on from this, the Shāh created in 1970 a Religious Corps (*Sipāh-i Dīnī*) and a Corps of Religious Propagandists (*Muravvijīn-i Dīn*). These were in even more direct competition with the village mullas.

Thus what came to be called the *Dīn-i Dawlat* (government's religion) was set up in competition with the *Dīn-i Millat* (people's religion) and had virtually a complete hierarchy; starting at the top with several influential religious figures, such as Āyatu'llāh Mahdavī and 'Allāma Vaḥīdī, who threw their weight behind it; a country-wide network of holders of government-appointed posts, such as the *Imām-Jum'as* of many of the most important mosques; the educational facilities of university theology faculties as well as the government-run college, the Madrasa Sipahsalār in Tehran; the efforts at the village level of the Literacy and Religious Corpsmen; and the financial backing of the Religious Endowments Department (see Table 10).

Indeed, although it was never explicitly claimed, the tenor of many of the Shāh's pronouncements, about how he was being guided by God and had seen visions of the Imams, implied that he regarded himself, rather than the ulama, as the true representative of the Hidden Imam (not unlike but less extreme than the claims of Shāh Ismā'īl, the first Safavid monarch, see p. 105) and therefore the *Dīn-i Dawlat* as the true form of Shi'i Islam.

However, the *Dīn-i Dawlat* had up to 1978 failed to win the allegiance of the masses who boycotted the government-controlled mosques in the cities and continued to turn to the traditional ulama and the independent mosques. Nevertheless, it was a serious threat to the ulama and may possibly have achieved its purpose had it continued longer. Its existence certainly explains the intense hostility of the ulama for the regime of the Shāh.[5]

During the 1960s there was an intense discussion among the ulama concerning their role in society. Āyatu'llāh Burūjirdī had always discouraged political involvement by the ulama but after his death a number of writers began to call for reforms within the religious establishment and for the ulama to take a more active social role. In

Table 10. Diagrammatic representation of Dīn-i Dawlat and Dīn-i Millat (*adapted from Braswell, 'Mosaic of Mullahs and Mosques', pp. 246–7*)

	Dīn-i Dawlat	**Dīn-i Millat**
	God Muhammad Imams	
Leadership	Shāh *Imām-Jum'as* *Sipāh-i Dīnī* and *Muravvijīn*	*Marāji' at-taqlīd* Mujtahids Mullas
Institutional Arrangements		
Education	Faculties of Theology Madrasa Sipahsalār	Qumm and other religious colleges
Legal	Secular courts	*Sharī'a* courts
Finance	Religious endowments	Some religious endowments
	Government support	Voluntary offerings of *khums* and *zakāt*
Centres: national	Tehran	Qumm
local	Government-controlled mosques	Independent mosques
Communications	Mass Media	Informal underground networks
Literature	Qur'an Shāh's autobiography	Qur'an Traditional Shi'i Literature
	White Revolution literature	Writings of *marāji' at-taqlīd* and some individual thinkers such as Sharī'atī
Ideology	White Revolution	Imam Husayn's Revolution
	Monarchy Modernisation (Westernisation)	Leadership of the ulama Traditionalism

December 1962, after Burūjirdī's death, there appeared a seminal publication *Baḥthi dar bāra-yi Marja'iyyat wa Rūḥāniyyat* (Discussion regarding the *marja'* and the Religious Classes) in which a number of leading ulama as well as prominent lay thinkers presented papers discussing the role of the ulama in Muslim society. This document urged the necessity of reform of the curriculum at the religious colleges so as to replace the centrality of *fiqh* (jurisprudence) in the curriculum with more socially-oriented subjects such as ethics. It considered that the main factor holding the ulama back from being a major social force was their financial dependence on the masses who always tend to conservatism. It also urged the ulama to resurrect the communal spirit among the Shi'i masses. Since Islam is a total way of life, there can be no separation between religion and social and political issues, therefore the ulama have no choice but to emerge, speak out on these issues and provide social leadership.[6]

Parallel with this reassessment of the role of the ulama in society was the attempt by a number of intellectuals to reinterpret some of the traditional concepts of Shi'i Islam in such a way as to make them more applicable to the modern world. In previous generations, intellectuals, seeing the backwardness of the Islamic world and the prosperity of the Western nations, had sought to bring modernisation to Iran and therefore had emphasised that Islam was compatible with modernisation (i.e. Westernisation). But now, seeing the regime pressing ahead with modernisation and the enormous social disruption that this was causing, the new generation of intellectuals looked back to a past that they imagined to have been free of such problems and therefore they sought to present Islam as a bulwark against the moral decay caused by Westernisation.

Among the first of this new generation of intellectuals who wrote of the need to resist the cultural penetration of Iran by the West were Dr Sayyid Fakhru'd-Dīn Shādmān, Prof. Iḥsān Narāqī and Jalāl Āl-i Aḥmad (d. 1969). The latter popularised the term *gharbzadigī* (spell-bound by the West) to describe the attitude of those who enthusiastically called for the uncritical and wholesale adoption of Western ways. Āl-i Aḥmad's line of thought was taken up and developed by Dr 'Alī Sharī'atī (1933–77). In 1965 an institute called the Ḥusayniyya Irshād was set up in Tehran to discuss modern social issues in an Islamic context. Sharī'atī lectured at this institute regularly from 1967 until it was closed by the government in 1973. These lectures were mimeographed and distributed and caused a great deal of discussion, eventually becoming one of the ideological bases of the 1979 Revolution.

Both Āl-i Aḥmad and Sharī'atī were very critical of the ulama for their obscurantism and passivity. Sharī'atī in particular presents a theory that the original 'pure' Shi'ism (which he calls 'Alawī Shi'ism) was perverted in Safavid times so that the socially-active 'Alawī Shi'ism in which each Muslim has an obligation to strive for achieving the ideal Shi'i society became the passive Safavid Shi'ism in which each Muslim was enjoined to sit back and wait for the advent of the Hidden Imam who would put everything right. The ulama of the Safavid period concerned themselves only with other-worldly matters and hence gave the state a free hand in politics and this tendency had persisted, Sharī'atī maintained, to the present day. Sharī'atī was also a sharp critic of the neo-colonialism of the West and sought in a revitalised Islam the means of combating this Western imperialism.

Although very popular with the masses and especially with the young, Sharī'atī's writings never found favour with the ulama. There was too much of an attack on the ulama themselves in his writings for their comfort, although they based their denunciations of Sharī'atī on his lack of traditional Shi'i learning and hence his liability to make mistakes in his presentation of Shi'i history and doctrine. Indeed, Sharī'atī and certain groups such as the Furqān terrorists who considered themselves his followers were accused of being crypto-Sunnis.[7]

Two other lay writers who were very influential at this time and who were later to play important political roles after the 1979 Revolution were Abu'l-Ḥasan Banī-Ṣadr (b. 1933) and Engineer Mihdī Bāzargān (b. 1905). The former was the leading economic thinker in the Revolution's ideology and later the first President of the Islamic Republic; the latter wrote mainly about Islam's adaptability and compatibility with modern science and technology and later became the Islamic Republic's first Prime Minister. Whereas in the 1950s the university students had been anti-religious, it was due to writers like Bāzargān that the interest of the students in Islam was rekindled in the 1960s and this paved the way for the alliance of the students with the ulama and Bazaar elements that was to be such an important factor in the 1979 Revolution. Another factor that contributed to the growing interest in Islam in the universities was the increasing number of students from the lower (and in general more rigidly Islamic) strata of society.

Among the ulama also there were several writers of importance in this process of rethinking the basis of Shi'i Islam. Leaving aside Khumaynī for the present, the most influential of these were Āyatu'llāh Maḥmūd Ṭālaqānī (1910–September 1979) who achieved a reputation of being liberal, progressive and sympathetic to minority groups and who was very popular with the students and the middle classes, and Āyatu'llāh Shaykh Murtaḍā Muṭahharī (assassinated May 1979) who was also very popular with the students and a leading advocate of reforms among the ulama.

The ulama within Iran had very limited opportunities for expressing opposition to the regime. Some protest did occur in 1970–72 when disturbances occurred in the universities especially at Tehran and also at Qumm. Two of the most outspoken ulama, Āyatu'llāhs Muntaẓirī and Ṭālaqānī, were arrested and exiled internally. Shortly afterwards in 1973, the Ḥusayniyya Irshād was closed down and Sharī'atī arrested. In June 1975, on the anniversary of Khumaynī's arrest in 1963, there was a demonstration by religious students at the Madrasa Fayḍiyya, the leading religious college in Qumm. Police invaded the building using tear gas and are said to have killed some of the students by throwing them off the roof. The Fayḍiyya was closed and remained so until the Revolution.

Āyatu'llāh Khumaynī, on the other hand, in exile in Iraq, did not have the same constraints upon him. His writings and talks in pamphlet form and on cassette were smuggled into Iran and distributed. He thus became a rallying point for the opposition to the regime among the religious elements of the population and, in particular, the lower-ranking ulama, the religious students and the Bazaar elements.

Until 1970, Khumaynī, while critical of the Shāh's government, had only called for its reform. But in that year, in a series of lectures given to his students in Najaf and later published in a book, *Ḥukūmat-i Islāmī* (Islamic Government), Khumaynī stated that the only acceptable form of Islamic government was government by an expert in Islamic jurisprudence (the *Vilāyat-i Faqīh*, see p. 196). The Shāh's government tried everything that it could to discredit Khumaynī and to prevent his messages from reaching his supporters, but its success was limited.

The Iranian population was left in the late 1970s with socialism and nationalism spent forces after the Muṣaddiq episode, with all forms of political expression suppressed by the state and with the Shāh's White Revolution in disarray. Of all of the groups that laid claim to leadership within the nation, only the ulama were still a creditable alternative with a viable organisation and so it was to this group that the people turned for leadership in the 1979 Revolution (see the last section of this chapter).

The population of Iran is about 38,000,000. The official statistics indicate that the vast majority of Iranians (92%, i.e. 35,000,000) are Twelver Shi'is although some observers have suggested a much lower figure. Almost all of the Persian-speaking population, both city-dwellers and the tribes of the south and south-west, are Twelver Shi'i. Several of the most important non-Iranian ethnic groups such as the Ādharbāyjānī Turks and the Arabs of the south-west are also predominantly Twelver Shi'i. Three important ethnic elements have remained Sunni: the Baluchis of the south-east, the Turkomans of the north-east, and the Kurds of the west (the latter also contain many Ahl-i Ḥaqq). The only important groups that are not Muslims are the Bahā'īs (numbering 350,000), the Christians (150,000), the Jews (50,000) and Zoroastrians (30,000).

Iraq

The First World War resulted in the British occupation of Iraq. The British were at first welcomed by the Shi'is of south Iraq as deliverers from the yoke of Turkish Sunni oppression. But from 1918 onwards, when it became clear that the British were not about to depart as quickly as they had arrived, the Shi'is, led by Shaykh Muḥammad Taqī Shīrāzī and Shaykh Abu'l-Ḥasan Iṣfahānī, began to oppose the British rule and, in particular, they issued *fatwās* against the appointment of a non-Muslim, Sir Percy Cox, as the British Governor of Iraq.

When in 1920 the British occupation appeared about to be formally institutionalised by the establishment of a League of Nations Mandate, the whole of Shi'i south Iraq erupted in a violent revolt which was only subdued with difficulty by the British. The Sunni elements in Iraq only played a minor role in this revolt. Even after the British had withdrawn the idea of ruling Iraq through a British governor, had put Faysal on the throne with an Iraqi government, and had produced a timetable that would lead eventually to full independence, the Shi'is remained implacably opposed to the British although most of the Sunni elements of the population accepted the position.

The opposition of the Shi'i mujtahids to the British reached its climax in 1922–3 when Nā'īnī and Iṣfahānī issued *fatwās* forbidding participation in the national elections. There were then some disturbances and three of the more politically-minded ulama were expelled from the country. In protest the leading ulama of Karbalā and Najaf, including Nā'īnī and Iṣfahānī, left Iraq for Iran in the summer of 1923. They went to the recently re-established centre of studies at Qumm as guests of Shaykh 'Abdu'l-Karīm Ḥā'irī-Yazdī. They had been expecting that their departure would provoke southern Iraq into revolt and would induce the Iraqi government to request their return on their terms. In the event, nothing happened and the Iraqi government was only too happy to have these mujtahids out of the country during the elections and only allowed their return afterwards in April 1924.

For a time Shi'i political activity was quiescent and when it re-emerged, in 1927, in protest at the publication of an anti-Shi'i book, it was now led by politicians rather than the ulama. In 1934–5 there was a further crisis caused by the resentment of the Shi'i tribes of the south at certain government actions. One of the leading ulama, Shaykh Muḥammad Ḥusayn Āl Kāshifu'l-Ghiṭā, acted as mediator in resolving these problems.

However, in the main, religious differences decreased in importance over the next decades and although individual Shiʿis were active in politics, they acted within the party political framework rather than representing the Shiʿi community. Most government cabinets had one or two Shiʿi members and Ṣālih Jabr and Sayyid Muḥammad aṣ-Ṣadr were Shiʿis who succeeded in becoming Prime Minister. Arab nationalism and party politics superseded the former Shiʿi political unity. The Shiʿi mujtahids were no longer politically active (although such figures as Nāʾīnī and Iṣfahānī, who had been active in the early 1920s, lived on for many years more) and even the renewed British occupation during the Second World War elicited surprisingly little reaction. The tribes, the main political weapon of the Shiʿi community, became less militant and less able to threaten the government.

The pace of secularisation was increased after the revolt of 1958 which overthrew the king and brought the socialists and communists into power. The Shiʿis, because of their poorer social and economic position supported the socialists. When the Baʿth party came to power in the coup of 1963, Shiʿis constituted 53% of the party. But gradually the Sunni element in the party predominated and by the time of al-Bakr's take-over of power in 1968, the Shiʿi representation in the party had fallen to 6%.

When Khumaynī first arrived in Iraq in 1965 after being expelled from Iran, ʿAbdu's-Salam ʿĀrif's regime was antagonistic to Shiʿis and Khumaynī was suppressed. Later, under ʿAbdu'r-Raḥmān ʿĀrif, Iraq established improved relations with Iran and once more Khumaynī's activity was kept under a tight rein.

It is said that at first Āyatu'llāh Muḥsin al-Ḥakīm, Iraq's foremost religious leader at the time, disapproved of Khumaynī's political stance but after Khumaynī's arrival in Najaf and meetings between the two, al-Ḥakīm reversed his opinion and supported Khumaynī. Āyatu'llāh Khūʾī, although al-Ḥakīm's successor as the leading *marjaʿ* of Iraq, is reported to have opposed Khumaynī's political activity.

In 1968, after Ḥasan al-Bakr took power, Āyatu'llāh al-Ḥakīm left Najaf for Baghdad in protest against the new regime's treatment of the Shiʿi ulama. It was about this time that, with the extinction of any hope of social improvement through political activity, the Shiʿi masses began to turn back to the ulama for leadership. It was out of this change that the Daʿwa party was formed and had the support of most of the minor ulama and the blessing of many of the more senior ulama.

In the early 1970s Khumaynī enjoyed a short period of favour with the regime of Ṣaddām al-Ḥusayn who took over from al-Bakr. This was during a period when there was increased tension between Iraq and Iran and Khumaynī was used by the Iraqi government as part of its campaign against the Shāh. In 1975, however, when Ṣaddām al-Ḥusayn came to terms with the Shāh, Khumaynī's activities were once more suppressed. The opening of the borders and the resumption of pilgrimages by Iranians to the Iraqi shrines, on the other hand, allowed Khumaynī to smuggle his messages and tape-recordings into Iran more easily.

The Shi'i population of Iraq became increasingly disaffected during the 1970s. The religious processions during Muḥarram in the shrine cities became occasions for political protests. In 1974 there was rioting after which five members of the Da'wa party were executed. In 1977 there were more serious disturbances and eight were executed.

The Iranian Revolution of 1979 was inevitably a severe test to Ṣaddām al-Ḥusayn's Ba'thist regime. Friction between the government and the Shi'is increased almost immediately. In June 1979 Āyatu'llāh Muḥammad Bāqir aṣ-Ṣadr was arrested and placed under house detention. During the same year another senior Iraqi religious figure, Āyatu'llāh Shīrāzī, who had close links with the Da'wa party, and Shaykh Ghulām-Riḍā Riḍwānī were expelled from Iraq and came to Iran where they began to organise the Shi'i resistance to Ṣaddām al-Ḥusayn. On 9 April 1980, after an attempt to assassinate Ṣaddām al-Ḥusayn, Āyatu'llāh Muḥammad Bāqir aṣ-Ṣadr was executed. Following this several hundred more Shi'is suspected of being associated with the Da'wa party were executed and several thousand Shi'is whose families had in some instances lived in Iraq for generations were pronounced to be Iranian and expelled across the border.

Various attempts have been made by the Iranian government to co-ordinate the different Iraqi opposition groups. The three main religious Shi'i groupings, the Da'wa party, the Paykar group (a guerilla organisation similar to the Iranian Mujāhidīn) and the Jamā'at al-'Ulamā (a grouping of pro-Khumaynī ulama) have been united and their activities co-ordinated from within Iran by Ḥujjatu'l-Islām Muḥammad Bāqir al-Ḥakīm, a son of Āyatu'llāh al-Ḥakīm.[8] But these Shi'i groups have not thus far managed to co-ordinate with the secular Syrian-backed opposition groups.

Meanwhile, the Iraqi leadership made a determined effort to woo support from Iraqi Shi'is. Resources were diverted to the Shi'i south. The official government propaganda has cast the war with Iran in terms of the struggle between the Arabs and the Iranians for supremacy that occurred in the early days of Islam, trying to make the Shi'is of south Iraq identify more closely with their being Arabs in the face of the Iranian foe rather than their being Shi'is. Thus the Iraqi official propaganda uses certain symbolic key-words such as Qādisiyya (the battle at which the Arab armies defeated the Iranian Empire in AD 637) while the Iranian propaganda seeks to win the support of south Iraq's Shi'is by using such key-words as Karbalā. Āyatu'llāh Khū'ī, the most senior of the Iraqi religious figures, has refused to commit himself politically but the regime did succeed in obtaining support from another important figure, Shaykh 'Alī Āl Kāshifu'l-Ghiṭā.

As the war with Iran has become prolonged, however, the Iraqi government has become more and more severe on the Shi'is in Iraq. Āyatu'llāh Khū'ī is now under virtual house arrest and Shī'īs in all walks of life are under suspicion and pressure. In June 1984 some 95 Shi'i ulama, and in particular members of the al-Ḥakīm family, were executed.

Most authorities are agreed that the Shi'is form the majority of Iraq's population and estimates of the proportion vary from 55% to 60%. Thus the Shi'is number approximately 7,000,000 of Iraq's total population of 12,000,000. With the Sunni population divided between the mutually-antagonistic Arabs and Kurds, this makes the Shi'i position even stronger. The Shi'is predominate in the southern half of the country as far north as Baghdad, which is a mixed Sunni-Shi'i city. Of the holy cities, Karbalā and Kāẓimayn, which is now a suburb of Baghdad, have a very strong Iranian influence while Najaf is much more an Arab city. Most of the tribes of the south are Shi'i and the largest town of the south, Baṣra, is predominantly Shi'i.

Lebanon

The Shi'i community in Lebanon has always been and largely remains to the present the poorest and least-educated among Lebanon's religious groups.[9] At the beginning of the 20th century it was predominantly a rural community occupying some of the poorest land. The majority were peasants dominated by a small number of rich land-owning Shi'i families. The Shi'is who lived in the towns tended to conceal their religious identity and conform outwardly to Sunnism.

During the 19th century the Ottomans had created a separately-administered Christian area on Mount Lebanon. Following the First World War the Christians succeeded in persuading the French, who were given control of Syria under a League of Nations Mandate, to create a separate state consisting of Mount Lebanon, Jabal 'Āmil and 'Akkār together with the central strip and the Biqā' valley. This area included a large number of Sunni Muslims who regarded themselves as Syrians and agitated against the proposed division into Syria and Lebanon.

It was as a result of this conflict that the Shi'is of Lebanon were suddenly forced into the centre of the political arena. The Sunnis claimed that they spoke for all Muslims, including the Druse and Shi'a, when they demanded to be rejoined to Syria. The Christians, however, realised that the Shi'is were unlikely to want to be drawn into a Sunni-dominated Syria when they could be a part of a multi-confessional Lebanon where they would not be forced to conceal their religion. Therefore it was largely due to the efforts of the Christians that the hitherto apolitical and largely forgotten Shi'i community was suddenly drawn into the limelight and in 1926 constituted as an official community separate from the Sunnis.

The Christians' assumption proved correct and the Shi'a gave their backing to an independent state. The Christians realised that the addition of large Muslim areas to the original Christian enclave to form the new state would threaten their numerical predominance but it was not until the 1932 Census that they realised to what extent. That Census revealed a Christian majority of only 266 in a total population of 793,226. The Christians had managed to persuade the French mandatory authorities to allow registration of some 67,403 citizens (i.e. about 8% of the electorate) who were resident abroad and predominantly Christians, thereby shoring up their figures. The Shi'is were numbered as 155,035 resident and 3,390 abroad. The Christians have blocked the taking of another Census since that time lest it show, as it almost certainly would, a Muslim predominance.

Based on the 1932 Census, an informal National Pact was worked out in 1943, just prior to full independence in 1944. According to this pact, virtually every aspect of public life would be arranged so as to maintain a confessional proportionality. The parliamentary seats were divided: Christians 54, Sunnis 20, Shi'a 19, Druse 6. It was determined that the President of the Republic would be a Maronite Christian, the Prime Minister a Sunni Muslim and the Speaker of the House a Shi'i. The Shi'a have usually been allocated the Agriculture Ministry.

During the 1950s the Muslims began to clamour for a fresh Census as they felt that they now outnumbered the Christians and resented the automatic predominance of Christians in all spheres of public life. Rising Arab nationalism under Nasser, the Suez crisis of 1956, and discontent with the rule of President Chamoun caused a political crisis in 1958 but Lebanon emerged from this with its power structure little altered.

The religious head of the Shi'i community at this time was Ḥajj Sayyid 'Abdu'l-Ḥusayn Sharafu'd-Dīn who had studied in Najaf under Ākhūnd Khurāsānī and Sayyid Muḥammad Kāẓim Yazdī and also under Sunni scholars in Egypt where he held some much-publicised debates with Sunni scholars at al-Aẓhar University between 1912 and 1919. He then returned to Tyre and became the head of the Shi'i community in the Jabal 'Āmil and was instrumental in setting up schools and a *madrasa* and building a mosque in Tyre. He died in 1377/1957.

In 1959 a leading Shiʿi scholar, Mūsā aṣ-Ṣadr (whose ancestors had been from the Jabal ʿĀmil) came to Lebanon from Iran and became the religious leader of Lebanon's Twelver Shiʿis. He took up residence in Tyre where he had been appointed the Shiʿi Mufti. The Shiʿis were still at this time, as they always had been, at the bottom of the social scale in Lebanon, occupying the poorest regions of the country and generally ignored by the government. So demoralised was the Shiʿi community that, in some villages, it is reported that Mūsā aṣ-Ṣadr even found Shiʿis burying their dead according to Christian rites.

Imām Mūsā aṣ-Ṣadr, as he came to be known, displayed considerable ability and was able to build up a community solidarity among the Shiʿis. In December 1967 the Shiʿi Supreme National Islamic Council was set up by an Act of Parliament and in 1969 Imām Mūsā aṣ-Ṣadr was elected as its President. The establishment of this Council completed the process begun in 1926 of separating the Shiʿi community entirely from the Sunnis.

Imām Mūsā aṣ-Ṣadr's new role thrust him into the political arena and at first he was opposed by the traditional Shiʿi feudal families who had always previously represented the Shiʿa politically. But by making his appeal direct to the Shiʿi masses he was able to neutralise this opposition. Politically, while confirming the basic Shiʿi support for an independent Lebanon, he criticised the Lebanese government's record with respect to the development of the poorer Shiʿi areas and also the failure of the Lebanese army to protect the Jabal ʿĀmil from repeated Israeli incursions.

In 1970 Imām Mūsā aṣ-Ṣadr was instrumental in setting up a Council of the South to develop the Jabal ʿĀmil region together with a large injection of government money. In 1974, when he saw that the money promised by the government for the south was not forthcoming, he mobilised the Shiʿa in the south and the Biqāʿ valley by holding a series of mass meetings to pressure the government, and also made an appeal to the Christians of Lebanon for a new supra-confessional approach. Parallel to this, however, aṣ-Ṣadr's supporters created the Amal, a partly-political, partly-military Shiʿi organisation. Although aṣ-Ṣadr was successful in mobilising the Shiʿis of the south, his success in the Biqāʿ valley was less marked. The Biqāʿ is notably less religious in its Shiʿism than the Jabal ʿĀmil. In the past there have been few notable ulama from this area compared to the Jabal ʿĀmil, and the usual Shiʿi commemorations of ʿĀshūrā, etc., are celebrated on a more modest scale. Aṣ-Ṣadr's appeal to religion was therefore less effective in this area.[10]

Then in August 1978, while on a trip to Libya, aṣ-Ṣadr mysteriously disappeared. The Libyans have failed to account satisfactorily for this disappearance and it must be assumed that the Imam was killed either deliberately or accidentally.

The disappearance of Imām Mūsā aṣ-Ṣadr led to a considerable amount of confusion among Lebanon's Shiʻis, particularly as it was closely followed by the Iranian Revolution and the Israeli occupation of southern Lebanon. After the beginning of the Irano-Iraqi War, the situation became even more confused with the pro-Khumaynī Amal organisation battling against the Lebanese branch of the Iraqi Baʻthists in the streets of Baʻālbakk and Beirut. There was also fighting between the Amal and Palestinian guerillas in south Beirut and southern Lebanon in April 1982 just prior to the second Israeli invasion. The Shiʻi militias around Baʻālbakk have been considerably reinforced by the Iranian military units stationed there. Many of the recent terrorist episodes directed against Israeli and other foreign forces have been attributed to Shiʻi groups and in particular one called the Islamic Jihād.

At present the leadership of Lebanon's Shiʻis is in the hands of a small group of individuals. Nabih Birri is head of the politico-military Amal organisation; Shaykh Muḥammad Mahdī Shamsu'd-Dīn holds a degree of religio-political leadership as Deputy Chairman (the Shiʻis have not as yet accepted Imām Mūsā aṣ-Ṣadr's disappearance sufficiently to allow his replacement as Chairman) of the Shiʻi Supreme National Islamic Council; Shaykh ʻAbdu'l-Amīr Qabalān is the Shiʻi Muftī. Considerable power, however, still remains in the hands of the old families of feudal overlords and notables, such as the al-Asʻad family in the Jabal ʻĀmil and the Ḥamāda in the Hirmal area.[11] Rapidly increasing in importance is the Ḥizbu'llāh party under Shaykh Muḥammad Husayn Fadlu'llah which is closely aligned to Khumaynī's ideology.

The question of how many Shiʻa there are in Lebanon is politically sensitive. As has been mentioned above, the Christians have maintained a political hegemony on the basis of the National Pact of 1943 which in turn was based on the Census of 1932. Although all attempts to have another Census taken have been blocked, it is almost universally acknowledged that, in the intervening period, the Shiʻa have grown proportionately more than the other communities and are now probably the largest group. The present estimated population of Lebanon is 3,500,000. The proportion of Muslims to Christians is much disputed but a 60–40 split in favour of the Muslims seems to be widely accepted by independent authorities. Of the Muslims, the Shiʻa probably represent 45% with the Sunnis 35%, Druse 17% and the remainder ʻAlawīs, Ismāʻīlīs, etc.

An-Nahār, Beirut's most prestigious daily newspaper, quoted on 5 November 1975 the following estimated figures:[12]

Total Population:	3,258,000	*Percentage of Total Population*
Christians:	1,250,000	38.4
Muslims:	2,008,000	61.6
Shi'a:	970,000	29.8
Sunnis:	690,000	21.1
Druse:	348,000	·10.7

Another more recent estimate gives the following figures:[13]

Total Population:	3,575,000	*Percentage of Total Population*
Christians:	1,525,000	42.7
Maronites:	900,000	25.2
Muslims:	2,050,000	57.3
Shi'a:	1,100,000	30.8
Sunnis:	750,000	21.0
Druse:	200,000	5.6

One area of Shi'i concentration is in the south of the country. Tyre (Ṣūr) with its hinterland, the Jabal 'Āmil, as far north as the Liṭānī River is predominantly Shi'i (80%), with Bint Jubayl, Mays al-Jabal and Tibnīn as the important inland Shi'i towns. Further north, Nabaṭiyya is the largest Shi'i centre in the district centred on Sidon which is 60% Shi'i. To the east of this area, the proportion of Shi'a in the district centred on Marj 'Ayūn drops to 40% and al-Khiyām is the only important Shi'i town in this region. Although the district of Jizzīn which includes the village of Juba' is historically important, it is now predominantly Christian with only 13% Shi'a.

The Shi'is in Beirut live predominantly in the southern suburbs around Ba'abda. Although earlier in the present century, the Shi'is constituted only 5% of the population of Beirut, recent events in south Lebanon have resulted in large numbers of refugees moving into the Beirut area with the result that Shi'is are now probably the largest religious community in Beirut. There is a small Shi'i population (7%) in the Kisrawān area, in the districts centred on Jubayl and Qarṭabā, including the resort villages of Afqā and Laqlūq on Mount Lebanon.

The other main Shi'i area is the northern Biqā' valley stretching from Ba'ālbakk to Hirmāl, both of which are important Shi'i towns. This area is 70% Shi'i. Further south in the Biqā' valley there are a small number of Shi'i villages in the area around Zahla.

The disturbances in Lebanon in the last decade have almost certainly made differences to the above figures (and to the map on pp. 270–71) which are calculated on the basis of the Censuses taken in 1921 and 1932. The area around Hirmal, for example, which was 70–80% Shi'i, is now almost 100% Shi'i due to the emigration of Maronites from there.

Syria

Once Lebanon had been carved out of the former Turkish *vilāyat* of Syria, there remained few Twelver Shi'is in the new state of Syria. Of the estimated 50,000 that remain, the majority live in villages in the region of Idlib to the south-west of Aleppo and in the region of Azaz to the north-west of Aleppo. These are the remnants of the once-large Twelver community centred on Aleppo that existed until the 12th century. There are also a few Twelver Shi'i villages in the area of Ḥumṣ and Ḥamā.

The present regime that controls Syria is dominated by the 'Alawīs (see p. 58) who predominate in the Latakia area of Syria and are considered heretical by many Muslims. In order to bolster the legitimacy of the regime, the 'Alawīs sought and obtained from Imām Mūsā aṣ-Ṣadr, the Twelver religious leader in Lebanon, a legal decision that they are a legitimate Muslim people.

Turkey

It is almost impossible to estimate the number of Twelver Shi'is in Turkey. This is for a number of reasons. Firstly, the official censuses make no differentiation between the various Islamic sects. Secondly, writers on Turkey usually make no attempt to differentiate between the various Shi'i sects but lump them all together as 'Alevi'. Thirdly, the Shi'is themselves probably recognise no distinct boundaries between the various sects and groupings. There are four main groups of Shi'is in Turkey: (a) the Arabic-speaking 'Alawī (Nusayri) community (see p. 58) centred on the Mediterranean coast between Antakya and Mersin; (b) the Turkish-speaking Turkomans who are scattered in villages throughout Turkey but especially in a band from the north of Ankara to Erzincan. These are mainly Bektāshī, while some still use the name Qizilbāsh; (c) the Kurds, who are mainly Ahl-i Ḥaqq and predominate in south-east Turkey; (d) the Ādharī (Azeri) Turkish refugees from Russian Ādharbāyjān.

Of these Shi'i groups all accept the Twelve Imams of the Twelver line. The first, the 'Alawīs, would be considered heterodox by most orthodox Twelver Shi'is although it is reported that they send students to the religious colleges in Najaf and Qumm. Among the second group can be found small numbers who call themselves Ja'farī and must presumably therefore be orthodox Twelvers but, in general, the standard of education among them is so low and their contacts with the rest of the Twelver Shi'i world so limited that they have little in common with the wider Twelver community. The majority of this second group subscribe to Bektāshī and other similar doctrines and would clearly be

MAP OF SOUTH LEBANON

Although strictly the Jabal ʻĀmil refers to the mountains south of the Līṭānī river as far as the international boundary, Shiʻi writers have traditionally referred to as *ʻĀmilī* ulama coming from any of the towns on this map and even from Karak-Nūḥ (home village of Muḥaqqiq al-Karakī and an important centre of learning in the 16th and 17th centuries) which is near Zahla in the southern Biqāʻ Valley, 50 kilometres to the north-west of Jizzīn. The Biqāʻ Valley is the other main Shiʻi area in Lebanon and is not shown on this map.

The figures after each name on the map refer to percentages of the population in each religious community according to censuses undertaken in the early part of the 20th century. Recent events in South Lebanon have undoubtedly altered some of these substantially but it remains to be seen whether these changes are permanent or temporary.

All towns and villages will usually have a small number of persons of religious groups other than the main religious group. For the purposes of calculating the percentages on this map, groups comprising less than 3% of a town or village have been ignored.

Sh	Shiʻi
Su	Sunni
M	Maronite
C	Greek Catholic
G	Greek Orthodox

Place-names underlined: Home-towns of famous ulama of the past or present
Place-names boxed: Centres of learning of the past or present

JIZZĪN – *madrasa* and important centre of learning 14th-17th century. Home of Shahīd al-Awwal and his descendants. Not a Shiʻi town since 19th century.

MASHGHARA – important centre of learning and home of al-Ḥurr family

JUBAʻ – *madrasa* and important centre of learning 15th-19th centuries. Home of Shahīd ath-Thānī, his son Ṣāḥibu'l-Maʻālim and his descendants, Sayyid Muḥammad Ṣāḥibu'l-Madārik and his descendants, Shaykh Bahā'ī, the al-Ḥurr family and Shaykh ʻAbdu'llāh Niʻma

TYRE – recent founding of *madrasa*. Home of ʻIzzu'd-Dīn and Mugniyya families and residence of Sayyid ʻAbdu'l-Ḥusayn Sharafu'd-Dīn

SHAQRĀ – *madrasa* and important centre of learning 18th-20th centuries. Home of al-Amīn family

ḤANAWAYA – *madrasa* founded by Shaykh Muḥammad ʻAlī ʻIzzu'd-Dīn 1841-1915

ḤĀNĪN – centre of learning 17th-18th centuries under Shaykh Ḥasan al-Ḥānīnī and his family

• villages
● towns

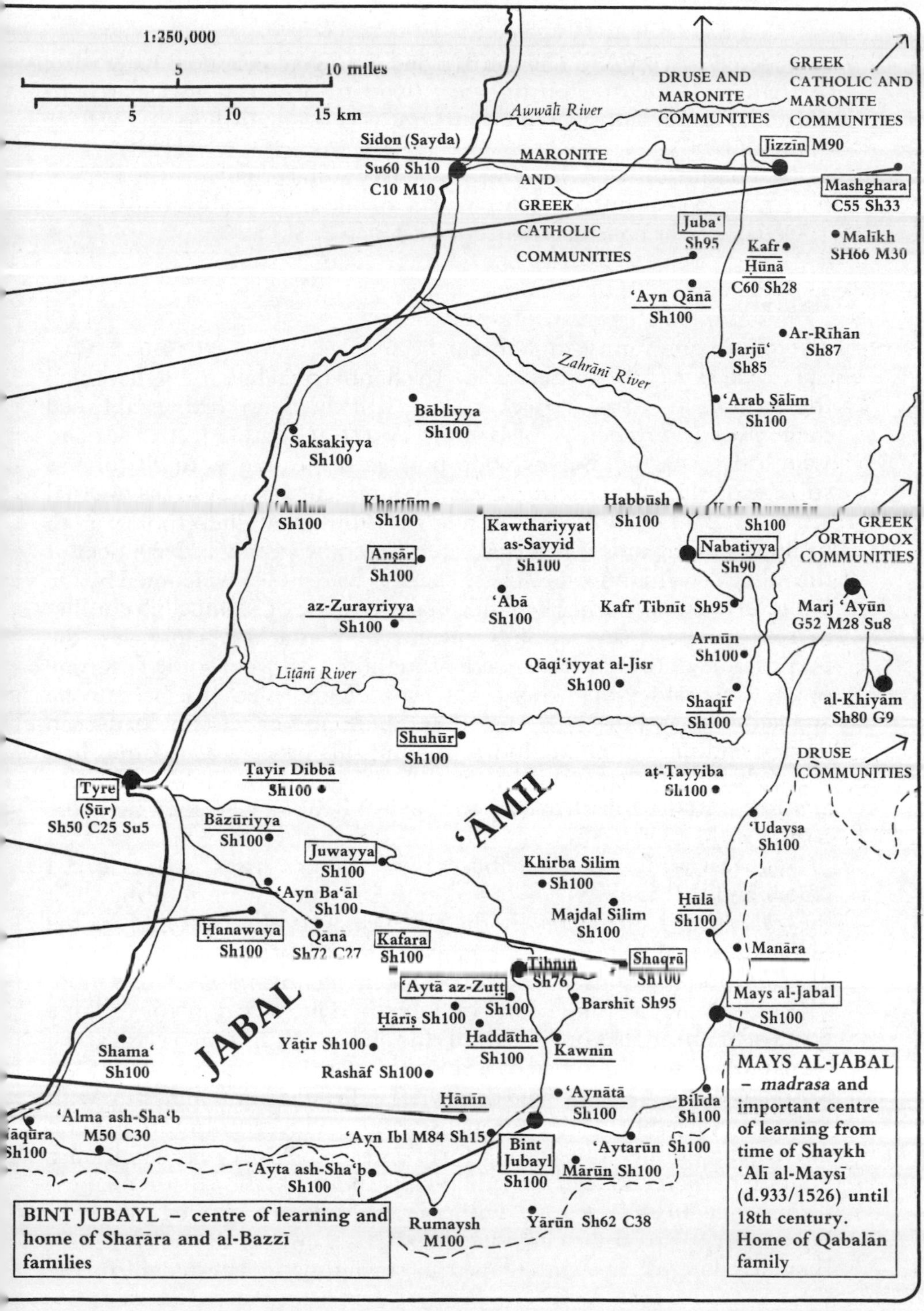

1:250,000
5
10 miles
5
10
15 km
Awwāli River
DRUSE AND MARONITE COMMUNITIES
GREEK CATHOLIC AND MARONITE COMMUNITIES
Sidon (Ṣayda)
Su60 Sh10
C10 M10
MARONITE AND GREEK CATHOLIC COMMUNITIES
Jizzīn M90
Mashghara
C55 Sh33
Juba‘
Sh95
Malikh
SH66 M30
Kafr Ḥūnā
C60 Sh28
‘Ayn Qānā
Sh100
Ar-Rīhān
Sh87
Jarjū‘
Sh85
Zahrānī River
‘Arab Ṣālīm
Sh100
Bābliyya
Sh100
Saksakiyya
Sh100
Sh100
Sh100
Ḥabbūsh
Sh100
Sh100
Kawthariyyat as-Sayyid
Sh100
Nabaṭiyya
Sh90
GREEK ORTHODOX COMMUNITIES
Anṣār
Sh100
‘Abā
Sh100
Kafr Tibnīt Sh95
Marj ‘Ayūn
G52 M28 Su8
az-Zurayriyya
Sh100
Arnūn
Sh100
Qāqi‘iyyat al-Jisr
Sh100
Līṭānī River
al-Khiyām
Sh80 G9
Shaqīf
Sh100
Shuhūr
Sh100
DRUSE COMMUNITIES
Ṭayir Dibbā
Sh100
aṭ-Ṭayyiba
Sh100
Tyre
(Ṣūr)
Sh50 C25 Su5
‘ĀMIL
Bāzūriyya
Sh100
‘Udaysa
Sh100
Juwayya
Sh100
Khirba Silim
Sh100
‘Ayn Ba‘āl
Sh100
Majdal Silim
Sh100
Ḥūlā
Sh100
Ḥanawaya
Sh100
Qānā
Sh72 C27
Kafara
Sh100
Manāra
Shaqrā
Sh100
Sh76
‘Aytā az-Zuṭṭ
Sh100
Barshīt Sh95
Mays al-Jabal
Sh100
JABAL
Ḥārīṣ Sh100
Ḥaddātha
Sh100
Kawnīn
Shama‘
Sh100
Yāṭir Sh100
Rashāf Sh100
MAYS AL-JABAL – *madrasa* and important centre of learning from time of Shaykh ‘Alī al-Maysī (d.933/1526) until 18th century. Home of Qabalān family
‘Aynātā
Sh100
Ḥānīn
Bilīda
Sh100
‘Alma ash-Sha‘b
M50 C30
Sh100
‘Ayn Ibl M84 Sh15
Bint Jubayl
Sh100
‘Aytarūn Sh100
‘Ayta ash-Sha‘b
Sh100
Mārūn Sh100
BINT JUBAYL – centre of learning and home of Sharāra and al-Bazzī families
Rumaysh
M100
Yārūn Sh62 C38

considered heterodox. The third group are also considered heterodox 'extremists'. Only the fourth group (who are not in any case native to Anatolia) can be considered an integral part of the orthodox Twelver community.

It has been estimated that some 15% of the total population of Turkey (i.e. 7,000,000 people) are Shi'i. But of these, probably only about 1,500,000 can be considered orthodox Twelver Shi'is.

Bahrain

The Shi'i community in Bahrain began the 20th century in a very oppressed situation, dominated by the Sunni tribal hierarchy that ruled the island. In 1919, however, the British, who had established themselves as 'protectors' of Bahrain by a treaty dating from 1861 and who had given themselves wide powers of dealing with all foreign subjects on the island in 1904, began to intervene actively in the internal affairs of Bahrain. One of the first measures they undertook was to institute administrative reforms, such as a court system independent of the ruling class's authority. These changes were much welcomed by the Shi'i community but sparked off a major episode of Sunni-Shi'i conflict in 1923 in which several Shi'i villages were attacked. However, the perpetrators of these attacks were brought to trial and for the first time public law, rather than the private law of the ruler, was seen to be applied. The authority of the ruling Sunni al-Khalīfa tribe had been limited and the Sunni attempt to disrupt this process overcome. It is somewhat ironic that at the time that the mujtahids of Iraq were issuing *fatwās* against the British in Iraq, the Shi'a of Bahrain were looking to the British as their protectors.

By 1932 a number of other abuses by the ruling classes, such as forced labour and the right to raise taxes on their estates, were abolished and these also principally benefited the Shi'i peasantry. In 1934 and 1935 the Shi'a protested vigorously against what they considered to be discriminatory actions by the court system against them. Much more serious was the uprising in the mid-1950s. This began in 1953 with a series of Sunni attacks on Shi'is and culminated in a sectarian clash at the oil refinery in 1954 followed by a Shi'i attack on the fort to free some Shi'i prisoners that were being held there. After this, the Shi'is joined up with a number of Sunni Arab Nationalists and a widespread more general movement aiming at political reform emerged. There was continuing political tension between the ruling class and the Nationalist reformers throughout 1955 and 1956 with periodic violent clashes. Then in November 1956, following the Suez Crisis and further violence in Bahrain, the government stepped in strongly and arrested all of the leading nationalists, imprisoning some and exiling others.

Although the Nationalist movement had been crushed, the episode created pressure on the ruling al-Khalīfa shaykhs to introduce some reforms and eventually, after independence from Britain in 1970, Shaykh 'Īsā permitted the election of an Assembly to determine the Constitution. This Assembly was elected in 1972 and sat in 1973. Fourteen Shi'is and eight Sunnis were elected but the ruler negated the Shi'i advantage through his appointment of eight additional members as well as the decision that the eleven Cabinet Ministers, also selected by the ruler, would have full voting powers in the Assembly. The Constitution was decided and in December 1973 there were further elections resulting in the formation of the National Assembly with thirty elected members and fourteen Cabinet Ministers acting *ex officio*. Ḥasan Jawād al-Jashī, a Shi'i, was elected Speaker of the Assembly. In 1975, however, in the midst of a clash with the government over security laws which the government was trying to introduce without the Assembly's approval, the Assembly was dissolved and the brief experiment with democracy ended.[14]

In 1971 the Shāh of Iran formally gave up Iran's long-standing claim to sovereignty over Bahrain and this move eased tension within Bahrain where the Shi'is were under suspicion of being sympathetic to Iran's claims (some 10% of Bahrain's Shi'is are of Iranian origin, having been resident in Bahrain for many generations, while there are some 5,000 recent Iranian immigrants).

After the Iranian Revolution of 1979, however, Sunni-Shi'i tensions re-emerged. On 14 July 1979 Āyatu'llāh Muḥammad Ṣādiq Rawḥānī, a senior member of the Iranian ulama, stated that the previous withdrawal of Iran's claim to Bahrain had been made by an illegitimate regime and was therefore illegal. Although the government of Bāzargān immediately repudiated this, his government fell shortly afterwards and, since Khumaynī has never pronounced on the issue, it remains 'in the air'.

On 20 September 1979 Ḥujjatu'l-Islām Hādī Mudarrisī and Shaykh 'Abdu'r-Razzāq Jawāhirī, Khumaynī's representatives in Bahrain, were arrested and expelled. Following this, all books and magazines from Iran were banned and pictures of Khumaynī in public places were torn down. In December 1981 a Shi'i plot to overthrow the government was discovered and some 73 people from the village of Jaw went on trial in Spring of 1982. Clearly the Bahrain government is nervous about the implications of the Iranian Revolution for its own Shi'i population which have been and continue to be an under-privileged section of society. There has been some attempt to improve relations with Iran and ambassadors have been exchanged but Bahrain remains very guarded in its relations with Iran, especially after the start of the Irano-Iraqi War, and is clearly seeking to shield its own Shi'i population from being influenced by the Iranian Revolution.

Bahrain, at present, has a population of about 290,000. Just over half of the population (55–60%, i.e. about 160,000) is Shi'i. The Sunni element of the population is mainly urban and strongly represented in the armed forces and the government. The Shi'a are the rural population, mainly peasants working the palm estates, and fishermen. In the 20th century large numbers of Shi'a did migrate to the towns and are increasingly represented in the professions and the lower echelons of the administrative bureaucracy. But in the main the Shi'a occupy the less-skilled, lower-income occupations.

Saudi Arabia

The Shi'is of Saudi Arabia live predominantly in the al-Aḥsā (or al-Ḥasā) province. At the beginning of the 20th century they were living under the comparatively tolerant Ottoman Empire. Then in 1913 the Wahhābīs under 'Abdu'l-'Azīz, Ibn Sa'ūd, reoccupied the area and the Shi'is were once again subjected to the harsh, puritanical, anti-Shi'i ideology of the Wahhābīs backed by the fanatical Ikhwān tribesmen. By 1925 Ibn Sa'ūd had taken Mecca and Medina and the Ikhwān damaged the important Shi'i tombs in the latter city and were only prevented from destroying the tomb of Muhammad himself by the personal intervention of Ibn Sa'ūd.

The harshness of Wahhābī rule was, however, considerably relaxed when, in 1929–30, Ibn Sa'ūd turned on the Ikhwān and destroyed them. From that time onwards, although open manifestations of Shi'ism are still prohibited in Saudi Arabia, the Shi'is are not molested.

The discovery of oil in large quantities in the Shi'i province of al-Aḥsā in 1938 changed the face of this area. There was an influx of foreigners and an introduction of all of the paraphernalia of Western (American) civilisation. The indigenous Shi'a only benefited to a small extent from this change. Some 8,000 of the 19,000 workforce of ARAMCO (Arab-American Oil Company) are local Shi'a but they are mainly employed in menial positions.

There are thus grounds for discontent among the Shi'a of al-Aḥsā and there were demonstrations in Sayhat and Qaṭīf in 1979 after the Iranian Revolution and in particular after the seizure of the Grand Mosque of Mecca by a group of Sunni fundamentalists on 20 November 1979 (the first day of the 15th Islamic century).

The Saudi government has clearly been worried about the possibility of Shi'i unrest in its vital oil province. It has increased security in the al-

Aḥsā province and has steadily been deporting Iranians whether or not these have been involved in political activity.

The population of Saudi Arabia is officially estimated at seven or eight million but is probably closer to five million, of which one million are immigrants. The Shi'is of al-Aḥsā province probably number in the region of 200,000. In addition there are about 50,000 Twelver Shi'i immigrants from India, Pakistan, Lebanon and Iran (there are also probably some 50,000 Ismā'īlī Shi'is and 200,000 Yemeni Zaydī Shi'is). Thus Twelver Shi'is probably number some 5% of the total population but a much greater proportion in the vital oil area.

Kuwait

In early 1979, shortly after the climax of the Iranian Revolution, there were Shi'i demonstrations in Kuwait. The Shi'is were protesting at being, in effect, second-class citizens with little share in the country's government or oil wealth. On 24 September 1979 Ḥujjatu'l-Islām Sayyid 'Abbās Muhrī, who had recently been appointed as Imām-Jum'a of Kuwait by Khumaynī, was arrested and together with nineteen others deprived of his Kuwaiti citizenship and expelled. Simultaneously all photographs of Khumaynī were collected from shops and other public places and destroyed. Muhrī went to Iran where he began to broadcast to the Gulf in Arabic promoting the Islamic Revolution. In November 1979, after the seizure of the Grand Mosque of Mecca by Sunni Islamic revolutionaries, there were further Shi'i demonstrations in Kuwait.

The government clearly remains nervous about the possibility of the importation of the Iranian Revolution, as witnessed by the deportation of numerous Iranians. In December 1983 a series of bomb blasts in Kuwait was attributed to a Shi'i group.

Although Kuwait is predominantly a Sunni country, the Shi'i tribes of southern Iraq and the al-Aḥsā province of Saudi Arabia overlap the borders of Kuwait and enter the country in considerable numbers during their seasonal migrations. Thus it has been estimated that some 20% of Kuwait's indigenous population is Shi'i. About 60% of Kuwait's population are immigrants and an estimated 20% of these are also Shi'i including a large Iranian community (1975 Census: 40,842).

	Total (1980 Census)	*Estimated Shi'is*
Indigenous Population	562,065	
Estimated 20% Shi'i		112,000
Immigrants	793,762	
Estimated 20% Shi'i		159,000
Total	1,355,827	271,000

Some have, however, estimated the proportion of Shi'is in Kuwait to be as high as 50%.

Other Gulf States

Although there are few indigenous Shi'is in the other Gulf states, the native populations of these states have in any case been inundated since the oil boom by large numbers of immigrants, among whom are many Shi'is. Thus, for example, so prominent are the Iranians among the merchant community in Dubai that much of the commercial transactions in the Bazaar is carried out in the Persian language. The Shi'is in these countries used to keep a low profile keeping all Shi'i observances in private and practising *taqiyya*. They have become a little more assertive since the Iranian Revolution of 1979 but most of them are in a vulnerable position, being liable to deportation by governments nervous of any disturbing ripples from the Iranian Revolution across the Gulf.

From the figures of Iranian, Iraqi, Lebanese, Indian and Pakistani immigrants it is possible to form a rough estimate of the numbers of Shi'is in each of these states:

	Total Population (1979 estimate)	*Estimated Shi'is*	*Shi'i % of Total*
Qatar	250,000	50,000	20
United Arab Emirates	900,000	60,000	6.6
Oman	800,000	1,000	0.1

India and Pakistan

In 1907 an All-India Shi'a Conference was established and thenceforward met annually. It devoted its attention to community projects (schools, hostels, orphanages, etc.) and to religious instruction. In some provinces there are also provincial Shi'a conferences.

Between 1904 and 1908 there were frequent Sunni-Shi'i clashes especially in the United Provinces area. These clashes were occasioned by public cursing of the first three Caliphs by Shi'is and their praise by the Sunnis. Such public demonstrations were banned in 1909 on the three most sensitive days: 'Āshūrā (10 Muḥarram), Chihilum (40th day after 'Āshūrā) and 'Ali's death (21 Ramaḍān). Intercommunal violence resurfaced in 1935–6 and again in 1939. Many thousands of Sunnis and Shi'is took to the streets on these occasions despite bans on public demonstrations.

When the issue of the separation of India and Pakistan came to the fore in the 1940s the Shi'a were at first reluctant to entrust themselves to a

Sunni-dominated state of Pakistan and so, in the main, opposed separation and supported the National Congress Party politically.

For the first decade of Pakistan's existence there was comparative peace between the Shi'i and Sunni communities. The first President of Pakistan, Iskandar Mīrzā, was a Shi'i. But the recent events in Iran have served to intensify Sunni-Shi'i differences. The present Pakistani regime has attempted to Islamicise itself and, as part of this, tried to organise state taxation on the basis of *zakāt*. This brought the Shi'is into the streets to protest, as they paid *zakāt* to their mujtahids. The state was eventually forced to alter its original plans, to allow for this. Since this episode there have been several occasions when Sunni mobs have descended upon Shi'i *Imāmbāras* and mosques and have destroyed them, especially in Karachi where the population that moved there from Oudh appears to have renewed its traditional Sunni–Shi'i feuding.

The total number of Shi'a in India and Pakistan is difficult to estimate since they do not exist as a separate identifiable community as in most parts of the Middle East but are intermingled with Sunnis and many practise *taqiyya* of their beliefs in the presence of the Sunni majority. There are moreover some difficulties of definition in that there appear to be large numbers who participate in the Muḥarram ceremonies, for example, and who venerate the Imam Husayn, but who are not otherwise identifiable as Shi'is. British censuses that attempted to differentiate Shi'is from Sunnis in the early 20th century are thought to have grossly underestimated the number of Shi'a on account of the practice of *taqiyya*.

Estimates of the proportion of the Shi'a of India vary from between ten and thirty-five per cent of the Muslim population. There are an estimated 80,000,000 Muslims in India; thus the number of Shi'a may be between 8,000,000 and 28,000,000. The lower estimate is more likely to be the more correct one.

The centre of Shi'sm in India is Lakhnau (Lucknow, the old capital of Oudh or Awadh). Here there are two religious colleges and the Madrasat al-Wā'iẓīn, a college for preachers. There are also Shi'i schools, secular colleges and publishing houses in this city. Most towns and cities in southern Uttar Pradesh (the former province of Oudh) have large Shi'i communities: Faizabad, Kanpur (Cawnpore), Varanasi (Benares), Allahabad and Jaunpur. There are also important Shi'i communities in the following cities: Bihara province: Patna and Muzaffarpur; northern Uttar Pradesh: Meerut, Saharanpur and Amroha; Andhra Pradesh province: Golconda and Hyderabad; Gujerat: Baroda and Bombay (Khoja converts). In the Punjab, before the partition of India, the Shi'is were probably the largest religious community after the Sikhs and are estimated to have constituted 20% of the population, but most of these

Shi'is are now on the Pakistan side of the frontier. In Kashmir the district of Baltistan with its capital Skardo is predominantly Twelver Shi'i and there are also many Shi'a in the Ladak district centred on Leh. In Nepal there are reported to be small communities of Twelver Shi'a in Ram Nagar, Bhutaha, Harnagara, Kaptanganj and the Bhokhra panchayat of the Sunsari district in the eastern region.

The Shi'a form an estimated 15% of the 80,000,000 Muslims in Pakistan. This gives a figure of about 12,000,000. The most important Shi'i area in Pakistan is the Punjab centred on Lahore. There are also large Shi'i communities in Sialkot and Khairpur. But after the partition of India a large number of Shi'is from Oudh moved to Karachi and this city now rivals Lahore as the centre of Shi'ism in Pakistan. Several of the tribes of north-west Pakistan, the Turis and part of the Bangash in the upper Karam, are Shi'i as are the Hazāras who live predominantly in Afghanistan but are to be found in large numbers in Pakistan now because of the situation in Afghanistan. The number of Shi'is in Pakistan has also been swelled by refugees from Iran. The refugees from Iran and Afghanistan may have increased the number of Shi'is in Pakistan by up to 1,500,000.

Afghanistan

Afghanistan is predominantly a Sunni country and its population has something of a reputation for fanaticism in its Sunnism. Therefore the Shi'is have always kept a low profile, especially in the towns. Among the tribes in the Afghanistan bordering Iran (the Fīrūzkūhī and Jamshīdī tribes) and also in the city of Herat, there is a substantial number of Shi'a. In addition, the Hazāra tribe of the Hazārajāt (numbering 80,000–100,000) and some of the mountain Tājīk tribe are Shi'i. In Kabul the descendants of the Shi'i Qizilbāsh who came with Nādir Shāh live in the Chindawal quarter of the city. An estimated 6% or 1,320,000 of Afghanistan's 22,000,000 population is thought to be Twelver Shi'i. However, many of these (perhaps as many as one-half) are at present refugees in Pakistan and Iran.

USSR

The USSR has a large Muslim population and a considerable proportion of these are Shi'is. In Central Asia some of the urban Tājīks are Twelver Shi'is, and descendants of Iranians who settled in cities such as 'Ishqābād, Bukhārā and Samarqand in the 19th and early 20th centuries form small Shi'i communities. But by far the largest number of Twelver Shi'is is in Azerbaijan (Ādharbāyjān) SSR where an estimated 4,000,000 of the total population of 6,000,000 are Shi'is.

A *qurultay* (council) of Muslims of Transcaucasia, convened in Baku on 28 May 1944, recognised the Shi'is as a separate community and created a joint Sunni-Shi'i Muslim Central Religious Administration. In Central Asia a similar *qurultay* in 1943 recognised the Shi'a as a fifth orthodox school of Islam, alongside the existing Sunni schools of law. Since the 1979 Revolution Iran has been aggressively beaming revolutionary radio broadcasts to these areas and it remains to be seen what effect this has.

Africa

Twelver Shi'ism was brought to East Africa in the middle of the 19th century by Iranians who came to serve the Sulṭān of Zanzibar and by Indian Khoja merchants. The Indian Khoja who settled in large numbers in the last half of the 19th century were Ismā'īlīs but included a number of Twelvers. The Twelvers petitioned Shaykh Zaynu'l-'Ābidīn Māzandarānī (d. 1309/1892) for a mulla to guide them and Sayyid 'Abdu'l-Ḥusayn Mar'ashī-Shushtarī was sent in 1885. Later Sayyid Ghulām Ḥusayn also came from Hyderabad.

Up to the time that the third Agha Khan, Sulṭān Muḥammad Shāh, visited East Africa in 1899 and 1905 there had not been much distinction between the Ismā'īlī and Twelver Khoja but, on the Agha Khan's orders, his followers separated themselves and the Twelvers found themselves cast out of the community with no mosques, cemeteries or meeting places. However, they rallied around and with help from India organised their communities.

From Zanzibar and other coastal towns like Mombasa, Tanga, Dar-es-Salaam, Lindi, Lamu and Bagamoyo, the Shi'a spread inland during the 20th century reaching Nairobi, Arusha, Bukoba, Moshi, Murunza, Kampala and Songea. In smaller numbers they even reached Usumbura in Zaire by 1920. In all these places they mainly engaged in trade and the size of each community varied from thirty to several hundred.

In 1945 the first effort was made to create a regional organisation when a delegate conference was held in Dar-es-Salaam. Following on from this, an organisation called the Federation of Khoja Shia Ithna-Ashari Jamaats of Africa was formed. The Supreme Council of this body consisted of the following representatives: Mainland Tanzania 26; Zanzibar and Pemba 4; Kenya 10; Uganda 15; Zaire 1; Rwanda-Burundi 1; Somalia 1; Mauritius 1; Malagassy Republic 4; and six others nominated by the President. The representation from each country was proportional to the number of Shi'a there.

The Federation has standardised the syllabus of religious instruction and promoted social, educational and other activities throughout the

THE SHI'I WORLD IN MODERN TIMES, AD 1500-1980
From the Safavid Period to the Present Day

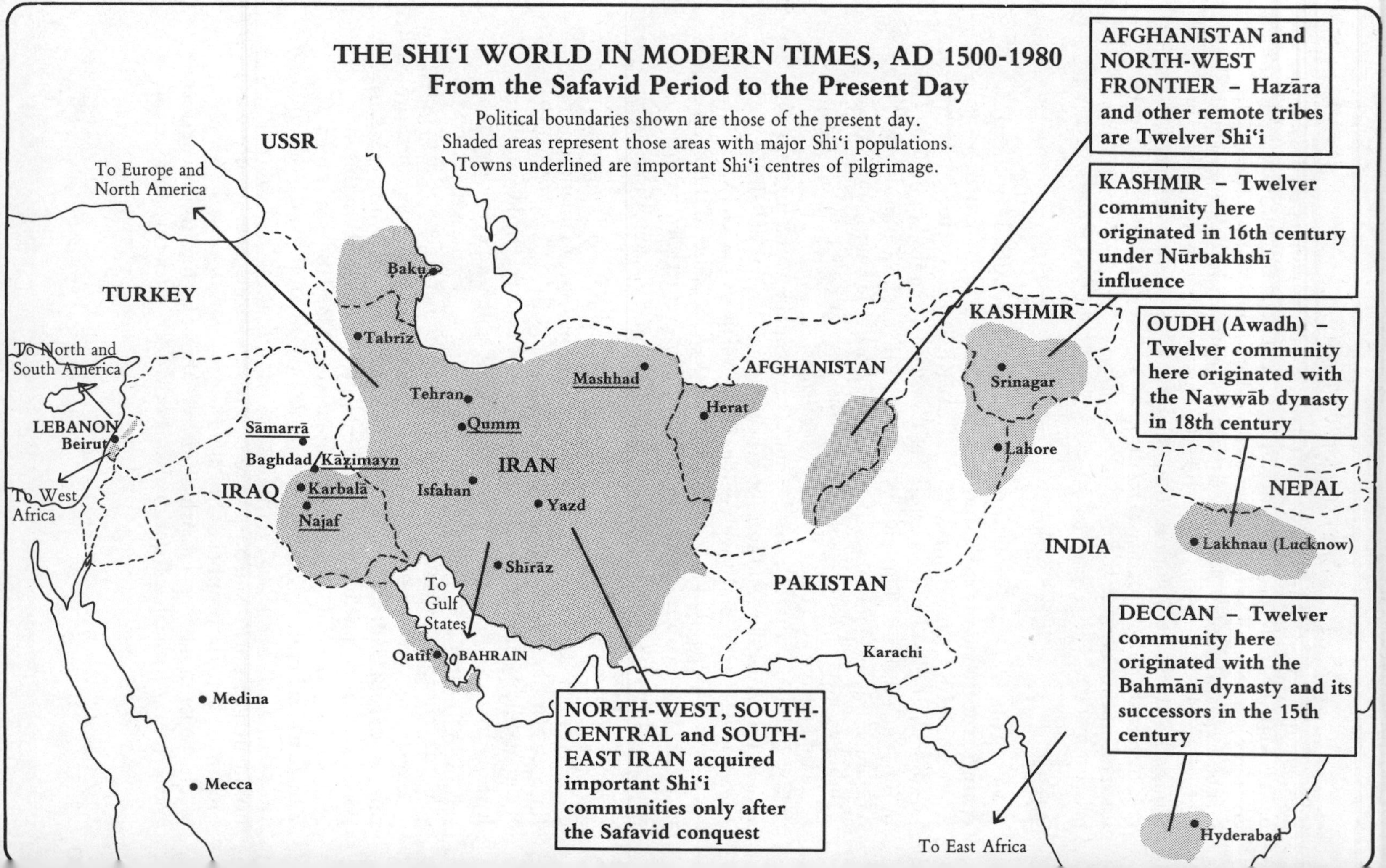
Political boundaries shown are those of the present day.
Shaded areas represent those areas with major Shi'i populations.
Towns underlined are important Shi'i centres of pilgrimage.
AFGHANISTAN and NORTH-WEST FRONTIER – Hazāra and other remote tribes are Twelver Shi'i
KASHMIR – Twelver community here originated in 16th century under Nūrbakhshī influence
OUDH (Awadh) – Twelver community here originated with the Nawwāb dynasty in 18th century
DECCAN – Twelver community here originated with the Bahmānī dynasty and its successors in the 15th century
NORTH-WEST, SOUTH-CENTRAL and SOUTH-EAST IRAN acquired important Shi'i communities only after the Safavid conquest
USSR
To Europe and North America
TURKEY
To North and South America
LEBANON
Beirut
To West Africa
Sāmarrā
Baghdad
Kāzimayn
Karbalā
Najaf
IRAQ
Baku
Tabrīz
Tehran
Qumm
IRAN
Isfahan
Yazd
Shīrāz
Mashhad
Herat
AFGHANISTAN
To Gulf States
Qatif
BAHRAIN
Medina
Mecca
PAKISTAN
Karachi
KASHMIR
Srinagar
Lahore
INDIA
NEPAL
Lakhnau (Lucknow)
Hyderabad
To East Africa

area. In 1964 the Bilal Muslim Mission was set up at Tanga to teach native Africans and a number have become Shi'is. Five of these went in 1968 to Najaf to study there, later moving to Lebanon and Qumm.

The largest Twelver community is in Tanzania and numbers some 10,000; Kenya has 3,000. Uganda did have some 4,000 but under the regime of Idi Amin most of these were expelled.

In West Africa the Lebanese emigrant community that dominates the trade of most of the area is composed of Christians and Shi'is. The latter predominate in Sierra Leone and Guinea. Although Shi'is probably do not number more than 20,000 their importance in the economic life of West Africa far outweighs their small numbers.

America and Europe

During the 19th and early 20th centuries large numbers of Lebanese emigrated to North and South America. Among these were a small number of Shi'is. In the United States their centre is in Detroit and they number some 50,000. The Shi'i communities in North America and Europe have been considerably increased by the influx of Iranians. Up to 1979 these numbered some 40,000 in the USA and between 7,000 and 15,000 in each of France, Germany and Great Britain. (The number of Shi'is in Britain was increased considerably after Idi Amin's expulsion of Asians from Uganda.) Since 1979, however, there has been a very large increase in the number of Iranians, mainly as refugees. Reliable estimates are difficult to obtain but it is estimated that there are probably 200,000 Iranians now in North America (100,000 in Southern California) and 100,000 in Western Europe, principally in France and Spain. Ethnic differences (Lebanese, East African Asians, Iranians) and political differences among the Iranians have prevented much cohesiveness among the Shi'is in Europe and North America although a number of 'umbrella' organisations have been set up. The Muhammadi Trust in Britain and the Mizan Press in California are publishing some Shi'i literature mainly in the form of translations. In South America, apart from the Lebanese Shi'i migrants in the southern half of the sub-continent, there are also some Shi'i migrants from the Indian subcontinent in the former British colonies of the West Indies and Guyana.

The Shi'i World

In each of the foregoing sections of this chapter an attempt has been made to estimate the number of Shi'is in each country and region dealt with. In most countries, no accuracy can be achieved because official censuses do not exist or do not single out Shi'is as a separate category. Bearing in mind the severe limitations of all such figures, Table 11 is a tentative attempt to estimate the total world Shi'i population in the year 1980:

Table 11: The Distribution of Shi'is throughout the world in 1980

Country	*Total Population*[15]	*Muslim Population*[16]	*Twelver Shi'i Population*[17]	*Twelver Shi'is as % of Total Population*
Iran	38,492,000	37,694,300	34,000,000	88.3
Pakistan	82,952,000	80,320,350	12,000,000	14.5
India	547,123,000	80,540,000	10,000,000	1.8
Iraq	13,145,000	12,589,200	7,500,000	57.1
USSR	268,115,000	30,297,000	4,000,000	1.5
Turkey	45,363,000	45,018,000	1,500,000	3.3
Afghanistan	22,038,000	21,885,280	1,300,000	5.9
Lebanon	3,360,000	2,000,000	1,000,000	29.8
Kuwait	1,439,000	1,368,600	270,000	18.8
Saudi Arabia	10,900,000	10,768,000	250,000	2.3
Bahrain	294,000	279,310	160,000	54.4
Syria	8,536,000	7,645,850	50,000	0.6
Other Asian countries			300,000	
Americas			270,000	
Europe			100,000	
Africa			40,000	
Australasia			10,000	

Total world population	4,374,000,000
Total Muslim population	723,000,000
Twelver Shi'i population	72,750,000
Percentage of world population	1.7

Iran: the 1979 Revolution and After

The 1979 Revolution

Between 1973 and 1977, although there were few disturbances in Iran that would be serious enough to feature in the world's press, there was increasing discontent seething below the surface. The grandiose promises made by the Shāh following the oil price rises in 1973 gradually turned into a nightmare of corruption and inflation. Attempts to control inflation and trim budgets to the falling real value of oil led in 1976–8 to a large rise in unemployment, particularly among the unskilled and semi-skilled. The two major urban terrorist groups which had been in existence since the 1960s (the Marxist-oriented Fidā'iyān-i Khalq and the Islamic leftist Mujāhidīn-i Khalq) suddenly increased in activity.

During this period between 1973 and 1977, the Bazaar and religious opposition continued covertly through distribution of Khumaynī's writings and tape-recordings (particularly after the resumption of pilgrimages to the Iraqi shrines in 1976); through allusions made by preachers and particularly by the *rawḍa-khāns* (implicitly identifying the Shāh's regime with the Umayyads who had caused the death of the Imam Husayn); by boycotting the *Dīn-i Dawlat* structure and by continuing to support the traditional ulama financially.

During 1977 there was a noticeable relaxation of censorship by the regime. This may have been caused by the initiation of President Carter's human rights policy with its attendant threat of withdrawal of American support from regimes that violated human rights. There had also been much pressure from international organisations such as Amnesty International and the International Commission of Jurists. The Shāh's illness with a lymphatic cancer may also have led to a weakening of his usual iron grip. He appeared to bow to public pressure and sacked Amīr-'Abbās Huvaydā, his Prime Minister, in August 1977, but little changed as the cabinet of the new Prime Minister was almost identical to that of his predecessor.

The result of the relaxation of censorship and a few human rights concessions by the regime was an immediate increase in the amount of protest material circulating and a subsequent heightening of the feeling of discontent. Almost every section of the Iranian population had grievances against the Shāh's regime by 1977. The ulama were alarmed by the increasing encroachment on their income and field of action by the *Dīn-i Dawlat* structure, the laws being passed by the regime which they considered anti-Islamic, and the wholesale importation of Western culture; the students were unhappy about government interference in the running of the universities and in the curriculum; the farmers and peasants had come to see that the propaganda of the White Revolution did not match the realities, the policies of the government were in fact favouring agricultural imports rather than the peasant farmers, many of whom drifted to the cities and became construction workers or unemployed; and the business community, the civil service and most of the middle class were unhappy about the increasing inflation and the pervasive corruption. Something of the complete disillusionment of the populace can be judged from the fact that in the last local elections before the Revolution, in Tehran, a city with 4,500,000 population, the top candidate received 7,000 votes. Thus with the relaxation of censorship, there were growing demands for reform and still greater freedom.

An incident in August 1977 when a number of slum-dwellers protesting about evictions were killed in clashes with the police increased tension. Then towards the end of 1977 the Shāh's regime tried to put the lid back on. Repressive measures were once again taken against a number of opposition leaders. On 23 October 1977 Khumaynī's son died under circumstances that led many to assume the involvement of SAVAK. There was a commemorative meeting in Tehran at which police clashed with mourners. A short time later large crowds attending a poetry recital began shouting anti-Shāh slogans and there was a further clash.

On 31 December President Carter visited Iran and expressed his support for the Shāh. This, together with an ill-conceived article on 7 January 1978 in the semi-official newspaper, *Ittilā'āt*, attacking Khumaynī in an undignified and obscene manner, led to a protest by several thousand students in Qumm on 9 January calling for the restoration of the Constitution, the re-opening of closed universities and religious colleges and the return of Āyatu'llāh Khumaynī. Police opened fire on the demonstrators causing much loss of life (no accurate figures are available but as many as 70 may have been killed).

The massacre at Qumm more than any other episode initiated the events that led to the overthrow of the Shāh. Khumaynī responded predictably by calling for the overthrow of the Shāh, but the importance of this episode was the widespread public indignation caused and the fact that it caused even the moderate Āyatu'llāh Sharī'atmadārī to declare the Shāh's government non-Islamic and to call for passive resistance.

These Qumm massacres initiated a pattern of events in which one massacre led to a commemoration of the martyrs after the traditional forty days which in turn led to a further clash, further deaths and another fortieth-day commemoration. At first these fortieth-day commemorations were local and sporadic but as time went by and the protests gained momentum, they became national and well-coordinated. On 18 February the fortieth-day commemoration of the Qumm massacre resulted in rioting and deaths in Tabrīz (as many as 100 may have been killed). On 30 March the fortieth day of the Tabrīz killings saw demonstrations in several Iranian towns. In Yazd perhaps as many as 100 were killed by troops firing on people as they emerged from one of the main mosques of the town. For the next fortieth day there were demonstrations in many towns on 8–11 May.

There was something of a lull in June when the fortieth day was commemorated by strikes and staying at home rather than street demonstrations but this was to be merely the prelude to an intensification of the protests during the holy month of Ramaḍān which began on 5 August that year. There were continuous demonstrations for most of that month, particularly after the Ābādān cinema fire on 19 August in which over 400 lost their lives.

In desperation the Shāh made Ja'far Sharīf-Imāmī, a politician with some religious credentials, Prime Minister. Sharīf-Imāmī was given leeway to make concessions to the opposition. A Ministry of Religious Affairs was set up and the Ministry of Women's Affairs disbanded, casinos were closed, a number of notoriously corrupt officials were dismissed and a number of Bahā'īs expelled from their jobs.

Ramaḍān ended on 3 September and on the following day, the Islamic festival 'Īd al-Fiṭr, there was a large, peaceful demonstration in Tehran. There were then several further demonstrations until the government banned demonstrations on 7 September. On 8 September, Black Friday as it came to be known, another demonstration in Tehran was fired on by troops and several hundred were killed. There was an immediate reaction by the crowds and the government imposed martial law on 9 September and detained opposition leaders.

Until this time there had been, in effect, two separate protest movements: the religious protest initiated by the ulama after the anti-Khumaynī articles in January, and the political agitation for greater liberalisation. From September onwards these two movements became increasingly merged and began to attract even middle-class support, thus broadening the basis of the protests considerably.

October saw the beginning of a major use of the strike weapon. Large sections of the work-force went on strike, including the economically important oil-workers and bank employees.

On 6 October Khumaynī was expelled from Iraq at the request of the Shāh's government, and moved to France. This proved another major miscalculation by the Shāh's regime in that from his residence at Neauphle le Chateau near Paris, Khumaynī was better able to communicate with his supporters in Iran as well as being in a better position to obtain publicity in the world's press and radio (in particular the BBC's Persian service which was eagerly listened to by the people of Iran and frequently broadcast Khumaynī's statements). Addresses by Khumaynī would be taped in Paris and then, via the telephone, transmitted to Iran where they were again taped, reproduced and distributed in large numbers. The Shāh tried to compromise with Khumaynī and even announced that he was free to return to Iran. Both the Shāh and the National Front sent messengers to Paris to negotiate. But Khumaynī announced that no compromise was possible and he would not return to Iran while the Shāh remained in power.

On 6 November Sharīf-Imāmī was replaced by a military government headed by General Azharī. At first the latter had some degree of success. He managed to get the oil-workers back to work and the demonstrations died down. But then a general strike was called for 26 November and the demonstrations began again. One group particularly hard hit at this time was the Bahā'ī community. Not only was it being attacked by the demonstrators urged on by the ulama, but it was also subjected at this time to a violent campaign against it organised by the Shāh's secret police, SAVAK, in order to try to shore up the regime's Islamic credentials.

It was clear to all that the month of Muḥarram with its Shi'i commemorations was to be the major test for the government. The month began on 2 December. Almost at once there were major demonstrations, while at night large numbers defied the curfew. The government attempted to negotiate but the opposition was now dictating the terms. There were massive demonstrations on the day of 'Āshūrā (11 December); more than a million people are estimated to have been on the streets of Tehran alone. More mass demonstrations, a hardening of the oil-workers strike and guerilla assassinations of government figures and foreign technical advisers followed. Towards the end of December the opposition groups began taking over institutions and government offices. The troops, increasingly isolated, either turned more brutal in their attacks on unarmed civilians, causing numerous deaths, or began to desert in increasing numbers, handing over their weapons to the revolutionaries. It became common to see youths dressed in white deliberately trying to provoke the troops into shooting them; the Karbalā theme and the Shi'i exaltation of martyrdom came very much to the fore.

On 29 December Dr Shāpūr Bakhtiyār, a long-time opponent of the Shāh's regime and formerly one of Muṣaddiq's aides, was asked to become Prime Minister in the hope of appeasing the crowds. But it was too late for even such a dramatic gesture to have any impact. The momentum of revolutionary fervour caused the crowd to turn even against Bakhtiyār for the simple reason that he had reached an agreement with the Shāh. The only question now was whether the military would stage a bloody coup in order to reassert order. Bakhtiyār persuaded them not to do this and also persuaded the Shāh to leave the country on 16 January. Bakhtiyār tried to block Khumaynī's return but to no avail.

On 1 February 1979 Khumaynī returned triumphantly to Iran welcomed by an estimated crowd of two million. Bakhtiyār, having tried to keep up a pretence of being in power for several days, finally gave up on 12 February and fled abroad. The Revolution was complete and Khumaynī was *de facto* ruler of Iran. The *Vilāyat-i Faqīh* (see p. 196) had begun.

Two years previously, almost no-one, not even the opposition, could have predicted the fall of the Shāh's regime so rapidly and so completely. It is of interest therefore to examine the factors that led to the success of the 1979 Revolution as compared to previous upheavals:

1. *The Shāh's lack of resolution*. During the crisis that lasted from late 1977

until his departure in January 1979, the Shāh displayed an uncharacteristic lack of resolution in dealing with the situation. At each stage he vacillated and did too little too late, neither being firm enough to crush the opposition as he had done in 1963 nor making enough concessions to satisfy them or at least to split them. It may be that, as has been suggested, the Shāh's illness or the drugs being used to treat it made it difficult for him to think clearly in the crisis, or alternatively that as he knew that he was dying he did not wish to cause a blood-bath which would have made the transition of power more difficult on his death.

It may also be that the Shāh felt somewhat insecure as to whether, if he acted firmly and many lives were lost, he would receive the backing of the USA where Carter was in the full swing of his human rights policy. Although it has been said that Carter let the Shāh down, it is difficult to see what America could have done, once events were in train, that would have saved the Shāh. Any direct interference by America would only have increased resentment. Although Carter was probably instrumental in encouraging the protest movement by his human rights policy, once the pattern of protests was under way nothing that Carter could have said or done would have saved the Shāh.

2. *The transfer of the allegiance of the middle classes.* It is doubtful whether the Revolution would have been successful if it had merely remained a protest of the religious classes, the Bazaar, the university students and the unemployed as the upheaval of 1963 had been. The movement towards revolution really picked up momentum when the middle classes began to desert the Shāh. This happened particularly from the late summer of 1978 onwards. The reasons for this switch are twofold. Firstly, the optimistic promises that the Shāh had made about the country's future were all beginning to look very hollow by 1977–8 and there was much discontent about corruption and inflation. Secondly, the intellectuals of the Revolution such as Banī-Ṣadr and Sharī'atī had succeeded in presenting an Islamic ideology that appeared modern, liberal and appealing by contrast to traditional Islam. By suppressing all free political discussion in the country, the Shāh forced the middle classes towards religiously-oriented opposition as that was the only form of discussion and protest left.

3. *Khumaynī's leadership.* The religious opposition was only one of many groups that were actively working against the Shāh, and in the 1960s and early 1970s it seemed much more likely that a leftist movement would overthrow the Shāh or that the liberals would wring concessions out of him. It was mainly Khumaynī's leadership that set the religious tone for the Revolution. Khumaynī succeeded in imposing his leadership on three main groups: the religious leaders, the political opposition, and the mass of the lower classes.

Firstly, he united the religious leadership behind him politically. The Shi'i mujtahids have been notorious for their factionalism and stubborn independent-mindedness. Therefore it speaks highly for Khumaynī's abilities that he was able to unite this disparate body behind him and get them to emerge from their traditional reticence to indulge in political activity. Secondly, Khumaynī was able to unite the various opposition groups, most of which had very diverse political aims, behind him in a concerted drive to get rid of the Shāh. Had the revolutionary ideology been expressed in political terms, it is doubtful if it would have had the mass support that it did. On the other hand, the organisational abilities of the political opposition and the military abilities of the guerilla groups undoubtedly played an important role in the revolutionary process. Thirdly, Khumaynī was able to inspire the masses of the people with his leadership. He succeeded in casting the struggle against the Shāh in cosmic terms in the minds of the people and especially the poorer classes. The Revolution became a struggle between good and evil; it became the re-enactment of Karbalā. Suddenly the wearing of the traditional *chādur* (veil) or the plain sombre dress with head-scarf, instead of being regarded as a symbol of religious obscurantism and reaction, became the symbol of protest against the regime and was adopted by many middle-class university students. Thus the language and imagery of the Revolution became predominantly religious rather than political. By stating that Khumaynī succeeded in imposing his leadership on these three groups it is not intended to imply that he deliberately planned this or did anything to attract these groups. Rather, he led the way and once the others saw that he was succeeding, they fell into line with him as the only way of ousting the Shāh. His stubborn refusal to compromise on his demands forced the other groups like the National Front to fall in behind him, thus ensuring that the Revolution went all the way to toppling the Shāh and did not come to any compromise short of that.

4. *The Karbalā factor*. Perhaps the critical deciding factor in the Revolution was the way in which Khumaynī was able to grip the imagination of the masses. Khumaynī's role in the Revolution became the embodiment and fulfilment of numerous Shi'i themes on which the people of Iran had been raised from childhood. The whole struggle became cast in terms of the struggles of the Imams against their enemies (the constant theme of the *rawḍas*) and, in particular, the battle of Karbalā. The Shāh and his powerful army were cast in the role of Yazīd and the Umayyad troops while Khumaynī became the Imam Husayn leading his people against overwhelming odds. The banners in the demonstrations proclaimed: 'Everywhere is Karbalā and every day is 'Āshūrā.' The demonstrators killed by the Shāh's troops were designated as martyrs (in parallel with the Shi'i martyrs at Karbalā and

elsewhere) and were buried in special cemeteries. Khumaynī in distant Paris was also like the Hidden Imam sending his messages through special representatives. Stories circulated among the crowd that Khumaynī had dreamed that he would be buried in Qumm and therefore it was inevitable that he would return to Iran. As the momentum of the Revolution increased, the anticipation of Khumaynī's return became like the anticipated return of the Hidden Imam; no sacrifice was too great to help to realise it. Then came the day of Khumaynī's return – the anticipated parousia. The crowds were shouting for 'Imam Khumaynī' and were confident that a new age had dawned with justice for all. Anyone who broke ranks with the Revolution and opposed Khumaynī after his return was likened to the *Nākithūn* (those like Talḥa, Zubayr and 'Ā'isha who broke their allegiance to 'Ali and fought against him at the Battle of the Camel). The commonest charge made against those executed by the Revolutionary courts was that of being *mufsid fi'l-arḍ* (a corrupter upon the earth) a vague and indefinable charge which, however, had strong Qur'anic overtones. Thus the Revolution became one long enactment of Shi'i themes and even the major participants in the events became more carried along by the momentum of the roles they were playing than able to initiate actions of their own free will.

Immediately after the success of the Revolution, there was an effort to cool religious fervour. It was firmly stated on several occasions that, of course, Khumaynī was not the Imam but the use of the designation Imam Khumaynī continued and so subsequently it was announced that Imam here was being used as meaning leader of the people – a usage familiar enough in Arabic but not hitherto made in Persian. Khumaynī has also allowed the designation of *Nā'ib al-Imām* (Deputy of the Imam) to continue[18] although it has been less used recently. If by this designation is meant the traditional *Nā'ib al-'Āmm* (general representative, see p. 190) of the Imam, then it applies equally to all mujtahids and Khumaynī is not even sole *marja' at-taqlīd*. If, on the other hand, a special representation of the Hidden Imam (*Nā'ib al-Khāṣṣ*) is intended, then this indeed is a radical change, for there has been no *Nā'ib al-Khāṣṣ* since the beginning of the Greater Occultation (see pp. 164, 190). One suspects that Khumaynī's aides would give the former interpretation but that the masses of the people infer the latter.

After the Revolution

Bāzargān, Khumaynī's appointee, took over as Prime Minister on 12 February 1979. But soon it became clear that there was a secret government in parallel, in the shape of the Revolutionary Council and the local Revolutionary Committees that were to a large extent directing the course of events. The identity of the members of the Revolutionary Council and the exact nature of its activities was to remain undisclosed to the public until early 1980 but it is now known that this Council was set up, on the orders of Khumaynī, in late October 1978, to coordinate the Revolution and to study and supervise what should be the form of government after the departure of the Shāh.

At first this Revolutionary Council was composed only of radical ulama such as Āyatu'llāhs Muṭahharī, Bihishtī and Mūsavī-Ardibīlī as well as Hashimī-Rafsanjānī and Bāhunar. When Āyatu'llāh Ṭālaqānī was freed from prison in November 1978, he became Chairman although in mid-1979 when he became unhappy with the direction that the Revolution was taking, he ceased to attend. Later a number of lay figures such as Engineer Bāzargān were added. In the final stages of the Revolution, the Council was in contact with Bakhtiyār, foreign ambassadors, and the army, while constantly receiving instructions from Khumaynī. Thus it is clear that it must have made a major contribution to the comparatively non-violent transfer of power and the forestalling of an army coup.[19]

Although the Revolution had a clear aim, the ousting of the Shāh, its ideology was far from clear and in some respects impractical. Everyone was in agreement that they wanted an Islamic government, but there was no consensus as to what an Islamic government was. Khumaynī's concept of *Vilāyat-i Faqīh* was that the Constitution and law of the country is already determined by the Islamic *Sharī'a* and only requires interpretation by the mujtahids and a planning council, also under clerical control, to determine priorities. There was really no place in Khumaynī's original scheme for any political parties, parliament or other democratic elements. But there was no consensus even among the ulama that Khumaynī's views were correct. Sharī'atmadārī, Ṭālaqānī and others favoured a constitutional democracy, patterned along the lines that Nā'īnī wrote of at the beginning of the 20th century, with multi-party political activity.

This split was reflected inside the Revolutionary Council where, although Bāzargān had left the Council on his appointment as Prime Minister, he had been replaced by a number of Khumaynī's lay associates from Paris such as Banī-Ṣadr, Yazdī, and Quṭbzāda, who together with Āyatu'llāh Ṭālaqānī were in favour of democratic government, while Āyatu'llāh Bihishtī and the other radical ulama wanted to pursue a rigidly Islamic policy along the lines of Khumaynī's *Vilāyat-i Faqīh*. However, the assassination of Āyatu'llāh Muṭahharī on 2 May and the death of Āyatu'llāh Ṭālaqānī on 10 September 1979 greatly strengthened the hand of the radical ulama on the Council.

The first clash between the radical and the liberal democratic elements on the Revolutionary Council came over the wording of the referendum which was held on 31 March 1979 on the question of whether the people wanted an Islamic Republic. Āyatu'llāh Ṭālaqānī and the liberal democrats (as well as Āyatu'llāh Sharī'atmadārī) wanted the people to have a free choice between several types of government in the referendum. But the final wording of the document gave only a choice between monarchy and an Islamic Republic.

The second major area of conflict to emerge was over the question of the Constitution of the new Islamic Republic. A draft Constitution, very similar to the 1905 Constitution (but without the monarchy), which had been drawn up largely by the secular democrats on the Council, was published in June 1979. But the draft was to be subjected to scrutiny by an Assembly of Experts and the radical ulama succeeded in getting a large number of their supporters onto this body. In order to facilitate this, the radical ulama had formed themselves into a political party, the Islamic Republican Party.

The final version of the Constitution that was published on 4 November 1979 was therefore much closer to what the radical ulama wanted. It contained provision for a supreme clerical guide, the *faqīh* or *rahbar* (leader), who together with a twelve-member Council would supervise the election and dismissal of a President and could veto any legislation of the National Assembly deemed to be contrary to Islam. It was, of course, a foregone conclusion that Khumaynī would occupy the position of supreme clerical guide. The Constitution was approved by a referendum in December 1979. This Constitution was opposed by the National Front and by Āyatu'llāh Sharī'atmadārī. The latter protested that the concept of *Vilāyat-i Faqīh* was not indisputably established in Shi'i jurisprudence, nor was there only one *marja' at-taqlīd* – indeed, if anything he was senior to Khumaynī. It should also be noted that the Constitution represents a considerable compromise from Khumaynī's original stance in favour of those wanting more democratic elements. What is not clear is whether this change of mind by Khumaynī occurred in Paris under the influence of lay democrats like Banī-Ṣadr or whether it occurred as a response to what Khumaynī found on his return to Iran.

The strain between the moderates and the radicals built up during the whole of 1979. In April 1979 Sharī'atmadārī's supporters formed a new party, the Islamic People's Republican Party in opposition to the radical ulama's Islamic Republican Party. Āyatu'llāh Ṣādiq Khalkhālī, one of the radical ulama, attacked Sharī'atmadārī publicly for dividing the Islamic movement and provoked pro-Sharī'atmadārī demonstrations, especially in Ādharbāyjān where most of Sharī'atmadārī's supporters live. This unrest continued for much of the year despite a much-publicised reconciliatory meeting between Khumaynī and Sharī'atmadārī on 18 June 1979 at the home of Āyatu'llāh Gulpāygānī in Qumm.

The Revolutionary Committees that were set up in every town to keep the Revolution on its Islamic course soon became an alternative government to Bāzargān and his Cabinet. These Committees began executing hundreds of people, some on comparatively minor charges and some without trial. It became clear that Bāzargān's government was unable to exert any control over these Committees.

Although freedom of speech and freedom of political activity had been one of the rallying points of the Revolution, it was soon evident that this did not include freedom to criticise the new regime. Those who spoke out against the actions of the Revolutionary Committees or against the restrictions that were being imposed soon themselves became victims of those Committees. The National Front disappeared from the ruling coalition and the liberal National Democratic Front headed by Muṣaddiq's grandson was suppressed in the summer of 1979. Sharī'atmadārī's Islamic People's Republican Party was outlawed in December 1979 and several of its leaders executed. Bāzargān's government became increasingly blocked in any action that it wished to take by the radical ulama's Islamic Republican Party, which effectively controlled the national Revolutionary Council, the Revolutionary Committees, the Revolutionary Guards and most of the mosques.

The situation of two governments in parallel was ended shortly after the take-over of the American embassy and the start of the holding of the American hostages on 4 November 1979. Two days later Bāzargān resigned and the Revolutionary Council took over as the government with Āyatu'llāh Bihishtī as secretary of the Council becoming *de facto* Prime Minister of the country.

Bihishtī and the Islamic Republican Party suffered some temporary setbacks between November 1979 and January 1980. In the first place, the students holding the American Embassy hostages refused to submit to the Revolutionary Council, nor did they consider themselves part of the Islamic Republican party. They maintained they were following 'the line of the Imam (Khumaynī)'. Bihishtī and the Islamic Republican Party had always considered themselves the true followers of Imam Khumaynī and were somewhat dismayed when Khumaynī refused to adjudicate on which group was following his 'line'. The question of 'the line of the Imam (*khaṭṭ-i Imām*)' and who was truly following it became a very heated point of discussion for many months. The second set-back for the IRP came when Khumaynī decided that the ulama, whose function he conceived to be supervising and guiding the government, could not themselves be candidates in the Presidential elections, thus barring the way to Bihishtī's candidature. To make matters worse, when the IRP did eventually choose another candidate, Khumaynī disallowed him on the grounds of his being found to be not of Iranian origin. Thus the IRP was only able to field a weak candidate for the Presidential election that was held on 25 January 1980.

Abu'l-Ḥasan Banī-Ṣadr won the Presidential election and was instated by Khumaynī on 4 February. However, Banī-Ṣadr had no real party political machine and in the elections for the National Assembly, the IRP by a number of tactics, such as announcing the need to screen all candidates on their Islamic credentials and pre-Revolution activities and suspending elections in some areas because of lack of security, succeeded in winning 130 of the 270 seats. This gave them a majority in the Assembly since 30 seats could not be filled because of unrest in Kurdistan and elsewhere. The Assembly began to function on 19 July 1980.

However, it is clear that there was among the people a growing disillusionment with the Revolutionary Government. Of a total electorate of about 24,000,000, about 20,400,000 had voted in the referendum for the Islamic Republic in March 1979; 14,000,000 in the Presidential election of January 1980; and only 6,100,000 in the first stage of the National Assembly elections in March 1980. After this punitive measures were decreed for failure to vote and numbers rose again.

During the summer of 1980 the split between Banī-Ṣadr and Bihishtī widened. Banī-Ṣadr had the support of most of the middle classes, the liberals and left-wing elements, especially among the students, the army, and urban women, all of whom were alarmed at the prospect of clerical domination. But they were poorly organised compared with Bihishtī's supporters who included the radical ulama, controlling most of the mosques, the Revolutionary Committees, Revolutionary Guards, the Islamic societies that had sprung up and now dominated many universities, factories and government offices and a group called the Ḥizbu'llāhīs (Followers of the Party of God) which was in fact only a new name for the street roughs (*lūṭīs*, see p. 199) who had always had a close relationship with the ulama. Bihishtī's IRP control of the National Assembly effectively blocked all of Banī-Ṣadr's political initiatives.

On 17 June 1980 Khumaynī tried to bring the two sides together in a 'charter of unity', but on the very next day Banī-Ṣadr's supporters revealed details of tapes made of a prominent IRP member discussing how to disrupt Banī-Ṣadr's control over the government.

Although Banī-Ṣadr had initially had Khumaynī's full support, at this critical juncture it became clear that Khumaynī himself was not at all happy with the progress of the Revolution and that a degree of tension was building up between him and Banī-Ṣadr. Khumaynī had envisaged an end to the complex, bureaucratic, Western-oriented state apparatus of the Pahlavī era, and its replacement by a much smaller number of administrators whose chief qualifications would be piety, Islamic knowledge, and justice rather than technical or managerial expertise, and who would be readily accessible to the people. This was Khumaynī's vision of returning Iran to governance in the mould of the Imam 'Ali.[20] But in practice, Banī-Ṣadr had found it impossible to make any progress on this front and even notoriously corrupt officials from the previous administration had found their way back to their old posts as it was found that the administration was grinding to a halt without their expertise.

Another aspect of Khumaynī's thinking that caused tension between him and the liberal-democratic elements that formed the majority of Banī-Ṣadr's supporters was Khumaynī's insistence that there should be ideological unity within the Revolution. Previously, as long as one observed the outward dictates of the religious law, orthodoxy of one's belief and thinking were not considered to be a matter of concern. But now, Khumaynī was insisting that to be a Shi'i involved not only observance of religious law but also that one's thoughts must be moulded by the socially-active Revolutionary ideology. With Shi'ism now rigidly defined, for Khumaynī, in terms of both action and ideology, any opposition, dissent or deviation must, by definition, originate from outside Shi'ism (i.e. from US Imperialism, Zionism, etc.).

Khumaynī decided to give a new impetus to the Revolution. In his Naw-Rūz (Iranian New Year, 21 March) speech, he called for a purge of the universities which had become increasingly dominated by left-wing elements. As a result, the Islamic Student Societies took over the universities and closed them down on 4 June until the 'leftist' and 'un-Islamic' elements could be screened out. Then in July there was a drive to screen all government offices and eliminate anyone whose pre-Revolutionary activities were considered to be unacceptable or who were found to be Bahā'īs. There was also a drive in the same month to get women to wear the veil. Unveiled women were attacked in the streets by Ḥizbu'llāhīs.

It was probably only the start of the Irano-Iraqi war on 22 September 1980 that saved Banī-Ṣadr's government from collapse under all these pressures at this time. Certainly control was increasingly slipping away from him as it had with Bāzargān.

During the last months of 1980 and almost the whole of 1981, the major drama that was being played out in the streets of the cities of Iran was the battle for supremacy between the left-wing Mujāhidīn guerillas and the Revolutionary Guards backed by the IRP. On 21 November 1980 Muḥammad Riḍā Sa'ādatī, the leader of the Mujāhidīn, was sentenced to ten years imprisonment on a charge of spying for Russia. During 1981 the Mujāhidīn staged several major demonstrations with as many as 10,000 participants but increasingly they were set upon by Revolutionary Guards and Ḥizbu'llāhīs and eventually, after Banī-Ṣadr's fall, they went underground.

During May and June 1981 the gradual erosion of Banī-Ṣadr's position reached critical proportions. In late May, Khumaynī made a speech in which he criticised him. This was the signal for his enemies to move in. During the first week of June several members of his staff were arrested and his newspaper closed. By 14 June he had gone into hiding, hoping to rally support. On 22 June Banī-Ṣadr was formally deposed as President, thus completing the triumph of Bihishtī and the IRP. Banī-Ṣadr and the Mujāhidin leader, Mas'ūd Rajavī, fled to Paris which now ironically became the centre of groups opposed to Khumaynī.

But Bihishtī's triumph was to be short-lived. On 28 June 1981 he and seventy-five members of the IRP were blown up by a bomb at the IRP headquarters. With Bihishtī's death went the only figure who looked likely to be able to emulate Khumaynī in political adroitness and leadership. Now the question of the succession to Khumaynī became problematical. But the immediate problem was the Presidential election to replace Banī-Ṣadr. Despite their losses in the bombing and other assassinations that occurred with alarming frequency throughout that summer, the IRP were able to reorganise themselves with great rapidity and their candidate, Muḥammad 'Alī Rajā'ī, received an overwhelming majority of the votes cast. Following this another leading member of the IRP, Muḥammad Javād Bāhunar, was made Prime Minister, replacing Rajā'ī who had occupied that position. Khumaynī's initial policy of not allowing clerics to hold executive governmental positions had been visibly faltering for some time and the appointment of Bāhunar, who was a member of the ulama, marked its final demise.

On 30 August 1981 another bomb blast killed Rajā'ī and Bāhunar. Following this, in October, another cleric, Khāmini'ī, was elected President and Ḥusayn Mūsavī was appointed Prime Minister.

Throughout the whole of 1980 and 1981, Khumaynī's relationship with the other major Āyatu'llāhs had been deteriorating. Sharī'atmadārī's Islamic People's Republican Party had in December 1979 threatened to take power in Ādharbāyjān, and Khumaynī asked Sharī'atmadārī to disperse his followers. After this the IPRP was outlawed and several of its leaders executed. Sharī'atmadārī was thus effectively silenced and, although subsequently frequently named by opposition groups as a figure-head around which a liberal democratic movement could be launched, he himself refrained from public political activity.

The two senior clerics of Mashhad, Āyatu'llāhs Qummī and Shīrāzī, delivered several attacks on the Revolutionary regime in the spring of 1981. Other senior clerics such as Āyatu'llāhs Zanjānī, Bahā'u'd-Dīn Maḥallātī-Shīrāzī and Shaykh 'Alī Ṭihrānī have also voiced opposition to Khumaynī, the IRP, the Revolutionary regime and the concept of

Vilayat-i Faqīh. At Qumm Āyatu'llāhs Sharī'atmadārī and Gulpāygānī were thought to be opposed to the IRP's domination while Āyatu'llāh Mar'ashī-Najafī tried to maintain a neutral stance. The senior Āyatu'llāhs were hit financially when it was announced by Khumaynī that the payment of *khums* and *zakāt* should be made to the *Imām-Jum'a* in each city, an official appointed by Khumaynī. If this measure were universally followed, the other Āyatu'llāhs would become unable to finance their students and their charitable works and would thus lose influence.

Then on 10 April 1982 it was announced that a plot had been discovered to overthrow the Islamic Government. Ṣādiq Quṭbzāda, formerly Foreign Minister, and Āyatu'llāh Sharī'atmadārī were accused of being the instigators. Later, in an unprecedented development, Sharī'atmadārī was declared to have been formally stripped of his position as *marja' at-taqlīd*.

One issue that came much to the fore in 1982 and 1983 was the discussion over the Ḥujjatiyya Society. In the 1950s this movement had been started by Shaykh Maḥmūd Ḥalabī in order to persecute and harass Bahā'īs. During the Pahlavī era it had confined itself to this and was called the Anti-Bahā'ī Society. But after the Revolution it began to take a wider, more political stance and assumed its new name. During 1982 and 1983 it was claimed that many members of this society had infiltrated the IRP and the government. It would seem, although this is a point that requires further careful analysis, that the intense discussion that went on about the Ḥujjatiyya at this time was an indirect way of conducting a debate about the concept of *Vilāyat-i Faqīh* (for no one would have dared to appear to be openly opposing Khumaynī from within Iran). Whether the issue was raised by the opponents of *Vilāyat-i Faqīh* in order to see what support they could raise, or by the supporters of the concept in order to flush out their last remaining opponents, is not clear. But in any case, the Ḥujjatiyya were said to be opposed to the concept of *Vilāyat-i Faqīh* and after many months of debate, the final victory of those opposing the Ḥujjatiyya Society (i.e. supporting *Vilāyat-i Faqīh*) was signalled by the fact that Shaykh Maḥmūd Ḥalabī was ordered to leave Tehran and retire to Mashhad.

In late 1982 it was announced that elections were to be held for an Assembly of Experts who would deliberate on the question of the succession to Khumaynī. Elections were held on 10 December 1982. This Assembly has considered a number of different proposals including the appointment of one named individual as Khumaynī's successor or the possibility of a council of mujtahids to take over the role. The deliberations of the Assembly were, however, upstaged when Khumaynī, with great ceremony, sent them his sealed will thus effectively forestalling any final decision being made until his death.

A few days after the elections for the Assembly of Experts, on 17 December, Khumaynī put forward what has become known as the Imam's eight-point decree. This decree was made in response to increasing complaints about the arbitrary nature of the proceedings of the Revolutionary Courts and the Revolutionary Guards. It laid down a number of principles which were intended to check abuses.

During February 1983 the leaders of the communist Tūdih Party, the last remaining active non-government party, were arrested and the Party disbanded, leaving Iran effectively a one-party state.

The Islamic Republican Party, although virtually unchallenged in the political sphere, is not as strong as it would appear to be. A number of factors have contributed to its decline: Khumaynī himself has recently shown no enthusiasm for the party but has rather tended to refer to the 'Party of God' (Ḥizbu'llāh);* several other influential figures such as Āyatu'llāh Ḥasan 'Alī Muntaẓirī (widely regarded as a possible successor to Khumaynī) have followed this trend; the party's leadership has never really recovered from the decimation it received at the hands of the Mujāhidīn and it has no one with the charisma of Bihishtī; some of the principal figures in the party appear to be intent on setting up independent power bases; some groups such as the 'students following the line of the Imam', who had previously aligned themselves with the party are now pulling away again.[21]

With the Revolutionary government much more secure than it has been since the Revolution, it has turned its attention to a number of other issues. Although the war with Iraq occupies a great deal of attention, the regime is also providing a great deal of support for the Shi'is of Lebanon in their conflict. At home, due to the shortages caused by the war and the poor state of the economy, the mosques have been able to consolidate their control over the population in that all rationing and relief supplies are distributed from there. A major drive has been launched to try to harass and pressure the Bahā'ī community into recanting their Faith and converting to Islam, but thus far few Bahā'īs have done so and the measures taken have produced widescale condemnation from such bodies as the United Nations Sub-Commission on Human Rights.

Developments in Shi'ism since the Revolution

Although it is perhaps too early to state for certain what permanent changes will remain in Shi'ism as a result of the 1979 Revolution, the trend of the changes can already be discerned. It can be stated with

* This is not a reference to the Ḥizbu'llāhīs (see p. 293) but rather to the idea that the divisiveness of political parties has no place among Muslims who all belong to the Party of God.

reasonable certainty that Khumaynī's Revolution will be seen as the final stage in the working out of the *Nā'ib al-'Āmm* concept. The right of the ulama to take over the religious functions of the Hidden Imam (the right to collect the *zakāt* and *khums*, the right to lead the Friday Prayers, etc.) and to give judgement on religious law through the use of *ijtihād* which had been gradually assumed by the ulama over the centuries and which had been confirmed by the Uṣūlī victory over the Akhbārīs was now completed by the victory of Khumaynī's concept of *Vilāyat-i Faqīh* which gave the ulama the right to deputise also for the political functions and authority of the Hidden Imam.

It may be argued that the triumph of Khumaynī's views is not yet complete and several of the most influential of the traditional ulama have expressed doubts on the subject. But one of the most surprising features of the last few years has been the ease with which many of the junior ulama have felt it possible to ignore the views of such senior figures as Āyatu'llāh Sharī'atmadārī, who was the most influential *marja' at-taqlīd* prior to the Revolution. Others have put into practice the idea of splitting the function of the *marja' at-taqlīd*; thus they follow Khumaynī in political matters but one of the other *marāji' at-taqlīd* in religious matters. It seems clear that among the present generation of students who are receiving training in the religious colleges at Qumm, most accept Khumaynī's views and the *Vilāyat-i Faqīh* will become an established doctrine within the next generation.

In parallel with this doctrinal development there has been a rapid and far-reaching institutional development. Previously Shi'ism had prided itself on its lack of institutionalisation. It had been very much a personal individual religion. There was no stress on attending the mosque even for the Friday prayers. Individual ulama rose in station according to personal charisma rather than any institutional structure. Following the Revolution, the mosque has become the centre of social life and is used not only for religious purposes but to distribute welfare supplies and even ration cards. The Friday prayers are now a major event in the week and attract hundreds of thousands in the large cities. The address at the Friday prayers has become an important politico-religious organ for carrying forward the Revolution, and government announcements are frequently made through this medium. There has evolved in a remarkably short time a formal hierarchy among the ulama with prefixed designations (see p.206). There is as yet no institutional procedure for ascending the hierarchy but no doubt this will come soon for, with the announcement of Āyatu'llāh Sharī'atmadārī's removal from the office of Grand Āyatu'llāh and the more recent (September 1984) decree from Khumaynī stating that certain persons who had been calling themselves Āyatu'llāh were not entitled to that designation and should henceforth be called Ḥujjatu'l-Islām, there is an unspoken assumption that it is possible to regulate such matters institutionally rather than leaving it to public acclaim. Nor is it yet clear what the implications are of the fact that the prefixed designation of Āyatu'llāh has been dropped for Khumaynī and he is now universally called Imam Khumaynī. Does this imply the creation of a new level in the spiritual hierarchy above *Āyatu'llāh al-'Uẓmā* (see p. 206) or is it merely an indication of his political function? Further evidence of the rapid institutionalisation comes with the election of the Assembly of Experts to decide on the successor to Khumaynī. Once again this represents a formalisation of what in previous generations had been left to public acclaim. The future will undoubtedly see a much greater development of this process.

The relationship of the individual believer to his religion has also undergone something of a change. The ulama have come to assert much more of a priestly intermediary role. It has become much more difficult for the individual to pursue a direct relationship with God. Whereas previously it was sufficient to conform to the precepts of the religious law and the individual's religious and political opinions were his own affair, what is now being increasingly insisted upon is a complete conformity, in both ideology and action, to a single view of what Shi'ism is.

Appendix I

A Chronology of Political and Religious Events in Shi'i History

Dates for dynasties are the dates of the start of the dynasty; dates of religious personages are dates of death. Place-names in parentheses after dynasties are capitals or areas of rule, and after persons are places of principal residence.

Political Events	Religious Personalities and Events
622 Hegira of Muhammad	
632 Death of Muhammad	
656 Beginning of Caliphate of 'Ali	
661 Assassination of 'Ali	
661 Umayyad Dynasty	
	669 Imam Hasan (Medina)
	680 Martyrdom of Imam Husayn at Karbalā
684 Revolt of Tawwābūn	
686 Revolt of Mukhtār	
	c.713 Imam Zaynu'l-'Ābidīn (Medina)
	c.735 Imam Muḥammad al-Bāqir (Medina)
740 Revolt of Zayd	
750 'Abbasid Dynasty	
758 Revolt of Muḥammad an-Nafs az-Zakiyya	
	765 Imam Ja'far aṣ-Ṣadiq (Medina)
	799 Imam Mūsā al-Kāẓim (Medina)
816 'Alī ar-Riḍā proclaimed 'Abbasid heir	
	818 Imam 'Alī ar-Riḍā (Medina)
	835 Imam Muḥammad at-Taqī (Medina, Baghdad)
	868 Imam 'Alī al-Hādī (Sāmarrā)

Political Events	**Religious Personalities and Events**
	873 Imam Ḥasan al-'Askarī (Sāmarrā)
	874 Occultation of Twelfth Imam
905 Hamdanid Dynasty (Mosul)	
934 Buyid Dynasty (Iran, Iraq)	
	940 Muhammad al-Kulaynī (Baghdad)
	941 Beginning of Greater Occultation
944 Hamdanid Dynasty (Aleppo)	
945 Buyids capture Baghdad	
990 'Uqaylid Dynasty (Mosul)	
	991 Ibn Bābūya (Qumm)
1012 Mazyadid Dynasty (S. Iraq)	
	1022 Shaykh al-Mufīd (Baghdad)
1023 Mirdasid Dynasty (Aleppo)	
	1044 'Alamu'l-Hudā (Baghdad)
1055 Seljuqs capture Baghdad	
	1067 Shaykhu't Ṭā'ifa (Baghdad, Najaf)
1079 'Uqaylid Dynasty (Aleppo)	
1101 Foundation of Ḥilla	
1128 'Imādu'd-Dīn Zangī captures Aleppo	
	1145 Shaykh Muḥammad, grandson of Shaykhu't-Ṭā'ifa (Najaf)
	1189 Ibn Zuhra Ḥalabī (Aleppo)
	1192 Ibn Shahrāshūb (Aleppo)
	1201 Ibn Idrīs (Ḥilla)
1225 Death of Caliph an-Nāṣir	
	1238 Ibn Nimā (Ḥilla)
1258 Mongols capture Baghdad	
	1265 Ibn Tāwus (Ḥilla)
	1274 Khwāja Naṣīru'd-Dīn Ṭūsī
	1277 Muḥaqqiq al-Ḥillī (Ḥilla)
1309 Oljeitu (Khudābanda) becomes Shi'i	
	1325 'Allāma al-Ḥillī (Ḥilla)
1336 Jalāyir Dynasty (Iraq)	
1337 Sarbadarid Rule (Sabzivār)	
1359 Mar'ashī Sayyid Dynasty (Māzandarān)	
	1370 Fakhru'l-Muḥaqqiqīn (Ḥilla)
1380 Timurid Dynasty (Iran, Iraq)	
	1384 Shahīd al-Awwal (Jabal 'Āmil)
1403 Execution of Faḍlu'llāh al-Ḥurūfī	
1409 Qarā-Quyūnlū Dynasty (Ādharbāyjān, Iraq)	

Political Events

1423 Revolt of Muḥammad Nūrbakhsh
1489 'Ādil Shāh Dynasty (Bijapur, India)
1490 Niẓām Shāh Dynasty (Ahmadnagar, India)
1501 Safavid Dynasty (Iran)
1512 Quṭb Shāh Dynasty (Golconda, India)
1597 Shāh 'Abbās moves capital to Isfahan
1602 Safavid force captures Bahrain
1722 Afghans capture Isfahan
1722 Nawwābs and Kings of Oudh (Lucknow)
1747 Nādir Shāh (Iran)
1750 Zand Dynasty (S. Iran)
1794 Qājār Dynasty (Iran)
1801 Wahhābīs sack Karbalā
1843 Najīb Pāshā sacks Karbalā

Religious Personalities and Events

1422 Al-Miqdād al-Ḥillī (Ḥilla)
1437 Ibn Fahd (Ḥilla)
1533 Muḥaqqiq al-Karakī (Jabal 'Āmil, Iran)
1558 Shahīd ath-Thānī (Jabal 'Āmil)
1602 Ṣāḥibu'l-Ma'ālim (Jabal 'Āmil)
1621 Shaykh Bahā'ī (Isfahan)
1623 Mullā Muḥammad Amīn Astarābādī, founder of Akhbārī school
1640 Mullā Ṣadrā of the *Ḥikmat-i Ilāhī* School of Isfahan
1659 Mullā Muḥammad Taqī Majlisī (Isfahan)
1699 Mullā Muḥammad Bāqir Majlisī (Isfahan)
1724 Fāḍil-i Hindī (Isfahan)
1760 Mullā Ismā'īl Khajū'ī (Isfahan)
1793 Vaḥīd Bihbahānī (Karbalā)
1797 Baḥru'l-'Ulūm (Najaf)
1812 Shaykh Ja'far Kāshifu'l-Ghiṭā (Najaf)
1815 Sayyid 'Alī Ṭabāṭabā'ī (Karbalā)
1816 Mīrzā-yi Qummī (Qumm)
1826 Shaykh Aḥmad al-Aḥsā'ī, founder of the Shaykhī School
1828 Mullā Aḥmad Narāqī (Narāq, Kāshān)

Political Events	Religious Personalities and Events
	1850 Shaykh Muḥammad Ḥasan Najafī (Najaf)
	1850 The Bāb, founder of the Bābī movement
1856 British end line of Nawwābs of Oudh	
	1864 Shaykh Murtaḍā Anṣarī (Najaf)
	1892 Bahā'u'llāh, founder of the Bahā'ī Faith
	1895 Mīrzā-yi Shīrāzī (Sāmarrā)
1906–9 Constitutional Revolution (Iran)	
1907 All-India Shī'a Conference established	
	1911 Ākhūnd Khurāsānī (Najaf)
1913 Wahhābīs occupy al-Aḥsā	
1918 Overthrow of Ottoman Empire ending Turkish rule over Lebanon, Syria and Iraq	1918 Sayyid Muḥammad Kāẓim Yazdī (Najaf)
	1920 Mīrzā Muḥammad Taqī Shīrāzī (Karbalā)
	1920 Shaykhu'sh-Sharī'a Iṣfahānī (Najaf)
1932 Iraq Independence	
	1933 Shaykh 'Abdu'llah Mamaqānī (Najaf)
	1936 Shaykh Muḥammad Ḥusayn Nā'īnī (Najaf)
	1937 Shaykh 'Abdu'l-Karīm Ḥā'irī-Yazdī (Qumm)
	1942 Shaykh Ḍiyā'u'd-Dīn 'Irāqī (Najaf)
1944 Lebanon Independence	
	1946 Sayyid Abu'l-Ḥasan Iṣfahānī (Najaf)
	1947 Āyatu'llāh Qummī (Karbalā)
1956 Suez Crisis causes upheavals in Lebanon and Bahrain	
	1961 Āyatu'llāh Burūjirdī (Qumm)
1963 Uprising against Shāh; Iraqi Revolution	
	1970 Āyatu'llāh Muḥsin al-Ḥakīm (Najaf)
	1978 Disappearance of Imam Mūsā aṣ-Ṣadr (Lebanon)
1979 Iranian Revolution topples Shāh	
	1980 Execution of Muḥammad Bāqir aṣ-Ṣadr (Iraq)
1983 Lebanon upheaval	

Appendix II

Shi'i Dynasties

Dates are for the start of the reign of each king or ruler. Where the name of a dynasty is preceded by an asterisk, this indicates a dynasty that was probably Shi'i but where it is not clear that they were orthodox Twelver Shi'i. Sources for this material include: Lane-Pole, *Muhammadan Dynasties*; Zambaur, *Manuel de Genealogie*; Bosworth, *Islamic Dynasties*; Shushtarī, *Majālis al-Mu'minīn*; and *Encyclopaedia of Islam*, articles under name of each dynasty.

* **Buyids** Iran and Iraq, an Iranian tribe from Daylām

Fars (Shīrāz)

320/923	'Imādu'd-Dīn 'Alī ibn Būya captured Shīrāz 322/934
338/949	'Aḍudu'd-Dawla Fanā-Khusraw ibn Ruknu'd-Dawla (nephew of above)
372/983	Sharafu'd-Dawla Shīrdil (Shīrzīl) ibn 'Aḍudu'd-Dawla
380/990	Ṣamṣāmu'd-Dawla Marzūbān ibn 'Aḍudu'd-Dawla
388/998	Bahā'u'd-Dawla Fīrūz ibn 'Aḍudu'd-Dawla
403/1012	Sulṭānu'd-Dawla Abū Shuja' ibn Bahā'u'd-Dawla
412/1021	Musharrafu'd-Dawla Ḥasan ibn Bahā'u'd-Dawla
415/1024	'Imādu'd-Dawla Marzūbān ibn Sulṭānu'd-Dawla
440/1048	Al-Mālik ar-Raḥim Khusraw Firūz ibn 'Imādu'd-Dawla
447/1055	Fulād-Sutūn Abū Manṣūr ibn 'Imādu'd-Dawla

—454/1062 power in Shīrāz taken by Kurdish chief Faḍlūya

Iraq (Baghdad)

334/945	Mu'izzu'd-Dawla Aḥmad ibn Būya captured Baghdad from 'Abbasids in 334/945
356/967	'Izzu'd-Dawla Bakhtiyār ibn Mu'izzu'd-Dawla
367/978	'Aḍudu'd-Dawla, see above
372/983	Ṣamṣāmu'd-Dawla, see above
376/987	Sharafu'd-Dawla, see above
379/989	Bahā'u'd-Dawla, see above
403/1012	Sulṭānu'd-Dawla, see above
412/1021	Musharrafu'd-Dawla, see above

416/1025 Jalālu'd-Dawla Abū Ṭāhir ibn Bahā'u'd-Dawla
435/1044 'Imādu'd-Dīn Marzūbān, see above
440/1048 Al-Mālik ar-Raḥīm, see above
—447/1055 Seljuqs capture Baghdad
Other branches of the family ruled in Kirmān, Hamadān, Rayy and 'Umān

* **Hamdanids** North Iraq and North Syria, of the Taghlib tribe of Arabs

North Iraq (Mosul)
292/904 Abu'l-Sajjād 'Abdu'llāh ibn Ḥamdān
made Governor of Mosul by 'Abbasids; deposed 303/915
318/930 Nāṣiru'd-Dawla Ḥasan ibn 'Abdu'llāh
358/968 'Uddatu'd-Dawla Abū Taghlib al-Ghaḍanfar
369/979 Buyids conquer Mosul
Abū Ṭāhir and Ḥusayn, brothers of Abū Taghlib, briefly reconquered Mosul 371/981 – 380/991

North Syria (Aleppo)
333/944 Sayfu'd-Dawla 'Ali ibn 'Abdu'llāh
captured Aleppo from Ikhshids
356/967 Sa'du'd-Dawla Abu'l-Ma'ālī Sharīf ibn Sayfu'd-Dawla
381/991 Sa'īdu'd-Dawla Abu'l-Faḍā'il ibn Sa'du'd-Dawla
died in 392/1001 leaving two small children who were dispossessed by their Mamluk guardian Lu'lu'; Aleppo eventually fell into Fatimid control in 406/1015

* **'Uqaylids** North Iraq (Mosul) and North Syria (Aleppo), of Banu Ka'b Arab tribe
380/991 Abū Dhawwād Muḥammad
occupied Mosul for one year then Mosul recaptured by Buyids
386/996 Ḥisāmu'd-Dawla al-Muqallad ibn Musayyib
captured Mosul and remained ruler as vassal of Buyids
391/1000 Mu'tamadu'd-Dawla Qirwāsh ibn Muqallad
442/1050 Za'īmu'd-Dawla Baraka ibn Muqallad
443/1051 'Alamu'd-Dīn Quraysh ibn Badrān (nephew of Za'īmu'd-Dawla)
453/1061 Sharafu'd-Dawla Muslim ibn Quraysh
captured Aleppo from Mirdasids 472/1079
—478/1085 Aleppo captured by Seljuqs
478/1085 Ibrāhīm ibn Quraysh
486/1093 'Alī ibn Muslim
—489/1096 Mosul captured by Seljuqs

Mazyadids South Iraq (Ḥilla), an Arab tribe of the Banī Asad
403/1012 Abu'l-Ḥasan 'Alī ibn Mazyād al-Asadī
created Amir by Buyids
408/1017 Nūru'd-Dawla Dubays ibn 'Alī

474/1081 Bahā'u'd-Dawla Manṣūr ibn Dubays
479/1086 Sayfu'd-Dawla Ṣadaqa ibn Manṣūr
built Ḥilla 495/1101
501/1107 Nūru'd-Dawla Dubays II ibn Ṣadaqa
529/1134 Ṣadaqa II ibn Dubays
532/1137 Muḥammad ibn Dubays
540/1145 'Alī II ibn Dubays
—545/1150 Ḥilla captured by Seljuqs

* **Mirdasids** North Syria (Aleppo), of Arab tribe of Kilāb
414/1023 Ṣāliḥ ibn Mirdās
captured Aleppo from Fatimids
420/1029 Shiblu'd-Dawla Abū Kāmil Naṣr
—Fatimid reoccupation of Aleppo 429/1037–434/1042
434/1042 Mu'izzu'd-Dawla Thamal
—Fatimid reoccupation of Aleppo 449/1057–452/1060
452/1060 Rashīdu'd-Dīn Maḥmūd
453/1061 Mu'izzu'd-Dawla, second reign
454/1062 'Atiya
457/1065 Rashīdu'd-Dīn, second reign
466/1074 Jalālu'd-Dawla Naṣr
468/1076 Sābiq
—472/1079 surrendered Aleppo to 'Uqaylids

* **Banū 'Ammār** Tripoli, Arabs
462/1070 Amīnu'd-Dawla Ḥasan ibn 'Ammār
took control of Tripoli from Fatimids
464/1072 Jalālu'l-Mulk 'Alī (nephew of above)
494/1100 Fakhru'l-Mulk 'Ammar (brother of 'Alī)
—501/1107 Tripoli captured by Crusaders

* **Chupanids** Ādharbāyjān (Tabrīz), a Mongol tribe
721/1321 Tīmūrtāsh ibn Chūpān
728/1328 Shaykh Ḥasan Kūchik ibn Tīmūrtāsh
744/1343 Malik al-Ashraf ibn Tīmūrtāsh
—756/1355 overcome by Qipchaq Turks

* **Jalayirids** Iraq and Ādharbāyjān (Baghdad), a Mongol tribe
736/1336 Tāju'd-Dīn Ḥasan Buzurg
757/1356 Uways ibn Ḥasan
776/1374 Jalālu'd-Dīn Ḥusayn ibn Uways
784/1382 Ghiyāthu'd-Dīn Aḥmad ibn Uways
813/1410 Shāh Walad ibn 'Alī (nephew of Aḥmad)
—814/1411–815/1412 Qarā-Quyūnlū ended Jalāyir control of all but south Iraq where Jalāyir Amirs continued until 835/1432

* **Sarbadarids** Khurāsān (Sabzivār), Iranians
737/1337 'Abdu'r-Razzāq ibn Amīr Faḍlu'llāh Bāshtīnī

738/1338	Amīr Vajīhu'd-Dīn Mas'ūd ibn Faḍlu'llah
745/1344	Muḥammad Āytīmūr
747/1346	Kulū Isfandiyār
748/1347	Amīr Shamsu'd-Dīn ibn Faḍlu'llāh
749/1349	Khwāja 'Alī Shamsu'd-Dīn
753/1352	Khwāja Yaḥyā Karāwī
759/1357	Khwāja Ẓahīru'd-Dīn (brother of Yaḥyā)
760/1359	Ḥaydar Qaṣṣāb
761/1360	Amīr Luṭfu'llāh ibn Vajīhu'd-Dīn
762/1361	Pahlavān Ḥasan Dāmghānī
763/1361	'Alī Mu'ayyad submitted to Tīmūr 782/1380 but continued to rule as Tīmūr's Governor until death in 788/1386

* **Mar'ashī Sayyids** Māzandarān (Āmul), Arab-Iranian

760/1359	Qavvāmu'd-Dīn, Mīr Buzurg Mar'ashī
781/1379	Kamālu'd-Dīn ibn Qavvāmu'd-Dīn
—794/1391 conquered by Tīmūr	
809/1406	Sayyid 'Alī ibn Kamālu'd-Dīn made Governor of Āmul, captured Sārī
820/1417	Sayyid Murtaḍā ibn 'Alī
830/1426	Sayyid Muḥammad ibn Murtaḍā
856/1452	Sayyid 'Abdu'l-Karīm ibn Muḥammad
865/1460	Sayyid 'Abdu'llāh ibn 'Abdu'l-Karīm
872/1467	Amīr Zaynu'l-'Ābidīn (cousin of 'Abdu'llāh)
880/1475	Mīr 'Abdu'l-Karīm ibn 'Abdu'llāh submitted to Safavids and governed as their vassals
933/1526	Mīr Shāhī ibn 'Abdu'l-Karīm
939/1532	Mīr 'Abdu'llāh grandson of 'Abdu'l-Karīm
969/1561	Mir 'Abdu'l-Karīm ibn 'Abdu'llāh d. 972/1564

* **Qarā-Quyūnlū** Ādharbāyjān and Iraq (Tabrīz), a Turkoman tribe

782/1380	Qarā Muḥammad Turmush
791/1389	Qarā Yūsuf ibn Qarā Muḥammad
823/1420	Jahān Shāh
872/1467	Ḥasan 'Alī
—873/1469 defeated by Aq-Quyūnlū	

'Ādil Shāhs Deccan, India (Bijapur), of Iranian or Turkoman ancestry

895/1489	Yūsuf 'Ādil Shāh proclaimed independence from Bahmānids
915/1510	Ismā'īl ibn Yūsuf
941/1534	Mallū ibn Ismā'īl
941/1535	Ibrāhīm ibn Ismā'īl
965/1557	'Alī ibn Ibrāhīm
987/1579	Ibrāhīm II, grandson of Ibrāhīm I

1035/1626 Muḥammad ibn Ibrāhīm I
1070/1660 'Alī II ibn Muḥammad
1083/1672 Sikandar ibn 'Alī II
—1097/1686 overrun by Moguls

Niẓām Shāhs Deccan, India (Ahmadnagar), Indian
896/1490 Aḥmad Niẓām Shāh
proclaimed independence from Bahmanids
914/1508 Burhān I ibn Aḥmad
961/1553 Ḥusayn ibn Burhān
972/1565 Murtaḍā I ibn Ḥusayn
996/1588 Mīrān Ḥusayn ibn Murtaḍā
997/1589 Ismā'īl ibn Burhān II
999/1590 Burhān II ibn Ḥusayn
1003/1594 Ibrāhīm ibn Burhān II
1004/1595 Aḥmad II
1004/1595 Bahādūr ibn Ibrāhīm
—1008/1599 overrun by Moguls

Quṭb Shāhs Deccan, India (Golconda), of Iranian ancestry
917/1512 Sulṭān Qulī
proclaimed independence from Bahmanids
950/1543 Jamshīd ibn Sulṭān-Qulī
957/1550 Suhān Qulī ibn Jamshīd
957/1550 Ibrāhīm ibn Sulṭān Qulī
989/1581 Muḥammad Qulī ibn Ibrāhīm
1020/1611 'Abdu'llāh, grandson of Ibrāhīm
1083/1672 Abu'l-Ḥasan ibn 'Abdu'llāh
—1098/1687 overrun by Moguls

Chak Kashmir (Srinagar)
969/1561 Ghāzī Khān Chak, son of Qādī Chak
971/1563 Naṣru'd-Dīn Ḥusayn Shāh, brother of Ghāzī
978/1570 Ẓahīru'd-Dīn 'Alī, brother of Ḥusayn
987/1579 Naṣru'd-Dīn Yūsuf ibn 'Alī
993/1585 Ya'qūb ibn Yūsuf
—994/1586 conquered by Moguls

Safavids Iran (Tabrīz, Qazvīn then Isfahan), probably of Kurdish or Turkoman ancestry
907/1501 Ismā'īl I, son of Ḥaydar
overcame Aq-Quyūnlū rulers
930/1524 Ṭahmasp I, son of Ismā'īl
984/1576 Ismā'īl II, son of Ṭahmasp
985/1578 Sulṭān-Muḥammad Khudābanda
996/1588 'Abbās I, son of Muḥammad
1038/1629 Ṣafī I, grandson of 'Abbās

1052/1642 'Abbās II, son of Ṣafī
1077/1666 Sulaymān
1105/1694 Sulṭān-Ḥusayn
—1135/1722 Afghans capture Isfahan ending effective Safavid rule although various Safavid princes continued to hold limited power.

Nawwābs and Kings of Oudh Oudh, India (Lucknow), of Iranian-Arab ancestry
1133/1720 Burhānu'l-Mulk Muḥammad Amīn Mūsawī Sa'ādat Khān
1152/1739 Ṣafdār Jang Abu Manṣūr Khān (nephew of above)
1167/1754 Shujā'u'd-Dawla, son of Ṣafdār Jang
1189/1776 Āṣafu'd-Dawla, son of Ṣafdār Jang
1212/1797 Wazīr 'Alī, adopted son of Āṣafu'd-Dawla
1213/1798 Sa'ādat 'Alī son of Āṣafu'd-Dawla
1229/1814 Ghāziyu'd-Dīn Ḥaydar son of Sa'ādat 'Alī
proclaimed independence from Moguls 1234/1819
1243/1827 Nāṣiru'd-Dīn Ḥaydar son of Ghāziyu'd-Dīn
1253/1837 Mu'īnu'd-Dīn Muḥammad 'Alī son of Sa'ādat 'Alī
1258/1842 Amjad 'Alī son of Mu'īnu'd-Dīn
1264/1847 Wājid 'Alī son of Amjad 'Alī
—1272/1856 deposed by British

Zand South Iran (Shīrāz), an Iranian tribe
1163/1750 Muḥammad Karīm Khān
1193/1779 Abu'l-Fatḥ and Muḥammad 'Alī
1193/1779 Ṣādiq (Shirāz) and 'Alī Murād (Isfahan)
1199/1785 Ja'far
1203/1789 Luṭf 'Alī
—1209/1794 defeated by Qājārs

Qājārs Iran (Tehran), a Turkoman tribe
1209/1794 Āghā Muḥammad Shāh
defeated Zand dynasty; crowned Shāh 1211/1796
1212/1797 Fatḥ 'Alī (nephew of above)
1250/1834 Muḥammad grandson of Fatḥ 'Alī
1264/1848 Nāṣiru'd-Dīn son of Fatḥ 'Alī
1313/1896 Muẓaffaru'd-Dīn son of Nāṣiru'd-Dīn
1324/1907 Muḥammad 'Alī son of Muẓaffaru'd-Dīn
1326/1909 Aḥmad son of Muḥammad 'Alī
—dynasty terminated 1344/1925

Pahlavis Iran (Tehran), Iranian
1344/1925 Riḍā Shāh
1360/1941 Muḥammad Riḍā, son of Riḍā
—dynasty overthrown 1399/1979

Appendix III

Biographies of Prominent Ulama

Look up ulama under commonest designation. Where this designation indicates place of origin, look up under this, e.g. for Muḥaqqiq al-Ḥillī look up under Ḥillī. Most of those listed here studied under many ulama, had numerous students and may have written up to 200 books, therefore only the most prominent in each category have been listed.

Āl Kāshifu'l-Ghiṭā. The descendants of Shaykh Ja'far Kāshifu'l-Ghiṭā (see below under Kāshifu'l-Ghiṭā) have produced mujtahids of the first rank in almost every generation from his time. The most notable of these were:
1. Shaykh Mūsā ibn Ja'far (1180/1766–1243/1827); eldest son of Kāshifu'l-Ghiṭā and took over his father's leadership after his death. Mediated between Turkey and Iran in 1821.
2. Shaykh 'Alī ibn Ja'far (d. 1253/1837); took over his brother's leadership at his death and shared religious leadership in Najaf with Shaykh Muḥammad Ḥasan an-Najafī. Was a teacher of Anṣārī.
3. Shaykh Ḥasan ibn Ja'far (1201/1786–1262/1846); was at first religious leader in Ḥilla but came to Najaf on his brother 'Alī's death and took over his religious leadership; shared religious leadership in Najaf with Shaykh Muḥammad Ḥasan an-Najafī. Negotiated with Najīb Pāshā in 1843 and saved Najaf from being occupied and plundered as Karbalā had been. Was a teacher of Anṣārī.
4. Shaykh Muḥammad ibn 'Alī ibn Ja'far (d. 1268/1851); after the death of Shaykh Muḥammad Ḥasan an-Najafī, became *marja'* for Iraq.
5. Shaykh Mahdī ibn 'Alī ibn Ja'far (1226/1811–1289/1872); one of the leading *marāji'* especially for Caucasus, Tehran, Isfahan, Tabrīz and the Sawad of Iraq during and particularly after the time of Anṣārī.
6. Shaykh Ja'far ibn 'Alī, known as Shaykh Ja'far aṣ-Ṣaghīr (d. 1290/1873); succeeded to his brother's leadership but died a year later.
7. Shaykh Hādī ibn 'Abbās ibn 'Alī ibn Ja'far (1289/1872–1361/1942); was a *marja'* but only of limited importance.
8. Shaykh Aḥmad ibn 'Alī ibn Muḥammad Riḍā ibn Mūsā ibn Ja'far (1292/1875–1344/1926); after the death of Sayyid Muḥammad Kāẓim Yazdī, became *marja'* for some Iraqi tribes and parts of Iran and Afghanistan.
9. Shaykh Muḥammad Ḥusayn, brother of (8) (1294/1877–1373/1954); was *marja'* for many of the Shi'is of Iraq and the other Arab countries as well as having some followers in India, Tibet, Afghanistan and Iran.

'Alamu'l-Hudā (Banner of Guidance), Abu'l Qāsim 'Alī ibn Ḥusayn al-Musawī, also known as Sharīf al-Murtaḍā or Sayyid al-Murtaḍā. b. Rajab 355/966, Baghdad. Studied in Baghdad under Shaykh al-Mufīd. Was Naqīb al-Ashraf (head of the 'Alids) in Baghdad and Amīr of the Ḥajj. Much respected and very wealthy resident of Baghdad. Author of many books especially on *kalām* and also much poetry. Teacher of Shaykhu'ṭ-Ṭā'ifa and Muḥammad ibn 'Alī al-Karāchakī. d. Rabī' I 436/1044, Baghdad; buried Karbalā. His brother was Abu'l-Ḥasan Muḥammad, Sharīf ar-Raḍī or Sayyid ar-Raḍī, the compiler of the *Nahj al-Balāgha*.

Anṣārī, Shaykh Murtaḍā ibn Muḥammad Amīn Anṣārī Tustarī Najafī. b. 1214/1799, Dizfūl. Studied under Sayyid Muḥammad Ṭabāṭabā'ī and Sharīfu'l-'Ulamā Māzandarānī in Karbalā, Mullā Aḥmad Narāqī in Kāshān and Shaykh Mūsā Āl Kāshifu'l-Ghiṭā, Shaykh 'Alī Āl Kāshifu'l-Ghiṭā and Shaykh Muḥammad Ḥasan Najafī in Najaf. Took up permanent residence in Najaf in 1249/1833. Became sole *marja' at-taqlīd* after death of Muḥammad Ḥasan Najafī in 1266/1850. Was famed for his memory, his speedy resolution of intellectual problems, his innovative teaching methods and his upright character. His life-style was that of the poor and, at his death, he left only 70 Qiran (£3.00 approx.). Author of *al-Makāsib* and *Farā'id al-Uṣūl* (known as *Rasā'il*). Students include Mīrzā-yi Shīrāzī, Sayyid Ḥusayn-i Turk (Kūhkamarī), Shaykh Muḥammad Ḥasan Mamaqānī, and Mullā Muḥammad Sharabiyānī. d. 18 Jamādī II 1281 18 November 1864, Najaf and buried there.

Ardibīlī, Muqaddas (Holy One), Aḥmad ibn Muḥammad, also known as Muḥaqqiq-i Ardibīlī. b. Ardibīl. Resident of Najaf. Became leading Shi'i scholar after death of Shahīd ath-Thānī in 966/1558. Was in communication with the Safavid monarchs Shāh Ṭahmāsp and 'Abbās I. Books include *Tafsīr Ayāt al-Aḥkām* and *Hadīqat ash-Shī'a*. Teacher of Shaykh Ḥasan Ṣāḥibu'l-Ma'ālim, Sayyid Muḥammad Ṣāḥibu'l-Madārik, and Shaykh 'Abdu'llah Shushtarī. d. Ṣafar 993/1585, Najaf and buried there.

Bahā'ī, Shaykh, Bahā'u'd-Dīn Muḥammad ibn Ḥusayn al-Ḥārithī al-Ḥamdānī al-'Amilī al-Juba'ī. b. 17 Dhu'l-Ḥijja 953/1547, Ba'ālbakk. When he was still young, his father moved to Khurāsān where he lived mainly in Herat. Shaykh Bahā'ī studied under his father who was himself a student of Shahīd ath-Thānī. Shaykh Bahā'ī became Shaykh al-Islām of Isfahan under Shāh 'Abbās, a position that was at that time the foremost clerical office in Iran. After a few years, during which Shaykh Bahā'ī assisted greatly in the building and development of Isfahan, he left everything for the life of a wandering darvish, a life which he led for thirty years. He was a great scholar in several fields such as mathematics, astronomy and jurisprudence as well as being an eminent poet, philosopher and mystic. His many books include *Jāmi' al-'Abbāsī*, on *fiqh*; *Kitāb az-Zubda* on *uṣūl al-fiqh*; and the *Kashkūl*, a *pot-pourri* of prose and poetry on various subjects. Among his students was Muḥammad Taqī Majlisī. d. Shawwāl 1031/1622 or 1032/1623, Isfahan and buried Mashhad.

Baḥru'l-'Ulūm (Ocean of the Sciences), Sayyid Muḥammad Mahdī ibn Murtaḍā Ṭabāṭabā'ī Burūjirdī. b. Shawwāl 1155/1742, Karbalā. Studied at

Karbalā under Shaykh Yusuf Baḥrānī and Vaḥīd Bihbahānī. Resident of Najaf. Became leading Shi'i mujtahid on death of Vaḥīd Bihbahānī. Many miracles related of him, including being in contact with the Hidden Imam. Teacher of Kāshifu'l-Ghiṭā, Mullā Aḥmad Narāqī, Ḥājj Mullā Ibrāhīm Kalbāsī, Shaykh Aḥmad al-Aḥsā'ī. d. 1212/1797, Najaf and buried there. The Baḥru'l-'Ulūm family has produced many important ulama down to the present day.

Bihbahānī, Vaḥīd (Unique One), Muḥammad Bāqir ibn Muḥammad Akmal, also known as Murawwij and Ustād-i Akbar, b. 1118/1706, Isfahan. Was descended from Shaykh al-Mufīd. Studied at Karbalā under his father Shaykh Muḥammad Akmal, Mullā Ṣadru'd-Dīn Tūnī and Shaykh Yūsuf Baḥrānī. After completing his studies, he returned to Bihbahān, near Isfahan. He remained there for thirty years before returning to Karbalā in 1159/1746. Was responsible for the Uṣūlī victory over the Akhbārī position and for defining the Uṣūlī system of jurisprudence and the role of the mujtahid. His works include *Risālat al-ijtihād wa'l-akhbār* and *Sharḥ Mafātīḥ*. His most important students include Baḥru'l-'Ulūm, Kāshifu'l-Ghiṭā, Mīrzā-yi Qummī, Mullā Aḥmad Narāqī, Ḥajj Muḥammad Ibrāhīm Kalbāsī, Sayyid 'Alī Ṭabāṭabā'ī and his own son Āqā Muḥammad 'Alī Bihbahānī. d. *c.* 1207/1792.

Burūjirdī, Āyatu'llāh Ḥusayn ibn 'Alī Ṭabāṭabā'ī Burūjirdī. b. 1292/1875, Burūjird. Studied at Isfahan and Najaf, at the latter place under Ākhūnd Khurāsānī and Sayyid Muḥammad Kāẓim Yazdī. Returned to Burūjird in 1328/1910. Moved to Qumm in Muḥarram 1364/December 1944–January 1945. Became sole *marja'* in 1947 on death of Āyatu'llāh Qummī. Books include *Ḥāshiyya al-Kifāya* and *Ḥāshiyya al-Nihāya*. Students include most of the leading ulama in the Revolutionary Islamic Government of Iran. d. 13 Shawwāl 1381/19 March 1962, Qumm.

Fakhru'l-Muḥaqqiqīn (Pride of the Investigators), Muḥammad, son of 'Allāma al-Ḥillī, also known as Fakhru'd-Dīn. b. 22 Jamādī I 682/1283, Ḥilla. Studied at Ḥilla under his father and uncle and is said to have achieved the rank of mujtahid at ten years of age. Resident of Ḥilla. Accompanied his father to the court of Sulṭān Khudābanda. Writings: is said to have been responsible for the completion of several of the works of his father; also wrote *Sharḥ al-Qawā'id* and *Ḥāshiyya al-Irshād*. Most of the important ulama of the next generation studied under him, including Shahīd al-Awwal, Ibn Ma'uya al-Ḥillī (d. 766/1364) and Sayyid Ḥaydar Āmulī. d. 25 Jamadī II 771/1370, Ḥilla.

Gulpāygānī, Āyatu'llāh Sayyid Muḥammad Riḍā ibn Muḥammad Bāqir. b. 8 Dhu'l-Qi'da 1316/1899, in a village near Gulpāygān. From 1336/1917 studied at Arāk under Āyatu'llāh Ḥā'irī-Yazdī and moved with him to Qumm in 1922. Began teaching *Dars al-Khārij* at Qumm in 1937 after death of Ḥā'irī-Yazdī. After death of Āyatu'llāh Burūjirdī became administrator of the Madrasa Fayḍiyya as well as building the modern Madrasa Gulpāygānī. Books include *Ḥāshiyyas* on the *Wasā'il* and *'Urwa al-Wuthqā*. At present resident in Qumm.

Ḥā'irī-Yazdī, Āyatu'llāh 'Abdu'l-Karīm ibn Muḥammad Ja'far. b. 1276/1859, in a village near Ardikān. Studied at Yazd, then at Sāmarrā under Mīrzā-yi

Shīrāzī and Najaf under Ākhūnd Khurāsānī and Sayyid Muḥammad Kāẓim Yazdī. Taught for a while at Karbalā until in 1332/1914 he was invited to teach at Arāk (Sulṭānābād). In Rajab 1340/March 1922 he travelled to Qumm intending only to stay there over Naw-Ruz but he was persuaded to remain there to teach. From this time on he devoted his energies to the building up of Qumm as a centre of studies. Books include *Durar al-Fawā'id*. Students include many of the present leading ulama including Āyatu'llāhs Khwānsārī, Mar'ashī-Najafī, Sharī'atmadārī, Gulpāygānī and Khumaynī. d. 17 Dhu'l-Qi'da 1355/28 February 1937, Qumm and buried there.

al-Ḥakīm, Āyatu'llāh Sayyid Muḥsin ibn Mahdī aṭ-Ṭabāṭabā'ī al-Ḥakīm an-Najafī. b. Shawwāl 1306/1889, Najaf. Studied at Najaf under Akhūnd Khurāsānī, Sayyid Muḥammad Kāẓim Yazdī, Nā'īnī and 'Irāqī. Taught at Najaf and after death of Āyatu'llāh Burūjirdī was the most widely-followed *marja'* of the Shi'i world. Was particularly active in opposing socialism and communism. Books include *Mustamsak al-'Urwa*. d. 27 Rabī' I 1390/2 June 1970, Najaf and buried there.

al-Ḥillī, 'Allāma (Very learned one), Jamālu'd-Dīn Abū Manṣūr Ḥasan ibn Yūsuf, also known as Ibn al-Muṭahhar. b. 29 Ramaḍān 648/1250, Ḥilla. Nephew of Muḥaqqiq al-Ḥillī. Studied under Khwāja Naṣīru'd-Dīn Ṭūsī, Muḥaqqiq al-Ḥillī, Ibn Ṭāwus, Ibn Nimā (Shaykh Ja'far) and Ibn Maytham al-Baḥrānī, as well as under a number of Sunni ulama. Resident of Ḥilla. Was responsible for conversion of Sulṭān Khudābanda to Shi'ism after debating with Qāḍī Niẓāmu'd-Dīn Shāfi'ī in 709/1309. Was the author of numerous books particularly on *uṣūl al-fiqh* and is specially noted for his development of the role of the mujtahid. Students include Fakhru'l-Muḥaqqiqīn and Ibn Ma'uya. d. 21 Muḥarram 726/1325, Ḥilla and buried in Najaf.

al-Ḥillī, Al-Miqdād ibn 'Abdu'llāh as-Sayyūrī al-Ḥillī al-Asadī. Studied under Shahīd al-Awwal. Resident of Ḥilla and Najaf. Books include *Kanz al-'Irfān*. Students include Ibn Fahd. d. 826/1423, buried in Baghdad.

al-Ḥillī, Muḥaqqiq Najmu'd-Dīn Abu'l-Qāsim Ja'far ibn Ḥasan, also known as Muḥaqqiq al-Awwal. b. 602/1205, Kufa. Studied under Shaykh Muḥammad, Ibn Nimā. Resident of Ḥilla. Most important book is *Sharā'i' al-Islām* on *fiqh*. Students include his nephew 'Allāma al-Ḥillī. d. 13 Rabī' II 676/1277, Ḥilla and buried there.

Hindī, Fāḍil-i (Distinguished one), Bahā'u'd-Dīn Muḥammad ibn Ḥasan Iṣfahānī. b. 1062/1652, Isfahan. While young, lived for a time in India and hence acquired the designation 'Hindī'. Studied under Muḥammad Bāqir Majlisī. Is said to have achieved the position of mujtahid while still a child, and, because of being learned while still a child, taught in the Royal Harem. Resident of Isfahan. Although some accounts state that he died before the fall of Isfahan to the Afghans in 1722, most agree that he witnessed this event. d. 25 Ramaḍān 1137/1725, Isfahan and buried there.

Ibn Bābūya Abu Ja'far Muḥammad ibn 'Alī al-Qummī, known as Ibn Bābūya (Bābawayh) and Shakyh aṣ-Ṣadūq. b. about 306/918, Qumm. Teachers include his father 'Alī ibn Ḥusayn. Resident of Qumm but travelled extensively collecting traditions. Between 352/963 and 368/978 travelled thus: Qumm, Rayy, Mashhad, Nīshāpūr, Rayy, Baghdad, Kūfa, Mecca, Hamadān, Baghdad, Mashhad, Rayy, Mashhad, Balkh, Samarqand. Approximately 300 works of his are listed. Among the most well-known are: *Man lā yaḥduruhu'l-faqīh*, *'Ilal ash-Sharī'a*, *Kamāl ad-Dīn wa Tamām an-Ni'ma* and *'Uyūn al-Akhbār ar-Riḍā*. His students include Shaykh al-Mufīd. d. 381/991, Rayy and buried there. His father, 'Alī ibn Ḥusayn, is also often called Ibn Bābūya and the two together are sometimes referred to as aṣ-Ṣadūqayn.

Ibn Fahd, Jamālu'd-Dīn Abu'l-'Abbās Aḥmad ibn Muḥammad al-Asadī al-Ḥillī. b. 757/1356, Ḥilla. Studied under al-Miqdād al-Ḥillī. Resident of Ḥilla. Students included Shaykh 'Alī ibn Halāl al-Jazā'irī (a teacher of Muḥaqqiq al-Karakī) and Muḥammad ibn Falāḥ, the founder of the Musha'sha'. Ibn Fahd tried to oppose Ibn Falāḥ's activities once it had become clear that he was deviating from orthodoxy, but was not successful. Books include *Al-Muhadhdhib*. d. 841/1437, Ḥilla, buried Karbalā.

Ibn Idrīs, Abu 'Abdu'llāh Muḥammad (ibn Aḥmad) ibn Idrīs al-'Ijlī al-Ḥillī. b. about 543/1148, Ḥilla. Studied under Ibn Zuhra at Aleppo. Resident of Ḥilla. In his book *As-Sarā'ir*, he strongly attacks Shaykhu'ṭ-Ṭā'ifa on many points. Teacher of Ibn Nimā. d. 18 Shawwāl 598/1202.

Ibn Nimā, Shaykh Muḥammad, Najību'd-Dīn Abū Ibrāhīm Muḥammad ibn Ja'far al-Ḥillī. Student of Ibn Idrīs. Resident of Ḥilla. Teacher of Muḥaqqiq al-Ḥillī and Ibn Ṭāwus. d. 4 Dhu'l-Ḥijja 636/1239 or 645/1248, Ḥilla, buried at Karbalā. His son, Najmu'd-Dīn Ja'far (d. 680/1281), author of the *Muthīr al-Aḥzān*, was also a prominent scholar and teacher of 'Allāma al-Ḥillī.

Ibn Shahrāshūb, Rashīdu'd-Dīn Abū 'Abdu'llāh Muḥammad ibn 'Alī ibn Shahrāshūb Sarawī Māzandarānī. b. about 489/1096, Sārī, Māzandarān. Teachers include Ḍiyā'u'd-Dīn Rāwandī and Faḍl ibn Ḥasan Ṭabarsī. Travelled to Baghdad and preached there in the time of the Caliph al-Muqtafī who is reported to have enjoyed his preaching. Then travelled to Aleppo and took up residence there. Was an important jurist but is chiefly remembered for his books on biography, *Ma'ālim al-'ulamā* and also the *Manāqib Āl Abī Ṭālib*. d. Sha'bān 588/1192, Aleppo and buried there.

Ibn Ṭāwus, Sayyid Raḍiyu'd-Dīn Abu'l-Qāsim 'Alī ibn Mūsā al-Ḥasanī al-Ḥillī. b. Muḥarram 589/1193, Ḥilla. Studied in Ḥilla under Shaykh Muḥammad, Ibn Nimā. Lived for 25 years in Baghdad and for short periods in Najaf, Karbalā and Kāẓimayn before returning to Ḥilla. Was Naqīb al-Ashraf (head of the 'Alids) for Iraq for a time. Was famed as a poet and ascetic. Is said to have met the Hidden Imam in Sāmarrā. Books include *Aṭ-Ṭarā'if* and *Kashf al-Yaqīn*. Teacher of 'Allāma al-Ḥillī. d. 5 Dhu'l-Ḥijja 664/1266, buried at Najaf.

Ibn Zuhra, Sayyid 'Izzu'd-Dīn Abu'l Makārim Ḥamza ibn 'Alī al-Ḥusaynī al-Ḥalabī. b. Ramaḍān 521/1127, Aleppo. Was said to have been in contact with the Hidden Imam and his frequent recourse to *ijma'* as the source of authority in his book on *fiqh*, *Ghaniyat an-Nuzu'*, is reported to be on account of the fact that it is material that he heard from the Hidden Imam but did not dare to attribute to him. Tried to rouse the population of Aleppo against Ṣalāḥu'd-Dīn Ayyūbī. d. 585/1189, Aleppo.

'Irāqī, Āqā Ḍiyā'u'd-Dīn ibn Muḥammad al-'Irāqī an-Najafī. b. 1278/1861. Studied at Najaf under Ākhūnd Khurāsānī and others. Was famed in teaching *uṣūl al-fiqh* but was considered poor in *fiqh*. Books include *Sharḥ at-Tabṣīra* and *Kitāb al-Qaḍā*. Was teacher of Āyatu'llāhs Khū'ī, Khwānsārī, Sharī'atmadārī, Mar'ashī-Najafī and Mīlānī. d. 28 Dhu'l-Qid'a 1361/1942, Najaf and buried there.

Isfahānī, Sayyid Abu'l-Ḥasan ibn Muḥammad Musawī Iṣfahānī Najafī. b. 1284/1867 in a village near Isfahan. Studied in Isfahan, Karbalā and finally in Najaf under Mīrzā Ḥabību'llāh Rashtī (d. 1312/1894) and Ākhūnd Khurāsānī. After political agitations, left Iraq for Qumm, 1923–4. After deaths of Nā'īnī and 'Irāqī became sole *marja'* of the whole Shi'i world. Author of *Risāla al-'Ilmiyya* and *Hāshiyya 'ala al-'Urwa*. Students include Āyatu'llāhs Sharī'atmadārī and Mar'ashī-Najafī. d. 9 Dhu'l-Ḥijja 1365/1946.

al-Karakī, Muḥaqqiq (Investigator), Nūru'd-Dīn 'Alī ibn 'Abdu'l-'Alī al-'Āmilī al-Karakī, also known as Muḥaqqiq ath-Thānī and Khātim al-Mujtahidīn. b. about 870/1465, Karak-Nūḥ in the Jabal 'Āmil. Studied under Shaykh 'Alī ibn Halāl Jazā'irī (a student of Ibn Fahd). Was invited to Iran by Shāh Ṭahmāsp and travelled to all parts of Iran, imposing Shi'ism on the population. Author of *Sharḥ al-Qawā'id*. Students include Shahīd ath-Thānī and Shaykh 'Alī al-Maysī. d. about 940/1533.

Kāshifu'l-Ghiṭā (Uncoverer of Error), Shaykh Ja'far ibn Khiḍr an-Najafī, from Janāja near Ḥilla. b. 1156/1743, Najaf. Studied at Karbalā under Vaḥīd Bihbahānī and at Najaf under Baḥru'l-'Ulūm. Became leading Shi'i scholar after death of Baḥru'l-'Ulūm. Was highly thought of by Fatḥ 'Alī Shāh. Intervened in hostilities between Iran and Turkey in 1806 in order to bring about the release of Sulaymān Pāshā who had been captured. Was involved in defence of Najaf against the Wahhābīs in 1803 and 1806. Travelled extensively in Iran. His most famous book, after which he is titled, is the *Kashf al-Ghiṭā* on *fiqh*. He also wrote a refutation of Mīrzā Muḥammad Akhbārī. His students include his sons (see Āl Kāshifu'l-Ghiṭā above), Shaykh Muḥammad Ḥasan Najafī, Ḥajj Muḥammad Ibrāhīm Kalbāsī and Shaykh Aḥmad al-Aḥsā'ī. d. 22 Rajab 1227/1812.

Khū'ī, Āyatu'llāh Ḥajj Sayyid Abu'l-Qāsim ibn 'Alī Akbar al-Musawī al-Khū'ī an-Najafī. b. Rajab 1317/1899, Khuy. Came to Najaf in 1912 and studied under Nā'īnī, 'Irāqī, and Shaykhu'sh-Sharī'a. After death of Āyatu'llāh al-Ḥakīm became leading *marja'* of Iraq and has religious leadership of most of the Shi'is of India, Pakistan and East Africa. Indeed, of the contemporary *marāji'*, Khū'ī probably has the greatest following outside Iran. Is now under virtual house-arrest. Is considered to be one of the leading exponents of *kalām*, *rijāl* as well as *fiqh*. Books include *Ajwad at-Taqrīrāt* and *Al-Bayān fi tafsīr al-Qur'ān*.

Khumaynī, Āyatu'llāh Ruḥu'llāh ibn Muṣṭafā Musawī Khumaynī. b. September 1902, Khumayn near Isfahan. His grandfather had traded for a time in India and therefore the family was sometimes called by the name Hindī. Studied under Ḥā'irī-Yazdī at Sulṭānābād from 1919 and at Qumm from 1922. After the death of Ḥā'irī-Yazdī in 1937, he began to teach. He specialised in *kalām*, *akhlāq* (ethics), philosophy and *'irfān* (mysticism, gnosis). In 1944 he published a book entitled *Kashf al-Asrār* (Discovery of Secrets) in which he condemned the government of Riḍā Shāh, stated that a monarchy should be limited by the provisions of the *Sharī'a* as interpreted by mujtahids and hinted that government by mujtahids was preferable. During the period of the leadership of Āyatu'llāh Burūjirdī, Khumaynī remained quiet politically in keeping with Burūjirdī's leadership. But from about 1960 onwards when Burūjirdī himself took a more politically active line, and particularly after Burūjirdī's death, his lectures at Qumm on ethics began to be openly critical of the government. Arrested 25 January 1963, 5 June 1963, 5 November 1963; arrested and exiled to Bursa, Turkey, in November 1964. Moved to Najaf, October 1965. In 1970, in the course of lectures delivered in Najaf, he developed the concept of *vilāyat-i faqīh*. Was the leading figure in the Iranian Revolution of 1978–9. In the Constitution inaugurated in December 1979, he became the *Rahbar* (Leader) of the Revolution. After living for a while in Qumm after his return to Iran, he moved to Jamarān, near Tehran.

Khurāsānī, Ākhūnd Muḥammad Kāẓim ibn Ḥusayn Harawī Khurāsānī Najafī. b. 1255/1839, Mashhad. Came to Najaf in 1279/1862 and studied under Anṣārī and Mīrzā-yi Shīrāzī. When Shīrāzī moved to Sāmarrā, Khurāsānī remained in Najaf and began to teach. He was the most prominent of Shīrāzī's successors and was particularly known for his innovative style in teaching *uṣūl al-fiqh*. His major book is the *Kifāyat al-Uṣūl*, completed in 1291/1874. Students include Iṣfahānī, 'Irāqī, Nā'īnī, Ḥusayn Qummī, Burūjirdī and Khwānsārī. d. 20 Dhu'l-Ḥijja 1329/1911.

Khwānsārī, Āyatu'llāh Ḥajj Sayyid Aḥmad ibn Yūsuf Musawī Khwānsārī. b. 1309/1891, Khwānsār. Studied at Khwānsār, Isfahan, and came to Najaf in about 1911, where he studied under Khurāsānī, Yazdī and 'Irāqī. In 1336/1917 he moved to Sulṭānābād and studied under Ḥā'irī-Yazdī, moving with him to Qumm in 1922. He began to teach in Qumm shortly afterwards. In 1369/1950 he was persuaded to move to Tehran and teach there. After Burūjirdī's death he became the main *marja'* for Tehran and other parts of Iran. Moved back to Qumm after the 1979 Revolution. d. 19 January 1985, Tehran, buried Qumm.

al-Kulaynī, Muḥammad ibn Ya'qūb, Abū Ja'far, al-Kulaynī (Kulīnī) ar-Rāzī al-Salsalī. Came from a village near Rayy called Kulayn. Lived in Baghdad near the Bāb as-Salsala (Kufa Gate) and hence is sometimes called Salsalī. Wrote *al-Kāfī* in twenty years. Students include Ibn Qūlūya. d. 328/939 or 329/940, Baghdad and buried there.

Majlisī, Muḥammad Bāqir ibn Muḥammad Taqī; b. 1038/1628, Isfahan. Studied under his father Muḥammad Taqī Majlisī, Mullā Muḥsin-i Fayḍ Kāshānī and al-Ḥurr al-'Āmilī. Became Shaykh al-Islām of Isfahan and foremost Shi'i scholar of his time. Was held in great respect by the Safavid king Shāh Sulṭān-Ḥusayn. Initiated campaign against Sunnis, Sufis and mystical philosophers. He wrote over 60 books, the most famous of which are the *Biḥār al-Anwār*, which consists of Traditions which are for the most part taken from books other than the four early canonical works; *Jalā al-'Uyūn*; *Ḥayat al-Qulūb*; *Ḥaqq al-Yaqīn*. Students include Fāḍil-i Hindī, Mīr Muḥammad Ṣāliḥ Khātūnābādī and Muḥammad Akmal Bihbahānī (father of Vaḥīd Bihbahānī). d. 27 Ramaḍān 1110/1699 or 27 Ramaḍān 1111/1700, Isfahan and buried there. His father Muḥammad Taqī ibn Maqṣud 'Alī Majlisī (*circa* 1003/1594–1070/1659) was also a prominent scholar having studied under Mullā 'Abdu'llāh Shushtarī, Shaykh Bahā'ī and Mīr Dāmād.

Mar'ashī-Najafī, Āyatu'llāh Abu'l-Ma'ālī Sayyid Shihābu'd-Dīn Muḥammad Ḥusayn ibn Maḥmūd Ḥusaynī Mar'ashī-Najafī; descended from Mar'ashī Sayyid dynasty of Ṭabaristān. b. 1318/1900, Najaf. Studied at Najaf under many teachers including 'Irāqī, Shaykhu'sh-Sharī'a, Iṣfahānī, Nā'īnī and Qummī, and also at Kāẓimayn and Tehran. In about 1924 he came to Qumm and began to study under Ḥā'irī-Yazdī and shortly afterwards began teaching there. Is at present the administrator of the Madrasas Mu'miniyya, Mar'ashī-Najafī, and Mahdiyya. Is considered the leading exponent of *uṣūl al-fiqh* at Qumm as well as teaching *fiqh*, *kalām* and *rijāl*. His books include *Ta'līqāt Iḥqāqu'l-Ḥaqq*, *Ghāyat al-Quṣwā* and on the the subject of genealogy *Mushajarāt Āl ar-Rasūl* as well as many biographical monographs.

Mīlānī, Āyatu'llāh Ḥajj Sayyid Muḥammad Hādī ibn Ja'far Ḥusaynī Mīlānī. b. 1313/1895, Najaf. Studied at Najaf under 'Irāqī, Shaykhu'sh-Sharī'a, and Nā'īnī. Taught at Najaf where his students included Āghā Buzurg Ṭihrānī. Came to Mashhad on a pilgrimage in 1954 and was persuaded to stay to teach. Built up Mashhad as a centre of studies. His own school there, however, was pulled down as part of road improvements around the Shrine of Imam Riḍā. His books include *Sharḥ Istidlālī* and *Ḥāshiyya 'ala al-'Urwa*. d. 29 Rajab 1395/1975, Mashhad and buried there.

al-Mufīd, Shaykh (the beneficial Shaykh), Abū 'Abdu'llāh Muḥammad ibn Muḥammad ibn Nu'mān al-'Ukbarī al-Baghdādī al-Karkhī, also known as Ibn al-Mu'allim. b. Dhu'l-Qa'da 336/948 or 338/950, 'Ukbarā in Iraq. Came to Baghdad at an early age and studied there under Ibn Bābūya and Ibn Qūlūya as well as a number of Mu'tazilī shaykhs. Became recognised by Sunnis and Shi'is alike as the leading Shi'i scholar of his time, but because of this, following Sunni-Shi'i clashes in Baghdad, he was expelled from the city for a time. Particularly important for his development of Shi'i *kalām*. His most important works include *al-Ikhtiṣāṣ*, *al-Irshād*, *al-Amālī* and *al-Fuṣūl*. His most important students include 'Alamu'l-Hudā, Sharīf ar-Raḍī, Shaykhu'ṭ-Ṭā'ifa, an-Najāshī, and al-Karāchakī. d. Ramaḍān 413/1022, Baghdad and buried there.

Muḥaqqiq (Investigator) **Ardibīlī** see **Ardibīlī, Muqaddas; al-Awwal** see **al-Ḥillī, Muḥaqqiq; Ath-Thānī** see **al-Karakī, Muḥaqqiq; Ṭūsī** see **Ṭūsī, Khwāja Naṣīru'd-Dīn.**

Nā'īnī, Shaykh Muḥammad Ḥusayn ibn 'Abdu'r-Raḥīm Nā'īnī Najafī. b. 1277/1860, Nā'īn. Studied at Nā'īn, then Isfahan, then at Najaf under Mīrzā Ḥabību'llāh Rashtī and Ākhūnd Khurāsānī and at Sāmarrā under Mīrzā-yi Shīrāzī. He lived for a time in Sāmarrā after the death of Shīrāzī and then in Karbalā before coming to Najaf. Was much involved in the Iranian Constitutional Movement and wrote a tract *Tanbīh al-Umma* supporting it. After the death of Khurāsānī, he became one of several *marāji'* in Najaf. Was involved in Shi'i agitations of 1922–3 and left for Qumm for eight months in 1923. His students include Āyatu'llāhs Mīlānī, Sharī'atmadārī, Khū'ī and Mar'ashī-Najafī. The most well-known of his writings are *Taqrīrāt fi'l-Uṣūl* and *Ḥāshiyya al-'Urwa al-Wuthqā*. d. 26 Jamādī I 1355/1936, Najaf and buried there.

an-Najafī, Shaykh Muḥammad Ḥasan ibn Bāqir. b. *c.* 1202/1787, Najaf. Studied under Kāshiful-Ghiṭā and his son Mūsā, Sayyid 'Alī Ṭabāṭabā'ī and Shaykh Aḥmad al-Aḥsā'ī. Became leading Shi'i scholar during his lifetime and taught most of the next generation of leading ulama such as Shaykh Raḍī an-Najafī, Shaykh Muḥammad Ḥusayn al-Kāẓimī, Mīrzā-yi Shīrāzī, Mīrzā Ḥabību'llāh Rashtī, Shaykh Murtaḍā Anṣārī and Shaykh Mahdī Āl Kāshifu'l-Ghiṭā. His most famous book is the *Jawāhir al-Kalām* on *fiqh*. d. 1 Sha'bān 1266/1850, Najaf and buried there. His descendants are called Āl al-Jawāhir and al-Jawāhirī and have included a number of prominent ulama.

Narāqī, Mullā Aḥmad ibn Muḥammad Mahdī Narāqī Kāshānī. Born in Narāq, resident of Kāshān. Studied under Vaḥīd Bihbahānī in Karbalā and later under Baḥru'l-'Ulūm and Sayyid 'Alī Ṭabāṭabā'ī. Made Kāshān a centre for teaching, attracting such students as Shaykh Murtaḍā Anṣārī. Was held in great respect by Fatḥ 'Alī Shāh. Was the author of a number of important books including *Mi'rāj as-Sa'āda* on ethics, *Miftāḥ al-Uṣūl* and the *Sayf al-Umma* written in refutation of Rev. Henry Martyn. d. *c* 1245/1829, Narāq.

Qummī, Āyatu'llāh Ḥasan ibn Ḥusayn Ṭabāṭabā'ī. b. 1329/1911, Najaf, the son of Āyatu'llāh Sayyid Āqā Ḥusayn Qummī. Studied at Mashhad and from 1348/1929 at Isfahan and from 1350/1931 at Najaf under the major teachers there such as Nā'īnī. He then returned to Mashhad until 1354/1935 when he left Iran with his father in protest at Riḍā Shāh's actions. He studied further at Karbalā and Najaf and soon began to teach as well. In 1368/1948 he returned to Mashhad and began to teach there. From 1383/1963 for a few years he lived at Karaj near Tehran but then he returned to Mashhad where, after the death of Mīlānī, he became the senior Āyatu'llāh and *marja'*.

Qummī, Sayyid Āqā Ḥusayn ibn Muḥammad Ṭabāṭabā'ī Qummī Ḥā'irī. b. 1282/1865, Qumm. Studied in Tehran under Mīrzā Ḥasan Āshtiyānī and Shaykh Faḍlu'llāh Nūrī; at Najaf under Ākhūnd Khurāsānī and Sayyid Muḥammad Kāẓim Yazdī; and at Karbalā under Muḥammad Taqī Shīrāzī. In 1331/1913, he settled in Mashhad and began teaching there. He became increasingly unhappy about the reforms initiated by Riḍā Shāh and in 1935 came to Tehran seeking an interview with the Shāh over the abolition of the veil and the mixing of the sexes in schools. However, the Shāh refused to meet him and invited him to leave the country. He left for Karbalā where he remained until his death except for a brief visit to Mashhad and Qumm in 1362/1943. Students include Mar'ashī-Najafī. His influence increased to such an extent that when Abu'l-Ḥasan Iṣfahānī died, he became the sole *marja' at-taqlīd* for the Shi'i world. But he survived Iṣfahānī by only three months and died on 14 Rabī' I 1366/1947, Karbalā, and was buried at Najaf.

Qummī, Mīrzā-yi Mīrzā Abu'l-Qāsim ibn Ḥasan Jīlānī Qummī. b. Jāpulaq, a village near Qumm. His father had moved to Qumm from Rasht. Studied at Khwānsār and under Vaḥīd Bihbahānī at Karbalā and under Shaykh Muḥammad Mahdī Fatūnī and Āqā Muḥammad Bāqir Hizārjarībī at Najaf. He then returned to the Qumm area and lived in one or other of the villages of that area for a time. He then moved to Isfahan where he taught at the Madrasa Kāsihgarān, but after a disagreement with the ulama there he moved to Shīrāz where Karīm Khān Zand held court. He remained there for a few years and then returned to Isfahan and eventually to the village of Qal'a-Bābū near Qumm. Later he moved into the town of Qumm itself and there set up a teaching circle that soon attracted a large number of students such as Sayyid Muḥammad Bāqir Shaftī and Ḥajj Muḥammad Ibrāhīm Kalbāsī. He became one of the leading mujtahids and *marāji'* of Iran and was held in great respect by Fatḥ 'Alī Shāh. His most famous book is the *Qawānīn al-Uṣūl* on the subject of *uṣūl al-fiqh*. d. 1231/1816, Qumm and buried there.

aṣ-Ṣadūq, Shaykh see **Ibn Bābūya**

Ṣāḥibu'l-Ma'ālim (Author of the *Ma'ālim*), **Shaykh Ḥasan** ibn Zaynu'd-Dīn al-'Āmilī al-Juba'ī, Abū Manṣūr Jamālu'd-Dīn, also known as Ibn Shahīd ath-Thānī and Khatīb al-Uṣūliyyīn. b. 959/1552, Juba' in Jabal 'Āmil; he was seven years old when his father, Shahīd ath-Thānī was martyred. He was a close and life-long friend of Sayyid Muḥammad Ṣāḥibu'l-Madārik with whom he studied under Muqaddas Ardibīlī at Najaf. He also studied in the Jabal 'Āmil under Shaykh Ḥusayn, the father of Shaykh Bahā'ī, and Sayyid 'Alī ibn Ḥusayn as-Sā'igh, a student of Shahīd ath-Thānī. Author of the *Ma'ālim fi'l-Dīn* from the introduction of which is taken the *Ma'ālim fi'l-Uṣūl*, one of the standard works for teaching *uṣūl al-fiqh*. Became the foremost Shi'i scholar of the Jabal 'Āmil and teacher of such persons as Shaykh 'Abdu's-Salām, the father of Shaykh Muḥammad al-Ḥurr al-'Āmilī. d. Muḥarram 1011/1602.

Shahīd al-Awwal (the First Martyr), Shamsu'd-Dīn Abū 'Abdu'llāh Muḥammad ibn Makkī al-'Āmilī al-Jizzīnī. b. 734/1333, Jizzīn in the Jabal 'Āmil. Studied at Ḥilla under Fakhru'l-Muḥaqqiqīn and Ibn Ma'uya and also under numerous Sunni teachers. Returned to Damascus and, through use of *taqiyya*, established himself as a leading scholar of that town, giving judgements on points of law for all four Sunni schools while at the same time being the head of the Shi'i community, and promoting Shi'ism. But eventually he was arrested, according to some accounts because of betrayal by a Shi'i and according to other accounts because of the jealousy of the Shāfi'ī *qāḍī*, Ibn Jamā'a. He made important contributions to *fiqh* and *uṣūl al-fiqh* and was the teacher of many Shi'i ulama, for example al-Miqdād al-Ḥillī. His most important book is the *al-Luma'a ad-Dimashqiyya*, which he wrote for Shamsu'd-Dīn Muḥammad Āwī, the emissary of 'Alī Mu'ayyad, the Sarbadarid ruler of Khurāsān. According to some accounts it was written in seven days during the year that he spent in prison prior to his execution but other accounts state that he completed it four years before his execution. He remained in prison one year and was then executed on the orders of the Governor of Damascus, Baydar, and the Mamluk Sulṭān, Barqūq, and on the *fatwās* of the Mālikī and Shāfi'ī *qāḍīs*. According to most accounts, he was kept in prison for one year and then executed by blows of the sword followed by crucifixion, stoning and then being burned. His death occurred on 9 Jamādī I 786/1384.

Shahīd ath-Thānī (the Second Martyr), Shaykh Zaynu'd-Dīn ibn 'Alī al-'Āmilī al-Juba'ī. b. Shawwāl 911/1506, Juba' in the Jabal 'Āmil. He studied in Juba' under his father and at Mays in the Jabal 'Āmil under Shaykh 'Alī al-Maysī; he may also have studied under Muḥaqqiq al-Karakī; then in about 937/1530 he went to Damascus, in 942/1535 to Egypt, and in 951/1544 to Istanbul, studying in each place under Sunni ulama. In 951/1544 he became a teacher at the Sunni Madrasa Nūriyya in Ba'ālbakk in the Biqā' Valley. Here he taught the four Sunni schools of law under *taqiyya* as well as Shi'i students. His major contribution was to standardise the subject of *Dirāyat al-Ḥadīth*, the study and classification of the *ḥadīth*, using largely his knowledge of Sunni scholarship on this subject. His major book is *Rawḍat al-Bahiyya* which is a commentary on Shahīd al-Awwal's *al-Luma'a ad-Dimashqiyya*. Among his students were Shaykh Ḥusayn, the father of Shaykh Bahā'ī, and Sayyid 'Alī ibn Ḥusayn as-Sā'igh, a teacher of both Muqaddas Ardibīlī and Shaykh Ḥasan Ṣāḥibu'l-Ma'ālim. A man whom he had given judgement against complained to the Wālī of Sidon and, as a result, Shahīd ath-Thānī was summoned to Istanbul. He was killed in 966/1558 either in or on his way to Istanbul.

Sharī'atmadārī, Āyatu'llāh Ḥajj Sayyid Kāẓim ibn Ḥasan Husaynī Burūjirdī Tabrīzī Qummī. b. 1322/1904, Tabrīz. Studied at Tabrīz, then in 1343/1924 he came to Qumm and studied under Ḥā'irī-Yazdī before going on to Najaf where he studied under Nā'īnī, Iṣfahānī and 'Irāqī. He returned to Tabrīz and taught *fiqh* there. Then in 1369/1949, he came once more to Qumm and began to teach there. After Burūjirdī's death he became one of the leading *marāji'* with followers in Iran, especially Ādharbāyjān, Pakistan, India, Lebanon, Kuwait and the Gulf. He was the founder of the *Dār at-Tablīgh Islāmī* (House of Islamic Propagation) which specialises in teaching students, and especially foreign students, at Qumm using modern educational methods, as well as distributing Shi'i literature throughout the world. He was also the administrator of the Madrasa Fāṭima in Qumm. He specialises in the teaching of *akhlāq* as well as *fiqh*. He was formally stripped of his rank of *Āyatu'llāh al-'Uẓmā* after the discovery in April 1982 of a plot against Khumaynī which was said to have had his support.

Sharīf al-Murtaḍā see **'Alamu'l-Hudā**

Shaykhu'sh-Sharī'a (Shaykh of the Sharī'a), Shaykh Fatḥu'llāh ibn Muḥammad Jawād Namāzī Shīrāzī, also known as Sharī'at Iṣfahānī. b. 1266/1849, Isfahan. Studied at Isfahan and, in 1295/1878, moved to Najaf where he studied under Mīrzā Ḥabību'llāh Rashtī and Shaykh Muḥammad Ḥusayn al-Kāẓimī. He participated in the Shi'i revolt against the British in 1920–23. His students include Āyatu'llāhs Mīlānī, Mar'ashī-Najafī and Khū'ī and Āghā Buzurg Ṭihrānī. He became sole *marja'* for the Shi'i world in August 1920 after the death of Mīrzā Muḥammad Taqī Shīrāzī but only survived the latter by four months and died on 9 Rabī' II 1339/20 December 1920, Najaf and was buried there.

Shaykhu'ṭ-Ṭā'ifa (Shaykh of the Sect), Abū Ja'far Muḥammad ibn Ḥasan aṭ-Ṭūsī, also known simply as ash-Shaykh. b. Ramaḍān 385/955, Ṭūs in Khurāsān. Studied at Ṭūs and then in 408/1017 moved to Baghdad where he studied under Shaykh al-Mufīd and 'Alamu'l-Hudā. After the death of the latter, Shaykhu'ṭ-Ṭā'ifa became the leading Shi'i scholar and taught in Baghdad where he had as many as 300 students. His most important works are the two collections of *ḥadīth* entitled *al-Tahdhīb* and *al-Istibṣār*, *an-Nihāya* on *fiqh*, *al-Ghayba* on the Occultation, and the bio-bibliographical works, *ar-Rijāl* and *al-Fihrist*. His students include his son, Shaykh Ḥasan. In 448/1056 his house was attacked and his library burned during Sunni-Shi'i riots in Baghdad and as a result of this he moved to Najaf. d. 22 Muḥarram 460/1067, Najaf and buried there.

Shīrāzī, Āyatu'llāh Sayyid 'Abdu'llāh ibn Muḥammad Ṭāhir Ṭāhirī Shīrāzī. b. 1309/1891, Shīrāz. Studied at Najaf and then became a teacher at Mashhad. After opposing the Shāh, he was jailed and later left for Najaf. He was one of the leading *marāji'* in Najaf after the death of Āyatu'llāh al-Ḥakīm and built three madrasas there. In 1975 he returned to Mashhad where he was one of the *marāji'*. d. 27 September 1984.

Shīrāzī, Mīrzā-yi Ḥājjī Mīrzā Sayyid Muḥammad Ḥasan ibn Maḥmūd Shīrāzī, Ḥujjatu'l-Islām. b. Jamādī I 1230/1815, Shīrāz. Studied in Isfahan and then in Najaf under Shaykh Murtaḍā Anṣārī as well as Shaykh Muḥammad Ḥasan Najafī and Shaykh Ḥasan Āl Kāshifu'l-Ghiṭā. After the death of Anṣārī, he became the leading Shi'i scholar and eventually sole *marja' at-taqlīd*. In 1292/1875 he moved to Sāmarrā and began teaching there. He is perhaps best known for his opposition to the Tobacco Regie in 1891. But he is also important for having reorganised and consolidated the teaching of *fiqh* along the lines that it has continued to be taught to the present day. However, he wrote no books of note. He was the teacher of the most prominent ulama of the next generation including Ākhūnd Khurāsānī, Muḥammad Kāẓim Yazdī, Muḥammad Taqī Shīrāzī, Nā'īnī and Ḥā'irī-Yazdī. d. 24 Sha'bān 1312/1895, Sāmarrā and buried in Najaf.

Shīrāzī, Mīrzā Muḥammad Taqī ibn Muḥibb 'Alī Shīrāzī Ḥā'irī. b. Ramaḍān 1269/1853, Shīrāz. Grew up in Karbalā where he began his studies, then moved to Sāmarrā where he studied under Mīrzā-yi Shīrāzī. After the death of Mīrzā-yi Shīrāzī, he remained in Sāmarrā for a while teaching but then moved to Karbalā. Became sole *marja'* after the death of Sayyid Muḥammad Kāẓim Yazdī in 1919. He led the start of the Shi'i revolt against the British Mandate in Iraq in 1920 but died in its early stages. His writings include *Ḥāshiyya 'ala al-Makāsib*. He was the teacher of many students including Āqā Ḥusayn Qummī. d. 13 Dhu'l-Ḥijja 1338/28 August 1920, Karbalā and buried there.

Shushtarī, Mullā 'Abdu'llāh ibn Ḥusayn Shushtarī (at-Tustarī). Born in Shushtar in south-west Iran. Studied under Shaykh Ni'matu'llāh ibn Khātūn 'Āmilī, a student of Muḥaqqiq Karakī, and Muqaddas Ardibīlī in Najaf from about 977/1569. After the death of Ardibīlī remained in Najaf teaching for about fourteen years until he moved to Isfahan in about 1007/1598. He was the leading teacher in Isfahan and was responsible for building up Isfahan as a centre of Shi'i scholarship. His books include *Sharḥ al-Qawā'id*. He was the teacher of Muḥammad Taqī Majlisī. d. 26 Muḥarram 1021/1612, Isfahan, and buried Karbalā.

Ṭabāṭabā'ī, Sayyid 'Alī ibn Muḥammad 'Alī Iṣfahānī. b. 12 Rabī' I 1161/1748, Kāẓimayn. Nephew of Vaḥīd Bihbahānī. Studied under Bihbahānī whose daughter he married. After the death of Bihbahānī, maintained the importance of Karbalā as a centre of teaching. Held a famous debate with Mīrzā Muḥammad Akhbārī. His best-known book is *Riyāḍ al-Masā'il*, known as *al-Sharḥ al-Kabīr*. Teacher of Mullā Aḥmad Narāqī and Shaykh Aḥmad al-Aḥṣā'ī. d. Muḥarram 1231/Dec. 1815, Karbalā.

aṭ-Ṭūsī, Shaykh Muḥammad see **Shaykhu'ṭ-Ṭā'ifa**

Ṭūsī, Khwāja Naṣīru'd-Dīn Muḥammad ibn Muḥammad, also known as Muḥaqqiq Ṭūsī. b. 11 Jamādī I 597/1201, Ṭūs in Khurāsān. Studied in Ṭūs under Shi'i ulama such as his father who was a student of Ḍiyā'u'd-Dīn Rāwandī and also under teachers of philosophy such as Farīdu'd-Dīn Dāmād who traced his teachers back to Abū 'Alī, Ibn Sīnā (Avicenna). However, he left home while still in his youth, possibly as a result of the Mongol advance towards Khurāsān, and then lived for over thirty years among the Ismā'īlīs at first in Qūhistān in east Iran and later at Alamūt. During this time Khwāja Naṣīru'd-Dīn wrote several important books in accordance with Ismā'īlī doctrines, and therefore he is also claimed by the Ismā'īlīs as one of their foremost exponents. After the fall of the Ismā'īlī strongholds to the Mongol leader Hulagū Khān, in 1256, Khwāja Naṣīru'd-Dīn became Hulagū Khān's astrologer and was able to save many of the valuable manuscripts in the libraries of Alamūt and Baghdad from destruction at the hands of the Mongols. After the fall of Baghdad in 656/1258, Khwāja Naṣīru'd-Dīn devoted his attention to the building of an astronomical observatory at Marāgha. He wrote on astronomy, mathematics, ethics, medicine, geography and history but his most important contribution to Twelver Shi'ism was his development of Shi'i *kalām* so as to incorporate philosophical concepts. His books include *Tajrīd al-I'tiqādāt* on *kalām* and *al-Akhlāq an-Naṣīriyya* on ethics. He was the teacher of 'Allāma al-Ḥillī. d. 18 Dhu'l-Ḥijja 672/1274, buried at Kāẓimayn.

Yazdī, Sayyid Muḥammad Kāẓim ibn 'Abdu'l-'Aẓīm Ṭabāṭabā'ī Yazdī Najafī. b. *c.* 1247/1831, Kasnū near Yazd. He travelled to Isfahan and then to Najaf in 1281/1864 where he studied under Mīrzā-yi Shīrāzī. He began to teach at Najaf after the death of Shīrāzī and became sole *marja'* after the death of Ākhūnd Khurāsānī in 1911. Unlike most of the other Iraqi ulama he was opposed to the Constitutional Movement in Iran. He lived in the village of Ḥuwaysh near Najaf. His most famous book is *'Urwa al-Wuthqā* on *fiqh*. He was the teacher of Āyatu'llāhs Burūjirdī, Khwānsārī and Ḥusayn Qummī. d. 28 Rajab 1337/1919, Ḥuwaysh, and buried in Najaf.

Notes

1. AN OUTLINE OF THE LIFE OF MUHAMMAD AND THE EARLY HISTORY OF ISLAM

There are numerous biographical accounts of Muhammad and histories of Islam. For someone who wants a detailed biography of Muhammad, Alfred Guillaume's translation of Ibn Hishām's *Sīra* entitled *The Life of Muhammad* can be recommended, as well as Montgomery Watt's two volumes, *Muhammad at Mecca* and *Muhammad at Medina*, and Martin Lings' *Muhammad*. Surveys of the course of Islamic history include Carl Brockelmann, *History of the Islamic Peoples*; M. G. S. Hodgson, *The Venture of Islam*, 3 vols.; and *Cambridge History of Islam*, 2 vols. A useful book that includes a fairly detailed biography of Muhammad and a survey of Islamic history is H. M. Balyuzi, *Muḥammad and the Course of Islam*.

More general works on Islam including doctrine and practice include: Kenneth Cragg, *The Call of the Minaret*; Frithjof Schuon, *Understanding Islam*; and for surveys of Islam written by Muslims see Syed Ameer Ali, *The Spirit of Islam*; K. Morgan (ed.), *Islam, the Straight Path*.

Of the numerous translations of the Qur'an that have been attempted, probably the best is that of A. J. Arberry.

For specific subjects a very useful source of information is the *Encyclopaedia of Islam*, 1st edition, 1913–34; new edition 1960–proceeding; although this source is relatively poor on Shi'i subjects. More information on Shi'i subjects will be provided in forthcoming issues of the *Encyclopaedia Iranica*.

2. THE QUESTION OF THE SUCCESSION TO MUHAMMAD

Sources

Arabic: A useful compilation of many of the Traditions cited in this chapter can be found in Ibn Ṭāwus, *al-Yaqīn*, and in a modern work, az-Zanjānī, *'Aqā'id al-Imāmiyya*, pp. 88–99. The Sunni Traditions relating to 'Ali can be found in most compilations of Traditions in the chapter on 'Ali in the section 'Faḍā'il or Manāqib as-Saḥāba' (The Virtues of the Companions). Concerning the events of the Saqīfa, Baladhūrī, *Ansāb al-Ashraf*, has a good cross-section of Sunni and Shi'i accounts of this episode.

European languages: A useful and detailed review of this subject can be found in Jafri, *Origins and Early Development of Shi'a Islam*. Some of the Traditions given here are also to be found in Ṭabāṭabā'ī, *Shi'ite Islam* (Chap. 6).

1 Or according to some sources, eleven years of age; see Ibn Athīr, *al-Kāmil*, Vol. 2, p. 42.

2 Some Sunni sources state that Abū Bakr was the first to believe in Muhammad. But even the most respected collections of Sunni Traditions contain examples giving 'Ali the credit for being first. See, for example, Tirmidhī, *Sunan*, Vol. 2, pp. 300, 301; Ibn Ḥanbal, *Musnad*, Vol. 1, pp. 209–210. The discrepancy can be accounted for by allowing that 'Ali preceded Abū Bakr, but that Abū Bakr was the first male adult to accept Muhammad, 'Ali being then only a child (see Tirmidhī, *Sunan*, Vol. 2, p. 301).

3 Qur'an 26: 214.

4 aṭ-Ṭabarī, *Ta'rīkh*, Vol. 1, pp. 1172–3.

5 Tirmidhī, *Sunan*, Vol. 2, p. 299.

6 Muslim, *Saḥīḥ*, Vol. 2, p. 324.

7 Ibn Ḥanbal, *Musnad*, contains more than 10 separate Traditions in which this sentence occurs with respect to 'Ali: Vol. 1, pp. 170, 173, 174–5, 179, 182–3, 184, 331; Vol. 3, pp. 32, 338; Vol. 6, pp. 369, 438. See also Tirmidhī, *Sunan*, Vol. 2, p. 301 (2 Traditions); Muslim, *Saḥīḥ*, Vol. 2, pp. 323–4 (4 Traditions); Ibn Māja, *Sunan*, Vol. 1, Bab 11, pp. 42–3, No. 115; p. 45, No. 121.

8 Ibn Ḥanbal, *Musnad*, Vol. 1, p. 151, similar Tradition in Vol. 1, p. 3[illegible]

9 Tirmidhī, *Sunan*, Vol. 2, p. 299.

10 Ibn Māja, *Sunan*, Vol. 1, Bab 11, p. 42, No. 114.

11 Tirmidhī, *Sunan*, Vol. 2, p. 299; Ibn Māja, *Sunan*, Vol. 1, Bab 11, p. 44, No. 119.

12 Tirmidhī, *Sunan*, Vol. 2, p. 298.

13 al-Ḥākim, *al-Mustadrak*, Vol. 3, pp. 126–7.

14 Tirmidhī, *Sunan*, Vol. 2, p. 299.

15 *ibid.* pp. 300, 319, 320.

16 *ibid.* p. 300.

17 *ibid.* p. 301.

18 *ibid.* p. 306.

19 Ibn Ḥanbal, *Musnad*, Vol. 4, p. 281; similar Traditions can be found in the same work: Vol. 1, pp. 84, 118, 119, 152, 331; Vol. 4, pp. 367, 370, 372; Vol. 5, pp. 347, 366, 419 and in many other works such as Ibn Māja, *Sunan*, Vol. 1, Bāb 11, p. 43, No. 116.

20 al-Bukhārī, *Saḥīḥ*, Kitāb al-'Ilm, Bāb 40, Vol. 1, p. 41.

21 Ibn Ḥanbal, *Musnad*, Vol. 1, p. 175.

22 Ibn Ḥanbal, *Musnad*, Vol. 3, p. 59. Similar *ḥadīth* in Vol. 3, pp. 3, 17, 26; Vol. 4, pp. 366–7; Vol. 5, pp. 151–2; also Tirmidhī, *Sunan*, Vol. 2, p. 308; Muslim, *Saḥīḥ*, Vol. 2, pp. 325–6.

23 Muslim, *Saḥīḥ*, Vol. 2, pp. 323–4; Tirmidhī, *Sunan*, Vol. 2, p. 300.

24 Tirmidhī, *Sunan*, Vol. 2, pp. 308, 320.

25 Ibn Ḥajar, *aṣ-Ṣawā'iq*, pp. 150, 184; al-Ḥākim, *al-Mustadrak*, Vol. 3, pp. 150–51.

26 Tirmidhī, *Sunan*, Vol. 2, p. 298.

27 Ibn Ḥanbal, *Musnad*, Vol. 1, p. 331.

28 Tirmidhī, *Sunan*, Vol. 2, p. 299; Ibn Māja, *Sunan*, Vol. 1, Bab 11, p. 44, No. 118.

29 Tirmidhī, *Sunan*, Vol. 2, p. 320.

30 al-Mufīd, *al-Ikhtiṣāṣ* quoted in Majlisī, *Biḥār al-Anwār*, Vol. 26, p. 30, Nos. 38–41.
31 Majlisī, *Biḥār al-Anwār*, Vol. 26, p. 6.
32 *ibid.* pp. 4–5; similar Tradition in Ibn Bābūya, *'Uyūn al-Akhbār ar-Riḍā*, quoted in *Biḥār al-Anwār*, Vol. 39, p. 36, No. 5.
33 Qur'an 13:7.
34 Suyūṭī, *ad-Durr al-Manthūr*, Vol. 4, p. 45.
35 Qur'an 5:55.
36 Rāzī, *at-Tafsīr al-Kabīr*, Vol. 12, p. 26.
37 For a review of these see Jafri, *Origins*, pp. 27–57.
38 Baladhūrī, *Ansāb al-Ashraf*, Vol. 1, p. 580.
39 al-Ya'qūbī, *Tārīkh*, Vol. 2, p. 137.
40 aṭ-Ṭabarī, *Ta'rīkh*, Vol. 1, pp. 2769–70; this phrase occurs several times.
41 Baladhūrī, *Ansāb al-Ashraf*, Vol. 1, pp. 581, 583.
42 *ibid.* p. 588 (2 Traditions).
43 But see, for example, aṭ-Ṭabarī, *Ta'rīkh*, Vol. 1, pp. 2769–70 where even in this source which is accepted by Sunnis, the mutual dislike of 'Umar and the house of Hāshim is clearly seen.
44 'Ali, for example, disagreed with 'Umar on the question of the distribution of money from the Central Treasury. The Sunni collections have numerous Traditions showing how 'Ali saved 'Umar from making erroneous legal decisions on several occasions. 'Umar is reported to have said: ''Ali is the best judge among us.'

3. THE LIVES OF THE IMAMS AND EARLY DIVISIONS AMONG THE SHI'IS

Sources

Arabic and Persian: Important sources on the lives of the Imams include Shaykh al-Mufīd, *Kitāb al-Irshād*; Ibn Shahrāshūb, *Manāqib Āl Abī Ṭālib*; al-Irbilī, *Kashf al-Ghumma*; and Majlisī, *Jalā' al-'Uyūn*.

On the Shi'i sects the most important non-Shi'i sources are: Ibn Ṭāhir al-Baghdādī, *Kitāb al-Farq bayn al-Firaq* (First part translated by Seelye and second by Halkin); ash-Shahristānī, *al-Milal wa'n-Niḥal* (Tr. Kazi and Flynn); Ibn Ḥazm, *al-Faṣl fi'l-Milal* (Tr. Friedlander); al-Khayyāt, *al-Intiṣār* (Tr. Nader); al-Ash'arī, *Maqālāt al-Islāmiyyīn*. Shi'i sources include: an-Nawbakhtī, *Firaq ash-Shī'a* (Tr. Mashkur) and al-Qummī, *al-Maqālāt*.

European languages: One of the most important Arabic sources on the lives of the Imams, al-Mufīd, *al-Irshād*, has been translated into English by Howard. Jafri, *Origins and Early Development of Shi'a Islam*, has given a detailed and thoughtful review of the traditional accounts for the period of the first six Imams. Hussain, *Occultation of the Twelfth Imam*, has useful information from the period of the last six Imams.

On the Shi'i sects several of the important sources have been translated as indicated above. See also Ivanow, 'Early Shi'ite Movements', for some additional information from Ismā'īlī sources.

1 For example al-Mufīd, *al-Irshād*; see notes 13 and 14 below.
2 Ibn Māja, *Sunan*, Vol. 1, p. 44, No. 118.

3 *ibid.* p. 51, No. 143.

4 'Āshūrā (10 Muḥarram) had been a Holy Day of atonement and fasting in pre-Islamic and Jewish custom, long before the martyrdom of Husayn on that day. Muhammad had ordained it as a day of fasting.

5 The al-Ḥurr family of Lebanon which has produced many prominent Shi'i ulama claims descent from this man.

6 al-Mufīd, *al-Irshād*, pp. 227–8 (Tr. pp. 364–5). Also quoted in Majlisī, *Biḥār al-Anwār*, Vol. 45, p. 116. Some of the Shi'i histories have a similar episode occurring when the head of Husayn reaches Damascus and is hit by Yazīd.

7 al-Mufīd, *al-Irshād*, pp. 228–9 (Tr. p. 366). Also quoted in Majlisī, *Biḥār al-Anwār*, Vol. 45, pp. 117–18.

8 Jafri, *Origins*, pp. 200–204.

9 The years AH 36, 37 and 38 are all mentioned by different sources. For the different versions of the dates of the births and deaths of the Imams, see the relevant sections in Majlisī, *Jalā'al-'Uyūn*.

10 al-Mas'ūdī, *Murūj adh-Dhahab* Vol. 5, pp. 467–8.

11 Jafri, *Origins*, pp. 290–3.

12 Hussain, *Occultation*, pp. 46–7.

13 al-Mufīd, *al-Irshād*, p. 308 (Tr. p. 495).

14 *ibid.* p. 314 (Tr. p. 506).

15 al-Kashshī, *Rijāl*, p. 48.

16 *ibid.* p. 70.

17 Ibn Ḥazm, see Friedlander, 'Heterodoxies' I, p. 45; Shahristānī, see Kazi, 'Shahristani', p. 76.

18 Ibn Ḥazm, see Friedlander, 'Heterodoxies' I, p. 45.

19 *ibid.*; Maqrīzī, *Kitāb al-Mawā'iz*, Vol. 2, pp. 356–7.

20 Ibn Ḥazm, see Friedlander, 'Heterodoxies' I, p. 66.

21 Shahristānī, see Kazi, 'Shahristani', pp. 56–7.

22 al-Mas'ūdī, *Murūj*, Vol. 6, p. 186.

23 Ibn Ṭāhir, *al-Farq*, pp. 242–3 (Tr. pp. 74–5).

24 *ibid.* p. 243 (Tr. pp. 75–8).

25 Ibn Ḥazm, see Friedlander, 'Heterodoxies' I, pp. 60–61.

26 *ibid.* p. 56.

27 al-Kashshī, *Rijāl*, p. 206.

28 Ivanow (ed.), 'Ummu'l kitāb', p. 11 of text, p. 97 of article

29 The Murji'ites were a group who took some of the important early steps towards what was to become the final Sunni position on matters of theology and politics. See Watt, *Islamic Philosophy*, pp. 32–5.

30 al-Mufīd, *al-Irshād*, p. 268 (Tr. pp. 432–3); also quoted in Majlisī, *Biḥār al-Anwār*, Vol. 47, p. 243.

31 It is said that in the course of argument, 'Alī al-Maythamī, one of the followers of Imam Ja'far aṣ-Ṣadiq, said to them: 'You are nothing but rain-drenched dogs' – it being considered that the smell of rain-drenched dogs was worse than that of rotting corpses.

32 al-Mas'ūdī, *Murūj*, Vol. 8, p. 40.

33 al-Qummī, *al-Maqālāt*, pp. 102–16.

34 an-Nawbakhtī, *Firaq*, p. 79.

4. EARLY HISTORY OF SHI'I ISLAM, AD 632–1000

Sources

Arabic and Persian: The heresiographers are an important source, see note on sources for the previous chapter. Of the Muslim historians, aṭ-Ṭabarī, *Ta'rīkh*; al-Ya'qūbī, *Ta'rīkh*; and al-Mas'ūdī, *Murūj adh-Dhahab* give the most information on Shi'ism.

European languages: No western scholar has produced an adequate survey of Shi'ism in this period. The articles by Hodgson, 'How did the early Shi'a . . .'; Kohlberg, 'From Imāmiyya to Ithnā-'Ashariyya'; Madelung, 'Imamism and Mu'tazilite Theology'; and Watt, 'The Rafidites' and 'Shi'ism and the Umayyads' provide valuable insights. See also note for previous chapter.

1 See, for example, Hodgson, 'How did the early Shi'a . . .', p. 1.
2 Watt, 'The Rafidites', p. 111; *idem, Islamic Philosophy*, p. 50.
3 Ṭabarī, *Ta'rīkh*, Vol. 2, pp. 131–2.
4 Jafri, *Origins*, pp. 200–205 quoted on pp. 31–2 of the present book.
5 Even the Zaydīs generally accept Hasan in spite of his resignation. They do not count the quietist Zaynu'l-'Ābidīn as an Imam.
6 This is confirmed in Kashshī, *Rijāl*, pp. 81–2, where it is stated that Muḥammad al-Bāqir said that after the death of Husayn all but three of the people apostasised (i.e. withdrew their allegiance from Zaynu'l-'Ābidīn) and only later did others join these three.
7 Hodgson, 'How did the early Shi'a . . .', p. 5.
8 See, for example, Ibn Ḥazm in Friedlander, 'Heterodoxies' I, p. 55.
9 Hodgson, 'How did the early Shi'a . . .', p. 6.
10 al-Khayyāt, *al-Intiṣār*, pp. 5ff., and al-Ash'arī, *Maqālāt al-Islāmiyyin*, quoted in Madelung, 'Imamism . . .', pp. 13–14.
11 al-Nu'mānī, *Kitāb al-Ghayba* (Tehran 1318/1900), pp. 4ff., quoted in Kohlberg, 'From Imamiyya . . .', p. 524.
12 Ibn Bābūya, *Kamāl ad-Dīn*, Vol. 1, p. 2.
13 This point has been fully argued by Kohlberg, 'From Imamiyya . . .', pp. 522–3, based on evidence from al-Barqī (d. 274/887 or 280/893), *Kitāb al-Mahāṣin,* and Muḥammad ibn al-Ḥasan al-Qummī (d. 290/903), *Baṣā'ir ad-Darajāt*.
14 See Kohlberg, 'From Imamiyya . . .', p. 523, who quotes as evidence 'Alī ibn Ibrāhīm al-Qummī (d. 307/919), *Tafsīr*, and Muḥammad al-Kulaynī (d. 329/940), *Uṣūl al-Kāfī*.
15 al-Nu'mānī, *Kitāb al-Ghayba*, cited in Majlisī, *Biḥār al-Anwār* (old ed.), Vol. 13, p. 142.
16 On al-Khayyāt and al-Ash'arī, see p. 74 and note 10 *supra*. On the differing agents of the Hidden Imam see Massignon, *Passion of al-Hallaj*, Vol. 1, pp. 306–7.
17 See Sahl ibn Ziyād al-Adamī (Najāshī, *Rijāl*, p. 132) and Muḥammad ibn 'Alī al-Qurashī (Najāshī, *Rijāl*, p. 234). Another resident of Qumm who was opposed for his *ghulāt* views was Muḥammad ibn 'Urama al-Qummī (Najāshī, *Rijāl*, p. 231).
18 Especially his *Kitāb at-Tawḥīd*; see MacDermott, *Theology of al-Shaikh al-*

Mufīd, pp. 323–40.

19 MacDermott, *Theology of al-Shaikh al-Mufīd*, pp. 341–6, quoting from Ibn Bābūya, *Kitāb al-Hidāya* and *Risalāt al-I'tiqādāt*.

20 MacDermott, *Theology of al-Shaikh al-Mufīd*, pp. 347–9, quoting from Ibn Bābūya, *Kitāb at-Tawḥīd*.

21 For a consideration of the relationships between the theologies of Ibn Bābūya, Shaykh al-Mufīd, 'Alamu'l-Hudā and the Mu'tazilites see MacDermott, *Theology of al-Shaikh al-Mufīd*.

22 Kulaynī, *al-Kāfī*, Vol. 1, pp. 228–9.

23 In fact the table is derived from Shaykhu'ṭ-Ṭā'ifa's *Fihrist* together with Muḥammad ibn Muḥammad Muḥsin 'Alamu'l-Hudā's supplement to this work, *Naḍad al-Īḍāḥ*, as published in the edition by A. Sprenger (ed. Maḥmūd Rāmyār).

24 Ṭihrānī, *Ṭabaqāt A'lām ash-Shī'a* (5th century).

5. SHI'I ISLAM IN THE MEDIEVAL PERIOD, AD 1000–1500

Sources

Arabic and Persian: Of contemporary sources, Qazwīnī, *Kitāb an-Naqd*, is one of the most useful. The great universal histories of Ibn al-Jawzī, Ibn al-Athīr, Abu'l-Fidā and Ibn Kathīr contain some useful information although each author tends merely to copy the previous author and only adds new material for the period following the previous author's death. Juwaynī, *Ta'rīkh-i Jihān-gushā* and Ḥamdu'llāh Mustawfī Qazwīnī, *Ta'rīkh-i Guzīdā*, are also of importance. Of modern works on this period, ash-Shaybī, *Fikr ash-Shī'ī*, is very useful for the connections between Shi'ism and Sufism throughout this period.

European languages: There has been very little research on Shi'ism during this period. The most useful sources are the two articles by Bausani in the fifth volume of the *Cambridge History of Iran*. Mazzaoui, *Origin of the Safawids*; Spuler, *Die Mongolen in Iran*; and Smith, *History of the Sarbadār Dynasty* also contain much useful information.

1 Ibn Athīr, *Kāmil*, Vol. 9, p. 11; regarding the year 456/1063.

2 Ibn Kathīr, *Bidāya wa Nihāya* Vol. 12, p. 152.

3 Nāṣir Khusraw, who travelled through the area in 439/1047, states that all of the inhabitants of Tripoli and most of those of Tyre and Tiberius were Shi'i (*Safarnāma*, pp. 18, 20–21, 25); Yāqūt quotes a letter from Ibn Buṭlān from about 440/1048 which states that the *fuqahā* of Aleppo gave their *fatwās* according to the Imāmī school (*Mu'jam al-Buldān* Vol. 3, p. 313).

4 Ibn Jubayr writes in the course of his description of Damascus (which he visited in 580/1184): 'The Shi'a in these lands have strange manifestations. They are more numerous than the Sunnis there and have spread their doctrines throughout the lands.' *Rihla*, p. 280.

5 Derived from Āghā Buzurg Ṭihrānī, *Ṭabaqāt* (6th century), Vol. 3, p. 313.

6 Majlisī, *Biḥār al-Anwār*, Vol. 1, pp. 209–10.

7 ash-Shaybī, *Fikr ash-Shī'ī*, pp. 82–4.

8 Ibn Ḥajār, *ad-Durar al-Kāmina*, Vol. 2, p. 72, n. 1.

9 Derived from Ṭihrānī, *Ṭabaqāt* (7th Century) and *Ṭabaqāt* (8th Century).

10 See Minorsky, 'Shah-Jihan'.

6. SHI'I ISLAM IN MODERN TIMES, AD 1500–1900

Sources

Arabic and Persian: The most important primary source for the Safavid period is Iskandar Beg Munshī, *Ta'rīkh-i 'Alam-ārā-yi 'Abbāsī*. For the period of Nādir Shāh, see Mīrzā Mahdī Khān, *Ta'rīkh-i Nādirī*. For the Qājār period, the court histories Sipihr, *Nāsikh at-Tawārīkh*, and Hidāyat, *Rawḍat as-Ṣafā*, are important sources. See also the biographical dictionaries of the ulama such as Tunukābunī, *Qiṣāṣ al-'Ulamā*, Kashmīrī, *Nujūm as-Samā*, and Khwānsārī, *Rawḍat al-Jannāt*.

European languages: There are several books that cover the Safavid period and the 18th century but none of them make much mention of religious issues: Savory, *Iran under the Safavids*; Lockhart, *The Fall of the Safavī Dynasty* and *Nadir Shah*. Much more useful for religious issues are the papers by Lambton, 'Quis Custodiet Custodes', and Arjomand, 'Religion, Political Action . . . ' and 'Religious Extremism . . . '. On the religious policy of Nadir Shāh, see Gursoy, 'Nadir Shāh's religious policy', and Algar, 'Shi'ism and Iran'. For the Qājār period there is a great deal of information on religious issues in Algar, *Religion and State*, and in Browne, *Literary History*, Vol. 4. For Shi'ism in India see Hollister, *Shi'a of India*, and Cole, Ph.D., 'Imāmī Shi'ism from Iran to North India'.

1 al-Ghazzī, *al-Kawākib as-Sā'ira* quoted in ash-Shaybī, *Fikr ash-Shī'a*, p. 409.
2 This threat was clearly perceived by those in neighbouring countries. See, for example, the reference by Ibn Ṭūlūn of Damascus to Ismā'īl as 'seeking to be a new Timurlane'; Hartmann, *Das Tübinger Fragment*, p. 61, and p. 24 of text.
3 See Arjomand, 'Religious Extremism', p. 31.
4 Khwānsārī, *Rawḍat al-Jannāt*, p. 404.
5 However, it should be noted that according to a twelfth-century source, some Shi'i *madrasas* existed in Iran at that time particularly at Rayy. See Qazwīnī, *Kitāb an-Naqḍ*, quoted in Bausani, 'Religion in Saljuq Period', p. 295. However, religious studies in the Shi'i field had virtually ceased in Iran by the start of the Safavid period.
6 Chardin, *Voyages*, Vol. 5, p. 208; Vol. 6, pp. 249–50. Du Mans, *Estat de la Perse*, p. 162.
7 Browne, *Literary History of Persia*, Vol. 4, p. 404; 'Risālat li-Muḥammad Taqī al-Majlisī', quoted in Lockhart, *Fall of the Safavī Dynasty*, p. 70.
8 Khwānsārī, *Rawḍat al-Jannāt*, pp. 336–7; Kashmīrī, *Nujūm*, pp. 64–5.
9 *ibid.* p. 185.
10 There is indeed a passing reference to Akhbārīs in the twelfth-century work, Qazwīnī, *Kitāb an-Naqd* (see Madelung, 'Imamism and Mu'tazilite Theology', pp. 20–21). The dispute between Shaykhu'ṭ-Ṭā'ifa and Ibn Idrīs in the 5th/11th and 6th/12th centuries (see p. 89) was probably in part a prodrome of the Uṣūlī-Akhbārī dispute in that Shaykhu'ṭ-Ṭā'ifa is considered to have taken an Akhbārī line in his book *Kitāb an-Nihāya* while Ibn Idris is described as a 'pure mujtahid' (Baḥrānī, *Lu'lu'āt Baḥrayn*, pp. 276, 297).

11 Khwānsārī, *Rawḍat al-Jannāt*, p. 405; ash-Shaybī, *Fikr ash-Shī'ī*, p. 416; ash-Shaybī, 'Ṣūfism and Shi'ism', Ph.D., p. 382. Al-Karakī was even called the 'inventor of Shi'ism' by Sunni writers perhaps on account of this innovative use of *ijtihād*, see Khwānsārī, *Rawḍat al-Jannāt*, p. 404.

12 Quoted in Kashmīrī, *Nujūm as-Samā*, p. 42. Among Majlisī's teachers were at least five Akhbārīs: a pupil and son-in-law of Muḥammad Amīn Astarābādī, Muḥammad Mu'min Astarābādī; the latter's son, Muḥammad Muḥsin; Muḥammad Ṭāhir Shīrāzī Qummī; Shaykh Muḥammad al-Ḥurr al-'Āmilī and Mullā Muḥsin-i Fayḍ (See Majlisī, *Biḥār al-Anwār*, Vol. 105, pp. 79, 82; Vol. 110, pp. 103–6, 124, 129–31); that is, if Majlisī's father who was probably an Akhbārī is not counted. In some recent works (see Morris, *Wisdom of the Throne*, p. 47 and note; Corbin, *En Islam iranien*, Vol. 4, p. 250) it has been implied that the Akhbārī viewpoint favoured mysticism and philosophical speculation and this would obviously militate against the possibility of Muḥammad Bāqir Majlisī being in favour of the Akhbārī school. But in fact, the Akhbārīs included among their number some prominent antagonists of Sufism and mysticism such as Muḥammad Ṭāhir Shīrāzī and al-Ḥurr al-'Āmilī. Thus it would appear that the Akhbārī-Uṣūlī dispute was purely about legal issues and did not affect this area. It is probably also of relevance to note that 'Alī Davvānī, in giving a list of the most important Shi'i mujtahids from earliest times to the time of Vaḥīd Bihbahānī, omits both Muḥammad Bāqir Majlisī and his father (*Vaḥīd Bihbahānī*, pp. 64–9).

13 Shaykh Yūsuf eventually abandoned his support for the Akhbārīs and adopted a neutral stance in face of the strong Uṣūlī advance in his time.

14 Khwānsārī, *Rawḍat al-Jannāt*, p. 39.

15 Muḥammad Taqī Majlisī quoted in Khwānsārī, *op. cit.*, pp. 38–9.

16 Lockhart, *Nadir Shah*, p. 60.

17 Kashmīrī, *Nujūm as-Samā*, pp. 316–17.

18 There is some uncertainty as to whether Shaykh Muḥammad Ḥasan Najafī, who held an *ijāza* from Shaykh Aḥmad, participated in the *Takfīr* or not. He did, however, come out against the Shaykhīs at a later date.

19 Algar, *Religion and State*, p. 109.

20 *ibid.* pp. 91–2.

21 Although it is usually stated in Shi'i historical works that Shaykh Murtaḍā Anṣārī was the sole *marja'* for the Shi'i world, there are indications that there were other *marāji'*. Anṣārī appears to have been followed throughout most of Iran but Shaykh Mahdī Āl Kāshifu'l-Ghiṭā (d. Ṣafar 1289/1872) was *marja'* for much of Iraq, the Caucasus and some parts of Iran, and after his death part of his following went to his brother Shaykh Ja'far (d. Jamādī I 1290/1873). After Shaykh Ja'far, Shaykh Rāḍī an-Najafī (d. 1290/1873) was *marja'* for part of Iraq and his following after his death went to Shaykh Muḥammad Ḥusayn al-Kāẓimī (d. 1308/1890). See Ḥirzu'd-Dīn *Ma'ārif ar-Rijāl*, Vol. 1, p. 309, and entries under each of these names in Ḥirzu'd-Dīn, *Ma'ārif ar-Rijāl*, and Ṭihrānī, *Ṭabaqāt* (13th cent.).

22 Although it is usually stated in Shi'i historical works that Mīrzā-yi Shīrāzī was sole *marja'* for the whole Shi'i world from about this date onwards, there

are indications that there were other *maraji'* during most of Shīrāzī's lifetime. Sayyid Ḥusayn Turk (Kūhkamarī) of Najaf was *marja'* for much of the Caucasus and Ādharbāyjān and he died in 1299/1882 although he was paralysed from 1291/1874 onwards. After the death of Sayyid Ḥusayn Turk, most of those who followed him turned to Shaykh Muḥammad Īrāvānī (d. 1306/1888) of Najaf. Shaykh Zaynu'l-'Ābidīn Māzandarānī, a resident of Karbalā, appears to have been regarded by Indian Shi'is as their *marja'* as well as being *marja'* for the Karbalā area. He died in 1309/1892 only two years before the death of Mīrzā-yi Shīrāzī. Shaykh Muḥammad Ḥasan Yā Sīn (d. 1308/1891), resident of Kāẓimayn, was *marja'* for the Kāẓimayn area. Another important figure was Shaykh Ḥabību'llāh Rashtī (d. Jamādī II 1312/1894) who, although he does not appear to have claimed the rank of *marja'*, was considered the leading scholar and teacher of Najaf. See Ḥirzu'd-Dīn, *Ma'ārif ar-Rijāl*, Vol. 1, pp. 204–5, and entries under each of these names in Ḥirzu'd-Dīn, *Ma'ārif ar-Rijāl* and Ṭihrānī, *Ṭabaqāt* (13th and 14th cent.).

23 Algar, *Religion and State*, p. 208.

7. THE IMAMATE

Sources

Arabic and Persian: For this chapter I have taken as the basis the section on the Imamate in Majlisī, *Biḥār al-Anwār* and Kulaynī, *al-Kāfī*.

European languages: There is no full account of the Imamate in any European language. Donaldson has a survey of some of the main points in the relevant chapter in his book *The Shi'ite Religion* (Chap. 29).

For these notes: Majlisī, *Biḥār al-Anwār* is abbreviated *BA*
Kulaynī, *al-Kāfī* is abbreviated *KK*

1 Ibn Bābūya, *'Ilal ash-Sharī'a*, quoted in *BA*, Vol. 23, p. 22, No. 25. See also *KK*, Vol. 1, pp. 178.

2 Ibn Bābūya, *'Ilal ash-Sharī'a*, quoted in *BA*, Vol. 23, p. 22, No. 24. See also *KK*, Vol. 1, pp. 178–9.

3 Ibn Bābūya, *'Ilal ash-Sharī'a*, quoted in *BA*, Vol. 23, p. 19, No. 14.

4 Ibn Bābūya, *Amālī*, quoted in *BA*, Vol. 23, pp. 57–8, No. 1.

5 al-Bursī, *Mashāriq al-Anwār*, quoted in *BA*, Vol. 25, p. 24, No. 42. See also *BA*, Vol. 26, p. 3.

6 Ḥasan ibn Sulaymān al-Ḥillī, *Muntakhab al-Baṣā'ir*, quoted in *BA*, Vol. 53, p. 46, No. 20; and al-Bursī, *Mashāriq al-Anwār*, quoted in *BA*, Vol. 25, p. 23, No. 39. See also *BA*, Vol. 25, pp. 15–25, Nos. 28–45, and Kirmānī, *Kitāb al-Mubīn*, Vol. 1, p. 242.

7 *BA*, Vol. 25, p. 17, No. 31.

8 Quoted in Kirmānī, *Kitāb al-Mubīn*, Vol. 1, p. 241.

9 aṣ-Ṣaffār, *Baṣā'ir ad-Darajāt*, quoted in *BA*, Vol. 25, pp. 10–13, Nos. 14, 16, 23–6.

10 *BA*, Vol. 25, p. 10.

11 aṣ-Ṣaffār, *Baṣā'ir ad-Darajāt*, quoted in *BA*, Vol. 25, p. 56, No. 22. See also *BA*, Vol. 25, pp. 56–7.

12 ‘Abdu’llāh al-Baḥrānī, *al-‘Awālim*, quoted in Kirmānī, *Kitāb al-Mubīn*, Vol. 1, p. 281. See also *BA*, Vol. 26, pp. 83–4. Indeed, in some Traditions the ‘Bee’ is interpreted as being the Imam; *BA*, Vol. 24, pp. 110–13.

13 aṣ-Ṣaffar, *Baṣā’ir ad-Darajāt*, quoted in Kirmānī, *Kitāb al-Mubīn*, Vol. 1, p. 283.

14 According to three Traditions quoted in *BA*, Vol. 26, p. 67, No. 5; pp. 69–70, No. 10; p. 74, No. 26, the phrase ‘or a speaker (*muḥaddith*, meaning the Imam)’ has dropped from and should be added on to the sentence ‘And whenever we sent an apostle or a prophet . . .’ (Qur’an 22:52).

15 aṣ- Ṣaffār, *Baṣā’ir ad-Darajāt*, quoted in *BA*, Vol. 26, pp. 75–6, No. 29. See also pp. 74–8, Nos. 27–34.

16 al-Qummī, *Tafsīr*, quoted in *BA*, Vol. 23, p. 206.

17 *KK*, Vol. 1, p. 187, No. 11.

18 Imam ‘Ali in the Tradition known as the *ḥadīth* an-Nūrāniyya; BA, Vol. 26, p. 7.

19 Furāt, *Tafsīr*, and other sources quoted in *BA*, Vol. 24, p. 305, Nos. 1–3.

20 al-Qummī, *Tafsīr*, and other sources quoted in *BA*, Vol. 23, pp. 209–19, Nos. 2–13, *KK*, Vol. 1, p. 207, Nos. 1–3; pp. 213–14, Nos. 1–5.

21 Ibn Bābūya, *Ma‘ānī al-Akhbār* and other sources quoted in *BA*, Vol. 24, pp. 9–17, 23–5, Nos. 1–5, 17–20, 23–7, 48–51. *KK*, Vol. 1, p. 419, No. 38. Ibn Shahrāshūb, *Manāqib*, Vol. 2, p. 271.

22 al-Qummī, *Tafsīr*, and other sources quoted in *BA*, Vol. 24, pp. 17–21, Nos. 28–32, 36–9. *KK*, Vol. 1, pp. 417, No. 24; p. 424, No. 63.

23 aṭ-Ṭabarsī, *Majma‘ al-Bayān*, quoted in *BA*, Vol. 24, pp. 51–2, 55, Nos. 2–4, 18–21; *KK*, Vol. 1, p. 217, Nos. 1, 4; p. 427, No. 77.

24 ‘Alam ibn Sayf al-Ḥillī, *Kanz Jāmi‘ al-Fawā’id*, quoted in *BA*, Vol. 24, p. 59, Nos. 34–6. *KK*, Vol. 1, p. 217, Nos. 2, 3.

25 ‘Alam ibn Sayf al-Ḥillī, *Kanz Jāmi‘ al-Fawā’id*, and other sources quoted in *BA*, Vol. 24, pp. 82–5, Nos. 1, 4, 7, 8.

26 Ibn Bābūya, *al-Amālī*, and other sources quoted in *BA*, Vol. 24, pp. 82–5, Nos. 2, 3, 5, 6, 9.

27 al-‘Ayyāshī, *Tafsīr*; Furāt, *Tafsīr*, and other sources quoted in *BA*, Vol. 23, pp. 308–25, Nos. 5–42. *KK*, Vol. 1, pp. 194–6, Nos. 1–6. Ibn Shahrāshūb, *Manaqib*, Vol. 2, p. 278.

28 Ibn Bābūya, *Ma‘ānī al-Akhbār*, and other sources quoted in *BA*, Vol. 23, pp. 279–83, Nos. 19–29. *KK*, Vol. 1, p. 413, No. 2.

29 al-‘Ayyāshī, *Tafsīr*, and other sources quoted in *BA*, Vol. 23, pp. 275–9, Nos. 2–18. *KK*, Vol. 1, p. 276, Nos. 1–4.

30 aṭ-Ṭabarsī, *Majma‘ al-Bayān*, and other sources quoted in *BA*, Vol. 24, p. 144, Nos. 4–11.

31 al-Qummī, *Tafsīr*, quoted in *BA*, Vol. 23, p. 191, No. 12.

32 *BA*, Vol. 23, p. 191, No. 11. *KK*, Vol. 1, p. 229, No. 6. Ibn Shahrāshūb, *Manāqib*, Vol. 3, p. 504.

33 al-Qummī, *Tafsīr*, and other sources quoted in *BA*, Vol. 23, pp. 191–2, 200–204, Nos. 10, 13, 14, 16, 34–50. *KK*, Vol. 1, pp. 213–14, Nos. 1–5.

34 al-Qummī, *Tafsīr*, quoted in *BA*, Vol. 23, pp. 212–23, Nos. 1–23, 28–33. *KK*, Vol. 1, pp. 214–15, Nos. 1–4.

35 al-'Ayyāshī, *Tafsīr*, quoted in *BA*, Vol. 23, pp. 189–90, No. 6.
36 aṭ-Ṭabarsī, *Majma' al-Bayān*, quoted in *BA*, Vol. 23, pp. 284–5. Ibn Bābūya, *'Uyūn al-Akhbār ar-Riḍā*, and other sources quoted in *BA*, Vol. 23, pp. 285–91, Nos. 2, 3, 13, 16–18, 26–32, 37–43, 47, 49–53.
37 aṭ-Ṭabarsī, *Majma' al-Bayān*, and other sources quoted in *BA*, Vol. 24, pp. 31, 33, Nos. 3–5, 8–10. *KK*, Vol. 1, p. 208, Nos. 1, 2. Ibn Shahrāshūb, *Manāqib*, Vol. 2, p. 288; Vol. 3, p. 314.
38 al-Qummī, *Tafsīr*, and other sources quoted in *BA*, Vol. 23, pp. 167–71, Nos. 1–12.
39 al-Qummī, *Tafsīr*, quoted in *BA*, Vol. 23, pp. 172–4, Nos. 1–4. *KK*, Vol. 1, pp. 210–12, Nos. 1–9.
40 aṭ-Ṭabarsī, *Majma' al-Bayān*, quoted in *BA*, Vol. 23, p. 212. al' Ayyāshī, *Tafsīr*, quoted in *BA*, Vol. 23, p. 225, Nos. 44–5.
41 aṭ-Ṭabarsī, *Majma' al-Bayān*, quoted in *BA*, Vol. 23, pp. 229–32. Furāt, *Tafsīr*; al-Qummī, *Tafsīr*, and other sources quoted in *BA*, Vol. 23, pp. 236–52, Nos. 2–31. al-Mufīd, *Ikhtiṣāṣ*, p. 63.
42 Bayḍāwī, *Anwār at-Tanzīl*, Vol. 5, p. 53. Rāzī, *Mafatīḥ al-Ghayb*, Vol. 7, pp. 273–5.
43 'Alam ibn Sayf al-Ḥillī, *Kanz Jāmi' al-Fawā'id*, quoted in *BA*, Vol. 23, pp. 257–8, No. 3.
44 'Alam ibn Sayf al-Ḥillī, *Kanz Jāmi' al-Fawā'id*, and other sources quoted in *BA*, Vol. 24, pp. 1–2, 4, 7–9, Nos. 1, 2, 4, 11, 13, 19, 22, 25. Ibn Shahrāshūb, *Manāqib*, Vol. 3, p. 403.
45 al-Qummī, *Tafsīr*, and other sources quoted in *BA*, Vol. 24, pp. 70–80, Nos. 4–10, 14–20. Some of the Traditions quoted here give slightly different interpretations to these verses.
46 Ibn Bābūya, *Al-Khiṣāl*, and other sources quoted in *BA*, Vol. 24, pp. 97–9, Nos. 1–7.
47 aṭ-Ṭabarsī, *al-Iḥtijāj*, quoted in *BA*, Vol. 24, p. 213, Nos. 6–7.
48 al-Qummī, *Tafsīr*, and other sources quoted in *BA*, Vol. 24, pp. 132–6, Nos. 1–11. *KK*, Vol. 1, p. 427, No. 8.
49 al-Qummī, *Tafsīr*, Furāt, *Tafsīr*, and other sources quoted in *BA*, Vol. 24, pp. 247–52, Nos. 1–20.
50 aṣ-Ṣaffār, *Baṣā'ir ad-Darajāt*, quoted in *BA*, Vol. 23, p. 73, No. 19.
51 aṣ-Ṣaffār, *Baṣā'ir ad-Darajāt*, quoted in *BA*, Vol. 23, p. 71, No. 9. Several other similar Traditions quoted on pp. 70–72. See also *KK*, Vol. 1, pp. 227–9, Nos. 2, 4.
52 aṣ-Ṣaffār, *Baṣā'ir ad-Darajāt*, quoted in *BA*, Vol. 23, p. 73, No. 17.
53 aṣ-Ṣaffār, *Baṣā'ir ad-Darajāt*, quoted in *BA*, Vol. 23, p. 53, No. 113. See also BA, Vol. 25, pp. 105–110, Nos. 1–8.
54 Muḥammad Javīrī, *Qiṣāṣ al-Anbiyā*, quoted in *BA*, Vol. 23, p. 33.
55 Majlisī, *Biḥār al-Anwār*, quoted in Kirmānī, *Kitāb al-Mubīn*, Vol. 1, p. 264.
56 Majlisī, *Biḥār al-Anwār*, quoted in Kirmānī, *Kitāb al-Mubīn*, Vol. 1, p. 265. Quotation from Qur'an 3: 101.
57 aṣ-Ṣaffār, *Baṣā'ir ad-Darajāt*, quoted in *BA*, Vol. 23, p. 196, No. 26.
58 aṣ-Ṣaffār, *Baṣā'ir ad-Darajāt*, quoted in *BA*, Vol. 23, pp. 198–9, No. 31. Similar Tradition from al-Qummī, *Tafsīr*, quoted in *BA*, Vol. 23, p. 191, No. 12.

59 aṣ-Ṣaffār, *Baṣā'ir ad-Darajāt*, quoted in *BA*, Vol. 25, p. 62, No. 40. Similar Traditions from various sources in *BA*, Vol. 25, p. 59, Nos. 27–45.
60 *KK*, Vol. 1, p. 255, No. 1.
61 MacDermott, *Theology*, pp. 107–9. See also *KK*, Vol. 1, pp. 256–7, Nos. 1–4.
62 *KK*, Vol. 1, pp. 274–5, Nos. 1–3.
63 'Abdu'llāh al-Baḥrānī, *al-'Awālim*, quoted in Kirmānī, *Kitāb al-Mubīn*, Vol. 1, p. 308.
64 *BA*, Vol. 23, pp. 79–95, gives this Tradition in 26 forms from nine different sources.
65 Commentary of Majlisī, *BA*, Vol. 23, p. 76.
66 'Alam ibn Sayf al-Ḥillī, *Kanz Jāmi' al-Fawā'id*, quoted in *BA*, Vol. 23, p. 93.
67 Ibn Bābūya, *Kamāl ad-Dīn*, quoted in *BA*, Vol. 23, p. 88, No. 31.
68 Al-Nu'mānī, *al-Ghayba*, quoted in *BA*, Vol. 23, p. 89, No. 34.
69 Ibn Bābūya, *Kamāl ad-Dīn*, quoted in *BA*, Vol. 23, p. 96, No. 2.
70 *ibid.*
71 Ibn Bābūya, *Kamāl ad-Dīn*, quoted in *BA*, Vol. 23, p. 97, No. 4.
72 Ibn Bābūya, *Ma'ānī al-Akhbār*, quoted in *BA*, Vol. 23, pp. 100–101, No. 4.

8. THE TWELFTH IMAM, HIS OCCULTATION AND RETURN

Sources

Arabic and Persian: There are a large number of sources for the doctrine of the Twelfth Imam. Some of the most important are the early works that sought to establish the legitimacy of the doctrine: al-Nu'mānī, *al-Ghayba*, Ibn Bābūya, *Kamāl ad-Dīn*, and Shaykhu't-Ṭā'ifa, *al-Ghayba*. I have also used the section on the Twelfth Imam in Majlisī, *Biḥār al-Anwār*. For a more recent view on the subject see Zanjānī, *'Aqā'id ul-Imāmiyya*.

European languages: There have recently appeared two good reviews of the doctrine of the Twelfth Imam and its place in Shi'ism. Hussain, *Occultation of the Twelfth Imam*, presents a review of the traditional historical accounts surrounding the Occultation. Sachedina, *Islamic Messianism*, concentrates on the doctrine itself and its significance for Shi'is. An important source for an understanding of events during the Lesser Occultation is Massignon, *Passion of al-Ḥallāj*.

1 Ibn Bābūya, *Kamāl ad-Dīn*, p. 516.
2 Sachedina, *Islamic Messianism*, pp. 86–7. Massignon suggests that the first Bāb, 'Uthmān al-'Amrī, died in 258/871 (i.e. during the lifetime of the Eleventh Imam and before the Occultation occurred) and that there were several agents until about 280/893 when the second Bāb, Muḥammad ibn 'Uthmān al-'Amrī, succeeded in consolidating his authority. *Passion of al-Ḥallāj*, Vol. 1, pp. 307–9.
3 See sources quoted by Kohlberg, 'From Imāmiyya . . .', p. 524. Also Hussain, *Occultation*, p. 143.
4 See, for example, the *risalā* by Ḥusayn ibn Muḥammad Taqī Nūrī entitled

Jannāt al-Ma'wā (appended to Majlisī, *Biḥār al-Anwār* (old ed.), Vol. 13) listing 59 such stories.

5 al-Mufīd, *al-Ikhtiṣāṣ*, quoted in Majlisī, *Biḥār al-Anwār* (old ed.), Vol. 13, p. 210.

6 For Sunni sources see Ibn Māja, *Sunan*, Bāb Khurūj al-Mahdī, pp. 1366, No. 4082; Abū Dāwud, *Sunan*, Kitāb al-Mahdī, Vol. 2, p. 422. Shi'i sources for this are numerous; see, for example, al-Mufīd, *al-Irshād*, p. 341 (Tr. 548).

7 az-Zanjānī, *'Aqā'id*, p. 255.

8 *ibid.* pp. 253–4.

9 *ibid.* p. 261, quoting Kulaynī, *al-Kāfī (Rawḍa)*. Zanjānī concludes this Tradition by stating that most of these signs are without doubt occurring today.

10 az-Zanjānī, *'Aqā'id*, pp. 258–9.

11 Ibn Bābūya, *Thawāb al-A'māl*, quoted in Majlisī, *Biḥār al-Anwār* (old ed.), Vol. 13, p. 152.

12 For Sunni sources see Ibn Māja, *Sunan*, p. 1367, No. 4085; at-Tirmidhī, *Sunan*, Vol. 2, p. 36; Abū Dāwud, *Sunan*, Vol. 2, p. 422. For Shi'is the Mahdī is the Twelfth Imam who was, of course, a descendant of Muhammad.

13 For Sunni sources see at-Tirmidhī, *Sunan*, Vol. 2, p. 36; Abū Dāwud, *Sunan*, Vol. 2, p. 420. For Shi'is the Mahdī is, of course, Muḥammad ibn Ḥasan al-'Askarī. However, interestingly, there are also numerous Traditions that state that no name should be attributed to the Hidden Imam prior to his advent; see Ibn Bābūya, *Kamāl ad-Dīn*, p. 648.

14 For Sunni sources see at-Tirmidhī, *Sunan*, Vol. 2, p. 36; Abū Dāwud, *Sunan*, Vol. 2, pp. 422–3. For Shi'i sources see, for example, al-Irbilī, *Kashf al-Ghumma*, Vol. 3, pp. 257, 269; al-Nu'mānī, *al-Ghayba* quoted in Majlisī, *Biḥār al-Anwār* (old ed.), Vol. 13, p. 178.

15 For Sunni sources see Ibn Māja, *Sunan*, p. 1367, No. 4084; see also p. 1366, No. 4082. For Shi'i sources see al-Irbilī, *Kashf al-Ghumma*, Vol. 3, pp. 262–3; Shaykhu't-Ṭā'ifa, *al-Ghayba*, quoted in Majlisī, *Biḥār al-Anwār* (old ed.), Vol. 13, p. 159.

16 For Sunni sources see at-Tirmidhī, *Sunan*, Vol. 2, pp. 36–7. For Shi'i sources see Ibn Bābūya, *Kamāl ad-Dīn*, pp. 525–32.

17 Taken from Majlisī, *Biḥār al-Anwār* (old ed.), Vol. 13; Shaykh al-Mufīd, *Kitāb al-Irshād*; al-Irbilī, *Kashf al-Ghumma*; and Ibn Bābūya, *Kamāl ad-Dīn*.

18 Ibn Bābūya, *Kamāl ad-Dīn*, p. 655; Shaykhu'ṭ-Ṭā'ifa, *al-Ghayba*, quoted in Majlisī, *Biḥār al-Anwār* (old ed.), Vol. 13, pp. 156–7; al-Mufīd, *al-Irshād*, p. 338 (Tr. 544).

19 al-Mufīd, *al-Irshād*, p. 336 (Tr. 541).

20 *ibid.* p. 336 (Tr. 541).

21 Ibn Bābūya, *Kamāl ad-Dīn*, pp. 650, 652; al-'Ayyāshī, *Tafsīr*, and other sources quoted in Majlisī, *Biḥār al-Anwār* (old ed.), Vol. 13, pp. 156, 160.

22 al-Mufīd, *al-Irshād*, p. 338 (Tr. 544).

23 *ibid.* p. 337 (Tr. 542, 548).

24 *ibid.* p. 341 (Tr. 548).

25 *ibid.* p. 341 (Tr. 548).

26 *ibid.* p. 341 (Tr. 549).
27 *ibid.* p. 342 (Tr. 551); al-Irbilī, *Kashf al-Ghumma*, Vol. 3, p. 254.
28 al-Nu'mānī, *al-Ghayba*, quoted in Majlisī, *Biḥār al-Anwār* (old ed.), Vol. 13, p. 191.
29 al-Nu'mānī, *al-Ghayba*, quoted in Majlisī, *Biḥār al-Anwār* (old ed.), Vol. 13, pp. 192, 194) al-Mufīd, *al-Irshād*, p. 343 (Tr. 552); al-Irbilī, *Kashf al-Ghumma*, Vol. 3, p. 255.
30 al-Nu'mānī, *al-Ghayba*, quoted in Majlisī, *Biḥār al-Anwār* (old ed.), Vol. 13, p. 192.
31 al-Nu'mānī, *al-Ghayba*, quoted in Majlisī, *Biḥār al-Anwār* (old ed.), Vol. 13, p. 193.
32 al-Mufīd, *al-Irshād*, pp. 343–4 (Tr. 552–3).
33 Quṭbu'd-Dīn Rāwandī, *al-Kharā'ij*, quoted in Majlisī, *Biḥār al-Anwār* (old ed.), Vol. 13, p. 187.
34 al-'Ayyāshī, *Tafsīr*, quoted in Majlisī, *Biḥār al-Anwār* (old ed.), Vol. 13, p. 222.
35 Ibn Bābūya, *'Uyūn al-Akhbār ar-Riḍā*, quoted in Majlisī, *Biḥār al-Anwār* (old ed.), Vol. 13, p. 214. For Sunni traditions see, for example, at-Tirmidhī, *Sunan*, Vol. 2, p. 36.
36 Ibn Bābūya, *Kamāl ad-Dīn*, p. 654; Ḥasan ibn Sulaymān al-Ḥillī, *Muntakhab al-Baṣā'ir*, quoted in Majlisī, *Biḥār al-Anwār* (old ed.), Vol. 13, p. 210.
37 al-Mufīd, *al-Ikhtiṣāṣ*, quoted in Majlisī, *Biḥār al-Anwār* (old ed.), Vol. 13, p. 210.

9. DOCTRINES, RITUAL PRACTICES AND SOCIAL TRANSACTIONS

Sources

Arabic and Persian: The manuals dealing with doctrine and points of jurisprudence are too numerous to mention. For this book reliance has been placed on Kulaynī, *al-Kāfī*, and Majlisī, *Biḥār al-Anwār*. These two works are notable in that they contain a section on the *uṣūl ad-dīn* which most legal works do not. Two relatively modern works are: Āl Kāshifu'l-Ghiṭā, *Aṣl ash-Shī'a*, which deals mainly with doctrine and, in particular, the five *uṣūl ad-dīn*, and al-Muẓaffar, *Aqā'id al-Imāmiyya*, which deals with ritual and legal points.
European languages: With respect to Shi'i jurisprudence, several of the manuals of Muslim law designed for use in British India contain a good deal of information about points of Shi'i law; see, for example, J. Baillie, *Digest of Mohummudan Law*; N. B. E. Baillie, *A Digest of Moohummudan Law*; and Querry, *Droit Musulman*, all three of which are based mainly on Muḥaqqiq al-Ḥillī's *Sharā'i' al-Islām*. Since the 1979 Revolution a number of translations of Shi'i works have appeared in Iran. The two works by Āl Kāshifu'l-Ghiṭā and al-Muẓaffar mentioned above are among these.

1 al-Qummī, *Tafsīr*, al-'Ayyāshī, *Tafsīr*, and other sources quoted in Majlisī, *Biḥār al-Anwār*, Vol. 23, pp. 222–8, Nos. 25, 26, 48, 49.
2 'Alam ibn Sayf al-Ḥillī, *Kanz Jāmi' al-Fawā'id*, quoted in Majlisī, *Biḥār al-Anwār*, Vol. 24, pp. 18–19, No. 31.

3 al-'Ayyāshī, *Tafsīr*, quoted in Majlisī, *Biḥār al-Anwār*, Vol. 24, p. 153, Nos. 1, 2.
4 aṭ-Ṭabarsī, *al-Iḥtijāj*, quoted in Majlisī, *Biḥār al-Anwār*, Vol. 24, pp. 195–6, No. 19.
5 See W. St. Clair Tisdall, 'Shi'ah additions to the Koran', and Eliash, 'The Šī'ite Qur'an'. For another example of material said to have been omitted from the Qur'an see the assertion that the names of six pseudo-prophets have been omitted from the Qur'an, al-Kashshī, *Rijāl*, pp. 187, 195. See also Chap. 7, note 14 *supra*.
6 See, for example, al-Bukharī, *Saḥīḥ*, Vol. 1, p. 146; Muslim, *Saḥīḥ*, Vol. 1, pp. 264–5.
7 See Muslim, *Saḥīḥ*, Vol. 1, pp. 534–8. Several of the Traditions quoted in this section state that temporary marriage was prohibited during the Prophet's lifetime but others confirm the Shi'i version.

10. SHI'I JURISPRUDENCE AND THE RELIGIOUS HIERARCHY

Sources

Arabic and Persian: Much information can be obtained from selective use of primary sources such as the biographies of the ulama (see Khwānsārī, *Rawḍat al-Jannāt*, Tunukābunī, *Qiṣaṣ al-'ulamā*, etc.) and comparisons of works on jurisprudence and the principles of jurisprudence from different periods (e.g. Shaykhu'ṭ-Ṭā'ifa, *Nihāya*, Shahīd ath-Thānī, *Rawḍa*, etc., see pp. 188–9).
European languages: The history of the development of Shi'i jurisprudence is poorly served in Western languages. The best work on the subject is the Ph.D. thesis, Calder, 'Structure of Authority . . . ', but see also Bellefonds, 'Droit imamite'. Concerning the ulama themselves see Fischer, *Iran*, and Arjomand, 'Shi'ite Hierocracy'. Concerning the programme of studies at the theological colleges see Fischer, *Iran*; Vahdati, 'Academies shiites'; Jamāli, 'Theological Colleges'; Mesopotamien, 'Programme des études'.

1 The old view of Shi'i jurisprudence was first put forward by Schacht, *Origins*; see also Bellefonds, 'Droit imamite', p. 185. The new view has been advanced by Coulson (see Coulson, *History of Islamic Law*, pp. 105ff.; *Conflicts and Tensions*, pp. 31–3; *Succession in the Muslim Family*, pp. 108–34). Nevertheless, it can still be said that in the field of ritual observances (*'ibādāt*) there is little significant difference between the Sunni schools and Shi'ism, whereas in the field of social transactions (*mu'āmalāt*) there are significant differences especially in three areas: marriage (with respect to temporary marriage), divorce (with respect to innovated divorce) and inheritance.
2 al-Ḥurr al-'Āmilī, *Amal al-'Āmil*, Vol. 2, pp. 81–5; Vol. 1, pp. 85–91 respectively.
3 al-Baḥrānī, *Lu'lu'āt Baḥrayn*, p. 14.
4 For example, using this Sunni-based terminology, 9,485 of the 16,199 Traditions in Kulaynī's *al-Kāfī* were found to be 'weak' (*ḍa'īf*) by one author; Tunukābunī, *Qiṣaṣ al-'ulamā*, p. 397.
5 Gibb, 'Government and Islam', p. 118.

6 Shaykhu'ṭ-Ṭā'ifa, *Nihāya,* cited in Calder, Ph.D., 'Structure of Authority', pp. 73–4, 110, 132–3, 160.

7 al-Ḥillī, *Sharā'i' al-Islām,* cited in Calder, Ph.D., 'Structure of Authority', pp. 77–8, 123.

8 al-Karakī, *Jāmi' al-Maqāsid,* cited in Calder, Ph.D., 'Structure of Authority', pp. 163–5.

9 Shahīd ath-Thānī, *Rawḍa al-Bahiyya*, sections: Kitāb az-Zakāt (3rd Chap.), Kitāb al-Jihād (Introduction), Kitāb al-Qaḍā. See also Calder, Ph.D., 'Structure of Authority', pp. 84–5, 112, 125–6, 147–51.

10 *Kitāb al-Jihādiyya* (Tabrīz, 1818), pp. 46–50, quoted in Arjomand, 'Shi'ite Hierocracy', pp. 57–8.

11 Tunukābunī, *Qiṣaṣ al-'ulamā*, p. 145.

12 Sayyid Ja'far Kashfī, *Tuḥfat al-Mulūk* (Tehran, 1857), p. 123a, cited in Arjomand, 'Shi'ite Hierocracy', pp. 53–5. On Mīrza Abu'l-Qāsim Qummī's political theory see Lambton, 'Some new trends . . . ', pp. 114–18.

13 Al-Ḥurr al-'Āmilī, *Wasā'il ash-Shī'a,* quoted in Khumaynī, *Ḥukūmat-i Islāmī*, pp. 100–101.

14. Ibn Bābūya, *Ma'anī al-Akhbār*, pp. 374–5, quoted in Khumaynī, *Ḥukūmat-i Islāmī*, p. 64.

15 Khumaynī, *Ḥukūmat-i Islāmī*, pp. 64–7.

16 Kulaynī, *al-Kāfī*, Vol. 1, p. 38, quoted in Khumaynī, *Ḥukūmat-i Islāmī*, pp. 70–71.

17 Kulaynī, *al-Kāfī*, Vol. 1, p. 46, quoted in Khumaynī, *Ḥukūmat-i Islāmī*, p. 75.

18 Al-Ḥurr al-'Āmilī, *Wasā'il ash-Shī'a*, quoted in Khumaynī, *Ḥukūmat-i Islāmī*, p. 86.

19 Ibn Bābūya, *Kamāl ad-Dīn*, pp. 283–5. Al-Ḥurr al-'Āmilī, *Wasā'il ash-Shī'a*, quoted in Khumaynī, *Ḥukūmat-i Islāmī*, p. 88.

20 Kulaynī, *al-Kāfī*, Vol. 1, pp. 24, 32, quoted in Khumaynī, *Ḥukūmat-i Islāmī*, pp. 111–12.

21 The following is a description of the relationship between the Bazaar and the ulama in the late Qājār period. Much of it remains true to the present day although the legal function of the ulama was much reduced in Pahlavī times. 'The relationship between the people of the bazaar (merchants, banker-changers, ambulatory changers, wholesale or retail merchants, bank messengers, intermediaries, bureaucratic functionaries, accountants, artisans, etc.) and the religious class was longstanding, close, and mutually beneficial. The people of the bazaars needed the services of the ulama to authenticate written contracts, to administer justice, to give reassurance of the orthodoxy of their actions, and to give clarification on casuistical and religious problems. They also sought the protection of the ulama, and, though the central government was making attempts to limit the practice, the bazaaris often turned to the men of religion for asylum. The merchants, both Muslim and non-Muslim, were dependent upon the services that the ulama provided, and could not do without them.

'But the ulama were dependent upon the merchants too, not least of all for financial support. Though merchants generally lived modestly, religious or secular feasts and ceremonies were occasions for generosity and display, especially on the part of the rich. But every merchant, whatever his economic situation, had to give alms during his life, or, through testamentary disposition, to make provision for donations after his death. Thus, a strong community of spirit and outlook was established between these two social categories, although it was never formally organized. This was so much the case, that during the period that concerns us, any action on the part of one group was often followed sympathetically by the other.' (Mahdavi, 'Significance of private archives', p. 259.)

22 See Fischer, *Iran*, p. 163.

23 See pathetic accounts of hardships endured by religious students in Browne, *Literary History*, Vol. 4, pp. 361–7; and Najafī-Quchānī, 'Zindigī-yi Ṭalabigī'.

24 Arjomand, 'Shi'ite Hierocracy', p. 69.

25 The role of a mujtahid as defined by such scholars as 'Allāma al-Ḥillī involved the forming of judgements on all legal points independently and indeed the following (*taqlīd*) by one mujtahid of another was, in some works, considered not permissible. But this position has undergone modification. In the 18th and early 19th centuries there were only a handful of people who were considered mujtahids. But as the number of mujtahids grew during the late 19th century and the 20th century, this independence and the ability to give judgements on all points was effectively passed upwards by most mujtahids and today only applies to the top-ranking *marāji'*. Lower-ranking mujtahids in effect practise *taqlīd* towards the judgements of these *marāji'*.

26 See, for example, Fischer, *Iran*, Appendix 2, pp. 252–4; and Hairi, *Shi'ism*, pp. 62–3. Although it has been stated that the concept of *marja' at-taqlīd* evolved during the 18th and 19th centuries, there is a hint of an earlier stage in the evolution of this concept in the designation of Shaykh 'Alī Muḥaqqiq al-Karakī as *mujtahid az-zamānī* (mujtahid of the age) in the Safavid history *Aḥsan at-Tawārīkh* (quoted in Savory, 'Principal Offices of the Safawid State', pp. 81–3).

27 Although it is not uncommon to find the phrase *Āyat Allāh fi'l-'ālamīn* among other similar phrases as part of an encomium extolling a prominent scholar in works dating from the 19th century or even earlier, its use as a prefixed designation denoting rank is a modern phenomenon. Ākhūnd Khurāsānī was sometimes referred to as Āyatu'llāh and there was sporadic use of the term in the early decades of the 20th century. It appears to have gained currency among Iranians in the 1940s and 1950s but Arabic books of even quite recent date do not use this designation.

28 Even these distinctions are not, however, clear-cut. There are, for example, some individuals such as Āyatu'llāh Āmulī, the head of one of the *madrasas* of Qumm, who obviously is in receipt of funds since he distributes money to the *ṭullāb* and who is called *Āyatu'llāh al-'Uzmā* but is clearly not considered of equal rank to such Āyatu'llāhs as Gulpāygānī and Mar'ashī-Najafī.

11. SUFISM, 'IRFĀN AND ḤIKMA

Sources

Arabic and Persian: Sources for the history of the Shi'i Sufi orders include Ma'sūm 'Alī Shāh, *Ṭarā'iq al-Ḥaqā'iq*; Humāyūnī, *Tārīkh-i Silsila-hā-yi Ṭarīqa-yi Ni'matu'llāhī*. For the history of the early connections between Sufism and Shi'ism see ash-Shaybī, *Fikr ash-Shī'a*. The writings of the philosophers of the School of Isfahan are very difficult for those not used to the vocabulary.

European languages: On the Sufi orders see Gramlich, *Die Schiitischen Derwischorden*. The Ni'matu'llāhī order has brought out a large number of tracts by their present Shaykh, Dr Javād Nūrbakhsh, in English. On *Ḥikmat-i Ilāhī*, the most important sources of information are the writings of Henri Corbin, see *En Islam iranien*, Vol. 4, and *La Philosophie iranienne islamique*. See also Fazlur Rahman, *The Philosophy of Mullā Ṣadrā*, and Nasr, *Ṣadr al-Dīn Shīrāzī and his Transcendent Theosophy*. One of Mullā Ṣadrā's works, *al-Mashā'ir*, has been translated into French by Corbin and his *al-Ḥikma al-'Arshiyya* into English by Morris (*The Wisdom of the Throne*). See also Dehbashi, Ph.D., 'Mullā Sadrā's Theory of Transubstantial Motion'.

1 See also comments on p. 90.
2 See, for example, Nūrbakhsh, *Murād wa Murīd*, and Miller, 'Shi'ah Mysticism'.
3 Gramlich, *Schiitischen Derwischorden*, Vol. 1, p. 90.
4 Ma'sūm 'Alī Shāh, *Ṭarā'iq al-Ḥaqā'iq*, Vol. 3, p. 215.
5 Sir John Malcolm (*History of Persia*, Vol. 2, pp. 382–426) gives a description of the revival of Sufism brought about by Ma'sūm 'Alī Shāh and also gives an account of Sufi doctrines and of the opposition of the ulama.
6 Gramlich, *Schiitischen Derwischorden*, Vol. 1, pp. 90–91.
7 *Ibid.* p. 91.
8 This summary is condensed from Nasr, *Ṣadr al-Dīn*, pp. 58–61.

12. SCHOOLS WITHIN TWELVER SHI'ISM

Sources

Persian and Arabic: Original Akhbārī works are difficult to obtain. On Shaykhīs the best source is Ibrāhīmī, *Fihrist*; see also al-Aḥsā'ī, *Ḥayāt an-Nafs*, and Rashtī, *Dalīl al-Mutaḥayyirīn*. No substantial work of the Bāb has been published in its original language. Many individual works and compilations of the writings of Bahā'u'llāh and 'Abdu'l-Bahā are available; for example, Bahā'u'llāh, *Kitāb-i Īqān* and *Muntakhabātī az āthār*.

European languages: Little work has been done on the Akhbārīs; see Scarcia, 'Interno alle controversie'. On Shaykhīs see Corbin, *L'Ecole Shaykhie* and *En Islam iranien*, Vol. 4; Nicolas, *Essai sur le Cheïkisme*; Bayat, *Mysticism and Dissent*; and the following Ph. D. theses: Rafati, 'Development of Shaykhī Thought'; MacEoin, 'From Shaykhism'; and Jalali, 'Shaikhiyya'. On the Bābīs and Bahā'īs see Balyuzi, *The Bāb*, and *Bahā'u'llāh*; Smith, *Bābī and Bahā'ī Religions*; and also the following Ph.D. theses: Amanat, 'Babi Movement'; Smith, 'Sociological Study of the Babi and Bahai Religions'. For Bābī and Bahā'ī doctrine see

Bausani, 'Bāb' and 'Bahā'ī' in *Encyclopaedia of Islam*, new edition. General introductory works on the Bahā'ī Faith include Esslemont, *Bahā'u'llāh and the New Era*; Huddleston, *The Earth is but One Country*;

1 See Khwānsārī, *Rawḍat al-Jannāt*, pp. 36–7, and Davvānī, *Vaḥīd Bihbahānī*, pp. 75–6.
2 Binder, 'Proofs of Islam', p. 125; Eliash, 'Misconceptions', p. 12.
3 I am grateful to Stephen Lambden of the University of Newcastle for the suggestion that in view of the intermediary position of Hūrqalyā, it may be a corruption of the Hebrew *Hā-Raqīa'* (or an equivalent word in another language) which is the word used in Genesis 1:6 for the firmament standing between heaven and earth.
4 When E. G. Browne was in Iran in 1887 he records having been told by a Shaykhī of Kirmān that the term *Rukn-i Rābi'* applied to a specific person: *Year among the Persians*, pp. 519–20.
5 See Kirmānī, *Hidāyat aṭ-Ṭālibīn*, pp. 135–6.
6 See, for example, Qur'an 32:6.
7 Amanat, Ph.D., 'Bābī Movement', pp. 75–90, surveys messianic expectation at this time in Iran, Iraq and the Caucasus. Mrs Meer Hasan Ali states that the Shi'is with whom she was in contact in Oudh in India in the 1820s were 'said to possess prophecies that led them to expect the twelve hundred and sixtieth year of the Hegirah [i.e. 1844] as the time for his [the Hidden Imam's] coming'. Mrs Meer Hasan Ali, *Observations*, p. 76, quoted in Cole, Ph.D., 'Imāmī Shi'ism from Iran to North India', pp. 348–9.

13. THE POPULAR RELIGION

Sources

A number of anthropological and other studies of Shi'i communities exist and the ones that have been of most use for this chapter include: *for Iran*: Thaiss, Ph.D., 'Religious Symbolism . . . '; Braswell, Ph.D., 'Mosaic of Mullahs . . . '; Fischer, *Iran*; *for Iraq*: Fernea, E.W., *Guests of the Sheik*; Fernea, A., *Shaykh and Effendi*; Thesiger, *Marsh Arabs*; *for Bahrain*: Khuri, *Tribe and State*; *for India*: Mrs Meer Hasan Ali, *Observations on the Musulmans*; *for Lebanon*: Adams, Ph.D., 'Shi'ite Community in Northern Lebanon', Peters, 'Aspects of Rank and Status'. I am also indebted for oral information to several persons including Prof. Emrys Peters and Dr Juan R. Cole.

Regarding the significance of the martyrdom of Husayn in the popular religion see Thaiss, Ph.D., 'Religious Symbolism . . . ', and Ayoub, *Redemptive Suffering*. For descriptions of the 'Āshūrā ceremonies see Gobineau, *Religions et Philosophies*, pp. 320–408; Pelly, *The Miracle Play of Hasan and Husain*; and Peters, 'A Muslim Passion Play'.

1 This paradox is closely linked to 'Alī Sharī'atī's concepts of Safavid Shi'ism and 'Alawī Shi'ism (see pp. 258–9). The attitude of *maẓlūmiyyat* is linked to an other-worldly intercessor role for the Imams which has as its counterpart a socially-passive role for the Shi'a (Sharī'atī's Safavid Shi'ism). The attitude of *qiyām*, on the other hand, involves bringing about social change and

demands an active role for the Shi'a (Sharī'atī's 'Alawī Shi'ism). It is clear, however, that these two attitudes are not, as Sharī'atī would have it, two opposed alternatives but rather they are two aspects of the same attitude (of love and reverence for the Imams) either of which may be manifested according to external (usually political) circumstances.

2 Thaiss, Ph.D., 'Religious Symbolism . . .', p. 230.

3 Although the *ta'ziya* is generally thought of as having evolved during the Qājār period, there is evidence of early forms of it in the late Safavid period (see Bruyn, *Travels*, Vol. 1, pp. 215–18).

4 Tancoigne, *Journey into Persia*, pp. 196–201.

5 There was one woman, Banū Amīn of Isfahan, who in recent years claimed the rank of mujtahid and held *ijāzas*. However, her ranking was never fully accepted by many of the ulama (see Fischer, *Iran*, p. 163). A recent analysis of the position of Banū Amīn suggests that women can achieve the status of being a mujtahid (in the sense of being able to follow their own independent judgement and not practise *taqlīd*, see p. 175), but they cannot act as *marja' at-taqlīd* (i.e. become a point of reference and imitation for others); see *Mahjubah* magazine for women, Vol. 3, Nos. 4, 5, 6, Aug.–Oct. 1983, pp. 60–64, and also Fischer, *Iran*, p. 279, n. 18. However, this is an area which is obviously still controversial among the ulama. On women under the present Revolutionary Government see Tabari, *Shadow of Islam*, and Nashat, *Women and Revolution*.

14. CONTEMPORARY SHI'ISM

Sources

On Iran see Akhavi, *Religion and Politics*; Hairi, *Shī'ism and Constitutionalism*; Braswell, Ph.D., 'Mosaic of Mullahs and Mosques'; Millward, 'Aspects of Modernism'. On Lebanon see Sicking and Khairallah, 'Shi'a awakening in Lebanon'. On Bahrain see Khuri, *Tribe and State in Bahrain*. On India and Pakistan see Hollister, *Shi'a of India*. On East Africa see Rizvi and King, 'Khoja Shia Ithna-Asheriya Community' and 'Some East African Ithna-Asheri Jamaats'. On the 1979 Revolution and after the most useful source of information is the *Iran Press Digest (Echo of Iran)*. See also Fischer, *Iran*; Keddie, *Roots of Revolution*; Akhavi, *Religion and Politics*; and Zabih, *Iran since the Revolution*.

1 On Burūjirdī's role in the 1950s see Akhavi, *Religion and Politics*, pp. 24, 77–9, 102.

2 There were also a number of slightly less important figures who were nevertheless regarded by some as *marāji'*: Āyatu'llāh Aḥmad Kafā'ī-Khurāsānī (d. 1971) in Mashhad; Āyatu'llāhs 'Abdu'l-Karīm Zanjānī (d. 1389/1969), Sayyid Muḥammad Javād 'Aynakī Ṭabaṭabā'ī Tabrīzī (d. 1387/1967) and his son Sayyid 'Alī (d. 1394/1974) and Ḥasan Bujnurdī (d. 1395/1975) in Najaf; and Āyatu'llāh Muḥammad 'Alī Shahristānī (d. 1385/1965) in Baghdad.

3 There are, however, a number of other cities with religious colleges: Isfahan, Shīrāz, Tabrīz, Karbalā, Lakhnau (Lucknow), etc. One recent

source states that whereas in the late sixties there had been 20,000 students at Najaf, as a result of the Iraqi government's persecution of the Shi'i *tullāb* there are now only 300 (Siddiqui, *Issues*, p. 319).

4 *Iran Press Digest*, No. 213, 22 Jan. 1978, pp. 5–6.

5 For a more detailed analysis of the *Dīn-i Dawlat*, see Braswell, Ph.D., 'Mosaic of Mullahs and Mosques'.

6 For a further discussion of this book, see Lambton, 'Reconsideration . . .'.

7 On Sharī'atī's thought see Akhavi, *Religion and Politics*, pp. 144–58. See also Sharī'atī, *On the Sociology of Islam*.

8 On Iraq's Shi'i opposition groups, see Batuta, 'Iraq's underground Shī'a movements'.

9 Chamie ('Religious Groups in Lebanon') has produced figures showing that Shi'is are at the bottom of the social scale in education, status of occupation and income. In all these areas the social scale runs: Christians, Druse, Sunnis, Shi'is. Even within the same occupation group, whether this be the professional/technical group at the top of the social status league or labouring occupations at the bottom, Shi'is tend to be paid less than other groups for the same kind of work.

10 See account of confrontation between aṣ-Ṣadr and Ḥamāda in the Hirmal area in Adams, Ph.D., 'Social Organisation of a Shi'ite Community'.

11 On Shi'i leadership in Lebanon see Deeb, 'Lebanon: Prospects', pp. 268–73.

12 Quoted in Betts, *Christians in the Arab East*, pp. 89–92.

13 McDowall, *Lebanon*, p. 9.

14 On Shi'i political activity in Bahrain see Khuri, *Tribe and State, passim* but especially pp. 66–84, 154–93, 225–9.

15 Derived from entries in Barrett, *World Christian Encyclopaedia* which are in turn based on United Nations Statistical Bulletins.

16 Derived from entries in Barrett, *World Christian Encyclopaedia*.

17 Author's estimates.

18 The edition of Khumaynī's important work *Ḥukūmat-i Islāmī* printed in Tehran shortly after the Revolution has the author's name as 'Nā'ib al-Imām Khumaynī' on the front cover.

19 On the role of the Revolutionary Council see *Iran Press Digest*, No. 268, 3 March 1980, pp. 2–10.

20 On Khumaynī's vision of governing in the mould of 'Ali see *Iran Press Digest*, No. 285, 7 July 1980, pp. 2–10; and Fischer, *Iran*, pp. 216–17.

21 On the decreasing cohesion of the IRP see *Iran Press Digest*, 15 March 1983, pp. 20–21.

Select Bibliography

In the course of this book, lists of the basic important Shi'i works have been given. The following will assist the reader to locate these lists, which can act as the basis for the drawing up of a Shi'i bibliography (the most comprehensive Shi'i bibliography is aṭ-Ṭihrānī, *adh-Dharī'a*, see below):

The rest of the Bibliography relates to books consulted by the author in the course of research for this book as well as a selection of other books on Shi'ism. As elsewhere in this book, the Islamic (Hijrī) dates precede the Gregorian. 'Sh' after a date indicates the Hijrī solar (Shamsī) calendar used in Iran. Otherwise Ḥijrī dates are according to the usual lunar calendar used in the rest of the Islamic world.

A. Arabic and Persian

Abū Dāwud Sulaymān as-Sijistānī. *Sunan*. 2 vols. Maṭba'a Muṣṭafā al-Bābī al-Ḥalabī, Cairo, 1371/1952.

al-Aḥsā'ī, Shaykh 'Abdu'llāh ibn Ahmad. *Risāla-yi Sharḥ Aḥvāl*. Trans. from Arabic by Muḥammad Ṭāhir Khān. Chāpkhāna Sa'ādat, Kirmān, 1387/1967.

al-Aḥsā'ī, Shaykh Aḥmad ibn Zaynu'd-Dīn. *Ḥayāt an-Nafs*. Trans. from Arabic by Sayyid Kāẓim Rashtī. Chāpkhāna Sa'ādat, Kirmān, 1353/1934.

Āl Kāshifu'l-Ghiṭā, Muḥammad Ḥusayn. *Aṣl ash-Shī'a wa Uṣūluhā*. 9th printing, Najaf, 1381/1962.

Āl Yā Sīn, Muḥammad Ḥusayn. *Tārīkh al-Mashhad al-Kāẓimī*. Maṭba'at al-Ma'ārif, Baghdad, 1387/1967.

al-Amīn, Muḥsin. *Khiṭaṭ Jabal 'Āmil*. Maṭba'at al-Inṣāf, Beirut, 1961.

—*A'yān ash-Shī'a*. Vol. 1. Matba'at al-Inṣāf, Beirut, 1960 proceeding.

al-Ash'arī, 'Alī ibn Ismā'īl. *Maqālāt al-Islāmiyyin*. Ed. Hellmut Ritter. Bibliotheca Islamica, Vol. 1a, b, c. Maṭba'at ad-Dawla, Istanbul, 1929–33.

al-Baghdādī, *see* Ibn Ṭāhir.

Bahā'u'llāh (Mīrzā Ḥusayn 'Alī Nūrī). *Kitab-i-Īqān*. Faraju'llāh Zakī, Cairo, 1934. RP Bahā'ī-Verlag, Hofheim-Langenheim, Germany, 1980.

—*Muntakhabātī az āthār-i Haḍrat-i Bahā'u'llāh*. Bahā'ī-Verlag, Hofheim-Langenheim, Germany, 1984.

al-Baḥrānī, Yūsuf ibn Aḥmad. *Lu'lu'āt Baḥrayn*. Ed. Muḥammad Ṣādiq Baḥru'l-'Ulūm. Maṭba'at an-Nu'mān, Najaf, 1386/1966.

Baladhūrī, Aḥmad ibn Yaḥyā. *Ansāb al-Ashraf*. Ed. Muḥammad Ḥamīdu'llāh. Vol. 1, Dar al-Ma'ārif, Cairo, 1960.

al-Bayḍāwī, 'Abdu'llāh ibn 'Umar. *Anwār at-Tanzīl*. 5 vols. Dār al-Kutub al-'Arabiyya al-Kubrā, Cairo, 1330/1912.

al-Bukhārī, Abū 'Abdu'llāh Muḥammad ibn Ismā'īl. *Saḥīḥ*. Ed. L. K. Krehl. 4 vols. E. J. Brill, Leiden, 1862.

Chahārdihī, Nūru'd-Dīn Mudarrisī. *Sayrī dar Taṣawwuf*. Intishārāt Ishrāqī, Tehran, 1359/1940.

Davvānī, 'Alī. *Vaḥīd Bihbahānī*. Mu'assisa Intishārāt Amīr Kabīr, Tehran, 1362 Sh/1983.

Dāwud, Nabīla 'Abdu'l-Mun'im. *Nashāt ash-Shī'a al-Imāmiyya*. Maṭba'at al-Irshād, Baghdad, 1968.

al-Ḥākim an-Naysābūrī. *al-Mustadrak*. 4 vols. Maktabat an-Naṣr al-Ḥāditha, Riyādh, n.d.

Hidāyat, Riḍā Qulī Khān. *Rawḍat aṣ-Ṣafā-yi Nāṣirī*. 2 vols. Lithographed Tehran, 1270/1853–1274/1857.

al-Ḥillī, Ja'far ibn Ḥasan, Muḥaqqiq. *Sharā'i' al-Islām fi masā'il al-ḥalāl wa'l-ḥarām*. Ed. 'Abdu'l-Ḥusayn Muḥammad 'Alī. 4 vols. Maṭba'at al-Adab, Najaf, 1389/1969.

Ḥirzu'd-Dīn, Muḥammad. *Ma'ārif ar-Rijāl fi tarājim al-'ulamā wa'l-udalā*. Ed. Muḥammad Ḥusayn Ḥirzu'd-Dīn. 3 vols. Maṭba'at an-Najaf, Najaf, 1383/1964.

Humāyūnī, Dr Mas'ūd. *Tārīkh-i Silsila-hā-yi Tarīqa-yi Ni'matu'llāhī dar Īrān*. Maktab-i 'Irfān, Tehran?, 1358 Sh/1978.

al-Ḥurr al-'Āmilī, Muḥammad ibn Ḥasan. *Amal al-'Āmil*. Ed. Aḥmad al-Ḥusaynī. 2 vols. Maktabat al-Andalūs, Baghdad, 1385/1965.

—*Wasā'il ash-Shī'a*. Ed. 'Abdu'r-Raḥīm ar-Rabbānī ash-Shīrāzī. 20 vols. Maktaba al-Islāmiyya, Tehran, 1383/1963.

Ibn Athīr, 'Izzu'd-Dīn Abu'l-Ḥasan 'Alī. *al-Kāmil fi't-Ta'rīkh*. Ed. C. J. Tornberg, E. J. Brill, Leiden, 1868.

Ibn Bābūya, Muḥammad ibn 'Alī. *'Ilal ash-Sharī'a*. Ed. Faḍlu'llāh Ṭabāṭabā'ī Yazdī. 2 vols. Maktaba Ṭabāṭabā'ī, Qumm, *c*. 1377/1957.

—*Kamāl ad-Dīn wa Tamām an-Ni'ma* (also called *Ikmāl ad-Dīn wa Itmām an-Ni'ma)*. Ed. 'Alī Akbar Ghaffārī. 2 vols. Maktabat aṣ-Ṣadūq, Tehran, 1390/1970.

—*Ma'ānī al-Akhbār*. Ed. 'Alī Akbar Ghaffārī. Maktabat aṣ-Ṣadūq, Tehran, 1379/1959.

—*'Uyūn al-Akhbār ar-Riḍā*. Matba'a al-Ḥaydariyya, Najaf, 1390/1970.

Ibn Ḥajar al-'Asqalānī, Shihābu'd-Dīn Aḥmad. *Durur al-Kāmina*. 4 vols. Matba'a Majlis Dā'irat al-Ma'ārif al-'Uthmāniyya, Hyderabad, 1348/1929–1350/1931.

Ibn Hajār al-Makkī, Aḥmad. *aṣ-Ṣawā'iq al-Muḥriqa*. Ed. 'Abdu'l-Wahhāb 'Abdu'l-Laṭīf. Maktabat al-Qāhira, Cairo, 1375/1955.

Ibn Ḥanbal, Aḥmad. *Musnad*. 6 vols. Maṭba'a al-Maymāniyya, Cairo, 1313/1896.

Ibn Ḥazm, 'Alī. *al-Faṣl fi'l-Milal*. Maṭba'a Muḥammad 'Alī Ṣabīḥ, Cairo, 1347/1928–1348/1929.

Ibn al-Jawzī, 'Abdu'r-Raḥmān ibn Alī. *al-Muntaẓam*. 5 vols. Maṭba'a Dā'irat al-Ma'ārif, Hyderabad, 1357/1938–1359/1940.

Ibn Jubayr, Muḥammad ibn Aḥmad. *Riḥla*. Ed. William Wright. Revised. M. J. de Goeje. E. J. W. Gibb Memorial Series, Vol. 5. E. J. Brill, Leiden, 1907.

Ibn Kathīr, Ismā'īl ibn 'Umar. *Bidāya wa Nihāya*, 14 vols. Maṭba'at as-Sa'āda, Cairo, 1351/1932–1358/1939.

Ibn Māja, Muḥammad ibn Yazīd. *Sunan*. Ed. Muḥammad Fu'ād 'Abdu'l-Baqī. 2 vols. Dar Iḥyā al-Kutub al-'Arabiyya, Cairo, 1372/1952–1373/1953, RP 1972.

Ibn Shahrāshūb, Abū 'Abdu'llāh Muḥammad. *Manāqib Āl Abī Ṭālib*. Ed. by a committee of scholars at Najaf. 3 vols. Maṭba'a al-Ḥaydariyya, Najaf, 1376/1956.

Ibn Ṭāhir al-Baghdādī. *Kitāb al-Farq bayn al-Firaq*. Maṭba'at al-Ma'ārif, Cairo, 1328/1910. For translation (designated 'Tr.') of last part, *see* Halkin in Section C.

Ibn Ṭāwus, Raḍiyu'd-Dīn 'Alī. *al-Yaqīn fi Imāra Amīr al-Mu'minīn*. Mu'assisa Dār al-Kitāb, Qumm, 1369/1950.

Ibn Ṭūlūn, *see* Hartmann in Section C.

Ibrāhīmī (Kirmānī), Abu'l-Qāsim. *Fihrist-i Kutub-i Mashāyikh 'Azzām*. 3rd ed., Chāpkhāna Sa'ādat, Kirmān, n.d.

al Irbilī, Abu'l-Ḥasan 'Alī ibn 'Īsā. *Kashf al-Ghumma*. 3 vols. Maktaba Banī Hāshim, Tabrīz, 1381/1961.

al-Iṣfahānī al-Kāẓimī, Muḥammad Mahdī. *Aḥsan al-Wadī'a*. 2 vols. Maṭba'at an-Najāḥ, Baghdad, 1347/1928?

Iskandar Beg Munshī. *Ta'rīkh-i 'Ālam-ārā-yi 'Abbāsī*. 2 vols. Chāpkhāna Mūsawī, Tehran, 1955–6.

Juwaynī, 'Alā'u'd-Dawla. *Ta'rīkh-i Jihān-gushā*. Ed. Mīrzā Muḥammad Qazwīnī. 3 vols. E. J. W. Gibb Memorial Series, Vol. 16. E. J. Brill, Leiden and Luzac & Co., London, 1912–37.

Kashmīrī, Muḥammad 'Alī. *Nujūm as-Samā*. Maṭba'a Ja'farī, Lucknow, 1303/1885.

al-Kashshī, Muḥammad ibn 'Umar. *ar-Rijāl*. Maṭba'a al-Muṣṭawiyya, Bombay, 1317/1899.

al-Khayyāṭ al-Mu'tazilī, Abu'l-Ḥusayn 'Abdu'r-Raḥīm. *Kitāb al-Intiṣār*. Ed. H. S. Nyberg. Dār al-Kutub al-Miṣriyya, Cairo, 1925.

Khumaynī, Nā'ib al-Imām Ruḥu'llāh. *Ḥukūmat-i Islāmī (Vilāyat-i Faqīh dar khuṣūṣ-i ḥukūmat-i Islāmī)*. No publisher, [Tehran, *c.* 1980].

Khwānsārī Iṣfahānī, Muḥammad Bāqir. *Rawḍat al-Jannāt*. Lithographed Tehran, 1306/1888.

al-Kilīdār, 'Abdu'l-Jawād. *Tārīkh Karbalā wa Ḥā'ir al-Ḥusayn*. Maṭba'a al-Ḥaydariyya, Najaf, 1386/1967.

Kirkush al-Ḥillī, Yūsuf. *Tarikh al-Ḥilla*. 2 vols. Maṭba'a al Ḥaydariyya, Najaf, 1385/1965.
Kirmānī, Muḥammad Khān. *Kitāb al-Mubīn*. 2 vols. 2nd printing, Chāpkhāna Sa'ādat, Kirmān, 1354 Sh/1975.
Kirmānī, Muḥammad Karīm Khān. *Hidāyat aṭ-Ṭālibīn*. Chāpkhāna Sa'ādat, Kirmān, 1380/1960.
Kulaynī, Muḥammad ibn Ya'qūb. *al-Kāfī*. Ed. 'Alī Akbar Ghaffārī. Vols. 1–2 (*Uṣūl*), Maktabat aṣ-Ṣadūq, Tehran, 1381/1961. Vols 3–8 (*Furū'* and *Rawḍa*), Shaykh Muḥammad al-Ākhūndī, Tehran, 1377/1957–1379/1959.
Mahdī Khān, Mīrzā. *Ta'rīkh-i Nādirī*. Lithographed Tehran, 1293/1876.
Māhir, Su'ād. *Mashhad al-Imām 'Alī fi'l-Najaf wa mā bihi min al-Hadayā wa'l-Tuḥaf*. Dar al-Ma'ārif, Cairo, 1969.
Majlisī, Muḥammad Bāqir. *Biḥār al-Anwār*. 110 vols. Matba'a al-Islāmiyya, Tehran, 1376/1956–1392/1972. Where access was not available to some volumes of this edition, the lithographed Tehran edition in 25 vols., 1301/1884–1315/1897 (designated 'old ed.'), has been used.
—*Jalā' al-'Uyūn*. Mu'assisa Matbū'ātī Amīr Kabīr, Tehran, 1332 Sh/1953.
al-Maqrīzī, Taqīyu'd-Dīn Aḥmad. *Kitāb al-Mawā'iz wa'l-I'tibār fi dhikr al-Khiṭaṭ wa'l-Āthār*. 2 vols. Dār aṭ-Ṭab'a al-Miṣriyya, Cairo, 1270/1853.
al-Mas'ūdī, 'Alī ibn Ḥusayn. *Murūj adh-Dhahab (Les Prairies d'or)*. Ed. and trans. C. Barbier de Meynard. 9 vols. Imprimerie Imperiale, Paris, 1861–77.
Ma'sūm 'Alī Shāh, Muḥammad Ma'sūm Shīrāzī. *Ṭarā'iq al-Ḥaqā'iq*. Ed. Muḥammad Ja'far Maḥjūb. 3 vols. Kitābfurūshī Bārānī, Tehran, 1345 Sh/1966.
Mudarrisī-Chahārdihī, *see* Chahārdihī.
al-Mufīd, Shaykh Muḥammad ibn Nu'mān. *Awā'il al-Maqālāt fi'l-Madhāhib al-Mukhtārāt*. Kitābfurūshī Ḥaqīqat, Tabrīz, 1371/1952.
—*al-Ikhtiṣāṣ*. Ed. 'Alī Akbar Ghaffārī, Maktabat aṣ-Ṣadūq, Tehran, 1379/1959.
—*Kitāb al-Irshād*, al-Ḥaydarī Press, Najaf, 1382/1963. For translation (designated 'Tr.') *see* Howard in Section C.
—*Sharḥ 'Aqā'id aṣ-Ṣadūq* or *Tasḥīḥ al-I'tiqād* published in same volume as *Awā'il al-Maqālāt, see above*.
Muslim, Abu'l-Ḥusain ibn al-Ḥajjāj. *Saḥīḥ*. 2 vols. Dār Iḥyā al-Kutub al-'Arabiyya, Cairo, 1349/1930.
al-Muẓaffar, Muḥammad Ḥusayn. *Tārīkh ash-Shī'a*. Dār az-Zuhrā, Beirut, 1399/1979.
al-Muẓaffar, Muḥammad Riḍā. *'Aqā'id al-Imāmiyya*. 3rd ed., Matbū'āt an-Najāḥ, Cairo, 1391/1971.
an-Najafī, Shaykh Muḥammad Ḥasan. *Jawāhir al-Kalām*. Ed. 'Abbās al-Qūchānī. 23 vols. Dār al-Kutub al-Islāmiyya, Tehran, 1392/1972.
Najafī-Qūchānī, S. Ḥasan. 'Zindigī-yi Ṭalabigī va Ākhūndī.' *Rāhnāma-yi Kitāb*, 14 (1971), pp. 267–73, 489–94, 779–89.
Najāshī, Aḥmad ibn 'Alī. *Rijāl*. Published by Ḥajj Shaykh 'Alī al-Maḥallātī al-Ḥā'irī, Bombay, 1317.
Nāṣir Khusraw. *Safar-nāma*. Ed. Maḥmūd Ghanīzāda. Chāpkhāna Kāviyānī, Berlin, 1341/1922.
an-Nawbakhtī, Abū Muḥammad Ḥasan. *Firaq ash-Shī'a*. Bibliotheca Islamica,

Istanbul, 1931.
Nūrbakhsh, Dr Jawād. *Murād wa Murīd/The Master and Disciple in Sufism*. Text and translation. Khānagāh Ni'matu'llāhī, Tehran, 1977.
al-Qazwīnī ar-Rāzī, 'Abdu'l-Jalīl. *Kitāb an-Naqḍ*. Ed. S. Jalālu'd-Dīn Ḥusaynī Muḥaddith. Chāpkhāna Sipihr, Tehran, 1371/1951.
al-Qazwīnī, Ḥamdu'llāh Mustawfī. *Ta'rīkh-i Guzīdā*. Ed. and trans. E. G. Browne. E. J. W. Gibb Memorial Series, Vol. 14, 2 vols. E. J. Brill, Leiden, 1910–13.
al-Qummī, Sa'd ibn 'Abdu'llāh al-Ash'arī. *al-Maqālāt wa'l-Firaq*. Ed. Muḥammad Javad Mashkūr. Maṭba'a Ḥaydarī, Tehran, 1963.
Rashtī, S. Kāẓim. *Dalīl al-Mutaḥayyirīn*. Chāpkhāna Sa'ādat, Kirmān, 2nd printing, n.d.
ar-Rāzī, Fakhru'd-Dīn. *Mafātīḥ al-Ghayb*. 8 vols. Maṭba'a al-Khayriyya, Cairo, 1308/1891.
—*at-Tafsīr al-Kabīr*, 32 vols. Maṭba'a al-Bahiyya al-Miṣriyya, Cairo, 1357/1938.
Rāzī, Muḥammad Sharīf. *Ganjīna-yi Dānishmandān*. 7 vols, Kitābfurūshī Islāmiyya Tehran 1352 Sh/1973
as-Sāmarrā'ī, Yūnis. *Tārīkh Madīna Sāmarrā*. Maṭba'at al-Umma, Baghdad, 1971.
Shahīd ath-Thānī, Zaynu'd-Dīn ibn 'Alī. *Rawḍa al-Bahiyya fi sharḥ al-Luma'a ad-Dimashqiyya*. Lithographed Tabrīz, 1271/1854.
ash-Shahristānī, Abu'l-Fatḥ Muḥammad. *Kitāb al-Milal wa'n-Niḥal*. Ed. Muḥammad Sayyid Kīlānī. Matba'a Muṣṭafā al-Bābī al-Ḥalabī, Cairo, 1967.
ash-Shaybī, Dr Kāmil M. *Fikr ash-Shī'ī wa'n-Naza'āt aṣ-Ṣūfiyya*. Maktabat an-Nahḍa, Baghdad, 1386/1966.
Shaykh al-Mufīd, *see* al-Mufīd.
Shaykh aṣ-Ṣadūq, *see* Ibn Bābūya.
Shaykhu'ṭ-Ṭā'ifa, Shaykh Muḥammad ibn Ḥasan aṭ-Ṭūsī. *al-Fihrist*. Published together with Muḥammad ibn Muḥammad Muḥsin 'Alam al-Hudā. *Naḍād al-Īdāḥ*. Ed. A. Sprenger. Revised Maḥmūd Rāmyār. Chāpkhāna Dānishgāh Mashhad, Mashhad, 1351 Sh/1972.
—*an-Nihāya fi mujarrad al-faqīh wa'l-fatāwī*. Trans. into Persian by Muḥammad Bāqir Sabzivārī. 2 vols. Intishārāt Dānishgāh Tehran, 1333 Sh/1954–1334 Sh/1955.
—*Tafsīr at-Tibyān*. 10 vols. Maktabat al-Amīn, Najaf, 1383/1963.
ash-Shidyāq, Ṭannūs. *Akhbār al-A'yān fi Jabal Lubnān*. 2 vols. Maṭābi' Simyā, Beirut, 1954.
Shushtarī, Nūru'llāh Mar'ashī. *Majālis al-Mu'minīn*. Lithographed Tehran, 1268/1852.
Sipihr, Muḥammad Taqī, Lisānu'l-Mulk. *Nāsikh at-Tawārīkh; dawra-yi kāmil-i tārīkh-i Qājāriyya*. Ed. Jahāngīr Qā'im-Maqāmī. Amīr Kabīr, Tehran, 1337 Sh/1958.
as-Suyūṭī, Jalālu'd-Dīn. *ad-Durr al-Manthūr*. 6 vols. Maṭba'a al-Maymāniyya, Cairo, 1314/1896, fascimile edition printed in Beirut, n.d.
aṭ-Ṭabarī, Abū Ja'far Muḥammad. *Ta'rīkh ar-Rusul wa'l-Mulūk*. Ed. M. J. de Goeje, 15 vols. E. J. Brill. Leiden, 1901.

aṭ-Ṭabarsī, Aḥmad ibn 'Alī. *al Iḥtijāj*. Dar an Nu'mān, Najaf, 1386/1966.

aṭ-Ṭabarsī, Faḍl ibn Ḥasan. *Majma' al-Bayān*. 5 vols. Maktaba al-'Ilmiyya al-Islāmiyya, Tehran, 1379/1959.

aṭ-Ṭihrānī, Muḥammad Muḥsin, Āghā Buzurg. *adh-Dharī'a ilā Taṣānīf ash-Shī'a*. 25 vols. distributed through author, Tehran and Najaf, 1355/1936–1398/1978.

—*Ṭabaqāt A'lām ash-Shī'a*. Volumes consulted: *Nawābigh ar-ruwāt fi rābi'a al-mi'āt* (4th cent.); *an-Nābis fi qarn al-khāmis* (5th cent.); *ath-Thiqāt wa'l-'uyūn fi's-sādis al-qurūn* (6th cent.); *al-Anwār as-sāṭi'a fi'l-mi'a al-sābi'a* (7th cent.); *al-Ḥaqā'iq ar-rāhina fi't-tarājim a'yān al-mi'a ath-thāmina* (8th cent). Above volumes published Dār al-Kutub al-'Arabiyya, Beirut, 1971–5. *al-Karām al-barara fi'l-qarn ath-thālith ba'd al-'ashara* (13th cent.); *Nuqabā al-bashar fi'l-qarn al-rābi' 'ashar* (14th cent). Above volumes published Matba'a al-'Ilmiyya, Najaf, 1954.

at-Tirmidhī, Abū 'Īsā Muḥammad. *Sunan* or *Saḥīḥ*. 4 vols. Maṭba'at al-Madanī, Cairo, 1292/1875.

aṭ-Ṭūsī, Shaykh Muḥammad, *see* Shaykhu'ṭ-Ṭā'ifa

Tunukābunī, Muḥammad. *Qisās al-'Ulamā*. Kitābfurūshī 'Ilmiyya Islāmiyya, Tehran, n.d.

al-Ya'qūbī, Aḥmad ibn Abī Ya'qūb. *Tārīkh*. Ed. M. T. Houtsma. 2 vols. E. J. Brill, Leiden, 1883.

Yāqūt ibn 'Abdu'llāh al-Baghdādī. *Mu'jam al-Buldān*. 10 vols. in 5. Maṭba'at as-Sa'ādat, Cairo, 1324/1906.

az-Zanjānī, Ibrāhīm al-Mūsawī. *'Aqā'id al-Imāmiyya al-Ithnā 'Ashariyya*. Mu'assisa al-A'lamī li'l-Maṭbū'āt, Beirut, 1393/1973.

B. Western languages, unpublished material

Adams, Raymond A. 'The Social Organisation of a Shi'ite Community in Northern Lebanon.' Ph.D., Univ. of Manchester, Dec. 1978.

Amanat, Abbas. 'The Early Years of the Babi Movement: Background and Development.' Ph.D., Univ. of Oxford, 1981.

Braswell, George W., Jr. 'A Mosaic of Mullahs and Mosques: Religion and Politics in Iranian Shi'ah Islam.' Ph.D., Univ. of North Carolina, 1975.

Calder, Norman. 'The Structure of Authority in Imāmī Shī'ī Jurisprudence.' Ph.D., School of Oriental and African Studies, Univ. of London, 1980.

Cole, Juan R. I. 'Imāmī Shi'ism from Iran to North India, 1722–1856: State, Society and Clerical Ideology in Awadh.' Ph.D., Univ. of California, Los Angeles, 1984.

Dehbashi, Mehdi, 'Mullā Sadrā's Theory of Transubstantial Motion: A Translation and Critical Exposition.' Ph.D., Fordham Univ., New York, 1981.

Faghfoory, Mohammad Hasan. 'The Role of the ulama in Twentieth Century Iran, with Particular Reference to Ayatullah Haj Sayyid Abul-Qasim Kashani.' Ph.D., Univ. of Wisconsin, Madison, 1978.

Garoussian, Vida, 'The *Ulema* and Secularization in Contemporary Iran.' Ph.D., Southern Illinois Univ., 1974.

Gedeon, George S. 'The "Ashura" Ceremonies in Lebanon.' Ph.D., School of Oriental and African Studies, Univ. of London, 1963.

Jalali, Aflatun, 'The Shaikhiyya of Hajji Muhammad Karim Khan in Kirman.' Ph.D., Univ. of Manchester, 1982.

MacEoin, Denis M. 'From Shaykhism to Babism: A Study in Charismatic Renewal in Shīʿī Islam.' Ph.D., Univ. of Cambridge, July 1979.

Rafati, Vahid, 'The Development of Shaykhī Thought in Shīʿī Islam.' Ph.D., Univ. of California, Los Angeles, 1979.

ash-Shaybī (el-Sheibi), Kāmil M. 'Studies in the Interaction of Ṣūfism and Shiʿism to the rise of the Ṣafavids.' Ph.D., Univ. of Cambridge, 1961.

Smith, Peter R. P. 'A Sociological Study of the Babi and Baha'i Religions.' Ph.D., Univ. of Lancaster, 1982.

Thaiss, Gustav E. 'Religious Symbolism and Social Change: The Drama of Husain.' Ph.D., Washington Univ., 1973.

C. Western languages, published material

Adams, Raymond. 'Paradoxes of religious leadership among the Shiʿites of Lebanon.' *MERA Forum*, Vol. 6, No. 4, Winter 1983 (ed. Dina Dahbany-Miraglia), pp. 9–12.

Akhavi, Shahrough. *Religion and Politics in Contemporary Iran: Clergy-State Relations in the Pahlavi Period*. State University of New York Press, Albany, N.Y., 1980.

Āl Kāshifu'l-Ghiṭā, 'Allamah Shaykh Muḥammad Ḥusayn. *The Origins of Shīʿite Islam and its Principles*. Ansariyan Publications, Qumm, 1982.

Algar, Hamid. *Religion and State in Iran 1785–1906: The Role of the Ulama in the Qajar Period*. University of California Press, Berkeley and Los Angeles, 1969.

—*The Islamic Revolution in Iran*. Ed. K. Siddiqui. Lectures given at the Muslim Institute, London. Open Press, London, 1980.

—'Shiʿism and Iran in the Eighteenth Century', in *Studies in Eighteenth Century Islamic History*. Ed. Thomas Naff and Roger Owen. Southern Illinois University Press, Carbondale and Edwardsville; Fefer and Simons Inc., London and Amsterdam, 1977, pp. 288–302.

Ameer Ali, Syed. *The Spirit of Islam*. Christopher, London, 1922.

al-Amin, Hassan. *Islamic Shiʿite Encyclopaedia*. Vols. 1–4. [Beirut, n.d.]

Anthony, John D. *Arab States of the Lower Gulf: People, Politics and Petroleum*. James Terry Duce Memorial Series, Vol. 3, Middle East Institute, Washington, D.C., 1975.

Arberry, Arthur J. *The Koran Interpreted*. George Allen and Unwin Ltd., London; the MacMillan Company, New York, 2 vols., 1955.

Arjomand, Said Amir. *The Shadow of God and the Hidden Imam*. University of Chicago Press, Chicago, 1984.

—'Religion, Political Action and Legitimate Domination in Shiʿite Iran: Fourteen to Eighteenth Century AD,' *Archives of European Sociology*, 20 (1979), pp. 59–109.

—'Religious Extremism (Ghuluww), Ṣūfism and Sunnism in Safavid Iran: 1501–1722.' *Journal of Asian History*, 15 (1981), pp. 1–35.

Arjomand, Said Amir. 'The Shi'ite Hierocracy and the State in Pre-Modern Iran: 1785–1890.' *Archives of European Sociology*, 22 (1981), pp. 40–78.

Arnold, Leon. 'Le Credo du Shi'isme duodecimain.' *Travaux et Jours*, 17 (1965), pp. 35–54.

Aubin, Jean, 'La politique religieuse des Safavides', in *Le Shi'isme imamite.* Colloque de Strasbourg 1968, Presses Universitaires, Paris, 1970, pp. 235–44.

Aucagne, Jean. 'L'Imam Moussa Sadr et la communauté chiite.' *Travaux et Jours*, 53 (1974), pp. 31–51.

Ayoub, Mahmoud. *Redemptive Suffering in Islam, a Study of the devotional aspects of 'Āshura' in Twelver Shī'ism.* Religion and Society Series, No. 10, Mouton Publishers, The Hague, 1978.

Baillie, John. *A Digest of Mohummudan Law according to the sect of the Twelve Imams* (compiled under the superintendence of Sir W. Jones). Calcutta, 1805.

Baillie, Neil B. E. *A Digest of Moohummudan Law. Imameea Code.* Smith, Elder & Co., London, 1869.

Balyuzi, Hasan M. *'Abdu'l-Bahā, the Centre of the Covenant of Bahā'u'llāh.* George Ronald, Oxford, 1971.

—*The Bāb, the Herald of the Day of Days.* George Ronald, London, 1973.

—*Muḥammad and the Course of Islam.* George Ronald, London, 1976.

—*Bahā'u'llāh, the King of Glory.* George Ronald, London, 1980.

Barrett, David (ed.). *World Christian Encyclopaedia.* Oxford University Press, Oxford, 1982.

Batuta, Hanna. 'Iraq's underground Shī'a movements; characteristics, causes and prospects,' *Middle East Journal*, 35 (1981), pp. 578–94.

Bausani, Alessandro. *Persia Religiosa.* Saggiatore, Milan, 1959.

—*The Persians.* Trans. J. B. Donne. Elek Books, London, 1971.

—'Religion in Saljuq Period', pp. 283–302; 'Religion under the Mongols', pp. 538–49; in *Cambridge History of Iran*; Vol. 5: *The Saljuq and Mongol Periods.* Ed. J. A. Boyle, Cambridge University Press, Cambridge, 1968.

Bayat, Mangol. *Mysticism and Dissent; socioreligious thought in Qajar Iran.* Syracuse University Press, Syracuse, N.Y., 1982.

Bellefonds, *see* Linant de Bellefonds.

Benjamin, Samuel G. W. *Persia.* T. Fisher Unwin, London, 1889.

Betts, Robert B. *Christians in the Arab East.* S.P.C.K., London, 1979.

Binder, Leonard. 'The Proofs of Islam: Religion and Politics in Iran', in *Arabic and Islamic Studies in honor of Hamilton A. R. Gibb.* Ed. George Makdisi. E. J. Brill, Leiden, 1965.

Bonine, Michael E., and Nikki R. Keddie (eds.) *Modern Iran: The Dialectics of Continuity and Change.* State University of New York Press, Albany, N.Y., 1981.

Bosworth, Clifford E. *The Islamic Dynasties.* Islamic Survey No. 5, Edinburgh University Press, Edinburgh, 1967.

—(ed.). *Iran and Islam: In Memory of the Late Vladimir Minorsky.* Edinburgh University Press, Edinburgh, 1971.

Braswell, George W. 'Civil Religion in Contemporary Iran.' *Journal of Church and State*, 21 (1979), pp. 223–46.

Brockelmann, Carl. *History of the Islamic Peoples*. Trans. Joel Carmichael and Moshe Perlmann. Capricorn Books, New York, 1960.

Browne, Edward G. *A Literary History of Persia*. 4 vols. Cambridge University Press, Cambridge, 1902–24.

—*A Year among the Persians*. New edition, Cambridge University Press, Cambridge, 1926.

—*The Persian Revolution, 1905–1909*. Cambridge University Press, Cambridge, 1910.

Brunschvig, Robert. 'Les *Uṣûl al-Fiqh* Imâmites à leur Stade ancien (Xe et XIe siècle)', in *Le Shīʿisme Imamite* (*see* Aubin), pp. 201–13.

Bruyn, Cornelius le. *Travels into Muscovy, Persia and part of the East-Indies*. Trans. from French. Published by A. Bettesworth et al., London, 1737.

Cahen, Claude 'Le Problème du Shīʿisme dans L'Asie Mineure Turque Préottomane', in *Le Shīʿisme Imamite* (*see* Aubin), pp. 115–29.

Calder, Norman. 'Accommodation and Revolution in Imami Shiʿi Jurisprudence: Khumayni and the Classical Tradition.' *Middle Eastern Studies*, 18 (1982), pp. 3–20.

Calmard, J. 'Le Chiisme en Iran à l'époque Seljoukide d'après le Kitab al-Naqḍ.' *Le Monde Iranien et l'Islam*, 1 (1971), pp. 43–67.

Cambridge History of Islam. Ed. P. M. Holt et al. 2 vols. Cambridge University Press, Cambridge, 1970.

Chamie, Joseph. 'Religious Groups in Lebanon.' *International Journal of Middle East Studies*, 11 (1980), pp. 175–87.

Chardin, Sir John. *Voyages du Chevalier Chardin en Perse, et autre lieux de l'Orient*. Ed. L. Langlès. 10 vols. Le Normant, Paris, new edition, 1811.

—*The Travels of Sir John Chardin into Persia and the East Indies*. Christopher Bateman, London, 1691.

Chelkowski, Peter J. (ed.). *Taʿziyeh: Ritual and Drama in Iran*. New York University Press, New York, 1979.

Cole, J. R., and M. Momen. 'Mafia, Mob and Shiism in Iraq: The Rebellion of Ottoman Karbala 1824–1843.' *Past and Present*. Forthcoming.

Corbin, Henri. *En Islam iranien; aspects spirituels et philosophiques*. 4 vols., Gallimard, Paris, 1971–2.

—*Avicenne et le Récit Visionnaire*. Bibliothèque Iranienne, Vols. 4, 5. 2 vols. Adrien Maisonneuve, Paris, 1954. Trans. by Willard R. Trask as *Avicenna and the Visionary Recital*, Routledge and Kegan Paul, London, 1960.

—*Terre céleste et corps de résurrection: de l'Iran mazdéen a l'Iran shîʿite*. Buchet-Chastel, Paris, 1960. Trans. by Nancy Pearson as *Spiritual Body and Celestial Earth*, Bollingen Series 91:2, Princeton University Press, 1977.

—*Histoire de la Philosophie islamique*. Vol. 1: *Des origins jusqu'a la morte d'Averroes (1198)*. Gallimard, Paris, 1964.

—*L'Ecole Shaykhie en Théologie Shiʿite*. Annuaire de l'Ecole Pratique des Hautes Etudes, Section des Sciences Religieuses, 1960–61. RP with Persian translation by Firaydūn Bahmanyār, Chāp-i Tābān, Tehran, 1967.

—*L'Homme de Lumière dans le Soufisme iranien*. Henri Viand, Paris, 1971. Trans. by Nancy Pearson as *The Man of Light in Iranian Sufism*, Shambala Publications, Boulder, Colorado, 1978.

Corbin, Henri. *La Philosophie iranienne islamique aux XVIIe et XVIIIe siècles*. Buchet-Chastel, Paris, 1981.

Coulson, Noel J. *A History of Islamic Law*. Islamic Surveys, No. 2, Edinburgh University Press, Edinburgh, 1964.

—*Conflicts and Tensions in Islamic Jurisprudence*. University of Chicago Press, Chicago, 1969.

—*Succession in the Muslim Family*. Cambridge University Press, Cambridge, 1971.

Cragg, Kenneth. *The Call of the Minaret*. Oxford University Press, New York, 1956.

Deeb, Marius K. 'Lebanon: Prospects for National Reconciliation in the mid-1980s.' *Middle East Journal,* 38 (1984), pp. 267–83.

Dieulafoy, Jane. *La Perse, la Chaldée et la Susianne*. Librarie Hachette, Paris, 1887.

Donaldson, Dwight M. *The Shi'ite Religion*. Luzac & Co., London, 1933.

—'The Shiah Doctrine of the Imamate.' *Moslem World,* 21 (1931), pp. 14–23.

Du Mans, Raphael. *Estat de la Perse en 1660*. Ed. C. Shefer. Ernest Leroux, Paris, 1890.

Eliash, Joseph. 'The Ithnā 'Asharī-Shī'ī Juristic Theory of Policial and Legal Authority.' *Studia Islamica,* 29 (1969), pp. 17–30.

—'The Šī'ite Qur'ān.' *Arabica,* 16 (1969), pp. 15–24.

—'On the Genesis and Development of the Twelver-Shī'ī three-tenet Shahādah.' *Der Islam,* 47 (1971), pp. 265–72.

—'Misconceptions regarding the Juridicial Status of the Iranian "Ulama".' *International Journal of Middle East Studies,* 10 (1979), pp. 9–25.

Enayat, Hamid. *Modern Islamic Political Thought: The Response of the Shi'i and Sunni Muslims to the Twentieth Century*. Macmillan, London 1982.

Encyclopaedia Iranica. Ed. Ehsan Yarshater. Routledge and Kegan Paul, 1982 proceeding.

Encyclopaedia of Islam. 1st ed. (ed. M. T. Houtsma et al.), 1913–34, 4 vols.; 2nd ed. (ed. H. A. R. Gibb et al.), 1960 proceeding. E. J. Brill, Leyden, and Luzac & Co., London.

Esslemont, John E. *Bahā'u'llāh and the New Era*. 4th rev. ed., Bahā'ī Publishing Trust, London, 1974.

Ezzati, Abu'l-Fadl. *An Introduction to Shi'i Islamic Law and Jurisprudence*. Ashraf Press, Lahore, 1976.

Fraser, James B. *An Historical and Descriptive Account of Persia*. Oliver and Boyd, Edinburgh, 1834.

Fernea, Elizabeth W. *Guests of the Sheik*. Robert Hale, London, 1968.

Fernea, Robert A. *Shaykh and Effendi*. Harvard University Press, Cambridge, Mass., 1970.

Fischer, Michael M. J. *Iran, from Religious Dispute to Revolution*. Harvard University Press, Cambridge, Mass., 1980.

Friedlander, Israel. 'The Heterodoxies of the Shiites in the presentation of Ibn Hazm.' *Journal of the American Oriental Society*, 28 (1907), pp. 1–80 (designated as Friedlander, 'Heterodoxies' I); 29 (1908), pp. 1–183 (designated as Friedlander, 'Heterodoxies' II).

Ghaffari, Salman. *Shia'ism or Original Islam*. no publisher, 2nd ed., Tehran, 1971.

Gibb, Hamilton A. R. 'Government and Islam under the early Abbasids: the political collapse of Islam', in *L'Elaboration de l'Islam*. Colloque de Strasbourg 1959, Presses Universitaires de Paris, Paris, 1961.

Gilsenan, Michael. *Recognising Islam: An anthropologist's introduction*. Croom Helm, 1982.

Gobineau, Joseph A., Comte de. *Religions et Philosophies dans l'Asie Centrale*. Gallimard, Paris, 1957.

Gramlich, Richard. *Die Schiitischen Derwischorden Persiens*. 2 vols. Deutsche Morgenlandische Gesellschaft, Wiesbaden, 1965–76.

Greussing, K. (ed.). *Religion und Politik im Iran*. Syndicat, Frankfurt am Main, 1981.

Guillaume, Alfred. *The Life of Muhammad, a translation of Iṣhāq's Sīrat Rasūl Allāh*. Oxford Univeristy Press, London, 1955.

Gursoy, Emine. 'An Analysis of Nadir Shah's religious policy.' *Bogazici Universitesi Dergisi (Humaniter Bilimler)*, 2 (1974), pp. 13–18.

Hairi, Abdu'l Hadi. *Shi'ism and Constitutionalism in Iran*. E. J. Brill, Leiden, 1977.

Halkin, Abraham S. *Moslem Schisms and Sects*. Trans. of Ibn Ṭāhir, *Farq bayn al-Firaq*, 2nd part. Palestine Publishing Co., Tel Aviv, 1935.

Hartmann, Richard (ed. and trans.). *Das Tübinger Fragment der Chronik die Ibn Ṭūlūn*. Deutsche Verlagsgesellschaft fur Politik und Geschichte, Berlin, 1926.

al-Ḥillī, 'Allāma Ḥasan ibn Yūsuf. *Al-Bābu'l-Hādī Ashar*. Trans. W. M. Miller. Royal Asiatic Society, London, 1928.

Hodgson, Marshall G. S. *The Order of the Assassins*. Mouton, The Hague, 1955.

—*The Venture of Islam*. 3 vols. University of Chicago Press, Chicago, 1974.

—'How did the Early Shī'a become Sectarian?' *Journal of the American Oriental Society*, 75 (1955), pp. 1–13.

Hollister, John N. *The Shi'a of India*. Luzac & Co., London, 1953.

Howard, I. K. A. (trans.). *Kitāb al-Irshād* (of Shaykh al-Mufīd). Balagha Books, Horsham, W. Sussex, and Muhammadi Trust, London, 1981.

Huart, Clement. *Textes persans relatifs a la secte des Houroufis*. E. J. Brill, Leiden, 1909.

Huddleston, John. *The Earth is but One Country*. Bahā'ī Publishing Trust, London, 1976.

Hussain, Jassim M. *The Occultation of the Twelfth Imam*. Muhammadi Trust, London, 1982.

Ibn Bābūya, Muhammad ibn 'Alī. *A Shi'ite Creed*. Trans. A. A. Fyzee. Oxford University Press, London, 1942.

Iran in der Krise. Verlag Neue Gesellschaft, Bonn, 1980.

Iran Press Digest (Echo of Iran), Tehran.

Ivanow, Vladimir (ed. and trans.). 'Umm al-Kitab.' *Der Islam*, 23 (1936), pp. 1–132.

—'Early Shi'ite Movements.' *Journal of the Bombay Branch of the Royal Asiatic Society*, 17 (1941), pp. 1–23.

Jafri, S. Husain M. *Origins and Early Development of Shi'a Islam*. Longman, London and New York, and Librarie du Liban, Beirut, 1979.

Jamāli, Fādil. 'The Theological Colleges of Najaf.' *Muslim World*, 50 (1960), pp. 15–22.

Kazemi, Farhad (ed.). *The Iranian Revolution in Perspective*. Special Edition of *Iranian Studies*, 13 (1980), nos. 1–4.

Kazi, A. K., and J. G. Flynn. 'Shahristani, *Kitab al-milal w'al-nihal* translated. VI: The Shi'ites.' *Abr Nahrain*, 15 (1975), pp. 50–98.

Keddie, Nikki R. *Religion and Rebellion in Iran: The Tobacco Protest of 1891–1892*. Frank Cass, 1966.

—(ed.). *Scholars, Saints and Sufis: Muslim Religious Institutions in the Middle East since 1500*. University of California, Berkeley and Los Angeles, 1972.

—*Iran: Religion, Politics and Society*. Frank Cass, London, 1980.

—*Roots of Revolution; an interpretative history of modern Iran*. With a section by Yann Richard. Yale University Press, New Haven and London, 1981.

—(ed.). *Religion and Politics in Iran: Shi'ism from Quietism to Revolution*. Yale University Press, New Haven and London, 1983.

— and J. R. I. Cole (eds.). *Shi'ism and Social Protest*. Forthcoming.

Khumaynī, Ruḥu'llāh. *Islam and Revolution: Writings and Declarations of Imam Khomeini*. Trans. and ed. Hamid Algar. Mizan Press, Berkeley, 1981.

Khuri, Fuad I. *Tribe and State in Bahrain*. Center for Middle Eastern Studies, No. 14, University of Chicago Press, Chicago and London, 1980.

Kohlberg, Etan. 'Some notes on the Imami attitude to the Qur'an', in *Islamic Philosophy and the Classical Tradition: Essays presented to R. Walzer*. Ed. S. M. Stern, A. Hourani and Y. Brown. Cassirer, Oxford, 1972, pp. 209–24.

—'Some Imāmī-Shī'ī views on taqiyya.' *Journal of the American Oriental Society*, 95 (1975), pp. 395–402.

—'From Imāmiyya to Ithnā-'Ashariyya.' *Bulletin of the School of Oriental and African Studies*, 39 (1976), pp. 521–34.

—'The Development of the Imāmī Shī'ī doctrine of jihād.' *Zeitschrift der Deutschen Morganländischen Gesellschaft*, 126 (1976), pp. 64–86.

—'The term "Rāfiḍa" in Imāmī Shī'ī usage.' *Journal of the American Oriental Society*, 99 (1980), pp. 677–79.

Lambton, Ann K. S. *State and Government in Medieval Islam; an introduction to the study of Islamic political theory: The jurists*. London Oriental Series, vol. 36. Oxford University Press, Oxford, 1981.

—'Quis Custodiet Custodes? Some reflections on the Persian theory of government,' *Studia Islamica*, 5 (1955), pp. 125–48; 6 (1955), pp. 125–46.

—'A Reconsideration of the position of *Marja' al-Taqlīd* and the religious institution.' *Studia Islamica*, 20 (1964), pp. 115–35.

—'A Nineteenth Century view of Jihād.' *Studia Islamica*, 32 (1970), pp. 181–92.

—'The Persian Ulama and Constitutional Reform', in *Le Shi'isme imamite* (see Aubin), pp. 245–69.

—'Some new trends in Islamic Political Thought in late 18th and early 19th Century Persia.' *Studia Islamica*, 32 (1974), pp. 95–128.

Lane-Poole, Stanley. *The Muhammadan Dynasties*. Archibald Constable & Co., London, 1894.

Laoust, Henri. *Les schismes dans l'Islam*. Payot, Paris, 1965.
—'Les Agitations religieuses à Baghdad aux IVe et Ve siècles de l'Hégire', in *Islamic Civilisation 950–1150*. Ed. D. S. Richards. Cassirer, Oxford, 1973, pp. 169–85.
Lewis, Bernard. *The Assassins: a radical sect in Islam*. Weidenfeld and Nicolson, London, 1967.
Linant de Bellefonds, Yvon. 'Le Droit imamite', in *Le Shi'isme imamite* (*see* Aubin), pp. 183–99.
Lings, Martin. *Muhammad, his life based on the earliest sources*. Islamic Texts Society and George Allen and Unwin, London, 1983.
Lockhart, Laurence. *Nadir Shah*. Luzac & Co., London, 1938.
—*The Fall of the Ṣafavī Dynasty and the Afghan Occupation of Persia*. Cambridge University Press, Cambridge, 1958.
Longrigg, Stephen H. *Four Centuries of Modern Iraq*. Clarendon Press, Oxford, 1925.
MacDermott, Martin J. *The Theology of al-Shaikh al-Mufīd*. Recherches, Nouvelle Série: A; Langue arabe et Pensée islamique 10; Persian Studies Series No. 9. Dar al-Machreq Éditeurs, Beirut, 1978.
Madelung, Wilferd. 'Imamism and Mu'tazilite Theology' in *Le Shi'isme imamite* (*see* Aubin), pp. 13–30.
—'Ibn Abī Gumhûr al-Ahsâ'i's synthesis of *kalam*, philosophy and Sufism', in *La Significance du Bas Moyen Age dans l'Histoire et la Culture du Monde Musulmane*. Actes du 8eme Congres de l'Union Européene des Arabisants et Islamisants. Aix-en-Provence, 1978, pp. 147–56.
—'A Treatise of the Sharīf al-Murtaḍā on the legality of working for the Government (*Mas'ala fī 'l-Amal ma'a 'l-Sulṭān*).' *Bulletin of the School of Oriental and African Studies*, 43 (1980), pp. 18–31.
Mahdavi, Asghar. 'The Significance of private archives for the study of the economic and social history of Iran in the late Qajar period'. *Iranian Studies*, 16 (1983), pp. 243–78.
Malcolm, Sir John. *History of Persia*. 2 vols. J. Murray, London, 1815.
Mashkur, Muḥammad Jawād. 'An-Nawbakhti, Les Sectes si'ites.' *Revue de l'Histoire des Religions*, 153 (1958), pp. 68–78, 176–214; 154 (1958), pp. 67–95, 146–72; 155 (1959), pp. 63–78.
Massignon, Louis. *La Passion de Husayn Ibn Mansur Hallaj*. New ed., 4 vols. Gallimard, Paris, 1975. Translated by Herbert Mason as *The Passion of al-Hallaj*. 4 vols. Bollingen Series 97, Princeton University Press, Princeton, N.J., 1983.
Mazzaoui, Michel M. *The Origin of the Safawids: Shi'ism, Sufism and the Ghulat*. Freiburger Islamica Studien, Vol. III, Franz Steiner, Wiesbaden, 1972.
McDowall, David. *Lebanon: a Conflict of Minorities*. Minority Rights Group, Report No. 61, London, 1983.
McLaurin, Ronald D. (ed.). *The Political Role of Minority Groups in the Middle East*. Praeger, New York, 1979.
Meer Hasan Ali, Mrs. *Observations on the Musulmans of India*. RP Oxford University Press, Karachi, 1974.
'Mesopotamien', 'Le Programme des études chez les chiites et principalement

chez ceux de Najaf.' *Revue de Monde Musulman*, 23 (1913), pp. 268–79.

Miller, William M. 'Shi'ah Mysticism; the Sufis of Gunabad.' *Moslem World*, 13 (1923), pp. 343–63.

Millward, William G. 'Aspects of Modernism in Shi'a Islam.' *Studia Islamica*, 37 (1973), pp. 111–128.

Minorsky, Vladimir. *Notes sur la secte des Ahle-Haqq*. E. Leroux, Paris, 1921.

—'The poetry of Shah Isma'il I.' *Bulletin of the School of Oriental and African Studies*, 10 (1942), pp. 1006a–53a.

—'Shah-Jihan Qaraquyunlu and his poetry.' *Bulletin of the School of Oriental and African Studies*, 16 (1954), pp. 271–97.

—'Iran: Opposition, Martyrdom and Revolt', in *Unity and Variety in Muslim Civilization*. Ed. G. E. von Grunebaum. University of Chicago Press, Chicago, 1955.

Molé, M. 'Les Kubrawiya entre Sunnisme et Shiisme aux huitième et neuvième siècles de l'Hégire.' *Revue des Etudes Islamiques*, 29 (1961), pp. 61–142.

Morgan, Kenneth W. (ed.). *Islam, the Straight Path*. Ronald Press Co., New York, 1958.

Morier, James. *A Journey through Persia, Armenia, and Asia Minor to Constantinople in 1808 and 1809*. Longman, Hurst et al., London, 1812.

—*A Second Journey through Persia, Armenia, and Asia Minor to Constantinople between the years 1810 and 1816*. Longman, Hurst et al., London, 1818.

Morris, James W. *The Wisdom of the Throne: an introduction to the philosophy of Mulla Sadra*. Princeton University Press, Princeton, N.J., 1981.

Mottahedeh, Roy P. *Loyalty and Leadership in an Early Islamic Society*. Princeton University Press, Princeton, 1980.

Muller, A. *Der Islam im Morgen- und Abendland*. 2 vols. G. Grote'sche Verlagsbuchhandlung, Berlin, 1887.

al-Muẓaffar, Muḥammad Riḍā. *The Faith of Shi'a Islam*. Ansariyan Publications, Qumm, 1982.

Nader, Albert. *Kitāb al-intiṣār – le livre du triomphe*. Text and translation into French of al-Khayyāṭ's work. L'Institut de Lettres orientales de Beyrouth, Editions des Lettres orientales, Beirut, 1957.

Nashat, Guity. *Women and Revolution in Iran*. Westview Press, Boulder, Col., 1983.

Nasr, S. Hossein. *Ṣadr al-Dīn Shīrāzī and his Transcendent Theosophy*. Imperial Iranian Academy of Philosohpy, Tehran, 1978.

—'Religion in Safavid Persia.' *Iranian Studies*, 7 (1974), pp. 271–86. See also Algar's reply to this paper in the same issue of *Iranian Studies*, pp. 287–93.

Nicolas, A. L. M. *Essai sur le Chéïkisme*. 4 vols. Paul Geuthner and Ernest Leroux, Paris, 1910–14.

Nizam al-Mulk. *The Book of Government or Rules for Kings*. Trans. H. Drake. Routledge and Kegan Paul, London, 1978.

Nurbakhsh, Dr Javad, *see also* Section A.

—*Masters of the Path; a history of the Masters of the Nimatullahi Sufi Order*. Khanigahi-Nimatullahi Publications, New York, 1980.

Pelly, Lewis. *The Miracle Play of Hasan and Husain*. 2 vols. William Allen, London, 1897.

Peters, Emrys L. 'A Muslim Passion Play.' *Atlantic Monthly – Perspective of the Arab World – a special Supplement.* 198, Oct. 1956, pp. 176–80.

—'Aspects of Rank and Status among Muslims in a Lebanese village', in *Mediterranean Countrymen.* Ed. J. Pitt-Rivers. Mouton, The Hague, 1963, pp. 159–200.

—'Shifts in power in a Lebanese village', in *Rural Politics and Social Change in the Middle East.* Ed. Richard Antoun and Iliya Harik. Indiana University Press, Bloomington, Ind., 1972, pp. 165–97.

Querry, Amédée. *Droit Musulman. Recueil de lois concernant les musulmans-schyites.* 2 vols. Imprimerie Nationale, Paris, 1871–2.

Rahman, Fazlur. *The Philosophy of Mullā Ṣadrā.* State University of New York Press, Albany, 1975.

Richard, Yann. *Le Shi'isme en Iran.* Jean Maisonneuve, Paris, 1980.

Rizvi, S. Saeed A. 'Ithna Ashariya Shias in India.' *Milla wa Milla*, 6 (1966), pp. 51–64.

—and Noel Q. King. 'The Khoja Shia Ithna-Asheriya Community in East Africa (1840–1967).' *Muslim World*, 64 (1974), pp. 194–204.

—and . 'Some East African Ithna-Asheri Jamaats (1840–1967).' *Journal of Religion in Africa*, 5 (1975), pp. 12–22.

Sachedina, Abdulaziz A. *Islamic Messianism: the idea of the Mahdi in Twelver Shi'ism.* State University of New York Press, Albany, 1981.

Sadighi, Gholam Hossein. *Les mouvements religieux iraniens au IIe et au IIIe siecle de l'hegire.* Les Presses Modernes, Paris, 1938.

Sarwar, Ghulam. *History of Shāh Ismā'īl Ṣafawī.* Privately published, Aligarh, 1939.

Savory, Roger M. *Iran under the Safavids.* Cambridge University Press, Cambridge, 1980.

—'The Principal Offices of the Safavid State during the reign of Isma'il I.' *Bulletin of the School of Oriental and African Studies*, 23 (1960), pp. 91–105.

—'The Principal Offices of the Safavid State during the reign of Tahmasp I.' *Bulletin of the School of Oriental and African Studies*, 24 (1961), pp. 65–85.

—'The Safavid State and Polity.' *Iranian Studies*, 7 (1974), pp. 179–212.

Scarcia, Gianroberto. 'Interno alle controversie tra Ahbari e Usuli presso gli Imamiti di Persia.' *Revista degli Studia Orientali*, 33 (1958), pp. 211–50.

—'Kerman 1905: la guerra tra seihi e balasari.' *Annali del Instituto Universitario di Napoli, 13* (1963), pp. 186–203.

Schacht, Joseph, *Origins of Muhammadan Jurisprudence.* Clarendon Press, Oxford, 1953.

Schimmel, Anne-Marie. 'The Ornaments of Saints: the religious situation in Iran in Pre-Safavid times.' *Iranian Studies*, 7 (1974), pp. 88–111.

Schuon, Frithjof, *Understanding Islam.* Trans. D. M. Matheson. George Allen and Unwin, London, 1963.

Shari'ati, Ali. *On the Sociology of Islam.* Trans. and biobibliographic sketch of author by Hamid Algar. Mizan Press, Berkeley, 1979.

Sharif, Ja'far. *Islam in India or Qānūn-i-Islām.* Trans. G. A. Herklots. Ed. William Crooke. Oxford University Press, Oxford, 1921.

Sharif, Miyan Muhammad (ed.). *A History of Muslim Philosophy.* Vol. 2. Otto

Harrassowitz, Wiesbaden, 1966. See in particular articles by S. H. Nasr, pp. 904–61.

Sicking, Thom, and Dr Shereen Khairallah. 'The Shi'a awakening in Lebanon: a search for a radical change in a traditional way', in *Vision and Revision in Arab Society*. CENAM Report, Vol. 2. Dar el-Mashriq Publishers, Beirut, 1974.

Siddiqui, Kalim (ed.). *Issues in the Islamic Movement, 1980–81.(1400–01)*. Open Press, London, 1981.

Smith, John M., Jr. *The History of the Sarbadār Dynasty 1336–81 A.D. and its sources*. Publications in Near and Middle East Studies. Columbia University, Series A, Vol. 11. Mouton, The Hague and Paris, 1970.

Smith, Peter. *The Bābī and Bahā'ī Religions: from Messianic Shī'ism to a World Religion*. Cambridge University Press, Cambridge, forthcoming.

Sell, Rev. Canon. *Ithna 'Asharīyya or the Twelve Shi'ah Imams*. Christian Literature Society for India, Madras, etc., 1923.

Sohrweide, Hanna. 'Der Sieg der Safaviden in Persien und seine Ruckwirkungen auf de Schiiten Anatoliens im 16 Jahrhundert.' *Der Islam*, 41 (1965), pp. 95–223.

Sourdel, Dominique. 'Les Conceptions Imamites au debut du XIe siècle d'après le Shaykh al-Mufid', in *Islamic Civilisation 950–1150* (*see* Laoust), pp. 187–200.

Spuler, Bertold. *Die Mongolen in Iran*. J. C. Hinrichs Verlag, Leipzig, 1939.

Strothmann, Rudolf. *Die Zwolfer-Schī'a*. Otto Harrassowitz, Leipzig, 1926.

Tabari, Azar, and Nahid Yeganeh. *In the Shadow of Islam: The Women's Movement in Iran*. Zed, London, 1982.

Ṭabāṭabā'ī, 'Allāmah S. Muḥammad Ḥusayn. *Shi'ite Islam*. Trans. and ed. by S. Hossein Nasr. George Allen and Unwin, London, 1975.

Tancoigne, J. M. *A Narrative of a Journey into Persia and Residence at Teheran*. Trans. from French. William Wright, London, 1820.

Thaiss, Gustav. 'The bazaar as a Case Study of Religion and Social Change', in *Iran faces the Seventies*. Ed. E. Yar-shater. Praeger, New York, 1971.

—'Unity and Discord: the symbol of Husayn in Iran', in *Iranian Civilisation and Culture*. Ed. C. J. Adams. McGill University, Montreal, 1972.

Thesiger, Wilfred. *The Marsh Arabs*. Longmans, London, 1964.

Tisdall, W. St. Clair. 'Shi'ah additions to the Koran.' *Moslem World*, 3 (1913), pp. 227–41.

Trimingham, J. Spencer. *The Sufi Orders in Islam*. Clarendon Press, Oxford, 1971.

Vahdati, Ataollah. 'Academies shiites.' *Objets et Mondes*, 11 (1971), pp. 171–80.

Vermeulen, Urbain. 'The Rescript against the Shi'ites and Rāfiḍites of Beirut, Saida and district (747 A.H./1363 A.D.).' *Orientalia Lovaniensis Periodica*, 4 (1973), pp. 167–75.

Watt, W. Montgomery, *Muhammad at Mecca*. Clarendon Press, Oxford, 1953.

—*Muhammad at Medina*. Clarendon Press, Oxford, 1956.

—*Islamic Philosophy and Theology*. Islamic Surveys, Vol. 1, Edinburgh University Press, Edinburgh, 1962.

—'Shi'ism under the Umayyads.' *Journal of the Royal Asiatic Society* (1960), pp. 158–72.

—'The Rafidites: a preliminary study.' *Oriens*, 16 (1963), pp. 110–21.
—'The reappraisal of Abbasid Shi'ism.' *Arabic and Islamic Studies in honor of Hamilton A. R. Gibb* (*see* Binder), pp. 638–54.
—'Sidelights on early Imamite doctrine.' *Studia Islamica*, 30 (1970), pp. 287–98.
Zabih, Sepehr, *Iran since the Revolution*. Croom Helm, London, 1982.
Zambaur, E. de. *Manuel de Genealogie et de Chronologie pour l'Histoire de l'Islam*. Librarie Orientaliste Heinz Lafaire, Hanover, 1927.

Index

Entries are alphabetised word by word. Component parts of compound names are treated as separate words and the Arabic definite article al- (as-, ar-, az-, etc.) is ignored. The contraction 'l is also ignored. Thus Abu'l-Qāsim follows Abū Muslim. To facilitate the location of entries thus affected, a space has been inserted between the root of the word and connecting material, e.g. Ṣafī yu'd-Dīn is listed before Safīna, and Nāṣir u'd-Dīn Shāh precedes Nāṣir Uṭrush. The term 'ibn' is ignored when it appears within a name, e.g. Ḥusayn ibn 'Alī, but is indexed when at the beginning of a name, e.g. Ibn 'Abbās.